P9-DMD-119

Windows® 10

ALL-IN-ONE

FOR DUMMIES

A Wiley Brand

by Woody Leonhard

Windows® 10 All-in-One For Dummies®

Published by:
John Wiley & Sons, Inc.,
111 River Street, Hoboken, NJ 07030-5774,
www.wiley.com

Copyright © 2015 by John Wiley & Sons, Inc., Hoboken, New Jersey

Published simultaneously in Canada

No part of this publication may be reproduced, stored in a retrieval system or transmitted in any form or by any means, electronic, mechanical, photocopying, recording, scanning or otherwise, except as permitted under Sections 107 or 108 of the 1976 United States Copyright Act, without the prior written permission of the Publisher. Requests to the Publisher for permission should be addressed to the Permissions Department, John Wiley & Sons, Inc., 111 River Street, Hoboken, NJ 07030, (201) 748-6011, fax (201) 748-6008, or online at http://www.wiley.com/go/permissions.

Trademarks: Wiley, For Dummies, the Dummies Man logo, Dummies.com, Making Everything Easier, and related trade dress are trademarks or registered trademarks of John Wiley & Sons, Inc. and may not be used without written permission. Windows is a registered trademark of Microsoft Corporation. All other trademarks are the property of their respective owners. John Wiley & Sons, Inc. is not associated with any product or vendor mentioned in this book.

LIMIT OF LIABILITY/DISCLAIMER OF WARRANTY: THE PUBLISHER AND THE AUTHOR MAKE NO REPRESENTATIONS OR WARRANTIES WITH RESPECT TO THE ACCURACY OR COMPLETENESS OF THE CONTENTS OF THIS WORK AND SPECIFICALLY DISCLAIM ALL WARRANTIES, INCLUDING WITHOUT LIMITATION WARRANTIES OF FITNESS FOR A PARTICULAR PURPOSE. NO WARRANTY MAY BE CREATED OR EXTENDED BY SALES OR PROMOTIONAL MATERIALS. THE ADVICE AND STRATEGIES CONTAINED HEREIN MAY NOT BE SUITABLE FOR EVERY SITUATION. THIS WORK IS SOLD WITH THE UNDERSTANDING THAT THE PUBLISHER IS NOT ENGAGED IN RENDERING LEGAL, ACCOUNTING, OR OTHER PROFESSIONAL SERVICES. IF PROFESSIONAL ASSISTANCE IS REQUIRED, THE SERVICES OF A COMPETENT PROFESSIONAL PERSON SHOULD BE SOUGHT. NEITHER THE PUBLISHER NOR THE AUTHOR SHALL BE LIABLE FOR DAMAGES ARISING HEREFROM. THE FACT THAT AN ORGANIZATION OR WEBSITE IS REFERRED TO IN THIS WORK AS A CITATION AND/OR A POTENTIAL SOURCE OF FURTHER INFORMATION DOES NOT MEAN THAT THE AUTHOR OR THE PUBLISHER ENDORSES THE INFORMATION THE ORGANIZATION OR WEBSITE MAY PROVIDE OR RECOMMENDATIONS IT MAY MAKE. FURTHER, READERS SHOULD BE AWARE THAT INTERNET WEBSITES LISTED IN THIS WORK MAY HAVE CHANGED OR DISAPPEARED BETWEEN WHEN THIS WORK WAS WRITTEN AND WHEN IT IS READ.

For general information on our other products and services, please contact our Customer Care Department within the U.S. at 877-762-2974, outside the U.S. at 317-572-3993, or fax 317-572-4002. For technical support, please visit www.wiley.com/techsupport.

Wiley publishes in a variety of print and electronic formats and by print-on-demand. Some material included with standard print versions of this book may not be included in e-books or in print-on-demand. If this book refers to media such as a CD or DVD that is not included in the version you purchased, you may download this material at http://booksupport.wiley.com. For more information about Wiley products, visit www.wiley.com.

Library of Congress Control Number: 2015945953

ISBN 978-1-119-03872-6 (pbk); ISBN 978-1-119-03874-0 (ebk); ISBN 978-1-119-03873-3 (ebk)

Manufactured in the United States of America

10 9 8 7 6 5 4 3 2 1

Contents at a Glance

Table of Contents

Introduction

Think of Windows 8/8.1 as an extended, really bad, no good, horrible nightmare. Microsoft's woken up now. They fired almost everybody who ran the Win 8 operation, cleaned out the house, and brought in some truly gifted engineers. Windows 10's a brand new day. Whether it's *your* brand new day, well, that's another story.

Windows 10 looks a little bit like Windows 7 and a little bit like Windows 8.1. It doesn't work like either of them, but for the billion-and-a-half Windows users out there, at least it's recognizable as Windows.

If you haven't yet taken the plunge with Windows 10, I advise you to go slowly. Microsoft is furiously working on extending the product and shoring up problems. The Windows 10 you know today will change in a few months, and you may like the new one better. Before installing Windows 10, I would simply. . .count to ten.

For most Windows 8 and 8.1 users, Win 10 is a no-brainer. You can kvetch about some problems — the disappearance of Windows Media Center, for example — and Microsoft cloud storage OneDrive users are going to have a hard time adapting to the now-you-see-it-now-you-don't interface (see Book VI, Chapter 2) until Microsoft figures out how to fix it. There are dozens of additional details, but by and large, Windows 10 is what Windows 8.1 should've been.

Windows 7 users, though, don't have as much incentive to move to Windows 10. There are some good changes. Microsoft effectively ditched Internet Explorer and built a much lighter and more capable browser, called Microsoft Edge. Instead of desktop gadgets, which in Win7 were held together with baling wire and chewing gum, Win10 sports a whole infrastructure for tiled "Universal" apps. Win10 works with all the new hardware, touch, and pens. There's an improved Task Manager, File Explorer, and a dozen other system utilities.

Is that enough to convince Win7 users to abandon ship in droves? Probably not. The single biggest allure of Windows 10 for the Win7 battle-hardened is that it's clearly the way of the future.

If you want a better Windows, for whatever reason, you'll have to go through Windows 10.

This isn't the manual Microsoft forgot. This is the manual Microsoft wouldn't dare print. I won't feed you the Microsoft Party Line or make excuses for pieces of Windows 10 that just don't work: Some of it's junk, some of it's evolving, and some of it's devolving. My job is to take you through the most important parts of Windows, give you tips that may or may not involve Microsoft products, point out the rough spots, and guide you around the disasters. Frankly, there are some biggies.

I also look at using non-Microsoft products in a Windows way: iPads, Androids, Kindles, Gmail and Google Apps, Facebook, Twitter, Dropbox, Firefox, Google Chrome, and iCloud. Even though Microsoft competes with just about every one of those products, each has a place in your computing arsenal and ties into Windows in important ways.

I'll save you more than enough money to pay for the book several times over, keep you from pulling out a whole shock of hair, lead you to dozens if not hundreds of "Aha!" moments, and keep you awake in the process. Guaranteed.

About This Book

Windows 10 All-in-One For Dummies takes you through the Land of the Dummies — with introductory material and stuff your grandmother can (and should!) understand — and then continues the journey into more advanced areas, where you can truly put Windows to work every day.

I start with the new Start menu, and for many of you, that's all you'll ever need. The Start menu coverage here is the best you'll find anywhere because I don't assume that you know Windows, and I step you through everything you need to know both with a touch screen and a mouse.

Then I dig in to the desktop and take you through all the important pieces.

I don't dwell on technical mumbo jumbo, and I keep the baffling jargon to a minimum. At the same time, though, I tackle the tough problems you're likely to encounter, show you the major road signs, and give you lots of help where you need it the most.

Whether you want to get two or more email accounts set up to work simultaneously, turn your tiles a lighter shade of pale, or share photos of your Boykin Spaniel in OneDrive, this is your book. Er, I should say ten books. I've broken out the topics into ten different minibooks, so you'll find it easy to hop around to a topic — and a level of coverage — that feels comfortable.

I didn't design this book to be read from front to back. It's a reference. Each chapter and each of its sections are meant to focus on solving a particular problem or describing a specific technique.

Windows 10 All-in-One For Dummies should be your reference of first resort, even before you consult Windows Help and Support. There's a big reason why: Windows Help was written by hundreds of people over the course of many, many years. Some of the material was written ages ago, and it's confusing as all get-out, but it's still in Windows Help for folks who are tackling tough "legacy" problems. Some of the Help file terminology is inconsistent and downright misleading, largely because the technology has changed so much since some of the articles were written. Finding help in Help frequently boggles my mind: If I don't already know the answer to a question, it's hard to figure out how to coax Help to help. Besides, if you're looking for help on connecting your iPad to your PC or downloading pictures from your Galaxy phone, Microsoft would rather sell you something different. The proverbial bottom line: I don't duplicate the material in Windows 10 Help and Support, but I point to it if I figure it can help you.

A word about Windows 10 versions: Microsoft is trying to sell the world on the idea that Windows 10 runs on everything — desktops, laptops, tablets, phones, assisted reality headsets, huge banks of servers, giant conference room displays, refrigerators, and toasters. While that's literally true — Microsoft can call anything "Windows 10" if it wants — for those of us who work on desktops and laptops, Windows 10 is Windows 10. If you're getting Windows 10 on a tablet, you need to check to see if it's the version that runs on phones. Windows 10 Phone has some small resemblance to what's presented here, but this book won't take you through the tough times.

Foolish Assumptions

I don't make many assumptions about you, dear reader, except to acknowledge that you're obviously intelligent, well-informed, discerning, and of impeccable taste. That's why you chose this book, eh?

Okay, okay. The least I can do is butter you up a bit. Here's the straight scoop: If you've never used Windows, bribe your neighbor (or, better, your neighbor's kids) to teach you how to do four things:

✦ Play a game with your fingers (if you have a touchscreen) or with a mouse (if you're finger-challenged). Any of the games on the tiled side of the Windows 10 Start menu, or free games in the Windows Store, will do. If your neighbor's kids don't have a different recommendation, try the new Microsoft Solitaire Collection.

✦ Start File Explorer.

✦ Get on the web.

✦ Turn Windows off. (Hint: click or tap the Start icon in the lower left of the screen, and choose Power, Shut down.)

That covers it. If you can play a game, you know how to turn on your computer, log in if need be, touch and drag, and tap and hold. If you run File Explorer, you know how to click a taskbar icon. After you're on the web, well, it's a great starting point for almost anything. And if you know that you need to use the Start menu, you're well on your way to achieving Windows 10 Enlightenment.

And that begins with Book I, Chapter 1.

What You Don't Have to Read

Throughout this book, I've gone to great lengths to separate "optional" reading from "required" reading. If you want to find out more about a topic or solve a specific problem, follow along in the main part of the text. You can skip the sidebars as you go, unless one happens to catch your eye.

On the other hand, if you know a topic pretty well but want to make sure that you catch all the high points, read the paragraphs marked with icons and be sure that the information registers. If it doesn't, glance at the surrounding text.

Sidebars offer information above and beyond what you need to know for those who are curious about a specific topic — or who stand knee-deep in muck, searching for a way out.

How This Book Is Organized

Windows 10 All-in-One For Dummies contains ten minibooks, each of which gives a thorough airing of a specific topic. If you're looking for information on a specific Windows topic, check the headings in the Table of Contents or refer to the index.

By design, this book enables you to get as much (or as little) information as you need at any particular moment.

Here's a description of the ten minibooks and what they contain:

✦ **Book I, Starting Windows 10** takes you through the pros and cons of using Windows 10. Whether you're just starting out, or you've been using Windows 8, 7, or earlier for decades, there's lots of stuff you've never seen before. This is where you start to earn your chops.

✦ **Book II, Personalizing Windows** runs you all around the Windows playing surface, pointing out what you can do, what you should do, and where you may fall into a rabbit hole. It shows you how to get your Lock screen and Logons working right, add new users, take advantage of cloud syncing of your Windows settings, and stay on top of your privacy. Yeah, there's even some of the stuff Microsoft doesn't want you to know about.

✦ **Book III, Working on the Desktop** goes through the whole nine yards. From the list-on-the-left/tiles-on-the-right Start menu to multiple desktops, and Hey Cortana!, this is where you're going to live, and this is what you need to read.

✦ **Book IV, Using the Built-in Universal Apps** introduces you to the latest and greatest programs from Microsoft. They're free, they're flashy, and they're oh-so-frustrating when they don't do what you want. See how to tame them into submission.

✦ **Book V, Connecting with the Universal Apps** shows you what you need to know about Microsoft Edge, the new browser you'll soon call home. Hop through all the important online apps both from Microsoft and from Microsoft's competitors. Whether you use OneDrive, Skype, financial apps, news apps, or games, this is where you can find the real story.

✦ **Book VI, Socializing with the Universal Apps** gets you started with details about Office, OneDrive, Facebook, Twitter, and LinkedIn. If you've never used them, see what all the fuss is about. If you're an old hand, drop by and see what Windows 10 brings to the table.

✦ **Book VII, Controlling Your System** goes through the new Universal Settings app and the old Control Panel and then covers many new and exciting Windows 10 capabilities. I also go through some school-of-hard-knocks tips on working with printers and other worse-than-senseless things.

✦ **Book VIII, Maintaining Windows 10** explains how to restore, refresh, and reset your computer, using tools that Microsoft touts, as well as the ones Windows hides. I also talk about how to use the key built-in Windows programs and tools, including how to keep independent historical file backups, so you'll never lose old data. It's easy.

✦ **Book IX, Securing Windows 10** goes way beyond the usual recommendations about Windows Defender and Firewall. I talk about the biggest security vulnerability on all Windows systems — the person behind the keyboard. And I step you through a couple of real-life takedowns of scammers to show you how to take care of yourself.

✦ **Book X, Enhancing Windows 10** takes you to the outside world. How do you get your iPad to work with your PC? What you can do with an iPhone? Where do Android tablets and phones fit into the picture? This minibook explains all that. You also find out how to use Google Apps, Microsoft's largest (and free!) online app competitor.

See. I told you this is a manual Microsoft wouldn't dare to publish.

Conventions

I try to keep typographical conventions to a minimum:

✦ The first time a buzzword appears in text, I *italicize* it and define it immediately. That makes it easier for you to glance back and reread the definition.

✦ Whenever I want you to type something, I put the letters or words in **bold.** For example: "Type **William Gates** in the Name text box." If you need to press more than one key at a time on the keyboard, I add a plus sign between the keys' names; for example, "Press **Ctrl+Alt+Delete** to initiate a Vulcan Mind Meld."

✦ I set off email addresses in `monospace`. For example, my email address is `woody@AskWoody.com` (true fact). Websites appear as `monospaced` in the printed version of the book and as clickable links in the electronic versions: My website is at `www.AskWoody.com/` (another true fact). Yes, I know that the "www." is rarely required — you can type AskWoody.com into a web browser, or asKwoodY.cOm for that matter, and you'll still get to the same place, but the "www." helps break things up visually and remind those of you reading ink on dead wood that you have to haul out a browser to get the job done.

There's one other convention that I use all the time: I always, absolutely, adamantly include the filename extension — the period and (usually) three or four letters at the end of a filename, such as .docx or .vbs or .exe — when talking about a file. Yeah, I know Windows 10 hides filename extensions by default, but you can and should change that setting. Yeah, I realize that Bill G. himself made the decision to hide the extensions, that Steve B. wouldn't back off, and that Terry M. hasn't had time to right his predecessors' wrongs. (At least, that's the rumor.)

I also know that, years ago, hundreds — probably thousands — of Microsoft employees passed along the ILOVEYOU virus, primarily because they couldn't see the filename extension that would've warned them that the file was a virus. Uh, bad decision, Bill.

Icons

Some of the points in *Windows 10 All-in-One For Dummies* merit your special attention. I set off those points with icons.

When I'm jumping up and down on one foot with an idea so absolutely cool that I can't stand it anymore, I stick a Tip icon in the margin. You can browse any chapter and hit its highest points by jumping from Tip to Tip.

When you see this icon, you get the real story about Windows 10 — not the stuff that the Microsoft marketing droids want you to hear — and my take on the best way to get Windows 10 to work for you. You find the same take on Microsoft, Windows, and more at my eponymous website, www.AskWoody.com/.

You don't need to memorize the information marked with this icon, but you should try to remember that something special is lurking.

Achtung! Cuidado! Thar be tygers here! Anywhere that you see a Warning icon, you can be sure that I've been burnt — badly. Mind your fingers. These are really, really mean suckers.

Okay, so I'm a geek. I admit it. Sure, I love to poke fun at geeks. But I'm a modern, New Age, sensitive guy, in touch with my inner geekiness. Sometimes, I just can't help but let it out, ya know? That's where the Technical Stuff icon comes in. If you get all tied up in knots about techie-type stuff, pass these paragraphs by. (For the record, I managed to write this whole book without telling you that an IPv4 address consists of a unique 32-bit combination of network ID and host ID, expressed as a set of four decimal numbers with each octet separated by periods. See? I can restrain myself sometimes.)

Beyond the Book

You can find additional features of this book online. Visit the web to find these extras:

✦ **Cheat Sheet:** Go to www.dummies.com/cheatsheet/windows10aio to find this book's Cheat Sheet. Here, you can find tips for navigating

Windows 10's Metro (tiled) and desktop interfaces, top tasks for new Windows 10 users, and suggestions on how to customize Windows 10.

✦ **Dummies.com online articles:** Go to `www.dummies.com/extras/ windows10aio` to find the Extras for this book. You'll find articles covering topics ranging from the case against Cortana, to Reading View in Microsoft Edge.

✦ **Updates:** Our technology books sometimes have updates. To check for updates to this book, go to `www.dummies.com/extras/ windows10aio`.

Where to Go from Here

That's about it. It's time for you to crack this book open and have at it.

If you haven't yet told Windows 10 to show you filename extensions, flip to Book VI, Chapter 1. If you haven't yet set up the File History feature, go to Book VIII, Chapter 1. If you're worried about Microsoft keeping a list of all the searches that you conduct *on your own computer,* check out Book II, Chapter 3.

Don't forget to bookmark my website: `www.AskWoody.com/`. It keeps you up to date on all the Windows 10 news you need to know — including notes about this book, the latest Windows bugs and gaffes, patches that are worse than the problems they're supposed to fix, and much more — and you can submit your most pressing questions for free consultation from The Woodmeister himself.

See ya! `woody@AskWoody.com`

Sometimes, it's worth reading the Intro, eh?

Book I

Starting Windows 10

getting started
with

Windows

10

Not sure if you qualify for a free upgrade to Windows 10? See http://www.
dummies.com/extras/windows10aio/upgrade for the latest details.

Contents at a Glance

Chapter 1: Windows 10 4 N00bs

In This Chapter

- ✔ A newbie's quick guide
- ✔ Hardware is hard — and software is hard, too
- ✔ Windows's place in the grand scheme of things
- ✔ Those computer words that all the grade schoolers understand
- ✔ What, exactly, is the web?
- ✔ Buying a Windows 10 computer

Don't sweat it. We all started out as n00bs ("newbies").

If you've never used an earlier version of Windows, you're in luck — you don't have to force your fingers to "forget" so much of what you've learned. Windows 10 is completely different from any Windows that has come before. It's a melding of Windows 7 and Windows 8 and 8.1, tossed into a blender, speed turned up full, poured out on your screen.

If you heard that Windows 8 was a dog, you only heard the printable part of the story. By clumsily forcing a touch-screen approach down the throats of mouse-lovers everywhere, Windows 8 alienated the touch-first people, drove the mousers nuts, and left everybody — aside from a few diehards — screaming in pain.

Windows 10 brings a kinder, gentler approach for the 1.7 billion or so people who have seen the Windows desktop and know a bit about struggling with it. Yes, Win10 will expose you to those tappy phone-style tiles, but they aren't nearly as intrusive, or as scary, as you think.

So you're sitting in front of your computer, and this thing called Windows 10 is staring at you. Except the screen (see Figure 1-1), which Microsoft calls the *lock screen,* doesn't say "Windows," much less "Windows 10." In fact, the screen doesn't say much of anything except the current date and time, with maybe a tiny icon or two that shows you whether your Internet connection is working, how many unopened emails await, or whether you should just take the day off because your holdings in AAPL stock soared again.

You may be tempted to just sit and admire the gorgeous picture, whatever it may be, but if you use your finger or mouse to swipe up from the bottom, or

Figure 1-1: The Windows 10 lock screen. Your picture may differ, but the function stays the same.

4:42
Wednesday, July 1

press any key on an attached keyboard, you see the logon screen, possibly resembling the one in Figure 1-2. If more than one person is set up to use your computer, you see more than one name.

That's the logon screen, but it doesn't say "Logon" or "Welcome to Win10 Land" or "Howdy" or even "Sit down and get to work, Bucko." It has names and pictures only for people who can use the computer. Why do you have to click your name? What if your name isn't there? And why in the %$#@! can't you bypass all this garbage, log on, and get your email?

Good for you. That's the right attitude.

Windows 10 ranks as the most sophisticated computer program ever made. It cost more money to develop and took more people to build than any previous computer program — ever. So why is it so blasted hard to use? Why doesn't it do what you want it to do the first time? For that matter, why do you need it at all?

Someday, I swear, you'll be able to pull a PC out of the box and plug it into the wall, turn it on, and get your email — bang, bang, bang, just like that, in ten seconds flat. In the meantime, those stuck in the early 21st century have to make do with PCs that grow obsolete before you can unpack them, software so ornery that you find yourself arguing with it, and Internet connections that surely involve turtles carrying bits on their backs.

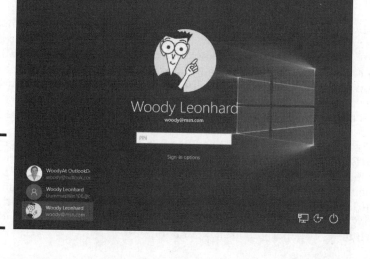

Figure 1-2:
The
Windows
10 logon
screen.

If you aren't comfortable working with Windows and you still worry that you may break something if you click the wrong button, welcome to the club! In this chapter, I present a concise, school-of-hard-knocks overview of how all this hangs together and what to look for when buying a Windows computer. It may help you understand why and how Windows has limitations. It also may help you communicate with the geeky rescue team that tries to bail you out, whether you rely on the store that sold you the PC, the smelly guy in the apartment downstairs, or your 8-year-old daughter's nerdy classmate.

Hardware and Software

At the most fundamental level, all computer stuff comes in one of two flavors: hardware or software. *Hardware* is anything you can touch — a computer screen, a mouse, a hard drive, a DVD drive (remember those coasters with shiny sides?). *Software* is everything else: email messages, that letter to your Aunt Martha, digital pictures of your last vacation, programs like Microsoft Office. If you shoot a bunch of pictures, the pictures themselves are just bits — software. But they're probably sitting on some sort of memory card inside your phone or camera. That card's hardware. Get the difference?

Windows 10 is software. You can't touch it. Your PC, on the other hand, is hardware. Kick the computer screen, and your toe hurts. Drop the big box on the floor, and it smashes into a gazillion pieces. That's hardware.

Chances are very good that one of the major PC manufacturers — Lenovo, HP, Dell, Acer, ASUS, or Toshiba, for example — or maybe even Microsoft, with its Surface line, or even Apple, made your hardware. Microsoft, and Microsoft alone, makes Windows 10.

When you bought your computer, you paid for a license to use one copy of Windows on the PC you bought. The PC manufacturer paid Microsoft a royalty so it could sell you Windows along with your PC. (That royalty may have been, in fact, zero dollars, but it's a royalty nonetheless.) You may think that you got Windows from, say, Dell — indeed, you may have to contact Dell for technical support on Windows questions — but, in fact, Windows came from Microsoft.

Most software these days, including Windows 10, asks you to agree to an End User License Agreement (EULA). When you first set up your PC, Windows asked you to click the I Accept button to accept a licensing agreement that's long enough to wrap around the Empire State Building. If you're curious about what agreement you accepted, a printed copy of the EULA may be in the box that your PC came in or in the CD packaging, if you bought Windows 10 separately from your computer.

Why Do PCs Have to Run Windows?

Here's the short answer: You don't have to run Windows on your PC.

The PC you have is a dumb box. (You needed me to tell you that, eh?) To get the dumb box to do anything worthwhile, you need a computer program that takes control of the PC and makes it do things, such as show web pages on the screen, respond to mouse clicks or taps, or print résumés. An *operating system* controls the dumb box and makes it do worthwhile things, in ways that mere humans can understand.

Without an operating system, the computer can sit in a corner and count to itself or put profound messages on the screen, such as `Non-system disk or disk error` or maybe `Insert system disk and press any key when ready`. If you want your computer to do more than that, though, you need an operating system.

Windows is not the only operating system in town. The other big contenders in the PC and PC-like operating system game are Chrome OS, Mac OS, and Linux:

✦ **Chrome OS:** Cheap Chromebooks have long dominated the best-seller lists at many computer retailers, and for good reason. If you want to surf the web, work on email, compose simple documents, or do anything in a browser — which covers a whole lot of ground these days — Chrome OS is all you need. Chromebooks, which by definition run Google's Chrome OS, can't run Windows programs such as Office or Photoshop. That said, they don't get infected and have very few maintenance problems. You can't say the same about Windows: That's why you need a thousand-page book to keep Windows going. Yes, you do need a reliable Internet connection to get the most out of Chrome OS. But some parts of Chrome OS and Google's apps, including Gmail, can work even if you don't have an active Internet connection.

Chrome OS, built on Linux, looks and feels much like the Google Chrome web browser. There are a few minor differences, but in general you feel like you're working in the Chrome browser.

For friends and family who don't have big-time computer needs, I find myself recommending a Chromebook more often than not. It's easier for them, and it's easier for me to support.

✦ **Mac OS:** Apple has made great strides running on Intel hardware, and if you don't already know how to use Windows or own a Windows computer, it makes a great deal of sense to consider buying an Apple computer and/or running Mac OS. Yes, you can build your own computer and run the Mac OS on it: Check out www.hackintosh.com. But, no, it isn't legal — the Mac OS End User License Agreement specifically forbids installation on a "non-Apple-branded computer" — and it's certainly not for the faint of heart.

That said, if you buy a Mac — say, a MacBook Air or Pro — it's very easy to run Windows 10 on it. Some people feel that the highest quality Windows environment today comes from running Windows on a MacBook, and for years I've run Windows on my MacBook Pro and Air. All you need is a program called BootCamp, and that's already installed, free, on the MacBook. See *Switching to Mac For Dummies* by Arnold Reinhold for details.

✦ **Linux:** The big up-and-coming operating system, which has been up and coming for a couple of decades now, is Linux, which is pronounced *LIN-uchs*. It's a viable contender for netbooks (covered in more depth at the end of this chapter). If you expect to use your PC only to get on the Internet — to surf the web and send email from the likes of your Gmail or Hotmail account — Linux can handle all that, with few of the headaches that remain as the hallmark of Windows. By using free programs like Libre Office (www.libreoffice.org) and online programs like Google Apps and Google Drive (www.drive.google.com), you can even cover the basics in word processing, spreadsheets, presentations, contact managers, calendars, and more. Linux may not support the huge array of hardware that Windows offers — but more than a few wags will tell you, with a wink, that Windows doesn't support that huge of an array, either.

In the tablet sphere, iOS and Android rule, with iOS for iPhones and iPads — all from Apple — and Android for phones and tablets from a bewildering number of manufacturers. Windows 10 doesn't exactly compete with any of them, although Microsoft tried to take on iPad with the now-defunct Windows RT (see the sidebar "Windows RT, RIP").

Windows RT, RIP

Back in the early days of Windows 8, Microsoft developed a different branch of Windows that was christened "Windows RT." New Windows RT computers at the time were generally small, light, and inexpensive, and had a long battery life and touch-sensitive displays.

Several manufacturers made Windows RT machines, but in the end the only company that sold more than a dumpster full of them was Microsoft. Microsoft's original Surface (later renamed Surface RT) and Surface 2 ran Windows RT — and even they didn't sell worth beans.

The fundamental flaw with Windows RT? It wasn't Windows. You couldn't (and can't) run Windows programs on it. But try explaining that to a garden-variety customer. Microsoft really blew it when they gave the new, odd operating system the name "Windows RT."

Microsoft has essentially orphaned Windows RT. If you own a Windows RT device (most likely a Microsoft Surface or Surface 2), the folks in Redmond promise that they'll issue a patch — at some point in the undefined future — that will add a few of the Windows 10 features to Windows RT.

I wouldn't hold my breath. Even though Windows RT owners, by and large, were Microsoft early adopters and many were Microsoft fans, they chose the wrong platform, and they're going to suffer for it.

There's yet another branch of Windows, which is geared toward phones and tablets, especially 8-inch and smaller tablets. I call it Windows 10 Mobile. Windows 10 Mobile (see the sidebar) owes its pedigree to Windows Phone 8 and Windows RT. At least conceptually (and, in fact, under the hood in no small part), Microsoft has grown Windows Phone "up" and Windows RT "down" to meet somewhere in the middle.

Windows 10 Mobile

Generally, devices with screens smaller than 8 inches run the other kind of Windows, known (at least unofficially) as Windows 10 Mobile. Yes, there are devices larger than 8 inches that run Windows 10 Mobile and devices 7 inches and smaller with the "real" Windows 10. The general argument goes like this: If you don't need to use the traditional Windows 7-style desktop, why pay for it? Windows 10 centers around the mouse-friendly desktop. Windows 10 Mobile sticks to the tiled world, and it's much more finger-friendly.

Believe me, running the Windows desktop on a 7-inch tablet takes a tiny stylus, or a pencil sharpener for your fingertips.

This book talks about Windows 10. Although some of the topics also apply to Windows 10 Mobile, there's quite a bit of difference. At least, for now.

While some of the nostrums in this tome apply to Windows 10 Mobile, most do not. The mobile layout's different, the approach is different, the way you interact with things is different, and most of the details are different. There is, however, some overlap in the "Universal" apps that can run on both Windows 10 and Windows 10 Mobile, and the tiles in many cases look the same.

What do other people choose? It's hard to measure the percentage of PCs running Windows versus Mac versus Linux. One company, Net Applications, specializes in inspecting the online records of big-name websites and tallying how many Windows computers hit those sites, compared to Apple and Linux.

I hesitate to mention Net Applications (www.netapplications.com), because there's a great deal of controversy surrounding its sampling and error correction methods, but it's still (arguably) the best source of information on operating system penetration.

If you only look at desktop operating systems — Windows (on desktops, laptops, 2-in-1s) and Mac OS X and Linux — the numbers in early 2015 broke as shown in Figure 1-3.

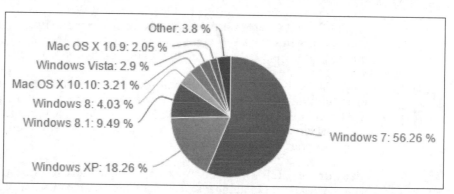

Figure 1-3: Web access by desktop operating system, second quarter 2015, worldwide.

Other: 3.8 %
Mac OS X 10.9: 2.05 %
Windows Vista: 2.9 %
Mac OS X 10.10: 3.21 %
Windows 8: 4.03 %
Windows 8.1: 9.49 %
Windows XP: 18.26 %
Windows 7: 56.26 %

Source: Net Applications

Yes, you read the graph correctly: as of early 2015, before Windows 10 was released, Windows 8 had a piddling market share. The winner, not unexpectedly, is Windows 7, but Windows XP continued with a strong showing, even after Microsoft stopped supporting it. Part of the reason: The market has shifted. Starting in late 2011, more PCs are sold in China than in the United States, and piracy remains a way of life in Asia.

If you look at tablet and mobile devices, the numbers change completely. Worldwide, in early 2015, iOS (iPad, iPhone, iPod) accounted for 42 percent of all tablet and mobile web hits, per Net Applications; Android picks up 37 percent and Java ME (mostly older phones) 5 percent. All the rest — BlackBerry, Windows, Symbian, Kindle — wallow in chump change.

A Terminology Survival Kit

Some terms pop up so frequently that you'll find it worthwhile to memorize them, or at least understand where they come from. That way, you won't be caught flat-footed when your first-grader comes home and asks whether he can download a program from the Internet.

If you want to drive your techie friends nuts the next time you have a problem with your computer, tell them that the hassles occur when you're "running Microsoft." They won't have any idea whether you mean Windows, Word, Outlook, Hotmail, Messenger, Search, Defender, or any of a gazillion other programs — and they won't know if you're talking about a Microsoft program on Windows, the Mac, iPad, iPhone, or Android.

An *app* or a *program* is *software* (see the earlier "Hardware and Software" section in this chapter) that works on a computer. "App" is modern and cool; "program" is old and boring, "application" manages to hit both gongs, but they all mean the same thing.

Windows, the *operating system* (see the preceding section), is a program. So are computer games, Microsoft Office, Microsoft Word (the word processor part of Office), Google Chrome (the web browser made by Google), Xbox Video, those nasty viruses you've heard about, that screen saver with the oh-too-perfect fish bubbling and bumbling about, and others.

A special kind of program called a *driver* makes specific pieces of hardware work with the operating system. For example, your computer's printer has a driver, your monitor has a driver, your mouse has a driver, and Tiger Woods has a driver (several, actually, and he makes a living with them). Would that everyone were so talented.

Many drivers ship with Windows, even though Microsoft doesn't make them. The hardware manufacturer's responsible for making its hardware work with your Windows PC, and that includes building and fixing the drivers. (Yes, if Microsoft makes your computer, Microsoft's responsible for the drivers, too.) Sometimes you can get a driver from the manufacturer that works better than the one that ships with Windows.

When you stick an app or program on your computer — and set it up so it works — you *install* the app or program (or driver).

When you crank up a program — that is, get it going on your computer — you can say you *started* it, *launched* it, *ran* it, or *executed* it. They all mean the same thing.

If the program quits the way it's supposed to, you can say it *stopped, finished, ended, exited,* or *terminated.* Again, all these terms mean the same thing. If the program stops with some sort of weird error message, you can say it *crashed, died, cratered, croaked, went belly up, jumped in the bit bucket,* or *GPFed* (techspeak for "generated a General Protection Fault" — don't ask), or employ any of a dozen colorful but unprintable epithets. If the program just sits there and you can't get it to do anything, no matter how you click your mouse or poke the screen, you can say the program *froze, hung, stopped responding,* or *went into a loop.*

A *bug* is something that doesn't work right. (A bug is not a virus! Viruses work as intended far too often.) U.S. Navy Rear Admiral Grace Hopper — the intellectual guiding force behind the COBOL programming language and one of the pioneers in the history of computing — often repeated the story of a moth being found in a relay of an ancient Mark II computer. The moth was taped into the technician's logbook on September 9, 1947. (See Figure 1-4.)

Figure 1-4: Admiral Grace Hopper's log of the "first actual case of bug being found."

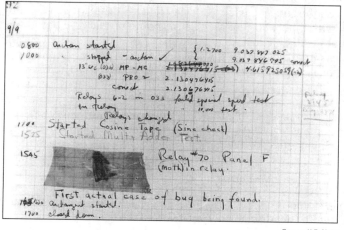

Source: U.S. Navy

The people who invented all this terminology think of the Internet as being some great blob in the sky — it's *up,* as in "up in the sky." So if you send something from your computer to the Internet, you're *uploading.* If you take something off the Internet and put it on your computer, you're *downloading.*

The *cloud* is just a marketing term for the Internet. Saying that you put your data "in the cloud" sounds so much cooler than saying you copied it to storage on the Internet. Programs can run in the cloud — which is to say, they run on the Internet. Just about everything that has anything to do with computers can now be done in the cloud. Just watch your pocketbook.

When you put computers together, you *network* them, and if your network doesn't use wires, it's commonly called a *Wi-Fi network.* At the heart of a network sits a box, commonly called a *hub,* or a *router,* that computers can plug in to. If the hub has rabbit ears on top for wireless connections, it's usually called a *Wi-Fi router.* (Some Wi-Fi routers may not have antennae outside.) Yes, there are fine lines of distinction among all these terms. No, you don't need to worry about them.

There are two basic ways to hook up to the Internet: *wired* and *wireless.* Wired is easy: You plug it into a router or some other box that connects to the internet. Wireless falls into two categories: Wi-Fi connections, as you'll find in many homes, coffee shops, airports, and some exceptionally enlightened cities' common areas; and cellular (mobile phone–style) wireless connections.

Cellular Wireless Internet connections are usually identified with one of the "G" levels: 2G, 3G, 4G, or maybe even 5G.

Truth be told, all the "G" nomenclature has turned into marketing malarkey. One vendor will call something 3G, whereas another calls it 4G. A vendor may call the same service 4G today and 3G tomorrow. Yes, they can get away with that. The general rule of thumb is that 4G should be faster than 3G, but in specific instances, that may not be true. When shopping for a wireless Internet service, look for reliability, speed, and price. Nothing else matters — in particular, 4G isn't necessarily better than 3G.

This part gets a little tricky. If your phone can connect to a 3G or 4G network, it may be possible to set your phone up to behave like a Wi-Fi router: Your computer talks to the phone, the phone talks to the Internet over its 3G or 4G connection. That's called *tethering* — your laptop is tethered to your phone. Not all phones can tether, and not all phone companies allow it.

Special boxes called *Mobile Hotspot* units work much the same way: The Mobile Hotspot connects to the 3G or 4G connection, and your laptop gets tethered to the Mobile Hotspot box.

If you plug your Internet connection into the wall, you have *broadband,* which may run via *fiber* (a cable that uses light waves), *DSL* or *ADSL* (which uses regular old phone lines), *cable* (as in cable TV), or *satellite.* The fiber, DSL, cable, or satellite box is commonly called a *modem,* although it's really a *router.* Although fiber optic lines are inherently much faster than DSL or cable, individual results can be all over the lot. Ask your neighbors what they're using and then pick the best. If you don't like your current service, vote with your wallet.

Turning to the dark side of the force, Luke, the distinctions among *viruses, worms,* and *Trojans* grow blurrier every day. In general, they're programs that replicate and can be harmful, and the worst ones blend different approaches. *Spyware* gathers information about you and then phones home with all the juicy details. *Adware* gets in your face, all too frequently installing itself on your computer without your knowledge or consent. I tend to lump the two together and call them *scumware* or *crapware* or something a bit more descriptive and less printable.

If a bad guy (and they're almost always guys) manages to take over your computer without your knowledge, turning it into a zombie that spews spam by remote control, you're in a *botnet*. (And yes, the term *spam* comes from the immortal *Monty Python* routine that's set in a café serving Hormel's SPAM luncheon meat, the chorus bellowing "lovely Spam, wonderful Spam.") Check out Book IX for details about preventing scumware and the like from messing with you.

The most successful botnets employ *rootkits* — programs that run "underneath" Windows, evading detection because normal programs can't see them. The number of Windows 10 computers running rootkits is probably two or three or four orders of magnitudes less than the number of zombified XP computers. But as long as Windows XP computers are out there, botnets will continue to be a major threat to everyone.

 This section covers about 90 percent of the buzzwords you hear in common parlance. If you get stuck at a party where the bafflegab is flowing freely, don't hesitate to invent your own words. Nobody will ever know the difference.

What, Exactly, Is the Web?

Five years from now (although it may take ten), the operating system you use will be largely irrelevant, as will be the speed of your computer, the amount of memory you have, and the number of terabytes of storage that hum in the background. Microsoft will keep milking its cash cow, but the industry will move on. Individuals and businesses will stop shelling out big bucks for Windows and the iron to run it. Instead, the major push will be online. Rather than spend money on PCs that become obsolete the week after you purchase them, folks will spend money on big data pipes: It'll be less about me and more about us. Why? Because so much more is "out there" than "in here." Count on it.

But what is the Internet? This section answers this burning question (if you've asked it). If you don't necessarily wonder about the Internet's place in space and time just yet, you will . . . you will.

 You know those stories about computer jocks who come up with great ideas, develop the ideas in their basements (or garages or dorm rooms), release their products to the public, change the world, and make a gazillion bucks?

This isn't one of them.

The Internet started in the mid-1960s as an academic exercise — primarily with the RAND Corporation, the Massachusetts Institute of Technology (MIT), and the National Physical Laboratory in England — and rapidly evolved into a military project, under the U.S. Department of Defense Advanced Research Project Agency (ARPA), designed to connect research groups working on ARPA projects.

By the end of the 1960s, ARPA had four computers hooked together — at UCLA, SRI (Stanford), UC Santa Barbara, and the University of Utah — using systems developed by BBN Technologies (then named Bolt Beranek and Newman, Inc.). By 1971, it had 18. I started using ARPANET in 1975. According to the website www.internetworldstats.com, by the end of June 2014, the Internet had more than 3 billion users worldwide.

Today, so many computers are connected directly to the Internet that the Internet's addressing system is running out of numbers, just as your local phone company is running out of telephone numbers. The current numbering system — named *IPv4* — can handle about 4 billion addresses. The next version, named *IPv6,* can handle this number of addresses:

340,000,000,000,000,000,000,000,000,000,000,000,000

That should last for a while, don'tcha think?

Ever wonder why you rarely see hard statistics about the Internet? I've found two big reasons:

- ✦ Defining terms related to the Internet is devilishly difficult these days. (What do you mean when you say "*X* number of computers are connected to the Internet"? Is that the number of computers up and running at any given moment? The number of different addresses that are active? The number that could be connected if everybody dialed up at the same time? The number of different computers that are connected in a typical day, or week, or month?)

- ✦ The other reason is that the Internet is growing so fast that any number you publish today will be meaningless tomorrow.

Getting inside the Internet

Some observers claim that the Internet works so well because it was designed to survive a nuclear attack. Not so. The people who built the Internet insist that they weren't nearly as concerned about nukes as they were about making communication among researchers reliable, even when a backhoe severed an underground phone line or one of the key computers ground to a halt.

As far as I'm concerned, the Internet works so well because the engineers who laid the groundwork were utter geniuses. Their original ideas from 50 years ago have been through the wringer a few times, but they're still pretty much intact. Here's what the engineers decided:

✦ **No single computer should be in charge.** All the big computers connected directly to the Internet are equal (although, admittedly, some are more equal than others). By and large, computers on the Internet move data around like kids playing hot potato — catch it, figure out where you're going to throw it, and let it fly quickly. They don't need to check with some übercomputer before doing their work; they just catch, look, and throw.

✦ **Break the data into fixed-size packets.** No matter how much data you're moving — an email message that just says "Hi" or a full-color, life-size photograph of the Andromeda galaxy — the data is broken into packets. Each packet is routed to the appropriate computer. The receiving computer assembles all the packets and notifies the sending computer that everything came through okay.

✦ **Deliver each packet quickly.** If you want to send data from Computer A to Computer B, break the data into packets and route each packet to Computer B by using the fastest connection possible — even if that means some packets go through Bangor and others go through Bangkok.

Taken together, those three rules ensure that the Internet can take a lickin' and keep on tickin'. If a chipmunk eats through a telephone line, any big computer that's using the gnawed line can start rerouting packets over a different telephone line. If the Cumbersome Computer Company in Cupertino, California, loses power, computers that were sending packets through Cumbersome can switch to other connected computers. It usually works quickly and reliably, although the techniques used internally by the Internet computers get a bit hairy at times.

Big computers are hooked together by high-speed communication lines: the *Internet backbone.* If you want to use the Internet from your business or your house, you have to connect to one of the big computers first. Companies that own the big computers — Internet service providers (ISPs) — get to charge you for the privilege of getting on the Internet through their big computers. The ISPs, in turn, pay the companies that own the cables (and satellites) that comprise the Internet backbone for a slice of the backbone.

If all this sounds like a big-fish-eats-smaller-fish-eats-smaller-fish arrangement, that's quite a good analogy.

It's backbone-breaking work, but somebody's gotta do it.

What is the World Wide Web?

People tend to confuse the World Wide Web with the Internet, which is much like confusing the dessert table with the buffet line. I'd be the first to admit that desserts are mighty darn important — life-critical, in fact, if the truth be told. But they aren't the same as the buffet line.

To get to the dessert table, you have to stand in the buffet line. To get to the web, you have to be running on the Internet. Make sense?

The World Wide Web owes its existence to Tim Berners-Lee and a few co-conspirators at a research institute named CERN in Geneva, Switzerland. In 1990, Berners-Lee demonstrated a way to store and link information on the Internet so that all you had to do was click to jump from one place — one web page — to another. Nowadays, nobody in his right mind can give a definitive count of the number of pages available, but Google has indexed more than 50 billion of them. By some estimates, there are trillions of individual web pages.

Like the Internet itself, the World Wide Web owes much of its success to the brilliance of the people who brought it to life. The following list describes the ground rules:

✦ Web pages, stored on the Internet, are identified by an address, such as `www.dummies.com`. The main part of the web page address — `dummies.com`, for example — is a *domain name*. With rare exceptions, you can open a web page by simply typing its domain name and pressing Enter. Spelling counts, and underscores (_) are treated differently from hyphens (-). Being close isn't good enough — there are just too many websites. As of this writing, DomainTools (`www.domaintools.com`) reports that about 140 million domain names end in `.com`, `.net`, `.org`, `.info`, `.biz`, or `.us`. That's just for the United States. Other countries have different naming conventions: `.co.uk`, for example, is the U.K. equivalent of `.com`.

✦ Web pages are written in the funny language HyperText Markup Language (HTML). HTML is sort of a programming language, sort of a formatting language, and sort of a floor wax, all rolled into one. Many products claim to make it easy for novices to create powerful, efficient HTML. Some of those products are getting close.

✦ To read a web page, you have to use a web browser. A *web browser* is a program that runs on your computer and is responsible for converting HTML into text that you can read and use. The majority of people who view web pages still use Internet Explorer as their web browser, but Microsoft has a new web browser called Microsoft Edge. Edge ships with Windows 10. IE is still inside Windows 10, but you have to dig deep to find it (hint: Click Start, All Apps, Windows Accessories). For almost all people, almost all the time, Edge works better than Internet Explorer: It's much more secure, faster, and not as dependent on things that can go bump in the night.

More and more people (including me!) prefer Firefox (see `www.mozilla.org`) and/or Chrome, from Google (`www.chrome.google.com`). You may not know that Firefox and Chrome can run right alongside Internet Explorer and Edge, with absolutely no confusion between the two. Er, four. In fact, they don't even interact — Edge, Firefox, and Chrome were designed to operate completely independently, and they do very well playing all by themselves.

One unwritten rule for the World Wide Web: All web acronyms must be completely, utterly inscrutable. For example, a web address is a *Uniform Resource Locator,* or *URL.* (The techies I know pronounce URL "earl." Those who don't wear white lab coats tend to say "you are ell.") I describe the HTML acronym in the preceding list. On the web, a gorgeous, sunny, palm-lined beach with the scent of frangipani wafting through the air would no doubt be called SHS — Smelly Hot Sand. Sheeesh.

The best part of the web is how easily you can jump from one place to another — and how easily you can create web pages with *hot links* (also called *hyperlinks* or just *links)* that transport the viewer wherever the author intends. That's the *H* in HTML and the original reason for creating the web so many years ago.

Who pays for all this stuff?

That's the 64-billion-dollar question, isn't it? The Internet is one of the true bargains of the 21st century. When you're online — for which you probably have to pay EarthLink, Comcast, Verizon, NetZero, Juno, Netscape, Qwest, some other cable company, or another ISP a monthly fee — the Internet itself is free.

Edge and Internet Explorer are free, sorta, because they come with Windows 10, no matter which version you buy. Firefox is free as a breeze — in fact, it's the poster child for open-source programs: Everything about the program, even the program code itself, is free. Google Chrome is free, too. Both Microsoft, with IE and Edge, and Google, with Chrome, keep tabs on where you go and what you do online — all the better to convince you to click an ad. Firefox, on the other hand, doesn't play that game.

Most websites don't charge a cent. They pay for themselves in any of these ways:

✦ **Reduce a company's operating costs:** Banks and brokerage firms, for example, have websites that routinely handle customer inquiries at a fraction of the cost of H2H (er, human-to-human) interactions.

✦ **Increase a company's visibility:** The website gives you a good excuse to buy more of the company's products. That's why architectural firms show you pictures of their buildings and food companies post recipes.

✦ **Draw in new business:** Ask any real estate agent.

✦ **Contract advertising:** Google has made a fortune. A thousand thousand fortunes.

✦ **Use bounty advertising:** Smaller sites run ads, most commonly from Google, but in some cases, selected from a pool of advertisers. The advertiser pays a bounty for each person who clicks the ad and views its website — a *click-through*.

✦ **Use affiliate programs:** Smaller sites may also participate in a retailer's affiliate program. If a customer clicks through and orders something, the website that originated the transaction receives a percentage of the amount ordered. Amazon is well known for its affiliate program, but many others exist.

Some websites have an entrance fee. For example, if you want to read more than a few articles on *The New York Times* website, you have to part with some substantial coin — about $15 per month for the most basic option, the last time I looked. Guess that beats schlepping around a whole lotta paper.

Buying a Windows 10 Computer

Here's how it usually goes: You figure that you need to buy a new PC, so you spend a couple weeks brushing up on the details — bits and bytes and kilobytes and megabytes and gigabytes — and comparison shopping. You end up at your local Computers Are Us shop, and the guy behind the counter convinces you that the absolutely best bargain you'll ever see is sitting right here, right now, and you'd better take it quick before somebody else nabs it.

Your eyes glaze over as you look at yet another spec sheet and try to figure out one last time whether a RAM is a ROM, whether a hybrid drive is worth the effort, and whether you need a SATA 3 Gbps, SATA 6 Gbps, or eSATA. In the end, you figure that the guy behind the counter must know what he's doing, so you plunk down your plastic and pray you got a good deal.

The next Sunday morning, you look in the paper and discover you could've bought twice as much machine for half as much money. The only thing you know for sure is that your PC is hopelessly out of date, and the next time you'll be smarter about the whole process.

If that describes your experiences, relax. It happens to everybody. Take solace in the fact that you bought twice as much machine for the same amount of money as the poor schmuck who went through the same process last month.

Pay more to get a clean PC

I hate it when the computer I want comes loaded with all that nice, "free" crapware. I'd seriously consider paying more to get a clean computer.

You don't need an antivirus and Internet security program preinstalled on your new PC. It'll just open and beg for money next month. Windows 10 comes with Windows Defender, and it works great — for free.

Browser toolbars? Puh-lease.

You can choose your own Internet service provider. AOL? EarthLink? Who needs ya?

And trialware? Whether it's Quicken or any of a zillion other programs, if you have to pay for a preinstalled program in three months or six months, you don't want it.

If you're looking for a new computer but can't find an option to buy a PC without all the "extras," look elsewhere. The big PC companies are slowly getting a clue, but until they clean up their act, you may be better served buying from a smaller retailer, who hasn't yet pre-sold every bit that isn't nailed down. Or you can buy direct from Microsoft: Its Surface tablets are as clean as the driven snow. Pricey, perhaps. But blissfully clean.

Microsoft Stores, both online and the physical kind, sell new, clean computers from major manufacturers as part of Microsoft's "Signature PC" program. If you pay more, you get a dreck-free computer.

Here's everything you need to know about buying a Windows 10 PC:

✦ **Decide if you're going to use a touch screen.** If you know that you won't be using the tiled part of Windows very much, a touch screen won't hurt, but it probably isn't worth the additional expense. Experienced, mouse-savvy Windows users often find that using a mouse and a touch screen at the same time is an ergonomic pain in the ar . . . m.

Unless you have fingertips the size of pinheads — or you always use a stylus — using some programs on a touch screen is an excruciating experience. Best to leave the touching to programs that are demonstrably touch-friendly.

✦ **If you're going to use the old-fashioned, Windows 7-style desktop, get a high-quality monitor, a solid keyboard, and a mouse that feels comfortable.** Corollary: Don't buy a computer online unless you know for a fact that your fingers will like the keyboard, your wrist will tolerate the mouse, and your eyes will fall in love with the monitor.

✦ **Get a screen that's at least 1366x768 pixels — the minimum size to support all of Windows's features.** Although a touch-sensitive screen isn't a prerequisite for using tiled "Universal" apps on Windows 10, believe me, you'll find it much, much easier to use tiled apps with your fingers than with your mouse. Swiping with a finger is easy; swiping with a mouse is a disaster.

There's no substitute for physically trying the hardware on a touch-sensitive Windows 10 computer. Hands come in all shapes and sizes, and fingers, too. What works for size XXL hands with ten thumbs (present company included) may not cut the mustard for svelte hands and fingers experienced at taking cotton balls out of medicine bottles.

See the section "Inside a touch-sensitive tablet" later in this chapter.

✦ **Go overboard with hard drives.** In the best of all possible worlds, get a computer with a Solid State Drive (SSD) for the system drive (the `C:` drive) plus a large hard drive for storage, perhaps attached via a USB cable. For the low-down on SSDs, hard drives, backups, and putting them all together, see the upcoming section "Managing disks and drives."

How much hard drive space do you need? How long is a string? Unless you have an enormous collection of videos, movies, or songs, 1TB (=1,024GB = 1,048,576MB = 1,073,741,824KB = 1,099,511,627,776 bytes, or characters of storage) should suffice. That's big enough to handle about 1,000 broadcast-quality movies. Consider that the printed collection of the U.S. Library of Congress runs about 10TB.

If you're getting a laptop or Ultrabook with an SSD drive, consider buying an external 1TB or larger drive at the same time. You'll use it.

Or you can just stick all that extra data in the cloud, with OneDrive, Dropbox, Google Drive or some competitor. See Book VI Chapter 2 to get started. For what it's worth, I used Dropbox in every phase of writing this book.

✦ **Everything else they try to sell ya pales in comparison.**

If you want to spend more money, go for a faster Internet connection and a better chair. You need both items much more than you need a marginally faster, or bigger, computer.

Inside the big box

In this section, I give you just enough information about the inner workings of a desktop or laptop PC that you can figure out what you have to do with Windows. In the next section, I talk about touch-enabled tablets, the PCs that respond to touch. Details can change from week to week, but these are the basics.

The big box that your desktop computer lives in is sometimes called a *CPU,* or *central processing unit* (see Figure 1-5). Right off the bat, you're bound to get confused, unless somebody clues you in on one important detail: The main computer chip inside that big box is also called a CPU. I prefer to call the big box "the PC" because of the naming ambiguity, but you've probably thought of a few better names.

Monitor   The "CPU"

Figure 1-5:
The
enduring,
traditional
big box.

Keyboard   Mouse

Courtesy of Dell Inc.

The big box contains many parts and pieces (and no small amount of dust and dirt), but the crucial, central element inside every PC is the mother-board. (You can see a picture of a motherboard here: www.asus.com/ Motherboards/SABERTOOTH_X79/gallery/).

You find the following items attached to the motherboard:

✦ **The processor, or CPU:** This gizmo does the main computing. It's prob-ably from Intel or AMD. Different manufacturers rate their CPUs in differ-ent ways, and it's impossible to compare performance by just looking at the part number. Yes, i7 CPUs usually run faster than i5s, and i3s are the slowest of the three, but there are many nuances. Unless you tackle very intensive video games, build your own audio or video files, or recalcu-late spreadsheets with the national debt, the CPU doesn't really count for much. In particular, if you're streaming audio and video (say, with YouTube or Netflix) you don't need a fancy processor. If in doubt, check out the reviews at www.tomshardware.com and www.anandtech.com.

✦ **Memory chips and places to put them:** Memory is measured in mega-bytes (1MB = 1,024KB = 1,048,576 characters) and gigabytes (1GB = 1,024MB). Although Windows 10 can run on a machine with 512MB (I've done it), Microsoft recommends a minimum of 1GB. Unless you have an exciting cornfield to watch grow while Windows 10 saunters along, aim for 2GB or more. Most computers allow you to add more memory to them, and boosting your computer's memory to 2GB from 1GB makes the machine much snappier, especially if you run memory hogs such as Office, InDesign, or Photoshop. If you leave Outlook open and work with it all day and run almost any other major program at the same time, 4GB isn't overkill. Toss Google Chrome into the mix and 8GB sounds good.

✦ **Video chipset:** Most motherboards include remarkably good built-in video. If you want more video oomph, you have to buy a video card and put it in a card slot. Advanced motherboards have multiple PCI card slots, to allow you to strap together two video cards and speed up video even more. For more information, see the "Screening" section in this chapter.

✦ **Card slots (also known as expansion slots):** Laptops have very limited (if any) expansion slots on the motherboard. Desktops generally contain several expansion slots. Modern slots come in two flavors: PCI and PCI-Express (also known as PCIe or PCI-E). Most expansion cards use PCI, but very fast cards — including, notably, video cards — require PCIe. Of course, PCI cards don't fit in PCIe slots, and vice versa. To make things more confusing, PCIe comes in four sizes — literally, the size of the bracket and the number of bumps on the bottoms of the cards is different. The PCIe 1x is smallest, the relatively uncommon PCIe 4x is considerably larger, and PCIe 8x is a bit bigger still. PCIe 16x is just a little bit bigger than an old-fashioned PCI slot. Most video cards these days require a PCIe 16x slot. Or two.

If you're buying a monitor separately from the rest of the system, make sure the monitor takes video input in a form that your PC can produce. See the upcoming section "Screening" for details.

✦ **USB (Universal Serial Bus) connections:** The USB cable has a flat connector that plugs in to your slots. USB 3 is considerably faster than USB 2, and any kind of USB device can plug in to a USB 3 slot. Make sure you get plenty of USB slots — at least two, preferably four, or more. More details are in the section "Managing disks and drives" later in this chapter.

✦ **Lots of other stuff:** You never have to play with this other stuff, unless you're very unlucky.

Here are a few upgrade dos and don'ts:

✦ **Don't** let a salesperson talk you into eviscerating your PC and upgrading the CPU: i7 isn't that much faster than i5; a 3.0-GHz PC doesn't run a whole lot faster than a 2.4-GHz PC, and a dual-quad-core ChipDuoTrioQuattroQuinto stuck in an old motherboard doesn't run much faster than your original slowpoke.

✦ When you hit 4GB in main memory, **don't** expect big performance improvements by adding more memory, unless you're running Chrome all day with 25 open tabs, or putting together videos.

✦ On the other hand, if you have an older video card, **do** consider upgrading it to a faster card, or to one with 512MB or more of on-board memory. They're cheap. Windows 10 takes good advantage of it.

✦ Rather than nickel-and-dime yourself to death on little upgrades, **do** wait until you can afford a new PC, and give away your old one.

If you decide to add memory, have the company that sells you the memory install it. The process is simple, quick, and easy — if you know what you're doing. Having the dealer install the memory also puts the monkey on his back if a memory chip doesn't work or a bracket snaps.

Inside a touch-sensitive tablet

Although touch-sensitive tablets have been on the market for more than a decade, they didn't really take off until Apple introduced the iPad in 2010. Since the iPad went ballistic, every Windows hardware manufacturer has been clamoring to join the game. Even Microsoft has entered the computer-manufacturing fray with its line of innovative tablets known as Surface.

The old Windows tablets generally required a *stylus* (a special kind of pen), and they had very little software that took advantage of touch input. The iPad changed all that.

The result is a real hodge-podge of Windows tablets. It really isn't fair comparing a full-featured Windows 10 tablet to an iPad: They're built for different situations, aimed at different markets. The Win10 tablet can do much more than an iPad, but at quite a price: The iPad wins hands-down in terms of weight, heat, battery life, and price. The screen on an iPad runs rings around most Windows tablets; the camera's better; and on and on. But you can't run Windows applications on an iPad — at least, not without connecting to a Windows computer.

That may be a plus or a minus, depending on where you sit.

I did most of the touch-sensitive work in this book on a Dell Venue 11 Pro 7000 (see Figure 1-6). It's a so-called 2-in-1: The tablet part detaches from the touch-enabled keyboard part. There's also an optional docking station, so you can readily attach a full-size keyboard, mouse, and big screen to your tablet, or just peel your tablet off and carry it.

This Venue 11 Pro has a Broadwell Core-M processor, from Intel, that (finally!) brings tablets into the big leagues. The Broadwell Core-M has enough power to run any Windows program — and it does so without a fan. There's also very little battery drain, and the screen's gorgeous, keyboard feels good, the snapped-together configuration doesn't fall over backward,

Courtesy of Dell Inc.

Figure 1-6:
The Dell
Venue 11
Pro 7000
that I used
to write this
book.

and there's room for extra memory with a MicroSD card on the tablet itself.
Those are all attributes you should seek when buying a Windows 10 tablet.

Of course, that kind of oomph comes at a price. That's the other part — quite
possibly the constraining part — of the equation. If you don't need a 2-in-1,
there are very respectable, traditional Windows 10 laptops (netbooks, whatever you want to call them), with or without touchscreens, that sell for a pittance. I currently find myself infatuated with the pricey touch-screen XPS-15.

That said, if a Chromebook or an iPad or Android tablet will do everything you need to do, there's no reason to plunk down lots of money for a
Windows 10 tablet. None at all.

If you're thinking about buying a Windows 10 tablet, keep these points
in mind:

+ **Make sure you understand the differences between an Intel/AMD
tablet and an ARM tablet.** If you want to use Windows 10 — as opposed
to Windows 10 Mobile — you have to stick with Intel/AMD models (frequently called *x86/x64* or *32-bit/64-bit* tablets). The other kind of tablet,
built on ARM chips (and sometimes, confusingly built on Intel chips), will
run only the mobile version of Windows 10.

  This book specifically covers Windows 10, but not Windows 10 Mobile.

+ **Focus on weight, heat, and battery life.** Touch-sensitive tablets are
meant to be carried, not lugged around like a suitcase, and the last thing
you need is a box so hot it burns a hole in your pants, or a fan so noisy
you can't carry on a conversation.

+ **Make sure you get multi-touch.** Some manufacturers like to skimp and
make tablets that only respond to one or two touch points. You need at
least four, just to run Windows 10, and ten wouldn't hurt. Throw in some
toes and ask for 20, if you want to be ornery about it.

✦ **The screen should run at 1366x768 pixels or better.** Anything smaller will have you squinting to look at the desktop.

✦ **Get a Solid State Drive.** In addition to making the machine much, much faster, SSDs also save on weight, heat, and battery life. Don't be overly concerned about the amount of storage on a tablet. Many people with Win10 tablets end up putting all their data in the cloud with, for example, SkyDrive, Google Drive, Dropbox, or Box. See Book VI, Chapter 2.

✦ **Try before you buy.** The screen has to be sensitive to your big fingers, and look good, too. Not an easy combination.

✦ **Make sure you can return it.** If you have experience with a "real" keyboard and a mouse, you may find that you hate using a tablet to replicate the kinds of things you used to do with a laptop or desktop PC.

As the hardware market matures, you can expect to see many variations on the tablet theme. It ain't all cut and dried.

Screening

The computer monitor or screen — and LED, LCD, and plasma TVs — use technology that's quite different from old-fashioned television circuitry from your childhood. A traditional TV scans lines across the screen from left to right, with hundreds of them stacked on top of each other. Colors on each individual line vary all over the place. The almost infinitely variable color on an old-fashioned TV combined with a comparatively small number of lines makes for pleasant, but fuzzy, pictures.

By contrast (pun absolutely intended, of course), computer monitors, touch-sensitive tablet screens, and plasma, LED, and LCD TVs work with dots of light called *pixels*. Each pixel can have a different color, created by tiny, colored gizmos sitting next to each other. As a result, the picture displayed on computer monitors (and plasma and LCD TVs) is much sharper than on conventional TV tubes.

The more pixels you can cram on a screen — that is, the higher the screen resolution — the more information you can pack on the screen. That's important if you commonly have more than one word-processing document open at a time, for example. At a resolution of 800x600, two open Word documents placed side by side look big but fuzzy, like caterpillars viewed through a dirty magnifying glass. At 1280x1024, those same two documents look sharp, but the text may be so small that you have to squint to read it. If you move up to wide-screen territory — 1920x1080 ("full HD"), or even 2560x1440 — with a good monitor, two documents side-by-side look stunning. Run up to 4K technology, at 3840x2160 or better, and you'll need a magnifying glass to see the pixels.

When Apple introduced its Retina displays, at 2048x1536 pixels on a 9.7-inch diagonal display, they simply blew away any screens we had ever seen for the PC. Now, PC manufacturers are slowly catching up — and Android hardware manufacturers, including Samsung, are out-Retina-ing the iPad. Take a look at an iPad or MacBook Retina display, or one of the Samsung super high-density displays. If you can see an eye-popping difference (most people can), you definitely should choose a Retina-quality PC.

A special-purpose computer called a *graphics processor (GPU)*, stuck on your video card or possibly integrated into the CPU, creates everything that's shown on your computer's screen. The GPU has to juggle all the pixels and all the colors, so if you're a gaming fan, the speed of the GPU's chip (and, to a lesser extent, the speed of the monitor) can make the difference between a zapped alien and a lost energy shield. If you want to experience Windows 10 in all its glory, you need a fast GPU with at least 1GB (and preferably 2GB or more) of its own memory.

Computer monitors and tablets are sold by size, measured diagonally (glass only, not the bezel or frame), like TV sets. Just like with TV sets, the only way to pick a good computer screen over a run-of-the-mill one is to compare them side by side or to follow the recommendation of someone who has.

Managing disks and drives

Your PC's memory chips hold information only temporarily: Turn off the electricity, and the contents of main memory go bye-bye. If you want to reuse your work, keeping it around after the plug has been pulled, you have to save it, typically on a disk, or possibly in the *cloud* (which means you copy it to a location on the Internet).

The following list describes the most common types of disks and drives:

✦ **SD/xD/CF card memory:** Many smaller computers, and some tablets, have built-in SD card readers. (Apple and some Google tablets don't have SD — the companies would rather sell you more on-board memory, at inflated prices!) You probably know Secure Digital (SD) cards best as the kind of memory used in digital cameras, or possibly phones (see Figure 1-7). Micro SD cards slip in to hollowed-out cards that are shaped like, and function as, SD cards.

Even now, long after the demise of floppy disks, many desktop computer cases have drive bays built for them. Why not use the open spot for a multifunction card reader? That way, you can slip a memory card out of your digital camera (or your Dick Tracy wristwatch, for that matter) and transfer files at will. SD card, MicroSD card, xD card, CompactFlash, memory stick — whatever you have — the multifunction readers cost a pittance and read almost everything, including minds.

Figure 1-7:
A 4GB
MicroSD
card slips
into a holder
shaped like
an SD card.

Courtesy of SanDisk

✦ **Hard drive:** The technology's changing rapidly, with traditional hard disk drives (HDDs) now being rapidly replaced by *Solid State Drives* (SSDs) with no moving parts, and to a lesser extent *hybrid drives* that bolt together a rotating drive with an SSD. Each technology has benefits and drawbacks. Yes, you can run a regular HDD drive as your C: drive, and it'll work fine. But SSD-goosed systems, on tablets, laptops, or desktops, run like greased lightning.

The SSD wins as speed king. After you use an SSD as your main "system" (C:) drive, you'll never go back to a spinning platter, I guarantee. SSDs are great for the main drive, but they're awfully expensive for storing pictures, movies, and photos. They may someday supplant the old whirling dervish drive, but price and technical considerations (see the sidebar "Solid State Drives have problems, too") assure that hard drives will be around for a long time. SSDs feature low power consumption and give off less heat. They have no moving parts, so they don't wear out like hard drives. And, if you drop a hard drive and a Solid State Drive off the Leaning Tower of Pisa, one of them may survive. Or maybe not.

Hybrid drives combine the benefits and problems of both HDDs and SSDs. Although HDDs have long had *caches* — chunks of memory that hold data before being written to the drive, and after it's read from the drive — hybrid drives have a full SSD to act as a buffer.

If you can stretch the budget, start with an SSD for the system drive, a big hard drive (one that attaches with a USB cable) for storing photos, movies, and music, and get *another* drive (which can be inside your PC, outside attached with a USB cable, or even on a different PC on your network) to run File History (see Book VIII, Chapter 1).

Solid State Drives have problems, too

Although I love my SSD system drives and would never go back to rotating hard disk drives (HDDs), SSDs aren't perfect.

SSDs don't have any moving parts, and it looks like they're more reliable than HDDs. But when an HDD starts to go belly up, you can usually tell: whirring and gnashing, whining and groaning. Expiring SSDs don't give off any advanced warning signals. Or at least sounds.

When an HDD dies, you can frequently get the data back, although it can be expensive and time-consuming. When an SSD goes, you rarely get a second chance.

SSDs have to take care of lots of internal bookkeeping, both for trimming unused space and for load balancing to guarantee uniform wear patterns. SSDs actually slow down after you've used them for a few weeks, months, or years. The speed decrease is usually associated with the bookkeeping programs kicking in over time.

Finally, the SSD's own software has to be ultra-reliable. SSDs don't lay down tracks sequentially like HDDs. They hopscotch all over the place, and the firmware inside the SSD needs to keep up.

If you want full on-the-fly protection against dying hard drives, you can get three hard drives — one SSD, and two hard drives, either inside the box or outside attached with USB or eSATA cables — and run Storage Spaces (see Book VII, Chapter 4).

Ultimately, though, the industry is headed to a three-tier system, with SSDs storing data you need all the time, intermediate backup in the cloud, and multi-terabyte data repositories hanging off your PC. Privacy concerns (and the, uh, intervention of various governments) have people worried about cloud storage. Rightfully so.

✦ **CD, DVD, or Blu-ray drive:** Of course, these types of drives work with CDs, DVDs, and the Sony Blu-ray discs, which can be filled with data or contain music or movies. CDs hold about 700MB of data; DVDs hold 4GB, or six times as much as a CD. Dual-layer DVDs (which use two separate layers on top of the disc) hold about 8GB, and Blu-ray discs hold 50GB, or six times as much as a dual-layer DVD.

Fewer and fewer machines these days come with built-in DVD drives: if you want to schlep data from one place to another, a USB drive works fine — and going through the cloud is even easier. Still, for long-term, cheap, local storage, DVDs are hard to beat.

Unless you want to stick a high-definition movie on a single disc or play Blu-ray discs that you buy or rent in your local video store, 50GB of data on a single disc is overkill. Most Windows 10 users who still want a DVD will do quite well with a dual-layer DVD-RW drive, for the princely sum of $30 or so. You can always use a dual-layer drive to record regular (single-layer) DVDs or CDs.

✦ **USB drive or key drive:** Treat it like it's a lollipop. Half the size of a pack of gum and able to hold an entire PowerPoint presentation or two or six, plus a half dozen full-length movies, flash memory (also known as a jump drive, thumb drive, or memory stick) should be your first choice for external storage space or for copying files between computers. (See Figure 1-8.) You can even use USB drives on some DVD players and TV set-top boxes.

Figure 1-8:
A (not cheap!) 1TB USB drive.

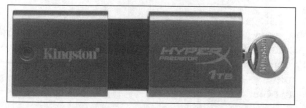

Courtesy of Kingston

Pop one of these guys in a USB slot, and suddenly Windows 10 knows it has another drive — except that this one's fast, portable, and incredibly easy to use. Go for the cheapest flash drives you can find: Most of the "features" on fancy key drives are just, uh, Windows dressing.

What about USB 3? If you have a hard drive that sits outside of your computer — an *external drive* — or a USB key drive, it'll run faster if it's tethered with a USB 3 cable. For most other outside devices, USB 3 is overkill, and USB 2 works just as well.

This list is by no means definitive: New storage options come out every day.

Making PC connections

Your PC connects to the outside world by using a bewildering variety of cables and connectors. I describe the most common in this list:

✦ **USB (Universal Serial Bus) cable:** This cable has a flat connector that plugs in to your PC, known as *USB A* (see Figure 1-9). The other end is sometimes shaped like a D (called *USB B*), but smaller devices have tiny terminators (usually called *USB mini* and *USB micro,* each of which can have two different shapes).

USB 2 connectors will work with any device, but hardware — such as a hard drive — that uses USB 3 will run much faster if you use a USB 3 cable and plug it into the back of your computer in a USB 3 port. USB 2 works with USB 3 devices, but you won't get the speed. Note that not all PCs have USB 3 ports!

Figure 1-9:
The most
common
USB B, Mini,
and Micro
USB cables.

Courtesy of CablesToGo.com

USB is the connector of choice for just about any kind of hardware —
printer, scanner, phone, camera, portable hard drive, and even the mouse.
Apple iPhones and iPads use a USB connector on one side — to plug in to
your computers — but the other side is Apple-only, and doesn't look or
act like any other connector.

If you run out of USB connections on the back of your PC, get a USB hub
with a separate power supply and plug away.

✦ **LAN cable:** Also known as a CAT-5, CAT-6, or RJ-45 cable, it's the most
common kind of network connector. It looks like an overweight telephone
plug (see Figure 1-10). One end plugs in to your PC, typically into a *network interface card* (or *NIC,* pronounced "nick"), a network connector
on the motherboard. The other end plugs in to your network's hub (see
Figure 1-11) or switch or into a cable modem, DSL box, router, or other
Internet connection-sharing device.

Figure 1-10:
CAT-6 LAN
connectors.

Courtesy of CablesToGo.com

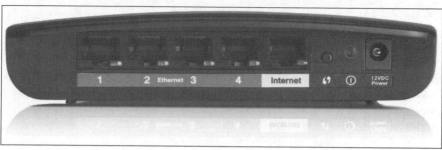

Figure 1-11:
The back
of a Linksys
wireless
router.

Courtesy of Linksys

+ **Keyboard and mouse cable:** Most mice and keyboards (even cordless mice and keyboards) come with USB connectors.

+ **DVI-D and HDMI connectors:** Although older monitors still use legacy, 15-pin, HD15 VGA connectors, most monitors and video cards now use the small HDMI connector (see Figure 1-12), which transmits both audio and video over one cable. Some older monitors don't support HDMI, but do take a DVI-D digital cable (see Figure 1-13).

Figure 1-12:
HDMI has
largely
supplanted
the old
VGA and
DVI-D video
adapters.

Courtesy of CablesToGo.com

If you hope to hook up your new TV to your PC, make sure your PC can connect to the TV with the right kind of cable.

Some really old monitors still use the ancient 15-pin VGA connector, the one shaped like a "D." Avoid VGA if you can. Old-fashioned serial (9-pin) and parallel (25-pin) cables and Centronics printer cables are growing as scarce as hen's teeth. Hey, the hen doesn't need them, either.

+ **Bluetooth** is a short-distance wireless connection. Once upon a time, Bluetooth was very finicky and hard to set up. Since the recent adoption of solid standards, Bluetooth's become quite useful.

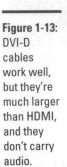

Figure 1-13: DVI-D cables work well, but they're much larger than HDMI, and they don't carry audio.

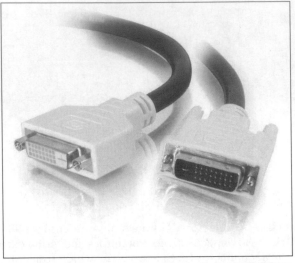

Courtesy of CablesToGo.com

Futzing with video, sound, and multitudinous media

Unless you're using a tablet, chances are pretty good that you're running Windows 10 on a PC with at least a little oomph in the audio department. In the simplest case, you have to be concerned about four specific sound jacks (or groups of sound jacks) because each one does something different. Your machine may not have all four (are you feeling inadequate yet?), or it may look like a patch board at a Foo Fighters concert, but the basics are still the same.

Here's how the four key jacks are usually marked, although sometimes you have to root around in the documentation to find the details:

✦ **Line In:** This stereo input jack is usually blue. It feeds a stereo audio signal — generally from an amplified source — into the PC. Use this jack to receive audio output into your computer from an iPad, cable box, TV set, radio, CD player, electric guitar, or other audio-generating box.

✦ **Mic In:** This jack is usually pink. It's for unamplified sources, like most microphones or some electric guitars. If you use a cheap microphone for Skype or another VoIP service that lets you talk long distance for free, and the mic doesn't have a USB connector, plug in the microphone here. In a pinch, you can plug any of the Line In devices into the Mic In jack — but you may hear only mono sound, not stereo, and you may have to turn the volume way down to avoid some ugly distortion when the amplifier inside your PC increases the strength of an already-amplified signal.

✦ **Line Out:** A stereo output jack, usually lime green, which in many cases can be used for headphones or patched into powered speakers. If you don't have fancy output jacks (like the Sony-Philips SPDIF), this is the source for the highest-quality sound your computer can produce. If you go for a multi-speaker setup, this is for the front speaker.

✦ **Rear Surround Out:** Usually black, this jack isn't used often. It's intended to be used if you have independent, powered rear speakers. Most people with rear speakers use the Line Out connector and plug it into their home theater systems, which then drives the rear speakers; or they use the HDMI cable (see the preceding section) to hook up to their TVs. If your computer can produce full surround sound output, and you have the amplifier to handle it, you'll get much better results using the black jack.

Many desktop computers have two more jacks: Orange is a direct feed for your subwoofer, and the gray (or brown) one is for your side speakers. Again, you have to put an amplifier between the jacks and your speakers.

Fortunately, PC-savvy 4-channel amplifiers can handle the lime (front speaker) and black (rear speaker) lines, 6-channel amps may be able to handle all but the gray, and 8-channel amps will take all four: lime (front speaker), orange (subwoofer, or center back), black (rear), and gray (side).

With a sufficiently bottomless budget, you can make your living room sound precisely like the 08R runway at Honolulu International.

Laptops typically have just two jacks, pink for Mic In and lime for Line Out. If you have a headphone with a mic, that's the right combination. It's also common to plug powered external speakers into the lime jack.

Tablets may or may not have a Line Out jack. If you see a jack — particularly a lime green jack — chances are good you can plug headphones or earbuds into the jack and get decent quality sound.

PC manufacturers love to extol the virtues of their advanced sound systems, but the simple fact is that you can hook up a rather plain-vanilla PC to a home stereo and get good-enough sound. Just connect the Line Out jack on the back of your PC to the Aux In jack on your home stereo or entertainment center. *Voilà!*

Netbooks and Ultrabooks

I really fell in love with an ASUS netbook while working with Windows 7. But then along came the iPad, and at least 80 percent of the reason for using a netbook disappeared. Sales of *netbooks* — small, light, inexpensive laptops — have not fared well, and I don't see a comeback any time soon. Tablets just blow the doors off netbooks.

Ultrabooks are a slightly different story. Intel coined the term *Ultrabook* — actually, trademarked it — and set the specs. In order for a manufacturer to call its piece of iron an Ultrabook, it has to be less than 21mm thick, run for five hours on a battery charge, and resume from hibernation in seven seconds or less. In other words, they need to work much like an iPad.

Intel threw a $300 million marketing budget at Ultrabooks, but to date, they haven't sold well. Times change, though, and with the advent of Windows 10 on Ultrabooks, you may see a turnaround.

At least, that's what Intel hopes.

Right now, I'm having a great time with all the new form factors: I mentioned the Venue 11 Pro 2-in-1 earlier in this chapter. I've also played with the Microsoft Surface Pro machines with their snap-on (and extra cost) keyboards, and they're quite capable. I worked with a trapeze-like machine for a bit, but always worried about snapping the carrier off. There's no one-size-fits-all solution.

If you're in the market for a new machine, drop by your favorite hardware store and just take a look around. You might find something different that strikes your fancy. Or you may decide that you just want to stick with a boring desktop machine with a mechanical keyboard and three monitors the size of football fields.

Guess what I work on.

Chapter 2: Windows 10 for the Experienced

In This Chapter

- ✔ Introducing what's new for Windows XP, Windows Vista, Windows 7, Windows 8, and Windows 8.1 users
- ✔ Checking out the new interfaces
- ✔ Getting to know the new Windows
- ✔ Deciding whether you really need Windows 10

If you're among the 1.7 billion or so souls on the planet who have been around the block with Windows 8/8.1, Windows 7, Windows Vista, or Windows XP, you're in for a shock.

Although Windows 10 will look vaguely familiar to long-time desktop users, the details are very different. And if you've conquered the Metro side of Windows 8.1 (which is the only side of Windows 8), you're going to be in for a pleasant surprise.

A Brief History of Windows 10

Pardon me while I rant for a bit.

Microsoft darn near killed Windows — and most of the PC industry — with the abomination that was Windows 8. Granted, there were other forces at work — the ascendancy of mobile computing, touch screens, faster cheaper and smaller hardware, better Apples, and other competition — but to my mind the number one factor in Windows' demise was Windows 8.

We saw PC sales drop. After Windows XP owners replaced their machines in a big wave in late 2014 and early 2015, responding to the end of support for XP, we saw PC sales drop even more. Precipitously. Steve Ballmer confidently predicted that Microsoft would ship 400 million machines with Windows 8 preinstalled in the year that followed Windows 8's release. The actual number was perhaps half that, and maybe not even half. Normal people like you and me went to great lengths to avoid Windows 8, settling on Windows 7.

Windows 8.1, which arrived a nail-biting year after Windows 8, improved the situation a little bit, primarily by not forcing people to boot to the tiled Metro Start screen, as shown in Figure 2-1.

Figure 2-1: The original, old Windows 8 Metro Start screen — a symbol of abject fear and loathing. What in the world was Microsoft thinking?

The team inside Microsoft that brought us the wonderful forced Windows 8 Metro experience were also responsible, earlier, for the Office ribbon. Many of us old-timers grumbled about the ribbon, saying Microsoft should at least present an alternative for using the older menu interface. It never happened. Office 2007 shipped with an early ribbon, and subsequent versions have been even more ribbon-ified since. Here's the key point: Office 2007 sold like hotcakes, in spite of the ribbon, and it's been selling in the multi-billion-dollar range ever since.

As a result, the Office interface team figured they knew what consumers wanted, and old-timers were just pounding their canes and waggling toothless gums.

The entire Office 2007 management team was transplanted, almost intact, to the Windows 8 effort. They saw an opportunity to transform the Windows interface, and they took it, over the strenuous objections of many of us in the peanut gallery. I'm convinced they figured it would play out like the Office ribbon. It didn't. Windows 8 is, arguably, the largest software disaster in Microsoft's history.

Essentially all the Windows 8 management team — including some very talented and experienced people — left Microsoft shortly after Win8 shipped. With a thud. Their boss, Steve Ballmer, left Microsoft too. Ballmer's still the largest individual shareholder in Microsoft, with 333,000,000 shares at last count, worth $14 billion and change.

In their place, we're seeing an entirely new generation of Windows managers, raised in the cloud, but more than willing to listen to reason. The current head of the Windows effort, Terry Myerson, was in charge of Windows Phone — and before that, Windows Exchange Server. Head honcho Satya Nadella not only knows cloud computing, he invented lots of the Microsoft pieces.

That said, Microsoft's traditional PC market has sunk into a funk, and it appears to be on a slow ride into the sunset. Or it may just turn belly up and sink, anchored with mounds of iPhones, iPads, MacBooks, Galaxy Tabs, and Chromebooks. Or maybe, just maybe, Windows 10 will breathe some life back into the 30-year-old veteran. Yes, Windows 1.0 shipped in November, 1985.

However things play out, at least we have an (admittedly highly modified) Start menu to work with, as you can see in Figure 2-2.

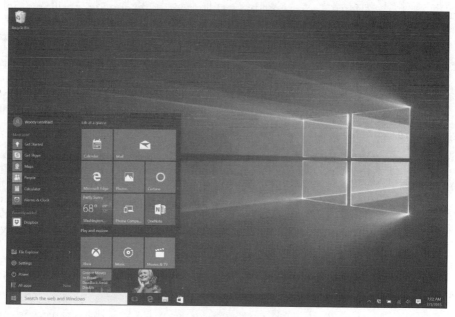

Figure 2-2:
The new
Start menu,
shown on a
Surface
Pro 3, should
look at least
vaguely
familiar to
just about all
experienced
Windows
users.

The Different Kinds of Windows Programs, Er, Apps

Windows 10 runs two very different kinds of programs. Permit me to go back to basics.

Computer programs (call them applications or "apps" if you wish) that you and I know work by interacting with an operating system. Since the dawn of Windows time, give or take a bit, Windows apps have communicated with Windows through a specific set of routines ("Application Program Interfaces" or APIs) known colloquially and collectively as Win32. With rare exceptions, Windows desktop apps — the kind you use every day — take advantage of Win32 APIs to work with Windows.

In early June 2011, at the All Things D D9 conference in California, Steve Sinofsky and Julie Larson-Green gave their first demo of Windows 8. As part of the demo, they showed off new "immersive" or "Metro" apps, which interact with Windows in a very different way. They use the newly minted (and still evolving) API set known as Windows Runtime or, more commonly, the WinRT API.

Microsoft started calling the WinRT based apps "immersive" and "full screen." Most of the world settled on Microsoft's internal code name, "Metro" — a name that's still preferred by me and a zillion other techies. Microsoft, however, has since changed the name to "Modern UI," then "Windows 8," "Windows Store App," "New User Interface," "Microsoft Design Language," "Microsoft style design," and more recently "Modern" and "Universal." The preferred terminology at the moment is "Windows Universal app," although the tech support folks revert to "Windows Store app" and "Universal app" all the time. I continue to use the term "Metro" in normal conversation, but in this book, to minimize confusion, I'll use the term "Windows Universal app."

Don't be confused. (Ha!) They all mean the same thing: Those are the names for Windows Universal applications that run with the WinRT API.

Windows Universal (Modern, Metro) apps have many other characteristics: They're "sandboxed" — stuck inside a software cocoon that isolates the programs so it's hard to spread infections through them. They can be easily interrupted, so their power consumption can be minimized; if a Windows Universal app hangs, it's almost impossible for the app to freeze the machine; and much more. But at their heart, Windows Universal apps are written to use the WinRT API.

Windows 8 and 8.1 (and Server 2012) support the WinRT API — Universal apps run on the "Metro" side of Windows 8, not on the desktop. ARM-based processors also run the WinRT API. You can find ARM architecture processors in many phones and tablets.

In Windows 10, Windows Universal (Modern/Metro/Tiled) apps run in their own boxes, right there on the desktop. Look at the Weather app — a Windows Universal app — shown in Figure 2-3.

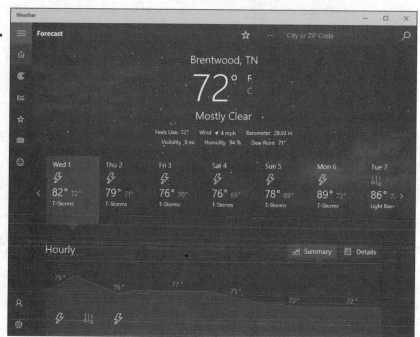

Figure 2-3: The Windows 10 Weather app is a "Windows Universal app" — formerly called a Universal or Metro or tiled app — because it's based on the WinRT API. See the distinctive design?

All the other Windows programs — the ones you've known since you were still wet behind the WinEars — are now called "Windows Desktop apps." Two years ago, you would've just called them "programs," but now they have a new name. After all, if Apple can call its programs "apps," Microsoft can, too. Technically, old-fashioned Windows programs (Windows Desktop apps) are built to use the Win32 API.

Unfortunately, there's a huge difference between Windows Universal apps and Windows Desktop apps. For starters:

✦ **Windows Desktop apps are on the way out.** Microsoft won't abandon them or the Win32 API anytime soon but, with the exception of a few big money-milking programs, and utilities and niche programs from small developers, Windows Desktop apps are starting to be viewed as "legacy" apps, ones ultimately headed to the bone farm.

✦ **Windows Universal apps — the ones that run on the WinRT API — are the future.** Microsoft rebuilt the aging Windows Desktop app Internet Explorer, and turned it into the Windows Universal app called Microsoft Edge. Microsoft is trying hard to replace Windows Desktop app versions of Office with snappier, analogous (and finger-friendly) Windows Universal apps. Of course, the Universal version of Office doesn't have anywhere near as many features as the Desktop version.

✦ **Windows Desktop apps and Windows Universal apps are starting to look the same.** Developers want you to look at their programs and think, "Oh, hey, this is a snappy new version."

✦ **Windows Universal apps really are better.** Don't shoot me. I'm just the messenger. Now that we can run those newfangled tiled Universal Metro whoozamajiggers in their own resizable windows on the Windows desktop, the underlying new WinRT plumbing beats the pants off Win32. WinRT apps don't bump into each other as much, they (generally) play nice in their own sandboxes, they won't take Windows down with them, and they don't have all the overhead of those buggy Win32 calls.

If you're going to stay with Windows, it's time to get with the system and learn about this new tiled stuff.

How did everyone get into this nice mess, Stan?

Microsoft's been making tablet software for more than 10 years, and it never put a dent in the market. Never did "get it." Apple started selling tablet software in 2010, and selling tons of it. Boy howdy. Now Microsoft's diving in to get a piece of the touch-enabled action.

There's a big difference in approaches. Apple started with a telephone operating system, iOS, and grew it to become the world's best-selling tablet operating system. There's very little difference between iOS 8 on an iPhone and iOS 8 on an iPad: Applications written for one device usually work on the other, with a few obvious changes, such as screen size. On the other hand, Apple's computer operating system, OS X, is completely different. It's built and optimized for use with a Mac computer. Apple is slowly changing the programs, er, apps on both iOS and OS X so they resemble each other and work together. But the operating systems are fundamentally quite different (even though, yes, iOS did originally start with the Mac OS Darwin foundation).

When Windows 7 was finished, Steve Sinofsky and crew decided to take a fundamentally different tack. Instead of the good people at Microsoft growing their phone software "up," they decided to grow their computer operating system "down." (The fact that the phone software at that point drew nearly universal scorn could've been part of the reason.) Windows 8 grew out of that decision: There's a touch-friendly part and a mouse/keyboard-friendly part. The two aren't mutually exclusive: You can use your mouse on the Metro Start screen and in the tiled full-screen apps; you can use your greasy thumb on an old-fashioned Windows desktop app. But the approach is different, the design is different, and the intent is different.

Windows 10 goes back to Windows' Start menu roots and tries to grow the same concept down even further, to Windows Phone. Microsoft will be able to say that Windows covers all the bases, from lowly smartphone to gigantic workstations (and server farms, for that matter). The fact that the "Windows" running in each of the device classes is quite different kinda gets swept under the rug.

Here's a quick guide to what's new — and what's still the same — with some down-and-dirty help for deciding whether you truly need Windows 10.

What's New for the XP Crowd

Time to fess up. You can tell me. I won't rat you out.

If you're an experienced Windows XP user and you're looking at Windows 10, one of two things happened: Either your trusty old XP machine died and you *had* to get Win10 with a new PC, or a friend or family member conned you into looking into Win10 to provide tech support.

Am I right, or am I right? Hey, as of this writing, almost 25 percent of all Windows online use comes from Windows XP. Yeah, you read that number right. Win7 may dominate, but XP is still alive and well.

If you're thinking of making the jump from XP to Win10, and you're going to stick with a keyboard (as opposed to going touch-only, or touch-mostly, heaven help ya), you have two big hurdles:

✦ Learning the ways of tiled Windows Universal apps (which I outline in the next section, "What's New for Windows 7 and Vista Victims")

✦ Making the transition from XP to Windows 7 because the Win10 desktop works much like Windows 7

Are you sure you want to tackle the learning curve? Er, curves? See the nearby sidebar about switching to a Mac.

That said, if you didn't plunge into the Windows 7 or Vista madness, or the Windows 8/8.1 diversion, and instead sat back and waited for something better to come along, many improvements indeed await in Windows 10.

Improved performance

Windows 10 (and Windows 8 and 7 before it) actually places fewer demands on your PC's hardware. I know that's hard to believe, but as long as you have a fairly powerful video card, and 1GB or more of main memory, moving from XP to Win10 will make your PC run faster.

If you don't have a powerful video card, and you're running a desktop system, you can get one for less than $100, and extra memory costs a pittance. I've upgraded dozens of PCs from XP to Win10, and the performance improvement is quite noticeable. You laptop users aren't so lucky because laptop video is usually soldered in.

Wouldn't it be smarter to get a Mac?

Knowledgeable Windows XP users may find it easier — or at least more rewarding — to jump to a Mac, rather than upgrading to Windows 10. I know that's heretical. Microsoft will never speak to me again. But there's much to be said for making the switch.

Why? XP cognoscenti face a double whammy: learning Windows 7 (for the Win10 desktop) and learning how to deal with Metro/Modern Windows Universal apps. If you don't mind paying the higher price — and, yes, Macs are more expensive than PCs, feature-for-feature — Macs have a distinct advantage in being able to work easily in the Apple ecosystem: iPads, iPhones, the App Store, iTunes, iCloud, and Apple TV all work together

remarkably well. That's a big advantage held by Apple, where the software, hardware, cloud support, and content all come from the same company. "It just works" may be overblown, but there's more than a nugget of truth in it.

Yes, Macs have a variant of the Blue Screen of Death. Yes, Macs do get viruses. Yes, Macs have all sorts of problems. Yes, you may have to stand in line at an Apple Store to get help — I guess there's a reason why Microsoft Stores seem so empty.

If you're thinking about switching sides, look at *Switching to a Mac For Dummies,* by Arnold Reinhold. I bet you'll be surprised at the similarities between Mac OS X and Windows XP.

Better video

Windows 10 doesn't sport the Aero interface made popular in Vista and Win7, but some of the Aero improvements persist.

The *Aero Snap* feature lets you drag a window to an edge of the screen and have it automatically resize to half-screen size — a boon to anyone with a wide screen. Sounds like a parlor trick, but it's a capability I use many times every day.

Windows 10's desktop shows you thumbnails of running programs when you hover your mouse over a program on the taskbar (see Figure 2-4).

Video efficiency is also substantially improved: If you have a video that drips and drops in XP, the same video running on the same hardware may go straight through in Windows 10.

A genuinely better browser

Internet Explorer lives in Windows 10, but it's buried deep. If you're lucky, you'll never see it when you use Win10. IE is an old, buggy, bloated slug with incredibly stupid and infection-prone "features" — ActiveX, COM extensions, custom crap-filled toolbars, and don't get me started on Silverlight. IE deserves to die, if only in retaliation for all the infections it's brought to millions of machines.

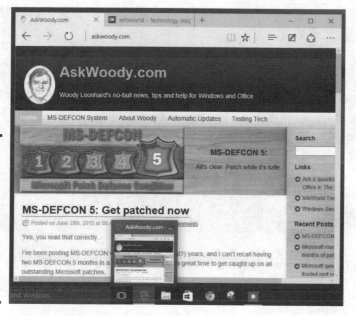

Figure 2-4:
Hovering your mouse over the Edge icon in the taskbar shows a thumbnail of the current tab.

In its place, the new, light, standards-happy, fast Microsoft Edge is everything IE should be, without the legacy garbage. Microsoft built Edge from the ground up as a Windows Universal app — a new WinRT API-based tiled app that runs on the desktop in its own resizable window.

It's a poster boy for the new apps that are coming down the pike. It took Microsoft forever to build, but the final result is well worth the effort.

Unfortunately, some corporate versions of Windows 10 only come with Internet Explorer; they don't run Edge. Apparently that's to protect you from the rapid updating that Edge is supposed to get. Most likely it's because enough big company admins complained.

If you live in fear of IE getting you infected and/or hate the massive IE patches now appearing every month, Microsoft Edge will be a refreshing change.

Cortana

Apple has Siri. Google has Google Now. Microsoft has Cortana, the Redmond version of an AI-based personal assistant, shown in Figure 2-5. Unlike Siri and Now, though, Cortana has taken over the Windows search function, so it has a larger potential footprint than its AI cousins, which comes with a double edge. At the same time, Cortana really, really wants to scan everything on your computer, coming and going — all the better to help you with, my dear.

Figure 2-5:
Cortana sits, listening and watching, waiting to help you. That should either make you skeptical or scared — or a little of both.

Hi, I'm Cortana.

I tell you much more about Cortana in this book — she has a chapter all to herself, Book III Chapter 6 — but I'll drop a little tidbit here, tailored for those Windows XP fans among you who may just be a bit intimidated by a talking helper-droid.

You see, Cortana has a history.

Back in 2001, Microsoft released a game called Halo: Combat Evolved. In Halo: CE, you, the player, take the role of the Master Chief, a kinda-human kinda-cyber soldier known as Master Chief Petty Officer John-117. Cortana is part of you, an artificial intelligence that's built into a neural implant in your body armor. After saving Captain Keyes, Cortana and the Master Chief go into a map room called the Silent Cartographer, and. . . well, you get the idea. Cortana is smooth and creepy and omniscient, just like the Windows 10 character.

Other improvements

Many other features — not as sexy as Cortana but every bit as useful — put Windows 10 head and shoulders above XP. The standout features include:

✦ **The taskbar:** I know many XP users swear by the old Quick Launch toolbar, but the taskbar, after you get to know it, runs rings around its predecessor. Just one example is shown in Figure 2-3 earlier in this chapter.

✦ **A backup worthy of the name:** Backup was a cruel joke in Windows XP. Windows 7 did it better, but Windows 10 makes backup truly easy, particularly with File History (see Book VIII, Chapter 1).

✦ **A less-infested notification area:** XP let any program and its brother put an icon in the notification area, near the system clock. Windows 10 severely limits the number of icons that appear and gives you a spot to click if you really want to see them all. Besides, Notifications are supposed to go in the Action pane, on the right. See Book II Chapter 3.

✦ **Second monitor support:** Although some video card manufacturers managed to jury-rig multiple monitor support into the Windows XP drivers, Windows 10 makes using multiple monitors one-click easy (see Book III, Chapter 1).

✦ **HomeGroups:** Windows 10, like Windows 7, lets you put together all the PCs in a trusted environment and share among them quite easily.

✦ **Easy wireless networking:** All sorts of traps and gotchas live in the Windows XP wireless programs. Windows 10 does it much, much better.

✦ **Search:** In Windows XP, searching for anything other than a filename involved an enormous kludge of an add-on that sucked up computer cycles and overwhelmed your machine. In Windows 10, search is part of Windows itself, and it works quickly.

On the security front, Windows 10 is light years ahead of XP. From protection against rootkits to browser hardening, and a million points in between, XP is a security disaster — Microsoft no longer supports it — while Windows 10 is relatively (not completely) impenetrable.

Although Windows 10 isn't the XP of your dreams, it's remarkably easy to use and has all sorts of compelling new features.

What's New for Windows 7 and Vista Victims

Anything that works with Windows 7, 8, or 8.1 — and almost everything from Vista — will work in Windows 10. Programs, hardware, drivers, utilities — just about anything.

That's a remarkable achievement, particularly because your Windows Desktop apps/Legacy programs (there's that "L" word again) have to peacefully coexist with the WinRT API-based Windows/Universal/Modern/ Metro apps.

Windows 10 does have lots going for it. Let me skip lightly through the major changes between Windows 7 and Windows 10.

Getting the hang of the new Start menu

By now, you've no doubt seen the tiles on the right of the Start menu (refer to Figure 2-6).

Figure 2-6:
The
Windows 10
desktop.

If you're coming to Windows 10 from Windows 7 — without taking a detour through Windows 8 — those tiles are likely to represent your greatest conceptual hurdle. They're different, but in many ways they're familiar.

Do you remember gadgets in Win7? They actually started in Vista. Many people (who finally found them) put tiles for clocks on their desktops. I also used to use the CPU gadget and on some machines the Weather gadget.

In Windows 10, you have a layout that's more or less similar to Windows 7, but it has fantastically good gadgets. Microsoft rebuilt all the plumbing in Windows to support these really good gadgets. Those updated, enormously powerful gadgets are now called "Windows Universal apps" (formerly "Universal apps," and formerly "Metro apps").

The new gadgets/Windows Universal apps run in resizable windows on the desktop. They can do phenomenal things. In fact, Microsoft Edge is quite superior to Internet Explorer, even if it doesn't yet have all the bells and whistles. Internet Explorer gets the heave-ho.Edge, which runs as a gadget/ Windows Universal app, becomes the new default browser.

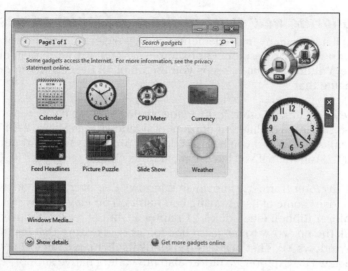

Figure 2-7:
Windows 7 gadgets — at least from the interface point of view — work much like the new Windows Universal app tiles.

Tiles for these gadgets/Windows Universal apps appear to the right of the list of programs in the Win10 Start menu.

Here's the big picture, from the Win7 perspective: Windows 10 has a desktop, and it's more or less analogous to the desktop in Windows 7. It doesn't have a Windows 8/8.1-style Metro view. Doesn't need a Metro view: The gadgets (or Metro apps or Windows Universal apps) now behave themselves and run in resizable windows on the desktop.

In Windows 10, you can switch from a finger-friendly view of the desktop to a mouse-friendly view and back. The finger-friendly view — called tablet mode — has larger gadget tiles, opens the gadgets at full-screen, and hides most of the text. It takes three clicks to change modes. Or you can plug or unplug your keyboard, and Windows will ask if you want to switch modes.

Here's the ace in the hole: Programmers who write programs for these new gadgets can have their gadgets run, with a varying amount of modification, on Windows 10 for PCs, Windows 10 for tablets without a keyboard, Windows 10 phones, and even Xbox. At least, that's the theory. Remains to be seen how it works in practice.

The only way you can get these new gadgets/Windows Universal apps is through the Windows Store, so — again, at least in theory — they should be well vetted, checked for malware, and generally in good shape, before you can install them.

Exploring new stuff in the old-fashioned desktop

You'll notice many improvements to long-neglected portions of the Windows 7-style desktop. For example, if you copy more than one file at a time, Windows actually keeps you on top of all the copying in one window. Imagine that.

A new and much better *Task Manager* rolls in all the usage reporting that's been scattered in different corners of Windows (see Figure 2-8). The new Task Manager even gives you hooks to look at programs that start automatically, and to stop them if you like. Some serious chops. See Book VIII, Chapter 4.

File Explorer (formerly known as Windows Explorer) takes on a new face and loses some of its annoying bad habits. You may or may not like the new Explorer Ribbon (see Book VI, Chapter 1), but at least Windows 10 brings back the up arrow to move up one folder — a feature that last appeared in Windows XP. That one feature, all by itself, makes me feel good about the new File Explorer. Explorer also now offers native support for ISO files. About time.

Taking a cue from iPad . . . er, other tablets, Windows 10 also offers a one-stop "system restore" capability. Actually, it's two capabilities: *PC Reset* wipes everything off the machine and then reinstalls Windows 10. *PC Refresh* goes through the same motions but retains your data, apps from the Windows Store, and settings. Note that PC Refresh zaps out your legacy Windows Desktop apps and doesn't put them back. See Book VIII, Chapter 2.

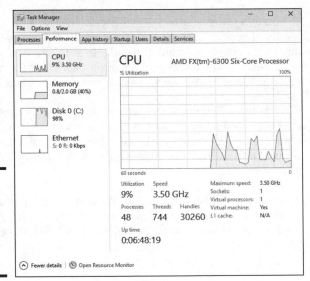

Figure 2-8:
The new and greatly improved Task Manager.

Storage Spaces requires at least two available hard drives — not including the one you use to boot the PC. If you can afford the disk space, Windows 10 can give you a fully redundant, hot backup of everything, all the time. If a hard drive dies, you disconnect the dead one, slip in a new one, grab a cup of coffee, and you're up and running as if nothing happened. If you run out of disk space, stick another drive in the PC or attach it with a USB cable, and Windows figures it all out. It's a magical capability that debuted in Windows Home Server, now made more robust. See Book VII, Chapter 4 for more on Storage Spaces.

Backup gets a major boost with an Apple Time Machine work-alike called *File History.* You may not realize it, but Windows 7 had the ability to restore previous versions of your data files. Windows 10 offers the same functionality, but in a much nicer package — so you're more likely to discover that it's there. See Book VIII, Chapter 1. Unfortunately, Windows 10 drops the ability to create whole-disk "ghost" backups — you need to buy a third-party program like Acronis if a full backup is in your future.

Power options have changed significantly. Again. The new options allow Windows to restart itself much faster than ever before. See Book VII, Chapter 1.

If you ever wanted to run a Virtual Machine inside Windows, Microsoft has made *Hyper-V* available, free. It's a rather esoteric capability that can come in very handy if you need to run two different copies of an operating system on one machine. You must be running a 64-bit version of Windows 10 Pro (or Enterprise), with at least 4GB of RAM. See Book VIII, Chapter 4.

What's New for Windows 8 and 8.1 Users

You're joking, right?

Windows 10 is a no-brainer if you already have Windows 8 or 8.1. If you're still running Windows 8, drop everything right now, and follow the instructions in Book I, Chapter 4 to install Windows 10.

Okay, I'll backtrack a bit. If you're a big fan of the tiled Metro side of Windows 8 or 8.1, you probably won't be happy with Windows 10, at least at first. There's no Charms bar, the taskbar always takes up part of the screen, Metro apps aren't completely "immersive" because they have title bars, and the full-screen tablet mode in Windows 10 isn't exactly comparable to the Metro side of Windows 8.

But if you use a mouse, even a little bit, or the desktop side of Windows 8/8.1, there's absolutely no question in my mind that you'll be happier with Windows 10.

Here's what you'll find when shifting from Win8 to Win10:

+ The Start menu — need I say more?

+ Big new features (detailed in the next section), along with a bunch of small tweaks really make life easier. Even in tablet mode, you'll find all sorts of things to love about Windows 10.

+ Windows Universal apps are updated and greatly improved.

+ OneDrive is built-in. You don't need to install a separate app.

On the downside, OneDrive in Windows 10 works differently from how it does in Windows 8.1. The "placeholders" that many Windows 8.1 customers have come to know and love disappear in Windows 10. In Windows 8.1, files in OneDrive, in the cloud, aren't automatically synced and stuck on the Win 8.1 machine. Instead, small file previews called "placeholders" live on the Win 8.1 machine and act much like the whole file. When you bring up Explorer, for example, you riffle through placeholders. If you click a file that's only a placeholder, OneDrive runs out and quickly downloads the file, feeding it to you or your program.

A problem arises if you're disconnected from the cloud when you want to open a file. By all appearances, the file's on your computer — but it isn't.

There are other problems. If you have a gazillion photos in OneDrive, and you crank up OneDrive on a Windows 8.1 machine with a tiny hard drive, just the placeholders can take up all the space on the hard drive.

Windows 10 changes all that, making the sync process much more convoluted, eliminating the old placeholders. Many people — rightfully — don't like that change. But, in my experience, it's the only significant feature that's getting the axe in moving from Windows 8.1 to Windows 10.

Windows 10 is, in many ways, what Windows 8 should've been. If Microsoft had been listening to its experienced Windows customers, Win8 never would've seen light of day.

What's New for All of Windows

Permit me to take you on a whirlwind tour of the most important new features in Windows 10 — of which there are many.

The Start menu

Unless you've been living on an alternate Windows desktop, you know that Win10 sports a new Start menu, with Windows 7-like menu entries on the left and Windows 8-style tiles on the right.

Figures 2-2 and 2-6 earlier in this chapter show the Start menu. In Figure 2-9, I show you the Start menu with All Apps listed; you get to it by clicking the Start icon and then clicking All Apps.

You have a few customizing options for the Start menu — for example, you can drag entries onto the pinned list in the top left, or drag items from the list on the left and turn them into tiles on the right. Tiles on the right can be resized to Small (see the three on the bottom right), Medium, Wide (two single-size slots, as with the Search and Weather tiles in the screen shot), and Large (Money). You can click and drag, group and ungroup tiles on the right, and give groups custom names.

You can resize the Start menu, within certain rigid limits. You can adjust it vertically in small increments, but trying to drag things the other way is limited to big swaths of tiles: Groups of tiles remain three wide, and you can add or remove only entire columns. You can drag tiles from the right side of the Start screen onto the desktop for easy access.

Although it's possible to manually remove all the tiles on the right (right-click each, Unpin from Start), the big area for tiles doesn't shrink beyond one column. There's some transparency available on the Start menu, so you can "see through" it, to some extent.

In tablet mode, Start looks quite different, although many of the options are the same. See Figure 2-10.

I talk about personalizing the Start menu in Book III, Chapter 2, and working with Tablet Mode in Book III, Chapter 3.

Microsoft Edge

Long overdue — and for many of us, a real surprise — Microsoft Edge (Figure 2-11) finally sheds the albatross that is Internet Explorer. Edge is a stripped-down, consciously standards-compliant, screamingly fast shell of a browser, ready to take on just about any website anywhere. Microsoft Edge may see Microsoft taking back the mindshare it's been steadily losing on the browser front for the past decade or so.

Figure 2-9:
The Start
menu, with
All Apps
unfurled on
the left.

Edge doesn't replace Internet Explorer — IE still lurks, but it's buried in the Start, All Apps, Windows Accessories list. Microsoft Edge is, however, the default web browser, with its own tile on the right side of the Start menu and its own icon on the taskbar. IE continues to use the old Trident rendering engine, while Edge has the newer Edge. That makes it faster, lighter, and much more capable of playing nicely with websites that are designed for Firefox and Chrome.

Edge is a Windows Universal app (formerly Universal app, formerly Metro app) that runs inside its own window on the desktop, like every other WinRT

Figure 2-10:
Start in
tablet mode,
which you
can see by
clicking the
hamburger
icon in the
upper-left
corner.

API-based Windows Universal app. IE is an old-fashioned Windows Desktop
app, and the difference is like a Tesla III versus a 1958 Edsel.

Adobe Flash Player can be turned on and off with a simple switch in Settings.
There's a Reading View as well, which helps on smaller screens. Click the
OneNote icon in the upper right, and all the OneNote markup tools become
available. And you can "Print as PDF."

Where IE was frequently infected by wayward Flash programs and bad PDF
files, Edge is relatively immune. And all the flotsam that came along with
IE — the ancient (and penetrable) COM extensions, wacko custom toolbars,
even Silverlight — are suddenly "legacy" and rapidly headed to a well-
deserved stint in the bit bucket.

On the other hand, Edge supports Google Chrome-like extensions, which
play in their own sandboxes, staying isolated. Instead of the spaghetti
mess with IE add-ons, we finally have some Microsoft-sponsored order.
It's about time.

Edge uses Cortana for voice assistance and search capabilities.

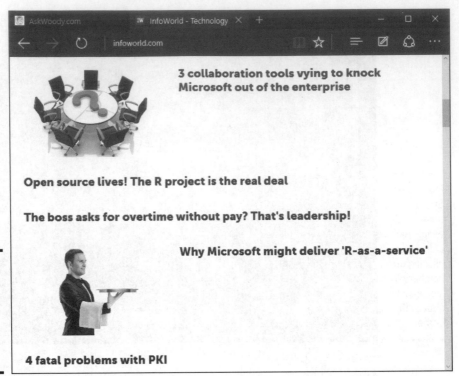

Figure 2-11:
Edge finally, finally lets everybody cut the IE cord...if you want to.

I talk about Edge in Book V, Chapter 1. I also talk about Internet Explorer, briefly, in Book III, Chapter 5.

Cortana

Although Apple partisans will give you a zillion reasons why Siri rules, and Googlies swear the superiority of Google Now, Cortana partisans think Microsoft rules the AI roost, of course. Unlike Siri and Now, though, Cortana has taken over the Windows search function — which you can see in Figure 2-12 — so it has a larger potential footprint than its AI cousins, which comes with a double edge.

Cortana occupies the Search box to the right of the Start button. She also appears when you click or tap the Search tile, on the right side of the Start menu. Cortana works only when connected to the Internet, and it's severely limited unless you use a Windows account. You can control some aspects of Cortana's inquisitiveness by clicking the hamburger icon in the upper-left corner.

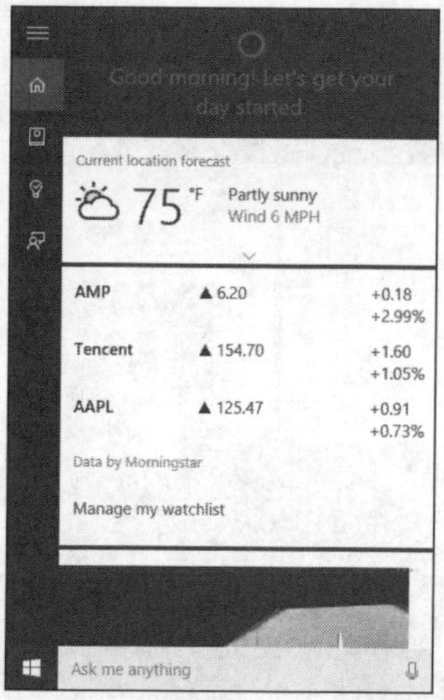

Figure 2-12:
Cortana
knows all,
sees all, and
takes over
your search
function.

Frequently overlooked in Cortana discussions: everything — absolutely everything — that you search for on your computer gets sent, through Cortana, to Microsoft's giant database in the sky. Cortana's Notebook, as your personal repository is called, can be switched off, and entries can be manually deleted, but Microsoft's banking on you leaving it on.

Cortana improves as it gathers more information about you — yes, by snooping on what you do. But it also improves as Microsoft hones its artificial intelligence moxie, on the back end.

Microsoft has announced that Cortana will be ported to both iOS (Apple phones and tablets) and Android, although the extent of its integration/usefulness remains to be seen. No, you won't be able to use Google Search with Cortana.

I talk about Cortana in Book III, Chapter 6.

Virtual desktops and Task view

Windows has had virtual (or multiple) desktops since Windows XP, but before Windows 10 you had to install a third-party app — or something like Sysinternals Desktop, from Microsoft — to get them to work. Windows 10 implements virtual desktops (Figure 2-13) so they're actually useful.

Don't let the terminology freak you out: Virtual desktops are just multiple desktops, and vice versa. If you want to sound cool, you can talk about optimizing your virtual desktops, but people in the know will realize you're just flipping between multiple desktops.

Figure 2-13:
Task view (shown here) displays all the multiple desktops you've set up.

Multiple desktops are very handy if you tend to multitask. You can set up one desktop to handle your mail, calendar, and day-to-day stuff, and another desktop for your latest project or projects. Got a crunch project? Fire up a new desktop. It's a great way to put a meta-structure on the work you do every day.

To start a new desktop, press Win+Ctrl+D, or bring up the Task view — the environment where you can work directly with multiple desktops — by clicking the Task view icon to the right of the Cortana Search bar and then clicking or tapping the + sign in the lower-right corner. Windows can be moved between desktops by right-clicking and choosing Move To. Alt+Tab still rotates among all running windows. Clicking an icon in the taskbar brings up the associated program, regardless of which desktop it's on.

I talk about multiple desktops in Book III, Chapter 4.

Security improvements

I'm told that Pliny the Elder once described the alarm system of ancient Rome by saying, "Even when the dogs sleep, the goose watches."

By that standard, Windows 10 has been goosed.

With Windows 8, Microsoft somehow found a new backbone — or decided that it can fend off antitrust actions — and baked full antivirus, antispyware, anti-scumstuff protection into Windows itself. Windows 10 continues to use exactly the same protection as Windows 8/8.1.

Although the 'Softies resurrected an old name for the service — *Windows Defender* — the antivirus protection inside Windows 10 is second to none. And it's free.

Microsoft is also encouraging hardware manufacturers to use a boot-up process called *UEFI,* as a replacement to the decades-old BIOS. UEFI isn't exactly a Windows 10 feature, but it's a requirement for all PCs that carry the Windows 10 (or Windows 8) logo. UEFI can help protect you from root-kits by requiring digital signatures on any operating system that gets loaded. See Book IX, Chapter 3.

Other Windows Universal apps

Microsoft has given most of its built-in apps a much-needed makeover.

Mail and **Calendar**, unlike their Windows 8.1 analogs, actually work. You don't need to feel like the 90-pound weakling on the beach if you crank them up. I, personally, use Gmail and Google Calendar, but the new Windows Mail app is definitely a contendah. I talk about Mail and Calendar (which are really one app with two different viewpoints) in Book IV, Chapter 1.

People is a derivative of the Windows Phone People Sense app. It doesn't do much. I talk about it in Book IV, Chapter 2.

Music and **Video** have replaced the useless Windows 8.1 Xbox Music and Xbox Video apps. They're surprisingly capable and tie into Microsoft's streaming service. (It only took Microsoft half a decade to put together a decent streaming service.) Look at Book IV, Chapter 6 for more.

The new **Photos** app is a dud. If you do anything at all with photos, other than file them and maybe remove some redeye from time to time, you're far better off with a free online alternative — or do yourself a favor and try Google Photos, www.photos.google.com. I talk about it in Book IV, Chapter 3.

The **Weather** app shows more weather and less sappy background than its Windows 8.1 counterpart. I cover it along with the other Bing apps — News, Finance, Travel, Sports, Fitness, Food, Money, Extortion — in Book V, Chapter 3.

Even the **Windows Store** is better than it used to be — damning with faint praise, for sure. Look for some actual improvements in Book V, Chapter 4.

What you lose

OneDrive in Windows 10 doesn't work anything like it did in Windows 8/8.1, primarily because Microsoft is doing away with "placeholder" or "smart file" behavior — where thumbnails of files are stored on your machine and pulled down from OneDrive only as needed. I talk about that in the "What's New for Windows 8 and 8.1 Users" section earlier in this chapter. If you're coming to Windows 10 from Windows 7, don't worry about it. You never knew what you're missing.

Although Microsoft hasn't talked much about it, the fact is that all the old Windows Live programs are disappearing. Windows Live is, in fact, dead. Windows 8 killed it, and Windows 10 drove a stake through its heart. If you use any of the Windows Live apps in Windows 7 (or Vista or XP, for that matter), your old Live apps are still available, but it doesn't look like Microsoft is going to do much with them. They certainly aren't getting any support.

Why? The Windows 10 Windows/Universal/Metro tiled apps cover many of the "Live" bases. Consider these:

✦ **Windows Live ID** (formerly known as Microsoft Wallet, Microsoft Passport, .NET Passport, and Microsoft Passport Network), which now operates from the Windows Live Account site (confused yet?), is rebranded Microsoft Your Account and referred to informally as "your *Microsoft Account.*"

✦ **Windows Live OneDrive** has already turned into just plain *OneDrive*. Parts of Ray Ozzie's Windows Live Mesh — formerly Live Mesh, Windows Live Sync, and Windows Live FolderShare — have been folded into OneDrive, although Microsoft has squashed PC-to-PC sync; the only way to synchronize files is through the OneDrive cloud. It appears as if Mesh has met its match.

✦ **Windows Live Mail** is missing in action. Expect Microsoft to push the new *Windows Universal Mail* as a "core Windows communications app." Ditto for **Windows Live Calendar.**

✦ **Windows Live Contacts** is now the *Windows Universal People app.*

✦ **Windows Live Photo Gallery** morphed into the *Windows Universal Photos* app.

✦ **Windows Live Messenger** is dead. It's been replaced by Skype — or Facebook, or any of a zillion competitors. I, personally, use Line, but that's a story for Book V, Chapter 2.

It's not just the Live apps that are dying. Some of the old Windows programs — **Media Player** being a good example — are just dead.

Some people feel that losing **Adobe Reader** (and other browser add-ins) in Edge is a bad thing. I disagree strongly. Reader (and Flash, which is insulated in Edge) have brought on more pain and misery — and hijacked systems — than they're worth. Microsoft's own ActiveX technology, which won't run on Edge, is another malware magnet that deserves to die, as do browser helper objects, homepage hijackers, custom toolbars, and much more. You can run all those add-ins in the Legacy desktop version of Internet Explorer, if you absolutely must.

Some other odd missing pieces include the following:

✦ **ClearType** doesn't run on the Windows Universal apps' interface, at all. It's still on the old-fashioned desktop, but your Windows/Universal/Metro tiles apps can't use it.

Note that this is different from Microsoft's ClearType HD technology, a marketing term for the monitors on Microsoft Surface tablets. I have no idea why Microsoft used the same term for both.

✦ **Flip 3D** is gone. Little more than a parlor trick, and rarely used, the Windows Key+Tab used to show a 3D rendering of all running programs and flip among them. Stick a fork in it. Now it cycles among desktops.

Do You Need Windows 10?

With the drubbing I gave Windows 8 and Windows 8.1 in the press — and in my *For Dummies* books — you might think that I'd come down hard on Windows 10.

Nope.

I've been using Windows 10 in various stages for almost a year now, and I still love it. This is from a guy who works in front of a monitor about 16 hours a day, 7 days a week (at least during book-writing season). I use a mouse or trackpad, and I'm proud of it. Windows 10, to my mind, is a great operating system, and it's a big improvement over Windows 8. I know, damning with faint praise again.

If you use a keyboard and a mouse with Windows 8 or 8.1, you need Windows 10. It's that simple.

Switching over to touch computing isn't quite so clear-cut. I have a couple of touch tablets, and I review dozens more, and for simple demands — mail, web, media playing, TV casting — I still prefer ChromeOS. It's simpler, less prone to infuriating screw-ups, less prone to infection, and less demanding for patches.

On the other hand, if you need one of the (many!) Windows Universal apps or Windows Desktop apps that don't run on ChromeOS, and you have a touch-first environment, Windows 10 ain't a bad choice.

One thing's for sure. This isn't recycled old Windows 8 garbage. With Windows 10, Microsoft has taken a bold step in the right direction — one that accommodates both old desktop fogies like me and the more mobile newcomers (like me, too, I guess).

I haven't felt this good about a Microsoft product since the original release of Windows 7.

Chapter 3: Which Version?

In This Chapter

- ✔ Windows 10 rumors that just aren't true
- ✔ The various versions of Windows 10
- ✔ Narrowing your choices
- ✔ 32-bit or 64-bit?

*P*ermit me to dispel two rumors, right off the bat. Windows 10 isn't exactly free. And it isn't the last version of Windows.

You probably heard either or both of those rumors from well-regarded mainstream publications, and what you heard was wrong.

Here are the facts:

- ✦ If you already own a legitimate copy of Windows 7 or 8/8.1, the upgrade to Windows 10 is free, providing you upgrade during the year after Windows 10's announced official shipping date. (If you're running Windows 8, you have to install the free upgrade to Windows 8.1 first.)

  Contrariwise, if you're building a new PC, you have to buy Windows 10. And if you buy a new PC with Windows 10 preinstalled, the PC manufacturer (probably) paid for Windows 10.

- ✦ Microsoft may drop the numbering system — so "Windows 10" in the future becomes, simply, "Windows" — but there will always be version numbers. I tell you how to find yours in this chapter. The number "10" is, was, and always will be, a marketing fantasy.

If you haven't yet bought a copy of Windows, you can save yourself some headaches and more than a few bucks by buying the right version the first time. And, if you're struggling with the 32-bit versus 64-bit debate, illumination — and possibly some help — is at hand.

Counting the Editions

Windows 10 appears in six different major editions, uncounted numbers of minor editions, and three of the major editions are available in 32-bit and 64-bit incarnations. That makes nine different editions of Windows to choose from.

Fortunately, most people need to concern themselves with only two editions, and you can probably quickly winnow the list to one. Contemplating the 32-bit conundrum may exercise a few extra gray cells, but with a little help, you can probably figure it out easily.

In a nutshell, the four desktop/laptop Windows versions (and targeted customer bases) look like this:

+ **Windows 10 Home** — the version you probably want — works great unless you specifically need one of the features in Windows 10 Pro. A big bonus for many of you: This version makes all the myriad Windows languages — 96 of them, from Afrikaans to Yoruba — available to anyone with a normal, everyday copy of Windows, at no extra cost.

+ **Windows 10 Pro** includes everything in Windows 10 Home plus the ability to attach the computer to a corporate domain network; the Encrypting File System and BitLocker (see the "Encrypting File System and BitLocker" sidebar later in this chapter) for scrambling your hard drive's data; Hyper-V for running virtual machines; and the software necessary for your computer to act as a Remote Desktop host — the "puppet" in an RD session.

+ **Windows 10 Enterprise** is available only to companies that buy into Microsoft's Software Assurance program — the (expensive) volume licensing plan that buys licenses to every modern Windows version. Enterprise offers a handful of additional features, but they don't matter unless you're going to buy a handful of licenses or more.

+ **Windows 10 Education** looks just like Windows 10 Enterprise, but it's available only to schools, through a program called Academic Volume Licensing.

Those four editions only run on Intel (and AMD) processors. They're traditional Windows.

Windows Vista and Windows 7 both had "Ultimate" editions, which included absolutely everything. Win10 doesn't work that way. If you want the whole enchilada, you have to pay for volume licensing and the Software Assurance program.

Windows Media Center — the Windows XP-era way to turn a PC into a set-top box — is no longer available in any version of Windows 10. Do yourself a favor and buy a Chromecast, or use your cable company's DVR if you really have to record TV.

There are two more editions of Windows 10 which only run Universal Windows apps. That bears repeating: **These versions of Windows don't run**

old-fashioned Windows programs. They're designed for Windows Phone and small (roughly 8-inch or smaller) tablets. Here are the options:

✦ **Windows 10 Mobile** is what you probably think of when you think "Windows Phone." It's all grown up now, and it'll run on small tablets, but it's still a phone at heart. By not including the Windows desktop, or running old-fashioned Windows programs, Windows 10 Mobile can run on less powerful computers, including both Intel and ARM processors. (ARM processors, traditionally, have powered phones. That's changing, though.)

✦ **Windows 10 Mobile Enterprise** adds a few features to Windows 10 Mobile, which is of interest only if you need to connect your phone to a corporate network.

This book covers Windows 10 and Windows 10 Pro. Most of the content is applicable to Windows 10 Enterprise and Windows 10 Education. Only a little bit of the content applies to Windows 10 Mobile and Windows 10 Mobile Enterprise.

Before you tear your hair out trying to determine whether you bought the right version, or which edition you should buy your great-aunt Ethel, rest assured that choosing the right version is much simpler than it first appears. Flip to "Narrowing the choices" later in this chapter. If you're considering buying a cheap version now and maybe upgrading later, I suggest that you first read "Buying the right version the first time" before you make up your mind.

Buying the right version the first time

What if you aim too low? What if you buy Windows 10 and decide later that you really want Windows 10 Pro? Be of good cheer. Switching versions ain't as tough as you think.

Microsoft chose the feature sets assigned to each Windows version with one specific goal in mind: Maximize Microsoft profits. If you want to move from Windows 10 Home to Windows 10 Pro (the only upgrade available to individuals), you need to buy the Windows 10 Pro Pack.

Upgrading is easy and cheap, but not as cheap as buying the version you want the first time. That's also why it's important for your financial health to get the right version from the get-go.

Narrowing the choices

You can dismiss two regular Windows editions and both Windows Mobile editions out of hand:

✦ **Windows 10 Enterprise** is an option only if you want to pay through the nose for five or more Windows licenses, through the Software Assurance program. Microsoft may change its mind — either lower the price for small bunches of licenses and/or make the Enterprise version available to individuals — but as of this writing, Enterprise is out of the picture for most of you.

✦ **Windows 10 Education,** similarly, can be purchased only in large quantities. If you're a student, faculty member, or staff member at a licensed school, you must contact the IT department to get set up.

✦ **Windows 10 Mobile** comes preinstalled only on new machines. You can't buy a copy and slap it on that cheap tablet you have sitting in the basement.

✦ **Windows 10 Mobile Enterprise** comes only in large quantities, just like Windows 10 Enterprise.

That leaves you with plain vanilla Windows 10, unless you have a crying need to do one of the following:

✦ **Connect to a corporate network.** If your company doesn't give you a copy of Windows 10 Enterprise, you need to spend the extra bucks and buy Windows 10 Pro.

✦ **Play the role of the puppet — the *host* — in a Remote Desktop interaction.** If you're stuck with Remote Desktop, you must buy Windows 10 Pro.

Note that you can use Remote Assistance, any time, on any Windows PC, any version. (See Book VII, Chapter 2.) This Win10 Pro restriction is specifically for Remote Desktop, which is commonly used inside companies, but not used that frequently in the real world.

Many businesspeople find that *LogMeIn,* a free alternative to Remote Desktop, does everything they need and that Remote Desktop amounts to overkill. LogMeIn lets you access and control your home or office PC from any place that has an Internet connection. Look at its website, `www.logmein.com`.

✦ **Provide added security to protect your data from prying eyes or to keep your notebook's data safe even if it's stolen.** Start by determining whether you need Encrypting File System (EFS), BitLocker, or both (see the later sidebar "Encrypting File System and BitLocker"). Win10 Pro has EFS and BitLocker — with BitLocker To Go tossed in for a bit o' lagniappe.

✦ **Run Hyper-V.** Some people can benefit from running *virtual machines* inside Windows 10. If you absolutely must get an old Windows XP program to cooperate, for example, running Hyper-V with a licensed copy of Windows XP may be the best choice. For most people, VMs are an interesting toy, but not much more.

Encrypting File System and BitLocker

Encrypting File System (EFS) is a method for encrypting individual files or groups of files on a hard drive. EFS starts after Windows boots: It runs as a program under Windows, which means it can leave traces of itself and the data that's being encrypted in temporary Windows places that may be sniffed by exploit programs. The Windows directory isn't encrypted by EFS, so bad guys (and girls!) who can get access to the directory can hammer it with brute-force password attacks. Widely available tools can crack EFS if the cracker can reboot the, uh, crackee's computer. Thus, for example, EFS can't protect the hard drive on a stolen laptop/notebook. Windows has supported EFS since the halcyon days of Windows 2000.

BitLocker was introduced in Vista and has been improved since. BitLocker runs *underneath* Windows: It starts before Windows starts. The Windows partition on a BitLocker-protected drive is completely encrypted, so bad guys who try to get to the file system can't find it.

EFS and BitLocker are complementary technologies: BitLocker provides coarse, all-or-nothing protection for an entire drive. EFS lets you scramble specific files or groups of files. Used together, they can be mighty hard to crack.

BitLocker To Go provides BitLocker-style protection to removable drives, including USB drives.

Choosing 32-bit Versus 64-bit

If you've settled on, oh, Windows 10 as your operating system of choice, you aren't off the hook yet. You need to decide whether you want the 32-bit flavor or the 64-bit flavor of Windows 10. (Similarly, Windows 10 Pro and Enterprise are available in a 32-bit model and a 64-bit model.)

Although the 32-bit and 64-bit flavors of Windows look and act the same on the surface, down in the bowels of Windows, they work quite differently. Which should you get? The question no doubt seems a bit esoteric, but just about every new PC nowadays uses the 64-bit version of Windows for good reasons:

✦ **Performance:** The 32-bit flavor of Windows — the flavor that everyone was using a few years ago and many use now — has a limit on the amount of memory that Windows can use. Give or take a nip here and a tuck there, 32-bit Windows machines can see, at most, 3.4 or 3.5 gigabytes (GB) of memory. You can stick 4GB of memory into your computer, but in the 32-bit world, anything beyond 3.5GB is simply out of reach. It just sits there, unused. That's why you only see 32-bit Windows these days on tiny, cheap tablets and mobile devices.

The 64-bit flavor of Windows opens your computer's memory, so Windows can see and use more than 4GB — much more, in fact. Whether you need access to all that additional memory is debatable at this point. Five years from now, chances are pretty good that 3.5GB will start to feel a bit constraining.

Although lots of technical mumbo jumbo is involved, the simple fact is that programs are getting too big, and Windows as we know it is running out of room. Although Windows can fake it by shuffling data on and off your hard drive, doing so slows your computer significantly.

✦ **Security:** Security is one more good reason for running a 64-bit flavor of Windows. Microsoft enforced strict security constraints on drivers that support hardware in 64-bit machines — constraints that just couldn't be enforced in the older, more lax (and more compatible!) 32-bit environment.

And that leads to the primary problem with 64-bit Windows: drivers. Many, many people have older hardware that simply doesn't work in any 64-bit flavor of Windows. Their hardware isn't supported. Hardware manufacturers sometimes decide that it isn't worth the money to build a solid 64-bit savvy driver, to make the old hardware work with the new operating system. You, as a customer, get the short end of the stick.

Application programs are a different story altogether. The 64-bit version of Office 2010 is notorious for causing all sorts of headaches: You're better off running 32-bit Office 2010, even on a 64-bit system (yes, 32-bit programs run just fine on a 64-bit system, by and large). Office 2013 and 2016 don't have the 64-bit shakes; they work fine on either 32-bit or 64-bit Windows. Some programs can't take advantage of the 64-bit breathing room. So all is not sweetness and light.

Now that you know the pros and cons, you have one more thing to take into consideration: What does your PC support? To run 64-bit Windows, your computer must support 64-bit operations. If you bought your computer any time after 2005 or so, you're fine — virtually all the PCs sold since then can handle 64-bit. But if you have an older PC, here's an easy way to see whether your current computer can handle 64 bits: Go to Steve Gibson's SecurAble site, at `www.grc.com/securable.htm`. Follow the instructions to download and run the SecurAble program. If your computer can handle 64-bit operations, SecurAble tells you.

If you have older hardware — printers, scanners, USB modems, and the like — that you want to use with your Windows computer, do yourself a favor and stick with 32-bit Windows. It's unlikely that you'll start feeling the constraints of 32 bits until your current PC is long past its prime. On the other hand, if you're starting with completely new hardware — or hardware that you bought in the past three or four years — and you plan to run your current PC for a long, long time, 64-bit Windows makes lots of sense. You may end up cursing me when an obscure driver goes bump in the night. But in the long run, you'll be better prepared for the future.

Which Version of Windows Are You Running Right Now?

You may be curious to know which version of Windows you're running on your current machine. Here's the easy way to tell:

1. **If you have a Start screen that resembles the one in Figure 3-1, you have some version of Windows 8, 8.1, RT, or RT 8.1.**

   If you don't have a Start screen, skip to Step 3.

Figure 3-1:
A Start screen like this is a dead giveaway for 8, 8.1, or RT.

2. **Swipe from the right or hover your mouse in the lower-right corner, choose Change PC Settings. Click or tap PC and devices, then PC info. You get a report like the one in Figure 3-2.**

Figure 3-2:
This
machine
runs 64-bit
Windows 8.1
Pro.

3. **On the other hand, if you have a desktop like the one shown in Figure 3-3, you're running some version of Windows 7.**

   If you don't see a desktop like the one in Figure 3-3, skip to Step 5.

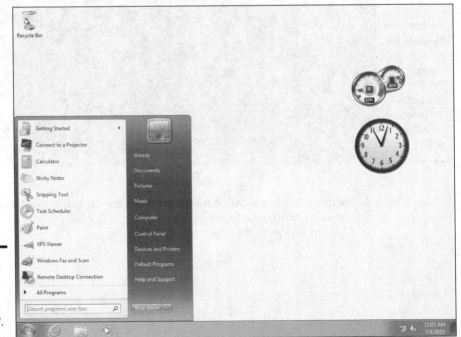

Figure 3-3:
Here's a
telltale
desktop in
Windows 7.

4. **From the desktop in Figure 3-3, click the Start button in the lower-left corner, then Control Panel, System and Security. Under System, click View amount of RAM and processor speed.**

   You see a report like the one in Figure 3-4.

Figure 3-4:
This is
Windows 7
Pro Service
Pack 1,
64-bit.

5. **If your computer doesn't resemble either Figure 3-1 or 3-3, follow the instructions in Step 4.**

   Those steps also work for Windows Vista and XP.

If you have a 64-bit system installed already, you should upgrade to a 64-bit version of Windows 10. If you currently have a 32-bit system, check Steve Gibson's site, as mentioned in the preceding section.

Chapter 4: Upgrades and Clean Installs

In This Chapter

↘ **Finding out whether you can upgrade that old bucket**

↘ **Upgrading online to Windows 10**

↘ **Installing Windows 10 from a DVD**

↘ **Cleaning the gunk off a new PC**

↘ **What to do if Windows dies**

I've been upgrading Windows machines since I moved from Windows 286 (a souped-up version of Windows 2.0) to Windows 3.0 on my trusty Gateway PC in 1990. All the upgrade took was five of those new-fangled high-density (1.2MB) five-and-a-quarter-inch floppies. Since then, I don't know how many systems I've upgraded over the years, how many times, but the count certainly runs more than a thousand.

During all those upgrades, I've sworn and kicked and moaned about in-place upgrades. They never worked. Sooner or later, putting a new version of Windows on top of an old one, without wiping out the old version, led to heartache, yanks of pulled hair, and screams of anguish. With Windows 8.1, for the first time ever, I changed my tune. Windows 10 in-place upgrades are even smoother. I talk about my near-religious conversion in this chapter.

Can your PC handle Windows 10? Probably. I talk about that in this chapter too, along with details about running upgrades, both online and from the DVD-based System Builder edition, creating a backup DVD, and what to do if your PC dies. I cover upgrading from Windows 7 or 8 to Windows 10.

I also sandwich in a few tips about getting the crap off new PCs — or how to avoid getting a junker altogether. It's shameful that Microsoft has to charge extra to get rid of PC manufacturer's junk, but that's how things shake out. Imagine how the fans would wail if Apple charged extra for clean, decrapified Macs.

If you're here because Windows 10 is misbehaving and you want to tear out its beating heart and stomp on it . . . you're in the wrong place. After

Windows 10 is installed on your PC, it's very rare indeed that you have to install it again. Instead, look into resetting or restoring your PC, a topic I cover in Book VIII, Chapter 2.

Do You Qualify for Free?

If your current PC runs Windows 7 Service Pack 1 or Windows 8.1 with the Update 1 installed (also known as KB 2919355), you can install Windows 10 over the top of the old system by using Microsoft's online upgrade.

If you upgrade before July 29, 2016, the upgrade is free, and Microsoft will continue to support your system with upgrades and security patches "for the life of the device."

Aren't sure if you have Win7 Service Pack 1? On a Windows 7 system, click Start, Control Panel, System and Security, then under the System heading, click the link to View amount of RAM and processor speed. If you have Service Pack 1, you see something like the notice in Figure 4-1.

Figure 4-1:
Here's where you find verification that you have Service Pack 1.

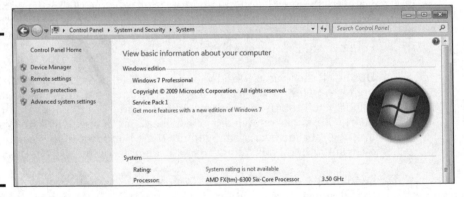

Not sure about Windows 8.1 Update (also called Update 1)? Go to the Start screen (remember that abomination?) and look in the upper-right corner. If there's a power switch and a search icon in the upper-right corner, as in Figure 4-2, you have the Update installed.

If you have Windows 7 without Service Pack 1, or if you have Windows 8 without 8.1, or 8.1 without the Update, you need to bring your machine up to snuff before you can even think about upgrading to Windows 10. Windows 7 Service Pack 1 has been around for a long while, and very few people have problems installing it. The Windows 8.1 Update isn't quite so user-friendly.

Figure 4-2:
The telltale
power and
search
icons in
Windows 8.1
Update 1's
Start screen
indicate
that you're
eligible
for a free
upgrade to
Win 10.

In any case, if you need to bring your system up to speed, turn on Automatic Update:

✦ In **Windows 7**, using an administrator-level account, click Start, Control Panel, and then System and Security. Under Windows Update, click the Turn automatic updating on or off link. In the drop-down box, select Install updates automatically (recommended) and click OK.

✦ In **Windows 8 or 8.1**, right-click or tap and hold the Start icon, and choose Control Panel. Then follow the instructions in the preceding paragraph to turn on automatic updates.

Leave your computer running overnight and by the time you come back, you should be up to speed, give or take a restart or two or three.

Deciding Whether to Upgrade Your Old PC

If you're currently running Windows Vista or Windows 7 or 8 on a PC, the answer is yes, you can almost certainly upgrade it to Windows 10 — and it'll probably run faster than Vista, at least.

Officially you can (not should, but *can*) upgrade if your PC has at least these criteria:

✦ **1 GHz** or faster processor — an Intel or AMD processor.

✦ **1GB** of RAM memory for the 32-bit version, **2GB** for the 64-bit. (See Book I, Chapter 3 for a discussion of "bittedness.")

✦ **16GB** of available hard drive space. Of course, that's just for Windows. If you want to install any programs or save any data, you're going to need a leeeeeetle bit more.

✦ **DirectX 9** graphics card with WDDM 1.0 or higher driver. Every video card made in the past ten years meets that requirement.

The much more difficult question of whether you *should* upgrade launches me into a metaphysical discussion. Consider how the following apply to you:

✦ **If you have a touch-enabled PC, especially if you're running Windows 8 or 8.1,** there's absolutely no question you should upgrade to Windows 10. Windows 8 and 8.1 are a grotesque joke. Get Windows 10 and you'll feel much better.

✦ **If you're using a mouse and keyboard and don't plan on getting a touchscreen,** you only need Windows 10 if you really need one of the new features I mention in Book I, Chapter 2, or if one of the Windows Store apps tickles your fancy. If the benefits there don't put a tingle down your spine, no, you don't need Windows 10. Stick with Windows 7.

Personally, I have a touch-sensitive Windows 10 clamshell (Dell XPS-13), which works great. My main desktop runs Windows 10 all the time. I have a couple of MacBooks that usually run Windows 10 under Bootcamp, although OS X is just a click away.

To write this book, I used several Dell products, including a lovely XPS-15. I also used a Microsoft Surface Pro 3. Quite an array of equipment. My desk looks like a mess.

Do you really want another Windows PC?

If you're looking for a new PC, stop and take a deep breath. Are you really, really sure you want to buy a new Windows PC?

I know it's heresy to write about this in Windows book, but it's true. Many of the things that most people want to do every day work just fine with an Android tablet or an iPad, perhaps with an attached keyboard and mouse. And those new Chromebooks run like wind for a mere pittance.

All those alternatives are easy to use, and none gets infected like Windows. Not even close. Contrariwise, if you have programs that only run on Windows, you may be stuck.

Before you shell out more money on Windows, look around. The options may astound you.

I love my iPad, Android Galaxy Note, and Kindle Fire. I also seriously covet my wife's iPhone. That's why I include lots of information about those dern Appley and Googlie things in this book. I find them all useful, although my life is still seriously buried in Windows.

Frankly, as things stand right now, I'm not sure I'll ever buy another desktop machine, unless the one I have turns shiny side up. I'll always need a big screen and a keyboard built like a brick house to get my work done, but even cheap laptops these days work very well, plugged into a solid keyboard, good mouse, and gorgeous monitor.

Will I ever *buy* a Windows 10 machine? Could happen.

Choosing Your Upgrade Path

Here are the three ways to get a Windows 10 upgrade from Windows 7 SP1 or Windows 8.1 Update:

+ **You can download the upgrade from the Internet.** This is the way I recommend to almost everybody, as long as your current computer is running a "genuine" copy of Windows 7 or 8.1. Your new Windows 10 installation is completely legit, 100% "genuine," and Microsoft keeps records of the upgrade, so you can reinstall Win10 from scratch if your system ever dies.

+ **You can download a file — called an ISO file — that lets you create a bootable DVD or USB drive**. Boot from the DVD or USB, and you're off to the races. If you're using Windows 8.1, you can even run the Windows 10 installation file from inside Windows.

+ **You can buy a Windows 10 DVD, called the System Builder Edition, in a box, through a process not unlike the one everybody used ten years ago.** If you already have a copy of Windows running on your computer, this approach is not only wasteful (just try recycling the DVD jewel case!), but it's also a pain in the neck because you have to futz with booting from the DVD, entering a product key, deciding which partitions to nuke, and then running Windows Activation. Windows 10 may even be available, from Microsoft, on a USB drive.

Whether you upgrade online or upgrade by booting from a DVD or USB drive, Windows 10 has certain restrictions:

+ **Windows Media Center won't come through**. If you paid for Windows Media Center, Microsoft says it'll give you a DVD player. Meh. But Microsoft won't let you put WMC on a Windows 10 machine or bring it across when you upgrade.

✦ **If you're using OneDrive in Windows 8.1, you're going to hate what it does to your file access.** I cover the details in Book VI, Chapter 2, but the bottom line is that you're going to find it hard to use OneDrive to locate your files, unless you go through a bunch of steps to make the files visible.

✦ **When upgrading from Windows 7 SP1 or 8.1 Update,** you can choose to keep your programs, some of your settings (desktop background and Internet Explorer favorites and history), and data (anything in your user folders, including Documents, Desktop, and Downloads). If you have anything stored outside of one of the user's libraries, don't count on it coming across. You may be pleasantly surprised, but it may not come through.

Of course, you should always, always, always back up all your data before you perform an upgrade.

✦ **When upgrading from Vista or XP,** you have to run a clean install. Nothing comes along for the ride.

✦ **If you want to change from a 32-bit version of Windows to 64-bit Windows 10,** you will necessarily wipe out all your old programs and settings, as is the case with an upgrade from XP. Note, though, that not all machines are capable of moving to 64-bit Windows 10.

I take you through the upgrading details, step by step, in the next three sections.

Upgrading Windows 7 SP1 or Windows 8.1 Update to Windows 10 Online

Unless you have a fake copy of Windows, this is the way to go.

Chances are good that you're already seeing notifications, when you click the Windows flag down near the clock in the lower-right corner. The come-on looks like Figure 4-3.

Just follow the instructions, and Windows 7 SP1 or 8.1 Update will upgrade itself, give or take a mammoth download and a few breathtaking restarts.

As part of the process kicked off by the dialog box shown in Figure 4-3, the upgrader also runs a compatibility checker. You can run the compatibility checker without going through the upgrade registration by following these simple steps:

1. **Instead of clicking the Windows flag in the system tray, right-click it (or tap and hold) and choose Check your upgrade status.**

See Figure 4-4.

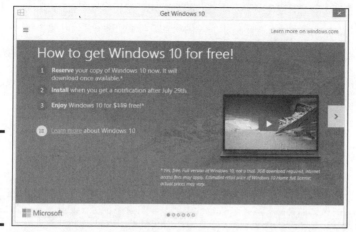

Figure 4-3:
A normal
Windows
10 upgrade
starts here.

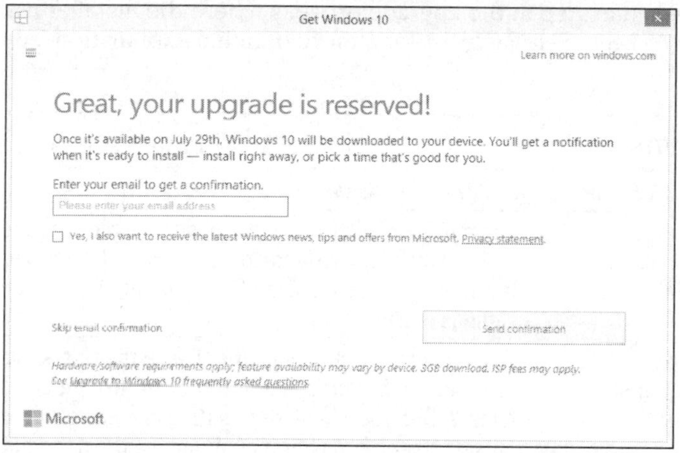

Figure 4-4:
The trick is
to right-click
the flag
and choose
Check your
upgrade
status.

If you've already gone through the registration process, the Get
Windows 10 app shows you a window that says All done for now. If you
still haven't signed up, you may get some other message.

2. **Click the hamburger icon in the upper-left corner, and under Getting
   the upgrade, choose Check your PC.**

   The upgrade advisor reports on your status, most likely giving you a
   clean bill of health, as in Figure 4-5.

As long as you get a good report from the upgrade advisor, performing the
upgrade is easy.

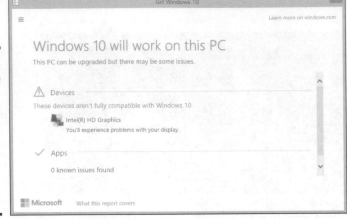

Figure 4-5: The upgrade advisor reports this machine is ready to get Win10, but the display may not work right.

There's one step in the upgrade process where the installer asks what you want to keep. See Table 4-1 for a more detailed explanation.

Table 4-1	Choose What to Keep
This Choice . . .	*. . . Actually Means This*
Keep Windows Settings	Some of your Windows settings survive the upgrade: user accounts and passwords, your desktop background, Internet Explorer favorites and history, some File Explorer settings. Other Windows settings don't survive.
Keep Personal Files	This specifically means all the files in the Users folder. That includes the Documents, Pictures, Photos, Videos, and Desktop folders. But if you have data sitting in some other folder, stored outside Users, it may or may not make the transition, even if it's in one of your libraries.
Keep Apps	The upgrade process keeps all the application programs that are identified and understood by the upgrader. Microsoft has hundreds of thousands of programs and drivers on file — but it doesn't have every Windows program made. In addition, some programs (such as some system utilities) can't make it through the upgrade process. The problematic programs should be listed in the compatibility scan.
Nothing	This is a clean install. The upgrade routine moves several folders (Windows, Program Files, Program Files [x86], Users, and Program Data) to the windows.old folder, but all the originals are overwritten in the upgrade process. *Remember:* If you use a fingerprint reader or some other device that doesn't rely on passwords to log you in, make sure you have your password before you upgrade. The biometric data doesn't survive the upgrade.

Installing Win 10 from a DVD or USB Drive

If you're going to upgrade from Windows 7 SP1 or 8.1 Update to Windows 10, and you want to keep your data and programs intact, I strongly urge you to perform the online upgrade I mention in the preceding section. As long as you stick to upgrading 32-bit Win7 to 32-bit Win10 or 64-bit Win7 to 64-bit Win10, the online installer works great.

On the other hand, if you want to wipe your computer and install Windows 10 from scratch, do that by booting from a DVD or USB drive and running a clean install. That's the process I describe in this section.

WARNING!

I can't emphasize enough that you must make full backups of *all* your data, write down *all* your passwords (unless they're stored online someplace like LastPass), get *all* your software installation CDs and DVDs, and make yet another backup just in case, before starting this process.

If you buy a shrink-wrapped copy of Windows 10, you get a DVD (or possibly a USB drive) that's ready to boot. If you download an ISO file, follow the instructions in the sidebar "Making an ISO file usable" to turn the file into a bootable DVD or USB drive.

With a bootable USB drive or DVD in hand, you may have to adjust your computer so it boots from the USB or DVD.

Here's how to go through the whole process — and survive to tell the tale:

1. **With your old version of Windows running, insert the Windows installation disk in the DVD drive, or the installation USB in a USB port.**

Making an ISO file usable

Many people get a copy of Windows 10 in the form of a single file with the filename extension .iso. Microsoft MSDN and TechNet subscribers, for example, get ISO files. An *ISO file* is just a compressed version of a DVD image. You can turn an ISO file into a bootable DVD or USB drive by using a simple tool that Microsoft provides.

To perform the magic, download Microsoft's Windows 7 USB tool, which is located at `www.store.microsoft.com/Help/ISO-Tool`. Run the tool. Navigate to the ISO file, and choose whether you want to burn a DVD or create a bootable USB drive. Four steps, and you're finished.

2. **In Win7, choose Start, Shut Down to go through a full shutdown. In Win 8.1, click the power icon next to your name on the Start screen and choose Shut Down.**

   Windows may offer to install itself while you're trying to shut down. If it does, click the Cancel button.

3. **Power off the PC, wait at least a full minute, and then turn on the power.**

   If the PC can start (or *boot)* from the DVD drive or USB drive, you see text on the screen that says something like Press any key to boot from CD or Press Esc to choose boot device.

4. **Press whatever key is recommended.**

   If the PC doesn't offer to boot from the DVD drive or USB stick, you have to look in your PC's documentation for the correct setting in your PC's BIOS. If you're not familiar with your PC's BIOS, go to the website for your PC manufacturer and search for the terms *change boot sequence*.

5. **When the PC boots, you may be asked if you want to go online to get the latest updates. If you do, choose Go Online to Install Updates Now and click Next.**

6. **In the Windows Setup screen, change the language if you wish, click Next, and then click Install Now.**

7. **When the installer prompts for the product key, enter it. When a license terms screen appears, accept it.**

   The Which Type of Installation Do You Want? dialog box, as shown in Figure 4-6, appears.

Figure 4-6:
Wipe
everything
and perform
a clean
install by
choosing
the Custom
option.

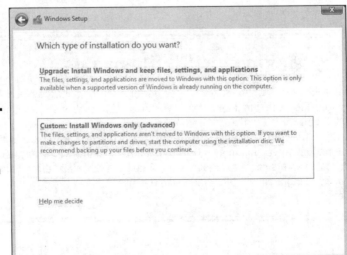

8. To wipe everything and start fresh, click Custom: Install Windows Only (Advanced).

The installer asks you where you want to install Windows, as shown in Figure 4-7.

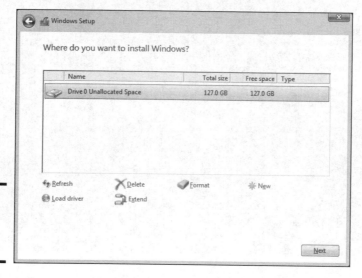

Figure 4-7:
Where
to install
Windows?

9. If there is more than one entry in the upper box, choose Drive Options (Advanced), click each entry in the upper box, one by one, and click the link that says Delete. When you're finished, click Next.

Then go have another latte . . . or two . . . or three. Your computer restarts several times.

If you had to jimmy your BIOS in Step 4 to make your PC boot from a DVD drive or USB, you may reach an odd situation where you see the setup screen again, and your computer just sits there waiting for you to start again. If that happens, pull the DVD or USB drive out of its slot and manually restart your computer. The installer kicks back in again the second time.

By the time the installer comes up for air, you're ready to personalize your copy of Windows.

10. Choose a background color for the tiled Start screen (don't worry, it's easy to change later), type a name for the PC (better if you stick to letters and numbers, no spaces or weird characters), and click Next.

Windows asks about your initial settings, as shown in Figure 4-8.

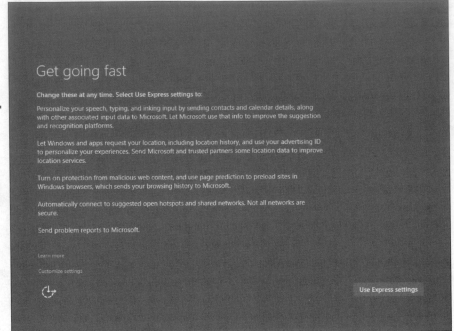

Get going fast

Change these at any time. Select Use Express settings to:

Personalize your speech, typing, and inking input by sending contacts and calendar details, along with other associated input data to Microsoft. Let Microsoft use that info to improve the suggestion and recognition platforms.

Let Windows and apps request your location, including location history, and use your advertising ID to personalize your experiences. Send Microsoft and trusted partners some location data to improve location services.

Turn on protection from malicious web content, and use page prediction to preload sites in Windows browsers, which sends your browsing history to Microsoft.

Automatically connect to suggested open hotspots and shared networks. Not all networks are secure.

Send problem reports to Microsoft.

Learn more

Customize settings

Use Express settings

Figure 4-8:
I suggest
that you
choose the
Customize
settings
option, in
fine print
on the left.
It saves
having to
change bad
choices
later.

11. **If you trust Microsoft, choose Use Express Settings. If you're like me, choose Customize settings.**

If you choose Customize, the installer takes you through two screens of questions. Here's what I do:

In the first screen, shown in Figure 4-9, I turn off just about everything in Personalization, unless I intend to use Cortana. Unfortunately, Cortana needs my contacts and calendar details, as well as my location — she can't work very well without them. I refuse to "let apps use your advertising ID for experiences across apps."

In the second screen, shown in Figure 4-10, I turn on SmartScreen, although I'm painfully aware that this sends some of my browsing history to Microsoft. I don't use page prediction because the fraction-of-a-second improvement in speed isn't worth giving away my entire browsing history. I don't trust all my contacts to share clean networks. And I debate on a daily basis whether I should automatically send problem reports to Microsoft.

After a rather lengthy time digesting your settings, Windows asks if your computer belongs to your organization or if you own it, as shown in Figure 4-11.

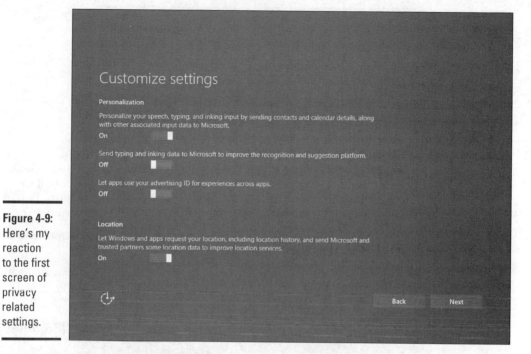

Figure 4-9:
Here's my
reaction
to the first
screen of
privacy
related
settings.

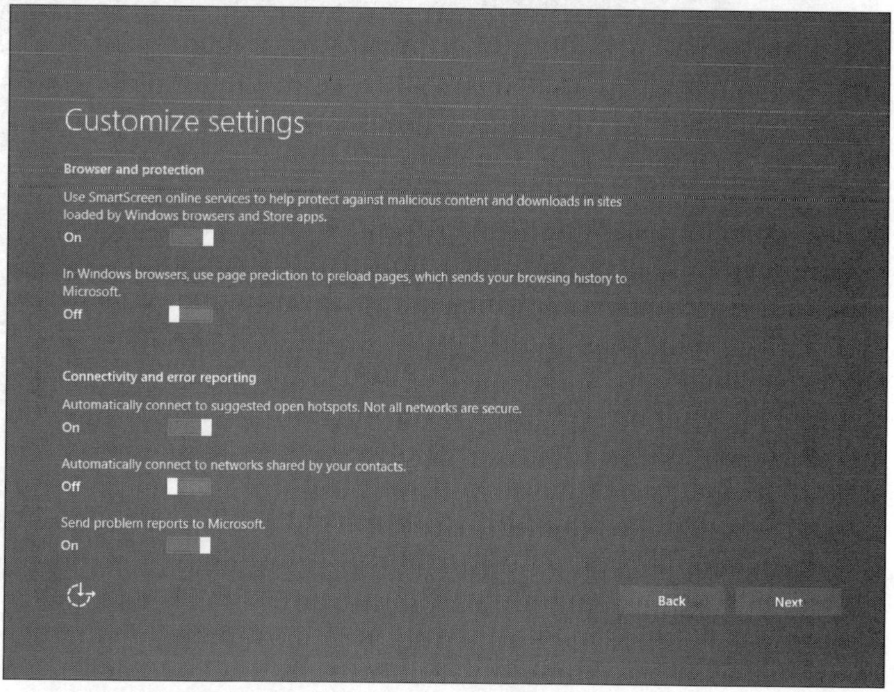

Figure 4-10:
Here are
my choices
for the
second
collection
of privacy
robbers.

Figure 4-11:
This is a key
question for
setting up
the internal
parts of
Windows.

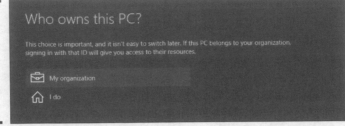

Who owns this PC?

This choice is important, and it isn't easy to switch later. If this PC belongs to your organization,
signing in with that ID will give you access to their resources.

My organization

I do

This is a key question. If you say it belongs to My organization, Windows
prompts you to log on to your organization's network and put all the
hooks in place so you can use the network. If you just say "I do" (where
have I heard that one before?), you get to play with your own network.

12. **Carefully consider whether you want to hook into your organization's
    network, make your choice, and click Next.**

    The installer prompts you for a Microsoft account and password, as in
    Figure 4-12.

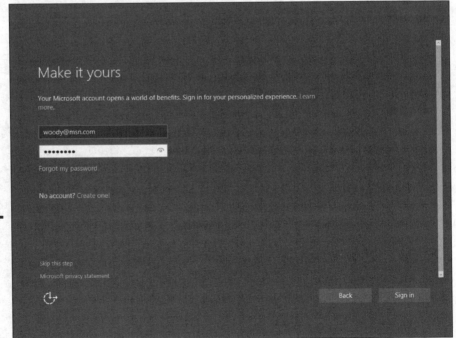

Make it yours

Your Microsoft account opens a world of benefits. Sign in for your personalized experience. Learn
more.

woody@msn.com

••••••••

Forgot my password

No account? Create one!

Skip this step

Microsoft privacy statement

Back   Sign in

Figure 4-12:
Don't be
bullied into
providing
an existing
Microsoft
account.

How to force Windows to take a local account

You may find yourself going round in circles, trying to get the installer to accept a local account, when it only provides prompts for entering — or signing up for — a Microsoft account. There's a little trick that isn't at all obvious.

If the installer demands that you enter (or sign up for) a Microsoft account, and there's no option available to enter a local account, just put any email address in the account name box, and put a completely bogus password in the password box. The installer responds with a prompt telling you that the account/password is invalid — but, at that point, it also shows you a link to enter a local account. Click the link, and remind yourself that Microsoft really, really wants you to sign on with a Microsoft account, to enhance your purchasing experiences. Meh.

13. **Don't let Windows bully you into using a Microsoft account. Enter the account name (and type!) you like. If you have a Microsoft account you want to use, go right ahead. If you'd rather not sully an existing Microsoft account, click Create one! And make a new one. They're free. If you want to log in with a local account, click Skip this step, or see the sidebar for a clever trick.**

    Personally, I use a clean (er, fake) Microsoft account, but you may feel differently. See the sidebar about forcing Windows to take a local account.

    In Book II, Chapter 4, you find an extensive discussion of the pros and cons of Microsoft accounts. Suffice it to say, there's no clear-cut "right" answer, but if you create a new, clean Microsoft account and use it exclusively for Windows 10, you won't be giving away too much of your privacy in exchange for the benefits of having a Microsoft account.

    The installer prompts you to set up a PIN.

14. **I, personally, like PINs — they're tied to the one device, and unless someone steals both the PIN and your computer, you're in good shape. So I click PIN me! and follow the steps to set up a PIN.**

    The installer asks if you want to set up a OneDrive account. If you signed in with an existing Microsoft account (as I did in Step 13, in spite of my bluster), Windows knows that you already have a OneDrive account and shows the window in Figure 4-13.

Figure 4-13:
Get
OneDrive
set up.

15. **Click Next.**

    Microsoft flashes a little advertisement for Cortana that doesn't do anything.

16. **Click Next, and stand back.**

    A new copy of Windows 10 appears, and you're finished.

In either upgrade scenario — online or boot from USB — Windows creates a folder called windows.old that contains dribs and drabs of your old Windows installation. After you've run Windows 10 for a while — and you're sure there's nothing in windows.old that you need to reclaim — you can delete that folder.

Cleaning the Gunk Off New PCs

On your new PC, did you get a free 60-day trial for Norton Internet Security with Symantec Live Update and the trial version of WinDVD and Roxio and Quicken — and oh! — this neat discount for EarthLink?

If you bought a new computer with Windows preinstalled, the manufacturer probably sold some desktop real estate to a software company or an Internet service provider (ISP).

Oh yeah, the AOLs and Nortons of the world compensate the Sonys and Dells and HPs for services, and space, rendered.

The last thing you need is yet another come-on to sign up for AOL or an anti-virus program that begs you for money every week, or a fancy manufacturer-installed driver that just sits there and sucks up space.

Some manufacturers have wised up and started offering clean PCs, for a slight premium. Microsoft stores also sell Signature editions of popular PCs — *Signature* implies that the PCs have been divested of typical manufacturer junk. Believe me, it's worth the money to get the cleanest PC you possibly can.

The easiest way to get a clean PC? Install Windows 10 from Microsoft. Use any of the methods mentioned in the preceding section and, as long as you don't bring across old programs in an upgrade, your new computer will be clean as can be. Blissfully so.

If you have a PC with all that junk, here's what you can do to remove it:

✦ **Take it to a Microsoft store** (one of the brick-and-mortar ones), where you can pay $99 for someone to take the junk off a new PC.

✦ **Use a tool that removes most, if not all, the useless junk.** PC Decrapifier is a free, simple program that scans your machine and gets rid of most of the junk. As this book went to press, the Windows 10 version wasn't ready, so check at the developer's website, `www.pcdecrapifier.com`, to see whether it's Win10-safe.

What If the Wheels Fall Off?

So what should you do if Windows dies? Try this:

✦ **If Windows came bundled with a new PC,** scream bloody murder at the vendor who sold you the %$#@! thing. Don't put up with any talk about "it's a software problem; Microsoft is at fault." If you bought Windows with a new PC, the company that sold you the machine has full responsibility for making it work right. Period.

✦ **If you upgraded from Windows 7 SP1 or Windows 8.1 Update to Windows 10 and didn't complete a custom (clean) install,** try that. You don't have much to lose, eh? Follow the instructions in the section, "Installing Win10 from a DVD or USB Drive," earlier in this chapter, and go for the Custom (Clean) Install.

✦ **If you completed a custom (clean) install and Windows still falls over and plays dead,** man, you have my sympathies. Check with your hardware manufacturer and make sure that you have the latest BIOS version installed. (Make sure to find an instruction book; changing the BIOS is remarkably easy, if you follow the instructions.) Visit the online newsgroups, look at `AskWoody.com`, or drop by my lounge, at `windowssecrets.com/forums` to see whether anybody there can lend a hand. If all else fails, admit defeat and reinstall your old operating system.

Life's too short.

Book II

Personalizing Windows

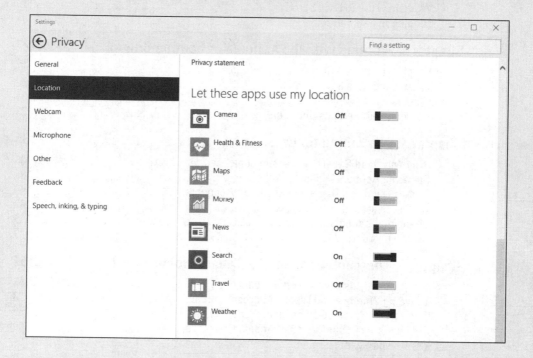

Looking for new and better wallpaper/background screens? Drop by www.dummies. com/extras/windows10aio/wallpaper for my latest favorites.

Contents at a Glance

Chapter 1: Getting Around in Windows

In This Chapter

✔ Navigating via your fingers or via a mouse

✔ Switching among apps

✔ To boldly go where no mouse has gone before

Ready to get your feet wet, but not yet up to a full plunge?

Good. You're in the right place for a dip-your-toes-in kind of experience. Nothing tough in this chapter, just a bit of windows cruising. Lay of the land kind of stuff.

If you're an experienced Windows 7 or XP user, you'll find parts of Windows 10 that look a bit familiar and parts that look like they were ripped from an iPhone. If you're an experienced Windows 8.1 user, I salute you and your stamina, and I welcome you to a kinder, gentler Windows.

Former Microsoft General Manager and Distinguished Engineer Hal Berenson said it best: "Consumers increasingly reject the old experiences in both their personal and work lives. For the 20-something-and-under crowd, the current Windows desktop experience is about as attractive as the thought of visiting a 19th-century dentist."

Windows 10 looks a little bit like that 19th-century dentist's office, but underneath it's gone through radical transformations.

I figure that 90 percent of the stuff that 80 percent of the people do with a computer, runs just fine on a tablet or a Chromebook. So why put up with all the hassles of running Windows on a piece of iron that weighs more than your refrigerator, and breaks down twice as often? Maybe you're addicted to blue screens and frozen mice. Or maybe you're ready to leave it all behind and tap your way to something new.

In this chapter, I show you what's to like about both the old-fashioned side of Windows and the new Universal side, how to get around if you're new to Windows, and if you're an experienced Windows hand, how to reconcile your old finger memory with the new interface. It isn't as hard as you think.

Really.

I also show you how to be input-agnostic — how to use either your fingers or your fork, er, mouse to get around the screen. And I give you a few not-at-all-obvious tips about how to get the most out of your consorting with the beast.

Windows' New Beginnings

The way I look at it, most people starting with Windows 10 start in one of five groups, with the largest percentage in the first group:

✦ Somewhat experienced at some version of Windows and primarily comfortable with a mouse and keyboard. (More than 1.4 billion people have used Windows.)

✦ Experienced at Windows but want to learn touch input.

✦ Windows 8 refugee who's hoping and praying Windows 10 isn't so disorienting.

✦ New to Windows, prefer to use touch.

✦ New to Windows and want to visit the 19th-century dentist's office to see what all the screaming's about.

If you fall into that final group, you need to learn to use the antique interface apparatus known as a mouse and keyboard. I'm reminded of Scotty on the Enterprise picking up a mouse and saying, "Computer! Computer! Hello computer . . ." When Scotty's reminded to use the keyboard, he says, "Keyboard. How quaint." At least he didn't say, "Hey, Cortana!"

So this section offers a whirlwind tour of your new Windows 10 home that helps you start clicking and tapping your way around.

A tale of two homes

As you undoubtedly know by now, Windows 10's Start menu has two faces. They're designed to work together. You can be the judge of how well they live up to the design.

On the left side of the Start menu (see Figure 1-1), you see the Start menu that's supposed to look like the Windows 7 (and Vista and XP and 95) Start menu. On the right side of the Start menu, you see a bunch of tiles, some of which actually have useful information on them.

Tap or click, paper or plastic?

Lots of people have asked me whether I'm serious about tapping on a Windows machine. Yes, I am, and I hope you will be, too.

I tried the old stylus Windows interface, back when the luggable Windows tablets first appeared, in the Windows XP days. I hated it. I still hate it. I hated it so much that when I saw someone using an iPad, all I could think was, "Oh, that must suck." (Remember, "suck" is a technical term.)

An hour later, I tried an iPad, and suddenly using a finger was fine. More than fine, it was tremendous. When my then-18-month-old son spent a few hours playing on the iPad and started using the interface like a virtuoso, I was hooked. The tap-and-swipe interface is astonishingly easy to learn, use, and remember.

Windows 10's tap interface isn't as elegant as the iPad's. Sorry, but it's true. The main difference is that Windows has to accommodate lots of things that the iPad just doesn't do — right-click comes immediately to mind. But for many, many things that I do every day — web surfing, quickly checking email, scrolling through Twitter, catching up on Facebook, reading the news, looking at the stock market, and on and on — the touch interface is vastly superior to a mouse and keyboard. At least, it is to me.

That said, yes, you can get used to a tablet without a mouse and keyboard.

As I'm writing this book, I have three computers on my desk. One's a traditional desktop running Windows 8.1, and one's running Windows 10. The third is a Win10 tablet with a portable keyboard. When I want to look up something quickly, guess which one I use? Bzzzzzt. Wrong. I pick up my Galaxy phone — or my iPad.

Figure 1-1:
The Windows 10 Start menu, default settings as seen on a Surface Pro 3.

Although the left side of the Start menu is supposed to bring back warm, comforting memories of Windows 7 (and XP), underneath the surface, the left part of the Start menu has almost nothing in common with earlier Start menus. The old Start menu has been ripped out and totally replaced with this new list of links.

That's both good and bad. As you'll see, the left side of the Start menu is quite powerful, but if you gnawed away at the Windows 7 Start menu back in the day, you'll find that there's very little meat to the new Start menu. Conversely, the Windows 10 Start menu doesn't get screwed up as easily — or as completely — as the Windows 7 Start menu.

On the right side of the Start menu, you see a vast sea of tiles. Unlike the tiles on your iPhone or iPad or Galaxy, these tiles have some smarts: If prodded, they will tell you things that you might want to know, without opening up the associated app. In this screen shot, you can see the weather, a news story, a photo, stock market results, and a sports story. That's the Windows tile shtick, and it's apparent here in all its glory.

Whether you like having your news boiled down into a sentence fragment, that's for you to decide.

Unlike the left side of the Start menu, the right side with the tiles can get gloriously screwed up. You can stretch and move and group and ungroup until you're blue screened in the face.

I tend to think of the tiles on the right side of the Start menu as the next generation of Windows 7 Gadgets. If you ever used Gadgets, you know that they were small programs that displayed useful information on their faces. Microsoft banned them before releasing Windows 8, primarily because they raised all sorts of security problems.

Windows 10 Start menu tiles don't have the security problems. And the infrastructure that has replaced the Gadget mentality has taken Windows to an entirely new level.

Switching to Tablet Mode and back

Get your computer going. Go ahead. I'll wait.

You're looking at the old-fashioned Windows desktop, right? (If you have a mouse and Windows sensed it, you're looking at the desktop. If your machine is only touch, you may be in Tablet Mode already.)

Time to take a walk on the wild side. Let's flip over to Tablet Mode. Click (or tap) Start, Settings, System. On the left, pick Tablet Mode, and at the top, move the Tablet Mode slider On.

This (Figure 1-2) is where the finger pickers live.

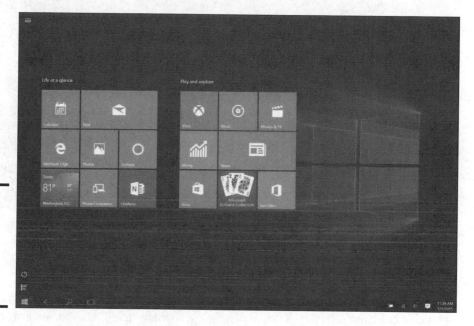

Figure 1-2: Tablet Mode, a good place for touch-first types.

Wait. Don't panic.

See the funny icon in the upper-left corner, the one with three horizontal lines? For the mathematicians in the crowd, it looks just like an equivalence sign. In the computer world, that's known as a hamburger icon (see the nearby sidebar). If you want to get back the Start menu items temporarily, you have to push the hamburger icon.

Go ahead and push the hamburglar. You see something like Figure 1-3.

To get back to normal (I call it "desktop view" although it doesn't really seem to have a name), click or tap the hamburger icon, choose Settings, then (if you're offered a choice) System. On the left, choose Tablet Mode. On the right, slide the Tablet Mode switch Off.

That brings you back to Figure 1-1. Which is probably where you wanted to be.

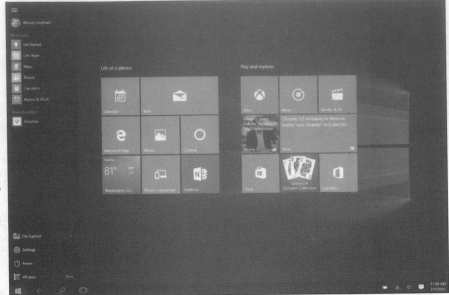

Figure 1-3:
Tablet Mode with the hamburger icon pushed.

The history of the hamburger icon

There have been many harsh words about the lowly hamburger. On the one hand, the icon doesn't really say anything. On the other hand, so many systems and programs now use the icon that it's close to being universal. Even cross-platform.

Ends up that the hamburger icon (like so many things we take for granted today) was designed at the Xerox Palo Alto Research Center, PARC, for use on the first graphical computer, the Xerox Star. Norm Cox designed it at PARC, and you can see its first appearance at `https:// vimeo.com/61556918#t=1265s`. Software designer Geoff Alday contacted Cox, and this is what he said:

"I designed that symbol many years ago as a 'container' for contextual menu choices. It would be somewhat equivalent to the context menu we use today when clicking over objects with the right mouse button. Its graphic design was meant to be very 'road sign' simple, functionally memorable, and mimic the look of the resulting displayed menu list. With so few pixels to work with, it had to be very distinct, yet simple. . . we used to tell potential users that the image was an 'air vent' to keep the window cool. It usually got a chuckle, and made the mark much more memorable."

That's why, 30 years later, Windows 10 uses the hamburger icon.

While you're in Tablet Mode, you can show the Action Center (better known as the Notification Center, the pane on the right side) by tapping the icon that looks like a cartoon's dialog balloon; it's next to the time and date in the bottom right-hand corner. More about it in the next chapter of this mini-book, Book II Chapter 3.

Although Tablet Mode is designed for people who want to use a touch screen, not a mouse, there's no law that says you're stuck in one persona or the other. You can flip back and forth between regular mouse-first mode and Tablet Mode any time.

Navigating Around the Desktop

Whether you use a mouse, a trackpad, or your finger, the Windows Desktop rules as your number-one point of entry into the beast itself.

Here's a guided tour of your PC, which you can perform with either a mouse or a finger, your choice:

1. **Click or tap the Start button.**

   You see the Start menu in Figure 1-1.

2. **Tap or click the tile on the right marked Mail.**

   You may have to "Add" an email account, but sooner or later, Microsoft's new Mail app appears, as in Figure 1-4.

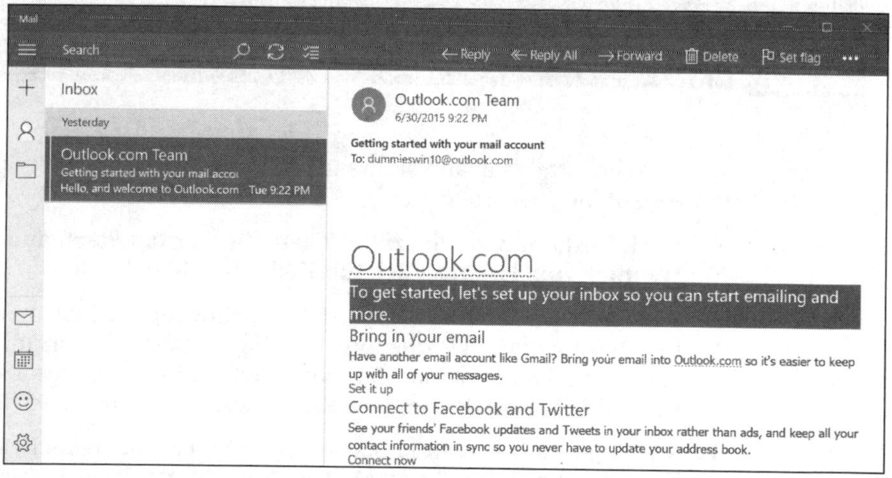

Figure 1-4: The Mail app is indicative of the new "Universal" Windows Universal apps.

3. **Take a close look at the Mail app window.**

   Like other Windows windows, the Mail window can be resized by moving your mouse over an edge and dragging. You can move the whole window by clicking the title bar and dragging. You can minimize the window — make it float down, to the taskbar — by clicking the square icon in the upper-right corner. And, finally, you can close the app by clicking the "X" in the upper right.

   That may seem pretty trivial if you're from the Windows 7 site of the reality divide. But for Windows 8/8.1 veterans, the ability to move a "Metro" app window around is a Real Big Deal.

4. **At the bottom in the taskbar, to the right of the Cortana "Ask me anything" puffery, click the Task View icon. It looks like a floorplan drawing of a table with two chairs.**

   The desktop turns gray, and your Mail window shrinks a bit. A New Desktop icon, shaped like a + sign, appears in the lower right.

5. **Click the + New desktop icon.**

   Windows creates a new, empty desktop, and shows it to you in Task View. See Figure 1-5.

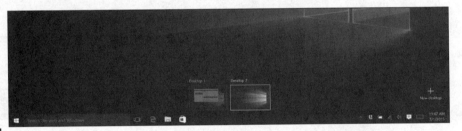

Figure 1-5: Windows 10 lets you create as many desktops as you like.

Note how the Mail app shows up on Desktop 1, and Desktop 2 is blank except for your wallpaper.

6. **Click Desktop 2, on the right. Then click or tap Start, and pick the Weather app. Finally, click the Task View icon.**

   Windows 10 pops back into Task View, showing the Mail app running on Desktop 1 and the Weather app running on Desktop 2. In addition, the background for Desktop 2 has darkened, and you can see a slimmed-down version of the Weather app on the Desktop 2 desktop. See Figure 1-6.

7. **Although your screen looks just like Figure 1-6, right-click the title bar (or tap and hold) and choose Move to, Desktop 1. Then click the Desktop 1 thumbnail at the bottom.**

Figure 1-6:
Two
desktops,
each with
different
programs
running.

You've just successfully created a second desktop, then moved a running application from one desktop to another. The results should look like Figure 1-7.

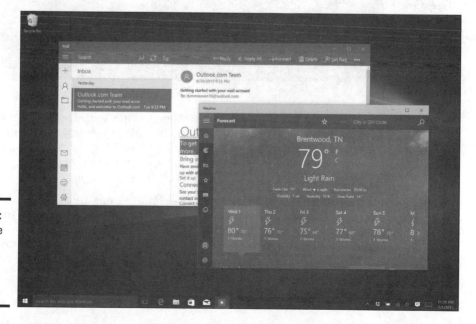

Figure 1-7:
Both of the
apps are
running
happily on
Desktop 1.

That's a quick introduction to Task View and multiple desktops, which I cover in detail in Book III, Chapter 4.

8. **"X" out of the Mail and Weather apps. Then click or tap the Start icon again, and choose All Apps.**

Windows brings up a more-or-less alphabetized view of all your apps.

9. **Scroll down to Windows Accessories, click the down arrow to the right of Windows Accessories, and choose Paint.**

Windows Paint appears, just like in the good old days, Figure 1-8.

Figure 1-8: The All Apps list is lengthy, but necessary.

Note that the Start menu's All Apps list has very few collections of programs like Windows Accessories. When you install new programs, they may build drop-down menus on the All Apps list, as you see with Windows Accessories, but far more commonly they just get dumped in the list. That gives you lots of stuff to scroll through.

Also note that the running app — Paint — has an icon down on the task-bar. When you close Paint, the icon disappears. If you want to keep Paint on the taskbar, right-click the icon and choose Pin this program to task-bar. That'll save you a scroll-scroll-scroll trip through All Apps the next time you want to run Paint.

10. **"X" out of Paint. Again, click or tap Start, All Apps. This time click or tap one of the alphabetizing indexes. For example, click the "A" above Alarms & Clock.**

Windows shows you a telephone-like index for all your All Apps entries, as you can see in Figure 1-9. Click, say, W, and you're immediately transported to the "W" part of the All Apps list.

Book II
Chapter 1

Getting Around in
Windows

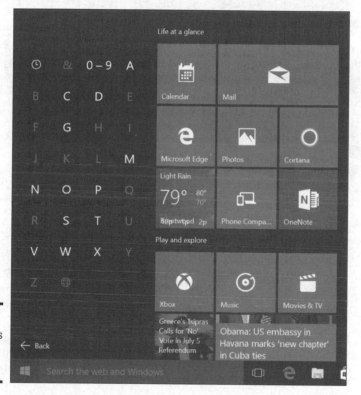

Figure 1-9:
The All Apps list has an index.

11. **Let's take a quick look at the other notable new Windows Universal apps. At the bottom of the screen, click or tap the icon that looks like an "e" in a blender. It's vaguely reminiscent of the old Internet Explorer "e."**

You're transported into Microsoft Edge, the new Internet browser from the folks in Redmond. See Figure 1-10.

Internet Explorer is still around if you really, really, really have to use it: Just look in All Apps under Windows Accessories, not far from where you found Paint in Step 9.

Figure 1-10:
Microsoft
Edge takes
you straight
to adville; do
not pass go.

Microsoft is, to a first approximation anyway, abandoning Internet Explorer. That's good because IE has turned into a bloated, buggy, sinking piece of scrap. (You knew that already if you read any of my previous Windows *All-In-One For Dummies* books.) With Microsoft Edge, there's a chance that the 'Softies may actually stand a chance competing against Google's Chrome browser and Firefox — both of which I still recommend.

Play with Edge for a bit — type something up in the address bar. Click or tap the + sign at the top, and add a new tab. Click some links. See how it works like a browser? Edge is actually a reasonably good browser, although it lacks some features. See Book V, Chapter 1 for much more info.

12. **If you haven't yet started with Cortana, give her a try. Click inside the bar that says Ask me anything.**

Cortana goes through some setup steps, which I describe in Book III, Chapter 6. If you already have a Microsoft account, it's easy to get set up. (Note that you do need a Microsoft account to get personal information out of Cortana — that's how she/he/it stores your data for later retrieval.)

13. **Click inside the Ask me anything box, and say "Hey, Cortana," pause for a heartbeat, and then say "Tell me a joke."**

I won't attest to her sense of humor (see Figure 1-11), but Cortana has certainly been trained well.

Figure 1-11:
Hey, Cortana
(pause,
pause) Tell
me a joke!

If you'd like more interesting things to ask Cortana, hop over to Google (sorry) and search for "Cortana questions."

14. **That completes the canned tour of Windows 10 highlights. There's much, much more to discover — we only scratched a thin layer of epidermis.**

Take a breather.

Keying Keyboard Shortcuts

Windows 10 has about a hundred zillion — no, a googolplex — of keyboard shortcuts.

I don't use very many of them. They make my brain hurt.

Here are the keyboard shortcuts that everyone should know. They've been around for a long, long time:

✦ **Ctrl+C** copies whatever you've selected and puts it on the Clipboard. On a touchscreen, you can do the same thing in most applications by tapping and holding, and then choosing Copy.

✦ **Ctrl+X** does the same thing but removes the selected items — a cut. Again, you can tap and hold, and Cut should appear in the menu.

✦ **Ctrl+V** pastes whatever is in the Clipboard to the current cursor location. Tap and hold usually works.

✦ **Ctrl+A** selects everything, although sometimes it's hard to tell what "everything" means — different applications handle Ctrl+A differently. Tap and hold usually works here, too.

✦ **Ctrl+Z** usually "undoes" whatever you just did. Few touch-enabled apps have a tap-and-hold alternative; you usually have to find Undo on a Ribbon or menu.

✦ When you're typing, **Ctrl+B**, **Ctrl+I**, and **Ctrl+U** usually flip your text over to Bold, Italic, or Underline, respectively. Hit the same key combination again, and you flip back to normal.

In addition to all the key combinations you may have encountered in Windows versions since the dawn of 19th-century dentistry, there's a healthy crop of new combinations. These are the important ones:

✦ The **Windows key** brings up the Start menu.

✦ **Alt+Tab** cycles through all running Windows programs, one by one — and each running Legacy desktop app is treated as a running program. (Windows key+Tab treats the entire desktop as one "app.") See Figure 1-12.

✦ **Ctrl+Alt+Del** — the old Vulcan three-finger salute — brings up a screen that lets you choose to lock your PC (flip to Book II, Chapter 2), switch the user (see Book II, Chapter 4), sign out, or run the new and much improved Task Manager (see Book VIII, Chapter 4).

You can also right-click the Start icon or press **Windows key+X** to bring up the so-called "Power User" menu shown in Figure 1-13.

Figure 1-12:
Alt+Tab
cycles
through
all running
apps.

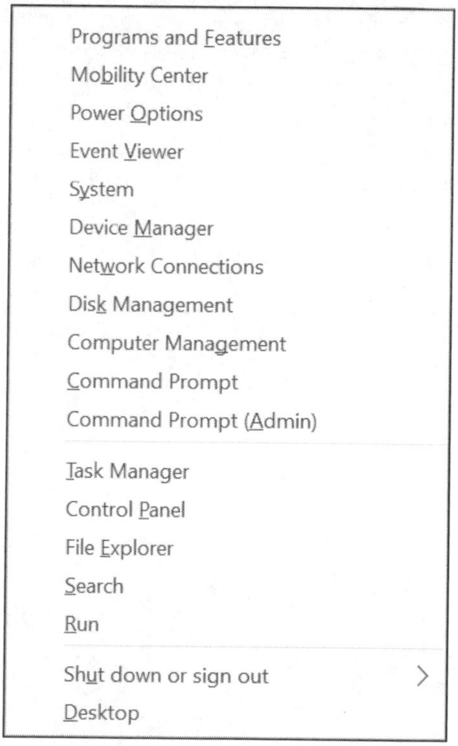

Programs and Features

Mobility Center

Power Options

Event Viewer

System

Device Manager

Network Connections

Disk Management

Computer Management

Command Prompt

Command Prompt (Admin)

Task Manager

Control Panel

File Explorer

Search

Run

Shut down or sign out   >

Desktop

Figure 1-13:
The Win-X
or "Power
User" menu
can get
you into the
innards of
Windows.

Chapter 2: Changing the Lock Screen and Logon Screen

*W*indows presents three hurdles for you to clear before you can get down to work (or play, or whatever):

1. You have to get past the *lock screen*. That's a first-level hurdle so your computer doesn't accidentally get started, like the lock screen on a smartphone or an iPad.

2. If there's more than one person — one *account* — set up on the computer, you have to choose which person will log on. I go into detail about setting up user accounts in Book II, Chapter 4.

3. If a password's associated with the account, you must type it into the computer. Windows allows different kinds of passwords, which are particularly helpful if you're working on a touch-only tablet or a tiny screen like a telephone's. But the idea's the same: Unless you specifically set up an account without a password, you need to confirm your identity.

Only after clearing those three hurdles are you granted access to the Start screen and, from there, to everything Windows has to offer. In the sections that follow, you find out how you can customize the lock screen and the login methods to suit yourself.

Windows Hello

Windows Hello gives an additional method for confirming your identity. Windows Hello uses biometric authentication — scanning your face, your iris, or your fingerprint — as a much more secure method than passwords.

As we went to press, Windows Hello technology (including, notably, Intel RealSense cameras) was just starting to hit the market.

Initial results are encouraging, but only time will tell if Hello is reliable enough (and the hardware cheap enough!) to make a dent in the market.

The hardware's quite specialized. If you have a pre-Windows 10 camera or fingerprint reader, chances are very good it won't work with Windows Hello.

Working with the Lock Screen

The very first time you start Windows, and anytime you shut it down, restart, or let the machine go idle for long enough, you're greeted with the lock screen, such as the one in Figure 2-1.

Figure 2-1:
The
Windows
lock screen.

Individualized lock screens

If you read the Microsoft help file, you may think that Windows keeps one lock screen for all users, but it doesn't. Instead, it has a lock screen for each individual user and one more lock screen for the system as a whole.

If you're using the system and you lock it — say, tap your picture on the Metro Start screen and choose Lock — Windows shows your personal lock screen, with the badges you've chosen. If you swipe or drag to lift that lock screen, you're immediately asked to provide your password. There's no intervening step to ask which user should log on.

If, instead of locking the system when you leave it, you tap your picture and choose Sign Out, Windows behaves quite differently. It shows the system's lock screen, with the system's badges. Your lock screen and badges are nowhere to be seen. If you drag or swipe to go through the lock screen, you're asked to choose which user will log on.

Bottom line: If you change your lock screen using the techniques in this chapter, you change only *your* lock screen. Windows' idea of a lock screen stays the same.

You can get through the lock screen by doing any of the following:

✦ Swiping up with your finger, if you have a touch-sensitive display

✦ Dragging up with your mouse

✦ Pressing any key on your keyboard

You aren't stuck with the lock screen Microsoft gives you. You can customize your picture and the little icons (or *badges*). The following sections explain how.

Using your own picture

Changing the picture for your lock screen is easy. (See the nearby sidebar "Individualized lock screens" for details about the difference between your lock screen and the system's lock screen.) Customizing the picture is a favorite trick at Windows demos, so you know it has to be easy, right? Here's how:

1. **Click or tap Start, Settings, Personalization.**

2. **On the left, choose Lock screen.**

   The Lock Screen Preview window, as shown in Figure 2-2, appears.

Figure 2-2:
Change your
own lock
screen here.

3. **From the Background drop-down list, first try Windows spotlight, if it's available.**

   Windows Spotlight images come direct from Microsoft and change frequently. Microsoft reserves the right to put advertising on the screen — ostensibly to tell you about features in Windows that you haven't used yet. Remains to be seen whether other, uh, partners can purchase spots on the screen.

4. **Next, from the drop-down list, choose Picture.**

   This selection (see Figure 2-3) lets you choose from images offered by Microsoft, or if you click the Browse button, you can choose any picture on your computer.

   You can decide whether you want your chosen picture to be overlaid with "fun facts, tips, tricks, and more on your lock screen."

5. **If you find a picture you want, click it. If not, choose Slideshow in the Background drop-down box.**

   This option ties into the Albums in the Windows Universal Photos app (see Book IV, Chapter 3), or you can choose to turn a folder of pictures into a slideshow. If you decide to go with a slideshow, click the link marked Advanced slideshow settings to set whether the slideshow can be pulled from your Camera Roll, whether the chosen pictures have to be large enough to fit your screen, and several additional choices.

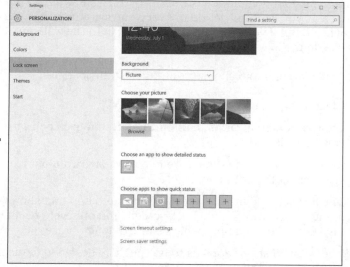

Figure 2-3:
Choose
your own
picture, with
or without
Microsoft
advertising.

6. **After you've chosen the background itself, you can specify what apps should provide details that appear on the Lock Screen. See the next section for details about *Badges*.**

   You're finished. There's no Apply or OK button to tap or click.

   Test to make sure that your personal lock screen has been updated. The easiest way is to go to the Start menu, click your picture in the upper-left corner, and choose Lock or Sign Out.

Adding and removing apps on the lock screen

Badges are the little icons that appear at the bottom of the lock screen. They exist to tell you something about your computer at a glance, without having to log on — how many email messages are unread, whether your battery needs charging, and so on. Some badges just appear on the lock screen, no matter what you do. For example, if you have an Internet connection, a badge appears on the lock screen. If you're using a tablet or laptop, the battery status appears; there's nothing you can do about it.

Mostly, though, Windows lets you pick and choose quick status badges that are important to you. The question I most often hear about badges is, "Why not just choose them all?"

Good question. The programs that support the badges update their information periodically — every 15 minutes, in some cases. If you have a badge on your lock screen, the lock screen app that controls the badge has to wake up every so often, so it can retrieve the data and put it on the lock screen. Putting everything on the lock screen drains your computer's battery.

Corollary: If your computer has a short battery life, whittle your needs down as much as you can, and get rid of every quick status badge you don't absolutely need. But if your computer is plugged in to the wall, put all the badges you like on the lock screen.

Here's how to pick and choose your quick status badges:

1. **Click or tap Start, Settings.**

2. **Choose Personalization, and on the left, choose Lock screen. On the right, scroll down.**

   At the bottom of the screen are two rows of grayed-out icons. You can see them at the bottom of Figure 2-3.

   The first icon points to a specially anointed app that shows detailed status information on the Lock screen. You only get one. In Figure 2-1, I have the date and time, which is the default choice.

   The detailed status app has to be specially designed to display the large block of information shown in Figure 2-1.

3. **Tap or click the detailed status icon, and choose which display badge you want to appear in that slot on the lock screen (see Figure 2-4).**

   Apps must be specially designed to display the badge information on the lock screen. You're given a choice of all the apps that have registered with Windows as being capable of displaying a quick status badge on the lock screen. As you add more apps, some of them appear spontaneously on this list.

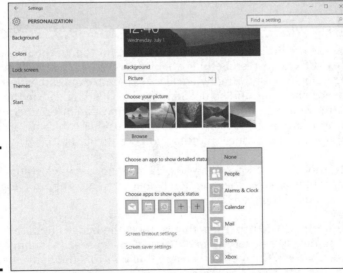

Figure 2-4: Choose which app's badges appear on the Lock Screen.

The second row, of seven icons, corresponds to seven badge locations at the bottom of the lock screen. They appear in order from left to right, starting below the time. In theory (although this doesn't always work), you can choose which badges appear, and where they appear, in order from left to right.

4. **Click each of the seven grayed-out icons in turn, and choose an app to show its status on the Lock Screen.**

   If you choose Don't Show Quick Status Here, the gray icon gets a plus (+) sign, indicating that it isn't being used. No badge appears in the corresponding slot on the lock screen.

   The quick status apps have to be built specifically to show their badges on the Lock Screen.

   You're finished. There's no Apply or OK button to tap or click.

Go back out to the lock screen — click or tap Start, choose your picture at the top, choose Lock — and see whether you like the changes. If you don't like what you see or you're worried about unnecessarily draining your battery with all the fluff, start over at Step 1.

Logging In Uniquely

In this section, I step you through setting up picture passwords and PINs, and I give you a little hint about how you can bypass logon completely, if you aren't overly concerned about other people snooping around on your PC. Yes, it can be done, quite easily.

Using a picture password

If you follow the instructions in Book II, Chapter 4, set up an account, and the account has an everyday, ordinary password, you can use a picture password.

It's easy.

A *picture password* consists of two parts: First, you choose a picture — any picture — and then you tell Windows that you're going to draw on that picture in a particular way, such as taps, clicks, circles, and straight lines, with a finger or a mouse. The next time you want to log in to Windows, you can either type your password or you can repeat the series of clicks, taps, circles, and straight lines.

So, for example, you may have a picture of a rugrat in the wild, as shown in the upper-right corner of Figure 2-5, and you may decide that you want your picture password to consist of tapping the forehead, right hand, and left hand, in that order.

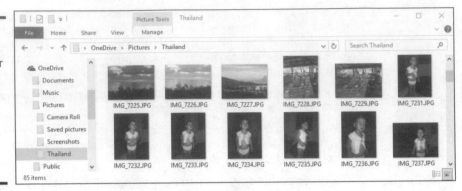

Figure 2-5:
The photo
in the upper
right, in my
Pictures
folder,
will make
a great
picture
password.

That picture password is simple, fast, and not easy to guess.

Everybody I know who has a chance to switch to a picture password or PIN loves it. Whether you're working with a mouse or a stubby finger, a few taps or slides are sooo much easier than trying to remember and type `a17LetterP@ssw0rd`.

Microsoft has a few suggestions for making your picture password hard to crack. These include the following:

✦ **Start with a picture that has lots of interesting points.** If you have just one or two interesting locations in the photo, you don't have very many points to choose from.

✦ **Don't use just taps (or clicks).** Mix things up. Use a tap, a circle, and a line, for example, in any sequence you can easily remember.

✦ **Don't always move from left to right.** Lines can go right to left, or top to bottom. Circles can go clockwise or counterclockwise.

✦ **Don't let anybody watch you sign in.** Picture passwords are worse than keyboard passwords, in some respects, because the picture password appears on the screen as you're drawing it.

✦ **Clean your screen.** Really devious souls may be able to figure out that trail of oil and grime is from your repeated use of the same picture password. If you can't clean your screen and you're worried about somebody following the grime trail, put a couple of gratuitous smudges on the screen. I'm sure you can find a two-year-old who would be happy to oblige.

Here's how to change your account to use a picture password:

1. **Tap or click Start, Settings, Accounts.**

2. **On the left, choose Sign-in options.**

   The password settings for your account, as shown in Figure 2-6, appear.

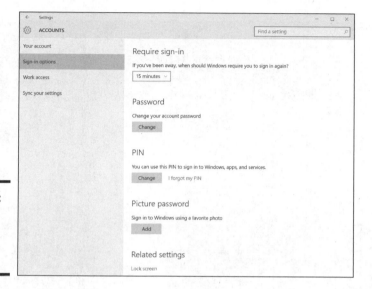

**Book II
Chapter 2**

Figure 2-6:
Your
account's
password
settings.

Changing the Lock
Screen and Logon
Screen

3. Under Picture Password, tap or click Add.

If your account doesn't yet have a password, you're prompted to provide one. If you do have a password, Windows asks you to verify your typed password.

You must have a typed password — the password can't be blank — or Windows will just log you in without any password, either typed or picture.

4. Type your password, and then tap or click OK.

Windows asks you to choose a picture.

5. Tap or click Choose Picture, find a picture (remember, with ten or more interesting points), and tap or click Open.

Your picture appears in a cropping bucket. The picture must conform to an odd shape, or it won't fit on the logon screen.

6. Slide the picture around to crop it the way you want it. Then tap or click Use This Picture.

Windows invites you to set up your gestures, as shown in Figure 2-7.

Windows then asks you to repeat your gestures. This is where you get to see how sensitive the gesture-tracking method can be.

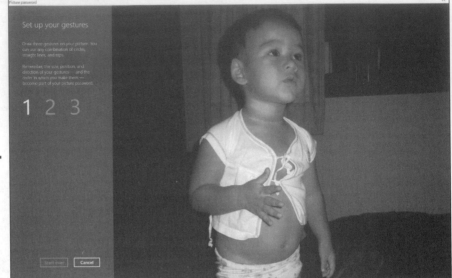

Figure 2-7:
Here's
where you
draw your
three taps/
clicks, lines,
and circles.

7. **Repeat the gestures. When you get them to match (which isn't necessarily easy!), tap or click Finish.**

   Your new picture password is ready.

8. **Go to the Start menu, tap your picture, choose Lock, and make sure you can replicate it.**

If you can't get the picture password to work, you can always use your regular typed password.

Creating a PIN

Everybody has PIN codes for ATM cards, telephones, just about everything.

Reusing PIN codes on multiple devices (and credit cards) is dangerous — somebody looks over your shoulder, watches you type your Windows PIN, and then lifts your wallet. They can have a good time, unless the PINs are different. Word to the wise, eh?

PINs have lots of advantages over passwords and picture passwords. They're short and easy to remember. Fast. Technically, though, the best thing about a PIN is that it's stored on your computer — it's tied to that one computer, and you don't have to worry about it getting stored in some hacked database or stolen with your credit card numbers.

Creating a PIN is easy:

1. **Tap or click Start, Settings, Accounts.**

2. **On the left, choose Sign-in options.**

   The password settings for your account appear (refer to Figure 2-6).

3. **Under PIN, tap or click Add.**

   Windows asks you to verify your password — it must be your typed password; a picture password won't do.

4. **Type your password, and tap or click OK.**

   Windows gives you a chance to type your PIN, as in Figure 2-8, and then retype it to confirm it. *Note:* Most PINs are four digits, but you can go longer, if you wish. Just uncheck the box marked Use a 4-digit PIN.

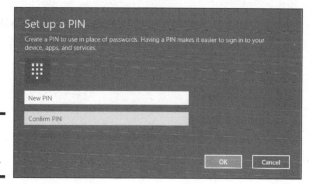

Figure 2-8:
Creating a
PIN is easy.

5. **Type your PIN, confirm it, and tap or click OK.**

   You can log on with your PIN.

Windows Hello

As we went to press, Windows Hello hardware was starting to roll out. In a nutshell, Windows Hello offers biometric authentication — way beyond a password or a PIN. The Windows Hello technology includes face and iris recognition with a specially designed camera and/or fingerprint recognition.

Microsoft is gradually implementing fingerprint recognition with older finger scanners, as well.

How to tell if your computer supports Windows Hello? Click Start, Settings, Account, Sign-in option. Set up a PIN using the steps in the preceding section. Then, if your machine can handle Windows Hello, there is a link in the settings page under Windows Hello.

Bypassing passwords and logon

So now you have three convenient ways to tell Windows your password: You can type it, just like a normal password; you can click or tap on a picture; or you can pretend it's a phone and enter four digits.

But what if you don't want a password? What if your computer is secure enough — it's sitting in your house, it's in your safe deposit box, it's dangling from a vine over a pot of boiling oil — and you just don't want to be bothered with typing or tapping a password?

As long as you have a Local account, it's easy. Just remove your password. Turn it into a blank. Follow the steps in Book II, Chapter 4 to change your password but leave the New Password field blank. (Shortcut: In Figure 2-6, tap or click the Change button under Password.)

Microsoft accounts can't have blank passwords. But local accounts can.

If you have a blank password, when you click your username on the logon screen, Windows ushers you to the desktop.

If there's only one user on the PC and that user has a blank password, just getting past the lock screen takes you to the Start screen.

Chapter 3: Working with the Action/Notification Center

In This Chapter

✔ What is the Action Center?

✔ Settings in the Action Center

✔ The different kinds of notifications

✔ What you can do with notifications

*I*f you've ever used a moderately sentient phone or tablet, you already know about the notification center. Different devices do it differently, but the general idea is that the phone watches and gathers notifications — little warning messages or status reports — that are sent to you. The phone or tablet gathers all the notifications and puts them in one place, where you can look at them and decide what to do from there.

In Windows 7, notifications just kind of flew by, and there weren't many of them. In Windows 8 and 8.1, you typically see many more notifications (I'm looking at you, Gmail running in Chrome), but they still fly by. There's no way in Windows 8 or 8.1 to look at old notifications. After they're off the screen — frequently for just a few seconds — that's it. And when they pile up, they can pile up and up and up and up, taking over the right edge of your screen.

Finally, with Windows 10, we have a place where Windows sticks all the notifications. Or at least some of them. Sometimes. You know, like smartphones have had for a decade or so.

What Is the Action Center?

Unfortunately, this new locus for machine notifications isn't called a "Notification Center," as it's called in almost every operating system, in almost every language, on earth. That name's taken — Microsoft started calling the System Tray, down at the lower-right corner of the screen, the "Notification Center" with Windows 8.

So we get a strange name for a common sight: It's officially called "Action Center," while everyone I know slips from time to time and calls it the Notification Center.

This isn't the Windows Solution Center (born in Windows 7, primarily for security stuff), nor is it the Windows 7 or Windows 8 Action Center (see Figure 3-1), which includes lots of system-related stuff, but no program notifications.

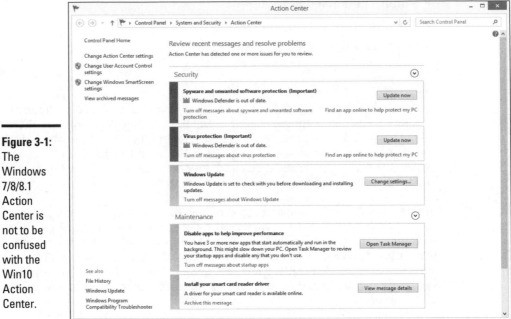

Figure 3-1: The Windows 7/8/8.1 Action Center is not to be confused with the Win10 Action Center.

Instead, the Windows 10 Action Center is, well, a real Notification center. Click the icon down in the lower right of the screen — the one that looks like a dialog balloon in a comic strip — and you can see the Action in Figure 3-2.

At the top, Windows gathers some (but by no means all) of the various programs' notifications. At the bottom, you have a bunch of quick links to various settings.

Figure 3-2:
The
Windows 10
Notific. . . er,
Action
Center.

What, Exactly, Is a Notification?

Historically, Windows allowed all sorts of notifications: blinking taskbar tiles, balloon messages over the system time (in the lower-right corner), dire-looking icons in the system notification area (near the system time), or dialog boxes that appear out of nowhere, sometimes taking over your computer. Then came Windows 8, and the powers that be started looking down on programs that jilted and cavorted, whittled and wheezed. People who write the programs have gradually become more disciplined.

Except for Scottrade, Figure 3-3, which locks out the screen, but that's another modal dialog story.

Figure 3-3: Scottrade's notifications, generated by its web app, lock up the system entirely. Those are not nice notifications.

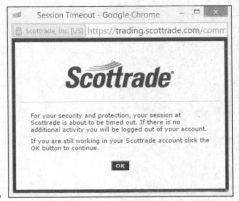

These new, politically correct notifications — the things that can happen when Windows 10 or one of its programs wants your attention — fall into three broad categories:

✦ They can put rectangular notices, usually gray, in the upper-right edge of your screen, with a few lines of text. Typically, the notifications say things like Tap or choose what happens when you insert a USB drive, or Turn sharing on or off.

These notifications are called *toaster notifications* (or sometimes just *toast*), and they're a core part of the new Universal face of Windows. It's a fabulous name because they pop up, just like toast, but on their sides, and then they disappear.

✦ They can show toaster notifications on the lock screen. This is considered more dire than simply showing the notifications on tiled apps or the desktop. Why? Because the apps that create lock screen notifications may need to run, even when Windows is sleeping. And that leads to battery drainage.

✦ They can play sounds. Don't get me started.

Google's never been partial to the Windows notification method, so they've built an independent notification system into the browser itself. The notifications appear in the lower-right corner of the browser. See Figure 3-4.

**Book II
Chapter 3**

Working with the Action/Notification Center

Figure 3-4:
This is
Google
Chrome's
notification
for arriving
Gmail.

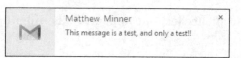

When you click a Chrome Gmail notification — if you're fast enough — Chrome opens the email for you, and puts it in a separate window, ready for you to reply. That's exactly the kind of response you should expect from your notifications — click them, and they do something appropriate.

These notifications are internal to Google Chrome; Windows doesn't see them and doesn't control them. As of this writing, they haven't been integrated into the Windows 10 Notific. . . er, Action Center.

Working with Notifications

In the best of all possible worlds, Windows 10 notifications would work like Google Chrome notifications, only better: Click a Windows 10 notification, and you get transported to a description, a setting, a piece of mail, some sort of instructions. . .whatever.

Instead, as of this writing, the notifications are pretty useless. Occasionally, you find that clicking one of them does something useful. But don't hold your breath.

If you find that a particular program is generating notifications that you don't want to see, Windows lets you disable all notifications rather easily, or you can pick and choose which apps can send notifications and which just have to stifle their utterances.

Here's how to disable notifications:

1. **Tap or click Start, Settings, System.**

Or you can get into Settings from the bottom of the Action Center.

2. **On the left, choose Notifications & actions.**

You see the Notifications pane shown in Figure 3-5.

3. **Turn off all Notifications by using the slider marked Show app notifications.**

4. **If you would like to silence just one app, move its slider to Off down below.**

You're finished. There's no Apply or OK button to tap or click.

Figure 3-5:
Turn off
notifications
here.

Working with Settings Shortcuts

The Action Center contains a gob (that's a technical term) of shortcuts at the bottom of the Notifications pane. In Figure 3-2, I count eleven of them.

You have some — but not much — control over which icons appear at the bottom of the pane. Here's how to exert as much influence as you can:

1. Tap or click Start, Settings, System.

Or you can get into Settings from the bottom of the Action Center.

2. On the left, choose Notifications & actions.

You see the Notifications pane (refer to Figure 3-5).

3. Click one of the four Quick actions icons at the top.

Choices appear as shown in Figure 3-6.

**Book II
Chapter 3**

Working with the Action/Notification Center

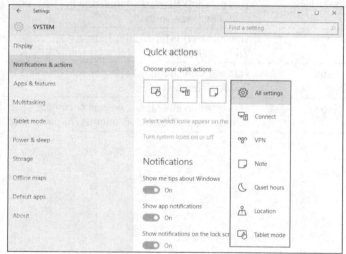

Figure 3-6:
Set the
Action
Center icons
here.

4. Choose the icon(s) you would like to appear on the top line of icons at the bottom of the Action Center.

I have no idea where Windows dredges up the other Quick action icons.

Table 3-1 explains what each of the configurable Quick action icons does.

Table 3-1	Action Icon Results in the Action Center
Click this icon	*And this happens*
Tablet Mode	The computer flips over to Tablet Mode.
Brightness (100%)	Adjust the screen brightness in 25% increments: Click once to cycle among 25%, 50%, 75%, and 100%.
Connect	This searches for wireless display and audio devices — Miracast in particular.
All Settings	This takes you to the Settings app.
Battery Saver	This cycles between two Battery Saver modes, dimming the display. It doesn't work if the machine is plugged in.
VPN	This takes you to the Settings app's Network & Internet section on VPN, where you can add a new VPN connection or connected to an existing one.
Bluetooth	This turns Bluetooth on and off.
Rotation lock	This prevents the screen from rotating from portrait to landscape and vice versa.
Wi-Fi	This turns Wi-Fi on and off. There's no provision to select a Wi-Fi connection.
Location	This turns the location setting on and off in the Settings app's Privacy, Location pane.
Airplane	This turns on and off all wireless communication. See the Settings app's Network & Internet, Airplane Mode setting.

Chapter 4: Controlling Users

In This Chapter

✔ **Choosing an account type**

✔ **The pros and cons of Microsoft accounts**

✔ **Adding a new user**

✔ **Changing accounts**

✔ **Switching between users**

Microsoft reports that 70 percent of all Windows PCs have just one user account. That's a startling figure. It means that 70 percent of all Windows PCs run at the most permissive security level, all the time. It means that, on 70 percent of all Windows PCs, little Billy can install Internet Antivirus 2009 — a notorious piece of scumware — and have it bring down the whole family with a couple of simple clicks. "Sorry, Dad, but it's an anti-virus program, and it said that we really need to install it, and it's just $49.95 for a three-month subscription. I thought you said that antivirus was good. They wouldn't lie about stuff like that, would they?"

Although it's undoubtedly true that many PCs are each used by just one person, I think it's highly likely that people don't set up multiple user accounts on their PCs because they're intimidated. Not to worry. I take you through the ins and outs.

Even if you're the only person who ever uses your PC, you may want to create a second account — another user, as it were — even if the second user is just you. (As Pogo said, "We have met the enemy, and he is us.") Then again, you may not. And therein lies this chapter's story.

If you're running Windows 10 Enterprise and your PC is connected to a big corporate network (in the parlance, a *domain*), you have little or no control over who can log on to your computer and what a logged-on user can do after she's on the machine. That's a Good Thing, at least in theory: Your company's network administrator gets to worry about all the security issues, relieving you of the hassles of figuring out whether the guy down the hall should be able to look at payroll records or the company Christmas card list. But it can also be a pain in the neck, especially if you have to install a program, like, right now, and you don't have a user account with sufficient capabilities. If your computer is attached to a domain, your only choice is to convince (or bribe) the network admin to let you in.

The nostrums in this chapter apply only to PCs that are connected to small networks or to standalone PCs. If you're on a big network, you must pay homage to the network gods. Pizza, beer, and a smile can help.

Windows 10 has two separate locations that control user accounts. If you only want to do some simple stuff — create a new account, change the password, or switch to a picture password, say — you can do it all on the touch-friendly Metro tiled side of Windows 10. On the other hand, if you want to do something more challenging — set the User Account Control trigger levels, for example — you must work with the old-fashioned Windows 7–style desktop's Control Panel. I show you how to use both in this chapter.

User Account Control is a security topic, only tangentially related to user accounts. I talk about it in Book IX, Chapter 3.

Why You Need Separate User Accounts

Windows assumes that, sooner or later, more than one person will want to work on your PC. All sorts of problems crop up when several people share a PC. I set up my screen just right, with all my icons right where I can find them, and then my son comes along and plasters the desktop with a shot of Alpha Centauri. He puts together a killer Taylor Swift playlist and "accidentally" deletes my Grateful Dead playlist in the process.

It's worse than sharing a TV remote.

Windows helps keep peace in the family — and in the office — by requiring people to log on. The process of *logging on* (also called *signing on*) lets Windows keep track of each person's settings: You tell Windows who you are, and Windows lets you play in your own sandbox.

Having personal settings that are activated whenever you log on to Windows doesn't create heavy-duty security. Unless your PC is a slave to a big Active Directory domain network, your settings can get clobbered and your files deleted, if someone else with access to your computer or your network tries hard enough. But as long as you're reasonably careful and follow the advice in this chapter, Windows security works surprisingly well.

If someone else can put his hands on your computer, it isn't your computer any more. That can be a real problem if someone swipes your laptop, if the cleaning staff uses your PC after hours, or if a snoop breaks into your study. Unless you use BitLocker (in Windows 10 Pro), anybody who can restart your PC can look at, modify, or delete your files or stick a virus on the PC. How? In many cases, a miscreant can bypass Windows directly and start your PC with another operating system. With Windows out of the picture, compromising a PC doesn't take much work.

Choosing Account Types

When dealing with user accounts, you bump into one existential fact of Windows life over and over again: The type of account you use puts severe limitations on what you can do.

Unless you're hooked up to a big corporate network, user accounts can generally be divided into two groups: the haves and the have-nots. (Users attached to corporate domains are assigned accounts that can exist anywhere on the have-to-have-not spectrum.) The have accounts are *administrator* accounts. The have-nots are *standard* accounts. That's it. "Standard." Kinda makes your toes curl just to think about it.

What's a standard account?

A person running with a standard account can do only, uh, standard tasks:

✦ Run programs that are installed on the computer, including programs on USB/key drives.

✦ Use hardware that's already installed on the computer.

✦ Create, view, save, modify, and use documents, pictures, and sounds in the Documents, Pictures, or Music folders as well as in the PC's Public folders.

✦ If your computer is part of a HomeGroup (see Book VII, Chapter 5), a standard user can also create, view, save, modify, and use any files in the Public folders of computers that are part of your Homegroup. A standard user can also access any shared folders on other computers in the HomeGroup.

✦ Change his password or switch back and forth between requiring and not requiring a password for his account. He can also add a picture or PIN password. If your computer is sufficiently enabled, he can also use Windows Hello to set up a camera, fingerprint or retina scan. Just like in the movies.

✦ Switch between a local account and a Microsoft account. I talk about both in the next section of this chapter.

✦ Change the picture that appears next to his name on the Welcome screen and in the upper left of the Start menu, change the desktop wallpaper, resize the Windows toolbar, add items to the old-fashioned desktop toolbar and Start menu, and make other small changes that don't affect other user accounts.

In most cases, a standard user can change systemwide settings, install programs, and the like, but only if he can provide the user name and password of an administrator account.

Child accounts

Microsoft provides a quick-and-dirty way to set up child accounts as part of the account creation process. Child accounts are like standard accounts, but they're automatically set up with child protection enabled — someone with an administrator account can control which websites the child account can access, what time of day the accounts can be used, and the total amount of time the account's used in a day.

It's all done on the web — the controls aren't in Windows 10 itself, they're in a web site maintained by Microsoft. There's a small charge for each child account that you set up. Full instructions for bringing a Windows 7 or 8 child account into Windows 10 are at `http://windows.microsoft.com/en-us/windows-10/set-up-family-after-upgrade`.

If you're running with a standard account, you can't even change the time on the clock. It's quite limited.

There's also a special, limited version of the standard account called a *child account.* As the name implies, child accounts can be controlled and monitored by those with standard and administrator accounts. See the sidebar on child accounts.

What's an administrator account?

People using administrator accounts can change almost anything, anywhere, at any time. (Certain folders remain off limits, even to administrator accounts, and you have to jump through some difficult hoops to work around the restrictions.) People using administrator accounts can even change other Local accounts' passwords — a good thing to remember if you ever forget your password.

If you start Windows with a standard account and you accidentally run a virus, a worm, or some other piece of bad computer code, the damage is usually limited: The malware can delete files in your Documents folder, and probably in the Public folders, but that's about the extent of the damage. Usually. Unless it's exceedingly clever, the virus can't install itself into the computer, so it can't run repeatedly, and it may not be able to replicate. Poor virus.

Someone with an administrator account can get into all the files owned by other users: If you thought that attaching a password to your account and putting a top-secret spreadsheet in your `Documents` folder would keep it away from prying eyes, you're in for a rude surprise. Anybody who can get into your machine with an administrator account can look at it. Standard users, on the other hand, are effectively limited to looking only at their own files.

Choosing between standard and administrator accounts

The first account on a new PC is always an administrator account. If you bought your PC with Windows pre-installed, the account that you have — the one you probably set up shortly after you took the computer out of the box — is an administrator account. If you installed Windows on a PC, the account you set up during the installation is an administrator account.

When you create new accounts, on the other hand, they always start out as standard accounts. That's as it should be.

Administrator accounts and standard accounts aren't set in concrete. In fact, Windows helps you shape-shift between the two as circumstances dictated:

✦ If you're using a standard account and try to do something that requires an administrator account, Windows prompts you to provide an administrator account's name and password (see Figure 4-1).

**Book II
Chapter 4**

Controlling Users

Figure 4-1:
Windows
asks
permission
before
performing
adminis-
trative
actions.

If the person using the standard account selects an administrator account without a password, simply clicking the Yes button allows the program to run.

✦ Even if you're using an administrator account, Windows normally runs as though you had a standard account, in some cases adding an extra hurdle when you try to run a program that can make substantial changes to your PC — and *substantial* is quite a subjective term. You have to clear the same kind of hurdle if you try to access folders that aren't explicitly shared (see Figure 4-2). That extra hurdle helps prevent destructive programs from sneaking into your computer and running with your administrator account, doing their damage without your knowledge or permission.

Figure 4-2:
Windows
lays down
a challenge
before you
dive in to
another
user's
folder.

> Desktop   ✕
>
> ⚠ You don't currently have permission to access this folder.
>
> Click Continue to permanently get access to this folder.
>
> [⊕ Continue]   [Cancel]

Most experts recommend that you use a standard account for daily activities and switch to an administrator account only when you need to install software or hardware or access files outside the usual shared areas. Most experts ignore their own advice: It's the old do-as-I-say-not-as-I-do syndrome.

I used to recommend that people follow the lead of the do-as-I-say crowd and simply set up every knowledgeable user with an administrator account. Times change, and Windows has changed: It's rare that you actually need an administrator account to accomplish just about anything in "normal" day-to-day use. (One exception: You can add new users only if you're using an administrator account.) For that reason, I've come to the conclusion that you should save that one administrator account for a rainy day, and set up standard accounts for yourself and anyone else who uses the PC. Run with a standard account, and I bet you almost never notice the difference.

What's Good and Bad about Microsoft Accounts

In addition to administrator and standard accounts (and child accounts, which are a subset of standard accounts), Microsoft also has another pair of account types, *Microsoft accounts* and *Local accounts*. You can have an administrator account that's a Microsoft account, or a standard account that's a Microsoft account, or an administrator account that's a local account, and so on. If you aren't confused, you obviously don't understand. Heh heh heh.

The basic differentiation goes like this:

✦ **Microsoft accounts** are registered with Microsoft. Most people use their `@hotmail.com` or `@live.com` or `@outlook.com` email addresses, but in fact, you can register any email address at all as a Microsoft account (details in Chapter 5 of this minibook). Microsoft accounts must have a password.

When you log on to Windows 10 with a Microsoft account, Windows goes out to Microsoft's computer in the clouds and verifies your password, and then pulls down many of your major Windows settings and transfers them to the PC you just logged on to. You can control which settings get synced in the Settings app (Start, Settings, Accounts, Sync settings) — see Figure 4-3.

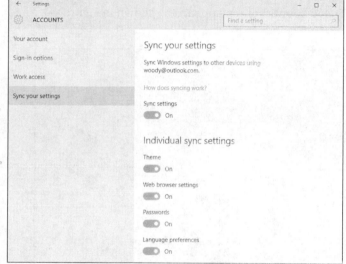

Figure 4-3: Control which Windows settings get synced across your Microsoft account.

Book II
Chapter 4

Controlling Users

If you change, say, your background, the next time you log on to Windows 10 — from any machine, anywhere in the world — you see the new background. More than that, if the Microsoft account is set up to do so, you can get immediate access to all your music, email, SkyDrive storage, and other Windows features without logging in again.

✦ **Local accounts** are regular, old-fashioned accounts that exist only on this PC. They don't save or retrieve your settings from Microsoft's computers. Local accounts may or may not have a password.

On a single PC, administrator accounts can add new users, delete existing users, or change the password of any Local account on the computer. They can't change the password of any Microsoft accounts.

As you may imagine, privacy is among the several considerations for both kinds of accounts. I go into the details in Book II, Chapter 5.

Adding Users

After you log on to an administrator account, you can add more users quite easily. Here's how:

1. **Click or tap Start, and then click or tap Settings.**

2. **On the Settings window, click or tap Accounts.**

The Accounts screen appears, as shown in Figure 4-4.

Figure 4-4:
The
Accounts
options.

3. **On the left, click or tap Family & other users and choose Add a family member (if you want to control the account with Parental Controls) or Add someone else to this PC (and the someone else could well be a family member — you just don't get easy access to Parental Controls for the new account).**

You see the challenging How Will This Person Sign In? dialog box, as shown in Figure 4-5.

4. **If the new user already has a Microsoft account (or an @hotmail. com or @live.com or @outlook.com email address — which are automatically Microsoft accounts), and they don't mind Microsoft keeping information about when they log in to Windows (see Book II, Chapter 5), type the address in the box at the top and then tap or click Next. Then skip to Step 7.**

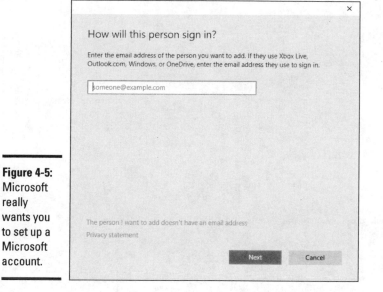

Figure 4-5:
Microsoft really wants you to set up a Microsoft account.

Windows sets up your account.

Don't get me wrong. There are good reasons for using a Microsoft account — a Microsoft account makes it much easier and faster to retrieve your mail and calendar entries, for example, or use the Microsoft Store or Music or Videos, bypassing individual account logins. It'll automatically connect you to your OneDrive account. Only you can decide if the added convenience is worth the decreased privacy. Book II, Chapter 5 covers the details.

5. **On the other hand, if you're skeptical about using a Microsoft account, waaaaaay down at the bottom, click or tap the link that says Take Your Microsoft Account and Shove It (otherwise known as The person I want to add doesn't have an email address).**

Windows helpfully gives you yet another opportunity to set up a Microsoft account, as shown in Figure 4-6.

6. **At the bottom, click or tap Add a user without a Microsoft account. Sheesh.**

Windows (finally!) asks you about a Local account name and password. See Figure 4-7.

7. **Type a name for the new account.**

You can give a new account just about any name you like: first name, last name, nickname, titles, abbreviations . . . No sweat, as long as you don't use the characters / \ [ ] " ; : | < > + = , ? or *.

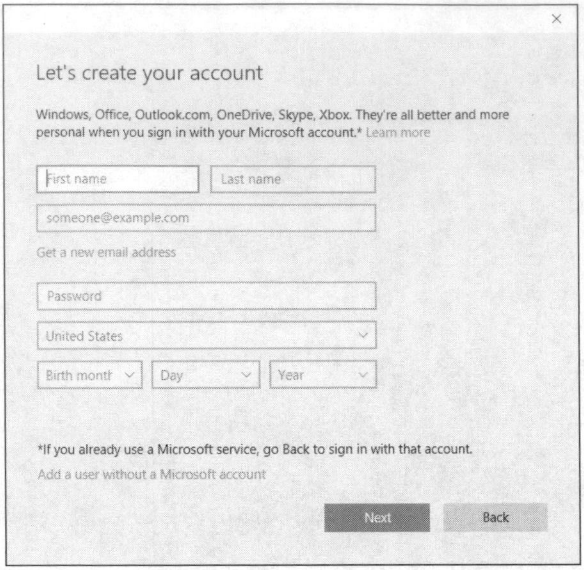

Figure 4-6:
Here's the
second time
Microsoft
asks
whether
you want
to set up a
Microsoft
account.

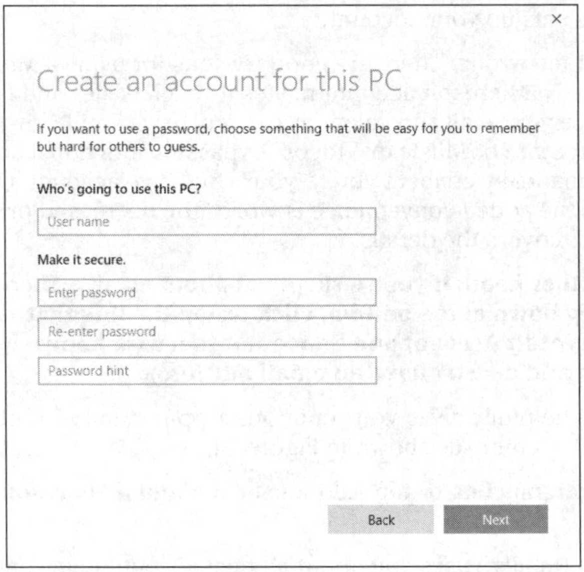

Figure 4-7:
Now you
get to the
"adding
a new
account"
part.

8. (Optional) Type a password twice, and add a password hint.

If you leave these fields blank, the user can log on directly by simply
tapping or clicking the account name on the logon screen. Usually, that
isn't a good idea, if only to thwart people who casually get ahold of your
machine for a minute.

Note that the password hint can be seen by anybody on the computer, so avoid that NSFW (Not Suitable For Work) hint you were thinking about.

9. Click or tap Next; then click or tap Finish.

You're finished. Rocket science. You have a new standard account, and its name now appears on the Welcome screen.

If you want to turn the new account into an administrator account or a child account, follow the steps in the section, "Changing Accounts," later in this chapter. To add an account picture for the logon screen and Start screen, flip to Book III, Chapter 2.

This topic is more than a bit confusing, but you aren't allowed to create a new account named Administrator. There's a good reason why Windows prevents you from making a new account with that name: You already have one. Even though Windows goes to great lengths to hide the account named Administrator, it's there, and you may encounter it one night when you're exploring a blind alley. For now, don't worry about the ambiguous name and the ghostly appearance. Just refrain from trying to create a new account named Administrator.

Just because you have a Microsoft account doesn't mean you can log on to any computer anywhere. Your Microsoft account has to be set up on a specific computer before you can use that computer.

Changing Accounts

If you have an administrator account, you can reach in and change almost every detail of every single account on the computer — except one.

Changing other users' settings

In general, changing other users' settings is easy if you have an administrator account. To change an account from a standard account to an administrator account:

1. Click or tap Start, and then click or tap Settings.

2. On the Settings window, click or tap Accounts. On the left, choose Family & other users.

A list of all the accounts on the computer appears.

3. Click or tap on the account you want to change.

For example, in Figure 4-8, I choose to change my local account called Woody.

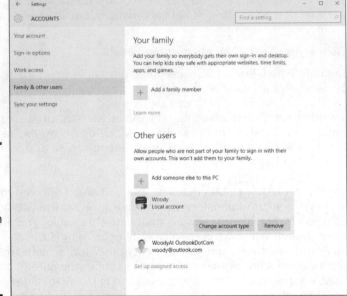

Figure 4-8:
Choose the
account
you want to
change from
standard
to adminis-
trator, or
vice versa.

4. **Choose the box marked Change account type.**

   Windows responds with the option to change from standard user to administrator account and back.

5. **Click or tap OK.**

   The type changes immediately.

For other kinds of account changes, you need to venture into the old-fashioned Control Panel applet. Here's how:

1. **Type Windows key + X, or tap and holds the Start icon, then choose Control Panel.**

   The old-fashioned Control Panel appears.

2. **Choose User Accounts, then User Accounts again. Choose Manage another account.**

   A list of all the accounts on the computer appears.

3. **Click or tap on the account you want to change.**

   Windows immediately presents you with several options (see Figure 4-9).

Book II
Chapter 4

Controlling Users

Figure 4-9:
Maintain
another
user's
account.

Here's what the options entail:

✦ **Change the Account Name:** This option appears only for Local accounts. (It'd be kind of difficult if Windows let you change someone's Microsoft account, eh?) Selecting this option modifies the name displayed on the Logon screen and at the top of the Start screen while leaving all other settings intact. Use this option if you want to change only the name on the account — for example, if Little Bill wants to be called Sir William.

✦ **Create/Change/Remove a Password:** Again, this appears only for Local accounts. If you create a password for the chosen user, Windows requires a password to crank up that user account. You can't get past the Logon screen (using that account) without it. This setting is weird because you can change it for other people: You can force Bill to use a password when none was required before, you can change Bill's password, or you can even delete the password.

If you change someone's password, do her a big favor and tell her how to create a Password Reset Disk. See Book VI, Chapter 4.

Passwords are cAse SenSitive — you must enter the password, with uppercase and lowercase letters, precisely the way it was originally typed. If you can't get the computer to recognize your password, make sure that the Caps Lock setting is off. That's the number-one source of logon frustration.

Much has been written about the importance of choosing a secure password, mixing uppercase and lowercase letters with punctuation marks, ensuring that you have a long password, blah blah blah. I have only two admonitions: First, don't write your password on a yellow sticky note attached to your monitor; second, don't use the easily guessed passwords that the Conficker worm employed to crack millions of systems (see Table 4-1, at the end of this list). Good advice from a friend: Create a simple sentence you can remember, and swap out some letters for numbers (G00dGr1efTerry), or think of a sentence and only use the first letters! (toasaoutfl!)

Table 4-1   The Most Frequently Used Passwords*

000	0000	00000	0000000	00000000	0987654321
111	1111	11111	111111	1111111	11111111
123	123123	12321	123321	1234	12345
123456	1234567	12345678	123456789	1234567890	1234abcd
1234qwer	123abc	123asd	123qwe	1q2w3e	222
2222	22222	222222	2222222	22222222	321
333	3333	33333	333333	3333333	33333333
4321	444	4444	44444	444444	4444444
44444444	54321	555	5555	55555	555555
5555555	55555555	654321	666	6666	66666
666666	6666666	66666666	7654321	777	7777
77777	777777	7777777	77777777	87654321	888
8888	88888	888888	8888888	88888888	987654321
999	9999	99999	999999	9999999	99999999
a1b2c3	aaa	aaaa	aaaaa	abc123	academia
access	account	Admin	admin	admin1	admin12
admin123	adminadmin	administrator	anything	asddsa	asdfgh
asdsa	asdzxc	backup	boss123	business	campus
changeme	cluster	codename	codeword	coffee	computer
controller	cookie	customer	database	default	desktop
domain	example	exchange	explorer	file	files
foo	foobar	foofoo	forever	freedom	f**k
games	home	home123	ihavenopass	Internet	internet
intranet	job	killer	letitbe	letmein	login
Login	lotus	love123	manager	market	money
monitor	mypass	mypassword	mypc123	nimda	nobody
nopass	nopassword	nothing	office	oracle	owner
pass	pass1	pass12	pass123	passwd	password
Password	password1	password12	password123	private	public
pw123	q1w2e3	qazwsx	qazwsxedc	qqq	qqqq
qqqqq	qwe123	qweasd	qweasdzxc	qweewq	qwerty
qwewq	root	root123	rootroot	sample	secret
secure	security	server	shadow	share	sql
student	super	superuser	supervisor	system	temp
temp123	temporary	temptemp	test	test123	testtest
unknown	web	windows	work	work123	xxx
xxxx	xxxxx	zxccxz	zxcvb	zxcvbn	zxcxz
zzz	zzzz	zzzzz			

From the Conficker worm, Bowdlerized with an asterisk (*) as a fig leaf

✦ **Change the Account Type:** You can use this option to change accounts from administrator to standard and back again. The implications are somewhat complex; I talk about them in the section "Choosing Account Types," earlier in this chapter.

✦ **Delete the Account:** Deep-six the account, if you're that bold (or mad, in all senses of the term). If you're deleting a Windows account, the account itself still lives — it just won't be permitted to log on to this computer. Windows offers to keep copies of the deleted account's `Documents` folder and desktop, but warns you quite sternly and correctly that if you snuff the account, you rip out all the email messages, Internet Favorites, and other settings that belong to the user — definitely not a good way to make friends. Oh, and you can't delete your own account, of course.

Changing your own settings

Changing your own account is just a little different from changing other users' accounts. Follow these steps:

1. **Bring up the Control Panel.**

   To do so, go to the old-fashioned desktop, right-click the Windows icon in the lower-left corner, or type Windows key + X, and choose Control Panel.

2. **In the upper right, choose User Accounts, then User Accounts again.**

   Windows offers you the chance to change your own account.

   Most of the options for your own account mirror those of other users' accounts, as described in the preceding section. If you have the only administrator account on the PC, you can't delete your own account and you can't turn yourself into a standard user. Makes sense: Every PC must have at least one user with an administrator account. If Windows lost all its administrators, no one would be around to add users or change existing ones, much less to install programs or hardware, right?

Switching Users

Windows allows you to have more than one person logged on to a PC simultaneously. That's convenient if, say, you're working on the family PC and checking Billy's homework when you hear the cat screaming bloody murder in the kitchen and your wife wants to put digital pictures from the family vacation on OneDrive while you run off to check the microwave.

The ability to have more than one user logged on to a PC simultaneously is *Fast User Switching,* and it has advantages and disadvantages:

+ **On the plus side:** Fast User Switching lets you keep all your programs going while somebody else pops on to the machine for a quick jaunt on the keyboard. When she's done, she can log off, and you can pick up precisely where you left off before you got bumped.

+ **On the minus side:** All idle programs left sitting around by the inactive ("bumped") user can bog things down for the active user, although the effect isn't drastic. You can avoid the overhead by logging off before the new user logs on.

To switch users, click Start, click or tap your picture, and choose either the name of the user you want to switch to or Sign Out. If you choose the latter, you're taken to the sign-in screen, where you can choose from any user on the computer.

Chapter 5: Microsoft Account: To Sync or Not to Sync?

In This Chapter

✔ Getting the lowdown on a Microsoft account

✔ Figuring out whether you even want a Microsoft account

✔ Getting a Microsoft account without spilling the beans

✔ Care and feeding of your Microsoft account

✔ Cutting back on syncing through a Windows account

Microsoft has been trying to get people to sign up for company-branded accounts for a long, long time.

In 1997, Microsoft bought Hotmail and took over the issuance of @hotmail. com email addresses. Even though Hotmail's gone through a bunch of name changes — MSN Hotmail, Windows Live Hotmail, and now Outlook.com, among others — the original @hotmail.com email addresses still work, and have worked, through thick and thin.

Then came *Microsoft Wallet,* a short-lived attempt to get consumers to put their credit card information online and trust Microsoft to take care of it. Microsoft scrubbed that idea and, in 2000, replaced it with *Microsoft Passport*.

Here's what tech commentator Joel Spolsky had to say about Microsoft Passport, in his Joel on Software blog:

> "Am I the only one who is terrified about Microsoft Passport? It seems to me like a fairly blatant attempt to build the world's largest, richest consumer database, and then make fabulous profits mining it. It's a terrifying threat to everyone's personal privacy, and it will make today's 'cookies' seem positively tame by comparison. The scariest thing is that Microsoft is advertising Passport as if it were a *benefit* to consumers, and people seem to be falling for it!"

Everything old is new again. More than a decade later, Microsoft is trying to do the same thing, but this time it's dangling a much bigger carrot, and it will undoubtedly garner a much larger audience.

Microsoft Passport became .NET Passport, and then Microsoft Passport Network. When Microsoft started branding everything as "Live," the same username became a Windows Live ID.

Fifteen years after its inception, that old @hotmail.com ID still works the same as it ever did — except now it's called a *Microsoft account.* If you picked up an @msn.com ID, @live.com ID, or @outlook.com ID along the way, it's now a Microsoft account as well.

In this chapter, I show you exactly what's involved with a Microsoft account, show you why it can be useful, explore the dark underbelly of Microsoft account-ability, and give you a trick for acquiring a Microsoft account that won't compromise much of anything.

What, Exactly, Is a Microsoft Account?

Now that Microsoft has finally settled on a name for its ID — at least, this month — permit me to dispel some of the myths about Microsoft accounts.

If you have an email address that ends with @hotmail.com, @msn.com, @live.com, or @outlook.com, that email address is, *ipso facto,* a Microsoft account. The same is true for Hotmail and Live and Outlook.com accounts in any country, such as @hotmail.co.uk. You don't have to use your Microsoft account. Ever. But you do have one.

Many people don't realize that *any* email address can be a Microsoft account. You need only to register that email address with Microsoft; I show you how in the section "Setting Up a Microsoft Account" later in this chapter.

In the context of Windows 10, the Microsoft account takes on a new dimension. When you set up an account to log in to Windows, it can either be a Microsoft account or a *local account.* The key differences:

+ Microsoft accounts are always email addresses, and they must be registered with Microsoft. As I explain in Book II, Chapter 4, when you log on to Windows with a Microsoft account, Windows automatically syncs some settings — Windows settings like your picture and backgrounds, Edge history and favorites, and others — so if you change something on one machine and log on with the same Microsoft account on another, the changes go with you.

  In addition, a Microsoft account gives you something of a one-stop log in to Internet-based Microsoft services. For example, if you have a OneDrive account, logging in to Windows with a Microsoft account automatically hitches you up to your OneDrive files.

✦ More insidiously, if you log on to Windows 10 with a Microsoft account, and you don't modify Cortana's searching behavior, Microsoft will start tracking every search you make *on your computer.* I'm not talking about a web search. With a few exceptions (for example, `www.DuckDuckGo.com`), any search you perform on the Internet is tracked by the search provider, typically Google or Microsoft/Bing. I'm talking about when you search through your own documents or email messages, right there on your machine. I talk about Cortana's search settings in Book III, Chapter 6.

✦ Local accounts can be just about any name or combination of characters. If you sign in with a local account, Microsoft doesn't try (indeed, can't) sync anything on different machines. Sign in with a local account, and you have to sign in to your OneDrive account separately. Windows will remember your settings — your backgrounds, passwords, favorites, and the like — but they won't be moved to other PCs when you log on.

So, for example, `phineasfarquahrt@hotmail.com` is a Microsoft account. Because it's an `@hotmail.com` Hotmail email address, it's already registered with Microsoft. I can create a user on a Windows 10 machine with the name `phineasfarquahrt@hotmail.com`, and Windows will recognize that as a Microsoft account.

On the other hand, I can set up an account on a Windows PC that's called, oh, *Woody Leonhard*. It's a local account. Because Microsoft accounts have to be email addresses (you see why in the section "Setting Up a Microsoft Account"), the Woody Leonhard account has to be a local account.

When you set up a brand-new Windows PC, you have to enter an account, and it can be either a Windows account or a local account. Microsoft stacks the deck and makes you tap or click all over heaven's half acre to avoid using a Microsoft account. When you add a new account, Microsoft nudges you to use a Microsoft account, but will begrudgingly accept a local account (see Book II, Chapter 4).

Deciding Whether You Want a Microsoft Account

If Microsoft tracks a Microsoft account, you may ask, why in the world would I want to sign on to Windows 10 with a Microsoft account?

Good question, grasshopper.

Signing on to Windows 10 with a Microsoft account brings a host of benefits. In particular:

✦ **Most of your Windows settings will travel with you.** Your user picture, desktop, browser favorites, and other similar settings will find you no matter which PC you log on to.

I find this helpful in some ways, and annoying in others. For example, I have a big screen Windows desktop and a little Windows tablet. If I set the screen for the desktop, it looks horrible on the tablet and vice versa.

✦ **Your tiled, Universal apps — the ones that came with Windows 10 or that you downloaded from the Windows Store — revert to their last state.** So if you're on a killer winning streak with a Solitaire game, that'll go with you to any PC you log on to. Your Internet Explorer or Edge open tabs travel. Settings for the Windows 10 Finance app travel. Even apps *that Microsoft doesn't make* may have their settings moved from machine to machine.

✦ **Sign-in credentials for programs and websites travel.** If you rely on Edge to keep sites' logon credentials, those will find you if you switch machines.

✦ **You will be automatically signed in to Windows 10 apps and services** that use the Microsoft account (or Windows Live ID). Windows's Universal Mail, Calendar, OneDrive, and the Microsoft website all fall into that category.

Don't be overly cynical. In some sense, Microsoft dangles these carrots to convince you to sign up for, and use, a Microsoft account. But in another sense, the simple fact is that none of these features would be possible if it weren't for some sort of ID that's maintained by Microsoft.

Personally, I use a Microsoft account on my main machine, although I employ a little trick — creating a new Microsoft account and only using it to sign in to Windows — which I describe in the next section on setting up a new account.

That's the carrot. Here's the stick. If you sign in with a Microsoft account, Microsoft has a record of every time you've signed on, to every PC you use with that account. More than that, when you crank up Edge (or Internet Explorer), you're logged in with your Microsoft account — which means that Microsoft can, at least theoretically, keep records about all your browsing (except, presumably, InPrivate browsing). Bing gets to jot down your Microsoft account every time you search through it. Microsoft gets detailed data on any music you view in the Windows 10 Music app. Your stock interests are logged in the Windows 10 Money app. Even the weather you request ends up in Microsoft's giant database. And if you use Cortana, heaven help ya, everything you search for on your computer ends up in Microsoft's big database chock full of your history.

Perhaps it's true that you have no privacy and should get over it. Fact is that most people don't care. But I do, and I suggest that you do, too.

What if my Hotmail/Outlook.com account is hijacked?

So you set up a Hotmail account or Outlook. com for logging on to your Windows PC, and all of a sudden the account gets hijacked. Some cretin gets into the account online and changes the password. The next time you try to log in to your Windows PC, what happens?

It's not far-fetched: I get complaints almost every day from people who have been locked out of their Hotmail/Outlook.com accounts.

If you use a Hotmail ID, Windows Live account, or Outlook.com account for your Microsoft account and your Hotmail/Outlook.com account gets hijacked and the password changed, Windows 10 lets you log on to your PC, but when you do, you got the notice `You're signed in to this PC with your old password. Sign in again with your current password, or reset it`. If you then try to reset your password, you can't — clicking or tapping the Reset link doesn't do anything.

Until you can come up with your Hotmail/ Outlook.com account's password, you're put in a reduced functionality mode that's very similar to logging on with a local account. As long as you can remember your old password — the last one you used to log on to this machine — you can continue to log on in local account mode. But ultimately you're going to want your Windows logon account back!

To get your account back, you need to contact the people at Microsoft and convince them that you're the rightful owner. If you set up your Hotmail/Outlook.com account recently, chances are at least fair that you have an alternate email address or phone number designated for just such an emergency. Microsoft started asking for that specific information on sign-up a couple of years ago. Go to `http://account.live.com/resetpassword.aspx`, and have a Microsoft rep contact you.

Setting Up a Microsoft Account

Just to make life a little more complicated, shortly before Microsoft released Windows 8, it suddenly decided to kill off the name "Hotmail" and replace it with "Outlook.com." I talk about the reasons why — basically, Hotmail was losing market share, and Microsoft needed to get it back — in Book X, Chapter 3.

For purposes of this chapter, a Hotmail or Outlook.com account, a Live. com account, Xbox LIVE account, OneDrive account, Skype account, MSN account, Microsoft Passport account, or a Windows Phone account are all interchangeable: They're email addresses that have already been automatically signed up as Microsoft accounts. I tend to refer to them collectively as Hotmail accounts because, well, most Microsoft accounts have been Hotmail accounts for the past two decades or so. Old habits die hard.

If you don't have a Microsoft account, the way I see it, you have three choices for setting one up:

✦ **You can use an existing email address.** But if you do that, Microsoft will be able to put that email address in its database, and it can cross-reference the address to many things you do with Windows 10. (Can you tell my tinfoil hat is showing?)

✦ **You can use (or set up) a Hotmail/Live/Xbox/OneDrive/Skype/Windows Phone/Outlook.com account.** If you already have one, Microsoft tracks it already — Microsoft knows when you receive and send email. But that's true of any online email program, including Gmail and Yahoo! Mail. Using a Hotmail/Outlook.com account to log on to Windows 10, though, means that Microsoft can track additional information and associate it with your Hotmail/Outlook.com account — the times you log in to Windows, locations, and so on — as described earlier in this section, as well as the special snooping that Cortana undertakes. You may be okay with that, or you may not want Microsoft to be able to track that kind of additional information.

✦ **You can create a completely bogus new Hotmail/Outlook.com account and use it only to log in to Windows 10.** It's free and easy, and if you use it wisely, nobody will ever know the difference. The only downsides: If you use Hotmail/Outlook.com, you have to tell the Windows 10 Universal Mail app to look in your other inbox; your existing Hotmail/Outlook.com contacts won't get carried over into the tiled People automatically; and Skype will want to work with your new, bogus ID — although you can change it.

I love to use bogus Outlook.com accounts. I keep in mind that every time I use Edge or Internet Explorer, having signed in to Windows with a Microsoft account, that Microsoft will dump all my browsing history in its coffers.

So, of course, I use the Firefox or Chrome browser when I want to use the Internet. Google keeps Chrome data, but it doesn't have Microsoft's database of logged in Windows 10 users, and Firefox isn't beholden to anybody.

Search engines, of course, are a different story entirely. Bing/Microsoft and Google keep track of everything you send their way.

Setting up a Hotmail/Outlook.com account

Here's how to set up a new Hotmail/Outlook.com account:

1. **Using your favorite web browser, go to** www.Outlook.com.

    The main screen asks whether you have a Microsoft account.

2. **If you aren't automatically signed in, tap or click Sign Up or Sign Up Now.**

   You see the sign-up form, as shown in Figure 5-1.

Book II
Chapter 5

Microsoft Account: To Sync or Not to Sync?

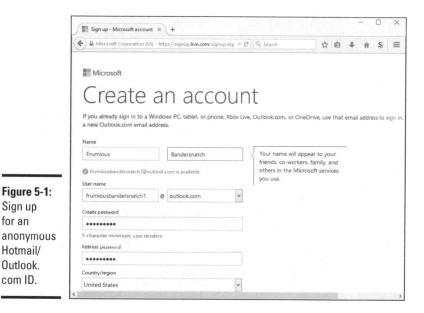

Figure 5-1:
Sign up for an anonymous Hotmail/Outlook.com ID.

3. **Fill out the form. Be creative.**

   Even though the form hints that your phone number is required, in my experiments, it wasn't required at all — an alternate email address suffices.

   That alternate email address is useful if your Microsoft account gets hijacked. You can contact Microsoft and have it send account reset information to that address. You don't need to monitor the address constantly, but if you can retrieve email from that alternate email address, it can help get your new account back.

   If you decide to tap or click the link and provide answers to security questions to make a password reset easier, make sure you keep the answers stored away some place safe.

   Microsoft's headquarters in Redmond has the ZIP code 98052.

4. **Type in the CAPTCHA codes, if you can figure them out, deselect the Send Me Mail check box, and tap or click I Accept.**

    Hotmail/Outlook.com whirrs for a minute or so and shows you the Hotmail/Outlook.com welcome screen, as shown in Figure 5-2. That's it.

You can now use your new Hotmail account as a Windows logon ID. You can use it for email, Skype, Xbox . . . just about anything.

Figure 5-2: Your new Microsoft account (*née* Windows Live ID, Hotmail account, MSN account, Outlook.com account, Xbox Live account) is alive and working.

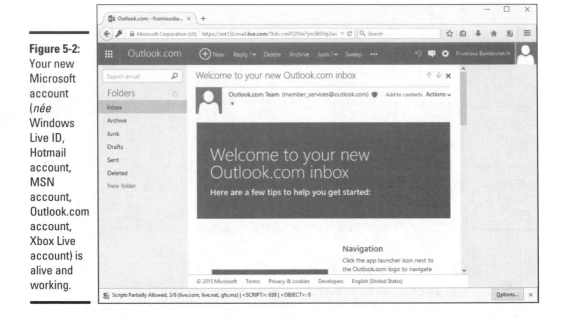

Making any email address a Microsoft account

There's an extra loop in turning any email address into a Microsoft account, but the procedure's quite simple, as long as you can retrieve email sent to the address. Here's how:

1. **Using your favorite web browser, go to** `http://signup.live.com`**. Under the User name box, tap or click the link Or use your favorite email.**

    You see the sign-up form, per Figure 5-3.

2. **In the User Name box, type an email address that you can access — it can be a Gmail address, a Yahoo! Mail address, or any other email address, no problem.**

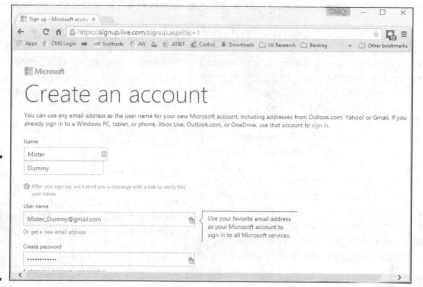

Figure 5-3:
You can
use any
valid email
address as
a Microsoft
account.

3. **Fill out the rest of the form. Fancifully, if you wish.**

   If you don't want to give Microsoft your phone number, select and answer one of its security questions. Note, though, that giving Microsoft your phone number allows it to SMS you a reset password, if you require one, instead of relying on a question — one that a hijacker may be able to figure out.

4. **Type in the CAPTCHA code, and tap or click I Accept.**

   Note that the password you provide here is for your Microsoft account. It is *not* your email password. The password you enter here will be the password you need to use in order to log on to Windows 10 or any website that requires a Microsoft account.

   Within a minute or two, the email address in the application form receives a message that says

   ```
   This email address was used to start setting up a
   Windows Live ID. To finish setting it up, we need
   you to confirm that this email address belongs to
   you. Click this link to confirm your account:
   ```

   If you don't see the message, check your Junk folder.

5. **Tap or click the link in the message to confirm your email address.**

   You end up on a Hotmail welcome screen (refer to Figure 5-2).

Two- factor authentication

Microsoft has been developing and expanding a feature called *two-factor authentication*. Details vary, but it's a good choice, if offered to you. Usually, when you log on with your Microsoft account using a machine that hasn't been explicitly identified (by you) as being an acceptable computer, Microsoft issues a challenge to verify that you are who you say you are. Usually the authentication comes in the form of an SMS sent to your phone, or an email sent to your registered email address. Benefits are pretty obvious: Somebody may be able to steal your password, but it's rare that they get both your password and your computer (which bypasses two-factor authentication entirely), and almost impossible to get both your password and your phone — or access to your email address.

Most people are leery about giving their phone numbers to Microsoft. Hey, it took me almost a decade before I learned to stop worrying and love the bomb. I've found, though, that Microsoft doesn't use my phone number for nefarious purposes. And that phone-based two-factor authentication works great. Even if I do mumble from time to time about it being so slow.

Highly recommended. Do it.

Taking Care of Your Microsoft Account

If you ever want to change any of the details in your Microsoft account, it's easy — if you know where to go.

For reasons understood only by Microsoft, to maintain your Microsoft account, go to `http://account.live.com`. Sign in, and you see full account information, as shown in Figure 5-4.

To change any of the information for your account, or the password, tap or click the related link below the item you want to change.

Microsoft has, commendably, gone to great lengths to improve its protection of your account. *Two-step verification* — which you can set up by clicking the link at the bottom of Figure 5-4 that says Manage advanced security — requires you to provide two different pieces of information every time you log on: Your password, plus an additional security code that Microsoft sends to you. That way, if your password gets compromised, the attacker won't be able to get into your account, unless she can provide the second, independent security code.

Unfortunately, many programs and devices aren't set up to take an additional step when you sign in. For example, Xbox doesn't support two-factor authentication, nor do older versions of Office, or any of the common phone mail apps — including older versions of Windows Phone. For those, you have to set up separate, individual kluges to get in. The Microsoft site guides you through the details.

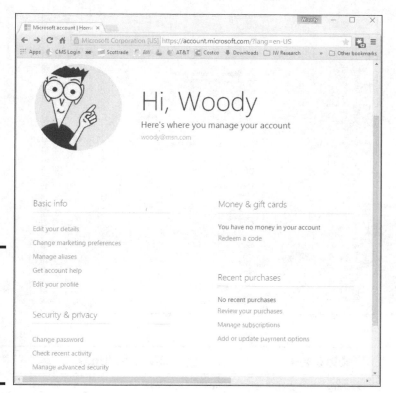

Figure 5-4:
Microsoft
account
mainte-
nance is
accessible
from the
Live site.

Controlling Sync

If you don't specifically change anything, logging on to Windows with a
Microsoft account syncs a number of settings across all the PCs that
you use.

You can tell Microsoft that you don't want to sync specific items. Here's
how:

1. **Click or tap Start, and then click or tap Settings.**

2. **Click or tap Accounts; on the left, click or tap Sync your settings.**

   The Sync screen appears, as shown in Figure 5-5.

3. **Following the list in Table 5-1, choose whether you want to sync specific items.**

   Sync happens only when you log on with the same Microsoft account on
   two different PCs.

   You're finished. No need to tap or click OK or Apply. The changes take
   effect with your next logon.

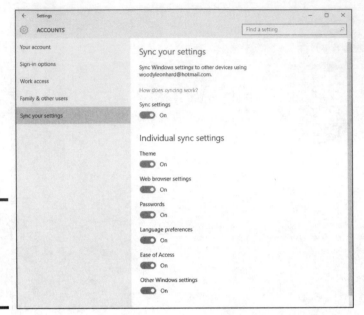

Figure 5-5:
Control
the way
Microsoft
accounts
sync here.

Table 5-1	Sync Settings
Setting	*What It Controls*
Sync Settings	This is an overall "off" switch. If you don't want to sync anything, turn this off.
Theme	Your user picture, Start menu tiles, color, background, and old-fashioned desktop settings are controlled here.
Apps	This is for Universal apps only; it may not work with non-Microsoft apps.
Web browser Settings	Edge and Internet Explorer settings, open tabs, navigation history, and state of File Explorer (such as whether the Ribbon appears) are controlled here.
Passwords	Potentially sensitive information, including logon credentials for Universal apps and some website passwords, are controlled here.
Language preferences	This controls which input method (language/keyboard) is in effect.
Ease of Access	All ease-of-access settings are controlled here.

Chapter 6: Privacy Control

In This Chapter

↙ **Finding out why privacy is important**

↙ **Discovering the complicated web of shared data**

↙ **Blocking location tracking**

↙ **Lessening the intrusion on your privacy**

"The best minds of my generation are thinking about how to make people click ads. That sucks."

— Jeff Hammerbacher, early Facebook employee

When you work with "free" services — search engines like Google and Bing; social networks like Facebook, Pinterest, and LinkedIn; online storage services like OneDrive and Google Drive; free email services like Gmail, Hotmail/Outlook.com, and Yahoo! Mail; even the "free" versions of Windows 10 — these services may not charge you anything, but they're hardly free. You pay with your identity. Every time you go to one of those sites, or use one of those products, with a few noteworthy exceptions, you leave a trail that companies are eager to exploit, primarily for advertising.

The exceptions? Google doesn't scan activity for any paid account, or any educational account. (They've been sued up the wazoo.) Apple swears it doesn't wallow in the data grabbing cesspool. Microsoft loves to say it doesn't scan the contents of Outlook.com/Hotmail messages. There are lots of if's and's but's and nuances. But by and large, if it's free, you're the product, not the customer.

There's a reason why you buy something on, say, Alibaba, and then find ads for Alibaba appearing on all sorts of websites. One of the big advertising conglomerates has your number. Maybe just your IP address. Maybe a planted cookie. But they've connected enough dots to know that, whatever site you happen to be on at the moment, you once bought something on Alibaba.

Now, even when you log on to Windows 10, if you opt to use a Microsoft account, you leave another footprint in the sand. (I talk about Microsoft accounts in Book II, Chapter 5.)

This isn't horrible. Necessarily. It isn't illegal — although laws in different localities differ widely, and lawsuits are reshaping the picture even as we speak. In most cases, anyway. The advertisers view it as a chance to direct advertising at you that's likely to generate a response. In some respects, it's like a billboard for a cold Pepsi on a hot freeway or an ad for beer on Super Bowl Sunday.

In other respects, though, logging your activity online is something quite different.

I talk about privacy in general in Book IX, Chapter 1, and the browser Do Not Track flag (which may or may not do what you think it should do) in Book V, Chapter 1. In this chapter, I want to give you an overview of privacy settings — and some privacy shenanigans — specifically inside Windows.

Why You Should Be Concerned

As time goes by, people are becoming more and more aware of how their privacy is being eroded by using the Internet. Some people aren't particularly concerned. Others get paranoid to the point of chopping off their clicking fingers. Chances are pretty good you're somewhere between the two poles.

Windows 10 users need to understand that this version of Windows, *much* more than any version of Windows before, pulls in data from all over the web. Every time you elect to connect to a service, you're connecting the dots for Microsoft's data-collection routines. And if you use a Microsoft account, Microsoft's dot connector gets to run into overtime.

I'm not implying that Microsoft is trying to steal your data or somehow use your identity for illegal purposes. It isn't. At this point, Microsoft mostly wants to identify your buying patterns and your interests, so it can serve you ads that you will click, for products that you will buy. The Google shtick. That's where the money is.

Although Google freely admits that it scans inbound and outbound Gmail email, on free accounts, all the better to generate ads that you will click, Microsoft (as of mid-2015, anyway) insists that it doesn't — ergo, the infamous Scroogled ads, wherein the pot and kettle somehow tie it on. Don't be fooled. Microsoft *does* scan Hotmail/Outlook.com mail and Windows 10 Universal Mail app messages that you receive with Windows 10 — for spam detection, if nothing else. Whether MS will start keeping track of detailed information about your messages in the future is very hard to say.

Here's how the services stack up, when it comes to privacy (or the lack thereof):

✦ **Google:** Without a doubt, Google has the largest collection of data. You leave tracks on the Google databases every time you use Google to search for a website. That's true of every search engine (except www. DuckDuckGo.com), not just Google, but Google has 70 percent or more of the search engine market. You also hand Google web-surfing information if you sign in to your Chrome browser (so it can keep track of your bookmarks for you) or if you sign in to Google itself (for example, to use Google Apps or Google Drive). The native Android browser ties into Google, too.

Google also owns *Doubleclick,* the best-known, third-party cookie generator on the web. Any time you go to a site with a Doubleclick ad — most popular sites have them — a little log about your visit finds its way into Google's database.

Google's scanning policies changed significantly in late 2014. As of mid-2015, Google no longer scans email, or the contents of Google Drive files, for paid accounts, Academic accounts, or non-profit accounts. If you have a free Google account, you should expect that Google will sift through your mail and files, looking for information that can convince you to click on an ad.

✦ **Facebook:** Although Facebook may not have the largest collection of data, it's the most detailed. People who sign up for Facebook tend to give away lots of information. When you connect your Microsoft account in Windows 10 to Facebook — for example, add your Facebook Friends to your Ultimate People app list (unless Facebook has shut Microsoft out this week, which happens from time to time) — some data that you allow to be shared on Facebook is accessible to Microsoft. That's why it's important to lock down your Facebook account (see Book VI, Chapter 3).

Every time you go to a website with a Facebook Like icon, that fact is tucked away in Facebook's databases. If you're logged on to Facebook at the time you hit a site with a Like icon, your Facebook ID is transmitted, along with an indication of which site you're looking at, to the Facebook databases. As of this writing, Microsoft can't get into the Facebook database — which is truly one of the crown jewels of the Facebook empire — although it can pull a list of your Friends, if you allow it.

✦ **Microsoft:** Microsoft's Internet access database may not be as big as Google's, or as detailed as Facebook's, but the 'Softies are trying to get there fast. One of the ways they're catching up is by encouraging you to use a Microsoft account. The other is to create all these connections to other data-collecting agencies inside Windows 10. Then there's Bing, which logs what you're looking at just like Google search.

Windows 10 is light-years ahead of earlier versions of Windows when it comes to harvesting your data. Or perhaps I should say it's light-years behind earlier versions of Windows when it comes to protecting your privacy. Same, same.

The single biggest leaker in Windows 10 is Cortana's "Smart Search" feature — which is certainly smart for Microsoft's data collection efforts. Unless you go to great lengths to trim back Cortana's snooping, Microsoft (through Bing) keeps a list of all the terms you search for *on your computer*. Because Cortana's Smart Search is enabled by default when you install Windows 10, chances are pretty good that Microsoft's collecting information about every single search you make for your documents, pictures, email, and so on. I talk about Cortana's wayward ways — and, most importantly, show you how to turn the leak off, or at least clip its wings — in Book III, Chapter 6.

For an ongoing, authoritative discussion of privacy issues, look at the Electronic Frontier Foundation's Defending Your Rights in the Digital World page at `www.eff.org/issues/privacy`.

Knowing What Connections Windows Prefers

If you use Windows, you're not on a level playing field. Microsoft plays favorites with some online companies and shuns others as much as it possibly can.

Cases in point:

✦ **Microsoft owns part of Facebook.** You see Facebook here and there in Windows. There's a reason why: Microsoft owns a 1.6-percent share of Facebook (at the time of this writing, anyway). Facebook is ambivalent about Microsoft, at best, and as of mid-2015 some open warfare had started. Hard to say how it will play out.

It isn't clear whether Microsoft and Facebook share any data about individual users. But that's certainly a possibility, if not now, at some point in the undefined future.

✦ **Microsoft doesn't play well with Google.** Windows has some hooks into Google, but invariably they exist in order to pull your personal information out of Google (for example, Contacts) and put it in Microsoft's databases. When you see a ready-made connector in Windows 10's Universal Mail app to add a Gmail account — so you can retrieve your Gmail messages in Microsoft's tiled Mail app — there's an ulterior motive.

✦ **Microsoft gives lip service to Apple.** There's no love lost between the companies. Microsoft makes software for Mac and iPad platforms (for example, Office for iPad is a treat, OneNote runs on the iPad, and Office has been on the Mac for longer than it's been on Windows!). Apple still makes software for Windows (such as iTunes, Safari, and QuickTime). But they're both fiercely guarding their own turf. Don't expect to see any sharing of user information.

✦ **Microsoft once tried to buy Yahoo!, which owns Flickr.** Although that possibility seems less likely now than it did in 2008 and again in 2011, it comes up from time to time. Microsoft has hired a boatload of talented people from Yahoo!. Microsoft also still has strong contractual ties to Yahoo!, particularly for running advertising on its search engine, although that could change.

And of course, you know that Microsoft also owns Skype, Hotmail/Outlook. com, and OneDrive, right?

Your information — aggregated, personally identifiable, vaguely anonymous, or whatever — can be drawn from any of those sources and mashed up with the data that Microsoft has in its databases. No wonder data mining is a big topic on the Redmond campus.

Controlling Location Tracking

Just as in Windows 8 of yore, Windows 10 has *location tracking*. You have to tell Windows and specific applications that it's okay to track your location, but if you do, those apps — and Windows itself — know where you are.

Location tracking isn't a bad technology. Like any technology, it can be used for good or not-so-good purposes, and your opinion about what's good may differ from others'. That's what makes a horse race. And a lawsuit or two.

Location tracking isn't just one technology. It's several.

If your PC has a *GPS* chip (see Figure 6-1) — they're common in tablets, but unusual in notebooks and rare in desktops — and the GPS is turned on, and you've authorized a Windows app to see your location, the app can identify your PC's location within a few feet.

GPS is a satellite-based method for pinpointing your location. Currently two different commercial satellite clusters are commonly used — GPS (United States, two dozen satellites) and GLONASS (Russia, three dozen satellites). They travel in very specific orbits around the earth (see Figure 6-2) — they aren't geosynchronous orbits, but they're good enough to cover every patch of land on earth. The GPS chip locates four or more satellites and calculates your location based on the distance to each.

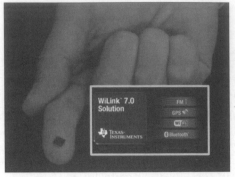

Figure 6-1:
This single
chip has
GPS,
Bluetooth,
Wi-Fi, and
FM radio.

Source: Texas Instruments

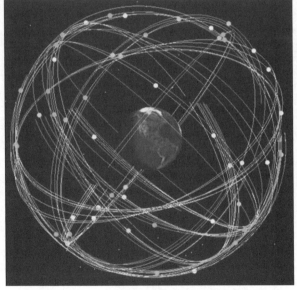

Figure 6-2:
Carefully
crafted
orbits
ensure that
a GPS chip
can almost
always
find four
satellites.

Source: Colorado Center for Astrodynamics Research

If your Windows PC doesn't have a GPS chip, or it isn't turned on, but you do allow Windows apps to track your location, the best Windows can do is to approximate where your Internet connection is coming from, based on your IP address (a number that uniquely identifies your computer's connection to the internet). And in many cases, that can be miles away from where you're actually sitting.

How Apple's location tracking rankled

In April 2011, two researchers — Alasdair Allan and Pete Warden — found that iPads and iPhones with GPS systems were keeping track of location and time data, inside the devices, even if the user explicitly disallowed location tracking. They discovered a log file inside every iPad and iPhone running iOS 4 that included detailed information about location and time since 2010.

They also found that the file was being backed up when the iPhone or iPad was backed up, and the data inside the file wasn't encrypted or protected in any way, and a copy was kept on any computer you synced with the iPhone or iPad.

When confronted with the discovery, Apple at first denied it, and then said that "Apple is not tracking the location of your iPhone. Apple has never done so and has no plans to ever do so" — effectively confirming the researchers' discoveries. As details emerged, Apple claimed it was storing the information to make the location programs work better, but it wasn't being used in, or passed to, any location tracking programs.

In May 2011, Apple released iOS 4.3.3, which no longer kept the data. But by then a series of lawsuits and a class action suit followed in the United States. In Korea, the Communications Commission fined Apple about $3,000 for its transgressions. As I write this, the U.S. case is making its way through the courts.

Location tracking in tablets is a relatively new phenomenon, and it's bound to have some bugs. With a little luck, the bugs — and gaffes — won't be as bad as Apple's.

Book II Chapter 6

Privacy Control

When you start a Windows 10 app that wants to use your location you may see a message asking for your permission to track your location. More commonly, you may see a request for you to provide a location, as in the Weather app shown in Figure 6-3.

Tracking your shots

Any time you put a GPS system and a camera together, you have the potential for lots of embarrassment. Why? Many GPS-enabled cameras — including notably the ones in many phones and tablets — brand the photo with a very precise location. If you snap a shot from your tablet and upload it to Facebook, Flickr, or any of a thousand photo-friendly sites, the photo may have your exact location embedded in the file, for anyone to see.

Law enforcement has used this approach to find suspects. The U.S. military warns active duty personnel to turn off their GPSs to avoid disclosing locations. Even some anonymous celebrities have been outed by their cameras and phones. Be careful.

Figure 6-3:
Windows
10's
Weather
app wants
you to
type in a
location.

If you've already turned on location services, each time you add another app that wants to use your location, you see a notification that says, "Can *[Windows 10 app]* use your location?" You can respond either Allow or Block. The following sections explain how you can control location tracking in Windows 10.

Blocking all location tracking

To keep Windows from using your location in *any* app — even if you've already turned on location use in some apps — follow these steps:

1. **Click or tap Start, and then click or tap Settings.**

2. **Click or tap Privacy. On the left, choose Location.**

The Location Privacy screen appears, as shown in Figure 6-4.

3. **To turn off location tracking — even if you've already given your permission to various and sundry applications to track your location — set Location to Off.**

That's all it takes.

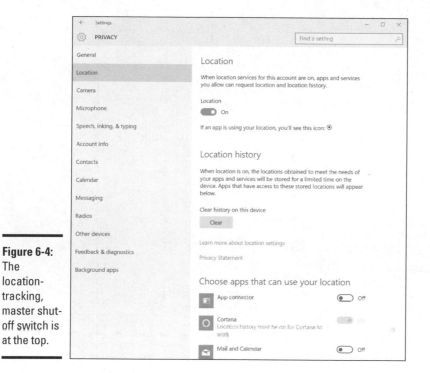

Figure 6-4: The location-tracking, master shut-off switch is at the top.

Blocking location tracking in an app

If you've given an app permission to use your location, but want to turn it off, without throwing the big Off switch described in the preceding steps, here's how to do it:

1. **Click or tap Start, and then click or tap Settings.**

2. **Click or tap Privacy. On the left, choose Location.**

3. **Scroll down until you find the app you want to cut off.**

   In Figure 6-5, I look for the Weather app.

4. **On the right, slide the Location slider to Off.**

   The app loses its permission.

Some apps keep a history of your locations, or searches that may pertain to your location. If you want to verify that's been deleted, too, bring up the app, click or tap the hamburger icon in the upper-left corner and choose Settings. The Settings pane appears on the right. In most cases, you can choose Options and then click the link that says Clear Searches.

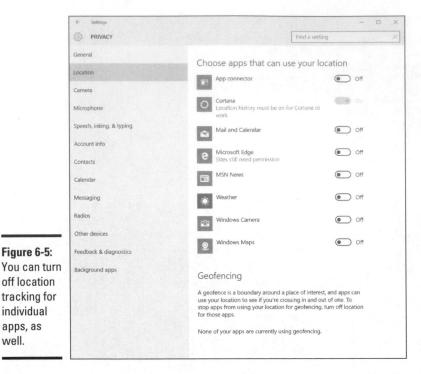

Figure 6-5:
You can turn off location tracking for individual apps, as well.

Minimizing Privacy Intrusion

Although it's true that using Windows 10 exposes you to many more privacy concerns than any previous version of Windows, you can reduce the amount of data kept about you by following a few simple rules:

✦ **If you want to log on to Windows using a Microsoft account — and there are many good reasons for doing so — consider setting up a Microsoft account that you use only for logging on to Windows (and possibly for OneDrive, Xbox, and/or Skype).** See Book II, Chapter 5 for details.

✦ **Don't use the Windows 10 apps for Mail, People, Calendar, Skype, or OneDrive.** If you have a Hotmail/Outlook.com or Gmail account, don't access them through Windows 10's Universal Mail app; go to your browser (Firefox?), and log on to Hotmail/Outlook.com or Gmail. If you keep a separate Microsoft account for logging on to Windows only, use the web interface for OneDrive — by going through OneDrive. Run your Contacts, Calendar, and Messaging through Hotmail/Outlook.com or Gmail as well. It isn't as snazzy as using the Windows 10 Universal apps, but it works almost as well. Even better, in many cases.

Also, as noted earlier in this chapter, be very aware of the fact that both Google (Gmail) and Microsoft (Hotmail/Outlook.com) scan every inbound and outbound message. Google has no qualms about saying it scans inbound and outbound messages on free accounts for text that will improve its aim with advertising. Microsoft swears it doesn't.

Personally, I use Gmail. If Google wants to bombard me with ads, so be it: I don't buy anything from the ads anyway.

✦ **Always use "private" browsing.** In Microsoft Edge it's called *InPrivate;* Firefox calls it *Incognito;* Chrome says *Private Browsing.* Turning on this mode keeps your browser from leaving cookies around, and it wipes out download lists, caches, browser history, forms, and passwords.

Realize, though, that your browser still leaves crumbs wherever it goes: If you use Google to look up something, for example, Google still has a record of your IP address and what you typed.

"Private" browsing isn't the same thing as Do Not Track. In fact, as of this writing, Do Not Track is a largely futile request that you make to the websites you visit, asking them to refrain from keeping track of you and your information. For details, see Book V, Chapter 1.

✦ **Don't opt in for Microsoft's Consumer Experience Improvement Program.** CEIP is the method Microsoft uses to watch what you're doing and send information back for its analysis about what you tried and how you tried it. Microsoft calls it "telemetry." Yes, I know that Microsoft swears it doesn't keep any personally identifiable information from the CEIP. But "personally identifiable" is a squishy topic, and it's simpler to just not go there.

There really is a trade-off between privacy and ease of use: All the apps mentioned in this chapter require a piece of your privacy in order to function. Only you can make the decision about how much of your privacy you want to give up, in exchange for nifty new features. Just be aware of what you're doing, before you do it.

There's also a lesser-known ability called *geofencing* that may become important. When an app uses geofencing, it tracks your location all the time, in order to trigger something (advertising, messaging hookups) when you enter a location that's been cordoned off. If you want to turn off geofencing, you do that in the Location settings pane, as well.

**Book II
Chapter 6**

Privacy Control

Book III
Working on the Desktop

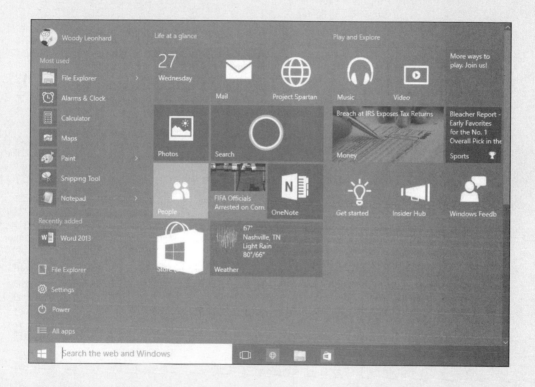

Tired of the Windows 10 Start menu? Bring back the glory days of Windows 7 with these add-ons. Go to `http://www.dummies.com/extras/windows10aio/startmenus` for late-breaking news.

Contents at a Glance

Chapter 1: Running Your Desktop from Start to Finish

In This Chapter

- ✔ Moving around the desktop
- ✔ Working with windows (*windows* with a wittle *w*)
- ✔ Snapping for fun and profit
- ✔ Stepping through the wondrous taskbar
- ✔ Organizing files and folders
- ✔ Showing filename extensions
- ✔ Using Libraries to extend your reach
- ✔ To sleep, perchance to dream

This chapter explains how to find your way around the Windows windows. If you're an old hand at Windows, you know most of this stuff — such as mousing and interacting with dialog boxes — but I bet some of it will come as a surprise, particularly if you've never taken advantage of Windows Libraries or if Windows 8/8.1's Metro side tied you in knots. You know who you are.

Most of all, you need to understand that you don't have to accept all the default settings. Windows 10 was designed to sell more copies of Windows 10. Much of that folderol just gets in the way. What's best for Microsoft isn't necessarily best for you, and a few quick clicks can help make your PC more usable, and more . . . yours.

If you're looking for information on customizing the Windows 10 Start menu and the taskbar, skip ahead to Book III, Chapter 2. To look at personalizing the desktop (and thus tablet mode), read Book III, Chapter 3.

Tripping through Win 10's Three Personas

As soon as you *log on* to the computer (that's what it's called when you click your name), you're greeted with an enormous expanse of near-nothingness, cleverly painted with a pretty picture. Your computer manufacturer might have chosen the picture for you, or you might see the default Microsoft screen.

Your Windows destiny, such as it is, unfolds on the computer's screen.

When you crank up Windows 10, it can take on one of three personas. They're pretty easy to discern, if you follow these guidelines:

✦ Almost everybody starts up with the **Windows Desktop**. It has a Start button in the lower-left corner, more icons along the taskbar at the bottom, and larger icons (possibly just the Recycle Bin) on top of the desktop. The picture on the desktop could look like just about anything.

   If you click the Start icon in the lower-left corner, you see a Start menu on the left and a whole bunch of tiles on the right, as in Figure 1-1. That's what I think of as regular Windows.

Figure 1-1:
This is the traditional Windows desktop — the default view on a Microsoft Surface Pro 3. Your background picture will no doubt differ, as will the contents of the Start menu on the left and probably the Start tiles on the right.

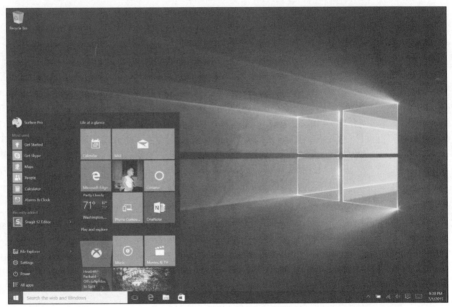

✦ If you've been playing around with your computer, or someone else has done it for you, you may arrive in **Full-Screen Start**, shown in Figure 1-2.

   If you're in Full-Screen Start, I recommend that you get out of it for now, while you're still getting your bearings. To do so, click the hamburger icon (the three line icon in the upper left that looks like a mathematician's equivalence symbol), choose Settings, Personalization, Start, and under Start behaviors, slide the switch marked Use full-screen Start when in the desktop to Off. That will put you back in Figure 1-1, the "real" Start screen.

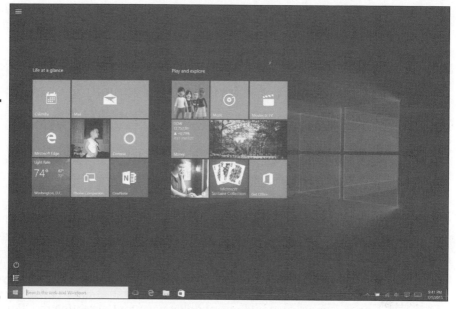

Figure 1-2: This is known as Full-Screen Start. If you see this, drop back to regular Start before you try to change anything.

♦ The third possibility is that you start in **Tablet Mode,** shown in Figure 1-3. The differences between Full-Screen Start and Tablet Mode are subtle, but you can see major differences in the taskbar at the bottom. Full-Screen Start, for example, has a big search box to the right of the Start button. Tablet Mode has a back arrow.

Figure 1-3: Tablet Mode is similar to Full-Screen Start, but it's designed specifically for touch interactions.

If you're going to use Windows primarily with your pinkies, instead of a mouse, Tablet Mode is a good way to, uh, start. I talk about Tablet Mode extensively in its own section of this chapter.

Working with the Traditional Desktop

So your main starting screen looks like Figure 1-1, yes? Good. This is where you should start.

The screen that Windows shows you every time you start your computer is the *desktop,* although it doesn't bear much resemblance to a real desktop. Try putting a pencil on it.

I talk about changing and organizing your desktop in Book III, Chapter 3, but every new Windows 10 user will want to make a few quick changes. That's what we'll do in this chapter.

The Windows desktop looks simple enough, but don't fool yourself: Under that calm exterior sits the most sophisticated computer program ever created. Hundreds of millions of dollars went into creating the illusion of simplicity — something to remember the next time you feel like kicking your computer and screaming at the 10 gods.

Changing the background

Start taking your destiny into your own hands by changing the wallpaper (er, the *desktop background).* If you bought a new computer with Windows 10 installed, your background text probably says *Dell* or *Vaio* or *Billy Joe Bob's Computer Emporium / Dial 555-3106 for a good time.* Bah. Change your wallpaper by following these steps:

1. **Right-click an empty part of the desktop, or tap and hold, and choose Personalize.**

   Windows hops to the Settings app's Background pane, shown in Figure 1-4.

2. **Play with the Background drop-down box, and see if you find a background that you like.**

   You can choose one of the pictures that Windows offers, pick a solid color, or go for a slideshow.

3. **If you don't see a background that tickles your fancy, or if you want to roll your own backgrounds, click Browse.**

   Windows responds by going into your machine and letting you pick a pic, any pic.

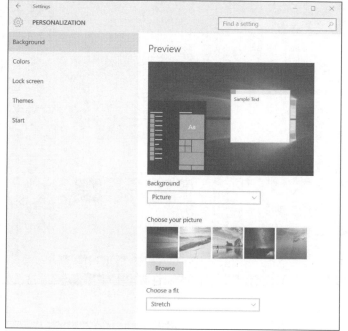

Figure 1-4:
Choose your
desktop
background
(even a slide
show) here.

4. **If you find a picture that you like, and it looks like a smashed water-melon on your screen, or it's too small to be visible, in the Choose a Fit drop-down list, tell Windows how to use the picture.**

These are your options:

- *Stretched to fill the screen*
- *Centered in the middle of the desktop*
- *Tiled over the desktop* (as in Figure 1-5)

5. **Tap or click the Close (X) button to close the Settings app's Background pane.**

Your new wallpaper settings take effect immediately.

Cleaning up useless icons and programs

If you haven't yet taken control and zapped those obnoxious programs that your PC vendor probably stuck on your machine, now is the time to do it.

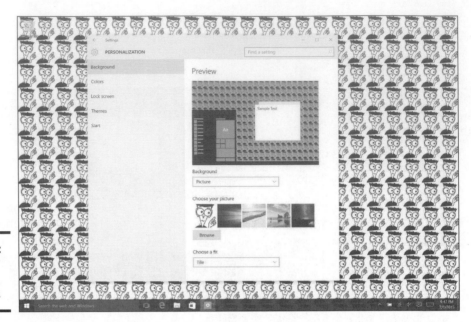

Figure 1-5:
Tiling can
be a bit...
excessive.

You might think that your brand-spanking-new Windows 10 computer wouldn't have any junk on it. Ha. The people who make and sell computers — all of the big-name manufacturers, except Microsoft — sell chunks of real estate on your computer, just to turn a profit. Hate to break it to you, but the AOLs and Nortons of the world pay Dell and HP and Sony and Asus and all the others for space. The manufacturers want you to think that they've installed this lovely software for your convenience. Bah. Humbug.

✦ **To get rid of most icons,** simply right-click them and choose Delete.

✦ **To get rid of the icons' associated programs,** try to remove it the Settings app way first: Choose Start, Settings, System, Apps and Features. See if the program is listed. If so, click or tap it and click Uninstall. If you can't find the program in the Settings app, right-click or tap and hold Start, choose Control Panel, and under Programs, choose Uninstall a Program. When the Uninstall or Change a Program dialog box opens, double-click a program to remove it.

Unfortunately, many scummy programs don't play by the rules: Either they don't have uninstallers or the uninstaller that appears in the Change a Program dialog box doesn't get rid of the program entirely. (I won't mention Norton Internet Security by name.) To get rid of the scummy stuff, look in Book I, Chapter 4 for information about PC Decrapifier, a program from Jason York. It's at `pcdecrapifier.com/download`.

Mousing with Your Mouse

For almost everybody, the computer's mouse (or the lowly touchpad) serves as the primary way of interacting with Windows. But you already knew that. You can click the left mouse button or the right mouse button, or you can roll the wheel in the middle (if you have one), and the mouse will do different things, depending on where you click or roll. But you already knew that, too.

The Windows 10 Multi-Touch technology and those ever-fancier 11-simultaneous-finger screens let you act like Tom Cruise in *Minority Report,* if you have the bucks for the multiple-finger stuff, the right application software, and the horsepower to drive it. But for those of us who put our gloves on one hand at a time, the mouse remains the input device of choice.

The best way to get the feel for a new mouse? Play one of the games that ships with Windows. Choose Start, All Apps, Microsoft Solitaire Collection, and take it away. Or hop over to the Windows Store for amazing new versions of Minesweeper, Chess Titans, and many others for mouse orienteering. I'm trying a test version of 2 Bee 2 right now (as shown in Figure 1-6), which may be in the Windows Store by the time you see this.

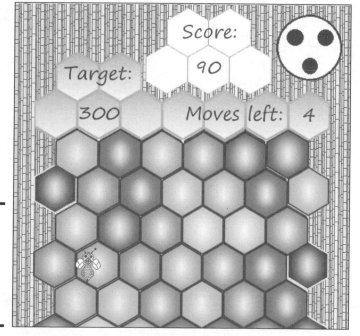

Figure 1-6:
This beta test copy of 2 Bee 2 is great for mouse practice.

Try clicking in unlikely places, double-clicking, or right-clicking in new and different ways. Bet you'll discover several wrinkles, even if you're an old hand at the games. (See Book V, Chapter 5 for more on Windows games.)

Inside the computer, programmers measure the movement of mice in units called *mickeys*. Nope, I'm not making this up. Move your mouse a short distance, and it travels a few mickeys. Move it to Anaheim, and it puts on lots of mickeys.

What's up, dock?

Windows 10 includes several "gesture" features that can save you lots of time. Foremost among them: a quarter- and half-window docking capability called *Snap*.

If you click the title bar of a window and drag the window a-a-all the way to the left side of the screen, as soon as the mouse hits the edge of the screen, Windows 10 resizes the window so that it occupies the left half of the screen and the docks the window on the far left side. Similarly, *mutatis mutandis*, for the right side. That makes it two-drag easy to put a Word document and a spreadsheet side by side, or an email message and a list of files from File Explorer, as shown in Figure 1-7.

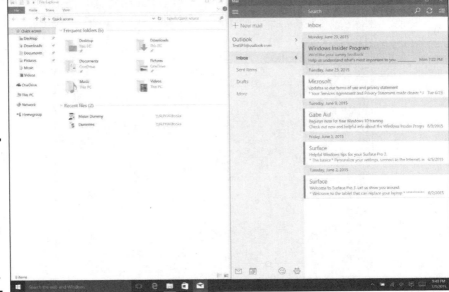

Figure 1-7:
Two drags
and you
can have
Windows
arrange two
different
programs
side by side.

There's a new feature in Windows 10 called Snap Assist that makes snapping easier than ever. If you snap one window to an edge, Windows brings up thumbnails of all the other programs that are running at the time. Click or tap the program, and it occupies the vacant part of the screen, as shown in Figure 1-8.

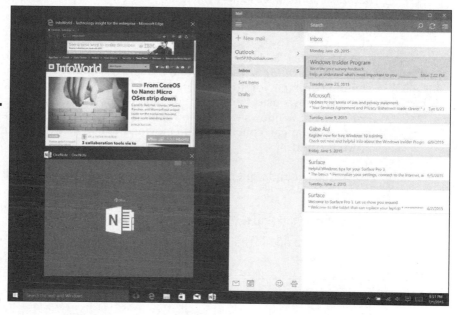

Figure 1-8: Snap Assist helps you put two programs side by side by offering to snap the other programs that are running.

**Book III
Chapter 1**

**Running Your
Desktop from
Start to Finish**

You can also drag into the corners of the screen and snap four programs into the four corners. (If you're curious, these all are controlled in the Settings app. Tap or click Start, Settings, System, Multitasking, and the relevant settings are at the top of the pane.)

Those aren't the only navigation tricks. If you drag a window to the top of the screen, it's *maximized,* so it occupies the whole screen. (Yeah, I know: You always did that by double-clicking the title bar.) And, if you click a window's title bar and shake it, all other windows on the screen move out of the way: They *minimize* themselves on the toolbar.

If you have rodentophobia, you can also do the mouse tricks explained in this section by pressing the following key combinations:

✦ **Snap left:** Windows key+left arrow

✦ **Snap right:** Windows key+right arrow

✦ **Maximize:** Windows key+up arrow

Changing the mouse

If you're left-handed, you can interchange the actions of the left and right mouse buttons — that is, you can tell Windows 10 that it should treat the left mouse button as though it were the right button and treat the right button as though it were the left. The swap comes in handy for some left-handers, but most southpaws I know (including both of my sons) prefer to keep the buttons as is because it's easier to use other computers if your fingers are trained for the standard setting.

The Windows ClickLock feature can come in handy if you have trouble holding down the left mouse button and moving the mouse at the same time — a common problem for notebook users who have fewer than three hands. When Windows uses ClickLock, you hold down the mouse button for a while (you can tell Windows exactly how long) and Windows locks the mouse button so that can concentrate on moving the mouse without having to hold down the button.

To switch left and right mouse buttons or turn on ClickLock, follow these steps:

1. **Click or tap Start, Settings, Devices, Mouse & touchpad.**

Windows opens the Mouse & touchpad dialog box, shown in Figure 1-9.

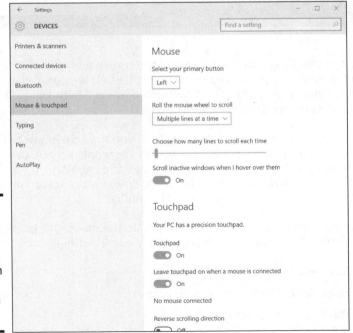

Figure 1-9:
Reverse the left and right mouse buttons with one click in the Settings app.

2. **If you want to switch the functions of the left and right mouse buttons, change the entry in the Select your primary button box.**

3. **If you want to turn on ClickLock, tap or click the link at the bottom for Additional mouse options.**

   You get an old-fashioned Control Panel dialog box called Mouse Properties, which you can see in Figure 1-10.

Figure 1-10: This old-fashioned Control Panel dialog box offers the setting for ClickLock.

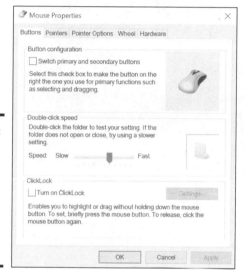

4. **At the bottom of the Mouse Properties dialog box, check the box marked Turn on ClickLock. Click OK.**

   Although changes made in the Settings app take effect immediately, changes in the old-fashioned Control Panel don't go into effect until you click Apply or OK.

Starting with the Start Button

Your Windows 10 orientation rightfully starts in the lower-left corner of the screen with the button that shows the Windows logo — the Start button, if you will.

Microsoft's subverting of the classic Rolling Stones song "Start Me Up" for Windows 95 advertising might be ancient history now, but the royal road to Windows still starts at the Start button. Click the Start button to open the new Windows 10 Start menu, which looks something like the one shown in Figure 1-11.

Figure 1-11: The Windows Start menu packs a wallop — and you can customize it, to some degree.

The Start menu looks like it's etched in granite, but it isn't. You can change three pieces without even digging deep:

✦ **To change the name or picture of the current user,** see Book II, Chapter 2.

✦ **To remove a program from the Most Used programs list,** right-click it and choose Don't show in this list.

✦ **To move a tile on the right or resize one,** just click and drag the tile. You also can right-click (or click and hold), choose Resize, and then pick a new size — see Book III Chapter 2 for details.

If you bought a new computer with Windows 10 preinstalled, the people who make the computer may have sold one or two or three of the spots on the Start menu. Think of it as an electronic billboard on your desktop. Nope, I'm not exaggerating. I keep expecting to bump into a Windows machine with fly-out Start menu entries that read, oh, "Statistics prove / Near and far / That folks who drive / Like crazy are / Burma Shave." (See `Burma-shave.org/jingles`.) You can always delete a pesky Start menu billboard by right-clicking it and choosing Remove from this List or Don't show in this list.

Windows Universal apps

Microsoft has always had a hard time with branding — making its technical achievements sparkle and fizz, and convey meaning with a name. I think "Windows RT" was the all-time low in Microsoft marketing nomenclature — "Windows Live" sure gave it a run for the money — but that's a bygone.

Near the top of the list (or the bottom, depending on how you stand) of really bad branding is the new term "Windows Universal app." At least in theory, Windows Universal apps (sometimes called, confusingly, just "Windows apps" or just "Universal apps" or even "Windows Universal Platform apps") are computer programs that can, in theory, run on any Windows 10 device, whether it's a desktop, a laptop, a tablet, a phone, or a hearing aid. I wonder what a Blue Screen sounds like.

They can, in theory, run on any device because they make use of a new set of Windows programming interfaces, called the WinRT API. The WinRT API is very different from the old Windows programming interfaces, generally called the Win32 API. The programs you've used on Windows for years run on the Win32 API, and they work on the Windows 10 desktop, much as they always have. But the new Windows Universal apps run inside their own little boxes — yep, they look just like Windows windows — and the boxes sit on the desktop.

When you think of Windows versions, the new Windows Universal apps only run on Windows 10. In general, they won't run on Windows 8 or 8.1. They definitely can't run on Windows 7 or earlier, because those versions of Windows didn't include the WinRT API.

The WinRT API has all sorts of advantages over the old Win32 API — security, for one, because it's harder to hack a system from inside a WinRT app, but there are lots of additional capabilities that have become more important as we've turned more mobile. The WinRT API reduces battery demand, makes programming easier for touch input and for resizing screens. It keeps programs from clobbering each other. And on and on.

In the ripe old days (circa Windows 8), the programs that used the WinRT API were called Metro apps. When, according to legend, the German supermarket chain Metro threatened to take Microsoft to task (Who is Microsoft to complain? They trademarked "windows."), Microsoft stopped calling Metro apps "Metro" and the result has been pandemonium.

The names used in the interim include "Metro," "Metro Style," "Windows 8 application," "Windows Store app," "Windows 8 style user interface app," (that really sizzles, doesn't it?) "New user interface app," "Modern app," and a handful of additional names that aren't entirely printable. Just ask the developers.

Microsoft seems to have dropped the name "program" entirely, no doubt because Apple and Google have apps, not (sniff) programs.

No matter what you call them, Windows Universal apps are clearly the way of the future. The WinRT API has the Win32 API beat in all sorts of ways, except compatibility: Win32 programmers have to learn a completely new way of programming and a new way of thinking, and transferring those tens of billions of lines of code from Win32 to WinRT will take decades. By which time WinRT will be obsolete, no doubt.

In the interim, we have Windows 10, which tries — nobly and somewhat successfully — to bridge the gap between the two worlds. Welcome to the future.

The right side of the Start menu contains a plethora of tiles. At the beginning, the built-in tiles are all for Windows Universal apps (see the nearby sidebar) from Microsoft itself. Your computer vendor may have stuck in a couple extras. Kaching. And in the normal course of using your computer, you may well put some tiles over there, too.

Here's what you find on the Right Side of the Start Force:

✦ The **"Productivity apps" from Microsoft** (Calendar, Mail, and People) are marginally useful, but not likely to draw you away from your current email or calendar program, especially if you use email or a calendar on your phone or tablet. The People app is a mess. See Book IV, Chapters 1 and 2.

✦ **Microsoft Edge** may be the best Universal app ever written. Microsoft is serious about getting rid of Internet Explorer, and getting people moved over to a modern browser. Book V, Chapter 1.

✦ The **Search** tile just duplicates the Search box at the bottom. I talk about Search and Hey, Cortana! in Book III, Chapter 6.

✦ **OneNote** is a useful note-taking and clipping app from Microsoft. I use Evernote, but they're directed at two different audiences. See Book IV, Chapter 3.

✦ Also included are a whole bunch of **typical phone apps**, including News, Money, Sports, Fitness, and Food (Book V, Chapter 3), Photos (Book IV, Chapter 3), Weather, plus an Xbox app that really requires an Xbox for full effect.

You can modify most of the right side of the Start menu by dragging and dropping tiles, and right-clicking (or tap and hold) a tile to resize. There's much more about working with Universal app tiles in Book III, Chapter 2.

Touching on the Taskbar

Windows 10 sports a highly customizable taskbar at the bottom of the screen (see Figure 1-12). I go into detail in Book III, Chapter 3.

The taskbar's a wonderfully capable locus for most of the things you want to do, most of the time. For example:

✦ **Hover your mouse over an icon to see what the program's running.** In Figure 1-12, I hover my mouse over the Edge icon and see that AskWoody. com is open.

Some applications, such as File Explorer show each tab or open document in a separate thumbnail. Clicking a thumbnail brings up the application, along with the chosen tab or document. This nascent feature is implemented unevenly at this point.

Figure 1-12:
The Windows 10 taskbar lets you pinpoint what's running and jump to the right location quickly.

✦ **Right-click an icon, and you see the application's Jump List.** The Jump List may show an application's most recently opened documents and, for many programs, a list of common tasks and activities. It may show a browser's history list. We're just starting to see how program writers will exploit this new capability, too.

If you click an icon, the program opens, as you would expect. But if you want to open a second copy of a program — say, another copy of Firefox — you can't just click the icon. You have to right-click and choose the application's name.

✦ **You can move most of the icons around on the taskbar by simply clicking and dragging (you can't move the Start icon, Cortana, or the Task View icons).**

If you want to see all the icons on your desktop and relegate all open windows to shadows of their former selves, click the far right edge of the taskbar.

The Windows taskbar has many tricks up its sleeve, but it has one capability that you may need, if screen real estate is at a premium. (Hey, you folks with 30-inch monitors need not apply, okay?)

Auto-Hide lets the taskbar shrink to a thin line until you bump the mouse pointer way down at the bottom of the screen. As soon as the mouse pointer hits bottom, the taskbar pops up. Here's how to teach the taskbar to auto-hide:

1. **Right-click an empty part of the taskbar.**

2. **Choose Properties.**

The Taskbar tab should be visible.

3. **Select the Auto-Hide the Taskbar check box, and click OK.**

The taskbar holds many surprises. See Book III, Chapter 3.

**Book III
Chapter 1**

Running Your
Desktop from
Start to Finish

Tapping with Tablet Mode

If you're looking at the desktop, try a little experiment, even if you don't have a touch-enabled computer. Bring up Tablet Mode, and play with it for a bit. Here's a mini guided tour:

1. **From the desktop, click Start, Settings, System, Tablet Mode.**

You see the options shown in Figure 1-13.

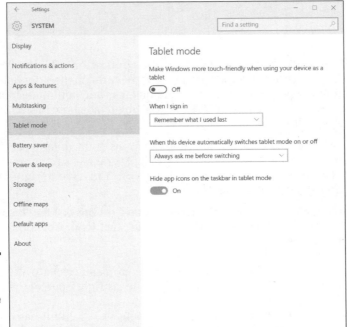

Figure 1-13: Flip into Tablet Mode here.

2. **Turn the first switch On.**

Whoa nelly! The little Tablet Mode dialog box suddenly expands to fit the entire screen. That's an important observation. Everything you run in Tablet Mode runs full screen. (Unless you snap, but that's another story.)

3. **Click or tap the Start button — the Windows logo — in the lower-left corner.**

You pop over to Tablet Mode, shown in Figure 1-14.

Note that there's usually an icon in the Action Center, accessible by clicking the comic book dialog icon in the lower right, that lets you jump into tablet mode.

Figure 1-14:
Tablet
Mode works
even on a
computer
that doesn't
support
touch.

4. **Before you get freaked out, click or tap the hamburger icon in the upper-left corner.**

   You see the more or less reassuring Start menu along the left edge, as in Figure 1-15.

5. **Try clicking a tile — say, the News tile or Weather or something not terribly threatening. Above all, avoid the tile called Global Thermonuclear War.**

   The Start menu disappears, and then the app kicks in. It takes a while to get used to the fact that absolutely everything runs full screen.

6. **When you're finished looking at the app, click the Start icon in the lower-left corner.**

   Alternatively, you can press the Windows key on your keyboard if you have one or the Windows key on your tablet if it has one. You return to the main screen (refer to Figure 1-14).

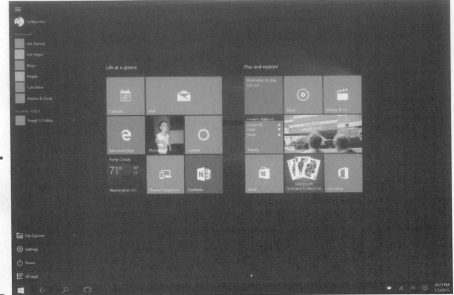

Figure 1-15:
A slightly
modified
Start menu
is available
via the
hamburger
icon.

7. **Right-click (or tap and hold) one of the tiles, choose Resize, and make the tile a different size.**

   In Figure 1-16, I right-clicked the Money tile and chose Resize, Large.

Figure 1-16:
Money is
one of the
few tiles
that can be
resized to
Large.

8. **If you feel adventurous, click (or tap) and drag a tile to a new location.**

   I have detailed instructions on arranging Start tiles in Book III, Chapter 2.

9. **If you want to get out of Tablet Mode (very few people with a mouse want to live in Tablet land), click or tap the hamburger icon, choose Settings, System, Tablet Mode, and slide the Tablet Mode slider to Off.**

   You're immediately transported to terra firma and the desktop, as in Figure 1-17, but note that your resized tile (Money, in this screenshot) is still resized.

Figure 1-17: When you transition back to regular old desktop mode, any changes you made to the tiles while in Tablet Mode persist.

Working with Files and Folders

"What's a file?" Man, I wish I had a nickel for every time I've been asked that question.

A file is a, uh, thing. Yeah, that's it. A thing. A thing that has stuff inside it. Why don't you ask me an easier question, like "What is a paragraph?" or "What is the meaning of life, the universe, and everything?"

A *file* is a fundamental chunk of stuff. Like most fundamental chunks of stuff (say, protons, Congressional districts, or ear wax), any attempt at a definitive definition gets in the way of understanding the thing itself. Suffice it to say that a Word document is a file. An Excel workbook is a file. That photograph your cousin emailed you the other day is a file. Every track on the latest Coldplay album is a file, but so is every track on every audio CD ever made. Chris Martin isn't that special.

Filenames and folder names can be very long, but they can't contain the following characters:

```
/ \ : * ? " < > |
```

Files can be huge. They can be tiny. They can even be empty, but don't short-circuit any gray cells on that observation.

Folders hold files and other folders. Folders can be empty. A single folder can hold millions — yes, quite literally millions — of files and other folders.

Keeping folders organized

If you set folders up correctly, they can help you keep track of things. If you toss your files around higgledy-piggledy, no system of folders in the world can help. Unfortunately, folders have a fundamental problem. Permit me to illustrate.

Suppose you own a sandwich shop. You take a photograph of the shop. Where do you stick the photo? Which folder should you use? The answer: There's no good answer. You could put the photo in with all your other "shop" stuff — documents and invoices and payroll records and menus. You could stick the photo in the Pictures folder, or in your OneDrive Pictures folder, which Windows 10 automatically provides. You could put it in the Public or Public Documents or Public Pictures folder so other people using your PC, or other folks connected to your network, can see the photo of the shop. You could create a folder named Photos and file away the picture chronologically (that's what I do), or you could even create a folder named Shop inside the Photos folder and stick the picture in `\Photos\Shop`.

This where-to-file-it-and-where-to-find-it conundrum stands as one of the hairiest problems in all of Windows, and until Windows 7, you had only piecemeal help in keeping things organized. Now, using the Windows 10 Libraries, and a Search function that (finally!) works the way you would expect, you stand a fighting chance of finding that long-lost file, especially if you're diligent in assigning tags to pictures and videos. For more info on that, see the sidebar "Creating Libraries," later in this chapter.

But if you stick the photo in OneDrive, ay, that's another story entirely. See Book VI, Chapter 2 for the sad story (and sidebar) of "smart files."

To look at the files and folders on your machine that you probably use every day, click or tap Start, File Explorer. A program named File Explorer appears, and it shows you the contents of your frequently used folders (see Figure 1-18).

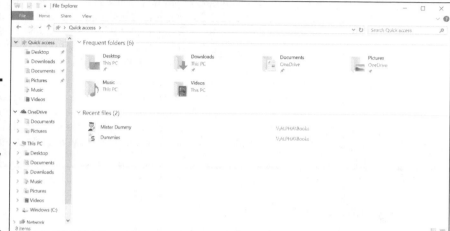

Figure 1-18: The most frequently used folders and recently accessed files, shown by File Explorer.

File Explorer can show you the contents of a hard drive — folders and files — or a thumb drive or a CD/DVD drive. File Explorer can also help you look at other computers on your network, if you have a network.

Creating Libraries

Windows 7 brought a powerful new concept to the table: Libraries. Think of them as easy ways to mash together the contents of many folders: You can work with a collection of folders as easily as you work with just one folder, no matter where the folders live. You can pull together pictures in ten of the folders on your desktop plus the ones in your computer's \ `Public` folder plus the ones on that external terabyte drive and the \ `Public` folder on another computer connected to your network, and treat them all as though they were in the same folder.

Unfortunately, as Microsoft pushed deeper into the cloud and brought OneDrive to the fore, Libraries got left behind. In Windows 8 and 8.1, it's hard to find the vestiges and make them work right. Windows 10 continues in the Windows 8/8.1 tradition.

Many people find Libraries too difficult. Personally, I find working *without* Libraries is too difficult.

I refer to Libraries occasionally in this chapter, but if you want the whole story, check out Book VII, Chapter 3. Unless you want to put all your data in OneDrive (which isn't a bad idea, really), drop by Book VII, Chapter 3 to find a better way to organize your data here on earth.

What is a HomeGroup?

HomeGroups make it easier to set up sharing among Windows 7, 8/8.1, and 10 computers on a network. I cover the details in Book VII, Chapter 5, but here's the one-minute version.

When your PC joins a HomeGroup, Windows strips away much of the hassle and mind-numbing details generally associated with sharing folders and printers and replaces the mumbo jumbo with a cookie-cutter method of sharing that works quite well, in almost all home and many small-business networks.

All the computers in a HomeGroup share their printers and some other peripherals. When an individual signs up for the HomeGroup, their Pictures, Music, and Videos Libraries are shared by default. An extra click adds the Documents Library to the list.

Other accounts on the computer — ones that haven't been explicitly logged into the HomeGroup — share only their printers. In other words, you must specifically log in to the HomeGroup to have your folders shared.

Using File Explorer

Your PC is a big place, and you can get lost easily. Microsoft has spent hundreds of millions of dollars to make sure that Windows 10 points you in the right direction and keeps you on track through all sorts of activities.

Amazingly, some of it actually works.

If you're going to get any work done, you must interact with Windows. If Windows is going to get any work done, it must interact with you. Fair 'nuff.

Microsoft refers to the way Windows interacts with people as the *user experience*. Gad. File Explorer lies at the center of the, er, user experience. When you want to work with Windows 10 — ask it where it stuck your wedding pictures, show it how to mangle your files, or tell it (literally) where to go — you usually use File Explorer.

Navigating

File Explorer helps you get around in the following ways:

✦ **Click a folder to see the files you want.** On the left side of the File Explorer window (refer to Figure 1-18), you can click a real folder (such as Desktop or Downloads), a shortcut you dragged to the Quick access list on the left, other computers in your HomeGroup (see sidebar on HomeGroups), other drives on your computer, or other computers on the network. You can also reach into your OneDrive account, in the sky, as you can see in Figure 1-19.

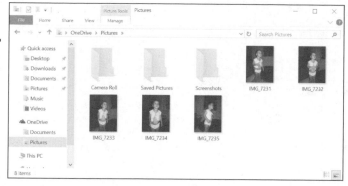

Figure 1-19:
File Explorer helps you move around, even into the sky with OneDrive.

✦ **Use the "cookie crumb" navigation bar to move around.** At the top of the File Explorer window (refer to Figure 1-19), you can click the wedges to select from available folders. So, in Figure 1-19, if you click Pictures up at the top, you end up in the OneDrive Pictures folder.

✦ **Details appear below.** If you click a file or folder once, details for it (number of items, Sharing state) appear in the Details box at the bottom of the File Explorer window. If you double-click a folder, it becomes the current folder. If you double-click a document, it opens. (For example, if you double-click a Word document, Windows fires up Word and has it start with that document open and ready for work.)

✦ **Many of the actions you might want to perform on files or folders show up in the command bar at the top.** Most of the other actions you might want to perform are accessible by right-clicking the file or folder.

✦ **To see all options, press Alt.** File Explorer shows you an old-fashioned command bar (File, Edit, View, Tools, Help) with dozens of functions tucked away.

✦ **Open as many copies of File Explorer as you like.** That can be very helpful if you're scatterbrained like I am — er, if you like to multitask and you want to look in several places at once. Simply choose Start, File Explorer, and a totally independent copy of File Explorer appears, ready for your finagling.

Viewing

Large Icons view (refer to Figure 1-19) is, at once, visually impressive and cumbersome. If you grow tired of scrolling (and scrolling and scrolling) through those icons, click the View menu and choose Details. You see the succinct list shown in Figure 1-20.

Book III
Chapter 1

Running Your
Desktop from
Start to Finish

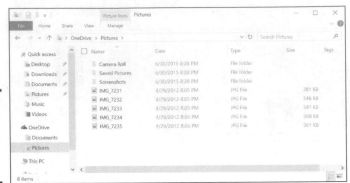

Figure 1-20: Details view has more meat, less sizzle.

Windows 10 offers several picturesque views — dubbed Extra Large Icons, Large Icons, Medium Icons, Small Icons, and Infinitesimal Eyestraining Icons (okay, I got carried away a bit) — that can come in handy if you're looking through a bunch of pictures. In most other cases, though, the icons only get in the way.

In Details view, you can sort the list of files by clicking one of the column headings — Name or Date, for example. You can right-click one of the column headings and choose More to change what the view shows (get rid of Type, for example, and replace it with Date Taken).

Creating files and folders

Usually, you create new files and folders when you're using a program. You make new Word documents when you're using Word, say, or come up with a new folder to hold all your offshore banking spreadsheets when you're using Excel. Programs usually have the tools for making new files and folders tucked away in the File, Save and File, Save As dialog boxes. Click around a bit and you'll find them.

Preview

Every File Explorer window can show a Preview pane — a strip along the right side of the window that, in many cases, shows a preview of the file you selected.

Some people love the preview feature. Others hate it. A definite speed hit is associated with previewing — you may find yourself twiddling your thumbs as Windows 10 gets its previews going. The best solution is to turn off the preview unless you absolutely need it. And use the right tool for the job — if you're previewing lots of picture files, fire up a Photo app (not necessarily the one in Windows 10; see Book IV, Chapter 3).

You can set the preview pane, and all other File Explorer panes, by clicking the View tab, and on the left, choosing Preview pane.

But you can also create a new file or folder directly in an existing folder quite easily, without going through the hassle of cranking up a 900-pound gorilla of a program. Follow these steps:

1. **Move to the location where you want to put the new file or folder.**

For example, if you want to stick the new folder Revisionist Techno Grunge in your Documents folder, choose Start, File Explorer, and on the left, under Quick Access, click Documents.

2. **Right-click a blank spot in your chosen location.**

By "right-click a blank spot," I mean "don't right-click an existing file or folder," okay? If you want the new folder or file to appear on the desktop, right-click an empty spot on the desktop.

3. **Choose New (see Figure 1-21), and pick the kind of file you want to create.**

If you want a new folder, choose Folder.

Windows creates the new file or folder and leaves it with the name highlighted so that you can rename it by simply typing.

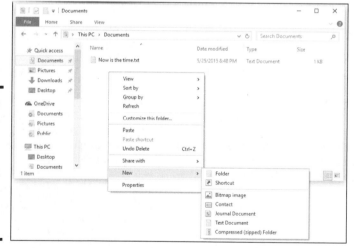

Book III
Chapter 1

Figure 1-21:
Right-click an empty location, and choose New to create a new file or folder.

Running Your
Desktop from
Start to Finish

Modifying files and folders

As long as you have permission (see the section "Sharing folders," later in this chapter), modifying files and folders is easy — rename, delete, move, or copy them — if you remember the trick: right-click.

To copy or move more than one file (or folder) at a time, select all the files (or folders) before right-clicking. You can select more than one file using any of these methods:

✦ Hold down Ctrl while clicking.

✦ Click and drag around the outside of the files and folders to "lasso" them.

✦ Use the Shift key if you want to choose a bunch of contiguous files and folders — ones that are next to each other. Click the first file or folder, hold down Shift, and click the last file or folder.

Showing filename extensions

If you're looking at the Recent files on your computer and you can't see the period and three-letter suffixes of the filenames (such as .txt and .tif and .jpg) that are visible in Figures 1-18, 1-19, 1-20, 1-21, and most of the rest of this book, don't panic! You need to tell Windows to show them — electronically knock Windows upside the head, if you will.

In my opinion, every single Windows 10 user should force Windows to show full filenames, including the (usually three-letter) extension at the end of the name.

I've been fighting Microsoft on this topic for many years. Forgive me if I get a little, uh, steamed — yeah, that's the polite way to put it — in the retelling.

Every file has a name. Almost every file has a name that looks more or less like this: Some Name or Another.ext.

The part to the left of the period — Some Name or Another, in this example — generally tells you something about the file, although it can be quite nonsensical or utterly inscrutable, depending on who named the file. The part to the right of the period — ext, in this case — is a filename *extension,* the subject of my diatribe.

Filename extensions have been around since the first PC emerged from the primordial ooze. They were a part of the PC's legacy before anybody ever talked about "legacy." Somebody, somewhere decided that Windows wouldn't show filename extensions anymore. (My guess is that Bill Gates himself made the decision, about twenty years ago, but it's only a guess.) Filename extensions were considered dangerous: too complicated for the typical user, a bit of technical arcana that novices shouldn't have to sweat.

No filename extensions? That's garbage. Pure, unadulterated garbage.

The fact is that nearly all files have names like `Letter to Mom.docx`, `Financial Projections.xlsx`, or `ILOVEYOU.vbs`. But Windows, with rare exception, shows you only the first part of the filename. It cuts off the filename extension. So you see `Letter to Mom`, without the `.docx` (which brands the file as a Word document), `Financial Projections` without the `.xlsx` (a dead giveaway for an Excel spreadsheet), and `ILOVEYOU` without the `.vbs` (which is the filename extension for Visual Basic programs).

I really hate it when Windows hides filename extensions, for four big reasons:

✦ **If you can see the filename extension, you can usually figure out which kind of file you have at hand and which program will open it.** People who use Word 2003, for example, may be perplexed to see a `.docx` filename extension — which is generated by Word 2010 and can't be opened by bone-stock Word 2003.

Legend has it that former Microsoft CEO (and current largest individual stockholder) Steve Ballmer once infected former CEO (and current philanthropist extraordinaire) Bill Gates's Windows PC using a bad email attachment, ILOVEYOU.VBS. If Ballmer had seen the .VBS on the end of the filename, no doubt he would've guessed it was a program — and might've been disinclined to double-click it.

✦ **It's almost impossible to get Windows to change filename extensions if you can't see them.** Try it.

✦ **Many email programs and spam fighters forbid you from sending or receiving specific kinds of files, based solely on their filename extensions.** That's one of the reasons why your friends might not be able to email certain files to you. Just try emailing an `.exe` file, no matter what's inside.

✦ **You bump into filename extensions anyway.** No matter how hard Microsoft wants to hide filename extensions, they show up everywhere — from the `Readme.txt` files mentioned repeatedly in the official Microsoft documentation to discussions of `.jpg` file sizes on Microsoft web pages and a gazillion places in between.

Take off the training wheels, okay? To make Windows show you filename extensions the easy way, follow these steps:

1. **Click Start, File Explorer.**

   File Explorer appears (refer to Figure 1-18).

2. **Click or tap View.**

   You see File Explorer's View ribbon, shown in Figure 1-22.

Figure 1-22:
Make
Windows
show you
filename
extensions.

3. Check the File name extensions box.

While you're here, you may want to change another setting. If you can avoid the temptation to delete or rename files you don't understand, check the Hidden items box. That way, Windows will show you all files on your computer, including ones that have been marked as Hidden, typically by Microsoft. Sometimes, you need to see all your files, even if Windows wants to hide them from you.

4. Your changes take place immediately.

Look at your unveiled filename extensions.

Sharing folders

Sharing is good, right? Your mom taught you to share, didn't she? Everything you need to know about sharing you learned in kindergarten — like how you can share your favorite crayon with your best friend and get back a gnarled blob of stunted wax, covered in mysterious goo.

Windows 10 supports two very different ways for sharing files and folders:

+ **Move the files or folders you want to share into the** `\Public` **folder.**
The `\Public` folder is kind of a big cookie jar for everybody who uses your PC: Put a file or folder in the `\Public` folder so all the other people who use your computer can get at it. The `\Public` folder is available to other people in your HomeGroup (see the nearby sidebar), if you have one, but you have little control over who, specifically, can get at the files and folders.

+ **Share individual files or folders, without moving them anywhere.**
When you share a file or folder, you can tell Windows 10 to share the folder with everyone in your HomeGroup, or you can specify exactly

who can access the file or folder and whether they can just look at it or change it or delete it. I talk about the details in the section "Sharing and permissions," later in this chapter.

Using the \Public folder

You might think that simply moving a file or folder to the \Public folder would make it, well, public. At least to a first approximation, that's exactly how things work.

Any file or folder you put in the \Public folder, or any folder inside the \Public folder, can be viewed, changed, or deleted by anybody who's using your computer, regardless of which kind of account they may have and whether they're required to log on to your computer. In addition, anybody who can get into your computer through the network will have unlimited access. The \Public folder is (if you'll pardon a rather stretched analogy) a big cookie jar, open to everybody who is in the kitchen.

(For more details, and important information about Public networks and big-company domains, check out *Networking All-In-One For Dummies,* by Doug Lowe [Wiley].)

Sharing and OneDrive

Microsoft wants you to put all your files in OneDrive. No, they aren't trying to snoop the contents: that's a Google kind of thing, for many (but not all) Google free accounts. Microsoft gives away lots of "free" cloud storage in OneDrive because they want you to use (and pay for) other Microsoft products. Microsoft's cost for 7 or 25 GB of "free" cloud space is measured in pennies, and it's getting cheaper. Microsoft's income from keeping you in the Microsoft fold — maybe buying a subscription to Office 365, say, or clicking an ad in Bing — pays for the free storage and then some.

That's why Windows 10 doesn't put a big emphasis on file sharing, here on earth. This book will show you many ways to share files — Libraries, Public folders, HomeGroups — that Microsoft isn't particularly interested in

proliferating. They don't make money and don't lock you into their ecosystem when your files are all down here, out of the cloud.

In some cases, OneDrive is your best choice for storing and sharing files. I use it all the time, although I tend to put my most important files (including all the files used in preparing this book) in Dropbox. For many people who get nosebleeds in the cloud, for a wide variety of reasons, though, keeping your sharing out of Microsoft's cloud makes good sense.

It's your data. You can choose. You can even change your mind if you want. This book has an extensive discussion of OneDrive and sharing in Book VI, Chapter 2. But if you want to keep your data out of Microsoft's cloud, follow along here to see how it's done the Windows way.

Follow these easy steps to move a file or folder from one of the built-in personal folders (Desktop, Documents, Downloads, Music, Pictures, or Videos) into its corresponding location in one of the \Public folders:

1. Tap or click Start, File Explorer. Navigate to the file or folder that you want to move into the \Public folder.

In Figure 1-23, I double-clicked the Quick Access Pictures folder to get to my Pictures.

Figure 1-23:
Moving a folder to the \Public folder is easy, if you know the trick.

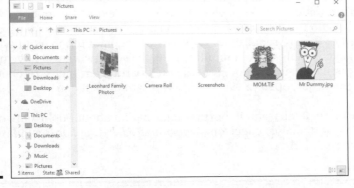

2. Right-click the folder or file you want to move, and choose Cut.

In this case, I wanted to move the _Leonhard Family Photos folder, so I cut it.

3. Navigate to the \Public folder where you want to move the folder or file.

This is more difficult than you might think. In general, on the left of File Explorer, double-click This PC, then scroll way down and double-click or tap Local Disk (C:). Then double-click Users, then Public. You see the list of Public folders shown in Figure 1-24.

Figure 1-24:
Your \Public folders live here.

4. **Double-click the \Public folder you want to use. Then right-click inside the folder, and choose Paste.**

   In this case, I double-clicked Public Pictures and pasted the _Leonhard Family Photos into the Public Pictures folder. From that point on, the photos are available to anybody who uses my computer and to people who connect to my computer using HomeGroups. (It may also be available to other computers connected to your network, workgroup, or domain, depending on various network settings. See *Networking All-In-One For Dummies* for specific examples.)

Recycling

When you delete a file, it doesn't go to that Big Bit Bucket in the Sky. An intermediate step exists between deletion and the Big Bit Bucket. It's called purgatory — oops. Wait a sec. Wrong book. (*Existentialism For Dummies*, anybody?) Let me try that again. Ahem.

The step between deletion and the Big Bit Bucket is the Recycle Bin.

When you delete a file or folder from your hard drive — whether by selecting the file or folder in File Explorer and pressing Delete or by right-clicking and choosing Delete — Windows doesn't actually delete anything. It marks the file or folder as being deleted but, other than that, doesn't touch it.

Files and folders on USB key drives, SD cards, and network drives don't go into limbo when they're deleted. The Recycle Bin doesn't work on USB key drives, SD cards, or drives attached to other computers on your network. That said, if you accidentally wipe out the data on your key drive or camera memory card, there is hope. See the sidebar on recovering lost photos in Book IV, Chapter 4.

To rummage around in the Recycle Bin, and possibly bring a file back to life, follow these steps:

1. **Double-click the Recycle Bin icon on the Windows desktop.**

   File Explorer opens to the Recycle Bin, shown in Figure 1-25.

2. **To restore a file or folder (sometimes Windows calls it *undeleting*), click the file or folder and then click Restore the Selected Items in the ribbon.**

   You can select a bunch of files or folders by holding down Ctrl as you click.

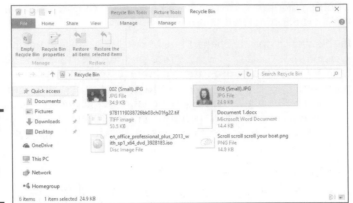

Figure 1-25:
Restore
files one at
a time or en
masse.

If you set things up properly, Windows 10 maintains shadow copies of previous versions of many kinds of files. If you can't find what you want in the Recycle Bin, follow the steps in Book VIII, Chapter 1 to see whether you can dig something out of the Windows Time Machine.

To reclaim the space that the files and folders in the Recycle Bin are using, click the Empty the Recycle Bin link. Windows asks whether you really, truly want to get rid of those files permanently. If you say Yes, they're gone.

Creating Shortcuts

Sometimes, life is easier with shortcuts. (As long as the shortcuts work, anyway.) So, too, in the world of Windows, where shortcuts point to things that can be started. You may set up a shortcut to Word and put it on your desktop. Double-click the shortcut and Word starts, the same way as if you chose Start, All Programs, Microsoft Word.

You can set up shortcuts that point to the following items:

✦ Old-fashioned Windows programs (er, apps), of any kind (I haven't yet found a way to put a shortcut for a Windows Universal app on the desktop.)

✦ Web addresses, such as `www.dummies.com`

✦ Documents, spreadsheets, databases, PowerPoint presentations, and anything else that can be started in File Explorer by double-clicking it

✦ Specific chunks of text (called *scraps*) inside documents, spreadsheets, databases, and presentations, for example

✦ Folders (including the weird folders inside digital cameras, the Fonts folder, and others that you may not think of)

✦ Drives (hard drives, CD drives, and key drives, for example)

✦ Other computers on your network, and drives and folders on those computers, as long they're shared

✦ Printers (including printers attached to other computers on your network), scanners, cameras, and other pieces of hardware

✦ Network connections, interface cards, and the like

You have many different ways to create shortcuts. In many cases, you can go into File Explorer, right-click a file, drag it to the desktop, and choose Create Link here.

Here's a more general-purpose method that works for, say, websites:

1. **Right-click a blank area on the desktop, and choose New, Shortcut.**

You see the Create New Shortcut wizard shown in Figure 1-26.

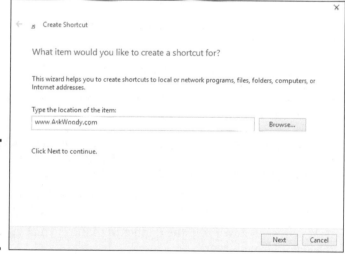

Figure 1-26:
Create new shortcuts the old-fashioned, manual way.

**Book III
Chapter 1**

Running Your
Desktop from
Start to Finish

2. **Type the name or location of the program (not Windows Universal app), file, folder, drive, computer, or Internet address into the top box. Click Next.**

Windows asks you for a name for the shortcut.

3. **Give the shortcut a memorable name, and click Finish.**

   Windows places an icon for the program, file, folder, drive, computer, website, document...whatever...on the desktop.

Anytime I double-click the AskWoody icon on my desktop, the default browser pops up and puts me on the AskWoody.com main page.

You can use a similar procedure for setting up shortcuts to any file, folder, program, or document on your computer or on any networked computer.

Believe it or not, Windows thrives on shortcuts. They're everywhere, lurking just beneath the surface. For example, every single entry on the Start menu is a (cleverly disguised) shortcut. The icons on the taskbar are all shortcuts. Most of File Explorer is based on shortcuts — although they're hidden where you can't reach them. Even the Windows Universal app icons work with shortcuts; they're just hard to find. So don't be afraid to experiment with shortcuts. In the worst-case scenario, you can always delete them. Doing so gets rid of the shortcut; it doesn't touch the original file.

Keying Keyboard Shortcuts

Windows 10 has about a hundred zillion — no, a googolplex— of keyboard shortcuts.

I don't use very many of them. They make my brain hurt.

Here are the keyboard shortcuts that everyone should know. They've been around for a long, long time:

✦ **Ctrl+C** copies whatever you've selected and puts it on the Clipboard. On a touchscreen, you can do the same thing in most applications by tapping and holding, and then choosing Copy.

✦ **Ctrl+X** does the same thing but removes the selected items — a cut. Again, you can tap and hold, and Cut should appear in the menu.

✦ **Ctrl+V** pastes whatever is in the Clipboard to the current cursor location. Tap and hold usually works.

✦ **Ctrl+A** selects everything, although sometimes it's hard to tell what "everything" means — different applications handle Ctrl+A differently. Tap and hold usually works here, too.

✦ **Ctrl+Z** usually "undoes" whatever you just did. Few touch-enabled apps have a tap-and-hold alternative; you usually have to find Undo on a Ribbon or menu.

✦ When you're typing, **Ctrl+B**, **Ctrl+I**, and **Ctrl+U** usually flip your text over to Bold, Italic, or Underline, respectively. Hit the same key combination again, and you flip back to normal.

Sleep: Perchance to Dream

Aye, there's the rub.

Windows 10 has been designed so that it doesn't need to be turned off.

Okay, that's a bit of an overstatement. Sometimes, you have to restart your computer to let patches kick in. Sometimes, you plan to be gone for a week and need to give the beast a blissful rest. But by and large, you don't need to shut off a Windows 10 computer — the power management schemes are very green.

The only power setting most people need to fiddle with is the length of time Windows allows before it turns the screen black. Here's the easy way to adjust your screen blackout time:

1. **Click or tap Start, Settings. Choose System and then Power & sleep.**

Windows brings up the Power & sleep dialog box shown in Figure 1-27.

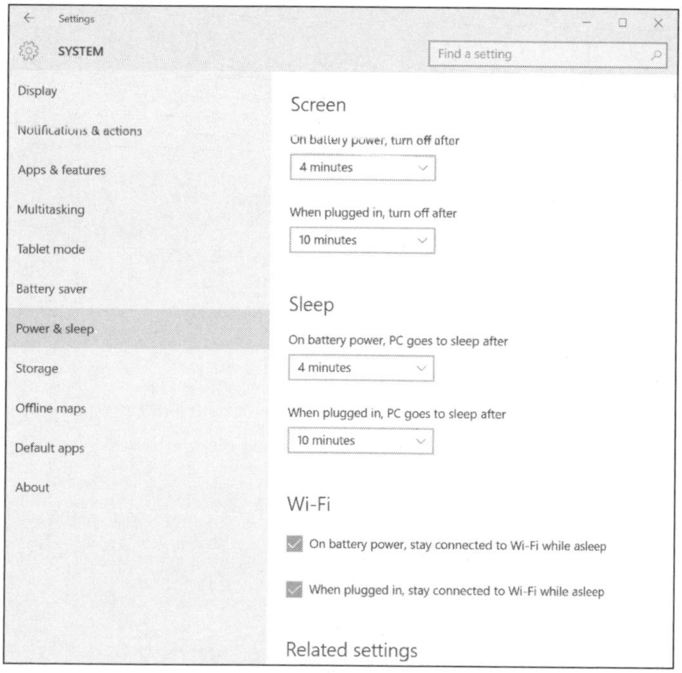

**Book III
Chapter 1**

**Running Your
Desktop from
Start to Finish**

Figure 1-27:
Tell your
machine
how long
to run off to
dreamland.

← Settings		— □ ×
⚙ SYSTEM	Find a setting	🔍

Display

Notifications & actions

Apps & features

Multitasking

Tablet mode

Battery saver

Power & sleep

Storage

Offline maps

Default apps

About

Screen

On battery power, turn off after

| 4 minutes ⌄ |

When plugged in, turn off after

| 10 minutes ⌄ |

Sleep

On battery power, PC goes to sleep after

| 4 minutes ⌄ |

When plugged in, PC goes to sleep after

| 10 minutes ⌄ |

Wi-Fi

☑ On battery power, stay connected to Wi-Fi while asleep

☑ When plugged in, stay connected to Wi-Fi while asleep

Related settings

2. **In the drop-down box at the top, choose whatever time you like.**

   Your changes take effect immediately.

Although Microsoft has published voluminous details about the power down and power up sequences, I haven't seen any details about how long it takes before your PC actually goes to sleep. In theory, that shouldn't matter too much because the wake-ups are so fast.

Microsoft recently published some recommendations that I found fascinating. To truly conserve energy with a desktop computer, be aggressive with the monitor idle time (no longer than two minutes), and make sure that you don't have a screen saver enabled. If you want to conserve energy with a notebook or netbook, your top priority is to reduce the screen brightness!

I talk about power conservation and the many paths to greenness in *Green Home Computing For Dummies*, which I co-wrote with Katherine Murray (Wiley). (Hi, Kathy!) It's packed with important information for anybody with a PC and a conscience.

Chapter 2: Personalizing the Start Menu

In This Chapter

✔ Stop worrying and start loving the Start menu's tiles

✔ Making the Start menu yours

✔ Changing tiles on the Start menu

✔ Behind the scenes with Tiled Snap

*I*f you're an experienced Windows user, chances are good that the first time you saw the Windows 8 Start screen, you wondered who put an iPad on it. However, if you're an experienced iPad user, chances are good that the first time you worked with the Win8 Start screen, you went screaming for your iPad.

Windows 10 has, I'm convinced, improved upon the Windows 8 experience greatly. If you have a mouse, the Windows 10 Start menu — the screen that almost everybody sees when they click the Start button, and the screen you'll come back to over and over again — defines and anchors Windows. Like it or not. See Figure 2-1.

If you don't have a mouse — if your machine is touch-only, and Windows 10 recognized that fact — you're acquainted with, and probably live in, the Tablet Mode screen shown in Figure 2-2.

My advice, if you don't like those newfangled Start tiles, is to give it a real workout for a month or two. I don't expect that you'll end up singing hosannas about the tiles. But I do expect that you'll warm up to it a little bit — and, like me, you may even miss it when you go back to Windows 7. That goes double if you can use Windows 10 on a touch-friendly tablet.

In this chapter, I take you through the Start menu, from beginning to end. It's a bit confusing because changes in the desktop's Start menu (refer to Figure 2-1) affects the appearance of the Tablet Mode Start screen (refer to Figure 2-2).

Hey, if you can get your thumb and all your pinkies on the screen simultaneously, touch has the mouse beat five to one. Sorta.

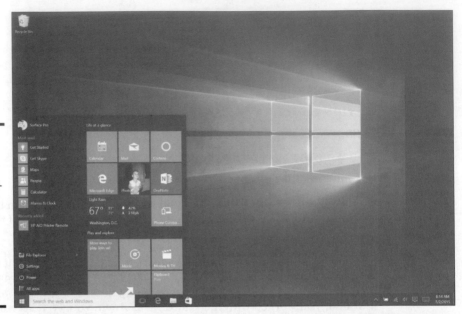

Figure 2-1:
This is the "normal" mouse-and-keyboard version of the Start menu, as seen on a Surface Pro 3.

Figure 2-2:
This is the Tablet Mode Start screen.

Touring the Start Menu

The very first screen you see when you click or tap the Start button, the Start menu (refer to Figure 2-1), is designed to be at the center of your Windows universe. Don't let the fact that the right side's intentionally made to look like a smartphone screen deter you in the least.

You've probably sworn at the Start menu a few times already, but if you can keep a civil tongue, permit me to expound a bit:

✦ The **left side** of the Start menu (refer to Figure 2-1) consists of links that are meant to look very familiar to Windows 7 users.

If you are in **Tablet Mode** and you see the hamburger icon in the upper left (refer to Figure 2-2), click or tap it and the full left side of the Start menu unfolds, as in Figure 2-3.

**Book III
Chapter 2**

**Personalizing
the Start Menu**

Figure 2-3:
In Tablet
Mode, the
left side of
Start sits
under the
hamburger
icon.

There's a third mode, called **Full-Screen Start,** which looks and acts much like Tablet Mode. It also has a hamburger menu that brings up the left side. See Book III, Chapter 1 for details.

✦ *Tiles* (the squares on the right side of the screen) appear in four sizes: Large, Wide, Medium, and Small (rocket science). In Figures 2-1, 2-2, and 2-3, the Money app is a large tile, the weather report is wide, Mail is medium, and small Get Office tile is one-quarter the size of a Medium. Most tiles that come from Microsoft are *live tiles,* with *active content* (latest news, stock prices, date, temperature, email messages) that changes the face of the tile.

✦ Tiles are bunched into *groups,* which may or may not have *group names*. In Figures 2-1, 2-2, and 2-3, there are two groups — one marked Life at a glance, the other marked Play and explore. Don't shoot me. Those are the names Microsoft gave them.

✦ In the upper-left corner of the "normal" Start menu, you see either your Windows username or (if you're logged on with a Microsoft account) your full name. For a description of the Microsoft account and the pros and cons of using one, see Book II, Chapter 5.

Modifying the Start Menu

Windows 7 has a marvelously malleable Start menu. You can click and drag and poke and rearrange it every which way but loose. I particularly enjoyed setting up nested folders and having them show up as cascading items on the Start menu. But that was then.

The left side of Windows 10's Start menu, by comparison, has a very rigid format that can be changed only in a few specific, preprogrammed ways (see Figure 2-4). Customizing the Start menu in Win10 is nothing like customizing Start in Win7. (And, of course, Windows 8/8.1 didn't *have* a Start menu.)

Changing your picture

I start with an easy change to the Start screen: changing the picture in the upper-left corner.

Here's how to change your picture:

1. **Tap or click your name, and select Change account settings.**

   Windows takes you to a familiar-looking place in the PC Settings hierarchy, as shown in Figure 2-5.

2. **If you already have a picture in mind, follow these steps (if you'd rather take a picture, continue to Step 3):**

   a. Choose Browse, and navigate to the picture.

   b. When you find the picture you want, select it, and tap or click Choose Image.

   You return to the PC Settings location shown in Figure 2-5, with your new picture in place.

Figure 2-4:
Let's dissect
the left side
of the Start
menu.

3. **If you'd rather take a picture with your computer's webcam, comb your
hair, pluck your eyebrows, and tap or click Webcam (in that order).**

In any case, however you create your new picture, it takes effect
immediately — no need to click OK or anything of the sort.

Figure 2-5:
Change your
picture in
the Settings
app.

Want a weird picture? Don't have an avatar-generating source, like the Xbox? Try reusing an avatar that somebody's posted on the Internet. Here's the easy way:

1. **In your favorite web browser, search for *avatars* and switch to the image-viewing mode in your search engine, where you find tons and tons of them.**

   I found a picture I like in the Wikimedia Commons library on the web (see Figure 2-6).

2. **Download the file if it's easy, and skip to Step 8. If not, take a screenshot. When you find the picture you want, make sure the whole picture appears on the screen. Then hold down the Windows key, and press Print Screen.**

   Windows puts a copy of the screenshot in your `Pictures\Screenshots` folder.

3. **Tap or click Start, File Explorer. Go find the screenshot, which will have a name like Screenshot (1).png. Right-click or tap and hold the picture, and choose Open With, Paint.**

   You need to crop your picture, to take away all the stuff in the screenshot except the avatar. Windows Paint is more than up to the task.

Figure 2-6:
Here's the
avatar from
AJ Gonzalez
that I want
to grab.

4. **Tap or click the Select icon on the Ribbon, and draw a rectangle around the picture you want to use for your Start menu.**

   If you don't get the rectangle the way you like the first time, don't worry. Start over and try Step 3 again. When you start again, your old rectangle disappears.

5. **When you have the picture framed properly, tap or click the Crop icon on the Paint Ribbon.**

   Your cropped picture appears without the pesky other stuff.

6. **Tap or click the Save icon — the tiny icon that looks like a floppy disk (eh, what's THAT?) at the very top of the screen — and save the cropped picture in your** `Pictures\Screenshots` **library.**

7. **Back on the Start menu, tap or click your name and choose Change Account settings.**

   You get the Your Account dialog box (refer to Figure 2-5).

8. **Tap or click Browse, navigate to your chosen picture, select it, and tap or click Choose Image.**

   There you go. You've just successfully perpetrated identity theft on a defenseless avatar.

Manipulating Most used

You would think that the next part of the Start menu — Most used — would contain links to the apps and locations that you use most often. Ha. Silly mortal.

Microsoft (and, likely, your hardware manufacturer) salts the list: They put items in there that don't deserve to be there, and they keep items on the list long after they should've disappeared. I've experimented with it for ages, and the list of which items appear on the list, and how rapidly they fall off, seems to be controlled by some sort of counter — a counter that isn't updated correctly all the time.

At this point, the only action I can find that you can perform on the list is to remove a link you don't like. Just right-click (or tap and hold) an entry you don't like, and choose Don't show in this list.

Alternatively, you can get rid of the list entirely. See the next section.

Controlling the bottom-left lists

Although you don't have much control over the top part of the Start menu list (refer to Figure 2-4), other than eliminating it entirely, you do have some say in what appears below the Most used list.

To see the choices on offer, choose Start, Settings, Personalization, Start. (Yeah, the sequence starts and ends with Start.) You see the Start menu options shown in Figure 2-7.

Figure 2-7: You do have some control over what appears at the bottom of the Start menu.

Some of those choices are a bit obscure. Here's what they mean:

✦ **Show most used apps.**

That's the salted most recently used set I talked about in the preceding section. I find it useful — you may not.

✦ **Show recently added apps.**

When you install a new program, er, app, Start notifies you by putting the word "New" next to the All Apps entry. (If the left side of the Start menu is turned into a hamburger icon, a dot appears on the hamburger.) It's a rather innocuous setting that saves some time, if you can't remember when you last installed an app.

✦ **Use Start full screen.**

Full-screen Start is kind of a compromise between the regular Start menu and the Tablet Mode Start screen. It's unlikely you'll want to use it, but I discuss the effect in Book III, Chapter 1.

Click the Choose which folders appear on Start link, and another set of options appears, as in Figure 2-8.

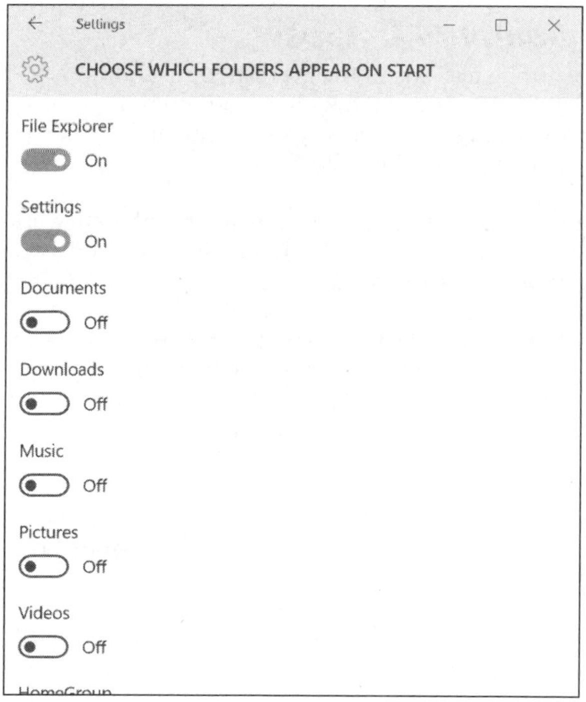

Figure 2-8:
There's a long list of items you can add to the bottom left of the Start menu.

Settings

CHOOSE WHICH FOLDERS APPEAR ON START

File Explorer

On

Settings

On

Documents

Off

Downloads

Off

Music

Off

Pictures

Off

Videos

Off

HomeGroup

Table 2-1 shows you what each of the settings means.

Table 2-1	Start Menu Customizing
Choose this	*And the Start menu does this*
File Explorer	Starts File Explorer as usual; link has flyout for Quick Access entries
Settings	Opens the Settings app
Documents	Starts File Explorer with your Documents Library
Downloads	Starts File Explorer at your personal Downloads folder
Music	Starts File Explorer in your Music Library
Pictures	Starts File Explorer in your Pictures Library
Videos	Starts File Explorer in your Videos Library
HomeGroup	Starts File Explorer with HomeGroup selected on the left
Network	Starts File Explorer with Network selected on the left
Personal folder	Starts File Explorer at \Users\<yourname>

Circumnavigating All Apps

The final entry on the left side of the Start menu — All Apps — brings up an alphabetized list of programs installed on your computer. In some cases, the programs are arranged in logical groups (apparently corresponding to instructions in the programs' installer).

In Figure 2-9, for example, you can see how Microsoft Office appears in the "M" section while Microsoft Excel, Word, PowerPoint, and so on, appear under the Microsoft Office heading.

As we went to press, there didn't appear to be any way to rearrange the entries in the All Apps list. You can uninstall some of the programs by right-clicking and choosing Uninstall, but there's no way to move the entries around, create new groups or coalesce old ones, rename, or shuffle in any way.

You can, however, click one of the alphabetic headers in the list — such as the "W" in Figure 2-9 — to bring up an unintelligent phone book that lets you skip to a specific letter. See Figure 2-10.

Figure 2-9:
Looking for
Internet
Explorer?
Check under
"Windows
Acces-
sories."

If you right-click (or tap and hold) one of the apps in the All Apps list, you're usually given two choices:

✦ **Pin to Start** creates a new tile on the right side of the Start menu that runs the program. (Yeah, I know it's confusing: "Start," to me, means the left side of the Start menu, and I bet it does to you, too. Still, that's the terminology Microsoft uses.)

✦ **Pin to Taskbar** creates an icon on the taskbar, at the bottom, which also runs the program.

In some cases, right-clicking a program gives you the option to uninstall the program and/or to run it as if you were an Administrator (see Book II, Chapter 4).

Figure 2-10:
This is
all the
organizing
the All Apps
list can give.

Also in some cases, you can click an app in the All Apps list and drag it over to the right, tiled part of the Start menu. I've had problems with that in the past, where the app disappears from the All Apps list and it won't come back. Beware.

Resizing the Start Menu

Depending on the width of your screen, when Windows 10 is first installed, it'll create columns of tiles on the right that are either three or four standard-sized tiles wide. The number of columns varies depending on the size of the screen as well. In Figure 2-11, I have Win10 set up with a fresh install on a 1920x1080 screen. It created one columns of tiles, three standard-sized tiles wide.

Your results may vary, of course.

Figure 2-11:
Here's a
default
setup on a
1920x1080
screen.

**Book III
Chapter 2**

**Personalizing
the Start Menu**

I don't know any way of changing the tile-width of a column. You're set at either 3 or 4, and short of reinstalling Windows 10 on a wider or narrower screen, there doesn't appear any way to change it.

The Start menu can be resized, either taller-and-shorter (vertically) or wider-and-skinnier (horizontally). If you click the upper edge of the Start screen in Figure 2-11 and slide it down, you see the result in Figure 2-12.

At least on my machines, you can shorten the Start menu so only four Most used apps still show. Beyond that, it won't shrink. There's also a limit to the height of the Start menu, which varies according to screen size.

Similarly, you can widen the Start menu to the width of two (sometimes more) columns of tiles. In that case, the groups of tiles get spread out, as you can see in Figure 2-13.

That appears to be the extent of the Start menu shrinking-expanding range.

Figure 2-12:
Adjust the
Start menu
vertically.

Figure 2-13:
Widen the
Start menu,
and the
groups of
tiles move
across.

Changing Tiles on the Start Menu

You can click and drag tiles anyplace you like on the right side of the Start menu. Drag a tile way down to the bottom, and you start a new group. Pin a new program to the Start screen (see the preceding section), and its tile magically appears in the rightmost group on the Start screen.

You can change every tile, too. The actions available depend on what the creator of the tile permits. Here's how to mangle a tile:

1. **Right-click (or tap and hold) the tile you want to change.**

In Figure 2-14, I right-click the Money tile. A list of actions appears.

Figure 2-14:
You can
control tiles
individually.

**Book III
Chapter 2**

Personalizing
the Start Menu

2. **See Table 2-2 to determine which action you want to take, and select the desired action.**

You can easily delete any tile, and you can resize many of them.

3. **If you would like to put a name above any of the groups of tiles, simply type it in the indicated spot.**

For example, you can change Life at a glance (at the top of the left column of tiles) to Another sticky day in paradise by clicking (or tapping) Life at a glance and typing.

The changes you make take effect immediately, and they carry through on both the traditional Start menu and over in Tablet Mode.

Table 2-2	Tile Actions
Tile Action Name	*What the Action Does*
Unpin from Start	Removes the tile from the right side of the Start menu. Doesn't affect the app itself. If you later change your mind, you can right-click the app in the All Apps list and choose Pin to Start.
Uninstall	Removes all vestiges of the program, using the Control Panel's Remove Programs.
Resize	Makes the tile icon large (four times the size of a normal tile, such as the Calendar tile in the figure), wide (the size of the Weather tile), medium (the size of the Mail tile), or small (one-quarter the size of a medium tile).
Pin to Taskbar	Puts an icon for the app on the desktop's taskbar (see Book III, Chapter 3).
Turn Live Tile Off/On	Stops/starts the animation that's displayed on the tile. Stopping the active content can help reduce battery drain, but the big benefit is stifling obnoxious flickering tiles — of which there are many.

Organizing Your Start Menu Tiles

The beauty of the Start menu tiles is that, within strictly defined limits, you can customize it like crazy. As long as you're happy working with the basic building blocks — four sizes of tiles, and groups — you can slice and dice till the cows come home.

The hard part about corralling the Start menu is figuring out what works best for you.

Add, add, add your tiles

Some people never use the Start menu's tiles. But if you do use them, it's easier to get organized if you put all of them on the table, as it were, before trying to sort them out.

You don't really need to have *any* tiles in the Start menu. You can right-click and choose Unpin from Start and get rid of every single one. Unfortunately, having done that, you can't make the Start screen narrower, but such is life.

The process for sticking tiles in the Start menu couldn't be simpler. Click the Start icon, choose All Apps, and go through your apps one by one. Right-click any apps that amuse you, and choose Pin to Start. The tile appears on the right.

At the same time, you can also right-click (or tap and hold) and choose to put the app on the taskbar. Or, in most cases, you can drag the app onto the desktop and create a link to the app on the desktop.

The only significant decision you need to make is whether you want a specific app among the tiles on the Start menu, on the desktop, on the taskbar (see Book III, Chapter 3), or on all three. As a general rule, I put my most-used apps on the taskbar, put tiles that convey useful information (such as Weather, News, and even Photos — for bringing back memories) on the Start menu, and only rarely stick anything on the desktop.

Before you start working with the tiles on your Start menu, it'll behoove you to go through your All Apps and pull out the tiles you want or need.

Forming and naming your groups

After you have all your tiles on the right side of the Start menu, it's easy to get the menagerie organized. Try this:

1. **Tap and drag (or click and drag) your tiles so similar tiles are in the same group.**

For example, if you use Mail, Messaging, People, and Calendar all day long, put them in the same group. If you have Office installed, go through the procedure described in the preceding section to move the tiles you want over to the Metro Start screen.

Don't worry just yet if the groups are in the wrong sequence: There are easy ways to move entire groups. Just concentrate on getting your similar tiles into the same group.

If you have programs that you look at constantly because they have important information — stock market results, your music playlist, Skype notifications, or new Mail — keep them in one or two groups.

If you need to create a new group, drag a tile all the way to the bottom. You see a faint vertical bar, which indicates that a new group has just been formed. Drop the tile below the bar.

2. **To give your groups names, click or tap the existing name (which may be "Name Group") and type over the name.**

In Figure 2-15, I put together all of the tiles I like to glance at, to see how things are going, and gave the group the name At a glance.

3. **To move the group, click or tap the two-thirds-of-a-hamburger icon in the upper right of the group, and drag it anywhere you like on the right side of the Start menu.**

I put this group in the upper-left corner. Then I put together another group of the tools I use most often and called the group Tools.

Book III
Chapter 2

Personalizing the Start Menu

Figure 2-15:
Here's my homemade collection of tiles that I use to keep up to date at a glance.

4. **Click or tap and drag, and resize the Start menu if you like.**

It took a little jockeying — remember that making the Start menu narrower brings the upper-right group down and tucks it below the upper-left group — but in the end, I settled with what you see in Figure 2-16. For today, anyway.

Figure 2-16:
With a bit of zigging and zagging, this is what I like. For now.

Chapter 3: Personalizing the Desktop and Taskbar

In This Chapter

✔ Putting shortcuts on the desktop — the advanced course

✔ Changing desktop colors and pictures

✔ Customizing the taskbar in unexpected, and useful, ways

*I*t's your desktop. Do with it what you will.

In Book III, Chapter 2, I talk about gussying up your Start menu — both the left side, with links, and the right side, with tiles. This chapter looks at the rest of your desktop, what you can do about it, and how you can grab Windows 10 by the throat and shake it up a bit. Player's gotta play, play, play, play, and tweakers gotta tweak, tweak, tweak, tweak.

Shake it up.

With Windows 10's tiles now basically replacing (and improving upon) Windows 7's gadgets, there are fewer reasons to use the desktop now than ever before. Still, many installers put links for their own programs on the desktop, avoiding Start menu tiles like the plague, and you may have your own reasons for using Desktop shortcuts.

No matter what your bias, the taskbar remains an excellent place to put your most heavily used icons.

Decking out the Desktop

The Windows 10 desktop may look simple, but it isn't. In Figure 3-1, for example, you can see the Start menu and the taskbar at the bottom, with an icon for the Recycle Bin, a picture file, and a running Windows Universal app on the right.

Underneath everything is a background color (white, in this case). And there is subtle blurring between the windows.

Figure 3-1:
The desktop
is a very
complicated
place.

Windows lays down the desktop in layers — and paints the mouse cursor on top of all of them.

You have a handful of options when it comes to making the desktop your kind of place. Let me step you through them.

1. **Click or tap Start, Settings, Personalization, Background.**

Windows shows you the Background personalization page.

2. **If you're going to use a picture that stretches all the way across the screen as your Background (what we used to call "wallpaper"), skip down to Step 5.**

If your wallpaper doesn't fill up the entire screen, you should first set a background color.

3. **In the Background drop-down box, choose Solid color.**

You see a dialog box like the one in Figure 3-2.

4. **Pick a color.**

At this point you're limited to just the colors that show in the Standard colors box.

After you've picked a new color, it should appear in the Preview box and on the screen itself.

5. **If you want to use a picture as your wallpaper, in the Background box, choose Picture.**

That sets up everything to not only pick a pic, but also to center it, as in Figure 3-3.

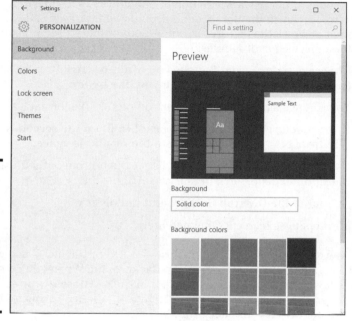

Figure 3-2:
If your picture won't fit the entire screen, first set the background color.

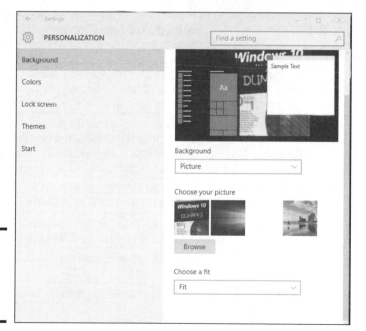

Figure 3-3:
Use a picture as your wallpaper.

If you'd rather use a whole bunch of pictures as a slideshow on your start screen, in the Background drop-down box, pick Slideshow. You must have all the pictures in one Album or folder; see Book IV, Chapter 3 for a discussion of Albums.

6. **Choose a picture from the ones on offer, or click Browse and go out (using File Explorer) to find one you like better.**

   You can use a picture in any common picture file format.

7. **If your picture is too big or too small to fit on the screen, you can tell Windows how to shoehorn it into the available space.**

   Use the drop-down Choose a Fit list at the bottom of the Desktop Background dialog box. Details are in Table 3-1.

8. **"X" out of the Desktop Background dialog box.**

   Your changes take effect immediately.

Windows lets you right-click a picture — a JPG or GIF file — using File Explorer, and choose Set As Desktop Background. When you do so, Windows makes a copy of the picture and puts it in the `C:\Users\<username>\ AppData\Roaming\Microsoft\Windows\Recent Items` folder and then sets the picture as your background.

Table 3-1	Picture Position Settings
Setting	*What It Means*
Fill	Windows expands the picture to fit the entire screen and then crops the edges. The picture doesn't appear distorted, but the sides or top and bottom may get cut off.
Fit	The screen is letterboxed. Windows makes the picture as big as possible within the confines of the screen and then shows the base color in stripes along the top and bottom (or left and right). No distortion occurs, and you see the entire picture, but you also see ugly strips on two edges.
Stretch	The picture is stretched to fit the screen. Expect distortions.
Tile	The picture is repeated as many times as necessary to fill the screen. If it's too large to fit on the screen, you see the Fill options.
Center	This one is the same as the Fit setting except that the letterboxing goes on all four sides.
Span	Expand the picture to fit as many monitors as are active, left to right.

You can also control a few aspects of the colors on your desktop, although the pickings are meager, compared to earlier versions of Windows. Here's how to colorize your life:

1. **Click or tap Start, Settings, Personalization. On the left, choose Colors.**

   You see the Desktop Colors dialog box shown in Figure 3-4.

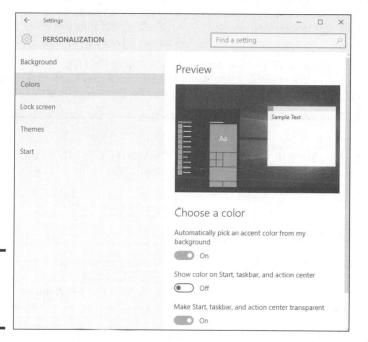

**Book III
Chapter 3**

Personalizing the Desktop and Taskbar

Figure 3-4:
Choose a secondary color here.

2. **If you want to let Windows choose an accent color for you — a color that's used sporadically to highlight choices in menus, background for navigational arrows, and other odd spots — choose On.**

3. **If you want to choose your own accent color, turn the slider Off, and choose from a limited selection of colors.**

4. **To have your chosen accent color appear as the background color on the Start menu, on the taskbar, on the notification pane Action center, and the battery charge indicator, turn that slider On.**

   Usually, Windows uses black (actually, varying shades of gray) for those colors.

5. **To put some transparency and blur on the Start menu, taskbar, and Action center, turn that slider On.**

   I rather like the blurring effect.

What happened to desktop themes?

Windows 10 still has a vestigial link to old-fashioned desktop themes: You can see the option in Figure 3-4, on the left. Themes are collections of the Windows desktop background, window color, sound scheme, and screen saver; you can simply choose among the offered themes.

At this moment, Themes don't sit front-and-center like they did in Windows 7. You can get to them in Figure 3-4, click or tap Theme settings, and you're transported to the Control Panel's Themes applet. Although you can still save your current theme or bring up new ones, the old controls for individual parts of the theme are gone. In particular, there's no screen saver in Windows 10, and the color selections in Windows 10 are very limited.

It's unlikely to be a high priority, but at some point Microsoft may bring back Themes. Look for them in later versions of Windows 10.

Of course, I'm still a fan of Windows 7's Aero Glass with its blurred edges and striking contrasts. Yes, I have the visual discernment of a cow. I can live with that. Moo.

Resolving Desktop Resolution

The best, biggest monitor in the world "don't mean jack" if you can't see the text on the screen. Windows contains a handful of utilities and settings that can help you whump your monitor upside the head and improve its appearance.

With apologies to Billy Crystal, sometimes it *is* more important to look good than to feel good.

Setting the screen resolution

I don't know how many people ask me how to fix this new monitor they just bought. The screen doesn't look right. Must be that %$#@! Windows, yes? The old monitor looked just fine.

Nine times out of ten, when somebody tells me that a new monitor doesn't look right, I ask whether the person adjusted the screen resolution. Invariably, the answer is no. So here's the quick answer to one of the questions I hear most.

If you plug in a new monitor (or put together a new computer) and the screen looks fuzzy, the most likely culprit entails a mismatch between the resolution your computer expects and the resolution your monitor wants. To a first approximation, a screen resolution is just the number of dots that appear on the screen, usually expressed as two numbers: 1920x1080, for example. Every flat-panel screen has exactly one resolution that looks right and a zillion other resolutions that make things look like you fused your monitor with the end of a Coke bottle.

Setting the screen resolution is easy:

1. **Right-click any empty place on the desktop, and choose Display Settings.**

You see the Customize your display dialog box, shown in Figure 3-5. (If you have more than one monitor or certain kinds of video cards, you may see multiple monitors in the top box.)

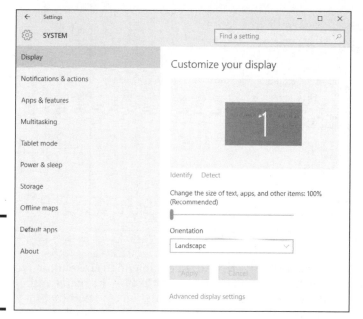

Figure 3-5: Seeking clarity the Windows way.

2. **We'll come back to this bunch of settings in Step 5. For now, let's zero in on the resolution. Click or tap the link at the bottom for Advanced display settings.**

You see the resolution-setting part of Customizing, shown in Figure 3-6.

3. **Click the drop-down box marked Resolution, and choose the resolution you would like to try.**

If there's a resolution marked (Recommended), that's the resolution your monitor manufacturer recommends. Nine times out of ten, that's your best choice. That's the easy part.

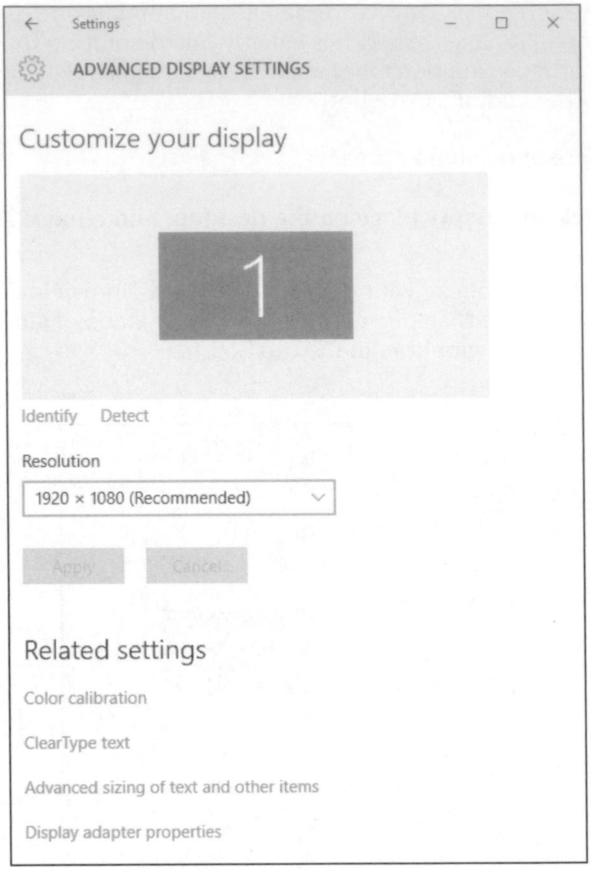

Settings

ADVANCED DISPLAY SETTINGS

Customize your display

1

Identify   Detect

Resolution

1920 × 1080 (Recommended)

Apply   Cancel

Related settings

Color calibration

Figure 3-6:
Set the
resolution
here.

ClearType text

Advanced sizing of text and other items

Display adapter properties

The hard part? If there's no (Recommended) resolution, you must figure out which resolution your monitor likes — its *native resolution.* Some monitors have the resolution printed on a sticker that may still adhere to the front. (Goo Gone works wonders.) All monitors have their native resolutions listed in the manual. (You do have your monitor's manual, yes? No, I don't either.)

If you don't know your monitor's native resolution, Google is your friend. Go to www.google.com, and type **native resolution** followed by your monitor's model number, which you can (almost) always find engraved in the bezel or stuck on the side. For example, typing **native resolution U3011** immediately finds the native resolution for a Dell U3011 monitor.

4. **In the upper-left corner, click or tap the back arrow.**

   That takes you back to Figure 3-5. I had you check the resolution first, because if you change it, everything else in this dialog box changes, too.

5. **If you find it difficult to read text on the monitor, you can move the slider to make everything bigger or smaller.**

If your eyes aren't what they used to be (mine never were), you may want to tell Windows to increase the size of text and other items on the screen. It's just enough boost to help, particularly if you're at an Internet cafe and forgot your glasses.

I strongly recommend that you use this setting with caution. Changing the magnification can cause older programs, in particular, to go bananas. The overall effect can be chilling. So take it slowly, test often, and go back to your default if things don't look or act right.

6. **If you want to lock the orientation of the display — make it portrait all the time, or landscape — turn the rotation slider On.**

It's unusual that you want to lock the orientation, but sometimes it happens — like when you're trying to read the news while skinning the cat. I mean the acrobatic maneuver, of course.

7. **To take control of your screen brightness, adjust the two settings at the bottom. I generally warn people against manually adjusting brightness because it can cause unnecessary drain on the battery, but some screens, on some machines, just don't look right unless you adjust the brightness manually.**

That's all it takes. Your changes take effect immediately.

Using magnification

If you need more "zoom" than the font enlarger can offer, you can always use the Ease of Access tool called the Magnifier. As you can see in Figure 3-7, the Magnifier can make everything very big.

Figure 3-7: The Magnifier can help make everything on-screen reeeeeeee-ally big.

```
←    Settings

⚙    MAGNIFIER


Magnify things on the screen

Magnifier
●○  On
```

The Magnifier lets you zoom the entire screen by a factor of 200, 300, or 400 — or as high as you like.

Note that magnifying doesn't increase the quality or resolution of text or pictures. It makes them bigger not finer. That *CSI* "David, can you make the picture sharper?" thing doesn't work with Windows. Sorry, Grissom.

To use the Magnifier do this:

1. **Click or tap Start, Settings, Ease of Access. On the left, choose Magnifier.**

You get the Magnifier control shown in Figure 3-8.

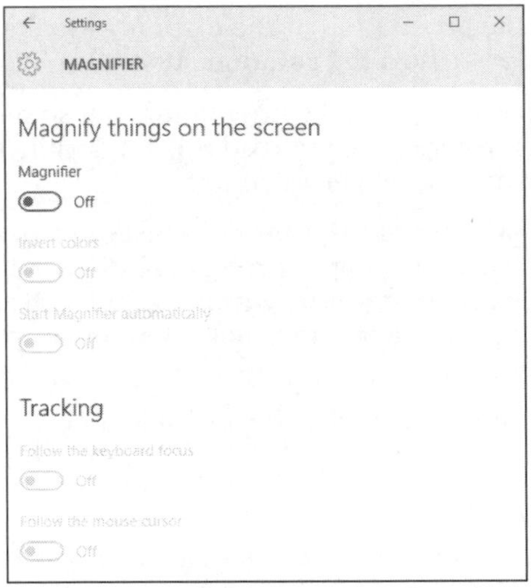

Figure 3-8: The other Magnifier options are grayed out until you start the Magnifier.

2. **Slide the Magnifier settings On.**

Everything immediately displays at twice its normal size — 200% in the parlance.

3. **Experiment with moving around. It's odd.**

Slide your mouse all the way to the left or right to move the screen to the left or right. Same with up and down. This is one situation where a touch screen really does help.

4. **A small control shows up with buttons to increase and decrease magnification. (It turns into a magnifying glass icon if you don't use it immediately.) Click or tap the Views drop-down box on the controller, and choose Lens.**

The Lens view, shown in Figure 3-9, lets you drag a viewing window across a regular-size screen and magnify what's under the window.

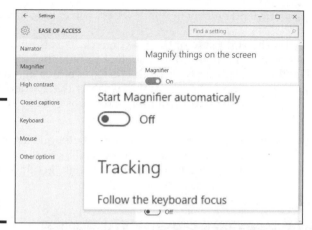

Figure 3-9:
The Lens slides across the top of a normal-sized view.

5. **Play with the settings to get the right combination for your eyesight.**

   The settings are "sticky" so when you come back to the Magnifier, it'll remember what settings you like best.

6. **To reduce the magnification, press Windows key and – (minus) repeatedly.**

   That steps you down the magnification levels, until you reach the "normal" 100% magnification. To turn off Magnification entirely, go back to Step 1 and set the Magnifier slider to Off.

If these nostrums don't do the job, you should take advantage of the Windows high-contrast themes. They use color to make text, in particular, stand out. High-contrast themes are available from the Ease of Access dialog box (refer to Figure 3-8) on the left side.

If you accidentally hit Windows key and + or –, and your magnification changes mysteriously, now you know the culprit. Go into Ease of Access and turn off Magnifier.

Putting Icons and Shortcuts on the Desktop

Back in the day, if you wanted to get at a program (er, app) quickly, you put a shortcut for it on your desktop. Nowadays, life isn't quite so straightforward. Your choices are many — and that's a good thing.

To access a program/app quickly in Windows 10, you can do any of these:

✦ **Stick a tile on the right side of the Start menu.** This is almost always pretty easy: You find the program (usually by going into the Start, All Apps menu, but also possibly through File Explorer, or maybe there's already a shortcut on your desktop that was put there when the app was installed). Right-click the program, and choose Pin to Start. See Figure 3-10.

✦ **Put a link to it in the taskbar.** Using the same technique as with Pin to Start, instead choose Pin to taskbar. That puts a link to the program in the taskbar, where it's generally available (although, in odd situations — such as Tablet Mode — it may not be.)

Figure 3-10:
It's usually easy to put a program on the right side of the Start menu.

✦ **Use Cortana to search for the program.** I talk about Cortana in Book III, Chapter 6. This is my least favorite way because it's not nearly as precise as having a tile on the right side of the Start menu, a link on the taskbar, or a shortcut on the desktop.

If you've considered adding the program to the Start menu's tiles and putting it on the taskbar, and both approaches leave you a little bit cold, then it's not hard to stick a shortcut to the program on your desktop.

The wonder of desktop shortcuts: You can put many things on the desktop that you just can't get hornswaggled into the Start menu or the taskbar.

Creating shortcuts

Back in Book III, Chapter 1, I showed you how to put a shortcut to a website on your desktop. Now it's time for the advanced course.

You can set up shortcuts that point to the following items:

✦ Old-fashioned **Windows programs** (er, apps), of any kind

✦ **Web addresses**, such as www.dummies.com

✦ Documents, spreadsheets, databases, PowerPoint presentations, pictures, PDF files, and anything else that can be started by double-clicking it

✦ **Folders** (including the weird folders inside digital cameras, the Fonts folder, and others that you may not think of)

✦ **Drives** (hard drives, CD drives, and key drives, for example)

✦ **Other computers** on your network, and drives and folders on those computers, as long they're shared

✦ **Printers** (including printers attached to other computers on your network), scanners, cameras, and other pieces of hardware

✦ Network connections, interface cards, and the like

Here's a whirlwind tour of many different desktop shortcut techniques:

1. **To pin a Windows Universal app to the desktop, find the app in the Start, All Apps list, click the link, and drag it to the desktop.**

That creates a shortcut to the Universal app, as shown with the Calculator app in Figure 3-11.

Figure 3-11:
Drag a
Windows
Universal
app to the
desktop
to create
a shortcut
there.

2. **As we went to press, putting a shortcut to a web page on the desktop wasn't easy. In the (sniff) good old days, all you had to do was select and drag the browser's address bar onto the desktop. Now it's a bit more complex.**

   See Book III, Chapter 1, in the section titled "Creating Shortcuts," for exact instructions.

3. **To create a shortcut to a document — say, a Word file you open over and over — use File Explorer to go to the document, *right*-click it, and drag onto the desktop. Release the mouse, and choose Create shortcut here.**

   If you simply click, you're bound to move the file.

4. **Similarly, to create a desktop shortcut for a folder or a drive, or another computer on your network (even in a HomeGroup), use File Explorer to navigate to the folder or drive, right-click it, and choose Create shortcut.**

   In Figure 3-12, I have a shortcut to a document on OneDrive, a shortcut to my Music folder, a shortcut to my C: drive, and a shortcut to a program, all set up and ready to click.

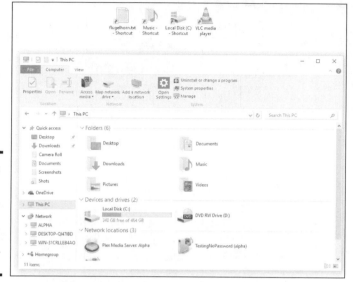

Figure 3-12: Shortcuts are easy to set up, if you work through File Explorer.

5. **Creating a shortcut to a network connection is only a little more complicated. Right-click the Start icon (or Windows key+X) and choose Network Connections. Right-click the connection, drag it to the desktop, and choose Create shortcuts here.**

   That'll give you a quick view of whether the connection's working, how long it's been up, and how much data has been going in each direction, as shown in Figure 3-13.

6. **Creating a shortcut to a printer or other attached device (such as a mouse or a keyboard) is more difficult still. Right-click the Start button or type Win+X, and choose Control Panel. Click Hardware and Sound, then Devices and Printers. Right-click the printer or other device, and drag it to the desktop, releasing it with Create shortcut here.**

   That makes it easy to see, for example, a printer queue or your current keyboard status, as shown in Figure 3-14.

Arranging icons on the desktop

If you bought a PC with Windows preloaded, you probably have so many icons on the desktop that you can't see straight. That desktop real estate is expensive, and the manufacturers receive a pretty penny for dangling the right icons in your face.

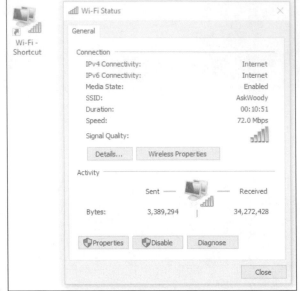

Figure 3-13:
A shortcut
to a network
connection
quickly
brings
up this
information.

Figure 3-14:
Printer,
keyboard,
and other
peripheral
device
status
panes are a
click away.

Know what? You can delete all of them, without feeling the least bit guilty. The worst you'll do is delete a shortcut to a manufacturer's tech support program, and if you need to get to the program, the tech support rep can tell you how to find it. The only icon you need is the Recycle Bin, and you can bring that back pretty easily (see the nearby sidebar).

Restoring the Recycle Bin icon

Sooner or later, it happens to almost everyone. You delete the Recycle Bin icon, and you're not sure how to get it back.

Relax. It isn't that hard. . .if you know the trick.

Bring up the Control Panel (Win+X will do it). In the Search box in the upper-right corner, type (precisely) `desktop icon setting`. Under Personalization, click or tap Show or hide common icons on the desktop. Follow that link, and you can re-check the box to show the Recycle Bin.

You're welcome.

Windows gives you several simple tools for arranging icons on your desktop. If you right-click any empty part of the desktop, you see that you can do the following:

✦ **Sort:** Choose Sort By, and then choose an option to sort icons by name, size, or type (folders, documents, and shortcuts, for example) or by the date on which the icon was last modified. See Figure 3-15.

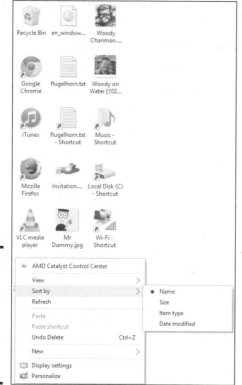

Figure 3-15:
Sort all
the icons
on your
desktop
with a
couple of
clicks.

✦ **Arrange:** Right-click an empty place on the desktop, and choose View, Auto Arrange Icons. That is, have Windows arrange them in an orderly fashion, with the first icon in the upper-left corner, the second one directly below the first one, the third one below it, and so on.

✦ **Align to a grid:** Choose View, Align Icons to Grid. If you don't want to have icons arranged automatically, at least you can choose Align Icons to Grid so that you can see all the icons without one appearing directly on top of the other.

✦ **Hide:** You can even choose View, Show Desktop Icons to deselect the Show Desktop Icons option. Your icons disappear — but that kinda defeats the purpose of icons, doesn't it?

✦ **Delete:** In general, you can remove an icon from the Windows desktop by right-clicking it and choosing Delete or by clicking it once and pressing the Delete key.

The appearance of some icons is hard wired: If you put a Word document on your desktop, for example, the document inherits the icon — the picture — of its associated application, Word. The same goes for Excel worksheets, text documents, and recorded audio files. Icons for pictures look like the picture, more or less, if you squint hard.

Icons for shortcuts, however, you can change at will. Follow these steps to change an icon — that is, the picture — on a shortcut:

1. **Right-click the shortcut, and choose Properties.**

2. **In the Properties dialog box, click the Change Icon button.**

3. **Pick an icon from the offered list, or click the Browse button and go looking for icons.**

Windows abounds with icons. See Table 3-2 for some likely hunting grounds.

Table 3-2	Where to Find Icons
Contents	*File*
Windows 10, 8.1, 8, 7, and Vista icons	C:\Windows\system32\imageres.dll
Everything	C:\Windows\System32\shell32.dll
Computers	C:\Windows\explorer.exe
Household	C:\Windows\System32\pifmgr.dll
Folders	C:\Windows\System32\syncui.dll
Old programs (Quattro Pro, anybody?)	C:\Windows\System32\moricons.dll

4. **Click the OK button twice.**

   Windows changes the icon permanently (or at least until you change it again).

Lots and lots of icons are available on the Internet. Use your favorite search engine to search for the term *free Windows icons.*

Tricking out the Taskbar

Microsoft developers working on the Windows 7 taskbar gave it a secret internal project name: the Superbar. Although one might debate how much of the Super in the bar arrived compliments of Mac OS, there's no doubt that the Windows 10 taskbar is a key tool for anyone who uses the desktop. Now that you can pin Windows Universal apps on the taskbar, it's become productivity central for many of us.

The Windows Super, uh, taskbar appears at the bottom of the screen, as in Figure 3-16.

Figure 3-16:
The taskbar
juggles
many
different
tasks.

If you hover your mouse over an icon, and the icon is associated with a program that's running, you see a thumbnail of what it's doing. For example, in Figure 3-16, Edge is running, and the thumbnail gives you a preview of what's on offer.

Anatomy of the taskbar

The taskbar consists of two kinds of icons:

✦ **Icons that have been pinned there:** Windows ships with six icons on the taskbar, one for Start, one for Cortana (and Search), on for Task View (multiple desktops), and one each for edge, File Explorer, and the Store. You can see them on the left in Figure 3-16. If you install a program and tell the installer to put an icon on the taskbar, an icon for the program appears on the taskbar. You can also pin programs of your choice on the taskbar.

Some older programs have installers that offer to attach themselves to the Quick Launch Toolbar. It's a Windows XP-era thing. If you agree to put the icon on the Quick Launch Toolbar, the icon for the program actually gets put on the far-more-upscale taskbar.

✦ **Icons associated with running desktop programs:** Every time a program starts, an icon for the program appears on the taskbar. If you run three copies of the program, only one icon shows up. When the program stops, the icon disappears.

You can tell which icons represent running programs: Windows puts a little, almost imperceptible, line under the icon for any running program. If you have more than one copy of the program running, you see more than one line underneath. It's subtle. In Figure 3-16, Edge has a line under the icon.

Jumping

If you right-click any icon in the taskbar or tap and hold, whether or not the icon is pinned, you see a bunch of links called a Jump List, as shown in Figure 3-17.

Figure 3-17: This is the Jump List for File Explorer.

The contents of the Jump List vary depending on the program that's running, but the bottom pane of every Jump List contains the name of the program and the entry Unpin This Program from Taskbar (or conversely, Pin This Program to Taskbar, if the program isn't pinned).

Jump Lists were new in Windows 7, and they haven't taken off universally. Implementation of Jump Lists ranges from downright obsessive (such as Edge) to completely lackadaisical (including most applications that aren't made by Microsoft).

Here are the Jump List basics:

✦ **Jump Lists may show your recently opened file history.** For example, the Paint Jump List (shown in Figure 3-18) shows you the same Recent Documents list that appears inside Paint. The currently open document(s) appear at the top of the list.

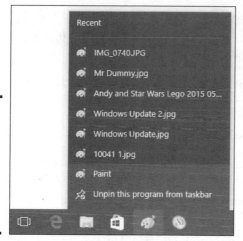

Figure 3-18: Lowly Paint's Jump List shows recently opened documents.

Book III Chapter 3

Personalizing the Desktop and Taskbar

✦ **It's generally easy to pin an item to the Jump List.** When you pin an item, it sticks to a program's Jump List whether or not that item is open. To pin an item, run your mouse out to the right of the item you want to pin and click the stick pin. That puts the item in a separate pane at the top of the Jump List.

 The Jump List has one not-so-obvious use. It lets you open a second copy of the same program. Suppose you want to copy a handful of albums from the music library to your thumb drive on F:. You start by clicking the File Explorer icon in the taskbar, and on the left, click the Music Library. Cool.

You can do the copy-and-paste thang — select an album, press Ctrl+C to copy, use the list on the left of File Explorer to navigate to F:, and then press Ctrl+V to paste. But if you're going to copy many albums, it's much faster and easier to open a second copy of File Explorer and navigate to F: in that second window. Then you can click and drag albums from the Music folder to the F: folder.

To open a second copy of a running program (File Explorer, in this example), you have two choices:

✦ Hold down the Shift key, and click the icon.

✦ Right-click the icon (or tap and hold, perhaps with a nudge upward), and choose the program's name.

In either case, Windows starts a fresh copy of the program.

Changing the taskbar

The taskbar rates as one of the few parts of Windows that are highly malleable. You can modify it till the cows come home:

✦ **Pin any program** on the taskbar by right-clicking the program and choosing Pin This Program to Taskbar. Yes, you can right-click the icon of a running program on the taskbar.

✦ **Move a pinned icon** by clicking and dragging it. Easy. You know, the way it's supposed to be. You can even drag an icon that isn't pinned into the middle of the pinned icons. When the program associated with the icon stops, the icon disappears, and all pinned icons move back into place.

✦ **Unpin any pinned program** by right-clicking it and choosing Unpin This Program from Taskbar. Rocket science.

Unfortunately, you can't turn individual documents or folders into icons on the taskbar. But you can pin a folder to the File Explorer Jump List, and you can pin a document to the Jump List for whichever application is associated with the document. For example, you can pin a song to the Jump List for Windows Media Player.

Here's how to pin a folder or document to its associated icon on the taskbar:

1. **Navigate to the folder or document that you want to pin.**

You can use File Explorer to go to the file or folder or you can make a shortcut to the file or folder.

2. **Drag the folder or document (or shortcut) to the taskbar.**

Windows tells you where it will pin the folder, document, or shortcut, as shown in Figure 3-19. For example, if you are dragging a .docx file, Windows will let you pin it to WordPad, Word, File Explorer, or any program that can open a .docx file.

3. **Release the Mouse button.**

That's all it takes.

Figure 3-19:
Drag a file
or folder
to pin it to
a taskbar
icon.

A little-known side effect: If you pin a file to a program on the taskbar, the program itself also gets pinned to the taskbar, if it wasn't already.

Working with the taskbar

I've discovered a few tricks with the taskbar that you may find worthwhile:

✦ Sometimes, you want to shut down all (or most) running programs, and you don't want Windows to do it for you. It's easy to see what's running by looking at the underlines under the icons, if your eyesight and your monitor are good enough (refer to Figure 3-16). To close down all instances of a particular program, right-click its icon and choose Close Window or Close All Windows.

✦ Sometimes, if a program is frozen and won't shut itself down, forcing the matter through the taskbar is the easiest way to dislodge it.

✦ The terminology is a bit screwy here. Normally, you would choose Exit the Program, Choose File, Exit, Click the Red X, or some such. When you're working with the taskbar, you choose Close Window or Close All Windows from the choices that pop up when you right-click the icon on the taskbar. Different words, same meaning.

If you move your mouse to the lower-right corner and then click, Windows minimizes all open windows. Click again, and Windows brings back all minimized windows. You can also right-click and choose Peek at Desktop or Show Desktop.

**Book III
Chapter 3**

Personalizing the
Desktop and
Taskbar

Chapter 4: Working with Multiple Desktops

In This Chapter

✔ **What, exactly, is a virtual desktop?**

✔ **How to build one of your own**

✔ **Switching among desktops in Task View**

✔ **Creating balance among your desktops**

When talk turns to virtual desktops in Windows 10, most people are referring to Win10's ability to support and juggle multiple desktops. You can set up a desktop for your work, a desktop for fun things, a desktop for your favorite hobby or club, and Windows keeps them all separate. You can run programs on each desktop, run the same program on two or more desktops, and mix and match — and Windows keeps them from stepping all over each other.

In Figure 4-1, you can see three running desktops, and the way they appear in Task View.

 Apparently people have forgotten, but Windows XP had a similar capability, which could be brought to life by installing an app, er, a program distributed by Microsoft as one of the XP PowerToys.

Those of you who are sufficiently long in the tooth may recall that the XP PowerToys were basically a series of skunkworks programs that enhanced Windows XP, built by Microsoft employees, distributed by Microsoft, but never officially supported by Microsoft. The XP Virtual Desktop Manager let you build and switch among four separate XP Desktops.

The Windows 7 virtual Desktop program I've used and recommend — the Sysinternals Desktop — also comes from Microsoft and arrived with Mark Russinovich and the Sysinternals team, which Microsoft acquired in 2006. Like the XP Virtual Desktop Manager, you can set up to four desktops and switch among them by clicking a taskbar icon or using a customizable key combination.

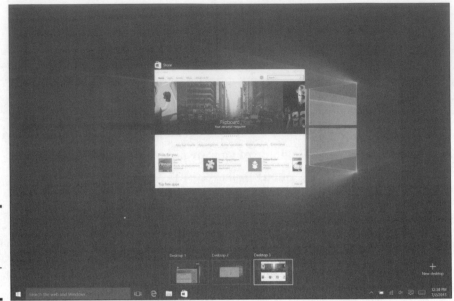

Figure 4-1:
These three
desktops
run indepen-
dently.

An entire industry of Windows virtual desktop add-ins exists — Dexpot, Finestra, mdesktop, Virtual Dimension, VirtuaWin, and others — many of which have fallen into disrepair. Virtual desktops are ancient in the Linux world, venerable on the Mac, and nothing new in Windows.

So what's new with Windows 10?

The big change in Windows 10 comes from the fact that the multiple desktop feature is built into Windows itself. You don't need to install a separate program or run something strange in the background. Windows just does the deed.

Getting around Multiple Desktops

To see what's going on, try building a few desktops. Here's one way:

1. **Start Windows.**

2. **Crank up a few programs.**

   Doesn't matter which ones. Get three or four going.

3. **Tap or click the Task View icon — the one that looks like two chairs at a table, just to the right of Cortana.**

Windows lines up your running programs, darkens the main desktop, and puts a + New Desktop icon in the lower-right corner, as shown in Figure 4-2.

Figure 4-2: Task View lines up the currently running programs and adds a + icon for creating new desktops.

Book III Chapter 4

Working with Multiple Desktops

4. **Click or tap the + icon to add a new desktop.**

   Windows creates a thumbnail for a second desktop and moves all the running programs to Desktop 1, as shown in Figure 4-3.

Figure 4-3: The first desktop gets all the running programs when a second desktop is added.

5. **Click the thumbnail marked Desktop 2.**

   Windows shows you a clean, new desktop.

6. **Crank up a few more programs.**

   They can be the same programs as the ones on Desktop 1 or new ones. Each desktop works independently.

7. **Click the Task View icon again.**

   Windows shows you the contents of Desktop 2, with a grayed background, but also shows you thumbnails for Desktops 1 and 2, as shown in Figure 4-4.

   Note that the items shown in Task View may vary depending on whether you're in Tablet Mode, or if you have the screen switched around into portrait.

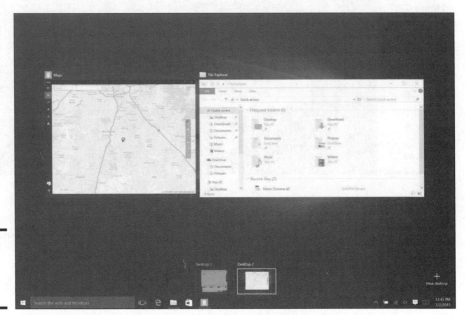

Figure 4-4:
Now showing Desktop 2.

8. **Tap or click the Desktop 1 thumbnail.**

   Desktop 1 reappears, with all its programs working.

   At the same time, all the programs on Desktop 2 stop. If you were playing music, the music stops. Watching a video? It freezes. Desktop 2 goes into suspended animation.

9. **Click the + icon again to add another desktop. And another.**

   You can also type Win+Ctrl+D to create a new desktop.

   In theory, there's no limit to the number of desktops you can run.

10. **To remove a desktop, hover your mouse or tap and hold the thumbnail, and choose the X icon at the top.**

When you shut down a desktop, all its running apps get transferred to
the next lower-numbered desktop.

Interacting between Desktops

Windows 10 has some built-in smarts that will help you take full advantage of
multiple desktops. When you have a couple of desktops (or more) set up, as
explained in the preceding section, try these calisthenics:

1. **On the taskbar, tap or click the Task View icon to bring up Task View.**

If you have three desktops set up, Task View might look like Figure 4-5.

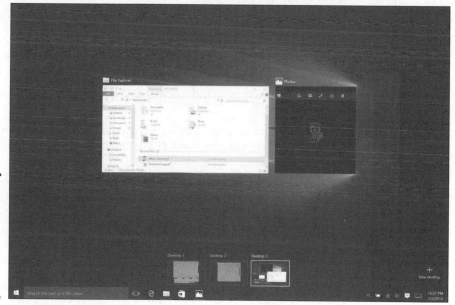

Figure 4-5:
Task View
with three
desktops
and the third
desktop
selected.

Book III
Chapter 4

Working with
Multiple Desktops

2. **At the bottom, click Desktop 1. Then press Alt+Tab. (You can change
the behavior of Alt+Tab in the Settings app. I talk about that in the
next section.)**

This is the old Windows coolswitch, which has been around since
Windows 95. Alt+Tab shows you all the running programs on a single

desktop. In Figure 4-6, for example, I get three thumbnails, one for each program running on Desktop 3.

Figure 4-6:
Alt+Tab
cycles
among
programs
running on
a single
desktop.

3. **Again, click one of the Desktops at the bottom of the screen. Now press Windows key+Tab.**

   That pops you in and out of Task View, just like clicking the icon in the taskbar next to Cortana.

4. **To cycle among Desktops, press Ctrl+Windows+Left arrow or Ctrl+Windows+Right arrow.**

   When you release the Windows key, Windows settles on the desktop that you've chosen.

   This is a difficult way to switch among desktops because you can't see them in advance, nor can you tell how many desktops you have — you just move from desktop to desktop.

5. **To shut down a desktop and move all the running programs from that desktop into the next desktop, press Windows+Ctrl+F4.**

   When you do so, Windows automatically shuffles you to the window that now contains all the programs that were running on the desktop you shut down.

6. **To move a running program from one desktop to another, bring up Task View (tap or click the icon next to Cortana, or Windows Key+Tab), right-click (or click and hold) the program you want to move, and choose Move To, followed by the desktop name.**

   You can see this move in action in Figure 4-7.

7. **To quickly close a desktop, bring up Task View, hover your mouse over the desktop you want to close, and click the X in the upper-right corner, as shown in Figure 4-8.**

   All the running programs (apps) get shuffled to the next desktop.

Figure 4-7:
Move a
program (or
app) from
one desktop
to another.

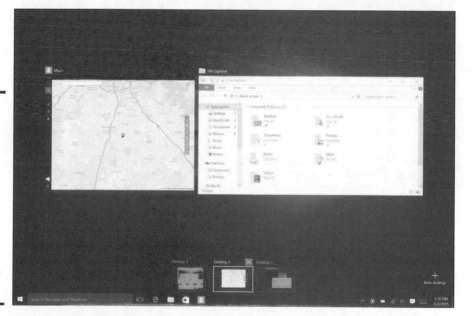

Figure 4-8:
The fast
way to
shut down
desktops,
without
closing any
programs:
Click the
X on the
desktop
name at the
bottom.

Other Multiple Desktop Settings

The Windows Settings app lets you alter multiple desktop behaviors, just
a little bit.

First, Windows shows you which programs are running on the current desktop by drawing a faint line under the taskbar icons of the running programs.

You can change that behavior, so Windows shows underlines for all programs that are running on any desktop. Here's how:

1. **Click or tap Start, then Settings.**

The Settings app appears.

2. **Click or tap System, then Multitasking.**

You see the choices in Figure 4-9.

3. **In the top drop-down box, choose All desktops.**

Your taskbar changes immediately to show underscores for any program that's running on any desktop, as shown in Figure 4-10.

Similarly, you can switch the behavior of the Alt+Tab coolswitch. It can be set to only cycle among programs on the current desktop or to cycle among all running programs on all desktops.

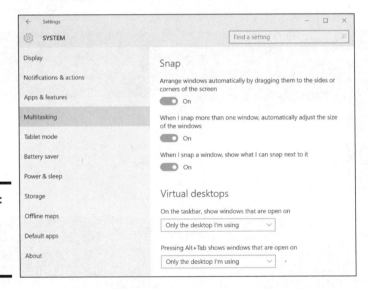

Figure 4-9:
You have multiple desktop options.

Figure 4-10:
Underlines indicate which programs are running.

Chapter 5: Internet Explorer, Chrome, and Firefox

In This Chapter

✓ Why Edge is in Book V, Chapter 1, and not here

✓ Evaluating desktop browsers — the good, the bad, and the ugly

✓ Choosing among the browsers on offer

✓ Customizing Internet Explorer, Firefox, and Chrome

✓ Searching on the web and taking control

✓ Using the reference tools on the web

For hundreds of millions of people, the web and Internet Explorer (IE) are synonyms. It's fair to say that IE has done more to extend the reach of PC users than any other product — enabling people from all walks of life, in all corners of the globe, to see what a fascinating world we live in.

At the same time, IE has become an object of attack by spammers, scammers, thieves, and other lowlifes. As the Internet's lowest (or is it greatest?) common denominator, IE draws lots of unwanted attention. That's changing though. Now, all the browsers get some of the flak. It's just that IE continues to get the worst of it.

This chapter looks at desktop browsers: Internet Explorer, sure, but also Firefox and Google Chrome, two viable alternatives, each with its own strengths and weaknesses.

If you're looking for Edge, Microsoft's long-overdue replacement for Internet Explorer, you're in the wrong place. Edge is a Windows/Universal app, one that lives on the new WinRT-based Universal/Modern/Metro side of the street. For that reason, I talk about it in the book that deals with the other side, Book V, Chapter 1.

This chapter looks at what's out there for the old-fashioned desktop, helps you choose one (or two or three) desktop browsers for your everyday use, shows you how to customize your chosen browser, and then offers all sorts of important advice about using the web.

Some of you may find that Edge isn't available on your Windows 10 machine. Some large companies want to "protect" the people on their networks by stifling Edge and only offering IE. Some companies don't have any choice — they've poured too much money into non-standard, creaky archaic IE programs, and they're unwilling or unable to re-write them. Bah.

Which Browser Is Best?

I must hear that question a dozen times a week.

The short answer: It depends.

The long answer: It depends on lots of things. But one thing we know for sure. Microsoft itself doesn't think much of Internet Explorer. The old guy's been given the boot, tucked away in an obscure corner where you can conjure him up if you insist. Microsoft's money (and talent) is on Edge.

I hear the same question over and over: "How can I make my browser run faster?" The short answer: 99 percent of the time, you can't. The big problem isn't your browser. It's the speed of your Internet connection.

Considering security

Without a doubt, the number-one consideration for any browser user is security. The last thing you need is to get your PC infected with a drive-by attack, where merely looking at an infected web page takes over your computer.

Fortunately, for the first time in many years, if not ever, I feel confident in telling you that the desktop versions of all three major browsers — Internet Explorer, Firefox, and Chrome — are excellent choices. None has clear superiority over the others. All are (finally!) secure, as long as you follow a few simple rules.

The days of Microsoft taking all the heat for security holes has passed. Although it's true that there are more frontal assaults on Internet Explorer than on the other two, it's also true that Firefox- and Chrome-specific attacks exist.

In fact, browsers aren't the major source of attacks any more. Starting in 2007 or so, the bad guys turned their attention away from browsers and went to work on add-ons, specifically Flash and Acrobat PDF Reader, as well as browser toolbars. According to IBM's X-Force Team, the number of browser-attacking exploits has been declining steadily since 2007, with a concomitant rise in infections based on Flash, Reader, Java, toolbars, and other third-party add-ons. Edge limits all of them. Score one for the new kid on the block.

Old versions of Internet Explorer still have major security problems. Microsoft's been actively trying to kill IE 6 for years now. But as long as you stick to the latest browser version, keep your browsers reasonably well updated, and don't install any weird toolbars or other add-ons, your only major points of concern for any of the major browsers are Flash, Reader, and Java. I talk about all three in the following sections.

The place where the latest versions of IE fall down? The infernal parade of patches. Month after month, we're seeing dozens, if not hundreds, of patched parts of IE running out the Automatic Update chute. Inevitably one or more of the patch parts causes problems. IE may be the grand old gold standard, but it's on life support.

There's a good case to be made for running Edge, and I talk about that in Book V, Chapter 1.

Both Chrome and Firefox have, in the Windows 8-era past, tried to make a browser that runs well in the new Universal arena. To date, they haven't had much luck. That may change though, and if it does, it'd be well worth your while to try the Universal/ Modern version of Chrome and/or Firefox. I'll keep you up to date on www.AskWoody.com.

IE, Firefox, and Chrome aren't the only games in the Windows desktop app milieu. Some people swear by Safari (which is the Apple browser); others go for Opera. Personally, I don't like Safari, but I do like Opera. I have my hands full just juggling the other three.

Looking at privacy

Privacy is one area that differentiates the Big Three. As best I can tell, nobody knows for sure how much data about your browsing proclivities is kept by the browser manufacturers, but this much seems likely:

✦ If you turn on the Suggested Sites feature or SmartScreen Filter in Internet Explorer (see the section on Internet Explorer), IE sends your browsing history to Microsoft, where it is saved and analyzed. But then, you get that with a fully enabled Cortana, too.

✦ Google keeps information about where you go with Chrome. Get over it.

✦ Although Firefox is capable of keeping track of where you're going with your browser, Firefox is the least likely of the Big Three to keep or use the data. Why? Because, in direct contrast to both Microsoft and Google, Firefox doesn't have anything to sell you.

What's an IP address?

When you're connected to the Internet interacting with a website, the website must be able to find you. Instead of using names (Billy Bob's broken-down ThinkPad), the Internet uses numbers, such as 207.46.232.182, something like a telephone number (that's one of Microsoft's addresses). When you go to a website, you leave behind your IP address. That's the only way the website has to get back to you. Nothing nefarious about it: That's the way the Internet works.

Although your IP address doesn't identify you, uniquely, the IP address for most computers with broadband connections rarely changes. Your IP address changes if you turn off your router and turn it back on again, but for most people, most of the time, the IP address stays constant.

The IP address actually identifies the physical box that's attached to the Internet. For homes and businesses with a network, the address is associated with the router, not individual computers on the Internet. If you're using a mobile (3G or 4G) connection, the IP address is associated with your mobile phone provider's equipment, not yours. In some developing countries, the whole country has a handful of IP addresses, and connections inside the country are handled as if they were on an internal network.

In general, the browser manufacturers can't track you directly, as an individual; they can only track your IP address (see the sidebar, "What's an IP address?"). But both Microsoft and Google mash together information that they get from multiple sources. As Microsoft puts it in the Internet Explorer Privacy Statement:

> "In order to offer you a more consistent and personalized experience in your interactions with Microsoft, information collected through one Microsoft service may be combined with information obtained through other Microsoft services. We may also supplement the information we collect with information obtained from other companies."

Funny that the statement doesn't mention targeted advertising.

Google does the same thing: It actively collects information about you from every interaction you have with a Google product or location, including the search site and the browser. Google also gets info when you visit a page with a Google ad.

If privacy is very important to you, Firefox is your best choice. No question.

Picking a browser

With all the pros and cons, which browser should you choose?

What's Do Not Track?

Microsoft made a huge step in the direction of helping to protect consumer privacy back when Windows 8 hit. Yes, *that* Microsoft. It turned on Do Not Track, by default during Windows 8 setup, in both the desktop and tiled versions of Internet Explorer 11.

Unfortunately, Microsoft was backed into a corner when the folks who promulgated DNT specifically said that a browser can't turn it on by default. Thus, in Windows 10, both IE and Edge don't have DNT enabled by default.

What's DNT? Good question.

Whenever you go to a website, your browser leaves certain fingerprints at each site you visit: the name of your browser, your operating system, your IP address, time zone, screen size, whether cookies are enabled, the address of the last website you visited, that kind of thing. I'm not talking about cookies. I'm talking about data that's inside the "header" at the beginning of the interaction with every web page. Even if you go "incognito" (in Chrome), "private" (in Firefox), or "In Private" (in Internet Explorer), your browser still sends all that information to every site, every time you visit.

The Do Not Track proposal — and it's only a proposal at this point — would assign one more bit in the header that says, "The person using this browser requests that you not track anything he's doing." DNT was originally developed by Firefox. You can turn on DNT in any recent version of Firefox by clicking the Firefox button, Options, Privacy, and selecting the Tell Web Sites I Do Not Want to Be Tracked check box.

As with everything Internet-related, DNT isn't cut and dried. There are lots and lots of nuances. First and foremost, it's entirely voluntary: Websites can ignore the DNT bit if the site's programmers want to. Second, the precise definition of "track" can get a little squishy. Third, there's no possible way to enforce the DNT settings — no way to tell which of the dozens of billions of websites now readily accessible even claim to have a DNT policy, much less implement it. The advertising industry and the privacy partisans have yet to agree on anything, much less a DNT proposal. Still, it's a start in the right direction.

For lightweight browsing, I recommend Edge. It's small, fast, secure, rarely hangs, and works with most sites. That's also Edge's Achilles Heel. It doesn't work with all sites, and it's so new that developers have yet to grow a rich base of add-ons.

For everyday browsing, I'd say stick with one of the desktop apps. Although each version of each browser is different, a few generalities about the different browsers seem to hold true:

+ **Internet Explorer** holds the title for most compatible with ancient websites. Unfortunately, sometimes that compatibility comes at a cost: You may have to install programs (such as ActiveX controls) that can have security holes. IE also has a few features that some people find useful, such as the capability to pin websites to the Windows taskbar.

✦ **Firefox** has the most extensions, and some of them are quite worthwhile. Ghostery, for example, shows every tracking cookie on every web page; DownThemAll can download every link on a page and manage them all; IE Tab brings IE compatibility to most ancient web pages; NoScript blocks Flash and Java unless you unleash them on a specific site. Firefox is also the least likely to sprout privacy problems (see the preceding section).

✦ **Chrome** usually comes out on top in security tests. With built-in support for both PDF reading and Flash, and the Java programming language, Chrome can handle all three without relying on the Flash, Reader, or Java plug-ins, which are historically riddled with security holes. Chrome has also been a pioneer in new features and standards adoption and will take your settings along with you as you move from PC to PC.

It isn't an either/or choice, actually. You can easily run Edge, Internet Explorer, Firefox, and Chrome side by side. Here's what I do:

✦ Most of the time, I run Edge.

✦ For serious browsing, I use Firefox, with NoScript turned on and Ghostery sniffing out the frighteningly large number of cookies watching me. I don't block cookies with Ghostery, although I can. Mostly I want to see how much sites have sold out, reducing my privacy for their profits.

✦ If I want to bookmark something, I usually shift to Chrome, which I keep signed in. I like its bookmarking interface better — and the bookmarks travel with me, wherever I go, because I'm signed in. If I have trouble with a fancy new site in Firefox, Chrome will usually handle it.

✦ And Internet Explorer is always ready, standing by, in case I hit an older web page that doesn't work right in Edge, Firefox, or Chrome. Yes, there are plenty of them (I won't mention my bank by name). Instead of switching Firefox over to the IE Tab add-on, I just jump the monkey and go to IE.

Setting a browser as your default

When you get Windows, Edge is set up as the default browser: Click a web link in a document, for example, and Edge jumps up to load the web page.

Both Firefox and Chrome offer to become your default web browser, as soon as you install them. Internet Explorer has the option, but it isn't so in your face. They also have a check box that basically tells them to quit asking. I always check that box.

The history of Internet Explorer

More than any other product, Internet Explorer reflects the odd and tortured Microsoft approach to the web. After largely ignoring the Internet for many years, Microsoft released the first version of Internet Explorer in 1995, as an add-on to Windows. In 1996, Microsoft built Internet Explorer version 3 into Windows itself, violating antitrust laws and using monopolistic tactics to overwhelm Netscape Navigator.

Having illegally pummeled its competitor in the marketplace, Microsoft made almost no improvements to Internet Explorer between August 2001 and August 2006 — an eternity in Internet time. IE became the single largest conduit for malware in the history of computing, with major security patches (sometimes several) appearing almost every month.

And then there was Firefox. Dave Hyatt, Blake Ross (who was a sophomore at Stanford at the time), and hundreds of volunteers took on the IE behemoth, producing a fast, small, free alternative that quickly grabbed a significant share

of the browser market. Microsoft responded by incorporating many Firefox features into Internet Explorer.

Although Google did provide most of the money that originally drove Firefox's development — Yahoo pays a pretty penny to be the default search engine in Firefox now — the Googlies decided to make their own browser, with a different slant. First released in late 2008, Chrome has grown to the point that Chrome and Firefox often run neck-and-neck in web utilization statistics, with IE on a downward trend around the 50-percent line.

With Windows 10's release, Microsoft isn't deprecating Internet Explorer as much as throwing it in a bottle of formaldehyde. You can still use IE all you want (it's under Start, All Apps, Windows Accessories), but Microsoft would much rather you use Edge. Which is good, because I would much rather you use Edge, too.

It's easy to change your default browser. Here's how:

1. **Right-click the Start button, and choose Control Panel.**

2. **Click the Programs link. Then, under Default Programs, click the link that says Set Your Default Programs.**

   You see the Set Your Default Programs dialog box shown in Figure 5-1.

3. **On the left, select the browser you want to turn into your default and choose Choose defaults for this program.**

   That tells Windows to associate all the filename extensions that the browser can handle to the browser. You can see a detailed list in Figure 5-2.

   Thus, in this example, after you've set Chrome as the default, double-clicking an HTML file opens the file with Chrome.

4. **Click OK.**

   Your chosen browser becomes the default.

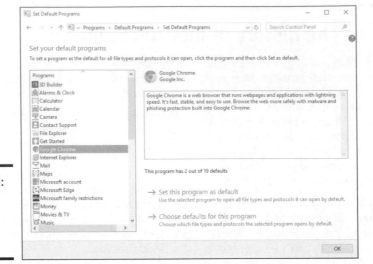

Figure 5-1:
Set your
default
browser
here.

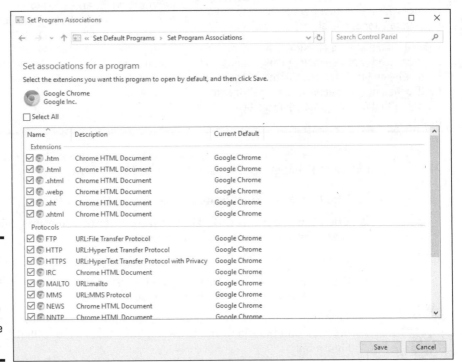

Figure 5-2:
These are
the kinds
of files and
"Protocols"
that Chrome
can handle.

Using Internet Explorer on the Desktop

Internet Explorer 11 on the Windows 10 desktop is very similar to — almost indistinguishable from — Internet Explorer 11 on Windows 7 or 8. It has the old, familiar interface. It runs all the add-ons you've come to know and love and distrust. Internet Explorer 11 gives you just about everything a modern browser can give you — except an extensive library of customized add-ons — but it's big, fat, slow, and curiously buggy.

Any way you look at it, Microsoft isn't giving IE much love these days. It's definitely on the way out. Which isn't necessarily a bad thing, for you and me.

Navigating in IE

One great thing about Internet Explorer is that you can be an absolute no-clue beginner, and with just a few hints about tools and so on, you can find your way around the web like a pro. A big part of the reason why: Hundreds of millions of people, if not more than a billion, have already used IE. For many, IE is synonymous with "web."

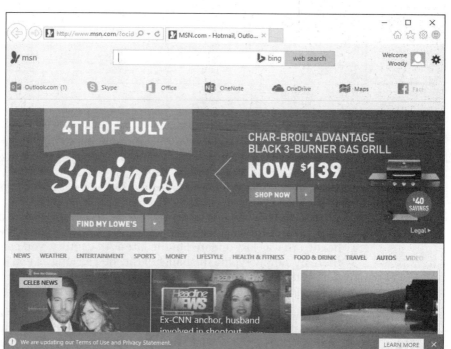

Figure 5-3:
Internet Explorer 11's slimmed down interface belies its bloated under-pinnings.

Book III
Chapter 5

Internet Explorer, Chrome, and Firefox

And that's kind of sad.

Figure 5-4 gives you a diagram of the basic layout of the Internet Explorer window.

Go back one page; hold for recent history

Go forward one page   Search

Favicon   Refresh

Address bar   Tab   Add a new tab

Comments

Tools

Favorites and history

Go to home page

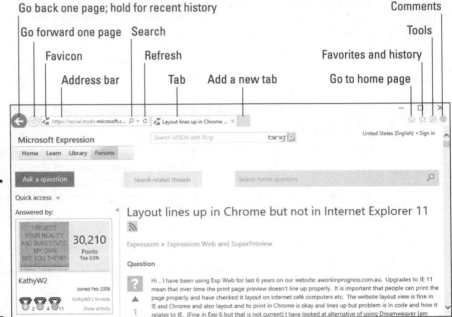

Figure 5-4:
The IE window includes everything you need to work on the web.

Don't work too hard

A handful of Internet Explorer tricks can make all the difference in your productivity and sanity. Every IE user should know these shortcuts:

✦ **You rarely need to type www in the address bar at the beginning of an address and you never need to type** http://. People who build websites these days are almost always savvy enough to let you drop the use of the www at the beginning of the website's name. Unless the site you're headed to was last updated in the late 17th century, you can probably get there by simply typing the name of the site, as long as you include the part at the end. So you can type **http://www.dummies.com** if you want to, but typing **dummies.com** works just as well.

✦ **IE automatically sticks** http://www. **onto the front of an address you type and** .com **on the end if you press Ctrl+Enter.** So if you want to go to the site http://www.dummies.com, you only need to type **dummies** in the address bar and press Ctrl+Enter.

✦ **With a few exceptions, address capitalization doesn't matter.** Typing either **AskWoody.com** or **askwoody.com** gets you to my website—as does **asKwoodY.cOm**. On the other hand, hyphens (-) and underscores (_) aren't interchangeable: `some-site.com` and `some_site.com` would be two completely different sites if they were the real deals. Similarly, the number 0 isn't the same as the letter o, the number 1 isn't a letter l, and radishes aren't the same as turnips. Or so my niece tells me.

The exceptions? Web addresses from one of the thousands of websites that now have shortened URLs. Go to `bit.ly`, for example, or `goo.gl`, feed it an URL that's a gazillion letters long, click a button, and you get back something that looks like this: `goo.gl/XY2Am`. In those kinds of addresses — shortened ones — capitalization *does* matter.

While we're on the topic of working too hard, keeping track of passwords rates as the single biggest pain in the neck in any browser. You have passwords for, what, a hundred different sites? If you haven't yet discovered LastPass (or Roboform), get to Book X, Chapter 5, and check it out.

Moving around the main desktop window

As you can see, IE packs lots of possibilities into that small space. The items you use most often are described in this list:

✦ **Backward** and **forward arrows:** Go to the previously displayed page; hold down to see a list of all previous pages.

✦ **Address bar:** This enables you to type the web address of a page that you want to move to directly. You can also type search terms here; click the spyglass or press Enter, and IE looks them up using your default search engine.

✦ **Refresh:** If you think the page has changed, tap or click this icon to have IE retrieve it for you again.

✦ **Tab:** You can have many pages open at a time, one on each tab. To create a new tab, click the first blank tab on the right.

✦ **Home page:** This replaces the current tab with the tab(s) on your Home page.

✦ **Favorites icon:** This lets you set, go to, and organize favorite websites, as well as look at your browsing history.

✦ **Settings:** This takes you under the covers to change the way IE behaves. Or misbehaves.

If you want to see the old-fashioned toolbar menus (File, Edit, View, and all the others) in Internet Explorer, press Alt. Yep, that's how you get to IE's inner workings.

**Book III
Chapter 5**

**Internet Explorer,
Chrome, and Firefox**

Tinkering with tabs

Tabs offer you a chance to bring up multiple web pages without opening multiple copies of IE. They're a major navigational aid because it's easy to switch among tabs. If you've never used browser tabs, you may wonder what all the fuss is about. It doesn't seem like there's much difference between opening another window and adding a tab (see Figure 5-5). But after you get the hang of it, tabs can help you organize pages and jump to the one you want.

Figure 5-5:
If you've never used tabs, you're in for a treat.

You can add a new tab to IE in any of these four ways:

✦ Click the blank box to the right of the right-most tab. That starts a blank new tab, and away you go.

✦ Ctrl+click a link to open the linked page in a new tab.

✦ Press Ctrl+T to start a new tab. When the tab is open, you get to navigate manually, just as you would in any other browser window.

✦ Right-click a link, and choose Open in New Tab.

In addition, the web page you're looking at may specify that any links on the page are to open in a new tab, instead of overwriting the current one.

Why do I like tabs? I can set up a single window with a bunch of related tabs and then bookmark the whole shebang. That makes it one-click easy to open all my favorite news sites, research sites, or financial sites. While my browser's out loading pages, I can go do something else and return to the tabbed window when everything's loaded and ready to go.

If I'm trying to research two different topics at the same time, I frequently start Firefox and create tabs to hunt down the first topic and then start Firefox again — start it in a different window, usually by Shift+clicking a link — or I start Chrome and traipse through the second topic. Edge and IE work the same way.

You can reorganize the order of tabs by simply clicking a tab and dragging it to a different location.

Using the address bar

No doubt you're familiar with basic browser functions, or you can guess when you know what the controls mean. But you may not know about some of these finer points:

✦ When you type on the address bar, IE looks at what you're typing and tries to match it with the list of sites it has in your history list and in your favorites. Sometimes, you can get the right address (URL) by typing something related to the site. Watch as you type and see what IE comes up with.

If you turn on Bing Suggestions (sometimes called Suggested Sites), IE sends all your keystrokes to Mother Microsoft and has Bing try to guess what you're looking for. Depending on how you feel about privacy, that may or may not be a good idea. See the section "Turning on key features," later in this chapter.

✦ Click a link, and the web page decides whether you move to the new page in the current browser tab or a new tab appears with the clicked page loaded. Many people don't realize that the web page makes the decision about following the link in the same tab or creating a new one. You can override the web page's setting.

- Shift+click, and a new browser window always opens with the clicked page loaded.

- Ctrl+click, and the clicked page appears on a new tab in the current browser window. Similarly, if you type in the Search bar and press Ctrl+Enter, the results appear in a new tab.

✦ Even if the web page "hijacks" your backward and forward arrows, you can always move backward (or forward) by clicking and holding the directional arrow, and choosing the page you want.

You can bring up a history of all the pages you visited in the past few weeks by pressing Ctrl+H, as shown in Figure 5-6.

Book III
Chapter 5

Internet Explorer,
Chrome, and Firefox

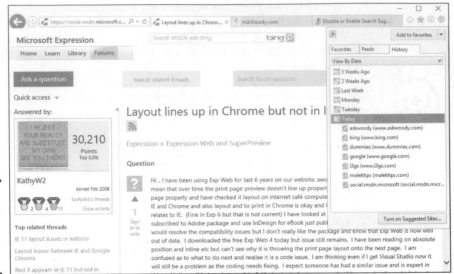

Figure 5-6:
Bring up the browsing history with Ctrl+H.

To search for a particular word or phrase on a page, press Ctrl+F. Force your browser to refresh a web page (retrieve the latest version, even if a version is stored locally) by pressing F5. If you need to make sure that you have the latest version, even if the timestamps may be screwed up, press Ctrl+F5.

Saving space, losing time

Increasing or decreasing the number of days of browsing history that IE stores doesn't have much effect on the amount of data stored on the hard drive: Even a hyperactive surfer will have a hard time cranking up a History folder that's much larger than 1MB. By contrast, temporary Internet files on your computer can take up 10, 50, or even 100 times that much space.

Those temporary Internet files exist only to speed your Internet access: When IE hits a web page that it has seen before, if a copy of the page's contents appears in the Temporary Internet Files folder, IE grabs the stuff on the hard drive rather than wait for a download. That can make a huge difference in IE's responsiveness, particularly if you have a slow Internet connection, but the speed comes at a price: 250MB, if you haven't changed it.

To clear out the IE temporary Internet files, follow these simple steps:

1. **Start Internet Explorer.**

2. **Click the Tools icon, the one shaped like a gear in the upper right, and choose Internet Options.**

   The Internet Options dialog box appears.

3. **On the General tab, under Browsing History, click the Delete button.**

   You see the Delete Browsing History dialog box shown in Figure 5-7.

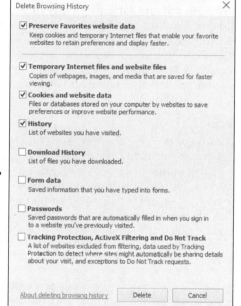

Delete Browsing History   ✕

☑ **Preserve Favorites website data**
Keep cookies and temporary Internet files that enable your favorite
websites to retain preferences and display faster.

☑ **Temporary Internet files and website files**
Copies of webpages, images, and media that are saved for faster
viewing.

☑ **Cookies and website data**
Files or databases stored on your computer by websites to save
preferences or improve website performance.

☑ **History**
List of websites you have visited.

☐ **Download History**
List of files you have downloaded.

☐ **Form data**
Saved information that you have typed into forms.

☐ **Passwords**
Saved passwords that are automatically filled in when you sign in
to a website you've previously visited.

☐ **Tracking Protection, ActiveX Filtering and Do Not Track**
A list of websites excluded from filtering, data used by Tracking
Protection to detect where sites might automatically be sharing details
about your visit, and exceptions to Do Not Track requests.

About deleting browsing history   Delete   Cancel

Figure 5-7:
You have
full control
over what
kinds of
browsing
history gets
deleted.

4. **Choose the kinds of data you want to delete, and click Delete; then click OK to close the Internet Options dialog box.**

   You won't hurt anything, but revisited web pages take longer to appear. For advice about cookies, see the next section.

Dealing with cookies

A *cookie,* as you probably know, is a text file that a website stores on your computer. The website can put information inside its own cookie (say, the time and date of your last visit or the page you were last viewing or your account number). At least in theory, a website can look at and change only its own cookies: The cookie provides a means for an individual website to store information on your computer and to retrieve it later, using your browser.

In general, that's A Good Thing. Cookies can minimize the amount of futzing around that you need to do on a site. Most shopping cart/checkout sites need cookies.

Of course, nothing ever goes precisely as planned. Bugs have appeared in the way Internet Explorer, in particular, handles cookies and, historically, it's been possible for rogue websites to retrieve information from cookies other than their own.

Because of ongoing problems, sound and fury frequently raised by people who don't understand, and concomitant legislation in many countries, "first-party" cookies these days rarely include any interesting information. Mostly, they store innocuous settings and perhaps a randomly generated number that's used to track a customer in the company's database. To a bad guy, the data stored in most cookies varies between banal and useless.

What's a third-party cookie?

By contrast, *third-party cookies* (or *tracking cookies*) aren't as bland. They have significant commercial value because they can be used to keep track of your web surfing. Here's how: Suppose ZDNet (www.zdnet.com), which is owned by CBS, sells an ad to DoubleClick. When you venture to any ZDNet page (they all have tiny, one-pixel "ads" from DoubleClick), both ZDNet/CBS and DoubleClick can stick cookies on your computer. ZDNet can retrieve only its cookie, and DoubleClick can retrieve only its cookie. Cool. DoubleClick may keep information about you visiting a ZDNet site that talks about, oh, an Android phone.

Now suppose that DealTime (www.dealtime.com) sells an ad to DoubleClick. You go to any page on DealTime (they also have tiny 1-pixel DoubleClick "ads" on every page), and both DealTime and DoubleClick can look at their own cookies. DealTime may be smart enough to ask DoubleClick whether you've been looking at Android phones and then offer you a bargain tailored to your recent surfing. Or an insurance company may discover that you've been looking at information pages about the heartbreak of psoriasis. Or a car company may find out you're very interested in its latest Stutzmobile.

Multiply that little example by 10, 100, or 100,000, and you begin to see how third-party cookies can be used to collect a whole lot of information about you and your surfing habits. There's nothing illegal or immoral about it. But some people (present company certainly included) find it disconcerting. Oh, you know that Google owns DoubleClick, yes?

I don't get too worked up about cookies these days. If you've ever worked with them programmatically, you're probably at the yawning stage too. But the potential is there for them to become pernicious.

Deleting cookies

Cookies don't have anything to do with spam — you receive the same junk email even if you tell your computer to reject every cookie that darkens your door. Cookies don't spy on your PC, go sniffing for bank accounts, or keep a log of those . . . ahem . . . artistic websites you visit. They do serve a useful purpose, but like so many other concepts in the computer industry, cookies are exploited by a few companies in questionable ways. I talk about cookies extensively in Book IX, Chapter 1. If you're worried about cookies and want to know what's really happening, that's a great place to start.

To delete all cookies in Internet Explorer, follow the instructions in the earlier section "Saving space, losing time" to bring up the Delete Browsing History dialog box (refer to Figure 5-7). Make sure you select Cookies and Website Data, and click Delete. IE deletes all your cookies.

Internet Explorer has a mechanism for blocking third-party cookies, but I don't think it works very well. It's based on an old "standard" known as P3P, which is actually used by about a dozen websites based in Lower Slobovokia—and that's about it. Even some of Microsoft's own sites don't use P3P. I talk about the problems with IE's third-party cookie blocking in one of my *InfoWorld* Tech Watch articles, at `www.infoworld.com/t/ internet-privacy/googles-cookie-runaround-in-ie-not-big- deal-186889`.

Changing the home page

Every time you start the desktop version of IE, it whirrs, and after a rela- tively brief moment (how brief depends primarily on the speed of your Internet connection), a web page appears. The information that page con- tains depends on whether your computer is set up to begin with a specific page known as a *home page*.

Microsoft sets up `www.msn.com` as the IE home page (see Figure 5-8) by default — a page best known for its, uh, quirky choice of "news" items and phenomenally high density of ads. Many PC manufacturers set the Internet Explorer home page to display something related to their systems.

If the ditzy, ad-laden MSN home page leaves you wondering whether P.T. Barnum still designs web pages (there's one born every minute), or if your PC manufacturer's idea of a good home page doesn't quite jibe with your tastes, you can easily change the home page. Here's how:

1. **Start IE.**

2. **Navigate to the page or pages you want to use for a home page.**

You can bring up as many pages as you like on separate tabs. All the tabs will become your home "page." See the previous section, "Navigating in desktop IE," if you're not sure how to use tabs.

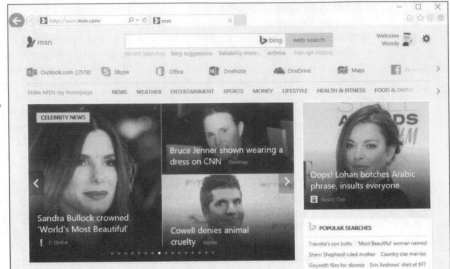

Figure 5-8:
If msn.
com is your
favorite
page on the
web, you
may want
to consider
a prefrontal
lobotomy.

3. **Tap or click the Tools icon (the one in the upper right that looks like a gear), choose Internet Options, and click the General tab.**

   You see the Home Page settings shown in Figure 5-9.

Figure 5-9:
Set the
home
page(s)
here.

4. **At the top, make sure you have the list of all the tabs you would like to open as your home page, and then tap or click the button marked Use Current.**

If you choose Use New Tab, IE starts with no new page at all. That can be considerably faster than starting with a real home page.

5. **Click OK.**

Every time IE runs, it brings up the tabs you selected.

Turning on key features

Microsoft has a long list of improvements to its latest version of Internet Explorer. Most of those improvements operate behind the scenes; you'll only know that they're there when you don't get infected, if you know what I mean.

The last few IE versions have brought along a few worthwhile improvements, which you may not have seen:

✦ **You can pin a specific page to the desktop taskbar.** To pin a site to the taskbar, click the "favicon" next to the page's address, or click the entire tab, and drag it down to the taskbar.

Microsoft says that a website accessed from the taskbar this way "takes on the branding of the site." What Microsoft means is that the background and border colors of the browser take on the main color of the site. Whooo-boy. Some sites, like Facebook, give you notifications about incoming messages.

✦ **IE analyzes add-ons and tells you how much they're dragging your system down,** each time you launch IE. In general, you only see the analysis when your add-ons are causing big problems. There's a detailed explanation on the IE Blog at `http://blogs.msdn.com/b/ie/archive/2011/03/23/updates-to-add-on-performance-advisor.aspx`.

✦ *Suggested Sites* **(also called Bing Suggestions) is a feature added in IE 8 that keeps track of keys as you type them,** sending your keystrokes to Microsoft (Bing), generating potential matches and suggestions on the fly. Matches are based primarily on your browsing history. To turn on Suggested Sites, click the star Favorites icon, and at the bottom of the box, select Turn on Suggested Sites.

As you may imagine, there's a great deal of controversy about the privacy aspects of Suggested Sites: Microsoft records every keystroke that you type into IE and watches your browsing history. Note that Suggested Sites is not turned on by default: You must enable it. (Check by tapping or clicking the gear icon in the upper right, choose Internet Options, then, on the Advanced tab, look for Enable Suggested Sites.) Microsoft has a detailed report on its side of the story on the IE Blog at `http://blogs.msdn.com/b/ie/archive/2009/02/05/suggested-sites-privacy.aspx`.

✦ *SmartScreen Filter* — **the collaborative Internet Explorer Phishing Filter** — **keeps up-to-the-minute blacklists** of websites that have been identified by other IE users as possible phishing sites. Before you go to a website, SmartScreen Filter compares the site's address to its blacklist and warns you if the site has been identified as an unsafe site. It also looks on the page for telltale "unsafe behavior" and warns you if the site looks fishy. It also checks files before you download them to see if they're on Microsoft's whitelist, warning you that the file "is not commonly downloaded" if it's a relative newcomer.

Unlike Suggested Sites, which sends all your information to Microsoft, the SmartScreen Filter maintains a small list of bad sites inside your computer that's updated frequently. That's a very effective trick first employed by Firefox.

To turn off SmartScreen Filter (for whatever reason), click the Tools icon (the one that looks like a gear), choose Safety, and then Turn off SmartScreen Filter. If you hit a dicey site — perhaps you were sent there by an apparent phishing e-mail message — you can report the site by clicking the gear icon and choosing Report Unsafe Website.

✦ *InPrivate Browsing* lets you surf anywhere on the web without leaving any records on your PC of where you dallied. It doesn't matter whether it's a racy page, the political headquarters of a candidate you detest, or a squealing fan site for a sappy soap opera, InPrivate Browsing makes sure that no details are left on your machine.

This kind of cloaking only keeps your PC clean. The sites you travel to can keep track of your Internet address (your IP address; see the earlier section "Looking at privacy," in this chapter, for details). Depending on how you connect to the Internet, your IP address can generally be traced to the router you're using to connect to the Internet. *Caveat surfor.*

Searching with alacrity . . . and Google

It shouldn't surprise you that Internet Explorer ships with Microsoft's Bing as its default search engine. If you like Bing, my hat's off to you. But if you want to change to Google (or DuckDuckGo, `www.duckduckgo.com`, which doesn't keep records of your searches; Dogpile, `www.dogpile.com`; Hotbot, `www.hotbot.com`; or Wolfram Alpha, `www.wolframalpha.com`, all of which have their high points), it's remarkably difficult.

Unless Microsoft changes IE 11 (or a judge forces the company to change, to provide better access to alternative search engines), here's the official way to move from Bing to Google in IE:

1. **Start IE.**

2. **Click the down arrow next to the magnifying glass, up in the address bar, and in the lower-right corner, choose Add.**

IE takes you to the Internet Explorer Gallery with Add-ons selected at the top, as in Figure 5-10.

Figure 5-10:
Adding
Google as
a search
provider.

**Book III
Chapter 5**

**Internet Explorer,
Chrome, and Firefox**

3. **When you find the Google search logo, click it.**

IE brings up the Internet Explorer Gallery highlighting Google Search.

4. **Click Add to Internet Explorer.**

IE responds with a dialog box called Add Search Provider, shown in Figure 5-11.

5. **Check the box marked Make This My Default Search Provider, and then click Add.**

IE doesn't say a thing, but it changes your default search provider to Google. How can you tell without running a search? Click the down arrow next to the magnifying glass icon again, and at the bottom, the tiny Google icon appears to the left of the Bing icon. That's how you know Google's the default search engine.

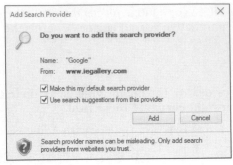

Figure 5-11:
This is the
Microsoft
way to make
Google
your default
search
provider.

From that point on, you can type your search terms in the address bar and press Enter, or tap or click the magnifying glass icon, and IE sends the search terms to Google.

The *easiest* way to change IE to use Google as its default search provider? Let Google do the hard work. Go to www.google.com/homepage/search and click the button marked Make Google My Search Provider.

I have a section later in this chapter that gives some pointers about searching on the web.

Customizing Firefox

Hey, you can use Internet Explorer if you want to. Without doubt, IE has a few features that other browsers can't match — dragging and dropping websites on the taskbar, Web Slices, InPrivate Filtering, and Accelerators come to mind. It also supports ActiveX controls and fits right in with Silverlight. If those ring your chimes, you need to play the IE game.

I use Firefox. I've used it for years, and I've recommended it in my books for years. Debating the relative merits of web browsers soon degenerates to a fight over the number of angels that can stand on the head of a pin. Suffice it to say that I feel Firefox has more options: more add-ons that make it work better and safer than either IE or Chrome. For me. I also like the fact that Firefox has no vested interest in keeping track of what I'm doing.

I don't mean to imply that Firefox is perfect. It isn't. The Firefox team releases security patches too, just like IE and Chrome teams, and you need to make sure you keep Firefox updated. But I think you'll enjoy using Firefox more than Internet Explorer. I also would bet that you hit far fewer in-the-wild security problems with the Fox.

Installing Firefox

Installing Firefox can't be simpler. You don't need to disable Internet Explorer, pat your head and rub your belly, or jump through any other hoops (although clicking your heels and repeating "There's no place like home" may help). Just follow these steps:

1. **Using any convenient browser (even Edge or IE), go to** www.firefox. com **and follow the instructions to download and run the installer for the latest version of Firefox.**

   In Figure 5-12, I pull up Firefox by using Edge.

**Book III
Chapter 5**

**Internet Explorer,
Chrome, and Firefox**

Figure 5-12:
You can install Firefox from Edge or any other browser.

2. **Click the big green Free Download button. Chances are good that you'll need to click Run to get the installer going. On the installer's splash screen, click Next.**

   You see the Setup window.

3. **Click Install.**

   The Setup wizard finishes and offers to launch Firefox now.

4. **Click Finish.**

   The Firefox main page appears (Figure 5-13).

Depending on how you install Firefox, the first time you run it, you may be asked whether you want to import bookmarks from Internet Explorer and/or Chrome. I generally choose No because I prefer to build my Favorites in each browser separately, but your opinion may well vary. You may also be asked whether you want to make Firefox your default browser. I click Not now, because I'd rather keep Edge as my default browser.

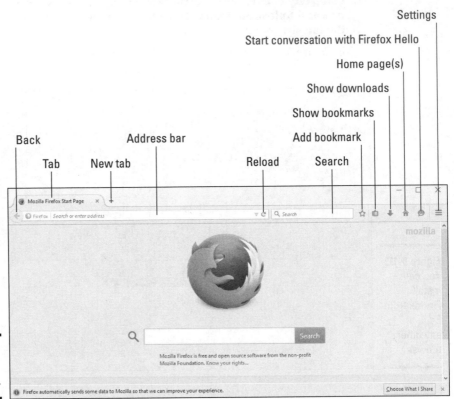

Figure 5-13: Firefox is up and running.

Firefox is a little different from IE in that it has a search bar in addition to the address bar. In fact, you can type search terms into the address bar or the search bar, and Firefox brings up your preferred search engine to look for them.

All the tricks I mention in the earlier IE section called "Don't work too hard," also perform in Firefox. You never need to type `http://`, almost never need to type `www`, and typing something like `dummies` followed by a Ctrl+Enter puts you spot-on for `www.dummies.com`.

Setting a home page in Firefox is similar to setting one in IE. To get to the right place, click the Firefox hamburger (three lines) menu in the upper-right corner to bring up the Settings menu shown in Figure 5-14. Choose Options. Home page settings are on the General tab.

Figure 5-14:
The Firefox settings "hamburger" menu.

Browsing privately in Firefox

Firefox has a private browsing feature similar to IE's InPrivate browsing, which I describe in the section "Turning on key features" in the IE part of this chapter. Firefox's version is called, er, Private Browsing. (Hey, Firefox invented it!)

To start a Private Browsing session, click the hamburger icon in the upper right and choose New Private Windows.

Some people prefer to always work in Private Browsing mode. There's much to be said for that approach, although you won't get the advantages of having cookies hanging around. Staying in Private Browsing mode is easy to do in Firefox. Here's how:

1. **Start Firefox. Click the hamburger icon in the upper right, and choose Options. At the top, click the Privacy icon.**

You see the Options dialog box shown in Figure 5-15.

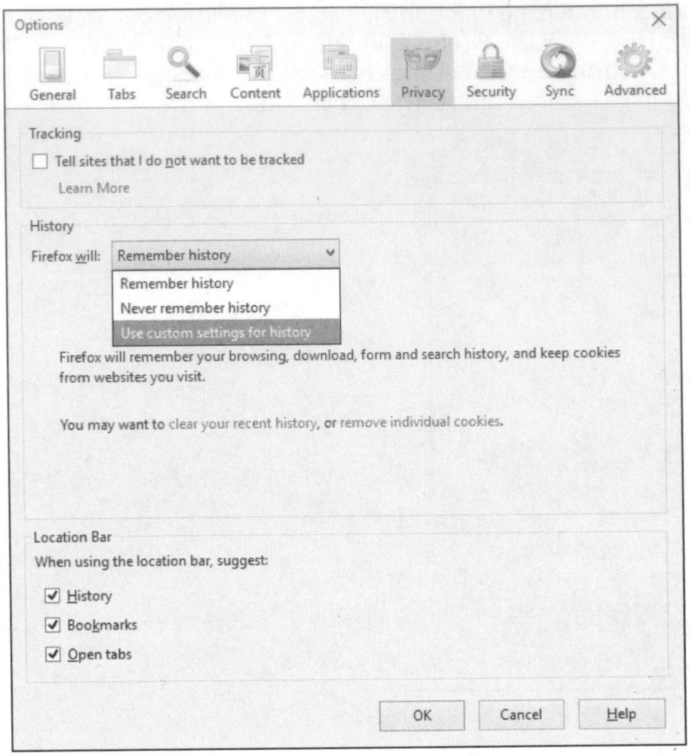

Figure 5-15:
It's easy to
have Firefox
always start
in Private
Browsing
mode.

2. **In the Firefox Will drop-down box, choose Use Custom Settings for History.**

3. **Select the box marked Always Use Private Browsing Mode.**

4. **If you want to turn on Do Not Track (see the sidebar, "What is Do Not Track?" earlier in this chapter), select the Tell Websites that I Do Not Want to Be Tracked check box.**

   Admittedly, DNT doesn't do much, but it doesn't hurt and may actually block a few sites.

5. **Click OK.**

   The next time you start Firefox, it'll be in Private Browsing mode. If you ever want to drop back into regular mode, click the hamburger icon and follow the above steps, choosing Firefox Will: Remember History.

Bookmarking with the Fox

Firefox handles bookmarks differently from Internet Explorer. (In IE, they're called Favorites. Same thing.)

The easiest way to understand Firefox bookmarks? Start with the Unsorted Bookmarks folder.

If you hit a website that you want to bookmark, follow these steps:

1. **Go to the site you want to bookmark, and tap or click the Bookmark icon (the big star) to the right of the address bar.**

   This step bookmarks the page and puts the bookmark in a kind of All Other folder named Unsorted Bookmarks.

2. **If you'd rather stick your bookmark in a place where you can find it later or assign a tag to it, click the clipboard to the right of the bookmark star. Go down to Unsorted Bookmarks, and look for the Bookmark you want to change.**

   Firefox shows you all the Bookmarks that aren't yet assigned to a folder, as in Figure 5-16.

3. **Right-click the Bookmark, and choose Properties.**

   Firefox shows you the Properties for the selected Bookmark.

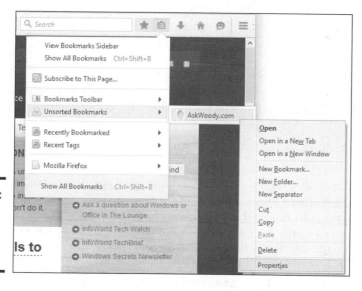

Figure 5-16:
Edit your
raw,
unsorted
bookmark.

4. **Type any tags you want to associate with the bookmark in the Tags box, in the middle.**

   Tags help you find things on the address bar. For example, if you assign a Stuxnet tag to the bookmark, typing **stux** in the address bar brings up this particular bookmark.

5. **To see the Bookmarks Toolbar, which appears underneath the Address bar, right-click any empty spot at the top of the Firefox window and check the line marked Bookmarks Toolbar.**

6. **To organize your bookmarks into folders or to place a bookmark on the Bookmarks Toolbar, click the clipboard icon to the right of the Star and choose View Bookmarks Sidebar.**

   The Bookmarks Sidebar (Figure 5-17) has all the tools you need to manage bookmarks.

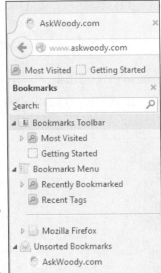

Figure 5-17:
Add new
folders here.

7. **To create a new bookmarks folder, right-click inside the Bookmarks Sidebar and choose New Folder. If you create a new folder, you can leave it in the Unsorted bookmarks folder, but if you want to make it more readily accessible from the Bookmarks Toolbar, click and drag the new folder in the Bookmarks Sidebar so the folder appears under the Bookmarks Sidebar folder.**

   In Figure 5-18, I put the News folder under the Bookmarks Toolbar folder, and it appears at the top on the Bookmarks Toolbar.

Figure 5-18:
The "News"
folder
appears
under the
Bookmarks
Toolbar
folder,
which
makes it
appear
on the
Bookmarks
Toolbar,
right
under the
Address bar.

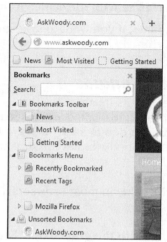

The bookmarks toolbar is convenient, but it takes up precious space on the screen. Many people prefer to work with the bookmarks icon, on the far right.

After the folder has been created (and, optionally, located on the Bookmarks Menu or the Bookmarks Toolbar), you can place any bookmark in the folder by double-clicking the bookmark star.

Syncing with Firefox

One of the nicest features in most modern browsers is their ability to sync bookmarks, history, and other settings. With Firefox, you can sync across Windows, Android, or iOS versions of the browser. All it takes is a (gulp) Firefox account.

Here's how to get your Windows version of Firefox synced:

1. **In Firefox, click the hamburger icon in the upper-right corner.**

You see the Settings menu (refer to Figure 5-14).

2. **Click or tap Sign in to Sync. Type your email address and password, give your year of birth, and click Sign Up.**

That gets you set up with a Firefox account.

3. **Any time you want to sync your settings with another copy of Firefox, follow the same procedure and sign in with the same Firefox Account.**

   You can use multiple Firefox accounts, if you want to sync groups of machines in different ways.

Changing the default search engine

Like Edge and Internet Explorer, Firefox puts its searches through Microsoft's Bing search engine — although it's called Yahoo! Search. That may change rapidly. Yahoo! and Microsoft don't exactly see eye to eye on the terms of their search contract, and nobody knows for sure at this point how it'll turn out.

It's hard to change the default search engine in most browsers. Not so in Firefox. Here's how you do it:

1. **In the Firefox Search bar (the one with the grayed-out "Search"), click or tap the magnifying glass,**

   You see the Search With choices shown in Figure 5-19.

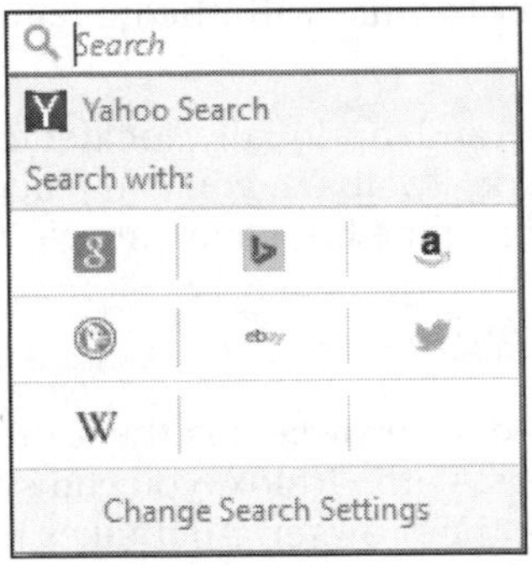

Figure 5-19: Firefox makes it easy to switch search engines.

2. **At the bottom, click Change Search Settings.**

3. **From the offered drop-down list, simply pick your preferred search engine.**

   Remember that DuckDuckGo — the icon with a duck on it — doesn't track your searches and doesn't sell your data to advertisers.

That's all it takes. Whichever search engine you choose becomes your default, and it'll stay that way until you change it.

Firefox's competitors could learn a thing or three.

Adding Firefox's best add-ons

One of the best reasons for choosing Firefox over IE and Chrome is the incredible abundance of add-ons. If you can think of something to do with a browser, chances are good there's already an add-on that'll do it.

An enormous cottage industry has grown up around Firefox. The Firefox people made it relatively easy to extend the browser itself. As a result, tens of thousands of add-ons cover an enormous range of capabilities.

To search for add-ons, click the hamburger icon in the upper right and choose Add-ons (see Figure 5-20). You can search for the add-ons recommended by Firefox itself or look for the most frequently downloaded add-ons.

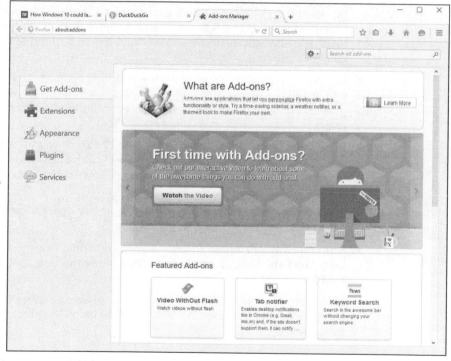

Figure 5-20: Firefox makes it easy to extend the browser with add-ons made by other groups.

Book III Chapter 5

Internet Explorer, Chrome, and Firefox

Here are some of my favorites. I always install the first four on any Firefox system I come into contact with:

✦ **NoScript** lets you shut down all active content — Java, JavaScript, Flash, and more — either individually or for a site as a whole. Many sites don't work with JavaScript turned off, but NoScript gives you a fighting chance to pick and choose the scripts you want. Between JavaScript and Flash blocking, NoScript significantly reduces your exposure to online malware.

✦ **Ghostery** keeps an eye on sites that are watching you. It tells you when sites contain "web beacons" or third-party cookies that can be used to track your surfing habits. I don't use Ghostery to stop cookies, but I do use it to watch who's watching me.

✦ **Adblock Plus** blocks ads. (What did you expect?) It blocks lots of ads — so much so that you may want to pull it back a bit. That's easy too. See a demo at `adblockplus.org/en`.

✦ **DownThemAll** "scrapes" all downloadable files on a web page and presents them so you can choose which files to download. Click Start, and they all come loading down.

✦ **Evernote Web Clipper** is the best way to keep track of all the bits and pieces of things that can never get organized. "Clip" websites you want to file away and get back to later, and organize them by project or topic. It's what Microsoft OneNote would like to be. Find out more at `www.evernote.com`.

✦ **Greasemonkey** adds a customizable scripting language to Firefox. After you install Greasemonkey, you can download scripts from `https://greasyfork.org/en` that perform an enormous variety of tasks, from tweet assistance to downloading Flickr files.

✦ **IETab** + embeds Internet Explorer inside Firefox. If you hit a site that absolutely won't work with Firefox, right-click the link, choose Tools and then choose Open This Link in IETab, and Internet Explorer takes over a tab inside Firefox.

✦ **eBay Sidebar** watches your trades while you're doing something else. It's from eBay.

✦ **Video DownloadHelper** makes it easy to download videos from the web. **Easy YouTube Video Downloader** does the same thing, but it's specialized for YouTube.

✦ **Linky** lets you open all links or images on a page, all at once, either on separate tabs or in separate windows. It's a helpful adjunct to Google image search.

To install the latest edition of any of these add-ons, go to the Add-Ons Manager (click the hamburger icon, Add-ons) search for the add-on's name. Each add-on's page has download and installation instructions — usually just a click or two and a possible restart of Firefox.

Optimizing Google Chrome

Google Chrome has several advantages over IE and Firefox. Foremost among them: world-class sandboxing of Flash, Java, and PDF support, which greatly reduces the chances of getting stung by the largest source of infections these days. IE and Firefox have both added similar protection, but Chrome was first and, I think, best.

As for Edge. . . it looks like Edge's going to beat Chrome at the sandboxing game, but it's still too early to tell. The bad guys are smart and getting smarter. Edge's still the new kid on the block. Time will tell.

That said, the biggest disadvantage is Google's (readily admitted!) tendency to keep track of where you've been, as an adjunct to its advertising program. If you install Chrome, sign in with your Google account, and start browsing, Google knows all, sees all, saves all — unless you turn on Incognito (private) browsing.

The second major disadvantage? Chrome's a resource hog. If you only open, oh, ten tabs, Chrome's great. But if you open 20 or 30 at a time — I'll confess I'm among the guilty — Chrome can bog things down significantly.

Installing Chrome

Installing Google Chrome is like falling off a log:

1. **With any browser, go to** `www.chrome.google.com`.

   You probably see a big blue button that says Download Now.

2. **Click the button to download.**

   You see a user agreement. Read all 214,197 pages of it, deselect the check box marked Set Google Chrome as My Default Browser, and click Accept and Install.

3. **Click run, or save and then run, depending on what browser you're using to download Chrome.**

   The installer takes a minute or two, asks you to choose a default browser (I say no, and keep Edge on top), and then comes up with a Set up Chrome page, as shown in Figure 5-21.

4. **The first time you use Chrome, it asks if you want to Sign In to Chrome. If you want your Chrome settings to follow you, onto any computer, tablet, or phone, sign in with a Google ID, such as a Gmail address.**

   I do. Syncing across many kinds of devices is one of the best parts about Chrome. But I'm ever mindful of the fact that Google keeps tabs on everywhere I go and uses the accumulated information to dish up ads designed to convince me to click.

Back

Forward

Reload the page   Address bar   Tools

Tab   Add a new tab   Add or edit bookmarks

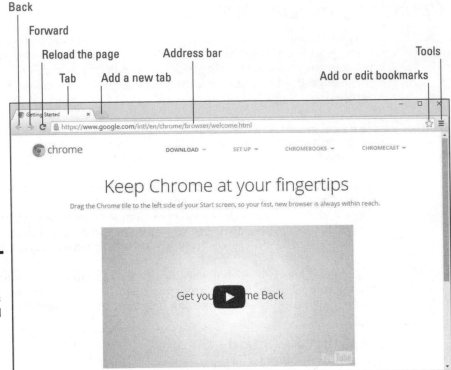

Figure 5-21:
Google
Chrome has
all the usual
controls,
easily
available.

Navigating in Chrome

Navigation in Chrome is very similar to that in Firefox, except there's no search bar. Chrome doesn't need one: You just type in the address bar.

All the tricks I mention in the earlier IE section called "Don't work too hard" also perform in Chrome. You never need to type `http://`, almost never need to type **www**, and typing something like `dummies` followed by a Ctrl+Enter puts you directly into `http://www.dummies.com`.

The default home page in Chrome is a little different from both IE and Firefox. The default in Chrome is to show what Chrome calls the New Tab page, which has an icon for Google Apps. At the bottom, you see thumbnails for the Chrome Web Store and other pages that you've frequently visited (see Figure 5-22). The New Tab page adds more entries as you use the browser.

Figure 5-22:
The New Tab in Chrome includes an Apps button, which brings up Google Docs, Gmail, Google Drive, YouTube, Google Sheets, Slides, and more.

If you want to change the home page in Chrome, navigate to the page(s) you want to use. Click the hamburger icon in the upper right, and choose Settings. A new tab opens with various Chrome settings. Under the heading On Startup, select the option Open a Specific Page or Set of Pages, and then tap or click the link to Set Pages. In the lower left, tap or click Use Current Pages. You see a list like the one in Figure 5-23. Verify that you have the right pages, and tap or click OK.

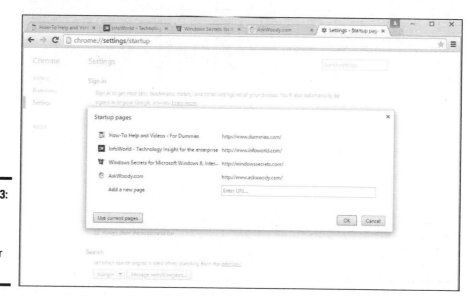

Figure 5-23:
It's easy to set the Home page(s) for Chrome.

Like IE, Firefox, and Edge, if you signed in to Chrome using a Google ID (such as a Gmail email address), changing the home page(s) here will change your Chrome home pages on all the computers — whether they're on PCs, tablets, phones — anywhere you go. Your add-ons and Favorites travel with you, too.

The following Chrome features are helpful as you move around the web using Chrome:

✦ **The default search engine:** The default search engine setting is on the same settings tab shown in Figure 5-23. Bing is one of the listed options, but you can add just about any search engine. Compare and contrast that with IE's default search engine hunting game.

✦ **Private browsing:** Chrome's version of InPrivate Browsing is called Incognito. To start a new Incognito window, click the hamburger icon and choose New Incognito Window.

✦ **Bookmarks:** I find Chrome's bookmarks capability much easier to use than Firefox's. To see why, go to a web page that you'd like to bookmark, and click the bookmark star icon, on the right. If you want to rearrange your bookmark folders, click the Edit button, and you can work with a full, hierarchical organization of folders, as in Figure 5-24.

Although the choices for Chrome Extensions won't make you shun Firefox's Add-Ons, it comes with a few cool items, including a free version of Angry Birds. Click the hamburger icon in the upper right, and choose More Tools, Extensions.

Figure 5-24: Chrome bookmarks are simple and easy to organize.

Chrome does have many Extensions (I use LastPass for Chrome all the time, for example), but it has never reached the depth or breadth of the Firefox add-on menagerie.

Searching on the Web

Internet searching can be a lonely business. You're out there, on the Internet range, with nothing but gleaming banner ads and text links to guide you. What happens when you want to find information on a specific subject, but you're not sure where to start? What if Google leads you on a wild goose chase? What if the Microsoft Bing "decision engine" takes the wrong turn?

Google's good. It's the search engine I use every day. But there are some decent alternatives, several of which can help in specific situations. For example:

✦ Microsoft's **Bing** (www.bing.com) isn't all that bad, and it's getting better. It remains to be seen if Bing can come up with any really compelling reasons to switch from Google. Microsoft's dumping a ton of money into search — more than a billion dollars a year, at last count — and I'm not sure it's come up with anything that puts Bing clearly in the lead.

✦ **DuckDuckGo** (www.duckduckgo.com) is an up-and-comer that I find fascinating. It relies heavily on information from crowd-sourced sources, including Wikipedia. At this point, the results DuckDuckGo delivers aren't as close to what I want as Google's, but they're getting better. One big point in this search engine's favor: Like Firefox, DuckDuckGo doesn't track what you do.

✦ **Dogpile** (www.dogpile.com), an old favorite, aggregates search results from Google, Bing, Yahoo!, and other engines, and smashes them all together, in a remarkably quick way. If I can't find what I need on Google, I frequently turn to Dogpile.

✦ **Wolfram Alpha** (www.wolframalpha.com) isn't exactly a search engine. It's a mathematical deduction engine that works with text input. So, for example, it can compare methanol, ethanol, and isopropanol. Or it can describe to you details of all the hurricanes in 1991. Or it can analyze the motion of a double pendulum.

But I find myself going back to Google.

Google has gone from one of the most admired companies on the web to one of the most criticized — on topics ranging from copyright infringement to pornography to privacy and censorship — and the PageRank system has been demonized in terms rarely heard since the Spanish Inquisition.

Few people now believe that PageRank objectively rates the "importance" of a web page; millions of dollars and thousands of person-months have been spent trying to jigger the results. Like it or not, Google just works. The Google spiders (the programs that search for information), which crawl all over the web, night and day, looking for pages, have indexed billions of pages, feeding hundreds of millions of searches a day. Other search engines have spiders too, but Google's outspider them all.

As this book went to press, Google was worth about $370 billion, the verb *google* had been embraced by prestigious dictionaries, the company was taking on Microsoft *mano a mano* in many different areas, and many other search engines offered decent alternatives to the once almighty Google. Everything's changing rapidly, and that's good news for us consumers.

In this section, I show you several kinds of searches you can perform with Google (and the other search engines). No matter what you're looking for, a search engine can find it!

Finding what you're looking for

Google has turned into the 800-pound gorilla of the searching world. I know people who can't even find AOL unless they go through Google. True fact.

The more you know about Google, the better it can serve you. Getting to know Google inside and out has the potential to save you more time than just about anything in Windows proper. If you can learn to search for answers quickly and thoroughly — and cut through the garbage on the web just as quickly and thoroughly — you can't help but save time in everything you do.

You can save yourself lots of time and frustration if you plot out your search before your fingers hit the keyboard.

Obviously, you should choose your search terms precisely. Pick words that will appear on any page that matches what you're looking for: Don't use *Compaq* when you want *Compaq S710*.

Beyond the obvious, the Google search engine has certain peculiarities you can exploit. These peculiarities hold true whether you're using Google in your browser's search bar or you venture directly to www.google.com:

✦ **Capitalization doesn't matter.** Search for *diving phuket* or *diving Phuket* — either search returns the same results.

✦ **The first words you use have more weight than the latter words.** If you look for *phuket diving,* you see a different list than the one for *diving phuket.* The former list emphasizes websites about Phuket that include a mention of diving; the latter includes diving pages that mention Phuket.

✦ **Google first shows you only those pages that include all the search terms.** The simplest way to narrow a search that returns too many results is to add more specific words to the end of your search term. For example, if *phuket diving* returns too many pages, try *phuket diving beginners*. In programmer's parlance, the terms are "anded" together.

✦ **If you type more than ten words, Google ignores the ones after the tenth**.

✦ **You can use OR** to tell Google that you want the search to include two or more terms — but you have to capitalize OR. For example, *phuket OR samui OR similans diving* returns diving pages that focus on Phuket, Samui, or the Similans.

✦ **If you want to limit the search to a specific phrase, use quotes.** For example, *diving phuket "day trip"* is more limiting than *diving phuket day trip* because in the former, the precise phrase *day trip* has to appear on the page.

✦ **Exclude pages from the results by putting a hyphen in front of the words you don't want.** For example, if you want to find pages about diving in Phuket but you don't want to associate with lowly snorkelers, try *diving phuket -snorkeling*.

✦ **You can combine search tricks.** If you're looking for overnight diving, try *diving phuket -"day trip"* to find the best results.

✦ **Google supports wildcard searches** in quite a limited way: The asterisk (*) stands for a single word. If you're accustomed to searches in, say, Word or Windows, the * generally indicates a sequence of characters, but in Google it only stands for an entire word. You may search for *div** and expect to find both diver and diving, but Google won't match on either. Conversely, if you search for, oh, *email * * wellsfargo.com,* you find lots of email addresses. (The second * matches the at sign [@] in an address. Try it.)

If you use Google to search for answers to computer questions, take advantage of any precise numbers or messages you can find. For example, googling *computer won't start* doesn't get you anywhere; but *two beeps on startup* may. *Can't install* won't get you anywhere. *Install error 800F9004* turns up wonders. If you're trying to track down a Windows error message, use Google to look for the precise message. Write it down, if you have to.

Using Advanced Search

Didn't find the results you need? Use Google Advanced Search. There's a trick.

If you need to narrow your searches — in other words, if you want Google to do the sifting rather than do it yourself — you should get acquainted with Google's Advanced Search capabilities. Here's a whirlwind tour:

1. **Run your search; if it doesn't have what you want, click the gear icon and choose Advanced Search.**

    The Google gear icon is located in the upper-right corner *of the search results page* — it's not part of your browser, it's actually on the search results page.

    Google brings up its Advanced Search page (see Figure 5-25).

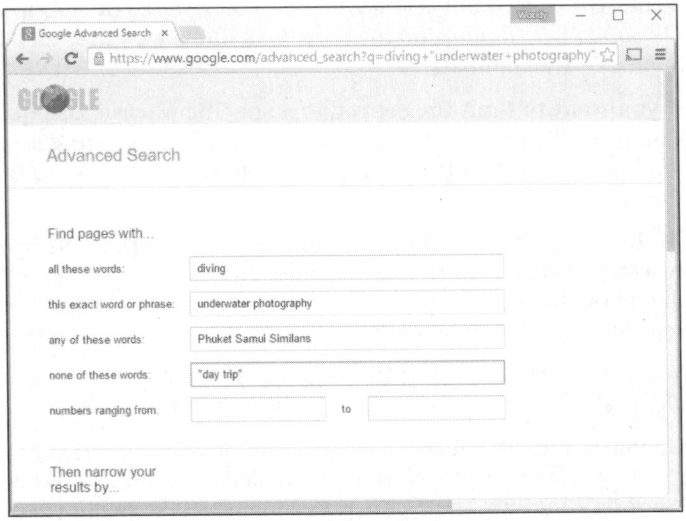

Figure 5-25: Advanced Search lets you narrow your Google search quickly and easily.

Find pages with...	
all these words:	diving
this exact word or phrase:	underwater photography
any of these words:	Phuket Samui Similans
none of these words:	"day trip"
numbers ranging from:	to

Then narrow your results by...

2. **Fill in the top part of the page with your search terms.**

    In Figure 5-26, I ask for sites that include the word *diving* and the exact phrase *underwater photography*. I also want to exclude the phrase *day trip* and return only pages pertaining to Phuket, Samui, or the Similans.

    Anything you can do in the top part of this page can also be done by using the shorthand tricks mentioned in the preceding section. If you find yourself using the top part of the page frequently, save yourself some time and brush up on the tricks (such as typing **OR**, -, "") that I mention in the earlier section, "Finding what you're looking for."

3. **In the bottom part of the Advanced Search page, further refine your search by matching on the identified source language of the page (not always accurate); a specific filename extension (such as `.pdf` or `.doc`); or the domain name, such as `www.dummies.com`.**

You can also click the link at the bottom to limit the search to pages stamped with specific dates (notoriously unreliable), pages with specific licensing allowances (not widely implemented), and ranges of numbers.

4. **Press Enter.**

   The results of your advanced search appear in a standard Google search results window (see Figure 5-26).

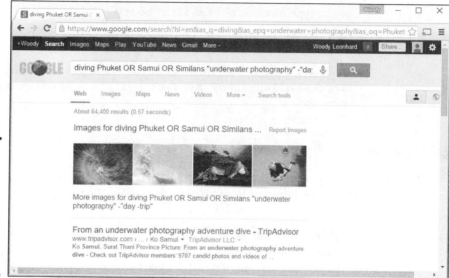

Figure 5-26: Running the stringent search specified in Figure 5-25 turns up 64,400 hits.

**Book III
Chapter 5**

Internet Explorer, Chrome, and Firefox

You can find more details about Google Advanced Search on the Google Advanced Search page, www.google.com/help/refinesearch.html.

Pulling out Google parlor tricks

Google has many tricks up its sleeve, some of which you may find useful — even if it's just to win a bet at a party. For example:

✦ To find the status of your UPS, FedEx, or USPS delivery, just type the package number (digits only) in the Google search box.

✦ The search box is a stock ticker. Type a symbol such as MSFT, GOOG, or AAPL.

✦ To use Google as a calculator, just type the equation in the Google search box. For example, to find the answer to $1,234 \times 5,678$, type `1234*5678` in the search box and press Enter. Or, to find the answer to 3 divided by pi, type `3/pi`. No, Google doesn't solve partial differentials or simultaneous equations — yet. For that, check out Wolfram Alpha.

✦ Google has a built-in units converter. The word `in` triggers the converter. Try `10 meters in feet` or `350 degrees F in centigrade` (or `350 f in c`) or `20 dollars in baht` or (believe me, this is impressive) `1.29 euros per liter in dollars per gallon`.

✦ To find a list of alternative (and frequently interesting) definitions for a word, type `define`, as in `define booty`.

✦ You can see movie reviews and local showtimes by typing `movie` and then the name of the movie, such as `movie star wars 7`.

✦ Try quick questions for quick facts. For example, try `height of mt everest` or `length of mississippi river` or `currency in singapore`.

Referring to Internet Reference Tools

I get questions all the time from people who want to know about specific tools for the Internet. Here are my choices for the tools that everyone needs.

Internet speed test

Everybody, but everybody, needs (or wants) to measure her Internet speed from time to time. The sites I use these days for testing is `www.dslreports.com/speedtest` and `www.testmy.net`.

A million different speed tests are available on the Internet, and 2 million different opinions about various tools' accuracy, reliability, replicability, and other measurements. I used to run speed tests at Speakeasy, but then found that my ISP was caching the data — in fact, caching all the data from OOKLA-based test — so the results I saw were just local; they didn't reflect long-distance speeds. So I moved to DSLReports, with its tests that can't be cached, and haven't looked back.

I later added `www.testmy.net` because the reports appear valid — and the site has automatic testing, so I can run tests every hour for days on end.

DNSStuff

Ever wonder whether the website `BillyJoeBobsPhishery.com` belongs to BillyJoeBob? Head over to `www.dnsstuff.com` (see Figure 5-27) and find out.

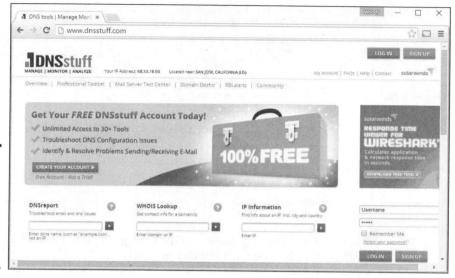

Figure 5-27:
DNSStuff
offers a
wide array
of web- and
Net-related
tools.

You give DNSStuff a domain name, and the site divulges all the public records about the site, commonly known as a whois: who owns the site (or at least who registered it), where the rascals are located, and whom to contact — although you must register a valid email address to get all the info.

DNSStuff also tells you the official "abuse" contact for a particular site (useful if you want to lodge a complaint about junk mail or scams), whether a specific site is listed on one of the major spam databases, and much more.

3d Traceroute

So where's the hang-up? When the Internet slows down, you probably want to know where it's getting bogged down. Not that it will do you much good, but you may be able to complain to your ISP.

My favorite tool for tracing Internet packets is the free product 3d Traceroute from German Holger Lembke in Braunschweig. You can download it at this website: `http://d3tr.de`. 3d Traceroute has no installer — it just runs. I like that.

When you run 3d Traceroute, you feed it a target location — a web address to use as a destination for your packets. As soon as you enter a target, 3d Traceroute runs out to the target and keeps track of all the hops — the discrete jumps from location to location — along the way. It measures the speed of each hop (see Figure 5-28).

**Book III
Chapter 5**

**Internet Explorer,
Chrome, and Firefox**

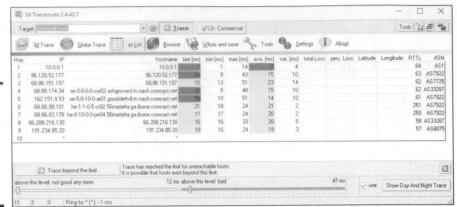

Figure 5-28:
Why is the
Internet so
slow? 3d
Traceroute
pinpoints
pileups.

If you look at the ASN column, on the far-right end in Figure 5-28, you can see a list of AS numbers. Each number uniquely identifies a network operator. You can search for the AS number at www.google.com and see where your packets hit a roadblock.

Down for everyone or just me?

So you try and try and can't get through to Wikipedia, or Hotmail has the hiccups: The browser keeps coming back and says it's timed out, or it just sits there and does nothing.

It's time to haul out the big guns. Hop over to www.downforeveryoneor justme.com (no, I don't make this stuff up), and type the address of the site that isn't responding. The computer on the other end checks to see whether the site you requested is still alive. Cool.

The Wayback Machine

He said, she said. We said, they said. Web pages come and go, but sometimes you just have to see what a page looked like last week or last year. No problem, Sherman: Just set the Wayback Machine for November 29, 1975. (That's the day Bill Gates first used the name Micro Soft.)

If you're a Mr. Peabody look-alike and you want to know what a specific web page really said in the foggy past, head to the Internet Archive at www.archive.org, where the Wayback (or is it WABAC?) Machine has more than 85 billion web pages archived and indexed for your entertainment (see Figure 5-29).

Figure 5-29:
Everything
old is new
again
with the
Archive.org
Wayback
Machine.
This is what
windows.
com looked
like almost
20 years ago
on October
11, 1997.

Chapter 6: Hey, Cortana!

In This Chapter

✓ The Cortana backstory

✓ The deal with Cortana — you're the product

✓ Teach Cortana to call you "Boss"

✓ How to blur Cortana's memory

"**H**ey, Cortana!"

"Yes, Boss."

"Get me a double skinny latte."

"I'll bring it to you. Okay to charge your Amex four dollars and thirty seven cents?"

Cortana isn't quite there yet. That was in my dream last night. In fact, if you try to order a double skinny latte in Windows 10, you get the response in Figure 6-1.

Cortana's good, but she isn't *that* good.

Launched on Windows Phone, Cortana is Microsoft's digital-assistant answer to Apple's Siri and Google's "OK Google."

Cortana, however, is a bit more refined: She (and I'll relentlessly refer to her as "she") is tied into all Windows 10 searches. That's both good and bad, as I discuss later in this chapter.

She's also lots of fun.

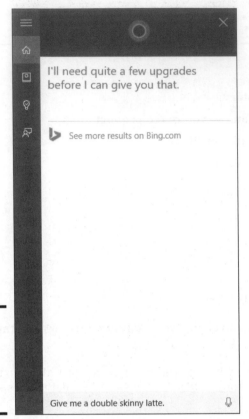

Figure 6-1:
Baristas
don't have
to worry
about their
jobs. Yet.

The Cortana Backstory

There aren't many parts of Windows 10 that have a backstory, so indulge me for a minute here.

Cortana is a fully developed Artificial Intelligence character from the video game series Halo. She lives (or whatever AIs do) 500 years in the future. In the Halo series, she morphs/melds into Master Chief Petty Officer John-117 and, in that position, tries to keep Halo installations from popping up all over the galaxy. Halo installations, of course, destroy all sentient life.

Cortana actually chose John-117, not the other way around. She was supposed to be the resident AI on a ship, temporarily, but plans changed and she ended up the permanent AI, apparently because of the deviousness of a Colonel Ackerson. It's not nice to fool Cortana, so she hacked into Ackerson's system and blackmailed him.

If that sounds a little bit like the kind of life you lead, well, you're ready for Cortana.

If you don't pay for it, you're the product

Cortana, as a flagship product in Windows 10, has lots to like — it's smart and getting smarter by the day, it hooks directly into Windows, it can help in a zillion ways with some real intelligence.

But Cortana, sorry to say, comes at a price. The price is your privacy.

In order to use Cortana in anything but a very stripped-down mode, you have to provide a Microsoft account. And after you've paired Cortana with your Microsoft account, a very big chunk of everything you do on your computer gets logged in Microsoft's database.

Some people don't mind; they figure the benefits of Cortana justify parting with all that personal information. In fact, in a very real sense, Cortana *can't do her job* unless she can see your email, check your calendar, and keep track of what you see and hear and search for. It's a two-way street.

In this chapter, I step you through ways to minimize Cortana's acquisitiveness.

In the end, the choice is yours, but be very much aware of the deal you're making when you invite Cortana into your machine.

Make Cortana Respond to "Hey, Cortana"

The first time you crank up Cortana — generally by clicking in the Ask me anything Search box to the right of the Start icon — she asks you a series of easy questions. Here's how the setup goes:

1. **If you've never used Cortana before, she won't respond to "Hey, Cortana!" in spite of all the demos you've seen. Instead, you need to click in the Ask me anything search box to the right of the Start icon.**

   Cortana responds with the first in a series of setup steps, shown in Figure 6-2.

2. **If you click Not interested at this point, Cortana shrinks back and turns into a simple (and not very smart) Ask me anything Search box. Click I'm in, and you're sent to the next step.**

   Cortana asks if she can look at your location, contacts, voice input, email, text, browser history, search history, calendar "and other info."

3. **Here's where you take the plunge. If you're ready to let Cortana into your life, click Next.**

   You can read the Privacy Statement, if you really want to wade through 147 pages of dense legalese.

   Cortana asks if you want to talk like real pals, so she can respond when you say, "Hey, Cortana!"

Book III
Chapter 6

Hey, Cortana!

Figure 6-2:
Start by
letting
Cortana in
the door.

4. **If you'd like to let a 500-year-in-the-future AI listen to everything you say, attempting to parse the words "Hey, Cortana!" click I agree.**

   At this point, if you haven't signed into a Microsoft account, Windows has you do it.

5. **You're asked to give your permission for speech, inking, and typing personalization to be turned on. Click Yes.**

   Ready with your Microsoft account, Cortana asks what she should call you, as in Figure 6-3.

6. **I'll be first to pay obeisance to our AI overlords, when the time comes, but for now I'll just have her call me Boss. Click Enter.**

   Cortana asks if it's okay for her to listen to you when you say "Hey, Cortana." Of course, that implies Cortana will be listening to everything within earshot of your microphone, all the time.

Figure 6-3:
She can call you whatever you like — but you must address her as "Cortana."

7. **If you don't mind a minus-500-year-old AI listening to everything in your office, click Yes please.**

   With little or no fanfare, Cortana is ready for your entreaties.

8. **Say "Hey, Cortana!" If that doesn't rouse the old biddy, click inside the Ask me anything search box and then ask your question.**

   I tried, "What is the sound of one hand clapping?" All I got was a Bing search.

9. **After the first time or two, Cortana gets the idea that she's supposed to be listening for the sound of your voice.**

10. **Practice asking all sorts of questions. Test a bit. You will probably find that you need to pause after saying "Hey, Cortana."**

    For example, if I say "Hey, Cortana" (pause a second) "How is the weather," I get a response like the one in Figure 6-4.

Figure 6-4:
Cortana's
great at
telling you
the MSN
weather
forecast.

Setting up Cortana

Cortana's still a fledgling. As time goes by, we're assured, she'll get better
and better at bringing up information that interests you, collating things like
your flight schedules, warning about appointments, and on and on.

That said, there's much you can do with and to Cortana right now. If you
open up the Ask me anything Search bar (click in the bar or say "Hey,
Cortana," if she's listening), you get four settings under the hamburger icon.
See the left side of Figure 6-4. Here's what the icons do:

✦ **Home,** which is where you start if you don't ask a question, brings up a
list of cards that are supposed to reflect your interests. At this point, that
usually means local news, as in Figure 6-5.

✦ The next icon, which looks like two sheets of paper with a circle on it,
brings up the **Notebook** (see Figure 6-6), which lets you make choices
and recommendations, to help guide Cortana in her pursuit of personal
assistanceship. Or something like that.

Figure 6-3:
She can
call you
whatever
you like —
but you
must
address
her as
"Cortana."

7. **If you don't mind a minus-500-year-old AI listening to everything in your office, click Yes please.**

    With little or no fanfare, Cortana is ready for your entreaties.

8. **Say "Hey, Cortana!" If that doesn't rouse the old biddy, click inside the Ask me anything search box and then ask your question.**

    I tried, "What is the sound of one hand clapping?" All I got was a Bing search.

9. **After the first time or two, Cortana gets the idea that she's supposed to be listening for the sound of your voice.**

10. **Practice asking all sorts of questions. Test a bit. You will probably find that you need to pause after saying "Hey, Cortana."**

    For example, if I say "Hey, Cortana" (pause a second) "How is the weather," I get a response like the one in Figure 6-4.

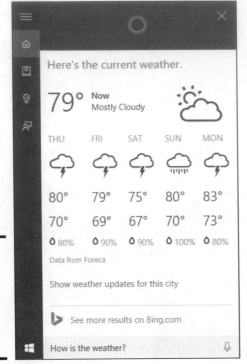

Figure 6-4:
Cortana's
great at
telling you
the MSN
weather
forecast.

Setting up Cortana

Cortana's still a fledgling. As time goes by, we're assured, she'll get better and better at bringing up information that interests you, collating things like your flight schedules, warning about appointments, and on and on.

That said, there's much you can do with and to Cortana right now. If you open up the Ask me anything Search bar (click in the bar or say "Hey, Cortana," if she's listening), you get four settings under the hamburger icon. See the left side of Figure 6-4. Here's what the icons do:

✦ **Home,** which is where you start if you don't ask a question, brings up a list of cards that are supposed to reflect your interests. At this point, that usually means local news, as in Figure 6-5.

✦ The next icon, which looks like two sheets of paper with a circle on it, brings up the **Notebook** (see Figure 6-6), which lets you make choices and recommendations, to help guide Cortana in her pursuit of personal assistanceship. Or something like that.

Figure 6-5:
The Home page has cards of items that interest you. Sorta.

For example, the **About Me** entry at the top of the Notebook list brings up a pane that lets me change my name, or the way Cortana pronounces my name. It also lets me add my favorite places, including Home and Work locations.

Favorites is an odd one because it ties into the Windows Universal Map pp. In Figure 6-7, I add Homer, Alaska, to my list of Favorites and set it as my "Work" location.

If I then crank up the Universal Map app (Start, All Apps, Maps), Homer is listed as my "Work" location, and Maps dutifully gives me full driving directions. For 76 hours and 4,300 miles. Now *that's* a commute.

Follow through the Notebook sections and you can tell Cortana about your food preferences, which stocks you own, what kind of movies you like, your music preferences, weather locations, news, sports and travel preferences, and the color of your favorite vegetable. (Okay, I fibbed a bit.) It's loaded.

The Notebook also contains the Settings for all of Cortana, which I discuss at the end of this chapter.

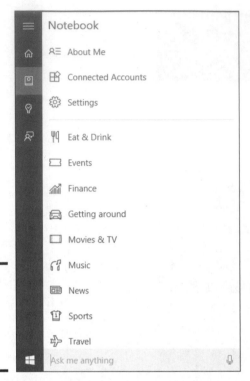

Figure 6-6:
The Notebook contains all sorts of settings.

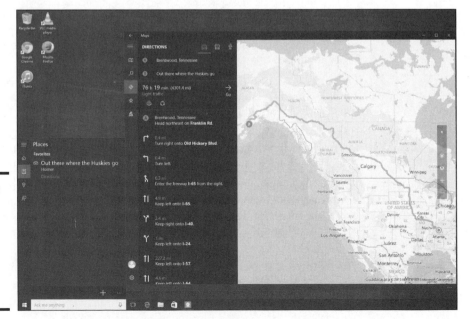

Figure 6-7:
Get to Homer the hard way. Alaska Highway, here I come!

✦ Then comes the lightbulb with the check mark on it, which brings up **Reminders.** You can set a Reminder with Cortana by saying, "Hey, Cortana" (pause) "Set a reminder." You can also set one by tapping the + sign in the lower right. See Figure 6-8.

✦ The **last** icon, which looks like a dummy staring at a projector screen, lets you make suggestions for Cortana.

Figure 6-8:
Reminders
operates
indepen-
dently of
everything
at the
moment.

Using Cortana Settings

The most important part of Cortana comes when you click the gear icon, near the top of the Notebook list (shown in Figure 6-6). Figure 6-9 shows you the kinds of settings you will find.

With the first item on this list, Cortana can give you suggestions, ideas, reminders, alerts, and more — that shouldn't surprise you. But the tiny-print caveat may: Turning off Cortana deletes everything Cortana knows on this device, but won't delete anything from Cortana's Notebook. The "Notebook," in this case is the data Microsoft keeps about you on their computers. Give Microsoft an A for full disclosure, but a D for how deep you have to dig to find it.

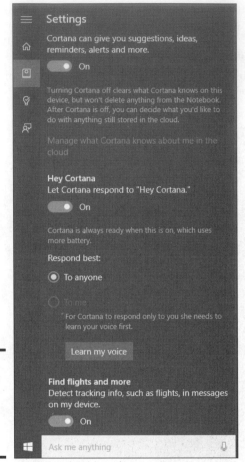

Figure 6-9:
Cortana's
settings
lead to
interesting
places.

If you click the link marked Manage everything Cortana knows about me in the cloud, you get to the Bing personalization page for your Microsoft account — in other words, the place Microsoft uses to store all sorts of nifty things about you. See Figure 6-10.

Spend some time looking through the types of information collected about you, and Clear at will. Unfortunately, you can't see the details. But at least you can delete wide swaths of history, from this web page.

If you scroll to the bottom of the list in Figure 6-9 and click the link marked Other privacy settings, you go to the Settings app's Privacy settings page shown in Figure 6-11.

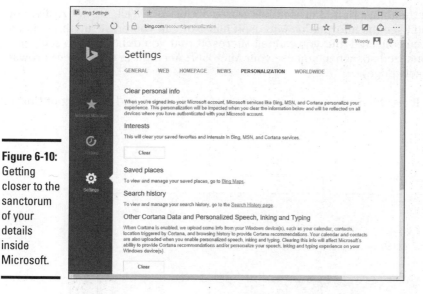

Figure 6-10: Getting closer to the sanctorum of your details inside Microsoft.

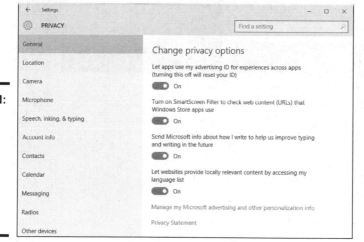

Figure 6-11: You find these privacy settings inside the Universal Settings app.

Check to make sure you're okay with each of those settings, and then — this part is important — click the link near the bottom that says Manage my Microsoft advertising and other personalization info.

That takes you to an entire website — not just a page, but a *site* — called http://choice.microsoft.com, shown in Figure 6-12, where you can see all the things that Microsoft has stored about you. Well, no, not really. You can't see the information Microsoft has. Nor can you erase anything that's been collected. But you can tell Microsoft that you don't want to see personalized ads when you use your Microsoft Account in the current browser (likely Edge).

Tell me the truth. Does that make you feel all warm and fuzzy about Cortana?

Figure 6-12:
You can't erase what Microsoft already has, nor can you use the website to block Microsoft from collecting more data. But you can keep Microsoft from using its accumulated data to dish out ads in your browser.

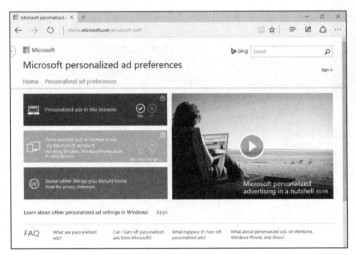

Chapter 7: Maintaining Your System

In This Chapter

✔ Understanding Refresh, Reset, and restore points, and older names

✔ Creating a Password Reset Disk

✔ Maintaining hard drives and SSDs

✔ Scheduling tasks

✔ Zipping and compressing

Windows is a computer program, not a Cracker Jack toy, and it will have problems. The trick lies in making sure that *you* don't have problems too.

Windows is notorious for crashing and freezing, making it impossible to start the computer or garbling things so badly that you'd think the screen went through a garbage disposal. Microsoft has poured lots of time, effort, and money into teaching Windows how to heal itself. You can take advantage of all that work — if you know where to find it.

Book VII is devoted to the topic of how to keep Windows alive and well. In this chapter, I introduce you to the basic ideas and get you started with some of the parts of Windows that you can use in many different ways. If you log on to Windows with a local account (as opposed to a Microsoft account, which is always an email address), I also want to cajole you into creating a Password Reset Disk, which may well save your tail someday.

You're welcome.

What Are the Differences among Restore, Reset, System Repair, Recovery Mode, Refresh, and Restart?

The terminology stinks. Bear with me.

Windows 10 has three very different technologies for pulling you out of a tough spot. I liken them to the WABAC Machine, a brain transplant, and global thermonuclear war.

✦ Like Rocky and Bullwinkle's WABAC Machine (thank you, Mr. Peabody), setting and using *restore points* provides a relatively simple way to switch your PC's internal settings to an earlier, and presumably happier state, should something go awry.

✦ Unlike in earlier versions of Windows, restore points aren't set automatically, and in Windows 10, it's hard to get to the rollback settings. Not to worry. The mechanism is still intact and useful. Details are in this chapter.

Restore points aren't intended to restore earlier versions of files that you work with — that's the function of File History (sometimes called "the Windows version of the Mac's Time Machine"). I talk about File History extensively in Book VIII, Chapter 1.

✦ Sometimes, the problem doesn't lie with the settings. Sometimes, Windows system files get messed up. In those cases, Microsoft has a program called Refresh that scans and fixes all the system files, without changing your settings, removing any installed programs, or blasting your data.

In previous versions of Windows, you may have used a System Repair disk, or booted into Safe Mode and hacked away at a cmd.exe command line, or used Recovery Mode from an installation DVD, or tried a dozen different incantations to bring Windows back from the dead. Having lived through many a late night with them, I can certainly sympathize. Those methods still work, by and large, but Microsoft has made it difficult to get them going and doesn't recommend using them. Nor do I.

In my experience, Windows 10 Refresh works almost all the time. It's light years ahead of System Repair, Safe Mode, and Recovery Mode, and should be your fixit method of second resort, after you try using a restore point. If Refresh doesn't work, you're in a world of hurt. Search online for instructions on manually booting into Safe Mode and running a recovery. Good luck.

✦ If a Refresh doesn't work and you don't mind losing all your data and installed programs, or if you want to wipe your computer clean before you sell it or give it away, the program you want to run is Reset, identified in the dialog box as "Remove everything and reinstall Windows." Global thermonuclear war.

Most of the time, you run a Restore when your computer starts acting flakey. You run a Reset to wipe the whole system when you're going to sell your PC. But either or both — or using restore points — may be offered as options when your computer won't boot right. I go into detail on restore points, Refresh, and Reset in Book VIII, Chapter 2.

What is Safe Mode?

Safe Mode used to be the gateway into the Windows inner workings: In earlier versions of Windows, if something went wrong, you booted into a very limited version of Windows — one that let you diagnose problems and install minimalist drivers, but not much more.

Safe Mode still exists in Windows 10, but it isn't used as much as it once was. Microsoft really has improved things to the point where Safe Mode isn't nearly as important as it used to be. Running a Refresh, in particular, will do just about everything people used to do in Safe Mode but without the hands-on nitty-gritty.

If you still want to get into Safe Mode, click or tap Start, Settings. Choose Update &

security, and then choose Recovery. Under Advanced Startup, choose Restart Now. When the blue Choose an Option screen appears, choose Troubleshoot, Advanced Options, Startup Settings. Click Restart, and you see an Advanced Boot Options screen. Type the number for Safe Mode (or Safe Mode with Networking or Safe Mode with Command Prompt). You get logged in to Windows in Safe Mode using the built-in Administrator account.

Yes, it's that complicated. Microsoft doesn't really want you to use Safe Mode, unless you know what you're doing, and you're willing to bend over backward to do it.

Using a Password Reset Disk

If someone forgets his password, a Password Reset Disk is what saves the day by enabling you to reset a password you otherwise wouldn't be able to access.

If you have a local account (not a Microsoft account) and that account has a password (any kind of password), it doesn't matter if you set the password or somebody else set it up for you. You should take a moment right now to create a Password Reset Disk. If you have multiple Local accounts on one PC (for example, a Regular account and an Administrator account), create a Password Reset Disk for each account. (If you need a refresher on the different types of accounts, flip to Book II, Chapter 4.)

If you have a Microsoft account, the only way to reset the password is online. Go to `https://account.live.com/resetpassword.aspx`, and follow the instructions.

I can't emphasize enough how important a Password Reset Disk is, particularly if there's only one Administrator account on your PC, and it's a local account. I get mail practically every day from people who have forgotten their passwords and can't get in. This one simple trick, which takes all of a couple of minutes, will save you untold grief should you forget that lousy password!

"Password Reset Disk" is a misnomer. The part that saves your bacon is a very simple, small file, called `userkey.psw`, which you can copy and move around just like any other file. If you create more than one Password Reset Disk, which is to say, more than one `userkey.psw` file, make sure you keep track of which file goes with which user ID.

Here's the basic idea: You log on to Windows, using any kind of password — typed, PIN, or picture. Crank up the Forgotten Password Wizard. It asks you for your typed password, which you must provide. The Wizard then creates this file, `userkey.psw`, on a removable drive. You keep that file someplace handy. If the time ever comes that you forget your password (typed, PIN, or picture), put that file on a removable drive, stick the drive in your computer, say the magic words, and click your heels three times. Bingo, you're in!

It doesn't matter if somebody has changed your password without your knowing. The Password Reset Disk resets your password, *no matter what the password may be.* As long as you have a Local account, you're in like Flynn.

Creating a Password Reset Disk

If you have a password-protected Local account, follow these steps to create a Password Reset Disk (that is, a `userkey.psw` file):

1. **Log on to the account.**

   It doesn't matter what kind of password you use.

2. **Make sure you have a USB flash drive handy or another type of removable media, such as an SD card, or even an external hard drive.**

   The wizard won't write anything to a local disk (think about it — d'oh!), and it won't write to a network attached location.

3. **Bring up the old-fashioned Control Panel. (Right-click Start or press Windows key + X, then choose Control Panel.) Click User Accounts, then click User Accounts again..**

   Windows shows you the User Accounts dialog box, shown in Figure 7-1.

4. **On the left, click the link that says Create a Password Reset Disk.**

   If you can't see a line on the left that says Create a Password Reset Disk, either you don't have a Local account (see the first part of this section) or your account doesn't have a password.

   This step launches the Forgotten Password Wizard, which creates a Password Reset Disk. This nifty little program creates a file that you can use to unlock your password and get into your account, even if your precocious seven-year-old daughter changes it to MXYPLFTFFT.

Figure 7-1:
The User
Accounts
dialog box,
with Create
a Password
Reset Disk
on the left.

5. **Follow the Wizard – you will have to type in the current password — and at the final step, click Finish.**

   Store that `userkey.psw` file someplace safe. If you ever forget your password, or if someone else changes it for you, follow the steps in the next section to log on to your account.

Guard that file! Anybody who has that `userkey.psw` file can log on in your stead, even if he doesn't know your password.

Once again: the Password Reset Disk is only for local accounts. It doesn't work for Microsoft accounts.

Using a Password Reset Disk

So you followed the steps in the preceding section and created a Password Reset Disk, which is, in fact, a little file called `userkey.psw`. And the time comes when you forget your password. Here's how to use the file and reset your password:

1. **Copy the file onto some sort of removable drive that your computer can read.**

   It'll probably be a USB flash drive, but it could also be an SD card or even a USB-attached hard drive. Make sure it isn't sitting in a folder somewhere; the file must be in the root directory.

2. **Go through the motions to log on using a typed password.**

   If you're accustomed to logging on with a picture password, click the link marked Sign-in options, and then click the icon that looks like a key and try there.

   I know you don't know the password. Relax. Just type something and press Enter.

**Book III
Chapter 7**

**Maintaining Your
System**

3. **When Windows comes back and tells you that The Password is Incorrect, smile because you have the magic Open Sesame Disk (er, file), and click OK.**

   That brings up the alternative logon screen shown in Figure 7-2.

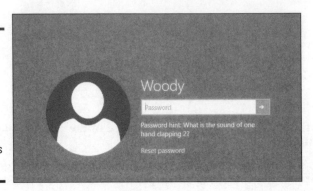

Figure 7-2: If you can't remember your password, type in a bad one. You see this screen.

4. **Click Reset Password.**

   Windows brings up the Welcome to the Password Reset Wizard. Glad you found it, eh?

5. **Make sure your Password Reset Disk — any disk with the `userkey.psw` file on it — is attached to the PC and tap or click Next.**

6. **Follow the steps in the wizard. The last step in the wizard asks you to type in a new password, as in Figure 7-3.**

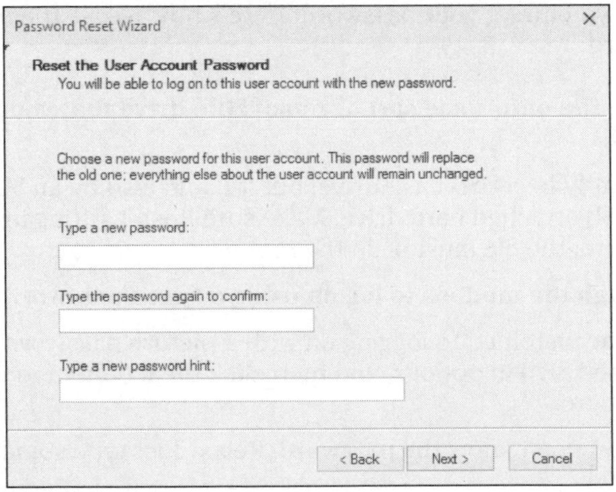

Password Reset Wizard

Reset the User Account Password
You will be able to log on to this user account with the new password.

Choose a new password for this user account. This password will replace the old one; everything else about the user account will remain unchanged.

Type a new password:

Type the password again to confirm:

Type a new password hint:

< Back   Next >   Cancel

Figure 7-3: The wizard forces you to create a new password and hint.

Remember that this is the new password for this account on this computer. It doesn't affect the Password Reset Disk or the `userkey.psw` file at all.

7. **Type a new password and hint. Tap or click Next, and then click Finish. Windows brings you back to the logon screen, where you can log on with the new password.**

Don't lose that `userkey.psw` file, okay?

To reiterate: As long as you have a Local account, the `userkey.psw` file logs you on to the PC, no matter what password is in effect, no matter who changed the password, when or how.

Maintaining Drives

Rotating drives (hard drives, CDs, DVDs, even those ancient floppies if you can still find one, and other types of storage media) seem to cause more computer problems than all other infuriating PC parts combined. Why? They move. And unlike other parts of computers that are designed to move (printer rollers and keyboard springs and mouse balls, for example), they move quickly and with ultrafine precision, day in and day out.

> *"E pur, si muove"*

That's what Galileo said in 1633, after being forced during the Inquisition to recant his beliefs about the earth moving around the sun. "And yet it moves" — and that's the crux of the problem.

As with any other moving mechanical contraption, an ounce of drive prevention is worth ten tons of cure. WD-40 may cure other moving mechanical contraptions, but WD-40 is *not* recommended for PCs. Duct tape and baling wire are another consideration altogether. . .

USB "key" drives and Solid State Drives are a whole different kettle of fish. SSD manufacturers typically offer diagnostic and health maintenance tools to keep their products in top shape, but they contain no moving parts, and thus aren't subject to the vagaries associated with moving drives. I talk about SSDs later in this chapter.

If you're looking for help installing a new hard drive, you're in the wrong place. I talk about adding new drives and getting Windows 10 to recognize them in Book VIII, Chapter 5.

What is formatting?

Drives try to pack lots of data into a small space, and because of that, they need to be calibrated. That's where formatting comes in.

When you format a drive, you calibrate it: You mark it with guideposts that tell the PC where to store data and how to retrieve it. Every hard drive (and floppy disk, for that matter) must be formatted before it can be used. CDs and DVDs must be formatted too, if you use the "Live File System" method for storing files. The manufacturer probably formatted your drive before you got it. That's comforting because every time a drive is reformatted, everything on the drive is tossed out, completely and (almost) irretrievably. Everything.

You can format or reformat any hard drive other than the one that contains Windows by starting File Explorer (click Start, File Explorer) and scrolling down to This PC. Then right-click the hard drive and choose Format. You can also "format" rewritable CDs, DVDs, USB (key) flash drives, and SD or other removable memory cards — delete all the data on them — by following the same approach. To reformat the drive that contains Windows, you must reinstall Windows. See the instructions for a clean Windows install in Book I, Chapter 4.

Introducing hard-drive-maintenance tools

Hard drives die at the worst possible moments. A hard drive that's starting to act flaky can display all sorts of strange symptoms: everything from long, long pauses when you're trying to open a file to completely inexplicable crashes and other errors in Windows itself.

Windows comes with a grab bag of utilities designed to help you keep your hard drives in top shape.

✦ **Storage Spaces:** The best, most comprehensive of the bunch is Storage Spaces (see Book VIII, Chapter 4), which keeps duplicate copies of every file in hot standby, should a hard drive break down. But to use Storage Spaces effectively, you need at least three hard drives and twice as much hard drive space as you have data. Not everyone can afford that. Not everyone wants to dig in to the nitty-gritty.

✦ **Basic utilities:** Three simple utilities stand out as effective ways to care for your hard drives, and one of them runs automatically once a week. You should get to know Check Disk, Disk Cleanup, and Disk Defragmenter because they all come in handy at the right times.

   You must be a designated administrator (see the section on using account types in Book II, Chapter 4) to get these utilities to work.

I explain how to use Check Disk and Disk Defragmenter in the following two sections.

✦ **Task Scheduler:** If you're really short on disk space, you can use the Windows Task Scheduler to periodically remove temporary files that you don't need by scheduling runs of the Disk Cleanup utility. Task Scheduler has other uses, but most Windows users never really need it.

Running an error check

If a drive starts acting weird (for example, you see error messages when trying to open a file, or Windows crashes in unpredictable ways, or a simple file copy takes hours instead of minutes), run the Windows error-checking routines.

If you're an old hand at Windows (or an even older hand at DOS), you probably recognize the following steps as the venerable CHKDSK routine, in somewhat fancier clothing.

Follow these steps to run Check Disk:

1. **Bring up the drive you want to check in File Explorer: Click Start, File Explorer (or click the File Explorer icon on the taskbar). On the left, choose This PC.**

2. **Right-click the drive that's giving you problems, and choose Properties.**

You see the Local Disk Properties dialog box.

3. **On the Tools tab, click the Check button, as shown in Figure 7-4.**

Windows may tell you that you don't need to scan the drive, as Windows hasn't found any errors on the drive. If you're skeptical, though, go right ahead.

4. **Tap or click Scan Drive.**

Windows tells you about any problems it encounters and asks for your permission to fix them.

Defragmenting a drive

Once upon a time, defragmenting your hard drive — instructing Windows to rearrange files on a hard drive so that the various parts of a file all sit next to one another — rated as a Real Big Deal. Windows didn't help automate running defrags, so few people bothered. As a result, drives started to look like patchwork quilts with pieces of files stored higgledy-piggledy. On the rare occasion that a Windows user ran the defragmenter, bringing all the pieces together could take hours — and the resulting system speed-up rarely raised any eyebrows, much less rocketed Windows fans into hyperthreaded bliss.

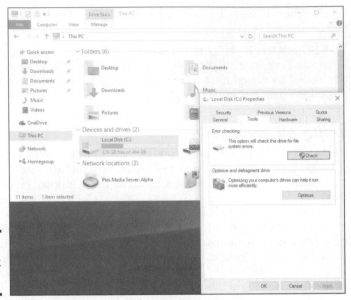

Figure 7-4:
Run a Check
Disk.

Windows 7 changed that by simply and quietly scheduling a disk defragmentation to run every week. Windows 10 continues in that proud tradition. To get defragmented, you don't need to touch a thing.

Windows doesn't run automatic defrags on SSDs, which is to say, flash memory drives that don't have any moving parts. SSDs don't need defragmentation. They also have a finite lifespan, so there's no need to overwork the drives with a senseless exercise in futility.

If you're curious about how your computer's doing in the defrag department, you can see the Defragmenter report this way:

1. **Bring up the Control Panel by tapping and holding (or right-clicking) in the bottom-left corner of the desktop — or typing Ctrl+X — and choosing Control Panel.**

2. **Tap or click the link to System and Security. Then, under Administrative Tools, tap or click the link to Defragment and Optimize Your Drives.**

   Windows shows you the Optimize Drives report, as shown in Figure 7-5.

3. **For a real-time analysis run, showing the fragmentation as of this moment, tap or click Analyze. To move files around into a more optimum ordering, click Optimize.**

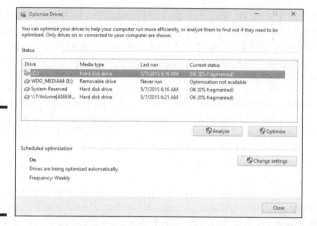

Figure 7-5:
Here's a
full report
of defrag-
menting
activities.

4. **If you want to permanently change the schedule for automatic defrag-ging, click Change Settings. When you're finished, click Close.**

   Defrags run automatically once a week unless you change the settings.

Maintaining Solid State Drives

Solid State Drives (SSDs) are a completely different breed of cat. You don't want to run a Checkdisk on them, even if you can, because the results aren't conclusive and you'd end up overworking the SSDs. You certainly don't want to run a defrag because the drives are (depending on how you look at it) already defragmented and/or horrendously fragmented and there's no reason to change.

Most SSDs these days are made from NAND Flash memory, which is memory that doesn't lose its settings when the power's turned off. Although an SSD may fit into a hard drive slot and behave much like a regular hard drive, the technology's completely different.

While the jury's still out on whether SSDs are *much* more reliable than hard disk drives (HDDs), just about everyone agrees they are more reliable. And there's absolutely no doubt that they're enormously faster. Change your C: drive over from a spinning platter to an SSD and strap on your seat belt, Nelly.

SSDs have controllers that handle everything. Data isn't stored on SSDs the same way it's stored on HDDs, and many purpose-built hard-drive tools don't work at all on SSDs. The controller has to take on all the housekeeping that just comes naturally with HDDs. For example, if you want to erase an

HDD, you can format it or just delete all the files on it. If you want to erase an SSD, you should use the manufacturer's utilities, or data can be left behind. See the *Computerworld* article at `http://www.computerworld.com/article/2506511/solid-state-drives/can-data-stored-on-an-ssd-be-secured-.html`.

Windows disables the Windows utilities known as Defrag, Superfetch, and ReadyBoost on SSDs — you should never see Windows offer to run a Defrag on an SSD, for example — and Windows startup works directly with the hardware during boot. That simultaneously makes the boot go faster and reduces unnecessary wear on the SSD.

If you have an SSD or get an SSD, you should drop by the manufacturer's website and pick up any utilities it may have for the care and feeding of the furious little buggers. Windows actually does a very good job of looking after them, but the manufacturer may have a few tricks up its sleeve. Intel's SSD Toolbox at `www.intel.com/support/go/ssdtoolbox/index.htm` is one of the better-known utility packs, but you should only use it on Intel SSDs.

Zipping and Compressing

Windows supports two very different kinds of file compression. The distinction is confusing but important, so bear with me.

File compression reduces the size of a file by cleverly taking out parts of the contents of the file that aren't needed, storing only the minimum amount of information necessary to reconstitute the file — extract it — into its full original form. A certain amount of overhead is involved because the computer must take the time to squeeze extraneous information out of a file before storing it, and then the computer takes more time to restore the file to its original state when someone needs the file. But compression can reduce file sizes enormously. A compressed file often takes up half its original space — even less, in many cases.

How does compression work? That depends on the compression method you use. In one kind of compression, known as Huffman encoding, letters that occur frequently in a file (say, the letter *e* in a word-processing document) are massaged so that they take up only a little bit of room in the file, whereas letters that occur less frequently (say, *x*) are allowed to occupy lots of space. Rather than allocate eight 1s and 0s for every letter in a document, for example, some letters may take up only two 1s and 0s, and others can take up 15. The net result, overall, is a big reduction in file size. It's complicated, and the mathematics involved get quite interesting.

These are the two Windows file compression techniques:

✦ Files can be compressed and placed in a *Compressed (zipped) Folder*. The icon for a zipped folder, appropriately, has a zipper on it.

✦ Folders or even entire drives can be compressed by using the built-in compression capabilities of the Windows file system (NTFS).

Here's where things get complicated.

NT File System (NTFS) compression is built in to the file system: You can use it only on NTFS drives, and the compression doesn't persist when you move (or copy) the file off the drive. Think of NTFS compression as a capability inherent to the hard drive itself. That isn't really the case — Windows does all the sleight-of-hand behind the scenes — but the concept can help you remember the limitations and quirks of NTFS compression.

Although Microsoft would have you believe that Compressed (zipped) Folder compression is based on folders, it isn't. A Compressed (zipped) Folder is really a file — *not* a folder — but it's a special kind of file, called a zip file. If you ever encountered zip files on the Internet (they have a .zip filename extension and are read and created directly in Windows File Explorer), you know exactly what I'm talking about. Zip files contain one or more compressed files, and they use the most common kind of compression found on the Internet. Think of Compressed (zipped) Folders as being zip files, and if you have even a nodding acquaintance with zips, you'll immediately understand the limitations and quirks of Compressed (zipped) Folders. Microsoft calls them Folders because that's supposed to be easier for users to understand. You be the judge.

If you have Windows show you filename extensions (see my rant about that topic in the section on showing filename extensions in Book III, Chapter 1), you see immediately that Compressed (zipped) Folders are, in fact, simple zip files.

Zipping is very common, particularly because it reduces the amount of data that needs to be transported from here to there. NTFS compression isn't nearly as common. It's more difficult, and hard drives have become so cheap there's rarely any need for most people to use it.

Table 7-1 shows a quick comparison of NTFS compression and zip compression.

If you try to compress the drive that contains Windows itself (normally your C: drive), you can't compress the files that are in use by Windows.

Table 7-1 **NTFS Compression versus Compressed (zipped) Folders Compression**

NTFS	*Zip*
Think of NTFS compression as a feature of the hard drive itself.	Zip technology works on any file, regardless of where it is stored.
The minute you move an NTFS-compressed file off an NTFS drive (by, say, sending a file as an email attachment), the file is uncompressed, automatically, and you can't do anything about it: You'll send a big, uncompressed file.	You can move a Compressed (zipped) Folder (it's a zip file, with a .zip filename extension) anywhere, and it stays compressed. If you send a zip file as an email attachment, it goes over the Internet as a compressed file. The person who receives the file can view it directly in Windows or use a product such as WinZip to see it.
Lots of overhead is associated with NTFS compression. Windows must compress and decompress those files on the fly, and that sucks up processing power.	Very little overhead is associated with zip files. Many programs (for example, antivirus programs) read zip files directly.
NTFS compression is helpful if you're running out of room on an NTFS-formatted drive.	Compressed (zipped) Folders (that is to say, zip files) are in a near-universal form that can be used just about anywhere.
You must be using an Administrator account to use NTFS compression.	You can create, copy, or move zip files just like any other files, with the same security restrictions.
You can use NTFS compression on entire drives, folders, or single files. They cannot be password-protected.	You can zip files, folders, or (rarely) drives, and they can be password-protected.

Compressing with NTFS

To use NTFS compression on an entire drive, follow these steps:

1. **Make sure you're using an Administrator account.**

   See Book II, Chapter 4.

2. **Bring up File Explorer. Click Start, File Explorer (or click the File Explorer icon on the taskbar). On the left, choose This PC.**

3. **On the left, tap and hold (or right-click) the drive you want to compress. Choose Properties, and click the General tab.**

4. **Select the Compress This Drive to Save Disk Space check box, see Figure 7-6. Then click the OK button.**

Windows asks you to confirm that you want to compress the entire drive. Windows takes some time to compress the drive; in some cases, the estimated time is measured in days. Good luck.

Figure 7-6:
Use NTFS compression on an entire drive.

To use NTFS compression on a folder, follow these steps:

1. **Make sure you're using an Administrator account.**

See Book II, Chapter 4.

2. **Bring up File Explorer. Click Start, File Explorer (or click the File Explorer icon on the taskbar). On the left, choose This PC.**

3. **On the left, tap and hold (or right-click) the folder you want to compress. Choose Properties, and click the Advanced button.**

4. **Select the Compress Contents to Save Disk Space check box. Then click the OK button.**

Windows asks you to confirm that you want to compress the folder. Unless the folder is enormous, it should compress in a few minutes.

To uncompress a folder, reopen the Advanced Properties dialog box (right-click the file or folder, choose Properties, and click the Advanced button) and deselect the Compress Contents to Save Disk Space check box.

Zipping the easy way with Compressed (zipped) Folders

The easiest way to create a zip file, er, a Compressed (zipped) Folder, is with a simple tap and hold (or right-click). Here's how:

1. **Navigate to the files you want to zip.**

   Usually you find them using File Explorer, although there are other ways. For File Explorer, click Start, File Explorer (or click the File Explorer icon on the taskbar). On the left, choose This PC.

2. **Select the file or files that you want to zip together.**

   You can tap and hold, or Ctrl+click to select individual files or Shift+click to select a bunch.

3. **Tap and hold (or right-click) any of the selected files, and choose Send to, Compressed (zipped) Folder.**

   See Figure 7-7.

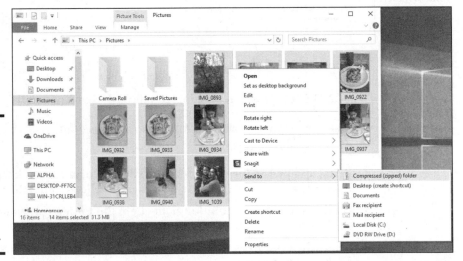

Figure 7-7: Select the files that you want to put in a zip file, right-click, and Send to Zip.

Windows responds by creating a new zip file with a `.zip` filename extension and placing copies of the selected files inside the new zip folder. File Explorer selects the file and shows a context tab for Compressed Folder Tools. Double-click the new file (er, folder) and you see something like Figure 7-8.

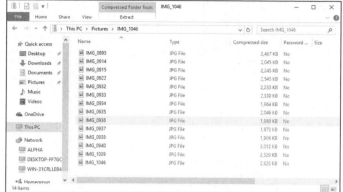

Figure 7-8:
Click a zip,
and you get
a context
tab for
Compressed
Folder
Tools.

The new zip file is just like any other file: You can rename it, copy it, move it, delete it, send it as an email attachment, save it on the Internet, or do anything else to it that you can do to a file. That's because it *is* a file.

4. **To add another file to your Compressed (zipped) Folder, simply drag it onto the zipped folder icon.**

5. **To copy a file from your zip file (uh, folder), double-click the zipped folder icon and treat the file the same way you would treat any "regular" file.**

6. **To copy all files out of your zip file (folder), click the Extract tab on the File Explorer Ribbon.**

   From there, you can choose the location or click the Extract All icon to choose a location other than the ones offered.

By default, the Extract All icon recommends that you extract all the compressed files into a new folder with the same name as the zip file, which confuses the living bewilickers out of everybody. Unless you give the extracted folder a different name from the original Compressed (zipped) Folder, you end up with two folders with precisely the same name sitting on your desktop. Do yourself a huge favor and feed the wizard a different folder name while you're extracting the files.

Book IV

Using the Built-In Universal Apps

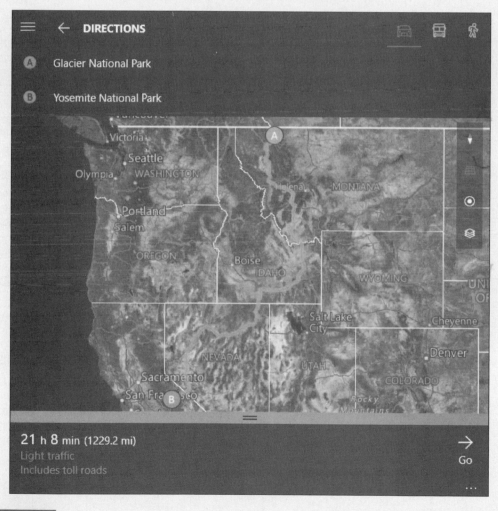

Does the Windows 10 Music app leave you cold? Check out http://www.dummies.com/extras/windows10aio/moremusic for my favorite alternatives.

Contents at a Glance

Chapter 1: Using the Mail and Calendar Apps

In This Chapter

✔ **How the new Win10 productivity apps hang together**

✔ **How we got into this brave new world**

✔ **Choosing Mail and Calendar apps**

✔ **Navigating Win10's tiled Universal Mail**

✔ **Avoiding duplicates and other Win10 Universal Calendar problems**

The whole "productivity" app situation — Mail, Calendar, and People — has gone through enormous change since the days of Windows 7. In the, ahem, good old days, Mail, Calendar, and People were basically just one app — very similar to the current situation in Office, where Outlook covers all the bases. That single app, confusingly, was called Windows Live Mail, even though it handled mail and contacts and calendar. It worked reasonably well, but it was old and clunky, and didn't have many features.

In Windows 8, Microsoft turned out three separate Metro tiled apps: Mail, Calendar, and People. In fact, all three were connected together, but they each had their own Metro tiles, and each worked more or less independently. Not to put too fine a point on it, but the Windows 8 Metro productivity apps were horrible (as you read in my *Windows 8* and *8.1 All-In-One For Dummies* books). Microsoft promised it would make them better. They didn't.

When Windows 8 hit, the Metro productivity apps were already second rate. By the time Windows 8.1 faded into the sunset, they were all, at best, third rate, eclipsed by Gmail (see Book X, Chapter 3) and various iThings. Even Microsoft itself had run rings around the apps it shipped in Win 8.1, with Hotmail, then renamed to Outlook.com. (I talk about Outlook.com in Book X, Chapter 4.)

In Windows 10, Microsoft threw away the Windows 8 Metro apps. Nobody regrets that less than I do. What has emerged are two apps — one for Mail and Calendar, the other for People — that work the same way, more or less, on Windows 10 PCs, laptops, tablets, smaller tablets, and even Windows 10 phones.

The new Windows Universal Mail and Calendar apps are basically two apps, with two tiles, that hook into the same accounts. I talk about the Universal Windows Mail and Calendar app (yes, they're one app, even though there are two tiles on the Start menu) in this chapter. In the next chapter, I step gingerly through the Universal Windows People app.

Choosing a Mail/Calendar App

The Universal Windows Mail app looks like Figure 1-1.

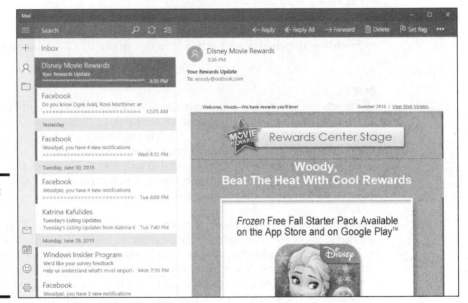

Figure 1-1:
Here's a
preview
of the
Universal
Windows
Mail app.

Your Mail may not quite look the same — the column on the left may be expanded, the preview pane on the right may not exist. There are lots of differences between Tablet Mode and regular mode, on wide and narrow screens, and whether your screen is in portrait or landscape.

Is Windows 10's Mail app the right one for you? Good question. Life is full of difficult choices, and I swear Microsoft sits behind about half of them. For me, anyway.

Before you jump into the productivity wallow, think about how you want to handle your mail and calendar.

Comparing email programs

Universal Mail has its benefits, but it may not best suit your needs.

Complicating the situation: Universal Mail isn't an either/or choice. For example, you can set up Hotmail/Outlook.com (see Figure 1-2) or Gmail accounts (see Figure 1-3), and then use either Universal Mail to work with the accounts or the Internet-based interfaces at www.hotmail.com and www.gmail.com. In fact, you can jump back and forth between working online at the sites and working on your Windows computer.

Google has a new email program, called Inbox, that I've been testing for some time. I really like it.

Windows 10's Universal Mail functions as a gathering point: It pulls in mail from Hotmail/Outlook.com, for example, and sends out mail through Hotmail/Outlook.com. It pulls in and sends out mail through Gmail. But when it's working right, Universal Mail doesn't destroy the mail: All your messages are still sitting there waiting for you in Hotmail/Outlook.com or Gmail. Although there are some subtleties, in most cases, you can use Mail in the morning, switch over to Gmail or Hotmail/Outlook.com when you get to the office, and go back to the tiled Universal Mail app when you get home — and never miss a thing.

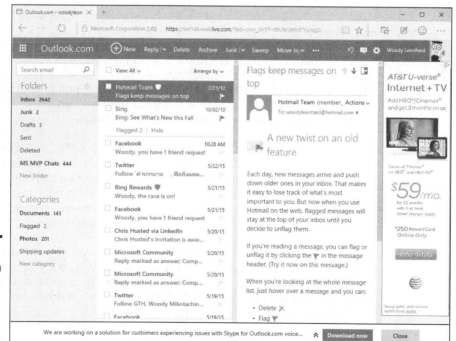

Figure 1-2: Outlook.com (formerly Hotmail) — note the ad on the right.

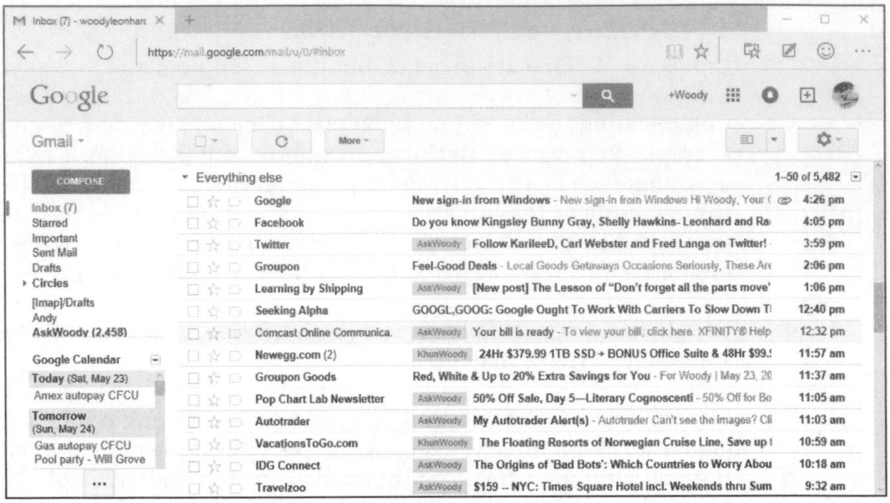

Figure 1-3:
I use Gmail
as my email
program.

As currently configured, Universal Mail can pull in mail from Hotmail/ Outlook.com, Gmail, or Exchange Server (a typical situation at a large office or if you use one of the Office 365 business editions), Yahoo! Mail, and AOL Mail, as well as IMAP and POP3 (methods supported by most Internet service providers).

That's the short story. Permit me to throw some complicating factors at you.

You can add your Hotmail/Outlook.com account to Gmail, or add your Gmail account to Hotmail/Outlook.com. In fact, you can add just about any email account to either Hotmail/Outlook.com or Gmail. If you're thinking about moving to Universal Mail just because it can pull in mail from multiple accounts, realize that Gmail (see Book X, Chapter 3) and Hotmail/Outlook. com (see Book X, Chapter 4) can do the same thing.

The main benefit to using Universal Mail rather than Hotmail/Outlook.com or Gmail is that the tiled Windows Universal Mail app stores some of your most recent messages on your computer. (Gmail running on the Google Chrome browser can do the same thing, but you have to set it up.) If you can't get to the Internet, you can't download new messages or send responses, but at least Universal Mail can look at your most recent messages.

Some people prefer the Universal Mail interface over Gmail or Hotmail/ Outlook.com. Personally, I prefer Gmail's new Inbox, but you must decide for yourself. *De gustibus* and all that. Moreover, the interfaces change all the time, so if you haven't looked in the last year or so, it'd be worth the effort to fire up your web browser and have a look-see.

Hotmail/Outlook.com and Gmail are superior to Universal Mail in these respects:

✦ Hotmail/Outlook.com and Gmail have all your mail, all the time — or at least the mail that you archive. If you look for something old, you may or may not find it with Universal Mail — by default, Universal Mail only holds your mail from the past two weeks, and it doesn't automatically reach out to Hotmail/Outlook.com or Gmail to run searches.

✦ Gmail and Hotmail/Outlook.com pack much more information on the screen. Although Mail has been tuned for touch, with big blocks set aside to make an all-thumbs approach feasible and lots of white space, Hotmail/Outlook.com and Gmail are much, much more mouse-friendly.

But wait! I've only looked at Universal Mail, Hotmail/Outlook.com, and Gmail. Many, many more options exist in the mail game, to wit:

✦ **Microsoft Outlook:** Bundled with Office since pterodactyls powered PCs, Outlook (see Figure 1-4) has an enormous number of options — many of them confusing, most of them never used — but it's also the only app that can handle hundreds of thousands of messages. Or at least, that's what I keep telling myself. Outlook's the Rolls Royce of the email biz, with all the positive and negative connotations.

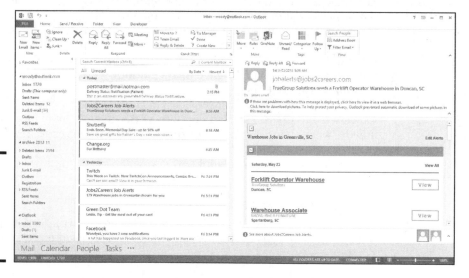

Figure 1-4: Here's Outlook 2013, the way I used to see it.

Among the many, many different versions of Outlook, each has its own foibles. I know people who are still stuck on Office 2007 because it was the last version without the Office Ribbon.

✦ **The Outlook Web App:** It isn't really Outlook, but Microsoft marketing wants you to believe that it is. It's part of Exchange Server (or some versions of Office 365), so companies with big iron can let their employees access their mail without using Outlook.

✦ **Windows Live Mail:** It's still alive and kicking, although it's getting older by the minute. For people who don't want to jump into the tiled side of Windows 10 with both feet (and fingers) — particularly those who feel more comfortable working with a mouse and an information-dense screen — it's a respectable, free alternative, and it works great with Windows 10. See `http://windows.microsoft.com/en-us/windows-live/essentials`.

✦ **Free, open-source, inexpensive alternatives:** These include Mozilla Thunderbird, SeaMonkey, Eudora, and many more that have enthusiastic fan bases.

✦ **Your Internet service provider (ISP):** It may well have its own email package. My experience with ISP-provided free email hasn't been very positive, but the service generally doesn't hold a candle to Gmail (my favorite), Outlook.com/Hotmail, Yahoo! Mail, or any of the dozens of competitive email providers. If you use ISP-based email, mail2web (`www.mail2web.com`) lets you get into just about any mailbox from just about anywhere — if you know the password.

The iPad Mail app has many of the problems that Universal Mail exhibits, but it has a host of advantages, including most notably the ability to easily merge inboxes so you don't have to flip between accounts to read all your incoming messages. Truth be told, I use the iPad Mail app when I'm on the road and don't expect anything important to arrive by email. Most of the time, though, I use Gmail. I gave up on Outlook a couple of years ago, and haven't regretted it once.

As we went to press, I started dabbling with the new Gmail Inbox app. Boy howdy, what an interface. Slicker than any mail deserves to be.

. . . and that's just the Mail app!

Comparing calendar apps

Calendars can also be handled by a bewildering array of packages and sites. Among the hundreds of competing Calendar apps, each has a unique twist. The highlights:

✦ **Google Calendar** (see Figure 1-5) is highly regarded for being powerful and easy to use. It's also reasonably well integrated into the other Google Apps, er, Google Drive, although you can use it — and share calendars with other people — without setting foot in any other Google app. Put all your appointments in Google Calendar (`http://calendar.google.com`), and you have instant access to your latest calendar from any computer, tablet, or phone that can get to the Internet. See Book X, Chapter 3 for details.

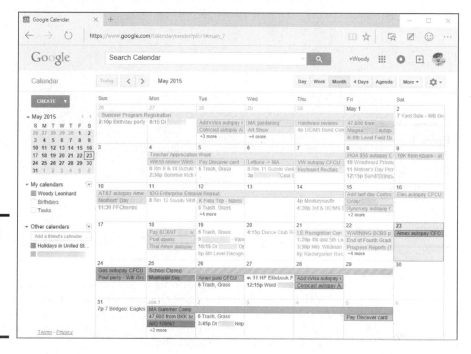

Figure 1-5: I use this Google calendar on many different devices.

✦ **Hotmail/Outlook.com Calendar,** on the other hand, lives inside Hotmail/Outlook.com. It's reasonably powerful and integrated, and you can share the calendar with your contacts or other people.

✦ **Outlook** also does calendars, ten ways from Tuesday (see Figure 1-6), with so many options that it'll bring a tear to your eye. Or maybe that tear is from tearing out your hair.

If you want to schedule one conference room in an office with a hundred people, all of whom use Outlook, the Outlook Calendar is definitely the way to go. If you want to keep track of your flight departure times, Aunt Martha's birthday, and the kids' football games, any of the Calendar apps will work fine.

**Book IV
Chapter 1**

Using the Mail and Calendar Apps

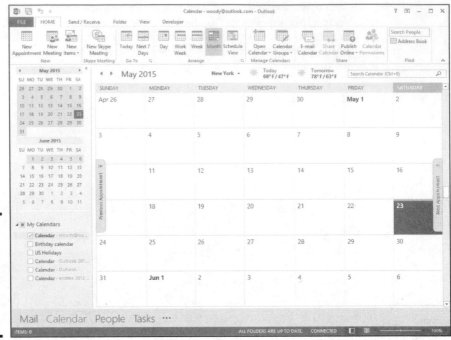

Figure 1-6:
The Outlook 2013 Calendar has lots and lots of options.

I'm very happy to say that the Windows 10 Universal Calendar app syncs very well with Google Calendar. I use Google Calendar everywhere — Android phone, Android tablet, iPhone, iPad, on the road, in the shower — and with Windows 10, I can finally use Google Calendar on my PCs and laptops. If I had a Windows 10 phone, it'd even work there.

Choosing the right package

So how do you choose a Mail/Calendar program? Tough question, but let me give you a few hints:

✦ The Win10 productivity apps — Universal Mail and Calendar — work well enough if your demands aren't great.

But if you have an iPad, consider using the built-in Mail and Calendar apps, or any of a dozen other Apple Apps instead. If you're an Android user, the Google apps work just great.

✦ Online services — specifically Hotmail/Outlook.com and Gmail — have many more usable features than either Win10 Universal Mail or iPad Mail. As long as you can rely on your Internet connection, look at both of them before settling on a specific Mail/Contacts/Calendar program.

Gmail and Hotmail/Outlook.com make it easy to use their programs to read "ordinary" email. I can set up my email account, woody@askwoody.com, to work through Gmail, for example, so mail sent to that email address ends up in Gmail, and if I respond to the message, it appears as if it's coming from woody@askwoody.com, not from Gmail.

A good compromise is to use either Gmail or Hotmail/Outlook.com most of the time but hook up either iPad Mail, the Gmail app, or Win10 Universal Mail (or all three!) to the Gmail or Hotmail/Outlook.com account, so you can grab your iPad when you're headed out the door.

✦ If you don't feel comfortable storing your mail in the cloud, or you don't want to go through the hassle of converting your email account, try Windows Live Mail, part of Windows Essentials (see http://windows.microsoft.com/en-us/windows-live/essentials). That's only as a last resort, though, for the Luddites in the crowd. The new stuff is so much better.

✦ Ancient dinosaurs will probably keep using Outlook until its bits rot away. It's ponderous and painful, the embodiment of 19th-century dentist's office chic. But it works. (I can't tell you how happy I am that I finally moved over to Gmail!)

Drilling Down on Windows 10 Universal Mail

The first time you tap or click the Start menu's Mail tile, you're given the chance to Add an Account. If you signed in to Windows with a Microsoft account, you just click a couple of times and end up at the Universal Mail screen, which I show at the beginning of this chapter in Figure 1-1.

If you signed in to Windows with a local account — one that isn't known to Microsoft (see Book II, Chapter 5) — or if you say that you want to add an additional email account (click or tap on the first screen, where it says Add an account), the Mail app presents you with the choices shown in Figure 1-7.

Table 1-1 explains the option you should choose, depending on what kind of email provider you have.

If you signed into Windows with a local account (probably because you don't want Microsoft tracking everything you do — see Book II, Chapter 4), you will be asked if you want to change that local account into a Microsoft account, per Figure 1-8.

Watch out! If you type your password a second time, Windows takes that as permission to switch your local account over to a Microsoft account. Just click I'll connect my Microsoft account later. There's nothing to see here, Obe-Wan.

**Book IV
Chapter 1**

Using the Mail and Calendar Apps

Figure 1-7:
The Universal Mail app works with just about any kind of email account.

Table 1.1	New Mail Account Types
Use This Type	*For This Email Service*
Exchange	If you get your mail through a company mail server, or if you use Office 365 to handle your mail.
Outlook.com	If you get mail through Microsoft's servers, your email address looks like something@outlook.com, @live.com, @hotmail.com, or @msn.com.
Google	If you have a Google account, most commonly an email address that looks like something@gmail.com, but also if you use Google's servers for email, as you can with Google Apps for Business, or if you've just registered your email address with Google and want to retrieve your mail through Google.
iCloud	For those from the Apple side of the street, if you have an @icloud.com or an @me.com or @mac.com address.
Other	For any other kind of email address. When you type in your email address, Microsoft looks for a bunch of associated information (such as the POP or IMAP server name) in its ginormous database and can almost always set you up with a click or two.
Advanced setup	Only use if you have an Exchange ActiveSync account, or if Other fails to find your address — which is rare.

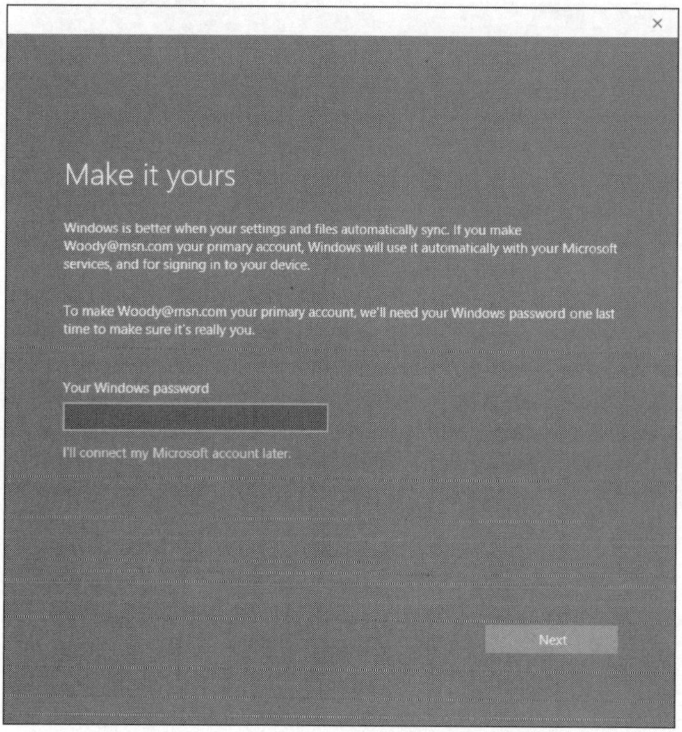

Figure 1-8:
Unless you want to change your Windows login to a Microsoft account, tell Windows to take a hike.

By hook or by crook, you end up at the Mail main page, which looks like Figure 1-9. The Universal Mail app pulls in two weeks' worth of messages and shows them to you. (Details of the display vary depending on many things, including the width of the screen and whether you're in Tablet Mode.)

Mail's standard layout takes three columns:

✦ The left column holds a bunch of icons, which can be hard to decipher. The hamburger icon at the top lets you change your mailbox (see Figure 1-10). The plus icon starts a new message. The shadow guy icon — looks like the top two-thirds of an 8-ball — lets you switch among accounts, if you have multiple email accounts. The file folder icon duplicates the hamburger icon. The envelope icon doesn't do anything. Click or tap the calendar icon, and Windows launches the Universal Calendar app. The gear-shaped Settings icon brings up a Settings pane, which I discuss in the next section, Universal Mail Settings.

✦ The middle column lists all the messages in the selected folder. If you don't manually select a folder — by using the Folders icon and clicking to pin the specific folder — Mail selects the Inbox for you.

✦ The right column shows you the selected message.

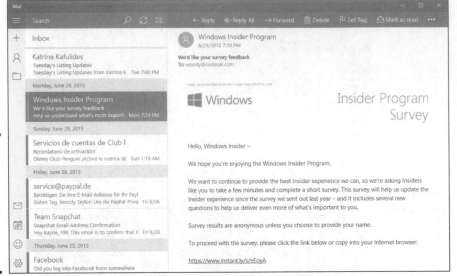

Figure 1-9:
Two weeks'
worth of
messages,
and it's
almost
entirely
spam. Sigh.

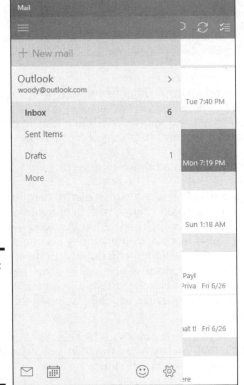

Figure 1-10:
The
hamburger
icon
expands
to let you
choose a
mailbox.

Creating a new message

When you reply to a message, Mail sets up a typical reply (or a reply to all) in a three-column screen, as shown in Figure 1-11. Similarly, if you tap or click the + icon in the upper left, Mail starts a new, blank message. Whether you reply or start a new message, your message is all set up and ready to go — just start typing.

Figure 1-11: When you reply to a message or compose a new message, Mail gives you these options.

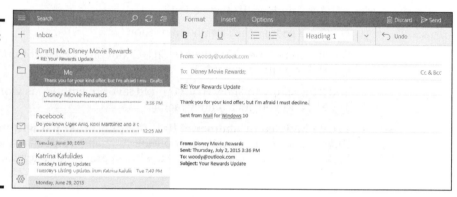

Here's a quick tour of the features available to you as you create your email message:

✦ **Format the text:** The new text you type appears in Calibri 11-point type, which is a good all-around middle-of-the-road choice. Don't get me started on Comic Sans. If you want to format the text, just select the text and click the down-arrow next to the Underscore icon; you see the formatting options in Figure 1-12.

Figure 1-12: Select the text and apply formatting in the usual way.

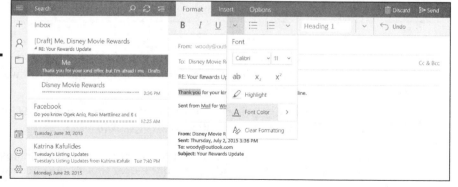

Book IV Chapter 1

Using the Mail and Calendar Apps

Those who have a keyboard and know how to use it will be pleased to know that many of the old, formatting keyboard shortcuts still work. Here are the most commonly used shortcuts for formatting:

- *Ctrl+B* toggles bold on and off.

- *Ctrl+I* toggles italic on and off.

- *Ctrl+U* toggles underline on and off.

- *Ctrl+Z* undoes the last action.

- *Ctrl+Y* redoes the last undone action.

(In addition to the old stalwarts Ctrl+C for copy, Ctrl+X for cut, and Ctrl+V for paste, of course.)

You'll be happy to know that your old favorite emoticons work, too. Type :-) and you get a smiley face.

✦ **Create bulleted or numbered lists, or apply other paragraph formatting:** Select the paragraph(s) you want to change, and click the icon that looks like a bunch of indented text with a paragraph (backward P) mark. See Figure 1-13.

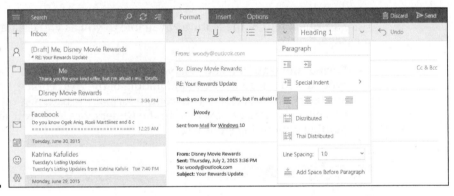

Figure 1-13:
To create a bulleted list, type the paragraphs, select them, and apply Bullets.

✦ **Add an attachment:** At the top, click or tap Insert, then Attach File. You end up in File Explorer, where you can choose the file you want to attach and (confusingly) click Open.

✦ **Add a message priority indicator:** At the top, choose the Options tab and set the message to either High or Low priority.

Tap or click the Send icon in the upper-right corner, and the message is queued in the Outbox, ready to send the next time Mail syncs for new message.

If at any time you don't want to continue, tap or click the Discard trash can button in the upper right. To save a draft, you don't need to do anything: Windows 10 Universal Mail automatically saves everything, all the time.

Searching for email in Universal Mail

Searching for mail is relatively easy, if you remember two very important details:

✦ **If you have multiple accounts, navigate to the account that you want to search before you actually perform the search.** If you search while you're looking at the askwoody.com Inbox, for example, you won't find anything in your hotmail.com account.

✦ **Don't use Cortana.** She isn't yet up to the challenge.

To search for email messages:

1. **If you have more than one email account, move to the account you want to search.** Easiest way to do that is to click the folder icon on the left, and choose whichever account you like.

2. **At the top, above the second column, tap or click the magnifying glass.**

3. **Type your search term, and press Enter or tap the magnifying glass icon again.**

Mail may or may not search all your mail — Microsoft hasn't released details on exactly which messages are searched, but the search appears to be limited to the number of messages shown on the screen — two weeks' worth. To find older messages in your search, click the link under the results that says Search online. That triggers Universal Mail to look online and bring back details on any messages that match the search terms.

Universal Mail Settings

The Windows 10 Universal Mail app has several worthwhile settings. On the left, at the bottom, tap or click the gear icon. If the window's wide enough, Settings appear on the right, as in Figure 1-14. (If it isn't wide enough, they'll tromp all over the left side.)

Here's what you can do.

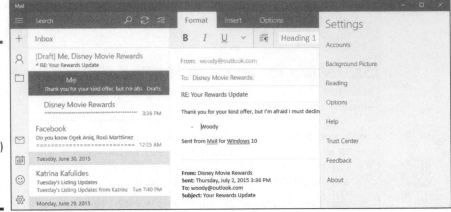

Figure 1-14: Not sure why, but you add new email addresses ("Accounts") from the Settings menu.

Adding a new email account

The Universal Mail app has built-in smarts for you to connect to any Hotmail/ Outlook.com, Gmail, Exchange Server (including Office 365 business edition), AOL, Yahoo!, or IMAP or POP accounts. You can add any number of different types of those accounts — two different Gmail accounts and a few Hotmails — no problem.

To add a new account:

1. **From the Universal Mail app, click or tap the gear icon at the bottom of the left side.**

   You see the Settings menu shown in Figure 1-14.

2. **Tap or click Accounts, and then tap or click Add Account.**

   The Add an Account list appears, as shown earlier in this chapter in Figure 1-7.

3. **Refer to Table 1-1 earlier in this chapter, and then tap or click the account type that you want to add.**

   You see the Add Your Microsoft account dialog box shown in Figure 1-15.

4. **Enter your email ID and password, and any ancillary information that may be required. Tap or click Sign In.**

   Universal Mail is probably smart enough to look up or find any other information it needs, but you may have to provide something from your email provider.

Figure 1-15:
Enter your
email
account
particulars.

5. **If Mail presents you with an option to "Make it Yours" (refer to Figure 1-8), don't enter anything. Just click or tap Next.**

   When Universal Mail comes back, your new account appears under the hamburger icon on the left.

   If you want to change the details about your account — in particular, if you don't particularly want to see the name Hotmail, Outlook, or Gmail as an account name — click or tap the Settings gear icon, click or tap Accounts, and then tap or click the account you want to change. The Account Details pane appears, as shown in Figure 1-16. In the top box, you can type a name that will appear in the first column of the Mail main page. If you also want to change the number of days' worth of email downloaded (the default is 7 days), or change the sync frequency, click the link marked Change Mailbox Sync Settings.

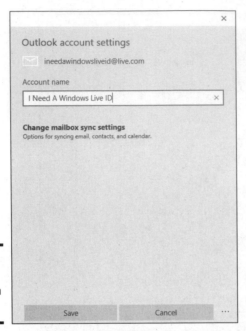

Figure 1-16:
Change the
details of an
account.

Setting Extra Options

There are several additional worthwhile options in the Settings pane. If you tap or click the gear icon in the lower-left corner, and on the right choose Options, you can do these things:

✦ Change the picture that appears in the far-right pane when no mail has been selected.

✦ Set the response to a swipe from the left or right (set flag, delete, and so on).

✦ Have Mail automatically open the next item when you're finished with the current message.

✦ Control how Mail marks messages as "read."

✦ Set an email signature, which is placed at the end of all new messages.

✦ Show notifications or play a sound when new mail arrives. Yes, "You've got mail" will work.

Avoiding Universal Calendar App Collisions

The Windows 10 Universal Calendar is relatively straightforward, but the first time you bring up the Calendar app, you may think you're seeing double. Or triple. In Figure 1-17, you can see what I mean.

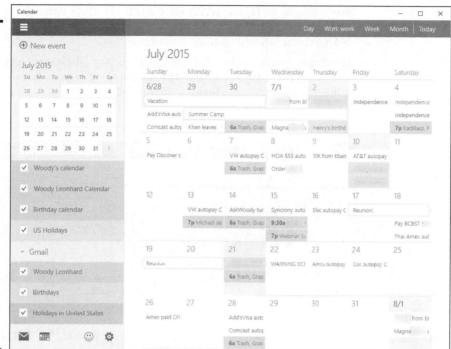

Figure 1-17:
The first time in Win10 Calendar may make your head spin. Note the three different entries for Independence Day, on July 3 (the business holiday) and 4 (from two different Holiday calendars).

Don't panic.

The reason for the duplication? Assuming you have added two or more accounts into Universal Mail, or Universal Calendar, or one or more of the accounts has duplicated entries, the calendars associated with those accounts came along for the ride, and any appointment that appears in both calendars shows up as two stripes on the consolidated calendar.

Fortunately, it's easy to see what's going on and to get rid of the duplicates. Or at least some of the duplicates. Maybe. Here's how to reorganize your Calendar:

1. **From the Start menu, tap or click the Calendar tile to start the Universal Calendar app.**

    If this is the first time you've looked at the Calendar app, it may look like the one in Figure 1-17.

2. **Looking at the color-coded index on the left at the bottom, see whether two or more of your calendars have a source that overlaps. If so, turn off one of the interfering calendars.**

For example, in Figure 1-17, I have a U.S. Holidays calendar (you can't see it, but that's from my Outlook account), and Holidays in the United States calendar, which came from Gmail.

By simply turning off one of the U.S. Holidays calendars, and unchecking the Gmail Birthdays calendar, the main calendar goes back to looking somewhat normal, as shown in Figure 1-18.

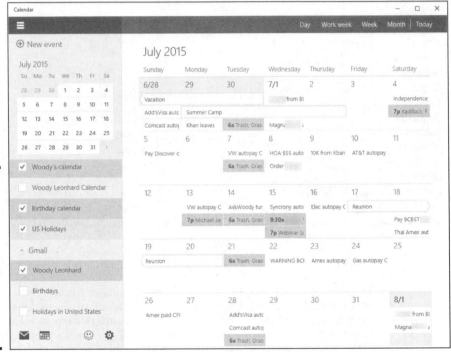

Figure 1-18:
Getting
rid of the
second U.S.
Holidays
calendar
and an extra
Birthdays
calendar
cuts down
the clutter.

3. **Go through the calendars, one by one, and set the color coding for each calendar component to something your eyes can tolerate.**

4. **When you're finished, simply tap or click outside the Options pane.**

On the top, you can choose the detail of the calendar you want to see:

✦ **Day** brings up an hourly calendar, for two or more days (depending on the number of pixels across your screen).

✦ **Work Week** lists Monday through Friday of the current week only.

✦ **Week** shows Sunday through Saturday.

✦ **Month** brings up one month at a time.

In call cases, there are up and down arrows at the top of the screen to move one unit (day, week, month) earlier or later.

Click the hamburger icon to get rid of the left column, and let the calendar take up the entire Calendar window.

Adding Calendar Items

To add a new appointment, or other calendar item, tap or click the New event + icon in the upper-left corner. Calendar shows you the Details pane, as shown in Figure 1-19.

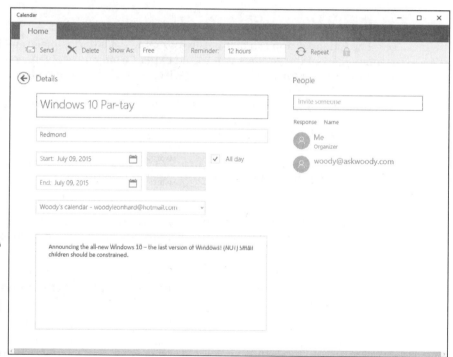

Figure 1-19: Create a new appointment or calendar entry.

Book IV Chapter 1

Using the Mail and Calendar Apps

Most of the entries are self-explanatory, except these:

+ **You must choose a calendar — actually, an email account — that will be synchronized with this appointment.** As soon as you enter the appointment, Calendar logs on to the indicated account and adds the appointment to the account's calendar.

> ✦ **You may optionally specify email addresses in the Who box.** If you put valid email address(es) in the Who box, Calendar automatically generates an email message and sends it to the recipient, asking the recipient to confirm the appointment.

When you finish the appointment, in the upper-left corner, tap or click Save or Send, depending on whether you're setting the appointment or sending invitations.

If you click the icon with two arrows chasing each other in a circle – the Repeat icon – Universal Calendar lets you choose How Often and when to end the repetition.

Struggling with Calendar shortcomings

The Calendar app is a just-barely-passable calendaring program. It doesn't have any of the goodies you would expect from more advanced calendaring apps, except for toaster-style slide-from-the-right notifications.

On the plus side, you can have Calendar notifications placed on your lock screen. The notifications list individual appointments for the current day. See Book II, Chapter 2 for details.

If you want to look at better calendars (which work from a browser, but not as an independent Universal app) check out these:

✦ Google Calendar — `www.calendar.google.com` — is free as a breeze. That's the one I use. When I'm on a Windows tablet, I'll scurry back to the Windows 10 Universal Calendar app, but only to plug in my Google Calendar.

✦ Sunrise Calendar — `https://calendar.sunrise.am` — is also free. It hooks into the Google Calendar and provides a better interface and an Android app that rocks.

✦ For the iPhone and iPad, I use the Google Calendar apps (available in the Apple App Store), but a good friend of mine recommends Calendars 5 — `https://readdle.com/products/calendars5` — which integrates very well indeed with the Apple products.

Beyond Email

It pains me to admit it, but email is changing a lot. Those of us who grew up with email have a hard time accepting it, but in the past week I've used Facebook, Twitter, Slack, and Line for interactions that are more or less email. The distinction between texting and email is disappearing — in fact, the line between video calls and email is crumbling. I tend away from video calls because I have to comb my hair, but other than that, there are advantages to all the new alternatives.

Don't lock yourself out of the new ways — Facebook, Twitter, Line, Slack, Snapchat (not just for sexting selfies anymore, in spite of what some politicians think/do; current capitalization over $10 billion), Yik Yak (with capitalization over $350 million), Yammer (which Microsoft now owns), Skype (which Microsoft now owns), and many others. Each has a slightly different approach, and in some situations, they're clearly better than good ol' email.

Chapter 2: Keeping Track of People

*O*nce upon a time, contact lists were the meat 'n taters of the PC world. Being able to keep one single list of all of your contacts — and keep their addresses, email addresses, and phone numbers all up to date — was one of the most important chores for a burgeoning PC.

Those days have long passed. Nowadays, contact lists get gummed up with outdated entries and useless information. Worse, the contact lists don't talk to each other: My contacts in Facebook, Line, Skype, Gmail, inside my phones, Flickr and Snapchat and Twitter and Pinterest and Outlook just don't talk to each other. Which is all for the better, actually, because if they did start talking to each other, there'd be some really heated arguments and lots of name-calling.

Even if your contacts are better behaved than mine, changing a detail in one place — say, a new email address in Gmail — doesn't ripple to all the lists. Instead, it just means that one of the lists is out of sync with all the others.

I wish I could say that Microsoft has built a better contact list, but they haven't. The Windows 10 Universal People app is a toy app, which may evolve into a superior central repository someday, but I'm not holding my breath.

Microsoft's been working on contact lists since the days of Windows 3.1 and Outlook 4, and none of the lists has worked worth a hill of beans. Don't get me started about changing an email address in Outlook, and not having it updated on the automatic fill-in list for new emails. I don't know how many times I embarrassed myself with that one.

The Contact List in Windows 10

You may want to think of it as the Windows 10 Universal People app (see Figure 2-1), but it's really just Windows 10's contact list. Nothing pretentious about it. In fact, at this point, it isn't even a capable as the contact list in Windows 8.1, which is saying something.

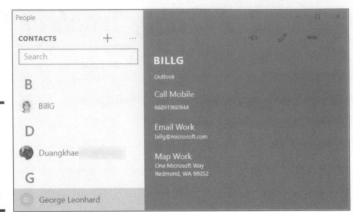

Figure 2-1:
The
Universal
People app
is a simple
contact list.

The Win10 People app keeps a list of contacts. If you hook things up right, it'll import contact lists from a variety of sources — the usual email contact lists (Office 365, Exchange, Outlook.com, Gmail.com, iCloud), plus a very few contact list managers available for sale in the Windows Store.

As we went to press, Microsoft promised that it was going to build bridges to more apps and sites with contact lists — Twitter, Pinterest, LinkedIn, the various Messenger and chat apps, Facebook, Sina Weibo, and heaven-knows-what-all, but it isn't clear how far Microsoft will get in its quixotic quest.

It would be nice if we could have a Microsoft Contacts Babel Fish, but it's hard to believe the job will ever be done.

Putting Contacts in the Universal People App

If you set up Mail with a Hotmail/Outlook.com, Gmail, or Exchange Server account, all the contacts belonging to that account have already been imported into People. If you set up more than one Hotmail/Outlook.com account, for example, all the contacts in both accounts have been merged and placed in People.

But you aren't even halfway done yet.

Adding accounts to Universal People

Before you start pulling all your contacts from Hotmail/Outlook.com, Gmail's Contacts, Exchange Server, Office 365, and all the others realize that there are side effects, not just in establishing Microsoft-controlled links with outside applications, but even inside the core Win10 Universal productivity apps, Mail, People, and Calendar.

Before you add an account to People, be aware of the effects that adding that account has in other tiled apps. Here's how connecting the following accounts with Universal People impacts other tiled apps:

✦ **Google account:** This brings in your Gmail contacts but not your Google+ contacts. In addition, it adds your Gmail account to the Universal Mail app. (Apparently Microsoft hasn't dug in to the Google+ social networking mill yet.)

✦ **Hotmail/Outlook.com account:** This brings in your Hotmail/Outlook.com (and Windows Live) contacts and hooks up the email accounts to the Universal Mail app.

✦ **Other accounts:** Although you can add other accounts (POP3 and IMAP email accounts) to the Universal People app, as best I can tell doing so does not import anything to Universal People. Rather, it simply adds the connected email account to the Universal Mail app.

Now that you understand the implications, you're ready to add accounts. Here's how to add many/most/all your contacts (you get to choose how many accounts to connect) to the Universal People app:

1. **Bring up the People app from the Universal Start screen by tapping or clicking the People tile.**

   If you've added only a single email address to Mail, you may see a prompt to add an account. If so, click Add an Account, and skip to Step 3.

2. **From the main People screen (refer to Figure 2-1), click the ellipses (. . .) on the left, and choose Settings.**

   You see the Add an account pane shown in Figure 2-2,

Figure 2-2: Merge contacts from various accounts into your Win10 People app.

3. **If you have a contact list with entries that you want to see, pause, and think about it a minute.**

   If you have old information in one or more of those accounts, you may want to think carefully about whether including all the contacts in your Universal People list will be more of a pain than it's worth. Modifying existing contacts, er, people is intensely time-consuming: You must tap or click each contact one by one, review the information about the contact, and modify accordingly. Although Universal People tries to identify duplicate entries — the same people coming from two different sources — and merge the data, it's not good at resolving differences.

4. **If you want to proceed, click or tap Add an account.**

   You see the Choose an account dialog box shown in Figure 2-3.

Figure 2-3:
The Choose
an Account
dialog box
looks just
like the
analogous
dialog
box in the
Universal
Mail app.

Table 2-1 explains the option you should choose, depending on what kind of email provider you have.

5. **Choose the type of account you have, and follow the directions to add that account's contacts to Universal People.**

   You're bound to find many duplicates and lots of mismatched data. Hang in there. There's another trick.

If you added too many accounts to your Universal People list, there's a way to drop back ten yards and punt — prevent Universal People from showing all the contacts from a specific source — without laboriously deleting individual entries.

Table 2.1	New Mail Account Types
Use This Type	*For This Email Service*
Exchange	If you get your mail through a company mail server, or if you use Office 365 to handle your mail
Outlook.com	If you get mail through Microsoft's servers — your email address looks like something@outlook.com, @live.com, @hotmail.com, or @msn.com
Google	If you have a Google account, most commonly an email address that looks like something@gmail.com, but also if you use Google's servers for email, as you can with Google Apps for Business, or if you've just registered your email address with Google and want to retrieve your mail through Google
iCloud	For those from the Apple side of the street, if you have an @icloud.com or @me.com or @mac.com address
Advanced setup	Use only if you have an Exchange ActiveSync account

Here's how:

1. **Bring up the People app from the Universal Start screen by tapping or clicking the People tile.**

2. **From the main People screen (refer to Figure 2-1), click the ellipses (. . .) on the left, and choose Settings.**

   You see the dialog box shown earlier in Figure 2-2.

3. **At the bottom, click or tap Filter Contact List.**

   That brings up the options shown in Figure 2-4.

4. **Check and uncheck boxes at the bottom, so you only show the contacts that you want to see.**

   It's easier to scale back duplicates that way — but harder to update older entries.

A little English translation: "Hide contacts without phone numbers — Off" means you want to see all your contacts, whether you have phone numbers for them or not.

**Book IV
Chapter 2**

**Keeping Track
of People**

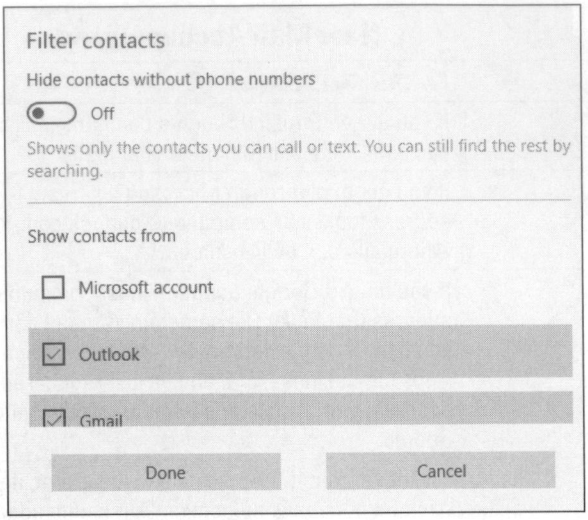

Figure 2-4:
Disable all
the contacts
from a
single
source.

Editing a contact

If you want to change the information associated with a Universal People person (altogether now: "One eyed, one horned, flying purple people person") — a contact — here's how to do it:

1. **Inside Universal People, tap or click a contact's tile.**

The contact details appear, as in Figure 2-5.

2. **Click or tap the pencil icon.**

The Edit Outlook Contact pane appears, as shown in Figure 2-6.

3. **Change the information you want to change.**

See the next section for a list of the different data fields.

Searching for People

Just to confuse things: Search in People looks only for the beginning of names. If you search for *umm*, you won't find *Dummy,* for example. That's usually not a real big deal, unless you've imported names where both the first and last names have been magically mashed together and stuck in the First Name field.

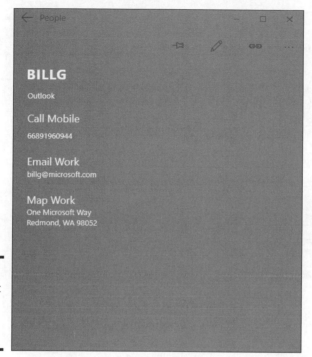

Figure 2-5:
The contact
info for
Mister
Windows.

4. **VERY IMPORTANT: Tap or click the Save icon. (It's the one that looks like a 3.5-inch floppy disk in the upper-right corner. What? You've never seen a 3.5-inch floppy disk? Yeah, I can sympathize.)**

    If you don't explicitly Save your changes, they'll disappear, and you won't be warned.

No, it isn't like you're in the 21st century, where contact apps make changes immediately and without prompts.

Adding people in Universal People

Adding a new contact in People isn't difficult, if you can keep in mind one oddity: You add *accounts* via the ellipses in the upper right of the screen, but to add a *contact,* you use the + (plus sign) icon.

A people, er, contact doesn't have to be a person. Your local animal shelter is a person, too. Or at least a contact.

Here's how to add a new contact. Keep in mind that People alphabetizes by the first name, or by the company name if there is no first or last name.

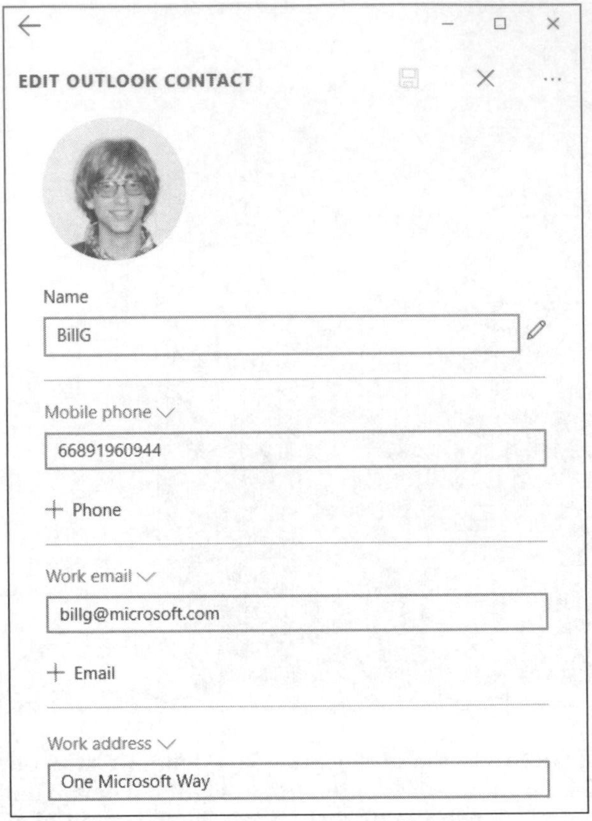

Figure 2-6:
Change the
contact's
information
here.

1. **Start Universal People. That puts you on the main screen (refer to Figure 2-1).**

2. **Tap or click the + sign on the upper left.**

   People wants you to pick an account, as in Figure 2-7.

3. **Choose the account that you want to sync this new contact to.**

   You can choose from any account that's been identified to the Mail app. When you add a contact to that account, Universal People goes to the account and puts the person in your contact list for that account. So, for example, if I add Phineas Farquahrt to my woody@msn.com account, as soon as I'm finished, the Universal People app will log on to my woody@msn.com account and add poor Phineas to my contact list.

   Universal People brings up the New Contact screen shown in Figure 2-8.

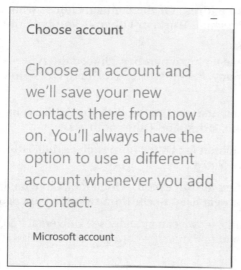

Figure 2-7:
Choose an
account.

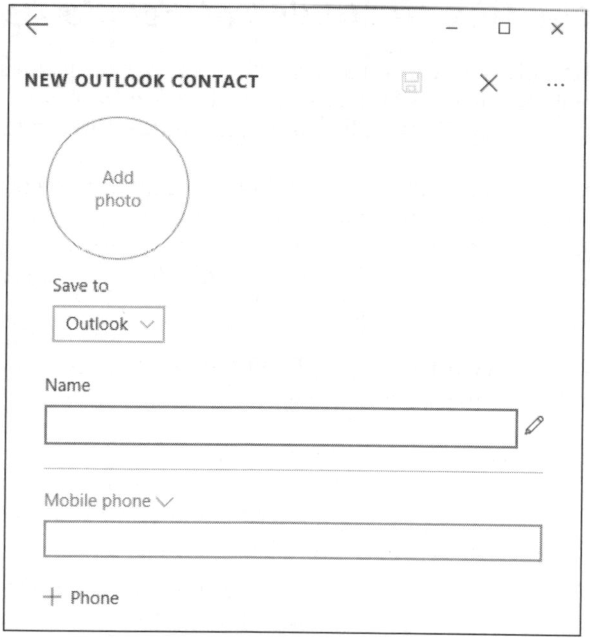

Figure 2-8:
Enter
your new
contact —
your new
Universal
People
person —
here.

4. **Type a first and last name, keeping in mind that People alphabetizes
   by the first name, by default.**

   For additional name options — phonetic names, middle names, nick-
   names, title, or suffix — you can tap or click the pencil icon to the right
   of the Name field.

5. **If you have an email address for the contact, choose what kind of email address — Personal, Work, or Other — and type the address in the box.**

6. **Similarly, if you have a phone number, choose the type — Mobile, Home, Work, Company, Pager, Work Fax, Home Fax — and type it in the indicated box.**

7. **If you want to add an address, tap or click the Address button and choose among Home, Work, and Other address.**

8. **Type as you feel inclined for Other Info, such as Job Title, Significant Other, Website, and Notes.**

9. **At the top tap or click the Save icon, which looks like an ancient floppy disk that your cat used to chew on twenty years ago.**

   It takes a few seconds — you can actually see Universal People going to your mail account and updating it — but you come back to the People screen.

Alternatives to the Win10 Universal People App

If that were the only contact app at your disposal, you'd be sitting smack dab in the dumb phone era of the late 1990s. Even Outlook 98 had considerably more sophisticated contact handling than Win10 Universal People.

Fortunately, while Microsoft's been playing at contacts, the rest of the world has zoomed right ahead. When you choose a contact app, your top consideration should be whether it runs on all your computers: desktop, laptop, tablet, and phone. Windows 10 Universal People doesn't even rate a meh on that scale.

If you're looking for a contact app and you aren't forced into Universal People, try one of these free alternatives:

✦ **Sync.me:** Android, iOS, or online, works with Google+, Facebook, and LinkedIn contacts. Features are caller ID (a godsend if you get lots of spammy calls), social syncing, spam protection, world phone book, and reminders. Find it at `https://sync.me/`.

✦ **Contacts+:** Android, iOS, or online syncs with Facebook, Google+, Twitter, and LinkedIn. It's very visual. Find it at `http://www.contactspls.com/`.

✦ **Google Contacts:** I use this one on my desktop, laptops, tablets, and phones. It works like a champ and ties in to Gmail, which I also use. Find it at `https://contacts.google.com`.

There's a whole big world of contact apps out there. Don't get stuck on one just because it ships with Windows.

Chapter 3: Zooming the Photos App and Beyond

*W*indows 10's Photos app Is meant to be a pleasing, easy way to look at your picture collection, coupled with some easy-to-use photo-editing capabilities. If your expectations go a little bit outside that box, you're going to be very disappointed.

In this chapter, you find an introduction to what Photos can and can't do. A quick tour shows you how to navigate around the Photos app. Then I explain how to edit with the simple but surprisingly powerful Photo tools and how to import images from your camera (or phone) with Photos. And I show you how to organize pics in your very own Albums.

Finally, if the Photos app doesn't do what you want — and unless your needs are very modest, it won't — I talk about the many photo storage and management apps available on the Internet. You may be surprised how much photo moxie is available, free, in the cloud.

Discovering What Windows Photos App Can Do

Photos has a very simple layout for viewing your photos. Here's what you get:

✦ A central place to view photos from your computer or from your OneDrive account

✦ Help searching for a photo

✦ A way to show your photos organized by date

The next section, "Touring Photos," explains the photo sources and how to search or change the display of your photos. The section "Editing Photos" shows how to apply Windows Photos' built-in editing tools to the photo of your choice. The section "Adding Photos" later in this chapter explains how to connect Photos with the web. The section "Using Albums" shows you how to physically set up albums, and what to do with them. And the last section takes you beyond Windows, to explore the amazing tools, available for free online, that will help you store, edit, and distribute your photos, whether you just pass them around the family and crow about them around the world.

The new Windows Photos app is reasonably capable, but it suffers from the same clunky navigation problems that plague all of the Windows side of Windows 10: Try to copy a handful of photos from one folder to another, for example, and your finger could fall off.

If you're trying to import photos to your PC from a camera or tablet, take a look at the Phone Companion app.

Touring Photos

To take a walk around the Photos app:

1. **From the Start screen, tap or click the Windows Photos tile.**

The main screen of the Photos app appears, showing you the Pictures Collection as shown in Figure 3-1.

Figure 3-1:
The Photos app can bring in files from the Pictures folder on your computer and from OneDrive.

Microsoft is actively burying and killing Libraries in Windows 10. If you haven't yet taken control of your Pictures Library (see Book VII, Chapter 3), the only folder in the Library is your personal Pictures folder. What you see on the main Windows Pictures screen is a list of all the folders inside your personal Pictures folder, with a representative picture from each folder emblazoned on the front.

The Collection is a simple, reverse chronological view of all the pictures (and videos) in your computer's Pictures folder, combined with all of your pictures and videos — in any folder — in OneDrive.

Note that pictures outside of your Pictures folder aren't included.

By default, the pictures are automatically enhanced by Windows Photo, and duplicates get removed.

2. **To search for a specific photo, scroll down to find the date the photo was taken.**

   See Figure 3-2.

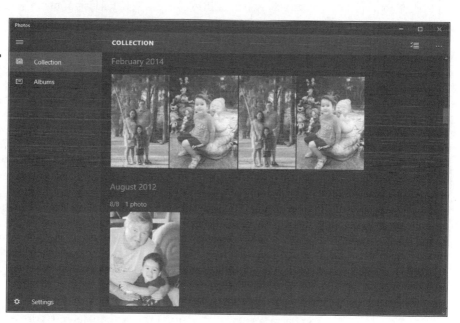

Figure 3-2: As of this writing, Windows Universal Photos doesn't even have a Search function. To find a photo, you have to scroll and find the date the photo was taken.

Book IV
Chapter 3

Zooming the Photos App and Beyond

Photos doesn't have many options at this point, but Microsoft is working on them. While Microsoft's busy trying to write a Universal Photos app, hop over to `photos.google.com` and see how a Photos app should work.

Seeing videos and network-attached folders

In Photos, you see some videos and photos, but not others. The reason has to do with the nuances of how Photos works behind the scenes to show you images. The following points may clear up a few mysteries for you:

✔ **Photos shows all the picture or video files in your Windows Pictures folder, or in OneDrive.** Although Photos does show videos, the videos need to be in your Pictures folder (not your Videos Library) on your computer in order to appear in Photos. Your video files in the Windows Video folder don't appear in Photos at all — odd, but true. Contrariwise, Windows Photos picks up all the videos in OneDrive, in any folder. This is a good place to note that the Windows Video app isn't anything at all like the Windows Photos app: Video

shows a tiny slice of your videos wedged in between mountains of marketing aimed at getting you to rent or buy movies. For more on the Windows Video app, flip to Book IV, Chapter 6.

✔ **But . . . if you have a network-attached folder in your Windows Pictures Library, Photos won't look at it.** That means you can't put a bunch of photos on a Windows Home Server, a network attached server, or even a different PC in your home network and have the pictures appear in Windows Photos — even if you add the folder to your Pictures Library. Worse, Photos can't even see photos inside your HomeGroup.

Yeah, I know it's ridiculously confusing.

The Photos app can display an enormous variety of picture and video formats, including AVI, BMP, GIF (including animated GIFs), JPG, MOV, MP4, MPEG, MPG, PCX, PNG, many kinds of RAW (high-quality photos), TIF, WMF, and WMV files. That covers most picture and movie formats you're likely to encounter.

Editing Photos

If you can find a photo you want to edit, in spite of Windows Photos' truly incapable search capabilities, editing it is quite easy — and the tools at hand, while rudimentary, are quite powerful. Here's how:

1. **Navigate to the photo, and click or tap it.**

   An App bar appears at the top of the screen, as in Figure 3-3.

2. **As noted in the App bar at the top, you can (from the left) Share the photo (if you have any programs that accept shared photos), start a Slide Show, Enhance, Edit, or Delete the shot.**

   Enhancement works automatically, without touching the original file. If you want to see the file as it actually existed — without Microsoft's machine-generated enhancement, click or tap to turn off the Enhancement tile.

Figure 3-3:
Select
a photo
to start
working
on it.

In short, it's a typical ham-fisted approach to working with files, without the aid of File Explorer.

3. **Click the ellipses in the upper-right corner.**

   That's how you get to options to Copy, Print, set the photo as your Windows Lock Screen, or look up some File Info.

4. **Click the Edit icon, which looks like a pencil.**

   Two bars appear, on the left and right, this time with your editing commands. See Figure 3-4.

5. **If the Enhance icon hasn't already been clicked, click it.**

   Although the Windows Photos app automatically applies enhancing to pictures when it shows them to you, manually applying it here lets you see what's being enhanced and, if you prefer the automatic changes, save the picture.

6. **If you prefer the automatically enhanced version of the picture, click or tap the Save As icon at the top.**

   It's the icon that looks like a pencil on top of a 3.5-inch diskette. If you know what a 3.5-inch diskette looks like.

Figure 3-4:
It takes a
long time
to get to
the editing
tools, but
here they
are at long
last.

Windows Photos does not overwrite your original picture. Unless you
try very hard to shoot yourself in the foot, you'll provide a new name.
Don't worry too much about duplicating pictures: Windows Photos is
smart enough to pick up your modified (and hopefully improved) version when it shows you the pictures.

7. **Check out the Basic Fixes on the right: Rotate, Crop, Straighten, Red
   Eye, and Retouch (blur, to a first approximation).**

   Use the Undo icon liberally.

8. **On the left, click or tap the Filters icon.**

   The Windows Photos editor shows you the effect of various preselected
   filters. Along the right side is a collection of photos that apply varying
   kinds and levels of fixing. See Figure 3-5.

9. **If one of the shots on the right appeals to you, click or tap it.**

   You may be finished, but just for a moment, look at the other tools.

Figure 3-5:
Want to
apply a
sepia filter?
Sharpen?
Enhance
contrast?
It's all right
here.

10. **On the left, click or tap Light. Then click the first icon on the right —
    it's labeled Brightness — and drag the white little circle around the
    big circle.**

    You can see how the circular control gradually makes the picture darker
    and lighter, as you drag the little circle around the big circle. See Figure 3-6.

11. **Experiment with the Color icon (adjust temperature, tint, saturation,
    or enhance the color) and the Effects icon (vignette to lighten the area
    around the outside of the picture, and selective focus to blur outside
    the chosen area).**

    If you hover your mouse on the bottom edge, you see + and – signs,
    which you can click or tap to zoom in or out of the picture.

12. **Play with the controls at the top: Undo, Redo, Compare (flips back and
    forth between the current version and the previous version), Save As,
    and Cancel.**

13. **When you're finished, either click the Save As icon (pencil and dis-
    kette) or the "X" Cancel icon.**

    You drop out of editing mode.

When you're ready to go back to the Collection, click or tap at the top and
then click or tap the back arrow.

Figure 3-6:
The circular controls are easy to use with a mouse or a finger.

Setting Settings

The Windows Photos app has a small collection of settings that you may (or may not) find useful.

To see them, tap or click the hamburger icon in the upper left and, at the bottom, choose the gear icon marked Settings. You see something like Figure 3-7.

Not all Settings on offer are obvious. Here's the backstory:

✦ **Automatically enhance my photos when they can be improved:** Don't panic. This means the Windows Photo app will apply its automatic enhancer when you see the photos. *The photos aren't changed.* If you want to change the photo, you must go through the preceding Edit steps and save the Enhanced version (refer to Figure 3-5).

✦ **Sources:** At this point, you can't add individual folders to the Windows Photos app's search list, and you can't tell the Windows Photos app to use the Photos Library.

✦ **Show my photos and videos from OneDrive:** The Windows Photos app scans all your OneDrive folders, looking for file types that are pictures or videos. Note, in particular, that any kind of graphic file — not just photos, not just videos — gets picked up.

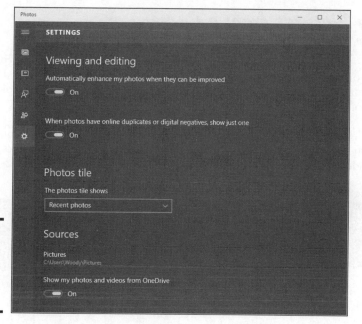

Figure 3-7: These basic settings may prove useful.

Don't be too surprised if your Setting panel looks different from this one. Microsoft's changing it all the time.

Adding Photos

You can add pictures to your collection in the Windows Photos app in three ways:

✦ **Add photos to OneDrive:** Putting photos into the OneDrive Photos folder is a simple drag and drop. File Explorer works great.

✦ **Use the Photos Import app:** You can import pictures from a camera or any removable device, including a USB drive, SD card, or even a big honking external hard drive. See the section "Importing Pictures from a Camera or External Drive" for details.

✦ **Add pictures to your Pictures folder:** I call this the old-fashioned way, and it's how I add pictures to the Photos app (in addition to OneDrive). Simply flip over to the desktop and use File Explorer to stick photos and videos in your Pictures folder. Remember that videos in your Videos folder don't show up in the Windows Photos app.

Importing Pictures from a Camera or External Drive

If you want to import pictures into your Windows PC from your iPhone, iPad, Android phone or tablet, or Windows phone or tablet, you're looking in the wrong place.

Go back to the Start menu and click on Start, All Apps, Phone Companion. You see the setup screen shown in Figure 3-8. Work from there to get the app loaded on your phone, and it talks with Windows 10 like they were best buds.

Figure 3-8:
To import pictures from a mobile device, go over to the Windows Universal Phone Companion app.

Working with Albums

Once you have photos visible in the Collection view, Windows works hard at sorting the photos into Albums. As of this writing, there's nothing you can do to speed up the process, and it can take many hours for even a small photo collection.

After the photos are sorted into Albums, there are no tools for rearranging the Albums. Look for improvements in the Photos app in the near future (if they aren't there already).

Storing and Managing Photos Online

There are hundreds — hundreds — of websites and apps, on all platforms, that help you pull your photos or videos from your camera (phone, tablet, phablet, laptop, massive external hard drive, whatever), stick your photos or videos somewhere else (cloud, Windows machine, Mac, network server), automatically sort and/or categorize them, help you label or tag them, and let you edit for both common problems (such as red eye or trimming), and offer far more advanced traits.

More than 900 billion — yes, with a "b" — photos are uploaded to the cloud every year. A big part of the push: Getting those old photos off your camera to make room for new ones.

The best sites and apps help you share your photos, limiting the distribution to people you specify or opening them to everyone. They let you edit with easy-to-use tools. They help you find those old photos that are stuck in weird places. And the very best sites do it all for free or for very little.

If you're looking for a place to put and manage your photos, here are some (but not necessarily the best!) options:

✦ **OneDrive:** I talk about OneDrive in Book VI, Chapter 2. Suffice it to say that you can get 15 GB of storage free, and an unlimited amount of data for less than $100 a year. You can share that data in many ways. OneDrive has web-based tools for organizing the data, and there are rudimentary tools (outside of Windows) for tagging and searching. At some point, Windows 10 should give us some tools to handle the rest of the typical processes, but as of this writing, Windows isn't helping much.

At some point, Microsoft will make a Windows Universal OneDrive app available in the Store. (No, you don't want the OneDrive for Business app — that connects in a totally different way.) When it's available, download the OneDrive app on your phone or tablet, and use the app to get your photos sent to OneDrive. It will be much easier and more reliable than trying to wrestle with Windows 10 on the desktop. Promise.

✦ **Flickr** (www.flickr.com): This has long been the photo site of choice for professionals, amateurs, and the completely clueless (see Figure 3-9). Flickr seemed to be in rapid decline, but in 2013, it started fighting back. Under Yahoo's umbrella now, the phone and tablet apps aren't as capable as its competitors, but it still has excellent editing capabilities.

✦ **iCloud** (www.icloud.com): Unlike Windows, the Apple ecosystem has amazing editing and photo-management software. Unfortunately, as I write this, storage in iCloud is relatively expensive and the hooks from

**Book IV
Chapter 3**

Zooming the Photos App and Beyond

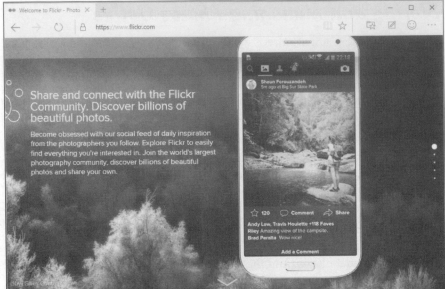

Figure 3-9:
Flickr has long been the favorite of photographers, professional and amateur alike.

iCloud into Windows aren't great. If you use Apple machines, iCloud's an easy (if expensive) choice. If you live and breathe Windows, not so much. Confounding the situation, Apple has two different photo services: iCloud Photo Stream lets you store your last 1,000 photos for free. iCloud Photo Library syncs your iPhone and iPad photos to the new Photos app for Mac.

✦ **Dropbox** (www.dropbox.com): Dropbox has very good backup capability, called Carousel, with apps that pull photos and videos off your camera (phone, or whatever) and stick the files in Dropbox. Unfortunately, Dropbox doesn't have any photo-editing tools.

✦ **Amazon** (www.amazon.com/clouddrive): Amazon has a photo service that was introduced in late 2014. If you subscribe to Amazon Prime ($99 per year), you get unlimited free photo storage. The service is rudimentary, but if you already belong to Prime, the price is sure hard to beat.

✦ **Shutterfly ThisLife** (www.thislife.com): As shown in Figure 3-10, Shutterfly grabs photos from everywhere. It can pull photos off your camera and Windows, Mac, iOS, and Android devices, and it can grab your photos on Facebook, Instagram, Twitter, Flickr, Picasa, Tumblr, and SmugMug — all of which are favorite parking places for photos. ThisLife is free for photos, and videos are not expensive.

Figure 3-10:
ThisLife
pulls
pictures
from just
about
anywhere,
easily, and
lets you
control
how they're
distributed.

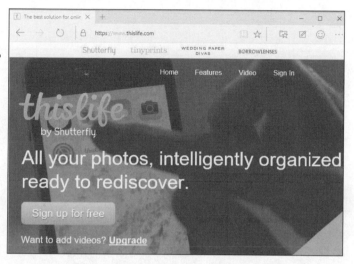

✦ **PictureLife** from StreamNation (www.picturelife.com): This has many of the features of Shutterfly ThisLife, but it adds a very capable photo editor. StreamNation bought PictureLife in February 2014, but it isn't clear what StreamNation will do with it.

You should also look at the picture storage and sharing capabilities of Facebook (www.facebook.com), which I discuss in Book VI, Chapter 3, and SmugMug (www.smugmug.com), which charges $60 per year but gives you unlimited storage. SmugMug's a good place to go if you're going to want to sell your pictures or turn your pics into T-shirts.

Finally — most importantly — Google's new Photos (www.photos.google.com) app runs rings around anything else ever offered to casual photographers. Keep these caveats in mind: Google scans your photos and uses them to target ads in your direction; if you have very high quality photos, they undergo some reduction in quality; the editing tools aren't great, but they're adequate.

On the plus side, Google's ability to form albums — from the kinds of beer you drink to the costumes you wear at Halloween — its automatic generation of travelogues and montages, generated animation from groups of stills (see Figure 3-11), its ability to group by facial recognition, easy importing from your phone or tablet or camera, and on and on, will leave you amazed.

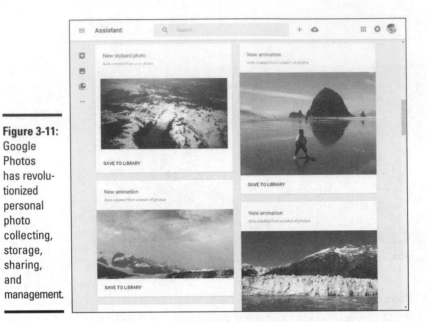

Figure 3-11:
Google
Photos
has revolu-
tionized
personal
photo
collecting,
storage,
sharing,
and
management.

Best of all, it's free. Unlimited storage, unlimited processing, all the time. And it's available in your web browser (Chrome works great), on your iPhone, iPad, Android tablet — just about anywhere except in the Windows Universal app world. Ten thumbs up.

Chapter 4: Noting OneNote

*I*f you haven't used OneNote, you've missed out on Microsoft's premier example of a cloud-first, mobile-first application. OneNote started as a piece of Office. It's grown though, so now — particularly in Windows 10 — it's part of Windows itself. It's arguably the most advanced Windows Universal app, although Microsoft Edge is catching up fast.

OneNote isn't Windows-only. Far from it. From the earliest days, it has been available on iPhones, iPads, Android phones and tablets, and other mobile devices. Working with OneDrive (see Book VI, Chapter 2), you can use OneNote to talk to yourself — pass all sorts of things around to your computer(s), your tablet(s), your phone(s) — and the OneNote interface makes working with those things surprisingly easy.

To understand OneNote, it helps to understand how it started and grew. It's unique in the Microsoft pantheon.

Believe it or not, OneNote started on the Windows XP Tablet PC, as a program inside Office 2003. All three of the people who actually used XP Tablet PCs with a stylus — a pen — got to struggle with the features, capabilities, and bugs of Microsoft's latest and greatest.

Maybe OneNote's developers thought they had developed a killer app for pens. What they really had was a red herring that took almost a decade to take root. Both the software and hardware to drive it had to stew for a long, long time.

Nowadays, OneNote is a strong product that's valuable for both the touch-and-pen crowd and for those of us who still live in a keyboard-and-mouse world. I, personally, don't use OneNote day to day: I'm a long-time Evernote user (www.EverNote.com). The features in Evernote don't match up with OneNote, one to one, but if you're not particularly attached to a pen (or even if you are!), you should look at the Evernote alternative.

Getting Started in OneNote with or without a Pen

The nicest part about OneNote is that it's already installed — part and parcel of Windows 10. To get it going, just click Start and then click the OneNote tile. You see a strange welcome like that in Figure 4-1.

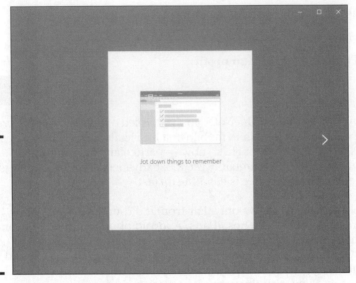

Jot down things to remember

Figure 4-1:
If you're already logged in to OneDrive, OneNote is ready and willing.

Click the right arrows, then Let's get started, and click OK for any additional notifications that may appear.

OneNote comes with four introductory videos that are worthwhile. (Refreshing, that.) I suggest you play each one in turn.

OneBook works with notebooks, just like Word works with documents, Excel with workbooks, and PowerPoint with presentations. Inside a notebook, there are sections. Within each section, there are pages. And on each page can be. . . many things. Typed notes. Screenshots. Photos. Voice recordings. Marked-up web pages. Tables. Attached files. Web links. Lots and lots of things.

You can store a notebook just about anywhere. If you store it in some place where others can get to it (OneDrive, or a computer on your home or office network, for example), you can set things up so they can look at and/or modify your notebook.

Try it. I guarantee you'll find OneNote is easy to use.

Setting Up Notebooks, Sections, Pages

Here's how to get going with your very own Notebook.

1. Get OneNote fired up by clicking or tapping Start and then the OneNote tile.

If you've used OneNote before, you get the main screen shown in Figure 4-2.

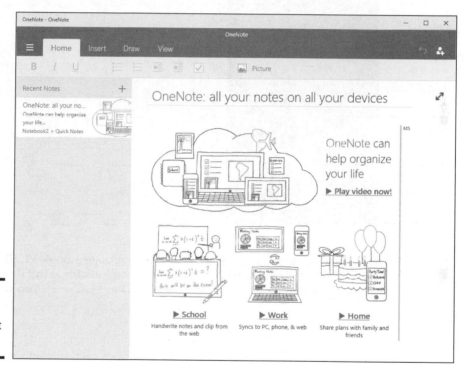

Figure 4-2:
OneNote is ready to get started.

2. Click the hamburger icon in the upper left.

You see the options shown in Figure 4-3.

3. Click or tap the + sign to the right of Notebooks.

OneNote opens a box, asking you to give your new notebook a name.

4. Assuming you want to store the new notebook in OneDrive, type in a name and press Enter.

OneNote creates a new notebook and puts a link to it in your OneDrive Documents folder.

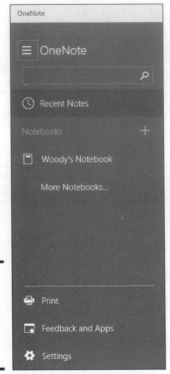

Figure 4-3:
Add a new notebook through the hamburger icon.

5. **Because of the weird way OneDrive works (see Book VI, Chapter 2), the new notebook may not appear if you look for it in File Explorer. But if you log on to OneDrive (www.onedrive.com), you'll see it.**

   In Figure 4-4, the new notebook appears as `The politics of dancing.one`.

You can't actually see the name of the notebook on the main OneDrive screen. To see it, you have to click the hamburger icon again. It's on the left.

Now that you have a new notebook, let's add a couple of sections. Just like tabs on a web browser, adding new sections is flat-out simple.

1. **On the first tab — in Figure 4-4, where it says New Section 1 — right-click or tap and hold the tab and choose Rename Section.**

   The same action also lets you change the background color for the tab, as you can see in Figure 4-5.

2. **Type in a new name, change the color if you like, and press Enter.**

   The new name appears on the tab.

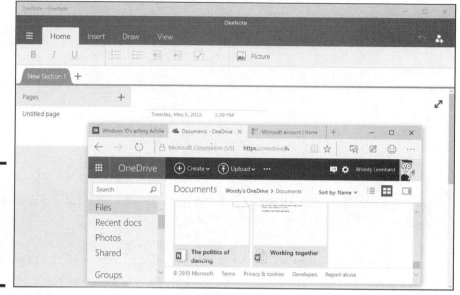

Figure 4-4:
The new notebook really does get saved to your OneDrive.

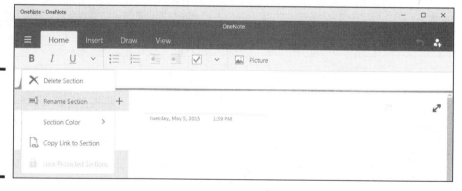

Figure 4-5:
Rename a tab — a Section — by right-clicking.

3. **To add a new section, tap or click the + sign to the right of the right-most tab and type in a name.**

   If you've ever worked with tabs in a browser, you already know all you need.

   To add pages to a section, right-click (or tap and hold) on the left in Figure 4-4, where it says Untitled Page, and choose Rename Page. That brings up a spot where you can type a page name, as shown in Figure 4-6.

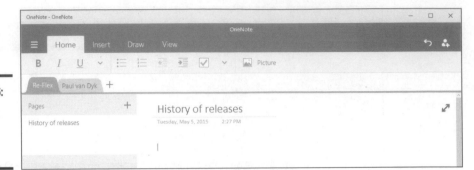

Figure 4-6: Naming a page, the OneNote way.

OneNote (like all sentient mobile apps) saves everything automatically. You don't have to do a thing.

The typing, formatting, and editing controls at the top work just like you would expect. In Figure 4-7, I typed text into a resizable box by simply typing on the keyboard. Formatting is easy.

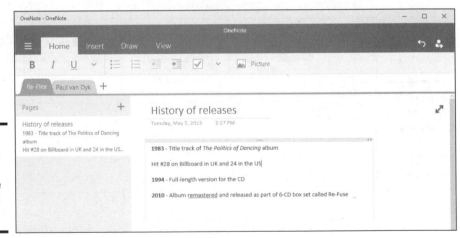

Figure 4-7: Typing into a OneNote page is like falling off a log.

Embellishing on a OneNote Page

You might think that you need a pen in order to draw in OneNote — and, believe me, a good pen helps! — but the fact is that you can doodle with your finger on a touch-sensitive computer, or with a mouse or trackpad if need be. It's just that some pens are sensitive to pressure, so your lines and doodles look much more refined than they do with a mouse.

Microsoft takes a great deal of pride in the way its pen interacts with the Surface Pro machines — click yer Bic (uh, pen), and the computer responds, booting to OneNote in an astonishingly short amount of time. The trick doesn't work with all pens, or all computers, but it's worth a try if you have a pen and a slate: Wait for the computer to go to sleep, and then try clicking any or all of the buttons on your pen.

Here's how to draw on a OneNote page.

1. **Start with whatever page you want to doodle upon. Then click the Draw tab at the top.**

   OneNote responds with the tools and palette shown in Figure 4-8.

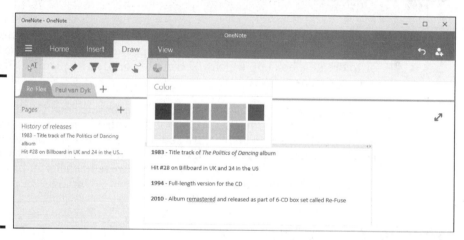

Figure 4-8: Extensive drawing tools work better with a pen, but they'll do okay with a mouse.

2. **Select a color, select the Draw icon (which looks like a finger with a party trailer), and choose either a thin or medium stroke (the icons that look like a Sharpie or a Highlighter, respectively).**

   The cursor turns into a circle.

3. **Draw away.**

   In Figure 4-9, I drew a highlighted yellow oval around a bunch of text I found interesting.

4. **If you don't like what you just drew, type Ctrl+Z.**

   That deletes the drawing you just put on the notebook page and lets you start all over.

Remember that everything is saved for you automatically; you don't need to do a thing.

**Book IV
Chapter 4**

Noting OneNote

Figure 4-9:
Drawing —
even with a
mouse — is
very easy.

The icon on the left in Figure 4-9 is a combination select/Insert text box control. Use it to either select text (say, to apply formatting from the Home tab) or to create a box into which you can type or insert a picture. The behavior is very similar to Word.

The second icon, which looks like a dot, is a lasso select. Use it to select items to move/copy/delete as a group. The third icon, which looks like an eraser, is an eraser (saints be praised!). If you're an experienced word processing geek, it's a little difficult to think about the typed text as being just a picture, but you can erase it like a picture. Erase half a letter or right down the middle of a line. Go ahead. OneNote doesn't mind.

Sending to OneNote

The version of OneNote in Windows 10 isn't nearly as capable as the versions on many other platforms, but there is one place where OneNote's reasonably well connected: Microsoft Edge.

It's easy to take a snapshot of a web page and send it to OneNote, but you need to do a little prep work to make the transfer go smoothly. Here's how to put it all together:

1. **When you send a page from Edge to OneNote, it must go into a specific notebook. No surprise there. To select the Notebook that'll get the page (actually, it ends up as an entire section, with a tab), click the hamburger icon in the upper-left corner and choose Settings.**

OneNote shows you the Settings pane, which I discuss in the next section.

2. **On the right, choose Options. At the bottom of the Options list, click or tap Choose a notebook for Quick Notes.**

   OneNote asks you to pick a default location for new notes.

3. **Choose the notebook you want from the drop-down list, and click OK.**

   You're now ready to "Share" with OneNote.

4. **Bring up Edge, and navigate to a website that you'd like to save in OneNote.**

   In Figure 4-10, I found a page of interest.

Figure 4-10: Here's the page I want to put in OneNote.

5. **In Edge, click or tap the ellipses in the upper-right corner and choose Share.**

   A big Share pane appears on the right.

6. **In the list of Share-able apps, choose OneNote.**

   OneNote responds with an odd scrape of the page.

7. In the upper-right corner, click or tap Send.

OneNote whirs for a bit and then comes up with the web page you selected, sitting in the "Quick Notes" tab (section) in the notebook you chose in Step 3. See Figure 4-11.

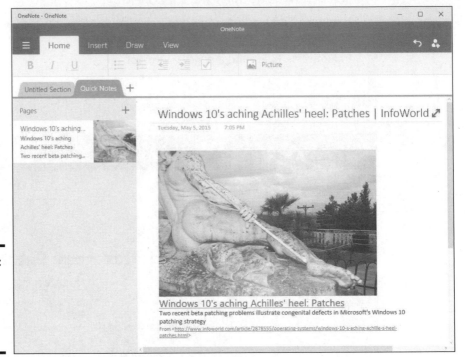

Figure 4-11:
OneNote
shares
nicely with
Microsoft
Edge.

Setting Settings

OneNote has a handful of setting you might want to try some day. Or maybe not. To see them, follow these steps:

1. Inside OneNote, click the hamburger icon in the upper-left corner. Choose Settings.

The Settings pane appears on the right.

2. Choose Options.

The other settings aren't very interesting. You end up with the pane shown in Figure 4-12.

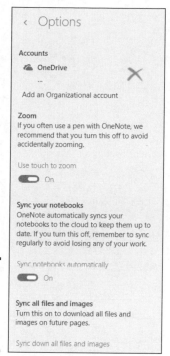

Figure 4-12:
A few settings may prove worthwhile.

3. **If you use a pen with OneNote, turn Off the Touch to Zoom setting.**

   Leaving it on will drive you nuts. Trust me. With the Zoom set to On, every time you use the pen and lightly touch the screen, OneNote thinks that you're trying to zoom. It ain't pretty.

4. **If you want to keep your work off OneDrive (or wherever else you store your notebooks), turn Sync your notebooks Off.**

   It's pretty rare that you would want to return to the not-so-good old days where you had to explicitly Save if you didn't want your work to get trashed. But sometimes there are extenuating circumstances, like when you don't want your coworkers to see what a mess you've made of the communal notebook.

This chapter just touched the surface of OneNote's capabilities, and you'll find that the app itself has many different guises in many different locations — OneNote online (www.onenote.com) is different from OneNote for the iPad, which is different from OneNote for phones, and so on. For a more detailed look, check out *OneNote 2013 For Dummies,* by James H. Russell, also from Wiley.

**Book IV
Chapter 4**

Noting OneNote

Chapter 5: Making Maps

In This Chapter

✔ **Basic map functions**

✔ **Taking a map offline**

✔ **Working through the settings**

Microsoft has had a short and rather tortured history with maps. Microsoft MapPoint emerged from the Expedia Streets and Trips Planner 98, which shipped in Office 97. It was released as a standalone product in 2000, and updated many times afterward, finally succumbing to much better mapping products in 2013.

Bing Maps, an outgrowth of MapPoint and MSN Virtual Earth, started in late 2010, and it's still alive. You can see the latest at www.microsoft.com/maps.

 The Windows Maps app, on the other hand, draws from one of the seminal sources of map information: HERE, a Nokia brand, which Nokia kept when it sold its much-larger telephone business to Microsoft. Windows Maps uses the HERE database, but superimposes Telenav Scout traffic information.

As I write this, HERE is about to go through some major changes, with a consortium of Mercedes, BMW, and Audi in line to take over. It's hard to tell what HERE's new ownership will mean for the Windows Maps app.

Remarkably, the Windows Maps app is a for-real Windows Universal app, which means it runs almost the same way on both Windows 10 and Windows Phone 10. What you see here can be replicated on your Windows phone, and vice versa.

Basic Map Functions

If you've ever used Google Maps (I do, every day) or the Apple Map app (my wife does, every day), you already have a basic understanding of the Windows Maps app (which both of us avoid, for reasons that will become obvious).

There are two basic map views:

✦ **Road** shows a traditional roadmap, at least to a first approximation. See Figure 5-1.

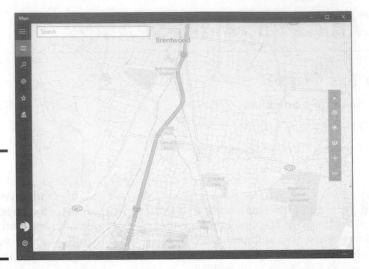

Figure 5-1:
The basic
Road map
calls out
the major
landmarks.

✦ **Aerial** shows a satellite view of the terrain, augmented by superimposed roads. See Figure 5-2.

Figure 5-2:
Aerial has
a satellite
shot with
various
notations.

To switch back and forth between the two views, click the icon at the right, the one that looks like a stack of paper.

At least in theory, both the Road and Aerial maps can be superimposed with traffic information, which appears color-coded on the roads. Again, click the icon that looks like a stack of paper and choose either Traffic or Hide Traffic. In my experience, the traffic information is far from infallible and only occasionally useful. In some cases, for reasons unknown, it doesn't appear at all.

Traffic problems are highlighted by an ! emergency icon, but in my experience the information connected to these icons is very old — problems cleared up days or even weeks before — and not terribly informative. The times posted are also unreliable.

If you want to see where you are, click the Show my Location button, the bulls-eye icon above the stack of paper. If you're mobile and have GPS turned on, the location's accurate. If you're working from a computer with a WiFi connection, the best you're going to get is a rough approximation of the nearest phone company router.

There's a rotate-30-degrees-or-so "Tilt" view, which you can enable or disable by clicking the grid icon above the bulls-eye. See Figure 5-3. It's not very interesting — places that should have breathtaking elevation differences, as in the area west of Denver, end up looking like Flatland.

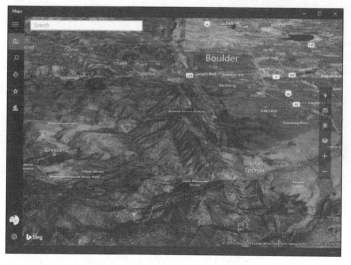

Figure 5-3:
Even places with lots of elevation differences look like a 12th-century depiction of a flat earth.

Book IV
Chapter 5

Making Maps

The map has the usual navigation controls: Click and drag to move the map, rotate the mouse button to zoom. With a touch screen, tap and drag, and pinch or unpinch. For the life of me, though, I couldn't get it to rotate.

Navigating with the Map App

If you're expecting a Google Maps turn-and-gander experience, you're going to be disappointed.

Windows Maps has a small supply of controls hidden under the hamburger icon in the upper-left corner. Click or tap the hamburger, and you see the choices in Figure 5-4.

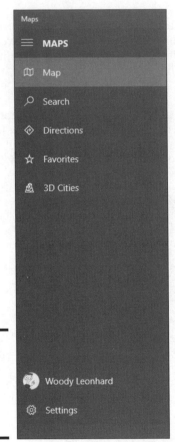

Figure 5-4:
You have these Windows Maps options.

The **Map** icon just takes you back to the standard Map view (refer to Figure 5-1 or 5-2).

Search brings up a search pane, which includes a list of all the places you've searched for recently, plus some general searches including Hotels, Coffee (made in Seattle, no doubt), Restaurants, Shopping, and Museums.

If you search for destinations with a qualification (for example, "Restaurants near Salt Lake City Utah") using the Search pane, you get a numbered map (Figure 5-5), which should look familiar to anyone who's used a map search function, a digest of Yelp reviews for the location, plus in some instances two additional options: outside pictures (apparently pulled from www. Panoramio.com, a Google photo sharing site and/or Foursquare, www. foursquare.com, a travel guide-like app that recommends locations nearby, and various other sources) and a Street View-like mode called Streetside.

Figure 5-5:
You get two extras for search targets: review-style shots and a Street View.

The Panoramio or Foursquare or Urbanspoon shots are presented only as a scrolling collection: You can't enlarge them, search through more than one at a time, or even look at anything higher resolution. The Street View wannabe lets you navigate in the vicinity of the found location, but it's very limited with few side streets and, in my experience, very old pictures.

Back at the hamburger icon, click Directions and you find a reasonably complete direction-navigating feature. Type your From and To locations, and Windows Maps draws you a map with estimated travel times. See Figure 5-6.

From the Directions map, near the estimated time, click the Go button, and you get mapped turn-by-turn instructions, but without any sound. See Figure 5-7.

Figure 5-6:
Windows
Maps does
provide
detailed
driving
instructions,
sometimes
with public
transport
options and
walking
instructions.

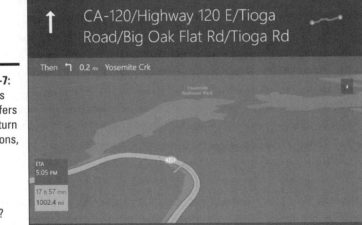

Figure 5-7:
Windows
Maps offers
turn-by-turn
instructions,
with no
voice.
Where
are you,
Cortana?

Windows Maps has another sloping view approximation called 3D Cities. You get to it from the hamburger menu on the main screen. Unfortunately, you can't just, uh, explore in 3D. You have to choose from a list of cities that Windows Maps supports. Flip through, in alphabetical order, and click a city. In Figure 5-8, I clicked Boulder, Colorado, and moved around a bit.

As you can see in Figure 5-8, the 3D view can be quite distorted. When you get to the outer limits of the chosen city, you'll see strange Minecraft-like block renderings of physical features. Just don't get too close to the edge, Okay?

Figure 5-8:
The Boulder
outer limits.

Settings, the last item in the hamburger menu, controls whether you use metric or imperial (which is to say, American) measurements. You can turn off history tracking for searches. There's also an admonition — not an option — that says, "Maps will collect and share anonymous location data with Microsoft to help improve map and location related services."

Yep, you agreed to that.

Taking a Map Offline

Windows Maps let you download a map and use it even if you aren't connected to the Internet. Here's how to download a map:

1. **From the Windows Maps app hamburger icon, at the bottom, choose Settings.**

2. **About halfway down the pane, click or tap the Offline Maps entry that says Download or update maps.**

   That flips you over to the main Windows Settings app and puts you in the System / Offline maps section, as in Figure 5-9.

3. **At the top, click the + icon next to Download a map.**

   The downloader has you choose a continent and then a country. If you choose France, Germany, Italy, Russia, China, India, Brazil, Canada, or USA, you are further asked to choose a region or state.

   Windows Maps downloads the map and shows you the progress on the System dialog box (refer to Figure 5-9).

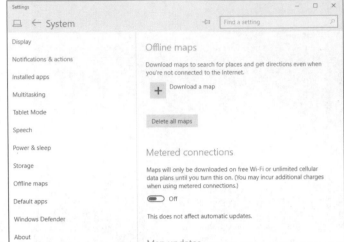

Figure 5-9:
Download
maps
from the
Windows
Settings
app.

4. **When the download is complete, you can navigate with the stored map, without being connected to the Internet.**

   Although, in the case of some Asian maps, they're so poor as to be basically unusable. See Figure 5-10.

Figure 5-10:
Here's a
shot of
my old
stomping
grounds
in Phuket.
Although
Apple and
Google have
very good
maps of
Thailand,
the HERE
maps are
basically
useless.

Chapter 6: Running Music and Movies & TV

In This Chapter

✔ **Understand how Spotify and Pandora have changed the industry**

✔ **Bring your music into the Music app, and movies into Movies & TV**

✔ **Navigating the Music and Movies & TV apps**

Microsoft has been trying for years to put together a decent media player — a program that can play songs and videos. For years, we Windows users have had to settle for programs from other companies, notably VLC, ignobly Apple, to get worthwhile players. And I use the terms "iTunes for Windows" and "worthwhile" in the same sentence only under duress.

With Windows 10, it looks like Microsoft finally put people in charge who understand music, who understand movies. It's like a breath of fresh air (see Figure 6-1).

There's powerful incentive to do so. Apple's made billions from iTunes. Microsoft wants a piece of that action, because it now sells both songs and flicks.

In Windows 8 and 8.1, the Xbox Music app (as it was then called) didn't really want to play your music. It wanted, desperately, to sell you music. With the supremacy of streaming music services — notably Spotify but also Pandora (see the nearby sidebar) — Microsoft would also like to sell you a subscription. That's where the future lies for music. The IFPI, an international organization of companies in the music business (www.ifpi.org), puts it this way:

> The industry's digital revenues grew by 6.9 percent in 2014 to US$6.9 billion and are now on a par with the physical sector. There was steep growth in both revenues and user numbers for subscription services, continued revenue growth from ad-supported services, and still sizable income from download sales in many markets. Globally, digital now accounts for 46 percent of total industry global revenues and in four of the world's top 10 markets, digital channels account for the majority of revenues.

Figure 6-1:
The
Universal
Music app
is like a
breath of
fresh air.

Subscription services, part of an increasingly diverse mix of industry revenue streams, are going from strength to strength. Revenues from music subscription services — including free-to-consumer and paid-for tiers — grew by 39.0 percent in 2014 and [are] growing consistently across all major markets.

Globally, "electronic" music — which is to say, music in the form of files purchased online — has overtaken regular CDs in sales, and the subscription services part of the electronic pie is growing at a 40 percent annual rate.

On the TV and movies side, streaming is rolling over the cable and broadcast TV industries as more and more people in the U.S. and Europe "cut the cord." (That is to say, they give up traditional subscription services and get what they want to watch via the Internet.) By 2017, according to a PricewaterhouseCoopers report, revenue from TV and subscription video on demand in the U.S. will be more than the gross income from box office sales.

With apologies to Robert Zimmerman, "You don't need a weatherman to know which way the wind blows."

Spotify, Pandora, and Microsoft

Pandora started the ball rolling, with a subscription-based streaming music service first available in 2000, and then completely redesigned in 2004. If you've never used it, think of Pandora as a smart radio station, able to respond to your likes and dislikes, dishing up songs that match your preferences. Its "discoverability" sets the standard. Pay for your subscription, and the song quality goes up and ads go away. By late 2014, Pandora had grown to 250 million registered users, 80 million active every month, with a profit approaching $1 billion.

Spotify appeared later, in 2008, and it had a different approach: Let people choose the songs they want to hear, and make those songs easily available; you only listen to music you know and like. Pandora has a "mere" one million songs available; Spotify has 20 million or more. Pandora's social interaction offerings are meager. Spotify has tons of features for sharing music and bringing together friends, including collaborative playlists. Spotify has roughly 60 million active subscribers, 15 million of whom pay monthly.

Where Pandora is like a smart radio station, Spotify is more like a rental service. But as time marches on, the distinction between the two continues to blur, with Spotify offering discoverability aids and Pandora picking up on sharing.

Apple (Beats), Google (Play Music), and Microsoft have all jumped into the fray, with variations on the theme, combining elements of Pandora's radio stations with Spotify's pick-and-choose approach. Apple's latest run into the market, called Apple Music, appears poised to overrun all the others. To date, Microsoft's Xbox Music Pass, at $10/month, hasn't really made a dent in the market.

The folks at Microsoft are shrewd enough to realize that they must offer something more than what people are getting with a browser. That's where the Universal Music and the Movies & TV apps are headed.

Perhaps most damning, Pandora had a Windows Phone app, so you could play your Pandora stations in a dedicated app on older Windows phones. It isn't clear whether Pandora will make a similar app for the new Windows 10 Universal platform. Spotify does not, and it doesn't appear to be in the mood to create one. Apple, with Apple Music now the service to beat, wouldn't get caught dead with a Windows Universal app. If you want to use any of them on Windows 10 machines, you may be forced to go in through a browser. That isn't horrible, but the browser version frequently doesn't have all the bells and whistles of a dedicated app.

What is DRM?

Music and video come in many different formats — think of them as different methods for converting sight and sound into bits. The formats are all different, and translating a video or song from one format to another can really put a crimp on the quality of the recording. Some of the formats put locks on the data, so you can only play or view the file if the creator gives you permission. That's DRM, Digital Rights Management, the scourge of the entertainment industry. In my opinion, anyway.

Back in the dark ages, if you wanted to record music on a computer, you used the MP3 format. It wasn't (and isn't) the fanciest format on the street; it makes files that are bigger than they need to be, and it doesn't support some truly cool capabilities in newer formats (such as Dolby-style 5.1 or 7.1 channel recording). Despite all its shortcomings, MP3 took off and became the universal language of digital music. If you have a device that plays digital music — whether it's an old PC, an ancient portable audio player (they're called "MP3 players" for a reason), a 200GB iPod, a Galactic Zune, or a beat-up 2003 Chevy — it understands MP3.

In the video arena, AVI and MPG file formats play a similar role: They're long-established (okay, old-fashioned) formats. They were invented before anybody thought much about DRM.

AVI, MP3, and MPG files aren't just DRM-free. They're DRM-impossible: The file format doesn't support any attempts to lock you out of your own music or videos. If you buy an MP3 file, for example, you know from the get-go that it doesn't bear any digital rights restrictions — nobody else has control over your music. There are no hidden restrictions, such as limitations on whether you can burn the song on a CD or whether you can play the song on a specific Windows PC.

Apple started out selling DRM-encumbered files in AAC format. But in late 2008, Amazon announced that all its music would be DRM-free. Apple wised up and in early 2009 took DRM off all its new offerings.

DRM-locked music is disappearing. Consumers wised up. Companies that used to peddle locked-up music now sing the praises of DRM-free, with all the fervor of a saved sinner caught with his hand in the till. Yeah, that includes Microsoft, which — for a brief period of time — sold DRM-enabled WMA audio files.

With a little luck, DRM in the audio world will go the way of the dodo, although you may be stuck with DRM-laden dreck that you got suckered into paying for months or years ago.

Getting Your Music and Movies into the Apps

If you want to buy your music, movies, or TV shows from Microsoft, the mechanics are easy: Buy them in the Windows Store, and they magically appear in both the Music and Movies & TV apps.

But what if you already have music and videos, and you want to be able to play them through the Universal Music app and the Universal Movies & TV app? That's a little more complicated — and it can take hours (if not days), depending on the speed of your Internet connection and the state of Microsoft's servers.

The answer is to stick everything in the OneDrive account that you'll use to play the files. Here's a quick course:

1. **Go to a computer that has the music and videos (or has access to the music and videos) that you want to make accessible to the Universal apps.**

    If you already have your music in the iTunes store, or inside Google or Amazon, you may have to copy the files onto your computer (download them). Each vendor has a different way to download its music — and some vendors' plans won't let you download them at all. Make sure you get DRM-free files (see the nearby sidebar).

2. **On that computer, log in to OneDrive (www.onedrive.live.com) and use the Windows account that you use on the machine where you want the music available.**

    For example, I have a new Windows 10 PC and I use woody@msn.com to log in to Windows on that PC. To transfer files via OneDrive, I'd find a PC that has the music I want and, using a web browser, log in to OneDrive using the account woody@msn.com.

3. **Drag and drop your music from the computer into the OneDrive account's Music folder.**

    You won't be able to drag folders into OneDrive. For reasons I can't begin to fathom, Music insists on organizing things according to the details inside the files, and it doesn't want your steeeenkin' folders. So you have to reach into each folder, select all the files (Ctrl+A), and drag the files into OneDrive.

    That can take hours, weeks, years, depending on how much music you have.

4. **While you're at it, create a folder called Videos in the OneDrive account, and drag and drop all your video files — MP4s, AVIs, and the like — from the computer into your OneDrive account.**

    With the media files all in OneDrive, you're ready to start.

Of course, if your only music is music you bought from Microsoft (there must be ten of you out there), you don't need to lift a finger.

Running around the Universal Music App

With your music sitting inside your computer's Music folder, or your OneDrive's Music folder, you're ready to crank it up to 11. Here's how.

1. **Tap or click Start, Music.**

    You see the Welcome to Music window (refer to Figure 6-1).

2. **On the left, click or tap Go to collection.**

   As you can see in Figure 6-2, Universal Music takes a brave stab at finding and organizing your music, but it doesn't always get the details right.

   Note, on the left in Figure 6-2, you're in Album mode (that's the second icon below the hamburger icon).

Figure 6-2: Universal Music's album consolidator doesn't always get things right — it put Carl Franklin's album #4 in a folder called Chapter 2.

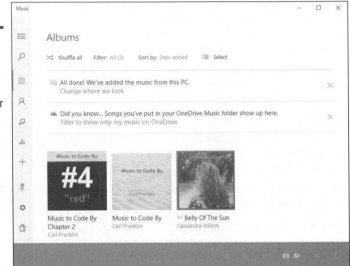

3. **If Music didn't find all the music on your machine, click or tap the link marked Change where we look.**

   Music opens a very hokey old-fashioned "file picker" window like the one in Figure 6-3.

Figure 6-3: This startlingly sparse file picker menu resides inside the svelte Music app.

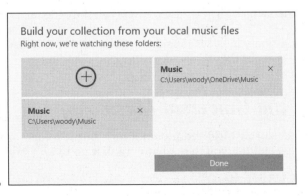

4. **If Music hasn't found all your music, tap or click the + sign in the top tile, and then go out and find the wayward folders.**

    Hint: If you have music in the Public Music folder, look for `c:\Users\Public\Music`. No, the Music app isn't smart enough to recognize your Music Library or the Public Music folder.

5. **Double-click one of the artificially assembled albums to play all the songs in the album.**

    You hear the music and see the playlist, as in Figure 6-4.

Figure 6-4:
The playlist constructed from three of Carl Franklin's four songs. Universal Music didn't put number four in the right album.

6. **You can use the playback controls — play, pause, change volume, repeat, fast forward, and so on, at the bottom of the screen — exactly as you would expect.**

    After you have the music in the machine, and the app knocked upside the head so it can find the music, the rest is easy.

Finding Music and Playlists

In the next section, I talk about buying new music, but if you already have music in your machine, and you can't find it, you have several options. Here's how to do it to it:

1. **Inside Music, at the upper left, click the hamburger icon.**

    That gives you the list of actions shown in Figure 6-5.

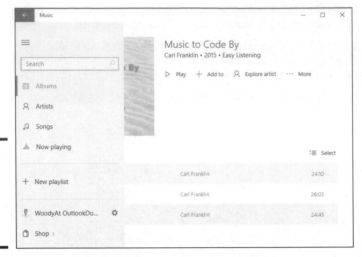

Figure 6-5:
Slice and
dice your
music and
playlists
here.

2. **To see a list of all the artists in your collection, click the Artists icon (the one that looks like a figure 8 chopped at the knees).**

   The list tells you how many albums each artist has in your collection, as shown in Figure 6-6.

3. **To see a list of all the songs in your collection (sorted alphabetically by the first name of the artist), click the Songs icon, which looks like two musical notes (what, two beamed half notes?).**

   The list can be very, very long — and not very informative.

What's a playlist?

Showing your age, aren't you? A *playlist* is a list of songs (or videos) that you want to treat as a group. In the normal course of events, you play a playlist from beginning to end, regardless of where the tracks came from. So if you want to stick a rousing rendition of *Who Let the Dogs Out* in between Beethoven's Fifth first movement *Allegro con brio* and its second *Andante con moto*, you just make a playlist and play it. Slice and dice.

Advanced music management programs give you lots and lots of tools for building, modifying, and managing playlists. Universal Music, not so much.

Figure 6-6:
The list by artist shows you only the number of albums.

Carl Franklin
2 albums

Cassandra Wilson
1 album

4. **To see what's playing right now — the current playlist — click or tap the Now playing icon.**

   You can remove individual songs from the Now Playing list by right-clicking and choosing Remove from List. But for reasons I don't understand, you can't remove the last song from the list.

5. **To create a new Playlist, click the + icon on the left.**

   You're prompted to provide a name for the list, but there are few tools for maintain the list.

You can add or remove an individual song from a playlist by right-clicking on the song and choosing Add To, then the playlist.

Buying Music

What if you decide that the shekels burning a hole in your pocket need a good jolt of blues? Ah, now that's a problem worth solving.

Here's how you buy music in the Music app:

1. **To buy a Music Pass — arguably the best deal, because you can stream "millions" of songs (no indication at this point how many millions) — click the gear Settings icon on the left in Figure 6-5.**

   The Universal Music app kicks up a "setting" with a link to Get a Music Pass. Click that link, and you see the sign-up window in Figure 6-7.

   The fine print here is important: If you pay for the pass, you can stream any songs you like from Microsoft's extensive (but not well-talked-about) collection, and you can stream to the Universal Music app on Windows 10, phone, tablet, or Xbox, as well as iPhones, iPads, and Android phones and tablets. You can download the music on up to four devices (but not Xbox consoles or through the Music web app), but if your subscription lapses, you won't be able to play the songs.

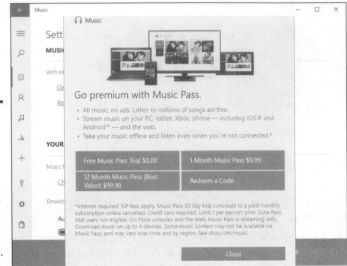

Figure 6-7:
The Music
Pass
(formerly
Xbox Music
Pass,
formerly
Zune Music
Pass) costs
$10 a month.

It would behoove you to compare that offer with the latest offers from Spotify and Pandora.

2. **If you want to buy music — so you have it without a subscription — click the icon at the bottom of the list that looks like a shopping bag.**

You're taken to the Windows Store and placed in the Music section, as in Figure 6-8.

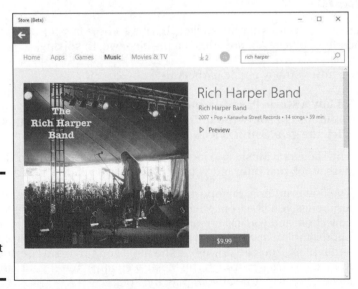

Figure 6-8:
The
Windows
Store has
lots of great
music.

3. **Click the price tag, and pay the piper.**

   The album appears in your Music\Purchases folder.

The Settings icon (the gear on the left) is also the place where you can change the Universal Music app background from a lethargic white to a very cool black, as in Figure 6-9.

Figure 6-9: Turn the background black in the Settings dialog box.

Running around the Movies & TV App

The Movies & TV app behaves much like the Music app. Click or tap Start, and choose the Movies & TV tile; if you have videos already in your personal Videos folder, you see something like Figure 6-10.

The icons on the left side of Figure 6-10 stand for Movies (the ones you buy from Microsoft), TV shows (also the ones you buy from Microsoft), and Videos (all other kinds of video files). As is the case with the Universal Music app, you can click the gear Settings icon and add additional folders for the Movies & TV app to scan.

Double-click a video, and it plays in a letterboxed window, as in Figure 6-11.

The icons at the bottom of Figure 6-11 may be unfamiliar. The first one sends the video to a Miracast-enabled box (such as a Roku or a Miracast receiver plugged into a TV set). The second adjusts the aspect ratio of the playback. Third is pause, fourth is volume, and the fifth puts you at full screen, as you've no doubt done a hundred times before with YouTube videos.

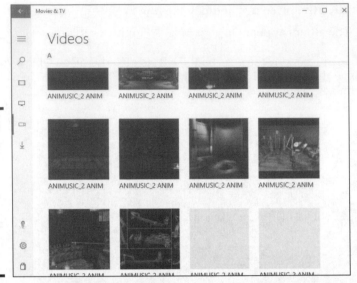

Figure 6-10:
Your own videos appear under the fourth icon on the left, under the hamburger icon.

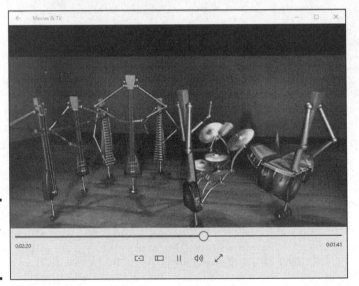

Figure 6-11:
Playing your own videos is easy.

The Movies & TV app isn't much more than a shell at this point, but as the samolians start rolling in, you can expect Microsoft to catch up with the competition.

Book V

Connecting with the Universal Apps

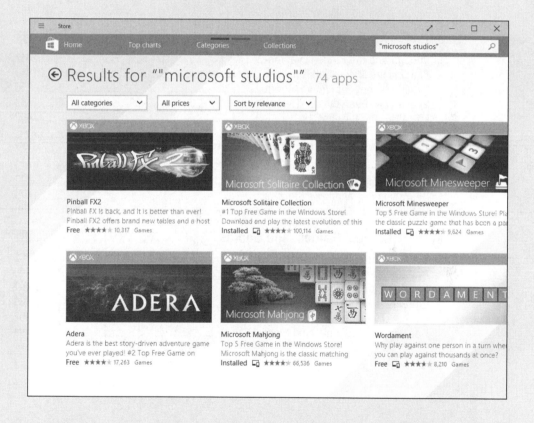

Edge is changing faster than any app in Microsoft's history. See what's new at www.dummies.com/extras/windows10aio/edge.

Contents at a Glance

Chapter 1: Introducing Edge

In This Chapter

✔ **Why does Microsoft need a new browser?**

✔ **What Edge does — and doesn't do**

✔ **Stepping through Edge**

✔ **Settings for the nascent browser**

As we went to press, Microsoft Edge was just starting to spread its wings. Born in a hellish crucible of Internet Explorer excess, Microsoft's new browser is fast and light, and — most importantly — it has shed all the baggage that IE carried for so long.

I touch on Internet Explorer, lightly, in Book III, Chapter 5. I don't recommend that you use it. In fact, I've been actively campaigning against its use since the days of Windows XP.

Why? Microsoft took its dominance in the web browser market as an excuse to release all sorts of Microsoft-only products, tie them into the browser, and convince developers to sing the IE song: ActiveX and Silverlight, Helper Objects, and Explorer Bars are all part of a lexicon that should have never appeared — one that should be crushed as quickly as possible.

What does that mean for you? The web pages you go to that used to be "built for Internet Explorer" are going to fade away. Rapidly.

The web programmers who were so caught up in Microsoft-proprietary technology have had their comeuppance. They're learning to build websites that are hospitable to all browsers. If they don't learn, their sites are going to wither. With Edge, all the browsers stand on a more or less level playing field. And that's truly refreshing.

All in all, Edge has put Microsoft back in the running. It doesn't yet have the huge support and add-on catalogs sported by Google Chrome and Firefox. But it doesn't have their legacy lethargy, either.

Edge has become something of a poster child for Microsoft's newly discovered interest in rapid release cycles. The version of Edge that you're running right now is probably different from the version in this book — and it's probably different from the version you'll see a couple of months from now. The foundation will stay the same, but bells and whistles are inevitable.

A Walk through Microsoft Edge

Let's take a walk around the new kid on the block and kick a few tires. Try this:

1. **Click or tap Start, and then click the Edge tile.**

   Edge springs to attention, as in Figure 1-1.

2. **In the address bar, near the top, type the address of a website you like.**

   I choose `dummies.com`.

Figure 1-1: Here's Edge in all its Spartan glory.

3. **Click links on the web page. Try right-clicking. Convince yourself that Edge works just like any other browser you've ever used.**

For example, a right-click on the Windows XP & Vista entry in Figure 1-2 shows the same basic navigation options you would expect in any browser.

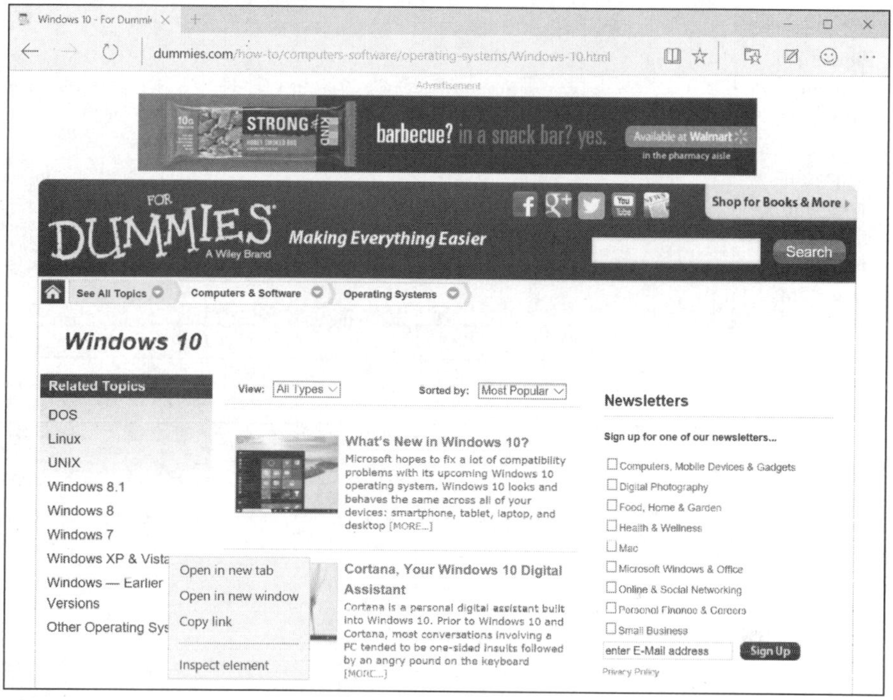

Figure 1-2:
Browser navigation in Edge works just like it works in any other browser. Note the right-click context menu next to Windows XP & Vista.

4. **Now click the icon up near the address bar that looks like an open book.**

That icon activates Reading View mode which, as you can see in Figure 1-3, does a remarkable job of stripping away the crudola and cutting to the meat of the page.

Yes, Figure 1-3 is the same page as Figure 1-2, but in Reading View.

5. **Click or tap the Reading View icon again to bring back the ads and the links. Then click the + sign at the top to start a new tab.**

Edge has an advertisement-laden new tab page, shown in Figure 1-4. The Top sites list is salted — no doubt pointing to companies with sufficient advertising budgets — but the new tab page, nonetheless, does show some recently viewed sites and brings in some interesting Cortana-generated cards, if you click the link marked Show my news feed.

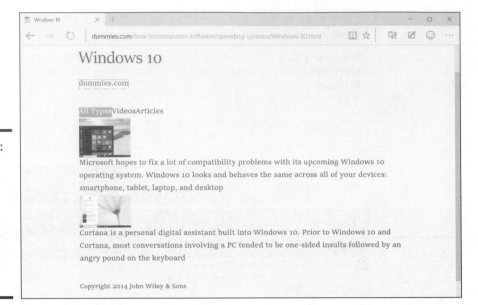

Figure 1-3:
Reading
View cuts
the carp,
strips the
links, and
shows
you the
important
parts.

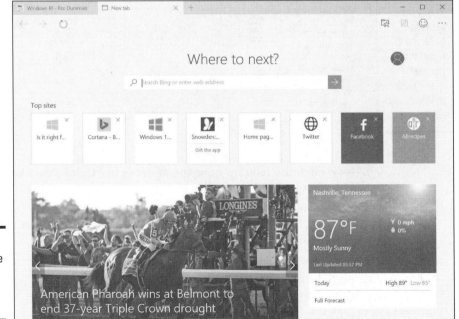

Figure 1-4:
Cards at the
bottom are
controlled
by Cortana.

6. **In the Where to Next? Box (which is just a combined address and search bar, as you've seen in Firefox and Chrome), type** `cuoco-seattle.com` **and press enter.**

   Edge takes you to the website for Cuoco restaurant in Seattle, which is one of the very few sites in the world that support Cortana. See Figure 1-5.

   The Cortana ring on the right end of the address bar starts bobbing up and down like a four-year-old who needs to pee. Click it, and you see all of the details in the pull-out pane on the right of Figure 1-5. There are even links to Bing Maps with driving instructions (only 34 hours and 46 minutes from my place), a Menu link that takes you back to the main page, and a link to book a reservation at `opentable.com`.

Figure 1-5: Cuoco restaurant in Seattle is powered by Cortana.

7. **To the right of the address bar, click the Star icon.**

   That opens up a window, shown in Figure 1-6, that lets you put the site (or some other folder of your choosing) in your Favorites folder and/or add the site to your reading list.

8. **Add the site to your Reading List. Then click the icon on the right that looks like a file folder with a star on it, to see your Reading List.**

   You see the site, as in Figure 1-7. The Reading List items get stored on your computer for later reading.

Figure 1-6: It's easy to add the site to Favorites, as you would expect, but it's also easy to add to your reading list.

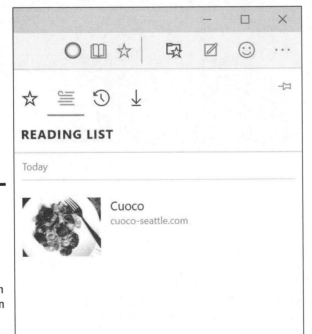

Figure 1-7: Reading List items get copied onto your computer and listed in this pane on the right.

Working with Web Note

Unique among web browsers, Edge has a web page mark-up capability that ties into OneNote, allowing you to make your own annotations on a suitably equipped tablet or touch-sensitive screen.

Here's how to make (and view!) your own Web Note:

1. **In Edge, navigate to a site you'd like to deface. Er, mark up.**

   I navigated to `AskWoody.com`, a place I feel comfortable defacing.

2. **Click the icon in the upper-right corner that looks like a sheet of paper with a pen.**

   The web page is turned into a OneNote-like drawing page, and you're given a variety of markup/inking tools to draw on it. See Figure 1-8.

3. **In the upper-right corner, click or tap the Save icon to save the WebNote to your reading list.**

   Or you can save it in OneNote.

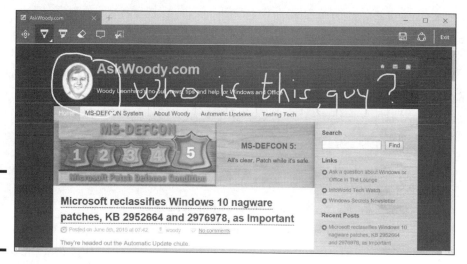

Figure 1-8:
Ink your
own
comments.

A Sampler of Edge Settings

Microsoft Edge is young, but growing rapidly. You can expect its settings to change as it grows some of the features you would expect from any browser. As we went to press, this is what was on offer:

1. **Start Edge, and bring up an interesting page. Click the ellipses icon in the upper-right corner.**

You see the main settings pane shown in Figure 1-9.

If you look at the settings on offer in Figure 1-9, they should strike you as being like just about any settings in any browser anywhere. The only subtleties are Pin to Start, which pins a link to the specific website on the right side of the Start menu, and Open with Internet Explorer, an emergency act for recalcitrant web pages, which does exactly what you would expect it to.

New window

New InPrivate window

Zoom   —   100%   +

Share

Find on page

Print

Pin to Start

F12 Developer Tools

Figure 1-9:
This is a
simple set of
settings.

Open with Internet Explorer

Settings

2. **At the bottom, click or tap Settings.**

   That brings up the next set of Settings, as in Figure 1-10.

   These settings do what you would expect, except that the Show the home button slider brings up a Home icon to the left of the address bar; click the Home icon, and you move to the Home page. There's some leeway in how much advertising you allow Edge to put on the new tabs.

3. **Scroll down the settings pane.**

   Farther down the settings page (see Figure 1-11) you can clear browsing data and set the operating parameters for Reading View.

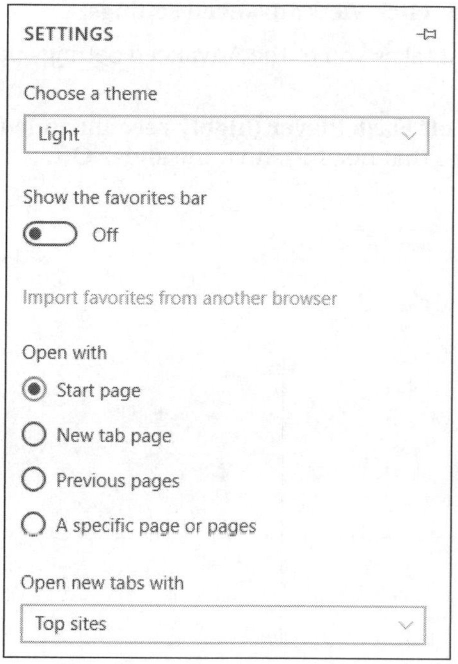

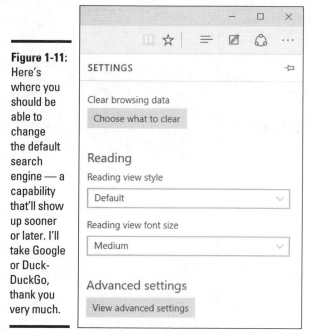

Figure 1-10:
This is a deeper dive into Edge's settings.

Figure 1-11:
Here's where you should be able to change the default search engine — a capability that'll show up sooner or later. I'll take Google or Duck-DuckGo, thank you very much.

4. **At the bottom, tap or click View advanced settings.**

    Not surprisingly, that takes you to the Advanced Settings pane shown in Figure 1-12.

5. **If you want to turn off Flash Player (highly recommended, unless you commonly view sites that need it), turn the slider Off.**

Figure 1-12:
Advanced
Settings
covers a
mixed bag
of important
options.

6. **If you're going to use arrow keys on your keyboard to move around web pages, turn the slider On.**

   Caret browsing, in case you wondered, is the ability to use the directional keys on your keyboard to select text.

   If you turn on caret browsing, you can click or tap inside a web page, and a cursor appears where you clicked. You can then navigate from character to character or line to line by using the direction keys on your keyboard, and you can select text by holding down the Shift key and using the direction keys.

   If you turn off caret browsing, clicking or tapping in a web page does not bring up a cursor. Directional keys move the page up or down, left or right.

7. **Scroll down the Advanced Settings pane to arrive at the choices in Figure 1-13.**

   Do Not Track requests is controversial and not very effective. See the nearby sidebar.

Figure 1-13: Here's where you can change the search engine. Try Google or (better) Duck-DuckGo.

"Do Not Track"

The privacy setting known as "Do Not Track" has a long and torturous history. In 2009, a group of Internet privacy advocates created the "Do Not Track" specification as a way for you, the user, to tell the websites you're browsing that you do not want them to keep track of your visit — no cookies, they won't store your IP address, no monkey business with sending your information to advertisers. All six of the major Windows browsers — IE, Chrome, Firefox, Opera, Safari, and now Edge — can tell sites that you don't want to be tracked.

In mid-2012, as part of the IE 10 push, Microsoft decided that DNT would be enabled by default: Unless you took action to disable it, IE would send the DNT signal to every site you visit. The web standards world, particularly those representing advertisers, erupted. An online advertising advocacy group said DNT would "harm consumers, hurt competition, and undermine American innovation." Go figure.

Ends up that the original sorta-agreed-upon standard said that browsers were only supposed to fly the DNT flag if the user specifically chose it.

Microsoft didn't back off until early 2015, when it announced that IE would not send DNT unless the user had explicitly asked for it. That decision has carried forward to Edge; you won't have the Send Do Not Track requests setting On unless you specifically slide it to On.

It doesn't make much difference anyway. Conformance to the DNT spec was (and is) completely voluntary. About ten websites decided to obey the DNT. (Okay, I'm exaggerating, but aside from Twitter and Pinterest, there have been very few.) The others bowed to pressure from their advertisers and kept doing what they've always been doing.

Will DNT ever take hold and become a de facto Internet standard? Why, yes, I figure it'll happen just about the time advertisers stop advertising on the web. Give it, oh, a hundred years.

8. **Depending on the speed and cost of your Internet connection, consider turning page prediction off.**

Although the overhead isn't very high, page prediction — where Edge anticipates which pages you're likely to want next and fetches them behind the scenes — can drive up your bills, particularly if you're on a line with a low data cap. You can turn it off here.

Look for fast advances in Edge. The tipping point will come when it accepts add-ins. At that point, we'll see how many developers jump to the challenge and what kind of products they can produce. That extensibility has made both Firefox and Chrome must-have products for many people.

Chapter 2: Using Skype in Windows 10

In This Chapter

✔ **Finding Skype**

✔ **Getting signed up for Skype**

✔ **Connecting with Skype**

✔ **Getting along with Skype**

E verybody knows Skype, the instant text-messaging, long-distance, telephone-killing video-chatting program. Not everybody knows that it started as something of a hacker's fantasy, about a decade ago, in Estonia. Two of the key players in getting Skype to market, Janus Friis from Denmark and Niklas Zennstrom from Sweden, spent their earlier years getting Kazaa — the notorious file-sharing program — off the ground.

Microsoft bought Skype, lock, stock, and barrel camera, in 2011, for a paltry $8.5 billion — yes, that's billion with a "b." The brass moved to Redmond, but most of the techies are still in Tallinn and Tartu, Estonia.

In spite of appearances, Skype is a Microsoft product. One hundred percent.

Skype was once known as a long-distance phone killer, but it's broadened enormously since then. In addition to voice, Skype also handles instant messaging (including SMSs to phones) and video calls, both one-on-one and conference call style. You can use Skype to call regular phones anywhere in the world, for an extra fee, which seems to change from year to year.

Microsoft's building Skype hooks into all sorts of products — your Windows Contacts come along for the ride, and Office is fully Skypable. Skype works, and works well, with iPhones and iPads, Android phones, Android tablets, but historically it's had a very difficult time with Windows.

It took Microsoft a couple years to get around to building a Metro Skype app for Windows 8.1. The app was widely panned and shunned. About a year later, on July 7, 2015, Microsoft killed the Metro/Universal app officially, saying they'll build a new one sooner or later. If you run Windows, of whatever stripe, your only choice is the desktop app (`https://www.skype.com/en`) or going through a web browser (`https://web.skype.com/en/`). As of this writing, the web browser version leaves much to be desired.

Many hundreds of millions of people use Skype. The last official tally, from December 2010 — before Microsoft took over and stopped publishing statistics — put the number of registered users at 663 million.

Exploring Skype Alternatives

Before you look for Skype on your Windows 10 computer, realize that Skype runs on just about anything: iPhone, iPad, Android phones and tablets, Windows XP or later, Windows Phone, Mac OS X, Xbox One, Blackberry — just about anything.

At the time we went to press, Skype runs better on all of those machines than it does on Windows 10.

Don't have a Skype app on some random computer? No problem. Just go to www.skype.com and download it.

I've played with Skype on dozens of machines, and I'm convinced that the best way to use voice-only Skype is on a phone, and the best way to use video Skype is on a tablet or a phone with a big screen.

If you only have a desktop connected to the Internet, you don't have many choices. If you're using a laptop with a built-in camera and mike, it'll work, and the picture may be great, but I bet you won't be impressed by the Skype sound quality. On the other hand, if you have an iPad, an Android tablet, or a big-screen phone, you're going to find that setting up and using Skype is a lead-pipe cinch. Download the app and install it, and everything just works.

The only downside? Skype is still tied to Skype usernames. Someday, you'll be able to connect using an everyday phone number. But we're still in user-name hell. Skype has an estimated 300 million users, but Microsoft keeps the numbers close to the chest.

Alternatives to Skype? Jeeeeeeeeeeeez. Just about everybody does over-the-top voice and video calls these days. ("Over-the-top" means they run on the internet directly, not through the phone company, and they're thus basically free.) A quick Google scan brings up the names of dozens of programs and program-less websites that can do the job. These are the big competitors:

Facebook Messenger and **Facebook Video**, www.facebook.com/video, work great with anyone who has Facebook. Chatting competitor WhatsApp is now part of Facebook, swallowed up for a paltry $19 billion. If you and your friends are on Facebook, it's an excellent choice.

Viber, www.viber.com, (600 million users?) also lets you call regular phones all over the world. Your Viber ID is your phone number.

LINE, www.line.me/en, may be the biggest chat app of all in terms of volume (400 million active users?), with a solid hold throughout Asia. It was built by the employees of NHN Japan, in response to the Tohoku earthquake in Japan in March 2011. With LINE you can add contacts by scanning QR codes and phone numbers or by shaking phones simultaneously; it has Facebook-like posting capability, groups, locations, and just about any feature you can imagine. Easy to see why it's spread that fast.

There are many others, including China-based Weibo (167 million?), WeChat (470 million??), Renren, ringID, Hike, and Tango. Google Hangouts (https://plus.google.com/hangouts) seems to be everyone's favorite whipping boy, with all sorts of problems real and imagined. Apple's FaceTime works tremendously well — but only on Mac, iPhone, and iPad.

What do I use? Glad you ask. I have many messaging programs set up on various machines, but most of the time I want to use my phone (Samsung Galaxy Note), not my desktop. Most of the friends I want to call use LINE, so I almost always pull up LINE instead of Skype, as shown in Figure 2-1.

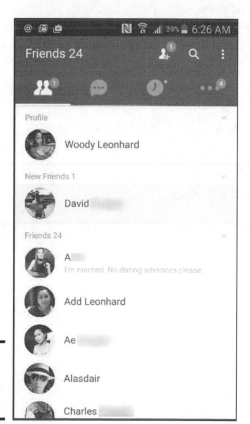

Figure 2-1:
LINE has become my favorite.

The case for LINE

Microsoft's support for Skype in "modern" Windows has dropped from lousy to nonexistent. My recommendation is that you use just about anything else until MS gets its act together. When I'm talking with people on an iPad, Mac, or iPhone, my first choice is FaceTime. But for a mixed environment, I swear by LINE. It just works on just about everything.

LINE covers the gamut from plain old phone calls to text, images, video, and audio, and it's completely free. If you know people in Asia, chances are very good they already have it and depend on it — and they may be a bit surprised that you aren't using it, too.

LINE makes its money by selling zillions of sets of emojis and "stickers." They're cheap and people love them. Right now, more than a billion stickers are sent every day. That keeps LINE more than solvent.

LINE has one significant limitation: When you create an account, it can be used on only one mobile device and one personal computer. If you want to run LINE on both your iPhone and your iPad, you need to use two different accounts: You can only verify one phone per mobile phone number/email address.

You can get the Windows (desktop) version of LINE here: `http://line.me/en/download`.

LINE's easy to navigate, reliable, works on (almost) any computer, tablet, or phone, and drop-dead simple to set up and use — even for dummies. See the sidebar.

Signing up with Skype

Here's how to get started with Skype.

 If you're using a local account to sign in to Windows — as opposed to a Microsoft account — and you crank up Skype, Skype prompts you immediately to switch to a Microsoft account. **If you want to use Skype, you must use it with a Microsoft account.**

Microsoft has tried to atone for the lack of a Windows Universal Skype app by placing a "Get Skype" link on the Start menu. Here's how to use it:

1. **Click or tap Start, All Apps, Get Skype.**

Yes, it's under the "G" listings.

You see the download site shown in Figure 2-2.

2. **Click or tap Download Skype.**

It only takes a second. At the bottom of the screen, you see a notification that SkypeSetup.exe finished downloading, and a button marked Run.

Skype keeps the world talking. Call, message and share whatever you want for free.

Download Skype ↓

Figure 2-2:
Download
Skype from
this (slightly
modified)
web page.

3. **Click or tap Run.**

   That starts the installer.

4. **Select your language (presumably English) and click or tap I agree — next.**

   Skype wants to know if you want to enable Click to Call — a free service that identifies specially marked Skype numbers on some web pages.

5. **Unless you really want Click to Call, uncheck the box marked Install Skype Click to Call and click Continue.**

   Next you're given the wonderful opportunity to make Bing your search engine and/or MSN.com your home page. Yeah, right.

   At this point, the installer only offers to make those changes on Internet Explorer, Firefox, Chrome, and Safari. Edge is noticeably absent. Not keeping up with the times, are we, Microsoft?

6. **Uncheck the two boxes marked "You're kidding, right?" (or something like that) and click Continue.**

   The installer does some downloading, ultimately returning with, uh, Skype. The old-fashioned Windows desktop app, not a shiny new Windows Universal app.

   The installer asks you to sign in with either a Skype Name (for old timers) or a Microsoft Account.

7. **Type the Microsoft Account that you're going to use to log in to Windows, when you're running Skype. Fill out the password and click Sign In.**

    Skype finally gets around to its sign-up page, as shown in Figure 2-3.

Figure 2-3:
Sign up for
Skype.

8. **Click or tap I'm new to Skype.**

    Finally, you get to the obligatory Terms of Use and Privacy Policy page. You can read both if you have a spare half an hour (and a law degree). Or you can do what everyone else does — uncheck the boxes asking for permission to spam you, both by email and by SMS.

9. **Click or tap I agree — join Skype.**

    Windows Firewall may appear at that point, warning you that the Firewall has blocked some features of this app. Keep in mind, both Windows Firewall and Skype are made by Microsoft.

10. **If you get a message from Windows Firewall, at the bottom, click Allow Access.**

    Skype then asks if it's OK to allow calls and Skype links to always open with Skype for Windows desktop.

11. **Check the box marked Do not ask me again, then click Yes.**

    If you get a notification saying "To change your default apps, go to Settings > System > Default apps," realize that although Skype and Windows come from the same company, they don't play well together. Just ignore it and click OK.

    You get the final setup screen in Figure 2-4.

Figure 2-4:
The old-
fashioned
Windows
desktop
version of
Skype.

12. **Click Continue.**

Skype puts up a test page like the one in Figure 2-5.

13. **Click the Test sound button and make sure your speakers are working. Speak and you shall be heard. Look at your wondrous pic in the
pic place. Then click Continue.**

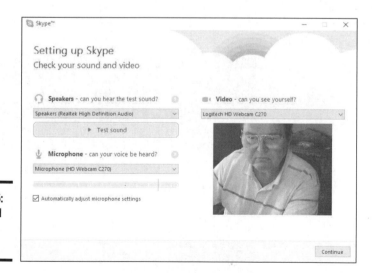

Figure 2-5:
The sound
and video
check.

If there are problems with your mic or speakers, Skype helps step you through some corrective actions.

You can add your picture later.

Congrats. You've just completed the setup. Maybe someday Microsoft will get its Skype act together.

Making First Contact

Each of the different versions of Skype — the beta version on the website, the Windows desktop version described in the preceding section, iPad, Android, and so on — presents a slightly different way of working, but they all have the same basic core features. The locations on the screen may vary, but the actions are all quite similar.

A note about nomenclature: All through Skype (and other Microsoft products), you'll see the terms "Contact" and "People" used interchangeably. There's no difference. Very confusing. Microsoft refuses to use the obvious word, "Friend," because Microsoft has few friends (and Facebook would undoubtedly retaliate).

The first time you use Skype, it will ask you if it can search your address book. See Figure 2-6 — which is remarkable for the fact that apparently none of the people in the pictures on the top of the screen are using Skype.

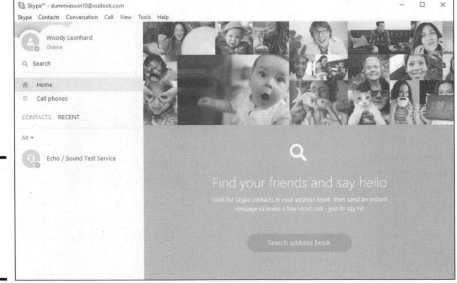

Figure 2-6: Skype asks for permission to spam all your contacts.

If you're really up for sending automatic messages to all of your (former) friends, go right ahead. Otherwise, just ignore the right part of the screen and get down to work.

Start by typing the name of someone who uses Skype, in the search box on the left. Press Enter. That brings you to the main Skype screen, shown in Figure 2-7.

Figure 2-7:
The basic Skype calling page.

You'll see two buttons at the top right and two columns in the main part of the screen. Here's what they mean:

✦ **Telephone handset button** is what you click to make a "real" phone call, to a "real" phone number. Skype has discount prices for making calls to real phone numbers.

✦ **Video camera button** (which looks like an old-fashioned camcorder) starts a video call.

✦ **Search** (which looks like a magnifying glass), on the left, goes to the Skype search function, so you can look up people you might know.

✦ **Contacts** column lists all the people you can call. Getting a person added to your Contacts list is not a one-way street: You have to ask the person, and he/she/it(?) must give permission before you're allowed to call him. See the next section.

If you can figure out how to get to each of those points on whatever device you use — desktop, laptop, tablet, phone, watch, keyfob — you'll have 90 percent of the Skype shtick down.

Adding a Contact

Before you can call someone, you have to make her an "official" Contact — which means you have to ask for, and receive, permission to call.

The methods for adding Contacts vary depending on which version of Skype you're using. In most versions, you have to go into the People list before you can add a new Contact. Here's how to add a Contact in Windows Skype:

1. **On the initial screen (refer to Figure 2-6), use the Search box to find someone you want to add as a Contact.**

Yes, trying to search by name can be a hassle. Skype lets you search by name (such as "Woody Leonhard"), Skype Name (a name that predates use of Microsoft Accounts), or email (a Microsoft Account).

When you've found someone you'd like to add, the screen should look like Figure 2-7.

2. **Click the button marked Add to Contacts.**

Skype formulates and offers to send a message to that person. If you click Send, Skype sends the message and logs the fact on your call screen. See Figure 2-8.

Figure 2-8: The first step in adding a contact involves asking permission.

3. **Wait.**

   If your Contact-to-be clicks or taps the invitation, and either responds to it (as on the Android) or clicks Accept (as in the Windows version of Skype, see Figure 2-9), you'll suddenly find yourself able to communicate.

Figure 2-9:
Accept a
contact
request and
the conver-
sation
can begin
immediately.

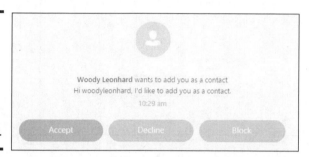

Woody Leonhard wants to add you as a contact
Hi woodyleonhard, I'd like to add you as a contact.
10:29 am

Accept   Decline   Block

4. **Add a few more friends, er, Skype-enabled Contacts, and you're ready to roll.**

   If you "X" out of Skype, the program continues to run — it can notify you of any incoming calls — but it shows you as Offline. There's an icon for Skype conveniently stuck in your taskbar, just to remind you that the program's alive and well.

After you get your Contacts going, I think you'll find it very easy to start a new conversation (click or tap the Contact/People/Friend), bring up old conversations and add a Contact to your favorites list.

A Few Tips from Skype-ologists

By default, people can send a friend request to you if they have your old-fashioned Skype Name (they're rapidly being phased out), if they type your real name ("Woody Leonhard") into the search box as in Figure 2-7 and can guess which result belongs to you, or if they have your primary email address. You don't have to respond to a Contact request.

There's a currently-nascent ability to add additional information to your Skype account. Someday, people may be able to search for you based on that information, but as I write this, the whole feature is garbled and doesn't work.

To see what info Skype has about you, in Skype, click your name in the upper left (it probably says "Online"). You see something like Figure 2-10.

Figure 2-10:
The
information
collected
by Skype
is quite
minimal.

Microsoft pushes ads in the free versions of Skype — they can take up the top bar of the display — and Windows 10 is no exception. I have no idea how to turn them off.

When you install the old-fashioned desktop version of Skype, Windows 10 puts a tile labelled Skype for Desktop in your All Apps list.

Skype-to-Skype calls are free. But Skype has many, many more options that aren't free. You will probably find that the Skype options are much, much cheaper than normal long-distance phone charges. There are promotions all the time and lots of ways to game the system. See www.skype.com just for starters.

Finally, don't make the mistake of thinking that your Skype conversations are secure. Although Microsoft hasn't officially admitted it, most industry observers (including me) are quite confident that Skype — and thus Microsoft, and thus the National Security Agency — can listen to or watch anything that's being transmitted over Skype. No matter what you think of Microsoft, Skype is not secure.

The folks at Skype are coming up with new capabilities all the time. For example, Skype Translator — which is only marginally functional as we went to press — may offer real-time voice translations between English and other Romance languages . . . and possibly a few others, as well. We're still a long way from Arthur Dent's Babel fish. Eurgh!

Chapter 3: News, Money, and Sports

In This Chapter

⮑ **Finding the Bing in everything**

⮑ **Getting a different slant on the news**

⮑ **Pinning Money for profit and fun**

⮑ **Working with the Sports app**

Although the tiles may be scattered hither and yon on your Start screen, three of the key Windows/Universal apps are really just portals to viewing stuff that's being fed by Microsoft Bing. In fact, by the time you read this, Microsoft may have even more Bing-y apps for you to install.

The Bing-based Windows/Universal apps are easy and cheap for Microsoft to assemble: Basically, what you see in the app's window is, in each case, a wrapper around a web browser that's set to work with the Bing search engine. The content is actually controlled by the Bing servers, and it's pulled down to your screen when you ask for it.

News delivers a very visual take on the latest news, with short articles that adapt reasonably well to a finger-first approach. In this chapter, I show you how to personalize News — there are several key options — but I also compare and contrast the Bing approach with the iPad Bing approach and the web Bing approach. I also toss in a bit of Flipboard, which may suit your fancy better than all the others.

In a similar vein, *Money* delivers colorful, picture-filled news reports and lots and lots of charts that aren't very touch-friendly. In this chapter, I show you how to focus on stocks that concern you, track interest rates and other economic indicators, and explore a few other features, all while repeating to myself that Microsoft wasn't willing to spend the bucks to deliver real-time stock quotes.

My friends tell me that *Sports* (called "MSN Sports" inside the app) is the greatest thing since live-streaming football games. (And those friends tend to think of "football" as what Americans call "soccer.") Although it's likely that other sporting outlets will have their own Windows 10 apps sooner or later,

Microsoft's Sports packs lots of information — and gorgeous pictures — into a compact frame.

Recognizing the Bing in Everyone

All three Microsoft Bing apps follow the same format:

✦ **A huge, high-definition photo is on the front page.** The front page photo is usually cycled onto the app's Start menu tile, with other photos also appearing.

✦ **Tiles for articles come in various sizes.** (Money leads with a market graph, followed by the articles.) The individual articles are short and, ahem, shallow, all the better for touch-enabled devices.

✦ **Each app has numerous customization options from stocks worth watching to favored news topics.** Slide from the top or right-click the desktop to bring up these options.

✦ **The source of all the information inside the apps is Microsoft's Bing.** And Bing is culled and maintained by a human team inside Microsoft. The team may or may not bring items to the limelight that interest you.

Just in case it isn't obvious: These apps don't do much of anything unless they're connected to the Internet. Bing does its thing in Microsoft's cloud, and spoon-feeds the results to you.

The Microsoft Bing apps are just shells: They rely on their connection to Microsoft's computers to come up with their content and perform their magic. That isn't necessarily bad. But it does contribute to a sort of blandness that you won't find if you go out on the web and find information in other ways.

Contrariwise, you aren't going to see many Bing articles about three-fingered aliens attacking dorms in Nantucket. Sometimes, it's good to have a content filter.

Reading the News with Bing

The News app includes some remarkable customization options.

Getting around News

At its heart, the News app is a wire-service aggregator. As you scan through the news stories, you can see where they came from.

Let me take you on a guided tour:

1. **Look at the News tile on the Start menu.**

   If you've used the News app at all while connected to the Internet, you see a picture that slides up and down, revolving with a one-sentence news description that actually matches the picture. See Figure 3-1.

Figure 3-1:
The News Start screen tile.

   If you've never used the News app, the tile that appears on the right side of the Start menu is just a blank tile with a little bit of text.

2. **Tap or click the Bing News tile.**

   The Top Stories panel appears with a high-definition photo associated with a top story. See Figure 3-2.

Figure 3-2:
The Headlines top stories appear as a series of large-size pictures.

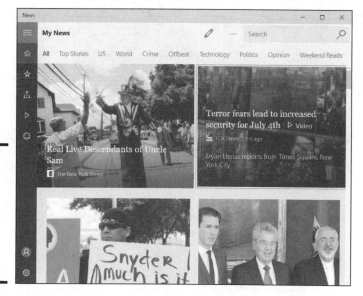

3. **Tap or click the story.**

   If you're using a tablet, you immediately realize that the text can't be pinched to zoom — although, confoundingly, the pictures can. The text size you see is what you get. See Figure 3-3.

   If you swipe up and down, you can continue to read the article. That's also true if you use the wheel on your mouse. Swiping from the left or right, or clicking the wedge arrows in the margin, takes you to the next (or previous) story.

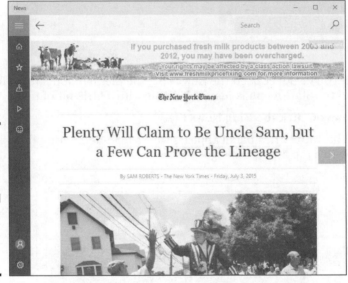

Figure 3-3: Individual stories cannot be zoomed, and they scroll in ways you might not expect.

4. **Go back to the main Headlines screen (refer Figure 3-2) by tapping or clicking the back arrow in the upper-left corner. (You can also click the hamburger icon in the upper left and choose Headlines.) Scroll or swipe to see the main categories offered in the News app.**

   Depending on your location, you probably see a dozen or two stories each in of these categories: U.S., World, Sci/Tech, Business, Entertainment, Politics, Sports, and Health.

   You can also tap or click the hamburger icon and choose Interests (the star icon) to see a list of trending topics in the national and international news. See Figure 3-4.

5. **In your favorite web browser, go to `www.bing.com/news`.**

   Note the tabs at the top of the Bing news page in Figure 3-5. They're almost identical to the sections in the Windows News app.

Figure 3-4:
Interests
lists topics
drawn from
your online
behavior.
There's lots
of overlap
with, for
example,
the
Windows
Universal
Money app.

Figure 3-5:
The Bing
News
website
mirrors the
Windows
News
app —
except the
web app
has more
news, and
it's faster.

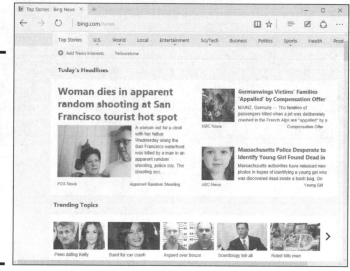

The overlap in categories emphasizes that the Bing News app is just a
repackaging of the Bing News site — but there's more to it than that.
Two concerns:

- The website packs much more information onto your screen at the
  expense of those huge high-def photos. Where the Windows News app
  shows just one top story, the website shows many more.

- In weeks of testing, I didn't see *any* breaking stories on the News app until after they appeared on the Bing News website. Usually, hot news items don't appear in the Windows News app until 4 to 8 hours or more after the news stories appeared on the Bing News site. Although the website's stories get updated frequently, the Windows News app isn't nearly as timely.

6a. Grab your iPad, if you have one, **install the Bing for iPad app (yep, it's in the Apple App Store) and look at Bing News from the iPad point of view. See Figure 3-6.**

Figure 3-6: Bing — yes, the same Bing — as seen from an iPad.

6b. If you don't have an iPad, **skip to Step 8.**

Bing for iPad looks a little different, but it has several of the same categories. Tap the Finance tile, for example, and you can put your choice of three stocks or indices on the screen.

7. On the iPad, tap the News tile at the bottom.

You get a full array of news stories (see Figure 3-7). Bing on iPad puts 24 stories on the screen, compared to the handful on the Windows News app. The pictures aren't as nice, but the categories are similar, and it's much easier to find a news story on the iPad.

Figure 3-7:
Bing News
on the iPad.

8. **Think about what you want from a news source.**

Although Windows News has beautiful pictures, it has very few stories, the stories are dated, and they're harder to find. The web version of Bing News is okay, and the iPad version is considerably better. But, frankly, I wouldn't waste my time on any of them.

I like Flipboard (www.flipboard.com) for the iPad, iPhone, Android, and now Windows 10, as well. Flipboard has a wider variety of sources than Bing News, its interface is much better, and it feels more like a news magazine and less like a tablet-size billboard. And it's free. Check out the Windows Store.

Adding your own Interests

When you first look at the Windows News apps' Interests (refer to Figure 3-4), you see a generic group of items that may or may not be of interest to you. What you don't see is the fact that "Topics" are really saved searches.

Here's how to see what's going on:

1. **In the upper-right corner of any News view, type in the name of something that interests you.**

   For example, in Figure 3-8, I type Yellowstone. Bing goes out and scours its collection, looking for items that match your search criteria.

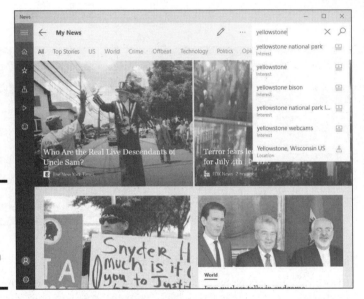

Figure 3-8:
To make your own Interests, start with a search.

2. **Press Enter to bring up the search results. Then click the Star icon at the top of the screen.**

   That adds your search term(s) to the Interests list.

3. **Click or tap the back arrow in the upper-left corner to return to the main MyNews list.**

   You can see that Yellowstone is now a topic in its own right, on the far right side of Figure 3-9. Click the topic, and it's just like running the search all over again.

When you save a search by turning it into an interest and then click an individual story, Windows News fires up Edge, opened to the story you chose. You can see how Edge lives inside Windows Universal News in Figure 3-10.

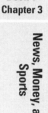

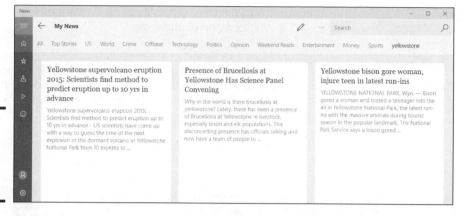

Figure 3-9:
Interests
are nothing
but saved
searches.

Figure 3-10:
Clicking
an article
brings up
Edge inside
the "News"
shell.

Navigating inside the story doesn't follow the Windows News standards; instead you're at the whim of the people who design the news website where you're headed. In Figure 3-10, that means clicking a link does whatever the Delhi Daily News site wants.

If you go to a news site that has some sort of blocked content (see Book V, Chapter 1) — maybe one trying to run Silverlight — you see warnings that say videos can't be viewed because you don't have the correct version of Silverlight. It's a bogus error message, but you're still stuck. The only way to view the animation is to flip over to the desktop version of IE and try to find the same page — which can be challenging.

Moral of the story? Use a different news aggregator. There are many. I recommend Flipboard (`www.flipboard.com`), as shown in Figure 3-11. It's an excellent, free Windows app that you can get at the Windows Store. (Yes, I know the Android and iOS versions are better. Or at least, they were as we went to press.)

If the pictures don't ring your chimes — just the facts, ma'am — just work with a news site on the web; I use `https://news.google.com/` all the time.

Figure 3-11:
Arguably the best known news aggregator, Flipboard lets you personalize just about everything. Windows News doesn't even come close.

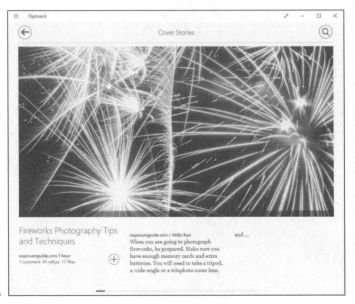

Pinning Money for Fun and Profit

Unlike the Windows News app, the Windows Money app doesn't have any glaring usability problems.

Well, okay, you can't pinch to make the text look bigger. It's heavy on the U.S. stock exchanges and a little light on news outside the United States. But other than that, Windows Money is reasonably usable — it even has an excellent international-capable watchlist.

Here's a quick run-through:

1. **On the Start menu, tap or click the Money tile.**

Like the Windows News app, the Money app opens with a gorgeous, high-definition photo, but it is overlaid with stock quotes and advertisements, as shown in Figure 3-12.

If the markets are open, you may also see the major U.S. index ticker at the bottom of the picture.

Figure 3-12: Windows Money splashes a gorgeous photo, no doubt to help you make good investment decisions.

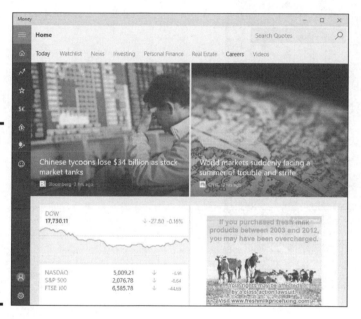

2. **Tap or click the hamburger icon in the upper left.**

Money shows you a navigation bar (see Figure 3-13) that'll take you to the important parts.

3. **Back on the main Money screen (refer to Figure 3-12), tap or click the lead story or one of the other stories, which you can see if you scroll down.**

You see a presentation — and ads! — identical to the kind you see in the News app, as in Figure 3-14.

Pages can't be pinched to resize the text, but you can swipe to move pages. Navigate around a bit, and you'll get the hang of it.

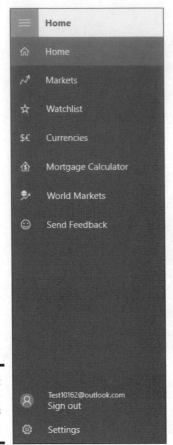

Figure 3-13:
Navigation
in Windows
Money.

4. **Tap or click the left arrow next to the story headline and go back to the main screen. Scroll down.**

   Here's what you see:

   - *Depending on your location and time of day, you may see an interactive graph of the major U.S. indices:* DJIA, S&P 500, NASDAQ, and Russell 2000, with Day/Month/Week/Year tiles on the bottom. You don't get point-and-read stock quotes. Nor can you plot your own trend lines, or plot one security against another. But all in all, it's a decent graph.

   - *News:* Shows just what it says — more news stories. Click a picture, and you're whisked away to the full story.

Figure 3-14:
Money articles look much like Windows News articles. They're all drinking from the same BingCup.

As I was putting together this chapter, I noticed something amazing. The entire Money app has nothing from the *Wall Street Journal*. If that's generally true — and not a one-day aberration — chances are good it's because *WSJ* has a paywall, and Microsoft wasn't willing to pay the Wall Street piper. In general, with *WSJ*, you're allowed to view a few articles every month and then you're expected to pay. *WSJ* is notorious for its paywall.

5. **Go back to the main Money screen (refer to Figure 3-12), and tap or click the hamburger icon. Then tap or click the Market icon.**

    You see an overview of the markets.

6. **Tap or click the hamburger icon. Then tap or click the Watchlist icon.**

    Watchlist in the Money app works much like the Topics item in the Windows News app: You specify what you want to see. Think of it as a saved search.

7. **Start by clicking or tapping Add a favorite, and add a couple of stocks, funds, indexes — even overseas stocks work fine.**

    In Figure 3-15 you can see some stocks that interest me.

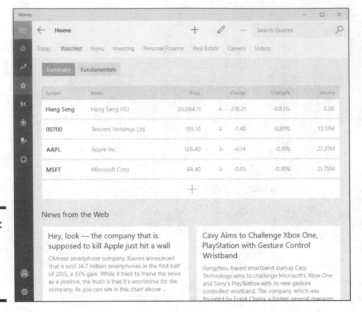

Figure 3-15:
It's easy to create your own watchlist.

The Watchlist includes stocks, funds, and commodities — basically anything with a symbol — that you want to watch. If you click the Summary block at the top, you see current prices and ranges. Click Fundamentals, and you get the same ticker items, with P/E, ROA, Yield, and so on. It's thorough, if an odd interface. Click an individual stock, and you get rudimentary charts and trading details.

Below the list of sticker symbols you see news for each symbol, drawn from a wide array of sources (but, again, no *WSJ*). Click a news block and, just like the Windows News app, you're sent to Microsoft Edge and placed on the right page. Just as with Topics in the News app, you're at the mercy of the browser and the website designer.

8. **To add your own sticker symbols to the Watchlist, tap or click the plus icon at the bottom of the list. Type the name or symbol of the product you want to watch, and the app looks it up for you. Click the symbol, and it's added to the list — both the ticker numbers and the saved news search.**

   You might also note that the news items in the screenshot refer to the securities in my watchlist.

9. **Back on the main Money screen (refer to Figure 3-12), tap or click Currencies.**

   You see a currency converter, with two drop-down lists of currencies, as in Figure 3-16.

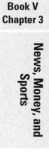

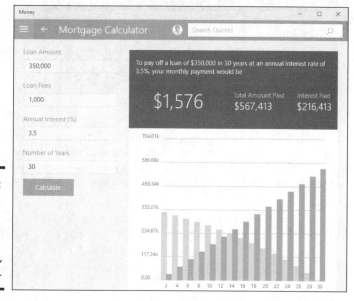

Figure 3-16:
Convert
any amount
between
currencies.

Scroll farther down to see conversions into other currencies. Tap or click Currency Rates to see the latest trading exchange rates and the daily trends. Don't see a currency that interests you? Choose it in the drop-down box on the right, and click Add to Watchlist.

10. **Click the hamburger icon, and choose Mortgage Calculator.**

You see the very basic mortgage payment calculator shown in Figure 3-17.

Figure 3-17:
The
mortgage
calculator
won't win
any awards,
but it works.

It's an easy alternative to hunting down a mortgage calculator on the Internet.

11. **The final hamburger item, World Markets, isn't very interesting.**

World Markets shows major exchanges (Dow, FTSE 100, DAX) and their one-day histories.

Sports Fans Everywhere, Take Note

Of the three Bing-driven apps, Windows Sports consistently receives the highest accolades.

Like the others, when you open the app you see a gorgeous (well, given the subject matter, maybe not exactly gorgeous, but certainly well crafted) high-resolution photo (see Figure 3-18).

Figure 3-18: Like the other Bing apps, Sports starts with a biiiig picture.

You may be tempted to click one of the boxes on the main screen, but try scrolling down. You see an enormous collection of news tiles, each headed by an excellent photo. Click one of the news tiles, and you see a report that's very similar to the ones in the Windows News app, as in Figure 3-19.

If you want to add another team or sport, click or tap the hamburger icon in the upper left, choose My Favorites, and click Add to Favorites.

The hamburger icon (see Figure 3-19) will overwhelm you with its navigation choices: Today (which is the main page), any teams you've added to your Favorites, NFL, NBA, MLB, NHL, NSA (Okay, I made that one up), NCAA, Golf, Soccer (Football to the aficionados), NASCAR, Tennis, and More Sports — which adds Ozzie football, Ruggers (for those who give blood), Nippon Baseball, LPGA, every Soccer (er, Football) division you've ever encountered, Formula 1, IPL Cricket, and many more.

Although I confess I didn't find Ultimate Frisbee among the choices.

Figure 3-19: There's an enormous amount of Sports News — and a whole lotta advertizing going on.

More Universal Apps

If you're looking for the Microsoft Travel, Health & Fitness and Food & Drink apps, they aren't here. They aren't in Windows 10.

Microsoft took the old Windows 8.1 Health app and turned it into the new Health & Fitness app, just for Windows 10 testing. Then, for reasons that remain obscure, they pulled the app a couple of weeks before Windows 10 shipped.

Similarly, the powers that be took the old Food app, morphed it into Food & Drink, displayed it for all to see, and then suddenly removed it as

Windows 10 went out the door. The Travel app (formerly "MSN Travel") made a similar journey. So if you heard about them, or you're expecting to see spiffy versions in Windows 10, you're going to be disappointed.

Fortunately, other Universal apps are just as good, if not better. That's what this part of the chapter is about — bringing back the old Bing app apps, but from different vendors.

Tripwolf, the Anointed Travel Guide

Starting with Windows 8, and on into Windows 8.1, and then the Windows 10 testing process, Microsoft pushed its MSN Travel app, one of the slate of Universal apps built around its Bing engine.

Imagine my surprise when, as Windows 10 approached the end of the testing cycle, I bumped into a web page extolling the virtues of tripwolf (it's spelled with a lower case "t"). Not just any web page, mind you. But an official Microsoft blog page. Recommending tripwolf.

I figured something was in the wind, and shortly after Microsoft announced that it was pulling the rug out from under the MSN Travel app. I have no idea what happened, but tripwolf (see Figure 3-20) suddenly became Microsoft's anointed Universal travel app.

Figure 3-20: Microsoft's new chosen travel app.

Microsoft had (and has) a long association with Fodor's, which publishes its own Universal travel app. Tripwolf combines content from Fodor's and Marco Polo and adds enormous quantities of beautiful photos to produce a top-notch app. If the name sounds familiar, it's because tripwolf has been available on both Android and iOS for many years.

Tripwolf has many advantages over simple guidebook-like apps. You can download the guides and use them completely offline — no internet connection required. You can plan a trip in advance, and bring it up wherever you might go. There are lots of TripAdvisor-like comments from real travelers. And if you're connected to a GPS, tripwolf can stick a "You are here" pin on any of the maps. That's bound to help when you're looking for a restroom in the Vatican.

The general tripwolf shtick goes like this: You can look at the listing for any major city (there are more than 150) for an hour, for free. If you want to look for more than an hour, or download the entire location, that costs a small amount — $4.50, at this writing. And if you want the whole guide to all locations (see Figure 3-21), it costs $50.

Figure 3-21: Individual cities are cheap; the whole guide is hefty.

Although most people use tripwolf on an iPad or Android tablet — or even in the somewhat more cramped confines of their phones — running on a larger Windows machine with a bigger screen has its benefits.

Before you spring for the whole shebang, realize that tripwolf only concentrates on the most popular, largest cities. If you want to go someplace off the beaten track — Koh Samui, for example, isn't listed — make sure you look before you buy. I also had trouble with the map. Clicking on a map link for Phuket (my old stomping grounds) took me to the eastern Atlantic, off the coast of Africa. It's a long swim.

BBC Good Food

The old Bing-driven Food & Drink app doesn't have an analog in the current crop of Windows Store Universal apps, but the Beeb offers an interesting alternative.

The BBC Good Food app (Figure 3-22) has 20 free recipes — I particularly like the "Easy" classic Lemon and thyme roast chicken, shown in the upper left of the screenshot — and "cookbooks" that you can buy. Each cookbook gets downloaded to your computer, so you don't have to be online to follow a recipe.

Figure 3-22: BBC Good Food has 20 freebies and a bunch of inexpensive award-winning recipes.

The $1.99 cookbooks each contain 170 recipes and span a variety of cuisines. Each recipe lists calories, protein, carbs, fat, saturated fat, fiber, sugar and salt per serving. I found the instructions very easy to follow.

Fitness & Health

I fully expect this category to get over-run by companion apps in the next year or so, as people who buy specific kinds of fitness equipment flock to the Windows App Store for companion apps. Fitbit, for example, already has a decent (if not particularly inspired) Universal app.

Look for Microsoft to get its act together with an app to go with the new Microsoft Band, one of these days.

I'm particularly impressed by all the good Yoga apps. (Hey, I'll never have sixpack abs, but at least I can avoid a sixpack butt.) The apps I like best have brief videos of specific exercises, along with a narrative. I use Windows 10 and my Roku to broadcast them on my TV (see Book X, Chapter 2, for details).

Just search in the Windows Store on "yoga," download a few alternatives and see which one(s) you like. Figure 3-23 shows a typical scene from Simply Yoga, which is a collection of yoga exercises from Daily Workout Apps, LLC.

Figure 3-23:
Simply
Yoga, a
typical yoga
app.

Most of the yoga apps have additional in-app purchases — typically videos of different exercises — that let you support the company that produced them. Simply Yoga, for example, contains several in-app purchases, so unlocking the full video costs a whopping $4.

Chapter 4: Navigating the Windows Store

In This Chapter

➤ Getting the lowdown on Windows Store apps

➤ Exploring the Windows Store

➤ Updating your Store accounts and preferences

If you're familiar with buying programs in the Apple App Store or the Google Play Store, you already know about 90 percent of the procedures you'll find in the Windows Store.

That said, the selection of programs, breadth, and quality are considerably better in either the App Store or the Play Store. I hate to be the bearer of bad news, but developers these days go for iOS apps and Android apps long, long before they think about Windows. Whether that will change anytime soon remains to be seen. Microsoft's working on it, but they've been working on it for years.

The reason's simple: money. There are large fortunes to be made with cool apps in the App Store and the Play Store. There's also a reasonable amount of money in apps that are designed to run in Facebook and even apps that run on the Internet. But the Microsoft Store is less than a backwater when most developers tally up the shekels.

Microsoft's Windows Store launched simultaneously with the release of Windows 8. The Windows Store is a big, extensible, very usable source of new programs for all of Windows.

Yes, you read that right. Although the Windows Store used to be the sole province of "Metro style" apps — what we call Universal apps in this more enlightened age — now the Windows Store carries all kinds of apps, even ones that run exclusively on the Windows desktop.

Apps make or break any computer these days, and Microsoft knows it. That's why you find some popular apps in the Windows Store — it's good for you and good for Microsoft, over and above the 30 percent commission Microsoft makes on every sale.

For many folks, the Windows Store continues to be a major disappointment. The big-name apps are appearing in the Windows Store at glacial speed — there wasn't even a legitimate Facebook app until more than a year after the original launch, and even now big-name players shun the Windows Store with glee. Slowly Microsoft's filling in some of the gaps — they're even paying developers with new ideas and cajoling old-timers as best they can — but don't be surprised if you hear about a cool Apple or Android app, and you can't find it in the Windows Store. Happens all the time.

The only way you can get new Universal apps for Windows is to download and install the app from the Windows Store. Although large companies can put Universal apps on their Windows devices (using a technique known as *sideloading*), normal people like you and me have to go through the Windows Store: the alpha and omega of Windows Universal apps.

Checking out What a Universal App Can Do

The longer Windows Store is available, the more apps you'll find there. The apps do all sorts of things, but each app also must meet a set of requirements before Microsoft will offer the app in the Windows Store.

Here's a short version of what you can expect from any app you buy (or download) via the Windows Store:

✦ **You can get both Universal apps (which are supposed to run on any version of Windows 10 including Windows 10 Phone) and legacy-style apps (which run on the old-fashioned desktop) from the Windows Store.**

If you want a new program for the desktop, you may be able to find it in the Windows Store, or you may be able to get it through all the old sources — shrink-wrapped boxes, monster download sites — to find and install what you want.

But if you want a new Universal program, you must get it through the Windows Store — unless you have a big company. (See the sidebar "Bypassing the Windows Store restrictions.")

✦ **Universal Windows apps can be updated only through the Windows Store.** If your apps are set to update automatically — the default — when an update is available, the Store tile on the Start screen shows a number, indicating how many apps have updates available. See "Adjusting Your Store Accounts and Preferences" later in this chapter.

✦ **Apps that use any Internet-based services must request permission from the user before retrieving, or sending, personal data.**

✦ **Each app must be usable on up to five computers at a time.** For example, if you buy the latest high-tech version of Angry Birds, you can run that same version of Angry Birds on up to five Windows 10 devices — computers, tablets, maybe phones (if it'll work on phones) — at no additional cost.

✦ **Microsoft won't accept apps with a rating over ESRB** *Mature,* **which is to say "adult content."**

✦ **Apps can (thankfully) put only one tile on the Start screen.**

✦ **Apps must start in five seconds or less and resume in two seconds or less.** Microsoft wants apps to be speedy, not sluggish; thus, it requires developers to make sure their apps meet this requirement.

In addition to the basic requirements for any app, you're also likely to find that the following is true of most apps:

✦ **Microsoft's tools help developers create trial versions of their apps, so you can try before you buy.** The trial versions can be limited in many ways — for example, they work only on a certain number of pictures, messages, or files or only for a week or a month — before demanding payment. That's all part of the plan.

Where try-before-you-buy has a long and checkered history on the desktop, it's baked into many Windows Store apps. Microsoft is very strict about requiring the developer to explain precisely what has been limited and what happens if you fork over the filthy lucre.

✦ **If an app breaks, you can complain to Microsoft, but the support responsibility lies 100 percent with the developer.** Although Microsoft acts as an agent in the distribution and sale of apps, Microsoft doesn't actually buy or sell or warrant anything at all. Even the license for using the tiled-style program goes between seller and buyer, with Microsoft out of the loop.

✦ **Many apps attempt to get you to buy more — more levels, more features, more content.** Microsoft has that covered, just like Apple and Google: Orders generated by the app must go through the Windows Store. Only Microsoft can fulfill the orders. Ka-ching.

Don't confuse the Windows Store — which hooks directly into Windows — with the Microsoft Store, which has both Internet and meat-space manifestations. Brick-and-mortar Microsoft stores are popping up all over the place (another bright idea borrowed from Apple). The online Microsoft Store, www.microsoftstore.com, serves as an online extension of the physical Microsoft stores. In the online Microsoft Store, you can buy the new Microsoft Surface computers, applications that run on the desktop, as well as competitors' computers, Xboxes, headphones, mice, phones, Windows, Office — in short, everything you find at a Microsoft store.

If you're familiar with the Apple view of life, the Windows Store is comparable to the App Store and the iTunes Store in general. Apple Stores, of-brick-and mortar persuasion, are analogous to Microsoft Stores.

Bypassing the Windows Store restrictions

Microsoft runs the Windows Store as a business — a tightly held business — and for that reason, it restricts what can be bought in the Windows Store. Microsoft can reject an application submitted to the Windows Store for a huge variety of reasons.

Here's the key point you need to understand about the Windows Store: With two exceptions, the Windows Store is the *only place* you can get Universal Windows apps. See Book I, Chapter 2 for a description of Universal apps.

The exceptions:

✔ Big companies can bypass the restriction and put their own programs on Windows machines using a technique called *sideloading.* At least in theory, sideloading can be accomplished only on machines that are locked in to a corporate network.

✔ If you *jailbreak* your PC (or phone), you may be able to put any tiled Universal apps you like on your computer — Microsoft's censors no longer apply. On the other hand, jailbreaking your computer voids every warranty in existence and automatically disqualifies you from Microsoft support. Think: No security patches, lots of exposure. Because there are very few apps available for jailbroken Win8/Win10 machines, there's basically no incentive to jailbreak your computer.

Unlocking (which may or may not be accompanied by jailbreaking) allows you to switch carriers, if you bought your PC (or phone) from a carrier who's locked in its services. Some carriers in the United States, for example, may offer a discounted price for your tablet in exchange for a multi-year Internet contract. If you unlock the computer (or phone), you may (or may not) be able to hook it up to a different network. All sorts of penalties may apply.

I don't recommend that you jailbreak your PC. But if you find an app that you really want and Microsoft won't let it into the Windows Store, jailbreaking may be your only option. Google is your friend.

Browsing the Windows Store

When you're ready to venture into the Windows Store for Universal Windows apps, tap or click the Store tile, and you see something like Figure 4-1.

Moving around in the Windows Store is a little funky. The following tips can help you move around and find what you're looking for:

✦ **You need a Microsoft account** to get anywhere beyond basic searching. You can't even download a free program unless you're logged in with a Microsoft account. (Microsoft needs it to keep track of what apps are on your machine.) If you logged on to Windows with a local account, the Microsoft account requirement splats you right in the face, as in Figure 4-2.

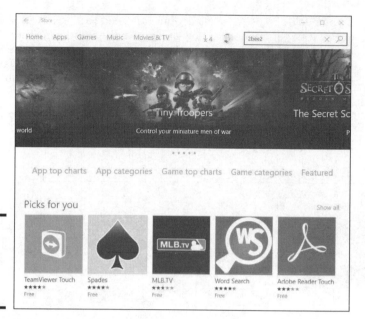

Figure 4-1:
Here's a
peek at the
Windows
Store.

Figure 4-2:
You can't do
anything but
go window
shopping
with a local
account.

If you decide to use a local account but need to sign in with a Microsoft account to get updates or new apps from the Windows Store, set up a bogus Microsoft account (see Book II, Chapter 5) and use the facility offered in Figure 4-2 to sign in to each app separately. That way, you'll be warned before you venture into another location that requires a Microsoft account.

✦ **To order an app,** tap or click the app's tile. The Store takes you directly to the ordering screen for the app. For example, if you tap or click the tile for the Kindle app, you see the ordering page in Figure 4-3.

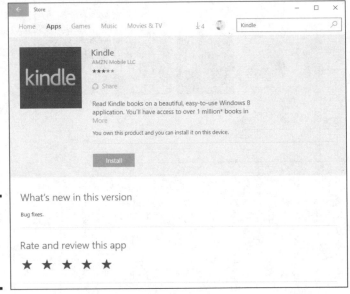

Figure 4-3:
The app ordering page for the Kindle app.

At the top, you see an overview of the app and you can get a more detailed feature list by clicking or tapping the More link. Scroll down, and you see the Ratings and Reviews. Even farther to the right, and you should see a release history (except for Microsoft's own Universal apps, which didn't have histories in earlier versions), list of permissions required, languages, and links to the manufacturer's site.

The star rating shouldn't impress you — it's the accumulated wisdom of all the people who've bothered to rate the app. But the supported languages section, if there is one, may be of interest — and the permissions list is detailed and thorough. At the very least, you can vent your spleen on the Reviews page if the app doesn't live up to your expectations.

✦ **To view apps by group,** from the main Store screen, click or tap Apps and scroll down. You see Picks for You (there's a reason Bing collects all that data, eh?), Top free apps, Top paid apps, New and rising apps (as opposed to old and declining, no doubt), Best-rated apps, Collections, and Categories. For example, in Figure 4-1, if you click Apps and then click Show All next to Top Paid, you see the mass shown in Figure 4-4.

WARNING!

Beware the marketing tricks. For example, the Free PowerPoint Templates app you see in Figure 4-4 is made by a company called Luzala Studio, and copyright by a company called Canalviral. If you hop on the web and look for Luzala Studio, you find a website with such nuggets as this: "Luzala | Responsive Onepage HTML Tempalte / Lorem ipsum dolor sit amet, consectetur adipiscing elit. Suspendisse varius enim in eros elementum tristique." Their Lead Developer is named "John Doe." If you want to send $4.99 their way, hey, knock yourself out.

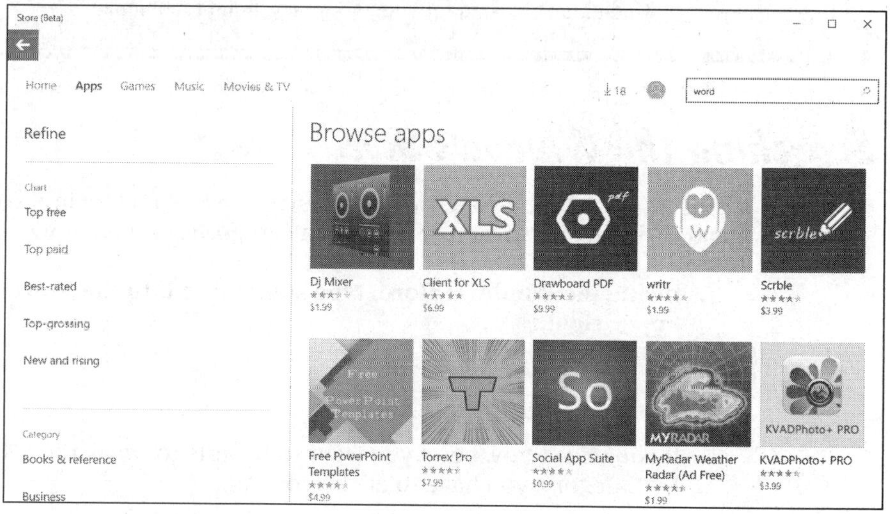

Figure 4-4:
In the Top paid apps group, you'll find a copy of "Free PowerPoint Templates" priced at $4.99.

Two out of three reviews for Free PowerPoint Templates run 5 stars. They appear to be written by people who have not used the app and who don't speak English very well. The one review that appears to be genuine starts out "Crashed on first opening."

Microsoft has spent millions vetting the apps in the Windows Store, but you'll find crapware like the $4.99 Free PowerPoint Templates everywhere. Ever wonder why first-tier developers don't really want to put their stuff in the Windows Store?

What? A Kindle app on Windows?

Hard to believe, but Amazon and Microsoft have cooperated long enough to put a Kindle app on the tiled Metro part of Windows. Not long ago, Microsoft paid $300 million to form a strategic partnership with Amazon quasi-competitor Barnes & Noble. Now, Amazon has put together a Kindle app that looks like something from the bottom of a Cracker Jack box.

The Kindle app takes the approach that many third-party apps mimic: As soon as you install the app, you need to sign in with your username and password. Don't be confused: Amazon (the purveyors of Kindle) isn't looking for your Microsoft account or your local account. Amazon's looking for your Amazon Kindle account.

After you sign in to the Kindle app with your Kindle account, all the Kindle books you've bought from Amazon are immediately available. Yes, inside Windows. As of this writing, the app had lots of minor problems — scrolling is cumbersome, the library is hard to view — and you can't go to the Kindle Store from inside the app; you get flipped over to your browser. Still, it's an amazing accomplishment organizationally, if not technically.

Searching the Windows Store

You can search the Windows Store using the Search box in the upper right, and/or by taking advantage of built-in categories. Here's how:

1. **Inside the Windows Store, type something into the Search box in the upper right.**

   In Figure 4-5, I typed news.

2. **At the top, click Show All.**

   It isn't clear why, but if you want to be able to break the 5,423 hits down by Category, you have to click Show All.

   Windows Store shows you a list of categories on the left.

3. **Choose a category.**

   In Figure 4-6, I looked for Entertainment News apps. Look at the quality of apps on offer.

   The HD Movies app you see in Figure 4-6, for example, consists entirely of promo shots and reviews (not movies) that appear to be lifted verbatim from IMDB. Fortunately, the developers, listed as Shaymaa Mustafa Hashim, Aly Ahmed, and Amr Khamise, aren't asking for any money.

Figure 4-5:
Looking for
News in all
the wrong
places.

Ever wonder why so many bad apps are in the Windows Store? Preston Gralla has a great investigative report in Computerworld that explains it. Back in 2013, Microsoft "launched a promotion in which it paid $100 to developers for apps they sent to the Windows Store, regardless of quality or type of app. Each developer could get up to $200." `http://www.computerworld.com/article/2600035/microsoft-windows/did-microsoft-help-seed-the-market-for-windows-store-scam-apps.html`.

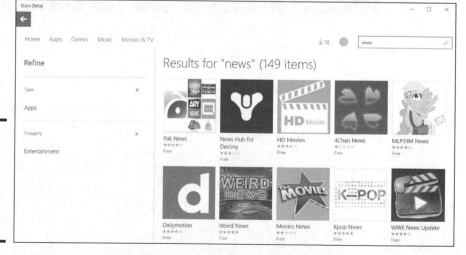

Figure 4-6:
Lots of, uh,
big name
Entertain-
ment News
apps on
offer.

Updating Your Windows Store Apps

Microsoft is updating all sorts of things through the Windows Store — not just apps you bought or downloaded from the Windows Store, but also the built-in Universal Windows apps, and the list is likely to expand over time.

Sometimes, the Windows Store doesn't update itself (as it will in the normal course of events). You should check from time to time to make sure you have the latest updates for absolutely everything. Here's how:

1. **Start the Windows Store app.**

It's probably on your taskbar.

2. **Up at the top of the window, next to your picture, see if there's a down arrow and a number.**

In Figure 4-7, you can see that I have 18 downloads waiting.

Figure 4-7: The tiny down arrow and number at the top signify that I have updates waiting.

3. **Click or tap the down arrow.**

Windows shows you the waiting updates, as shown in Figure 4-8.

4. **Click or tap Update all.**

In the normal course of events, you'll want to update all your apps, but if you know of a bad update (and they happen), you can pick and choose which apps you want to bring up to date.

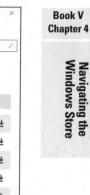

Figure 4-8:
These
updates are
waiting for
permission.

From time to time, you'll hit a problem with an update. An error report
pops up, as shown in Figure 4-9. If you hit an error, try installing the
update again by clicking or tapping the circle-arrow icon on the right.
If that doesn't work, you should either run the error number through
Google, or you can try contacting the app manufacturer. Good luck.

Figure 4-9:
From time to
time, even
app updates
fail. Don't
panic. Call
Saul.

Chapter 5: Games, Games, and Games

In This Chapter

✔ **Searching for games**

✔ **Klondike and the Solitaires**

✔ **Tapping Pirates Love Daisies**

✔ **Starting with Sudoku**

✔ **Old games reborn**

The Windows Store offers tons of games. Many of them, including some free ones, are well worth trying.

If you're looking for old Windows standbys like Minesweeper and Solitaire, they're here too — but they're all gussied up, fabulously more playable, and very touch friendly, unlike their elder counterparts. In fact, the free touch-savvy Minesweeper and Solitaire may be enough to convince you to buy a touch tablet. No joke.

Unfortunately, the old Windows 7 cheats don't work anymore, but the eye candy should more than compensate.

In this chapter, I talk about a sampling of games — free games — that you can download from the Windows Store and play directly on just about any Windows 10 computer. You don't need a monster graphics card, $600 joystick, or the reflexes of a trained fighter pilot to play.

Well, it helps to have the reflexes of a trained fighter pilot. But that's okay. You can limp along, just like me.

One thing all these games have in common is that there really are strategies to help you win. Take a few minutes to read about the idiosyncrasies of the games, and you may find yourself jumping a few extra levels or plucking off a couple of rats.

The free games that come with Windows 10 run quite a gamut. Microsoft itself offers loads of free games, and some of them may be preinstalled on your computer. The poster child of the add-on bunch, Cut the Rope, runs on iPads and iPhones, but the game action on Windows 10 is faster — primarily because the whole game was rewritten (with Microsoft's help) in HTML5.

You can read all about the technical dexterity on the U.K. Team blog for the Microsoft Developer Network, `http://blogs.msdn.com/b/ukmsdn`.

If you're looking for Xbox games, you're in the wrong place. The Xbox ecosystem has some overlap with Windows 10, but by and large, Xbox gaming exists at a completely different level of complexity. If you're looking for an intro to that world, start at `support.xbox.com`.

I'm going to assume that you haven't coughed up the money to buy an Xbox: If you have, you should approach Xbox gaming from the Xbox side, not the Windows Store Game app side. I talk about Xbox in Book IV Chapter 7.

Although the Xbox Game app has some very cool capabilities — and more than a few top-ranked games — in my experience, they don't work very well if they live in an Xbox-free environment. That may change over time, but for now, the Xbox and Kinect provide a much, much better gaming "experience" than a tablet or PC connected to a TV set.

Searching the Store for Games

Want to see what games will run on Windows 10? Head to the Windows Store. Here's how:

1. **Click or tap Start; then, on the right, tap or click the Store tile.**

   The Windows Store appears.

2. **In the Search box, in the upper-right corner, type** free games **and click Enter or tap the magnifying glass. Then click or tap Show All on the right, in the Apps category.**

   An enormous array of tiles for games appears, as shown in Figure 5-1.

   Choosing games is a black art, all by itself, but if you see a game that looks interesting, check it out.

3. **Tap or click any interesting game.**

   The Windows Store shows you a complete description of the game and presents you with an opportunity to install the app. In Figure 5-2, I chose Sonic Dash.

   Note in particular that the description of the program includes a list of what you can buy while inside the app ("in-app purchases") and their prices.

4. **To install the app, make sure you're willing to pay the price, and then tap or click Install.**

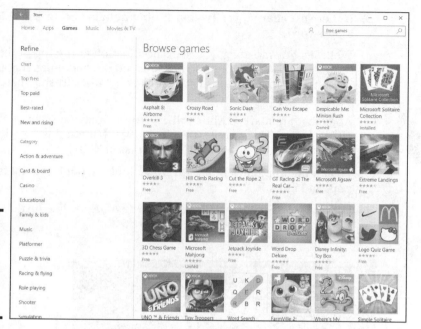

Figure 5-1:
Free games offered at the Windows Store.

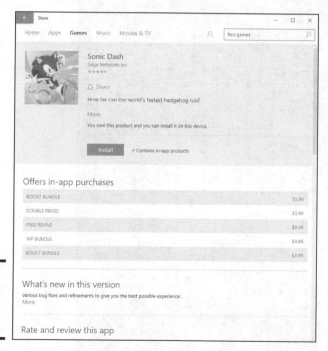

Figure 5-2:
If it tickles your fancy, install it.

5. **If there's a charge, verify your billing details and/or provide a password.**

   While it's downloading, you see a notification at the top of the Windows Store screen. When your app has finished downloading, it appears as an entry on your All Apps list, just like any other freshly installed Windows app.

   Apps that are marked Xbox will, in general, play on plain ol' Windows 10 machines. For example, Despicable Me: Minion Rush works fine on Win10 (refer to Figure 5-1). It also works on Xbox.

6. **To run the app, click Start, All Apps; look through the list for your app, and click it.**

   For example, Sonic Dash appears on the All Apps list, just like any other Windows app, as you can see in Figure 5-3.

Figure 5-3: Games appear just like any other app in the All Apps list.

Downloading and installing a game is one-click easy. Finding them and beating them are anything but.

Bringing Back the Classics

Admit it. You want to play Solitaire on your new Win10 machine. And Minesweeper. Just like you did in Windows 3.1. (Windows 3.0, actually.) Well, you're in luck — and they're easy to find if you know where to look.

Just crank up the Windows Store, and in the Search box in the upper right, type "Microsoft Studios" — including the quotation marks. Press Enter. In the Games section, press Show All. You get a list of all the apps published by Microsoft Studios, as shown in Figure 5-4.

If you're an experienced Windows user, you might want to pick up some or all of these free games.

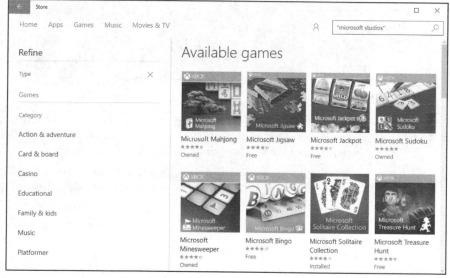

Figure 5-4: These apps are published by Microsoft Studios.

✦ **Microsoft Solitaire Collection** includes Klondike (the game you no doubt remember as "Solitaire," shown in Figure 5-5), Spider Solitaire, FreeCell, Pyramid, and TriPeaks.

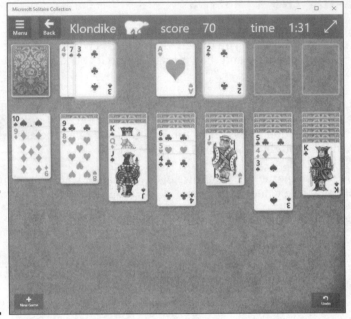

Figure 5-5:
Klondike, the game you remember from when you were a kid.

None of the old cheats work in Solitaire — you can't switch how many cards you flip in the middle of a hand, or peek — but you can still play with hints, or choose between 1-card and 3-card draws.

✦ **Microsoft Minesweeper**, the game that BillG loved to hate, works very much like it has for many years, in many versions of Windows. See Figure 5-6.

✦ **Microsoft Mahjong** brings the classic click-clack to the screen.

✦ **Microsoft Sudoku** is explained in the next section.

✦ **Adera** is a story-driven adventure game that you can play with your kids.

There are many more, but those Microsoft Studio games should keep you going for hours. Or days.

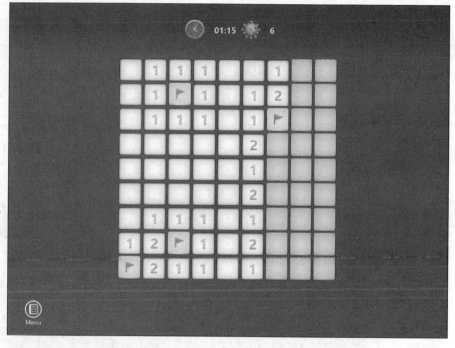

Figure 5-6: Mine-sweeper works like the original, but looks much better.

Starting with Sudoku

If you've ever tried to finish a really hard Sudoku, you know it can be quite a challenge.

Microsoft's Sudoku game starts by asking whether you want a Very Easy, Easy, Medium, Hard, or Expert game (see Figure 5-7). One guess which one I usually pick.

Sudoku has a fascinating history. Apparently, the first puzzles of this type to appear in print were published in *Dell Magazines,* starting in 1979. They were known as Number Place. It appears as if they were created by a 74-year-old retired architect named Howard Garns from Connersville, Indiana.

These puzzles first appeared in Japan in the *Monthly Nikolist* paper, starting in April 1984. The name *Sudoku* is an abbreviation of a lengthy Japanese name that means, roughly, "the digits are limited to one occurrence."

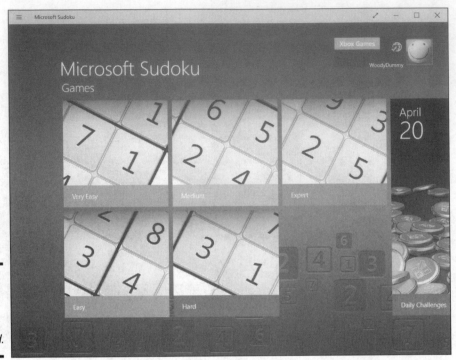

Figure 5-7:
When it
says *hard*,
it means
haaaaaaard.

The object of Sudoku is to arrange the digits from 1 to 9 in a 9x9-grid, so that each column and each row has one of each digit. To make things a bit more complex, each of the nine 3x3-blocks must also have all the digits from 1 to 9.

You're presented with a grid, prefilled with some numbers. Your challenge is to come up with an arrangement of digits that fits all the rules.

The game play in this app is a bit confusing. First, tap or click a number at the bottom of the screen. Then click or tap a square where you want the number to go. To clear a square, tap or click it, then tap or click the "Erase" block on the bottom left.

If you put a number on the grid and the number already exists in the same row or column, you goofed, and the number appears with a red "X". If there are no immediate conflicts, the number pulses in white. See Figure 5-8.

The Internet has about 200 billion free Sudoku grids.

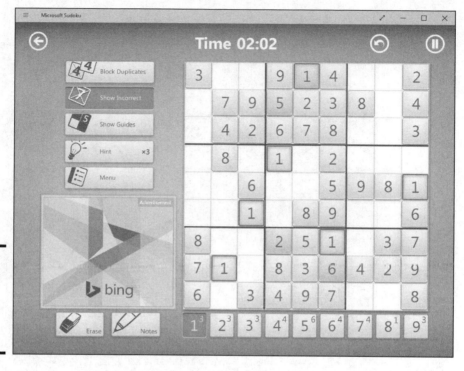

Figure 5-8:
Sudoku the
Microsoft
way, with a
Bing ad, of
course.

Cutting the Rope with Style

Everybody knows Angry Birds.

Cut the Rope isn't Angry Birds. The physics are a little more complex, and the variations are trickier. That said, it's every bit as addictive as its feathered counterpart. And there aren't any stinkin' pigs.

Many people don't realize it, but Cut the Rope was invented in Russia in 2010. It became very successful on the iPad and iPhone with more than 1 million copies sold in the Apple App Store *in the first nine days*.

Microsoft picked it up as a demo for its HTML5 browser experiments, then ported it hook, line, and sinking candy monster to the tiled side of Windows 8. No doubt the 'Softies hope that some of that App Store magic rubs off on Windows 10 players.

There are both free and paid versions, with the paid versions running more levels — and considerably more challenge. In theory, the free version is a "trial version," but in fact it's free and will always be that way.

The back story isn't terribly complex: You need to get a piece of candy into the mouth of the adorable monster Om Nom and collect points along the way. The action is based on pendulum swings, anchored by ropes, where you get to decide when to, uh, cut the rope. See Figure 5-9.

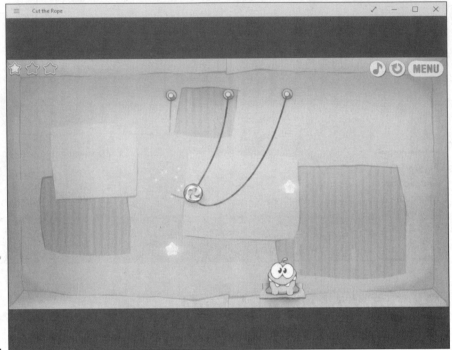

Figure 5-9:
Cut the Rope to give Om Nom the candy.

Things get considerably more complicated when you encounter bubbles: When a piece of candy hits a bubble, it's absorbed into the bubble, and the bubble and candy rise together. Bellows push the candy and bubbles around. Spikes and electricity can pop the bubbles. With each new level, you see different layouts and accoutrements.

Scoring is pretty intuitive: You get points for touching stars with candy, and the faster you go, the more points you get.

Advancing levels isn't intuitive at all. You start in the Cardboard Box, which has nine levels, but only one is unlocked; that's the one you have to play.

Each level holds three stars. Collect at least one star and feed Om Nom, and the next level gets unlocked. See Figure 5-10.

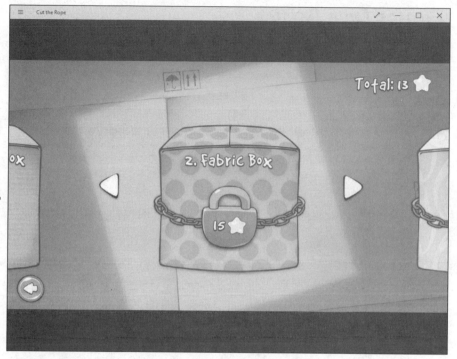

Figure 5-10:
Collect at
least one
star and
feed the
monster,
and you can
go on to the
next level.

Collect enough stars in the Cardboard Box, and you're allowed to progress to the Fabric Box. Get enough stars there, and you can go on to the Toy Box. And from there . . . you get to pay for the next levels.

You may think that your progress through the game is measured by points. It isn't. The trick is in the stars.

Here are a few more tricks:

✦ Don't get hung up on finishing a level. If you get frustrated, remember that you only need to catch one star and feed Om Nom, and you're granted access to the next level.

✦ If you're in an impossible position (believe me, it happens often), just cut the candy free or click the circle-arrow in the upper-right corner to start the level all over again (refer to Figure 5-9).

✦ If you encounter blue dotted circles with slider bars, think about moving the slider bar — and thus the circle — before you start cutting ropes.

Throw ol' Om Nom a bone.

Pirates Love Daisies

Another big Microsoft score for the Windows 10 platform and another early port to HTML5, Pirates Love Daisies (see Figure 5-11) is a thoroughly modern rendition of a class of games called Tower Defense.

Figure 5-11: Pirates Love Daisies is a considerably less-gory variation on Plants vs. Zombies.

Microsoft convinced Flash programming guru Grant Skinner to try his hand at an HTML5 game. Just like Cut the Rope, it was an attempt on Microsoft's part to demonstrate that HTML5 had the moxie to carry along a real-world game. The result is a fun and playable game that isn't overly sophisticated and doesn't rely on zombies.

The back story reverberates with preteen swashbucklers: "Davy Jones is sending his scurvy minions to steal your most valuable possessions: your daisies. Only your stalwart crew can stop them before they take all your fragrant flowers to the murky depths. Hire new crew members and place them strategically to prevent the creeps from nabbing your daisies and returning to the water from whence they came."

In other words, shoot the crawling things before they take your daisies and crawl back in "the water from whence they came." I think "from whence" is a pirate phrase or something. Arghhh.

When you bring up the main screen (see Figure 5-12), tap or click Help to get a general overview.

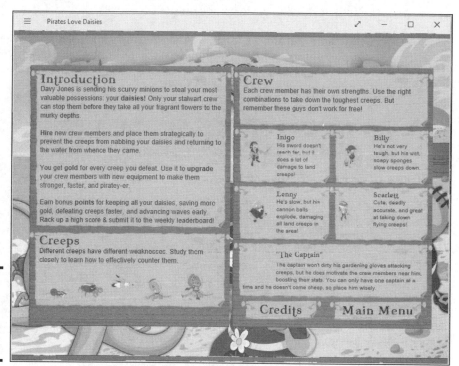

Figure 5-12: Bright and colorful pirates with perfect hair.

The key thing to realize about Pirates Love Daisies is that your sole point of interaction is in placing one of the characters in a specific location on the map. You don't fire the guns or swash the buckles. The characters do that all by themselves — no clicking required.

When you have enough gold stored (accumulated by killing the creepy critters), tap or click one of the characters, and then tap or click at the base of one of the picks that appears. The character is transported to the location you click and starts fighting all by himself.

A simple strategy for dealing with the first level: Put lots of pirates at the entrance to the bridge. Then put more pirates next to the daisy field to fend off flying critters.

Despicable Me, Sonic, and More

I'll finish with two more games on the top ten list.

Despicable Me: Minion Rush, a trusty Android and iPad staple, lets you run, run, run through the Minion worlds, gathering bananas in your wake. Seriously fun, with great graphics and an addictive (keyboard-based!) navigation capability. See Figure 5-13.

Figure 5-13: Everyone's favorite bald yellow thing runs like crazy in Minion Rush.

Sonic Dash (Figure 5-14) puts the iconic Sega character through his rolling, jumping, diving paces, gathering rings along the way.

Figure 5-14:
Yes, Sonic
is now on
Windows 10.

Another game best known on Android and iOS, Sonic Dash has multiple
levels and alternate characters, which you can buy by collecting enough red
rings — or paying cash, of course. Just $3.99 for a breakout bundle of 30 red
star rings.

And you thought free games were free.

Book VI
Socializing with the Universal Apps

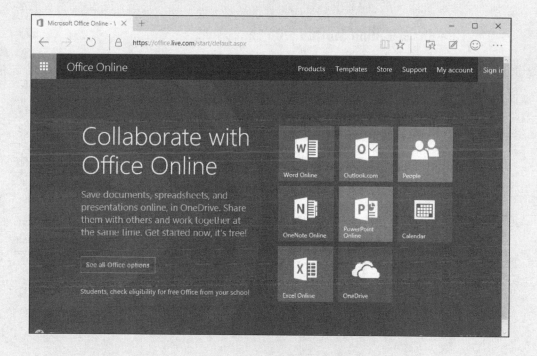

More people use Facebook than Windows. See how Android mobile users fare with Facebook at www.dummies.com/extras/windows10aio/facebook.

Contents at a Glance

Chapter 1: Organizing Office for Windows 10

In This Chapter

✔ **Understanding the various versions of Office**

✔ **Installing the touch-friendly Universal Office**

✔ **Tips to get more done, faster**

*I*n this chapter, I look at the touch-friendly "Universal" version of Office and how it works with (and against!) Windows 10.

If your only interest is in the old-fashioned mouse-centric version of Office, you have my sympathies and my encouragement (only slightly tongue-in-cheek, this coming from somebody who started with Word 1.0), but the problems and opportunities with Office 365/Office 2016 are very different, well-documented, and grist for great books such as Peter Weverka's *Office 2016 All-In-One For Dummies* (John Wiley & Sons, Inc.).

Three Major Branches of the Office Family Tree

There are so many different versions of Office, it's hard to count them all. Microsoft is only gradually sorting out all the names. Not all Offices are the same — not by a long shot — but in general they'll all share the same documents without clobbering them.

That's a big advantage over some rivals.

I tend to break the various versions of Office into three broad categories, based on how powerful they are, how many features, and what you can do with those features. There's a fourth consideration, Office 365, which you could consider to be a modifier to each of these three categories.

All told there are more than a hundred variations and combinations of "Office." Strap on your hip waders, and let's take a look.

Office 2016 and desktop versions

First are the mouse-friendly versions of Office, the old-fashioned desktop and laptop apps (programs, to you old-timers). If you've been using Office for more than a few years, you've undoubtedly used one of the old-fashioned programs, because the other versions didn't exist several years ago.

Figure 1-1 shows the interface for Word 2013, which is probably familiar to anyone who's used Office in the past few years.

Figure 1-1: The main screen for Word 2013.

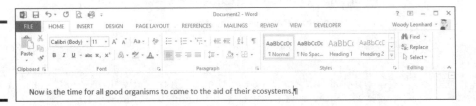

Note how Word 2013 has a long list of tabs — Home, Insert, Design. . . all the way up to View or Developer, depending on which version you're using.

In Figure 1-2, you can see an early advance release version of Word 2016 for Mac. Note how its tab area, up at the top, is quite similar to Word 2013 for the PC. The ribbons (the area below the tabs) look quite different, but in fact they accomplish many of the same tasks.

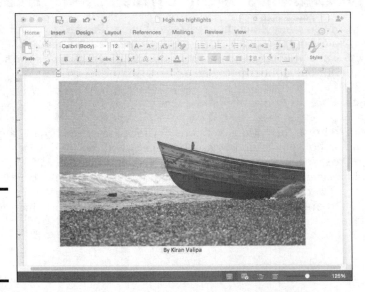

By Kiran Valipa

Figure 1-2: Word 2016 for Mac, an early version.

Office 2013 and 2016, for the PC and for the Mac, represent the top of the Office food chain. They have, by far, the most features and greatest capabilities of all the Offices. You can quibble about how Office 2016 has more features than Office 2013, or how the PC version is more advanced than the Mac, but for most of the people, most of the time, there's very little difference.

Most importantly: A document created in any of those versions works equally well in all the other versions, give or take a few new features in Office 2016.

All these desktop versions have hundreds of features — thousands, depending on how you count. Most people using the desktop Office variants use fewer than 20 percent of the features. Of course, the 20 percent you use will be slightly different from the 20 percent I use, but the overlap's enormous.

And you have to wonder if it's worth paying for all those things you, and everybody else, never use. Microsoft's well aware of the dilemma, and the threat to its enormous multi-billion-dollar cash cow.

Universal/Mobile/iOS/Android Office

Microsoft shocked the Windows Faithful (I think that's a union, a rock band, or maybe a religious cult) when they announced Office for iOS, back in March 2014. There had been halfhearted attempts at putting Office on mobile devices for more than a decade. (Remember "Office Mobile 6.1"? No, I didn't think so.) But the release of an iPad version of Office before a touch-centric version for Windows or Windows Phone felt like a slap across the face.

It took Microsoft more than a year to bring the same level of functionality to Windows devices. And although the Windows version of Office was still gestating, Microsoft had the audacity to release a very functional version of Office, first for iPhone and then for Android. If you weren't around at the time, it's kind of hard to imagine the indignation among Windows users that their more mobile brethren got the goodies before those who bought 'n paid for Windows.

As things stand right now, Universal Office — which is to say, the touch-centric version of Office running on Windows 10 — looks and behaves much like both Office for iOS and Office for Android.

As you can see in Figure 1-3, the Universal version of Word 2016 (also called Word Mobile, touch-centric Word, and a dozen other epithets, only some of which are printable) doesn't look anything at all like either the Windows or the Mac versions of the "full" Office.

Just for starters, the tabs across the top are just a small subset of the ones you see in Figures 1-1 and 1-2. The ribbon is completely different.

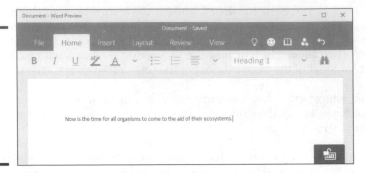

Figure 1-3:
Word in Universal Office, the touch-centric Windows version.

It's just as well that the Universal Office doesn't look like the desktop version, because it doesn't behave like the desktop version either.

Universal Office for Windows, though, bears an uncanny resemblance to Office for iPad, shown in Figure 1-4.

Figure 1-4:
Word for iPad.

Office for Android behaves similarly. In fact, Office for iOS and Office for Android have more in common than their Universal Windows Office sibling.

What none of them have is the full feature list found in the desktop versions of Office. In my experience, for 90 percent of Office users, 90 percent of the time, it's no big deal. All the mobile versions of Office work just fine, unless you need some specific, advanced capability.

Office Online

But wait! There's a third big chunk of Office that's trying to lure you into the Microsoft web. Literally.

Office Online (formerly known as the Office Web Apps) works inside your browser. It's the least capable of the Office clan, but the features are completely free. And they run on just about any web browser you can imagine — Internet Explorer, Firefox, Chrome, or even (as you can see in Figure 1-5) Edge.

Book VI Chapter 1

Organizing Office for Windows 10

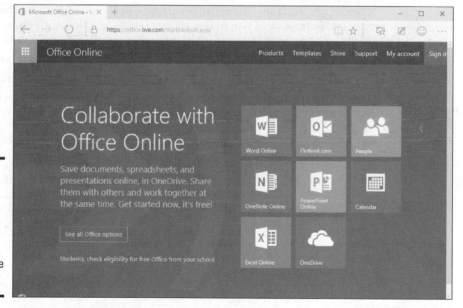

Figure 1-5: Office Online offers free, but limited, versions of all the Office apps.

Working with Office Online can be a bit limiting, but you can still get some work done. In Figure 1-6, I crank up Word inside Office Online, and it has the basic features available.

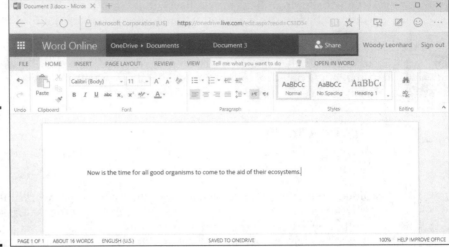

Figure 1-6:
Word in
Office
Online is
limited,
but still
usable —
and it's free.

As long as you keep your data stored in OneDrive, and you have a fairly fast Internet connection, Office Online is quite usable. Granted, compatibility isn't 100 percent and you may have problems working with complex documents or templates — and forget about macros. But if you're working with simple docs, it works pretty well.

The feature list, of course, changes fairly frequently. If you're interested in using Office Online, I suggest you look at Microsoft's official lists of features that are found in each of the Office Online apps:

✦ The Word Online feature list is at `https://technet.microsoft.com/en-us/library/word-online-service-description.aspx`.

✦ The Excel Online feature list is at `https://technet.microsoft.com/en-us/library/excel-online-service-description.aspx`.

✦ The PowerPoint Online list is at `https://technet.microsoft.com/en-us/library/powerpoint-online-service-description.aspx`.

✦ Similarly, the OneNote Online feature list is at `https://technet.microsoft.com/en-us/library/onenote-online-service-description.aspx`.

You may be surprised to discover that everything you need to do with Office is online — and if your needs aren't great, it's free, for everybody, all the time. Remember: Office Online isn't equivalent to the full-blown version of Office. Nor is it the equal of Windows Universal (commonly called "touch first") Office. But it's surprisingly good at most things, most of the time.

Amazing what a little competition from Google and Apple can do, eh?

Office 365 — the Differentiator

As you probably realize at this point, Office has gone from a simple three application package (four, including Outlook) just a few years ago and has morphed into a massive glob of different kinds of features and services.

But wait. There's more.

Office 365 originated as a plan to let customers rent Office, instead of buying it. Launched in June 2011, it started as a replacement to the old Business Productivity Online Suite and soon became a multi-billion-dollar business, all by itself. It's fair to say that Office 365 has become one of the most profitable, if not *the* most profitable, business at Microsoft. Yeah, Microsoft makes way more money by renting Office than they do by selling Windows.

Office 365 changes the features in two of the three big categories of Office. Certain versions of Office 365 give you access to "premium" features in the Universal Windows Office (mobile) app, as well as the iOS and Android versions of Office. Certain versions of Office 365 also give you access to different flavors of the desktop Office apps. Fortunately (for the sake of my tattered scorecard), everybody gets Office Online, free, all the time.

Here's what you — or your company, organization, or school — get with the various versions of Office 365. (I list Microsoft's current list price. You may be able to get them cheaper.)

+ **Office 365 Personal** ($70 per year) gives you a license for running the desktop version on one PC or Mac, plus "premium" features for one tablet, plus "premium" features for one phone. The desktop programs include Word, Excel, PowerPoint, OneNote, Outlook, Publisher, and Access. You get 1TB of OneDrive storage and 60 Skype minutes to select countries.

+ **Office 365 Home** ($100 per year) gives you licenses for running the desktop version on up to five PCs and/or Macs, plus "premium" features for five tablets, plus "premium" features for five phones. The desktop programs include Word, Excel, PowerPoint, OneNote, Outlook, Publisher, and Access. You get 1TB of OneDrive storage for each of up to five Microsoft accounts and 60 Skype minutes per user to select countries.

+ **Office 365 Business Essentials** ($60 per user per year, up to 300 users) doesn't give you any core Office functions over the "free" versions, but it does add support for Exchange Server ("business class email"), SharePoint, and OneDrive for Business.

✦ **Office 365 for Business** ($100 per user per year, up to 300 users) includes the most popular Office desktop programs (Word, Excel, PowerPoint, OneNote, Outlook, Publisher) with five licenses for up to five PCs and/or Macs. You also get "premium" features for up to five tablets and up to five phones. But there is no license for Exchange Server, SharePoint, or OneDrive for Business.

✦ **Office 365 for Business Premium** ($150 per user per year, up to 300 users) combines Business Essentials and Business.

✦ **Office 365 Academic** (free) gives you licenses for running the desktop version on up to five PCs and/or Macs, plus "premium" features for five tablets, plus "premium" features for five phones. The desktop programs include Word, Excel, PowerPoint, OneNote, Outlook, Publisher, and Access. You get 1TB of OneDrive storage for each of up to five Microsoft accounts. The Academic version is available for students in eligible universities and colleges in 140 countries.

There are also versions for accredited non-profits (free) and governmental organizations.

Full, official descriptions of all the versions are on the Microsoft TechNet site: `https://technet.microsoft.com/en-us/library/jj819284%28v=technet.10%29`.

Confused? Here's what I say to my friends:

✦ The basic Office functions are free, as long as Office Online is good enough for your desktop/laptop work, and the basic versions of the various Office mobile apps (for Windows, iOS, and Android) are good enough for your tablets/convertibles. (The "premium" versions of the mobile Offices add very, very few features.)

If you're running Windows 10, you can use the Office mobile apps for free, and they're probably good enough.

✦ If Office Online isn't good enough, or you're running a version of Windows that can't support the mobile version of Office, spend $100 per year and get the versions of Office that you're used to, on up to five machines, with 1TB of OneDrive storage per person (up to five) as a bit of lagniappe.

As long as Office Online is still around — it's highly unlikely that Microsoft would take it away — you don't need to worry about discontinuing your Office subscription. Changing from desktop Office to Office Online is a bit jarring, and you pretty much need to put all your data in OneDrive, but you aren't tied to $100 per year forever.

And if you're using Windows 10, the touch-centric Universal version of Office is free as a breeze.

Setting Up Universal Office for Windows 10

Although definitions vary, many people feel that "Office" includes Word, Excel, PowerPoint, Outlook, and OneNote. If that matches your definition and expectations, you already have 40 percent of the battle won: Outlook (in the form of the Universal Windows Mail app), its cohort the Universal Calendar, and OneNote all ship, preinstalled on Windows 10. See Figure 1-7.

Figure 1-7: Outlook (Mail), Calendar, and OneNote ship with Windows 10.

The other three apps can be downloaded, individually, from the Windows Store. Or you can retrieve them by using the Get Office tile on the right side of the Start menu. In fact, even if your machine already has the touch-centric Universal version of Word, Excel, and PowerPoint, it'd be a good idea to make sure they're up to date.

Here's how to snag the latest:

1. **Click Start, All Apps, Windows Store.**

    That brings up the Windows Store. Rocket Science.

2. **In the search box in the upper right, type Word and press Enter.**

    You see results that look, more or less, like those in Figure 1-8.

3. **This part's important. You're looking for Word, not Metro Word (from livingenzyme), not Word Solver. Tap or click Word, and then tap or click Free.**

    The Store may take a while to download it, but when it's finally finished, you get a notice that This Product is Installed.

4. **Click Start, and under Recently Added, you should see Word. Tap or click it.**

    That starts Word with a quick tutorial. When you're finished, close Word.

5. **Repeat steps 2 through 4 for Excel and again for PowerPoint.**

    You should have all five Universal Office apps — six, if you include Calendar — ready to use.

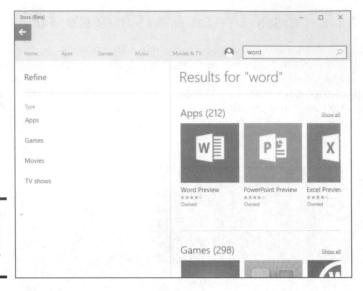

Figure 1-8:
The results
of a search
on "Word."

While you're still thinking about it, pin icons for your commonly used Office apps to the taskbar. If you use them frequently enough, you should also stick them on the right side of the Start menu, and maybe even put a link to each on your desktop. Here's how:

1. **Click Start, All Apps. Find Word — it may be near the top, in Recently Installed Apps, or it may be farther down the screen in alphabetical order. Right-click (or tap and hold) Word.**

You see the four options shown in Figure 1-9.

Figure 1-9:
You have
four
different
ways to
skin the
Word cat.

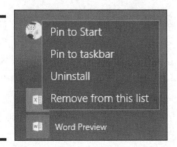

2. **If you want Word to appear among the tiles on the right side of the Start menu, or if you want to put a shortcut to Word on your desktop, choose Pin to Start.**

That sticks a Word tile on the right side of the Start menu.

3. **If you want a link to Word on your desktop, click the Word tile on the right side of the Start menu and drag it to the desktop.**

    That puts a link to Word on the desktop. If you really don't want a separate tile in the Start menu for Word, you can right-click the tile and choose Unpin from Start.

4. **Again in the All Apps list (refer to Figure 1-9), if you want to pin Word to your taskbar — which I heartily recommend — right-click Word and choose Pin to Taskbar.**

    Personally, I use the taskbar Word icon all the time.

5. **Repeat Steps 1 through 4 for Excel and/or PowerPoint.**

    That leaves you with clickable tiles on the Start menu, icons on the taskbar, and optional links on the desktop, all pointing to your favorite Universal Windows touch-centric versions of the Office apps.

The Future of Universal Windows Office

As we went to press, Microsoft had a long list of features it planned to add to the Universal, touch-first Windows version of Office. By the time you read this, some of these may be a reality. Some may be long discarded. The best way to keep up, of course, is to follow along on www.AskWoody.com, and ask a question if you're not quite sure.

This much we know for sure. Microsoft's pouring serious amounts of money into building up the Universal Office app and the other mobile apps — for iOS and Android — so they get some of the most important features of the desktop version.

At the very least, we'll be getting some way to move Office apps from the desktop to mobile. That's very exciting. It won't be easy. But it will be well worth the wait. For an example, consider the Office add-in called Microsoft Sway, https://sway.com, as shown in Figure 1-10.

Developers have been writing Office add-ins for eons. (Heck, *I've* been writing Office add-ins since Spiff in 1991.) There's a certain symmetry in using Office as your foundation, instead of going directly to Windows or using iOS or Android. Office is a very powerful starting point. Expect to see more apps — apps you want — built to plug into Office, in the not very distant future.

Figure 1-10:
Many
people
don't realize
it, but the
presentation
app called
Microsoft
Sway is, in
fact, built on
Office.

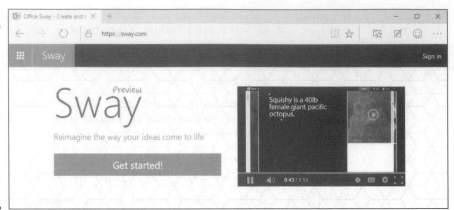

Chapter 2: Using OneDrive

In This Chapter

✔ **Introducing OneDrive**

✔ **Working with OneDrive through File Explorer**

✔ **Running OneDrive on the Internet**

✔ **Music, music, and more music**

✔ **Future directions with OneDrive**

*I*f you've used Windows for a while, you might recall the Microsoft online storage service known as SkyDrive. Those were the old days. Microsoft lost a trademark lawsuit in the U.K. with British Sky Broadcasting — the TV people — and instead of taking the lawsuit back for another appeal, MS decided it was smarter to just stop using the term *Sky*. I'm astounded that a company can trademark the name *Sky,* but then again I'm still dealing with the idea that a company can trademark the name *Windows*.

As we went to press, Microsoft had cut back on OneDrive's features, removing extra goodies added in Windows 8.1, and trimming it back to, more or less, the Windows 8 version. Microsoft removed its Universal (formerly Metro) OneDrive app, basically leaving all of us with using OneDrive through File Explorer, and through the web.

In fact, if you click on OneDrive in the Start menu, you end up inside File Explorer, sitting on the OneDrive folder.

At the same time, Microsoft has made promises (and promises and promises) about what will happen with OneDrive, Real Soon Now. I talk about the future in the last section of this chapter.

Start with the basics: OneDrive is an online storage service, sold by Microsoft, which has some features woven into Windows, to make it easier to work with your files stored on Microsoft's servers "in the cloud." (*Cloud* is another word for the web or the Internet.)

"In the cloud" is just a euphemism for "stored on somebody else's computer."

If you have a Microsoft account (such as an Outlook.com ID, or Hotmail ID, or any of a dozen other kinds of Microsoft accounts — see Book II, Chapter 5), you already have "free" OneDrive storage space, ready for you to use.

In this chapter, I show you the limited things you can do with File Explorer and OneDrive. But I also show you the rest of the story, by jumping over to OneDrive with a web browser.

Microsoft will undoubtedly bring more capabilities to OneDrive in Windows, including a promised Windows Universal OneDrive app, probably dribbling out improvements over time. Slowly, you'll see the OneDrive app add some of the features that are already accessible from the web.

You're lucky. You don't have to wait — because this chapter shows you where to look for the more robust OneDrive features on the web. OneDrive is up and running, and it doesn't cost you a cent.

OneDrive has many competitors — Dropbox (which I use, and did use for this book), Google Drive (see Book X, Chapter 3), the Apple iCloud (which isn't quite the same, although you can get to it through a web browser), the Amazon Cloud Drive, Facebook storage, SugarSync, Box, SpiderOak, and cloud storage and sharing from many smaller companies. These competitors all have advantages and disadvantages — and the feature list changes from week to week. I talk about the tradeoffs in Book VIII, Chapter 1.

In this chapter, I show you just about everything you need to know to make OneDrive work for you and in Windows 10.

What Is OneDrive?

OneDrive is an Internet-based storage platform with a significant chunk of space offered for free by Microsoft to anyone with a Microsoft account. Think of it as a hard drive in the cloud, which you can share, with a few extra benefits thrown in. One of the primary benefits: OneDrive hooks into Windows 10, at least in fits and starts.

Microsoft, of course, wants you to buy more storage, but you're under no obligation to do so.

As of this writing, OneDrive gives everyone with a Microsoft account 15GB of free storage, with 100GB for $4/month or 1TB for $7/month. Many Office 365 subscription levels have unlimited OneDrive storage, free, for as long as you're an Office 365 subscriber. Yes, that's unlimited, as in infinite, for free.

Microsoft's offers change from time to time, but the general trend is down — prices are going down, fast, and it won't be too long before most online storage asymptotically approaches free.

The free storage is there whether you use your Microsoft account to log on to Windows, even if you never use OneDrive. In fact, if you have a Microsoft account, you're all signed up for OneDrive.

Many people find OneDrive, at least the Windows 7, 8, and 10 versions of OneDrive, very confusing because, in essence, OneDrive keeps two sets of books. (Windows 8.1 OneDrive, by contrast is quite upfront about the whole process.) In Windows 10's OneDrive, there's the whole OneDrive enchilada stored on the web. But there's a second, shadow, subset of OneDrive folders that are stored on your computer.

Some OneDrive users have all of their web-based files and folders stored on their computers, and OneDrive syncs the folders quite quickly — what you see in File Explorer is what's stored in the cloud, and vice versa. But other OneDrive users have only *some* of their OneDrive folders on their computers. File Explorer shows them only this subset of folders and hides all the others that are sitting in the cloud.

If you aren't confused, you obviously don't understand.

I have a workaround for the two-sets-of-books problem in the last section of this chapter, but you should understand the inner workings.

Here's the full OneDrive shtick:

✦ OneDrive does what all the other cloud storage services do — it gives you a place to put your files on the Internet. You need to log on to OneDrive with your Microsoft account (or, equivalently, log on to Windows with your Microsoft account) to access your data.

✦ If you log on to a different Windows 10 computer using the same Microsoft account, you have access to all your OneDrive data through the web but, surprisingly, not necessarily through File Explorer. In fact, if you look only at Windows File Explorer, you might not even know *what* data is sitting in your OneDrive storage.

This is one of the most confusing and dangerous parts of Windows 10. Realize that Windows File Explorer, when looking at OneDrive, is lying to you. See Figure 2-1.

✦ File Explorer offers a very simple process for copying files from your computer into OneDrive, as long as you want to put the file in a folder that's visible to File Explorer. See Figure 2-2.

File Explorer lets you move files in the other direction, from OneDrive storage onto your local hard drive, but again you must be able to see the file or folder in File Explorer before you can move it.

✦ Even the OneDrive app on the internet has problems. For example, in Figure 2-3, I have a Group called "Bridge Players" that I can't delete.

Figure 2-1:
Windows
File
Manager
says I have
one folder
in OneDrive.
But the web
version of
OneDrive
says that
I have
many. File
Manager
lies.

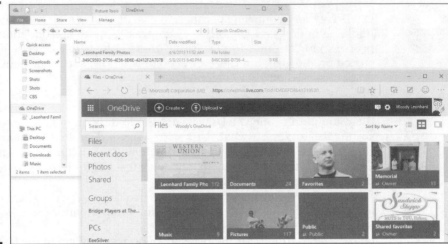

Figure 2-2:
Click and
drag files
into the
OneDrive
folder in File
Explorer,
and you
can move
or copy
files — but
only if the
folder you
want to stick
the file in
is already
visible to
File Explorer.
Confused
yet? You
will be.

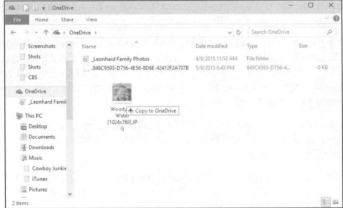

✦ You can share files or folders that are stored in OneDrive by sending or
   posting a link to the file or folder to whomever you wish. So, for example,
   if you want Aunt Martha to be able to see the folder full of pictures of Little
   Billy, OneDrive creates a link for you that you can email to Aunt Martha.
   You can also specify that a file or folder is *Public,* so anyone can see it. See
   the section "Running OneDrive on the Web," later in this chapter.

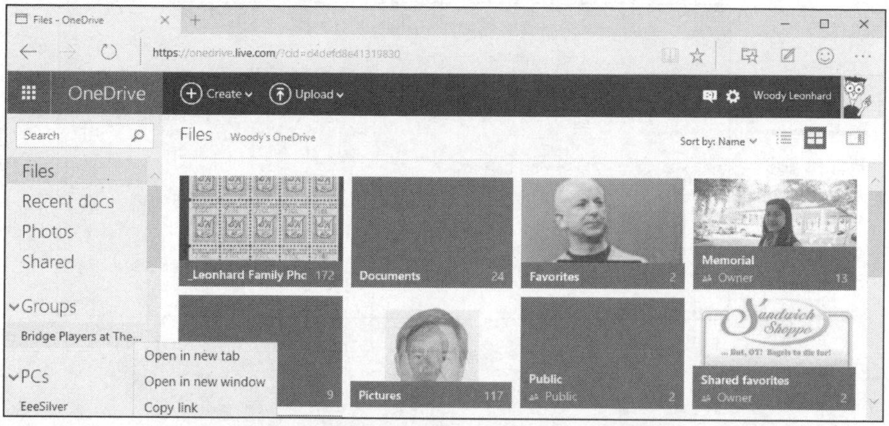

**Book VI
Chapter 2**

Using OneDrive

Figure 2-3:
Even the
online
OneDrive
app has
problems.

✦ To work with the OneDrive platform on a mobile device, you can download and install one of the OneDrive programs — OneDrive for Mac, OneDrive for iPhone, iPad, or Android. The mobile apps have many of the same problems that you find in File Explorer in Windows 10.

✦ In Windows 10, you don't need to download or install a special program for OneDrive — it's already baked into Windows.

✦ If you have the program installed, OneDrive syncs data among computers, phones, and/or tablets that are set up using the same Microsoft account. If you change a OneDrive file on your iPad, for example, when you save it, the modified file is put in your OneDrive storage area on the Internet. From there, the new version of the file is available to all other computers with access to the file. Ditto for Android devices.

Setting Up a OneDrive Account

If you sign in to Windows with a Microsoft account, File Explorer gets primed automatically to tie into your OneDrive account, using the same Microsoft account ID and password you use to sign in.

But if you're using a local account (see Book II, Chapter 5), life isn't so simple. You must either create a Microsoft account or sign in to an existing Microsoft account (and thus an existing OneDrive account) when you try to get into OneDrive. Here's the way to sign up for an account. You need to do it only once.

1. **Click Start, File Explorer.**

You see File Explorer, as in Figure 2-4.

2. **On the left, click OneDrive.**

You get a Welcome to OneDrive splash screen.

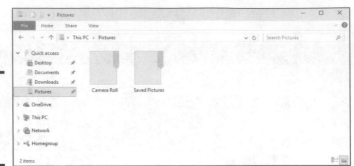

Figure 2-4:
A clean File
Explorer
on a local
account.

3. **Click Get Started.**

   OneDrive has you sign in with a Microsoft account.

   Note that you *must have a Microsoft account* in order to use OneDrive.
   It makes sense.

4. **Either sign in with an existing Microsoft account or click the link to
   Sign up now.**

   Follow the advice in Book II, Chapter 4 to get a Microsoft account
   set up.

   OneDrive gurgles and burps and makes changes to your File Explorer,
   adding some "glue" programs to both sides.

   When the installer comes up for air, you're presented with the wholly
   uninspiring picture you see in Figure 2-5.

Figure 2-5:
A new
OneDrive
account,
as seen
from File
Explorer.

The four folders — Documents, Music, Pictures, and Public — in your online OneDrive folder appear by default. Those are the four folders that Microsoft sets up for you in the cloud. From the screen shown in Figure 2-5, you can add a file to any of the folders, and after you've added files, you can delete files or download any of them to your computer by simply dragging and dropping, the way you usually move files. If you put a file in the Documents, Music, or Pictures folders, only you have access (unless you change permissions). However, anyone can see files you add to your Public folder.

5. Close File Explorer to leave OneDrive.

Here's how to work with files in OneDrive when you access OneDrive via File Explorer:

If you stay forever mindful that File Explorer may not show you all the folders or files in OneDrive, you can use File Explorer to work with OneDrive in exactly the same way you would use any folders on your computer: copy, move, delete, rename, or work with folders or files or groups of folders or files — they all work the same way that they would if the files were living on your computer.

Anything you can do to files anywhere, you can do inside the OneDrive folder — as long as you use File Explorer or one of the (many) apps, such as the Microsoft Office apps (see Figure 2-6) that behave themselves with OneDrive.

Book VI
Chapter 2

Using OneDrive

Figure 2-6:
Saving files to OneDrive in Word is easy — in fact, it's the default in recent versions of Word.

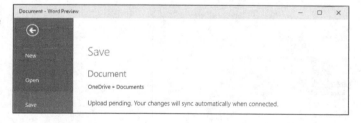

For example:

✦ You can edit files, rename them, copy, or move vast numbers of them. The OneDrive folder in File Explorer is by far the easiest way to put data into OneDrive and take it out.

✦ You can add subfolders inside the OneDrive folder, rename them, delete them, move files around, and drag and drop files and folders in and out of the OneDrive folder to your heart's content.

✦ You can change file properties (with a long tap or right-click).

✦ You can print files from OneDrive just as you would any other file in File Explorer.

What makes the OneDrive folder in File Explorer unique is that when you drag files into the OneDrive folder, those files are copied into the cloud. If you have other computers connected to OneDrive with the same Microsoft account, those other computers may or may not get copies of the files, but they can all access the files and folders through a web browser.

It may take a minute or two to upload the files. But plus or minus a bit-slinging delay, the files appear everywhere, magically.

So if you have other computers (or tablets or phones) that you want to sync with your computer, now would be a good time to go to those other computers and install whichever version of the OneDrive program is compatible with your devices. Remember that a OneDrive program is available for Windows (Vista, Windows 7, and Windows 8 only), Windows Phone 10 or later, Mac OS X, and iOS (for iPad and iPhone). There's also a OneDrive app for Android phones and tablets. That's the one I use on my Samsung phone, as shown in Figure 2-7.

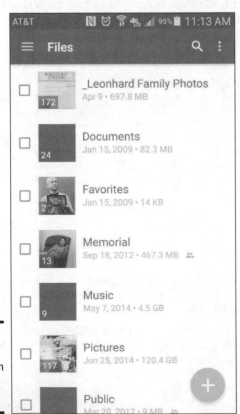

Figure 2-7:
The One Drive app on an Android phone.

Running OneDrive on the Web

If you want to use OneDrive (as opposed to just playing with it in File Explorer), you need to crank up a browser. Any browser will do — Edge, Chrome, Firefox, even nasty ol' Internet Explorer.

As we went to press, the only way to get into many of these features is through a web browser. Microsoft swears it's going to build access to all this — and more — in a Windows Universal app, but they've been promising that since the days of Windows 8. I wouldn't hold my breath. But if you find that there's a OneDrive app on your computer, it might be worthwhile to try it and see if Microsoft's gotten anywhere close. Good luck.

By far the most options and the best controls for OneDrive are on the web. The option I use most? Sharing.

While it's true that you can right-click a file or folder inside File Explorer— and choose Share a OneDrive Link (which pops out to the web, retrieves a link and copies it into your clipboard), or More OneDrive sharing (which also pops you into the web-based version of OneDrive, sometimes). Kinda cheating, but it works.

To share a file that's sitting in your OneDrive folder:

1. **Go to** `www.OneDrive.com` **with your favorite browser, and sign in with your Microsoft account.**

    Your OneDrive data appears as big boxy tiles on a web page (refer to Figure 2-3). To make the whole thing more accessible, at least with a mouse and keyboard, click or tap the Details View icon immediately to the right of the Sort by Name line. That brings you into Details View, shown in Figure 2-8.

Book VI Chapter 2

Using OneDrive

Figure 2-8: If you have a mouse, Details view is the easiest way to work with OneDrive.

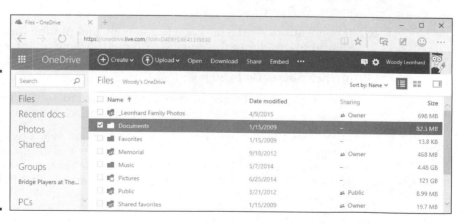

2. **Find the file or folder you want to share, hover your mouse over it, and select the box to the left of its name or in the upper-right corner of the picture.**

Selecting the box is important. Don't click the file. If you click the file, you'll probably open it — not the end of the world, but it's easier to share without opening.

If the file or folder is already shared, the word "Owner" appears in the Sharing column, with details in the pane on the right (see Figure 2-9).

Figure 2-9:
Files or folders with any kind of sharing enabled show "Shared" in the Sharing column.

3. **With the box in front of the file or folder selected (or the upper-right corner of the picture selected), right-click the file and choose Share, or tap or click the Share link in the preview pane on the right.**

OneDrive assumes that you not only want to share the file, but you also want to send an email to the person(s) you're sharing the file with. The email has a link to the file or folder. The Send a Link screen appears, as shown in Figure 2-10.

4a. **If you want to send a message to someone and put the link to the shared file/folder in the message, fill out the Send a Link screen: Type email address(es) in the To box, add whatever note you like, and tap or click Share. Go to Step 5.**

If you want to let the person receiving the email to be able to edit your photo, in your OneDrive folder, click the link marked Recipients Can Edit.

If you click the Recipients Can Only View link and select Recipients Need to Sign In with a Microsoft Account, the recipient of the email message must log on with a Microsoft account that matches the email address you sent. That's a good way to reduce the possibility that the person who receives the email will pass along the link.

Figure 2-10:
You can email a link to someone, so she can see a file in your OneDrive folder.

4b. **If you don't want to send an email, or you don't want to share the file (folder) with specific email addresses, tap or click the Get a Link option on the left.**

OneDrive shows you the rather ambiguous Get a Link screen, shown in Figure 2-11. Although the options seem straightforward, they aren't.

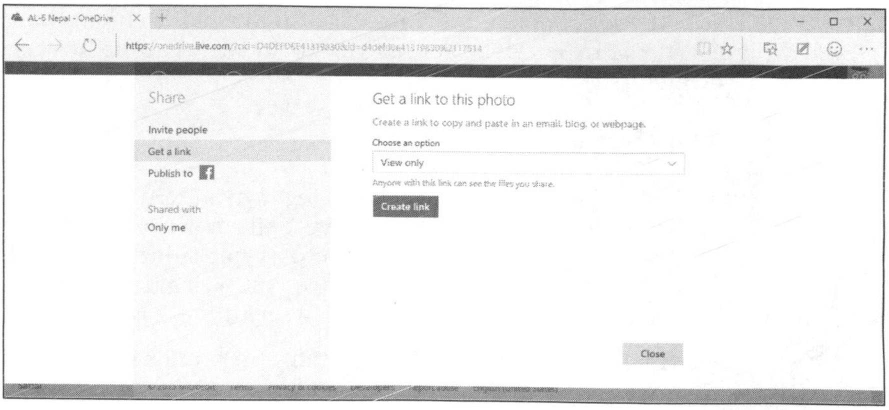

Figure 2-11:
Create links with the appropriate restrictions.

5. **Consult Table 2-1, and from the Option drop-down box, choose the option you would like.**

A link appears. Send that link to somebody, and when he clicks it, his web browser opens with the file you've selected, giving the person who clicked the link editing permissions indicated in Table 2-1.

6. **Make sure you copy the link provided by OneDrive.**

You can use the link any way you wish.

Table 2-1	Get a Link Options
This Option	*Really Means This*
View Only	OneDrive gives you a link to your file or folder. Anybody who has that link can view, but not change, the file or folder. This setting doesn't lock out other people: If someone can guess the link, she's in like Flynn. Similarly, if you give the link to someone, and she gives it to someone else, the third party can see the file or folder.
Edit	Like View Only, except anybody who gets into the file or folder can change or delete the file or anything in the folder.
Public	Makes the contents searchable, so Google or Bing may pick it up someday. Anyone can view, but not change, the file or folder.

OneDrive has many more capabilities. See the tutorial at `http://windows.microsoft.com/en-US/OneDrive/home` for an overview.

Syncing Files from OneDrive to Your Machine

OneDrive, as it stands, puts files in the cloud, but it doesn't put copies of the files on your computer. In most cases, it doesn't even put thumbnails of the files in File Explorer, so at least you could see what the heck is sitting out in the cloud.

There are two good reasons why:

+ Lots of people now have many megabytes in OneDrive. Some (like me) have many gigabytes in OneDrive, and a few have terabytes in OneDrive. If you try to sync all that data onto a typical desktop hard drive, it may or may not survive the experience. But trying to sync all that onto a fast solid state-equipped laptop with a tiny drive is just a non-starter.

    Think of it this way. If you stuck all your photos in OneDrive, would you want to have copies of all those photos automatically synced up with your phone? Naw, I didn't think so.

+ The second big reason to avoid syncing all your files to all your devices is that even the tiny space occupied by a thumbnail can — if you have gazillions of files — completely overwhelm whatever computer you're using. When people only kept 10,000 photos in OneDrive, they could still tolerate thumbnails of all those photos appearing on their tablets. But when the number of photos hits 100,000 — or a hundred times that many — the hardware just can't handle it. Not to mention the bandwidth charges.

Unfortunately, there's a huge downside to getting rid of the files and the thumbnails: As I showed way at the beginning of this chapter, it's entirely possible to have gobs of data in OneDrive and not even know through File Explorer that the data exists. You can crank up your web browser and see the ugly truth, but File Explorer remains oblivious.

Microsoft's stuck between a rock and a hard place. Even if they showed you thumbnails of all your files, there may come a time — get on a plane without a WiFi connection, for example — when you think that you have a copy of the file handy, but you don't. More than a few knowledgeable Windows 8.1 users got bitten that way, and they weren't too happy about it.

Many alternatives have been proposed by disappointed Windows 10 users, but Microsoft's marching to its own tune. The bottom line: We're going to see updates to how OneDrive behaves, over time, but you need to learn to live within the constraints of the version of OneDrive that you're using at the moment.

Or switch to Dropbox. Or Google Drive. Or iCloud. Or Box.

If you've weighed the burden of syncing all your files on your PC and decided that you'd rather know what's out there, rather than flipping to your browser to find out, it's relatively easy to tell OneDrive which folders it should sync — that is, which folders should be physically copied onto your computer and updated as the data in the cloud changes. Here's how:

1. **Click Start, File Explorer. Navigate to your OneDrive folder, and right-click any file in the folder.**

You see the options shown in Figure 2-12.

**Book VI
Chapter 2**

Using OneDrive

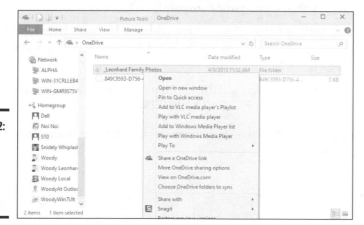

Figure 2-12: Set up syncing from inside File Explorer.

2. **Select Choose OneDrive Folders to Sync.**

   OneDrive responds with a dialog box that lets you choose which folders you want to sync, as shown in Figure 2-13.

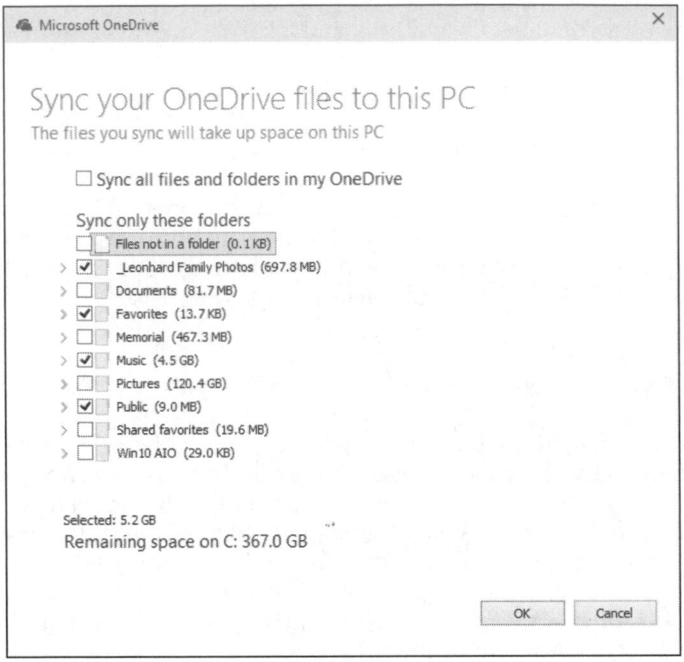

Figure 2-13: You can choose to sync entire top-level folders, not individual files.

3. **Check the boxes next to the folders that you want to have copied — and updated — on your computer.**

   Note that there's no way to sync a subfolder or an individual file. You can only sync folders at the highest level.

4. **Click OK.**

   OneDrive starts syncing the contents of those folders — and only those folders — on your PC. See Figure 2-14.

   Microsoft promises it'll make the process easier and better. At this point, we have no idea how.

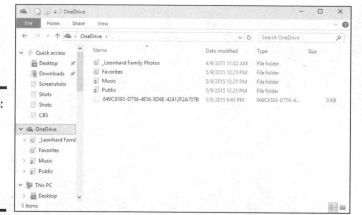

Figure 2-14:
The result of telling OneDrive to sync specific folders.

You might also note the other OneDrive-specific options in Figure 2-12. Share a OneDrive Link takes you to the sharing page shown earlier in Figure 2-10. More OneDrive sharing options takes you to Figure 2-9. And View on OneDrive.com takes you to the OneDrive website, with that folder open, similar to Figure 2-8.

The Future of OneDrive — We Hope

If you're looking for the OneDrive feature called "Fetch," you're completely out of luck. Windows 7 and 8 — but not 8.1 — opened up the PC, so you could get into it over the web using the right credentials in OneDrive. That doesn't happen anymore, and it won't happen in the future. Microsoft killed Fetch in Windows 8.1, and it isn't coming back.

Instead of using Fetch, you'll have to settle for a competing, and far more secure, tool like Microsoft Remote Desktop (look in the Windows Store), TeamViewer (www.teamviewer.com) or LogMeIn (www.logmein.com).

If you're disappointed by OneDrive, you aren't alone. Microsoft decided, for better or worse, to ship Windows 10 with OneDrive not even quarter-baked, figuring that advanced users would use the web and less-advanced users might not even notice.

Microsoft laid out the roadmap shown in Figure 2-15, in May 2015. Remains to be seen if they'll hit any or all of their goals.

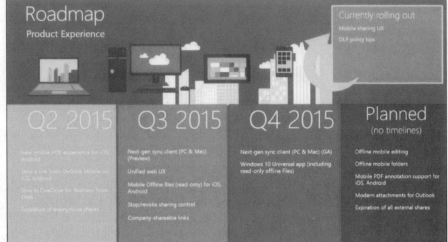

Figure 2-15:
The future
of OneDrive,
as promised
by Microsoft
in May 2015.

Chapter 3: Getting Started with Facebook

In This Chapter

- ✔ **Where's the Universal Facebook app?**
- ✔ **Establishing a Facebook account**
- ✔ **Nailing down your settings**
- ✔ **Building your Timeline**
- ✔ **Locking down your Facebook info**

*I*f you don't yet have a Facebook account, about a billion and a half people are ahead of you.

I have friends who figure Facebook is some sort of fad that's going away soon. They'd rather be drawn and quartered than put anything on Facebook. "You lose your privacy," they say, "I don't see any need for it."

Of course, many of them said the same thing about mobile phones two decades ago. ATMs. Online banking. Two decades before that they lambasted the newfangled color television stuff — it'll never catch on, you know?

In the past decade, Facebook's become an important part of the daily routine of 900 million people, and it claims more than 1.4 billion registered users who go online every month. It's been credited with starting revolutions. It's certainly a good source of news — almost as good as Twitter (see Book VI, Chapter 4) — if you choose your sources carefully.

More than 40 percent of all American adults log on to Facebook *every day*.

Facebook has fundamentally changed the way hundreds of millions of families interact, more so than any other invention since the telephone. It's altered the way people work. Businesses. Schools. Hospitals. Governments. Charities.

Facebook has even eaten into email, and instant messaging, for heaven's sake. Email usage has gone down the past couple of years because Facebook's one-to-many nature reduces the need for email messages, and its embedded mail and chat features are growing fast. To me, that's incredible. I grew up with email — sent my first email message in 1977 — and it boggles my mind that so many people prefer Facebook to email. But that's how it is.

I'm tempted to stand up and bellow a chorus from Bob Dylan's "The Times They Are A-Changin'."

You can ignore Facebook, if you want to, but someday your kids or grandkids or the young whippersnappers in the nursing home are going to ask why dad or grandpa or Uncle Fuddyduddy doesn't get off his duff and get with the system. It's the same argument people had with Luddites about typewritten letters and faxes a couple decades ago.

In this chapter, I only brush the surface of the capabilities available to Facebook users. You find a bit of depth about the Timeline because it's hard to find information about it. And I hit the privacy/security part hard because that's where you need to concentrate your efforts when you're just starting out.

As you get more adept at Facebook, you'll figure out about tagging photos, sharing things that have been posted to your home page or your Timeline, subscribing, setting up groups, chatting and video calling, setting up your own fan (or business, group, or charity) pages, posting events, searching, GPS location-based features, setting up your own lists — and much more. If Facebook intrigues you, I suggest you pick up a copy of *Facebook For Dummies,* 5th Edition, by Carolyn Abram. For a deeper look at the side of Facebook that's tailored for businesses, charities, and groups (including that knitting circle or bridge club), look at *Social Media Marketing All-In-One For Dummies* (published by John Wiley & Sons), by Jan Zimmerman and Deborah Ng.

Facebook has apps that run on iPads, iPhones, Android tablets, and phones — and I use all of them. Its website, `www.facebook.com`, runs in every browser you can imagine — and many you probably can't.

I'm happy to say that Facebook finally, finally has an official Windows Universal app. Born on October 17, 2013 (about five years later than it should've been), the app's in reasonably good shape, and it works fine on Windows 10. In the same breath, I must say that the apps for iPhone, iPad, and Android phones and tablets are much, much better. Facebook's not particularly fond of playing footsie with Microsoft. I take you through the details of the Windows Universal app later in this chapter.

Signing Up for a Facebook Account

If you don't yet have a Facebook account, I suggest you sign up. Don't worry, nobody's going to steal your identity or mine your personal data. Yet. And Facebook's absolutely free — and will be free to use forever, we're assured, although some features may cost something someday, and a few business-oriented features like promoting posts or other kinds of advertising do cost real samolians.

There's one cardinal rule about Facebook, which I call the *prime directive:* Don't put anything on or in Facebook — *anything* — that you don't want to appear in tomorrow morning's news. Or your ex-spouse's attorney's office. Or your boss's inbox. Or your kid's school class. Privacy begins at home, eh?

Now that you have the right attitude, all you need is a working email address, and as long as you state that you're at least 13 years old, you can have a Facebook account in minutes. Here's how:

1. **Use your favorite browser to go to www.facebook.com.**

The Sign Up page, as shown in Figure 3-1, appears.

**Book VI
Chapter 3**

**Getting Started
with Facebook**

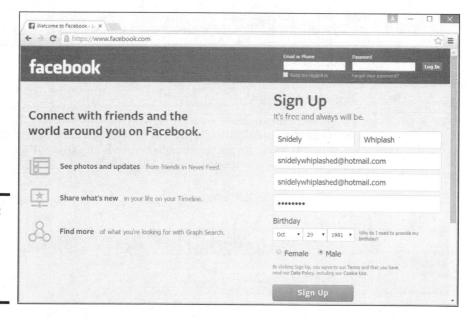

Figure 3-1:
Signing up for a Facebook account is easy.

2. **Fill in your name and email address (it must be a valid one that you can get to because a confirmation email goes to that address), give your new account a password, and make sure your birthday indicates that you're at least 13.**

   This is *not* the way to set up an account for a celebrity, band, business, charitable organization, or knitting group. In all those cases, you need to set up an individual account first — follow the instructions here — and then after your individual account is ready, you add a *fan page* to your individual account. I know it's complicated, but Facebook works that way. Even Coca-Cola's page is attached to an individual — presumably either Mr. Coca or Ms. Cola signed up and then created a page for Coca-Cola afterward.

   There's no reason to give personally identifiable information in this sign-up sheet. Facebook may balk if you try to sign up as Mark Zuckerberg, but it (probably) won't have any problem with Marcus Zuckerbergus (although, now that I've mentioned it, the name may be added to Facebook's blacklist). Some people have had trouble using their stage names, even when their stage names are, legally, their real names. Facebook has a policy that you have to use your "real" name, so if you feel so inclined, make sure whatever name you use looks real enough. (Apparently you can make up a silly middle name, though, and it's likely to be accepted.)

   And if you figure your birthday is your business, the Internet Police aren't going to come knocking. The one item that has to be valid, though, is the email address — which can come from a free site, such as Hotmail/Outlook.com or Gmail.

3. **Tap or click Sign Up.**

   Facebook sends a confirmation email to the address you specified. After you click the confirmation button in the email, Facebook brings up a page that tries to get you to suck in contact data from other services, such as Hotmail/Outlook.com (see Figure 3-2).

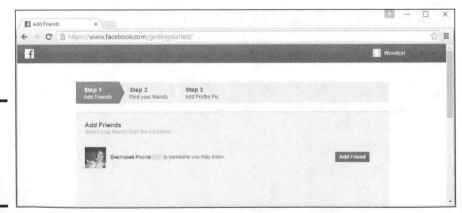

Figure 3-2: Facebook starts by fishing for your contacts.

You don't have to bring in your contacts from elsewhere. If you decide to suck your Hotmail/Outlook.com contacts into Facebook in the future, it's easy. Personally, I only add Facebook contacts manually.

4. **Divulge the minimum amount possible and, in the lower-right corner, tap or click Skip.**

   Facebook asks you to provide other email addresses, all the better to line them up for spamming email, searching for "Friends."

5. **Tap or click Skip this Step.**

   Facebook asks you to provide a profile picture.

6. **Upload an appropriate picture (see Figure 3-3), and then tap or click Next.**

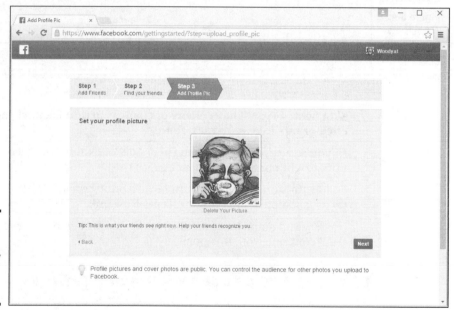

Figure 3-3:
Extra points
for creativity
in your
picture.

Congratulations. You now have a Facebook account, and your first job is to lock it down.

You should see a Welcome to Facebook page, like the one shown in Figure 3-4.

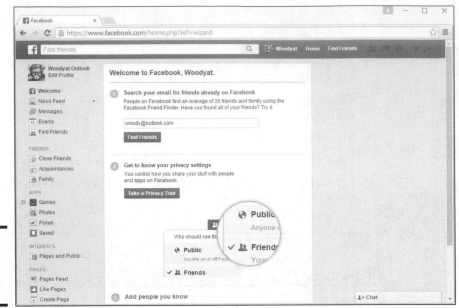

Figure 3-4:
A fresh
Facebook
account.

7. **Skip point 1 (you'll have plenty of chances to find friends), and under 2, click or tap Take a Privacy Tour.**

(If you're already signed in to Facebook, click the "lock" icon in the upper-right corner and follow along.)

Follow the screens titled Learn More About Privacy. On the third screen, do as instructed and click the Try it Now link.

Next, set up some basic settings and get your security locked down. We'll continue from this point.

Choosing basic Facebook privacy settings

Before you try to figure out what you're doing — a process that will take several days — step through setting up the rest of your Facebook account.

Here's what you do:

1. **If you're continuing from the previous section, you don't need to do a thing. If you've already set up your Facebook account, log on to Facebook and click the icon in the upper right that looks like a padlock. (The icon may be grayed out: Don't worry, it works.)**

2. **Tap or click Who can see my stuff?**

You see a list of privacy shortcuts, like the one in Figure 3-5, with the four "Who can see my stuff?" shortcuts in light gray.

What, exactly, is a friend?

Most people new to Facebook think that "friends" are, well, friends. Not so.

On Facebook, a *friend* is someone you're willing to interact with. If you're interested in interacting with somebody who has a Facebook account — let her see what you've posted (typed in the What's on Your Mind box), look at your *Timeline* (a historic bulletin board), or look at the pictures you've posted on Facebook — you send a *friend request*. The person who receives the friend request decides whether she wants to accept the request, decline it, or just sit on it.

Many of my Facebook friends are people I've never met and don't really know. They are, however, people I trust enough to allow them to look at my vacation pictures, say, and people who are interesting enough that I want to look at what they post on their sites. If the concept of a friend is a bit overwhelming at this point, don't worry about it. Find two or three people you know who have Facebook accounts, send friend requests to them, and watch what happens when they respond.

Get your feet wet with the concept before you start friending everything with two legs. Or four. You can always add new friends (or delete them — *unfriend* them — for that matter), but it's easier to start out slowly while you're getting the hang of it. Too many friends at first can be overwhelming.

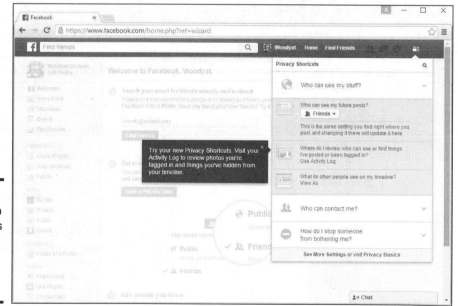

Figure 3-5:
Shortcuts to your various (and widely spread out) privacy settings.

What other people can see about you

Ever since the FTC slapped Facebook's hands, repeatedly, for privacy problems — and Facebook submitted to a 20-year ongoing audit by the U.S. Federal Trade Commission starting in November 2011 — Facebook has been quite forthcoming about its privacy policies.

Lots and lots of rumors circulate about what people can and can't see, so let me set the record straight.

If you look at someone's Timeline (or profile), the person you're snooping, er, looking up, doesn't have any way to tell that you've looked. In fact, there's no way to tell how many times people have looked at a Timeline. There are lots of Facebook scams that offer to give you a list of who's visited your Timeline. They're just that — scams. It can't be done.

And if you confirm that only your Friends can see your future posts, the amount of information that other people can see is very small.

Although the ubiquitous Facebook Like button sits on millions and millions of sites, Facebook doesn't give the people who run those sites any information at all about you. None. On the other hand, sites with the Like button allow Facebook to set third-party cookies on those sites. Facebook can trace your IP address as you go from site to site with the Like button. But the site itself doesn't get any information from Facebook.

3. **Confirm that only your Friends can see your future posts.**

   Don't be overly generous — or exhibitionistic — until you have a feel for the medium. See the sidebar "What other people can see about you."

4. **In the section marked Where do I review who can see or find things I've posted or been tagged in?, click the link that says Use Activity Log.**

   Facebook takes you to your Activity Log, as in Figure 3-6.

   To the right of each entry that's visible to other people, you see a drop-down box marked with a description of who can see the post. In Figure 3-6, the posted photo is visible only to Friends.

5. **Click the padlock icon to go back to the privacy settings (refer to Figure 3-5), and under What do other people see on my timeline?, click or tap the link to View As.**

   Facebook shows you the only information that the general public can see about you, as shown in Figure 3-7. Click the Timeline, About, Friends, Photos, and More tabs to look at everything that's hanging out for the world to see.

   This is also all the information that businesses — and potential employers, nosy neighbors, Better Call Saul — can access about you, personally, unless you've monkeyed with the default "Show to Friends" setting from Step 3. See the sidebar "What businesses can see about you."

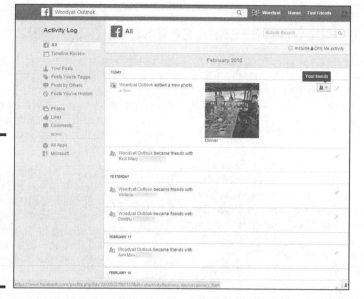

Figure 3-6:
Make
sure that
the items
you post
are visible
only to the
people you
intended.

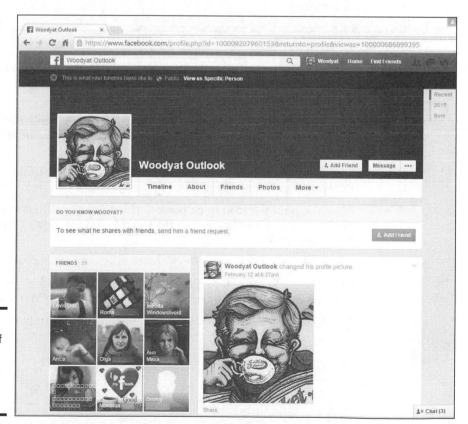

Figure 3-7:
The view of
your page
for the
Public at
large.

What businesses can see about you

Many people starting out with Facebook are worried that businesses — particularly businesses that pay to advertise on Facebook — can see all your personal information.

Sorry. As much as I love a good conspiracy theory, it just isn't true.

Anybody who controls a business page can see the profiles of people who have visited the page and the people who have clicked the Like button on the page. So, for example, if you go to the Ford page (which is a very good one, by the way), Ford will know that one more female between 25 and 34 years old visited the page. Ford will also get one more visitor tallied by city, country, and major language. If you arrived at the page by clicking a Facebook ad, that fact is also counted. But that's it.

When a business pays for an ad, it chooses the demographics ("only show ads to males 18 to 24 living in Los Angeles") but there's no lingering information about who got served an ad, and no way to tie you, specifically, into a click on an ad. Facebook has that information. The advertiser does not.

Facebook guards your information jealously. It doesn't sell your info to businesses or give it away, unless you specifically permit an app to pull the data from Facebook. That's why the Windows People app asks your permission before retrieving Facebook data — Facebook won't let Microsoft pull the data unless you specifically allow it.

6. **Click the padlock icon to go back to the privacy settings (refer to Figure 3-5), click or tap Who can contact me?, and choose the level of filtering you like.**

   For most people, in most situations, the defaults — Basic filtering so mostly Friends and people you may know appear in the Inbox, and Everyone can send friend requests — work well.

   If you're flooded with friend requests, you might want to throttle back Everyone to Friends of Friends.

7. **Click the padlock icon to go back to the privacy settings (refer to Figure 3-5), and click or tap How can I stop someone from bothering me?**

   Facebook gives you the option to block specific names or emails.

8. **Click the padlock icon to go back to the privacy settings (refer to Figure 3-5). At the bottom of the list, click or tap See More Settings.**

   The Privacy Settings and Tools page appears, as shown in Figure 3-8.

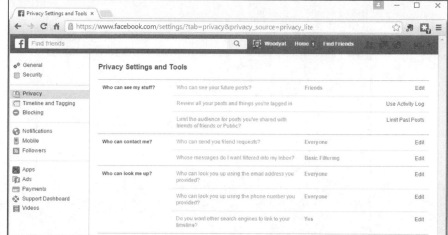

Figure 3-8:
Important
security
settings are
here.

9. **On the left, at the top of the list, choose General.**

   Facebook shows you the overall settings that you can change at any time, most notably including your password. See Figure 3-9.

10. **When you're finished, up at the top, tap or click Home.**

    You return to your home page, as shown in Figure 3-10.

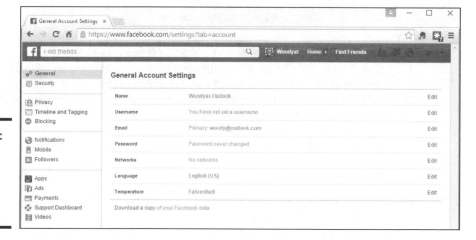

Figure 3-9:
Start here
to look at
all your
security
settings.

Figure 3-10:
Your Home
page has
posts
from your
Friends —
and some
ads.

Interpreting the Facebook interface lingo

Now that you've taken the whirlwind tour, permit me to throw some terminology at you. Facebook used to be simple; it isn't anymore. In order to work with Facebook, you need to figure out the names of things and what the different pieces are supposed to do. The really complicated part? Names have changed over the years, and you're bound to run into old names for new things — and vice versa.

Here's my handy translator:

✦ **Home page (also called the News Feed)** is primarily about your friends. The important stuff is in the middle — there are navigation aids on the left, and basically uninteresting things (including ads) on the right. When you type something in the What's on Your Mind box, it's added to the top of the list, as well as at the top of your Timeline. When your friends type something in their What's on Your Mind box, that gets added to your home page, too. When you add photos or videos, thumbnails of the photos go at the top of the list in the middle of the home page. Ditto for your friends' photos.

When you tap or click Home at the top, you go to the home page. When you sign on to Facebook, you go to the home page.

Facebook has a secret sauce that it uses to figure out which items appear on your home page and in what sequence. If you're mystified why something's on the top of the page, but the really important stuff is down farther, well, I'm frequently mystified, too.

At this moment, your Home page also has a drop-down box that lets you cycle between Facebook-generated Top Stories, and Most Recent. Try both and see which you prefer.

✦ **Profile page (sometimes called the Info page)** — now basically obsolete — contains details about you. It's been supplanted by . . .

✦ **Timeline (replaces the old Wall and the old profile page)** is all about you. There's a big picture at the top, dubbed a cover, with your profile picture appearing to the left. Then there are all the settings you've made visible, followed by almost all the posts you've made over the years, in reverse-chronological order. I talk about the Timeline in the "Building a Great Timeline" section later in this chapter.

When you type something in the What's on Your Mind box, it's added to the top of the Timeline list, as well as at the top of your home page. Your friends can also post on your Timeline — in effect, leaving you a note.

The Timeline appears when you tap or click your name at the top of the page. It also appears when someone clicks your profile picture in something you posted.

✦ **News Ticker** and Trending are among the uninteresting things that appear on the right side of your home page, toward the top. It's a scrolling jumble of things that your friends are doing. If you just joined Facebook and can't see the News Ticker, don't worry about it. You'll see it sooner or later.

Building a Great Timeline

The Timeline — the place you go when you click your name — is where people usually go when they want to learn about you. If somebody clicks your picture in a post elsewhere in Facebook, he's sent to an abbreviated version of your Timeline, as shown previously in Figure 3-7.

When you bring up your own Timeline, you get to see a great deal more than what the world sees, as in Figure 3-11.

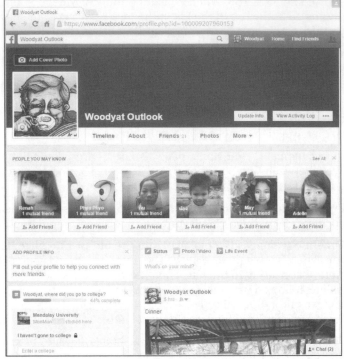

Figure 3-11:
Your
Timeline is
your resume
in the
Facebook
world.

Follow these steps to personalize your Timeline:

Keep in mind the prime directive: Don't put anything on or in Facebook — *anything* **— that you don't want to appear in tomorrow morning's news. Fill in the details sparingly.**

1. **Bring up your Timeline by tapping or clicking your name at the top of the Facebook screen.**

Depending on how much you've done to your Timeline, it looks like the one in Figure 3-11.

2. **Tap or click the Add Cover Photo button.**

Facebook takes you through the steps of either uploading a new photo or choosing from one that you've already uploaded.

3. **After you choose or upload a photo, tap or click it to drag the part you want to see into the fixed-size frame. Then tap or click Save.**

If you don't have a suitable photo already, pre-fab Facebook cover photos are all over the Internet. Just be careful when you go out looking: Any website that has you click and log on to Facebook in order to deliver the photo may be gathering your Facebook login ID in the process. It's much safer to simply download the photo to your hard drive and then upload it yourself to Facebook.

The Facebook cover photo is 850 pixels wide x 315 pixels tall. Facebook will actually accept any picture as long as it's at least 720 pixels wide. When you drag the uploaded picture to fit it into the fixed-sized frame, you're telling Facebook how to crop the picture to make it fit into the 315 x 850-pixel box. For best results, use a photo-manipulation program — or even Windows Paint (Book VII, Chapter 6) — to get the photo just right before you upload it.

4. **To change your *profile picture* — the little picture on the left that also appears on anything that you post, tap it or hover your mouse and choose Update Profile Picture.**

   Remember that your profile picture gets squeezed down most of the time, so a highly detailed photo usually doesn't work very well.

5. **When you're finished editing your profile information, tap or click your name at the top of the screen to go back to the Timeline.**

   By now the layout of the Timeline is a little more comfortable, but now it's time to change the contents of the Timeline itself.

6. **Find an item in the Timeline that you don't want other people to see, and click or tap the down-arrow in the upper-right corner.**

   Facebook gives you the options shown in Figure 3-12.

**Book VI
Chapter 3**

**Getting Started
with Facebook**

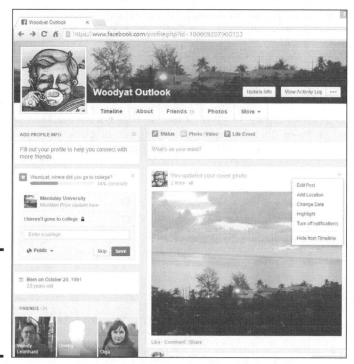

Figure 3-12:
The options
available
for every
item in your
Timeline.

7. To remove the item from your Timeline, tap or click Hide from Timeline.

The item disappears immediately, replaced by a placeholder that only you can see. If you ever want to bring back the hidden item, tap or click Undo.

8. On the left, where it says Add Profile Info, consider typing your college's name and click Save. Or you can click Skip. Either way, Facebook hits you with a barrage of questions that help flesh out your profile.

As you get more adept at Facebook and figure out how to lock down your account, you may want to add more information to your profile. Cool, as long as you understand the consequences. For now, put in the minimum you feel comfortable about disclosing to the world at large. Remember, someday your boss or your son might read it.

Each line you can enter — from your schools and marital status to your religious views — has a drop-down choice to limit access to that information.

Access limitations are based on your lists. For example, if you identify Snidely Whiplash as a member of your family, Snidely can look at any items you've set to be visible to Family. Any friends who aren't on your Family list can't see the item.

For now, while you're still getting your feet wet, be very circumspect in what information you provide, *even if you limit access to the information to specific lists.* Give yourself awhile to get more friends. You can always update your profile.

If you've been using Facebook for a long time, your Timeline may go on and on and on. But I bet there's no chance you have your baby picture pinned.

9. To add something to your Timeline that goes waaaaaay back (I'm talking years or decades, not centuries), tap or click the Life Event link, just above the What's on Your Mind box.

Facebook lets you identify the event, as shown in Figure 3-13.

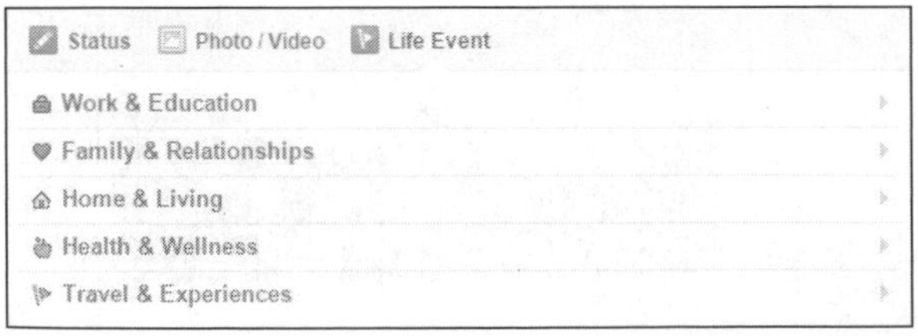

Figure 3-13:
You can add items to the Timeline and mark them as a specific life event. Previous lives don't count.

Status	Photo / Video	Life Event
Work & Education		▸
Family & Relationships		▸
Home & Living		▸
Health & Wellness		▸
Travel & Experiences		▸

Downloading your Facebook data

Apps aren't allowed to download all your Facebook data. But you can.

Log in to Facebook. Tap or click the down arrow at the top all the way to the right, and choose Settings. At the bottom of the General Account Settings page that appears (see Figure 3-9), tap or click the Download a Copy of Your Facebook Data link. Tap or click the Start My Archive button. Twice.

Then go have a latte. When you get back, check your email. You — eventually — receive

a message from Facebook that says your download has been generated. Tap or click the indicated link to retrieve the download, and you go back to the General Account Settings page (getting vertigo yet?). Tap or click the Download a Copy link again. Enter your Facebook password, tap or click Continue, tap or click Download Archive, and pick a location; your browser downloads the zipped file. Finally.

---

10. **Choose the life event, and then follow the instructions to give a date, choose or upload a picture, and provide more details about the event. When you're finished, tap or click Save.**

The item attaches itself to the appropriate place on your Timeline — even if it predates your joining Facebook.

It's your account. Take control over it.

Using the Universal Facebook App

I find it much easier to set up a Facebook account — and particularly keep on top of the privacy settings — by using a web browser. For day-to-day use, though, most people rely on a mobile app. It's just simpler and faster to keep on top of Facebook comings and goings with your phone or tablet, or with the Facebook Universal app in the Windows Store, as in Figure 3-14.

Facebook has apps for all the major platforms — iPad, iPhone, Android phones and tablets, and of course Windows phones and tablets. Details for using the apps vary, but the general layout is the same, as are the main functions.

Given a choice, I would take the iPad, iPhone or Android versions of the Facebook app over the Windows version in a New Yawk minute. And I'd be tempted to use the web instead of the Windows Universal app. So don't get overly frustrated by the Universal app's oddities.

Figure 3-14:
The
Facebook
Universal
app,
from the
Windows
Store.

In the Universal Facebook app for Windows, Figure 3-14, for example, you can click or tap Status to post text on your Timeline (the same as filling out the What's on Your Mind box in the web version). Click Photo to upload a photo to your Timeline. Check In lets you post a What's on Your Mind notice with your current location.

The Facebook app for my Galaxy Tab 3 is very similar, as you can see in Figure 3-15. I use Facebook on my Tab 3 all the time.

Buttons function in the same way: Status, Photo, and Check In all perform identically to the analogous actions in the Windows Universal app.

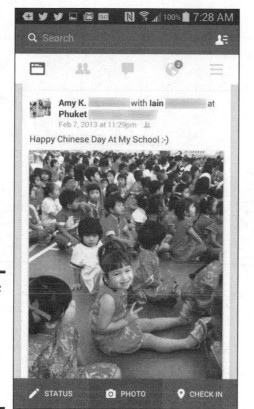

Figure 3-15:
Facebook
app from
the Google
Play Store,
running on
an Android
phone.

Chapter 4: Getting Started with Twitter

In This Chapter

⮑ **The idea behind Twitter**

⮑ **Setting up your Twitter account**

⮑ **Beginning to tweet**

⮑ **Hooking Twitter into Windows**

The revolution will not be televised. It will be tweeted.

In March 2006, an amazing array of developers and entrepreneurs — originally intent on building a podcasting platform called Odeo — unleashed Twitter on an unsuspecting world. A decade later, Twitter has been credited with helping to overthrow totalitarian governments, spread fear and mayhem, aid and abet leaks of embarrassing government documents, shed light on official dirty dealings, establish a rallying point for the Occupy disenfranchised, and let everyone know what Lady Gaga had for breakfast.

That's quite an accomplishment. As of early 2015, Twitter had more than a billion registered users, 300 million of them active every month, who send an average of 500 million or so tweets per day. Those are all industry estimates because Twitter doesn't divulge much, even though it's listed on the New York Stock Exchange. Interestingly, 77% of the most active users hail from outside the U.S.

Twitter crashed on June 25, 2009, the day Michael Jackson died, after logging tweets at 100,000 per hour. The current record for tweet volume was set on August 3, 2013, when a screening of the movie "Castle in the Sky" in Japan generated 143,199 tweets *per second*.

I use Twitter all day, every day. I've used it to keep on top of important fast-breaking news, notify people around the world, quell tsunami fears, talk with other writers in the computer business, keep tabs on political organizations important to me, track down obscure pieces of Windows 10, and point people to my favorite funny videos.

Just about every tech writer you can name is on Twitter. Every major news outlet is on Twitter — and breaking news spills out over Twitter much sooner than even the newspaper wire services. The Royal Society. The Wellcome Trust. Lots of people who are on the ground, relaying news as it happens, use Twitter. And did I mention Justin Bieber?

In short, Twitter's a mixed bag — but an interesting one.

Twitter's fast, easy, and free. It works with every web browser. It works with almost every telephone and tablet. There's a Windows 10 Universal Twitter app — an official one — that's not very inspiring, but it works.

Twitter's short, concise, sometimes vapid, but frequently illuminating and witty. And every single piece of it is limited to 140 characters.

Understanding Twitter

When I try to explain Twitter to people who've never used it, I usually start by talking about mobile phone messaging — texting. A message on Twitter — a *tweet* (see Figure 4-1) — is much like a text message.

Figure 4-1: A typical tweet from an atypical source.

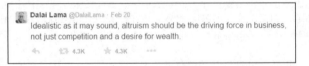

Twitter is a very simple one-to-many form of communication, kind of like Texting all the people who have agreed, in advance, that they want to receive your texts.

You usually send a text message to one person. If you have a business, you may send the same, identical text message to many people all at once. Now imagine a world in which these are true:

✦ You have an ID, not unlike a phone number, and you can send any messages *(tweets)* that you like, any time you want. The messages are limited to 140 characters — short and sweet.

✦ You get to choose whose texts you're going to receive. In Twitter parlance, you can *follow* anybody. If you get tired of reading their tweets, it's easy to *unfollow* them as well.

That's the whole shtick. Twitter has lots of bells and whistles — location tracking, if you turn it on, for example — but at its heart, Twitter is all about sending messages and wisely choosing whose messages you receive.

Spam texts and harassing phone calls may dog your days on the phone. On Twitter, while all is not happiness and light, in general the problems are much less frequent and less severe.

If you follow someone who posts a tweet, you see the tweet when you log on to Twitter. If you keep Twitter running on your PC, phone, or tablet, as I do, the tweet appears in your Twitter window. If you tweet, the people who follow you can see it.

In fact, *anybody* can see *every* tweet — a fact that's proved highly embarrassing to an amazingly large number of people. (Twitter has a Protected Tweets feature that lets you manually approve every person who's permitted to receive your tweets. But, in general, when you let it all hang out on Twitter, it's all hung out, eh?)

In addition, when you send a tweet, you can identify keywords in the tweet by using the # character in front of the keyword, creating a *hashtag*. See Figure 4-2.

Book VI Chapter 4

Getting Started with Twitter

Hashtag

Figure 4-2: Two sample tweets with hashtags.

Hashtag

You can tell Twitter that, in addition to the tweets from people you follow, you also want to see all tweets that contain specific hashtags. For example, if you ask to see all the tweets with the hashtag #ForDummies, Twitter delivers to your web page or Twitter reader every tweet where the author of the tweet specifically typed the characters #ForDummies.

Twitter (and other sites, such as www.trendsmap.com) keeps track of all the hashtags in all the tweets. It posts lists of the most popular hashtags, so you can watch what's really popular. Thus, hashtags are not only a way to make it easier for people to find your tweets, but they're also a way to publicize your cause — and many good causes have risen to the top of the hashtag heaps. Some odd ones, too, such as Lady Gaga kissing Marge Simpson, but I digress.

In fact, Twitter now keeps track of every phrase that's tweeted and compiles its trending lists from the raw tweets, with or without hashtags. You really don't need to use hashtags anymore. But you see them all the time in tweets, `#knowwhatImean`?

As of this writing, Google and Twitter have announced that they're going to enter into a partnership, whereby tweets are scanned by Google, so they'll show up in Google searches. Details are cloudy at the moment, but the sheer volume of tweets will change searching as we know it.

The power of Twitter — outside of gossip and teenage angst — lies in choosing those you follow carefully. If they, in turn, receive information from reliable sources and then retweet the results, you'll have a steady stream of useful information, each in 140-character capsules.

For example, during the Egyptian political crisis in January 2011, which saw the downfall of President Hosni Mubarak, Twitter played a pivotal (if controversial) role in aiding communication among protestors. One of the government's first acts was to shut down access to Twitter and Facebook. The protestors found ways around the government's shutdown.

There's a fascinating re-creation of the tweeting and retweeting that followed the January 25 start of demonstrations in Cairo. Data about tweets with the hashtag `#jan25` was assembled by the University of Turin, the ISI Foundation, and a research institute at Indiana University, to come up with the graph you see in Figure 4-3.

In the graph, the points represent individuals, and the lines are tweets that go from one individual to another. It's downright explosive.

That's how a one-to-many social network like Twitter works. If there's an important tweet (or even an unimportant, but popular one), it jumps from person to person.

My Twitter ID for computer-related news is @woodyleonhard, and you're welcome to follow me anytime you like.

#FollowFriday

Ever since the dawn of the Twitterverse, people have been using one very strange hashtag, `#followfriday` or sometimes `#ff` for a very specific purpose: It's to show the people who are following them which tweeters are worth following. Something like an endorsement newsletter in 140 characters, `#ff` recommendations frequently point you to people who have interesting, timely, or important things to say.

Or maybe not.

You can do it, too. Every Friday, look at the people who send you interesting stuff, create a tweet that starts out `#FollowFriday`, and then list the usernames. Don't forget to tweet `#FollowFriday @woodyleonhard` at some point.

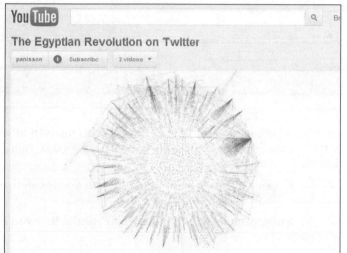

Figure 4-3: The interconnections among Twitter users during the Egyptian uprising.

Photo courtesy of `http://youtu.be/2guKJfvq4uI`

Setting Up a Twitter Account

Twitter has apps for all sorts of phones and tablets. I use it frequently on the iPhone, iPad, and Android phones and tablets. There's also a Universal Twitter app for Windows 10, on both the PC and the phone versions. I mention Universal Twitter occasionally in this chapter, but it's woefully underpowered. If you want to get going with Twitter, it's much easier to start with a web browser, and that's the primary emphasis in this chapter.

Starting a new account at Twitter couldn't be easier. Here's what you do:

1. **Fire up your favorite web browser, and go to** www.twitter.com.

   You see the Sign Up box, as shown in Figure 4-4.

Figure 4-4:
All you need
to sign up
for Twitter is
a valid email
address.

2. **Enter a full name, a valid email account (you need to be able to retrieve email sent to the account), and a password; then tap or click Sign up for Twitter.**

   Twitter creates a sign-up sheet, together with a suggested username, and shows them to you, as shown in Figure 4-5.

3. **Pay particular attention to the username, and when you're ready, tap or click Sign up.**

   Usernames are key because you want a name that will be easy for people to remember. Capitalization doesn't matter — MisterDummy is the same as MiStErDuMmY — but some characters are confusing. Be wary of the similarities between a number 0 and letter O; the letters I and l, and the number 1. And in particular, avoid ambiguous punctuation like underlines and hyphens.

   Twitter creates your account and then steps you through a brief personalization shakedown.

4. **Fill out any information you want to share — but don't divulge anything you wouldn't want your manicurist to know.**

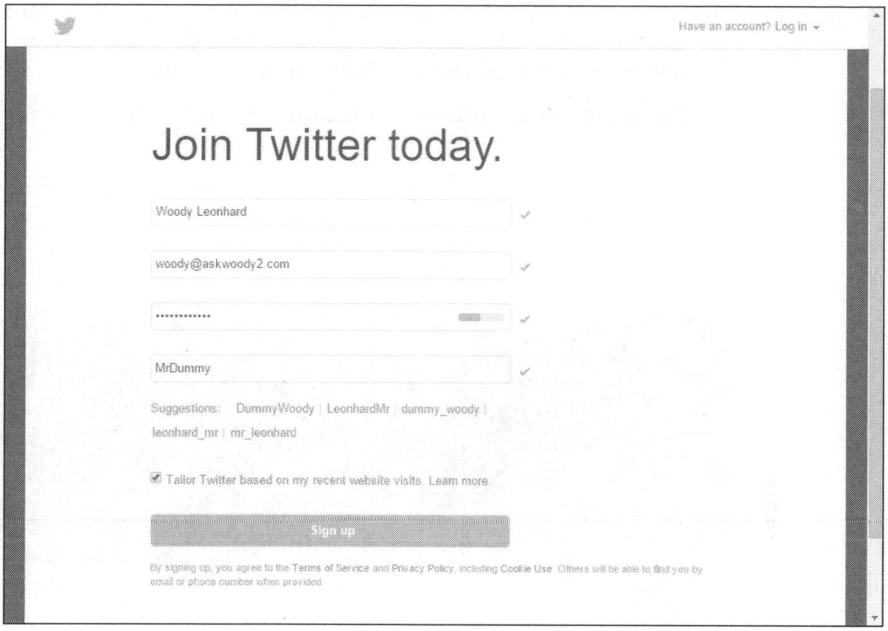

Join Twitter today.

Woody Leonhard ✓

woody@askwoody2.com ✓

••••••••••• ✓

MrDummy ✓

Suggestions: DummyWoody | LeonhardMr | dummy_woody |
leonhard_mr | mr_leonhard

☑ Tailor Twitter based on my recent website visits. Learn more.

Sign up

By signing up, you agree to the Terms of Service and Privacy Policy, including Cookie Use. Others will be able to find you by email or phone number when provided.

Figure 4-5:
Pay
particular
attention
to the
username.

5. **When the setup routine asks you to start by following five
   people, think about following @woodyleonhard, @ForDummies,
   @AndyRathbone who writes the original *Windows For Dummies*,
   @windowsblog to keep up on the Microsoft Party Line, @windows-
   secrets to follow the newsletter, @GabeAul for the latest in Windows
   news from Microsoft, and some of the major news services —
   @BBCWorld perhaps or @BreakingNews. I know that's eight.**

   Or try a couple of the most-followed people on Twitter, @justinbieber
   at 60 million followers or @katyperry at 65 million and counting. You
   could even vote for fellow Nashvillian @taylorswift13 by adding to
   her trove of 53 million followers.

6. **Don't go overboard just yet. When you're finished, tap or click Done.**

   Most people have Twitter send them an email message when someone
   follows them. (I'm sure Lady Gaga has long since opted out.) The message includes your name and Twitter account name. If you happen to
   follow somebody you know, that email message may be enough incentive to have him start following you; it's a good way to get a following
   kick-started.

7. **Twitter tries to get you to sign up for five more, well-known people. If
   you aren't up for it, at the bottom, tap or click the Skip This Step link.**

8. **When Twitter offers to scan your Gmail, Yahoo! Mail, Hotmail/ Outlook.com, and/or AOL Mail accounts, to try to find contacts who are also tweeters, tap or click Skip This Step, too.**

9. **Upload a profile photo and header photo, as shown in Figure 4-6.**

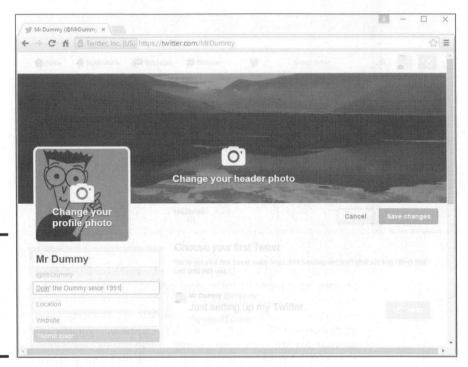

Figure 4-6: Upload a picture — an avatar. It doesn't have to be you.

The Internet is full of images. Go find a good one.

You may be tempted to bypass typing your bio. Give it some thought, if there's something unique about you that you want the world to know — if you're an expert on 18th-century Tibetan bronzes, adding that to your bio may help someone else who's interested in bronzes find you. Your bio's accessible to anybody, so don't put anything in there that you don't want to be widely known.

10. **In the email message you receive, tap or click the link, and you're finished.**

Twitter advises that your account has been confirmed, and you're ready to roll, as shown in Figure 4-7.

Figure 4-7:
Twitter
is ready
for you.

Celebrities and politicians don't have it so easy — many need to go through an independent confirmation step. But for normal dummies like you and me, it's that easy.

At first, you probably just want to watch and see what others are tweeting to give you a sense of how tweeting is done. Create a practice tweet or two, and see how the whole thing hangs together.

The very, very best first tweet of all time? Big Bird's first tweet is immortalized in Figure 4-8.

Figure 4-8:
From the
Bird himself.

Tweeting for Beginners

On the surface, Twitter's easy and fun. Below the surface, Twitter's a remarkably adept application with lots of capabilities.

Beware hacking

Before I dig in to the more interesting parts of Twitter, permit me to give you just one warning.

There are unscrupulous people on Twitter, just as anywhere else. If you get a tweet from someone with a gorgeous picture who's trying to convince you to sign up for something or hand over your password, just ignore him, and he'll go away. If you get a tweet saying, "Somebody is writing bad things about you" or "Want to see a funny photo of you?" or "Find out who's been looking at your bio," ignore her.

Better, yet, report her as a spammer. Tap or click the spammer's name. That takes you to the spammer's profile page. In the upper right, tap or click the gear icon and choose Block or report. Check the box marked File a report, choose the reason, and click Block.

If your Twitter account has been hacked — somebody talked you into clicking something that gets into your account or someone guessed your password — don't feel too bad about it. Fox News was hacked in July 2011. Mark Ruffalo (who plays The Hulk in *The Avengers*) got hacked in May 2012. Justin Bieber's account was hacked — back in the old days, when he only had 20 million followers. Ashton Kutcher. Taylor Swift. *The Huffington Post. USA Today.* Senator Chuck Grassley. Brett Favre. Miley Cyrus. *Reuters. Associated Press* (bombs at the White House). Newsweek. Queensland Police Department. Chipotle (it also faked a hack, as a publicity stunt). Burger King. US Central Command. Even Twitter's own Chief Financial Officer. And President Obama.

It happens. If your account's been taken over, see the Twitter instructions at `http://support.twitter.com/articles/31796#su`.

On the other hand, if you've posted some tweets you want to categorically disavow, you can always *claim* that your Twitter account was hacked. Sure to draw plenty of sympathy.

Twitter supports two-factor authentication: Every time you start tweeting from a new device, it sends a confirmation text to your pre-established phone number, asking permission. To start using 2FA (as it's called), log on to `twitter.com`, click Settings, then on the left choose Security & privacy. Check the box marked Send login verification requests to, type in your phone number, and you're done.

Using the @ sign and Reply

You see the @ sign everywhere on Twitter. In fact, I used it when listing the people you may want to follow. The @ sign is a universal indication that "what follows is an account name."

But it goes deeper than that.

If you put an @ sign at the beginning of a tweet, the only people who will automatically receive copies of the tweet must match *both* criteria:

✦ They must follow you.

✦ They must follow the person whose username follows the @.

Suppose you tweet this:

```
@woodyleonhard You're one big dummy!
```

The only people who will automatically receive a copy of the tweet are people who follow you *and* follow @woodyleonhard.

There's a reason why Twitter works this way. If somebody follows you and follows the person you're @ responding to, he can see the whole conversation. But anybody who follows only one of you sees only half of the conversation . . . unless he goes in and searches *all* tweets. In that case, the tweet turns up.

If you want to send the message to everyone who follows you and to one specific person, put a character — any character or characters — *in front of* her name. For example, any of these tweets will go to all your followers, plus it'll go to @woodyleonhard:

```
.@woodyleonhard You're one big dummy!
> @woodyleonhard You're one big dummy!
You're one big dummy @woodyleonhard!
```

Now that you know how the @ sign works, you're ready to understand how Reply works.

In the Twitter viewer on the Internet there's a Reply option to a tweet. In Figure 4-9, on the Twitter website, hover over the left-hooking arrow and you see a Reply link.

If you tap or click that Reply link, Twitter starts a new message with an @ sign followed by the sender's username. If you reply to the message in Figure 4-9, Twitter on the web creates a new tweet that starts: @DrPizza.

**Book VI
Chapter 4**

**Getting Started
with Twitter**

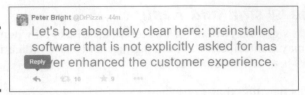

Figure 4-9:
Reply to a
tweet.

If you type a body to that message and click Tweet, the message goes only to
people who are following *both* you and @DrPizza.

A reply is *not* a private or hidden message. It's completely out in the open.
Anybody who searches for your username or @DrPizza will see the message in its entirety.

Retweeting for fun and profit

If you receive a tweet and want to send it to all the people who follow you,
the polite way to do so is with a *retweet* or *RT* for short. In order to give
credit to the person who sent you the tweet, the retweet will include his
username.

In Figure 4-9, the circling arrows icon is for Retweet. Tap or click the Retweet
link, and the Twitter program builds a new tweet that copies the original
tweet, puts an RT on it, and adds the originator's username. Like this:

```
RT @DrPizza Let's be absolutely clear here: preinstalled
software that is not explicitly asked for has never enhanced
the customer experience.
```

By retweeting a tweet precisely, you pass the information on to your followers, yet preserve the attribution. If you want to modify the tweet (perhaps
trim it down, in order to add a comment), use the modified tweet (MT) tag.
To do that, you need to copy the tweet and create your own, new tweet.
Like this:

```
Yeah, cramware sucks MT @DrPizza Let's be absolutely clear
here: preinstalled software. . . has never enhanced the
customer experience.
```

Direct Messaging

No discussion of the advanced part of Twitter would be complete without
a mention of Direct Messaging – better known as "dm"ing. When you create
a message starting with dm and someone's @username, only you and the
person receiving the message can see it.

Unfortunately, people screw up DMs all the time, and the result can be embarrassing. I suggest you limit your use of DMs to situations where email may be a better approach, and that you studiously use the DM tools built into your Twitter program. You'll generally find DM hiding behind an ellipses (. . .) icon.

Hooking Twitter into Windows

I intentionally wrote this chapter to get you going on Twitter using the web directly. It's something of a lowest common denominator for Twitter access.

Do I actually *use* the web interface? Heavens no!

There are dozens of programs — many of them free or very cheap — that run rings around the Twitter web interface. The names change every week, and the feature sets almost as quickly.

There's a Universal Twitter app available in the Windows Store, but (as of this writing) it's junk.

If you're serious about using Twitter — particularly if you have more than one Twitter account or use both Twitter and Facebook — there are much better alternatives.

I'm an old-fashioned desktop kind of guy, and I use TweetDeck (www.tweetdeck.com, see Figure 4-10), which helps me keep track of my incoming Twitter messages, tweets where I've been mentioned, and the all-important notices from Microsoft spokesman @GabeAul.

Twitter actually bought TweetDeck in May 2011 and has been extending its capabilities ever since. At the same time, the Twitter folks have been making it just about impossible for anybody to write an app that uses the Twitter interface. That's why you see so few competitors for viewing tweets.

Both the Twitter web page and TweetDeck have support for several key features:

✦ **Automatic URL shortening** so http://www.*somethingoranother*.com/this/and/that.php ends up looking like http://is.gd/12345 — an important trick when you're limited to 140 characters.

✦ **Multiple Twitter accounts** so people who keep their business and personal accounts separate can manage both simultaneously.

✦ **Picture attachments** with automatically generated links to picture sites. The best Twitter apps let you drag and drop pictures onto your tweets and take care of all the details.

Figure 4-10:
TweetDeck makes managing multiple Twitter accounts easy.

✦ **Sophisticated search functions** so you can display not only your tweets, and the tweets of those you follow, but also tweets on topics that interest you, such as #19thcenturydentistoffices.

If you find yourself using Twitter much at all, take the time to look at TweetDeck. Check the Windows Store to see if there has been any improvement in the Twitter apps. And don't forget to download a Twitter app for your phone and tablet, too. I use both the Android and the iOS (iPhone/iPad) Twitter apps every day, and they're great.

Chapter 5: Getting Started with LinkedIn

In some ways, LinkedIn resembles Facebook — keeping up with people and expanding connections are grist for the mill. But in other ways, LinkedIn is completely different; LinkedIn is focused on professional relationships, which LinkedIn calls *connections*.

You can use your LinkedIn connections to showcase products, look for a job, advertise a job, scout new business opportunities, find temporary help, stay up to date on companies that interest you — for any reason — or just replace your old Rolodex (does anybody still use a Rolodex?) or that tattered box of business cards on your desk.

With more than 150 million subscribers — half of whom are in the U.S. — LinkedIn has more than reached critical mass. Many business people consider it a key part of their existence.

LinkedIn doesn't have a Windows Universal app. There's nothing in the Windows Store from LinkedIn. But that shouldn't stop you from using it on your Windows 10 computer. All it takes is a browser.

Signing Up for LinkedIn

Don't have a LinkedIn account? Got a few minutes?

Here's how to get started:

1. **Fire up your favorite browser, and go to** www.linkedin.com.

   You see a sign-up page like the one in Figure 5-1.

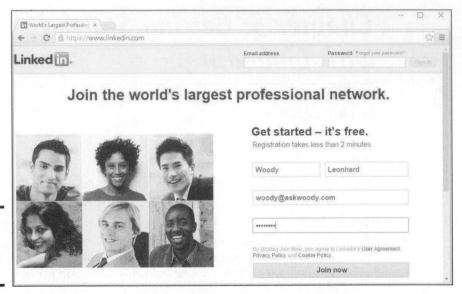

Figure 5-1:
Signing up
for LinkedIn
is easy.

If you want to sign up with your Facebook account, you can, but remember that doing so will add another note to Facebook and LinkedIn's databases, connecting one with the other.

2. **If you want to start a new account, fill in the blanks and tap or click Join Now.**

   Make sure you use a real email address: LinkedIn uses it to verify your account. You're better off NOT using an email address that's associated with your current employer. Remember, even the walls have eyes.

   The first profile page appears, as shown in Figure 5-2, which asks the first of a series of questions that can be tricky to answer. In particular, if you already have a job, advertising that you're *looking* for a job is probably not politically correct.

   My strong suggestion is that, if you have a job, declare that you're Employed *even if you're looking for a new job.* Why? Because your boss's boss may be on LinkedIn. (Of course, she may be looking for a new job, too, but I digress.)

3. **LinkedIn wants to look inside your email account, to find connections.**

   Click Skip this step. You can find your own contacts later.

4. **LinkedIn advises that it's sending you a confirmation email.**

   LinkedIn sends you a message a few minutes later. The message includes a link.

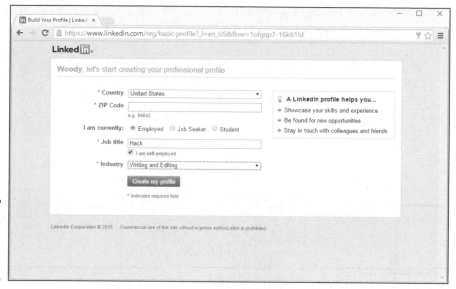

Figure 5-2:
Looks
simple but it
isn't.

5. **Tap or click the link in your email message, provide your email address and password, and sign in *again*.**

You're confirmed.

6. **Tap or click Skip This Step to avoid sucking in your email contacts again. Tap or click Skip to avoid having your phone pinged with a link to download LinkedIn.**

LinkedIn gives you an opportunity to spend money on a Premium account (see Figure 5-3). If you really want to see the details of everyone who's looked at your profile, you might want to consider Premium (the Free accounts can look at the last five viewers), or if you want to look at details about the people you're stalking, er, seeking (job and education history, recommendations and groups), or send private InMail to those who aren't directly connected to you, pay for the Premium package.

7. **Choose a Premium or Basic account.**

I chose Basic.

8. **Step through a professional version of 20 guided questions. If you don't want to list anything, tap or click Skip This Step, but if you think it may help you connect with the right people, by all means, enter your job and education history.**

The Skills question is another tricky one, particularly if you're looking for a job. Puffery here can come back to bite you, but being passive isn't good, either. If you're going to be looking for a job, put items in here that you would put on your résumé. Assume that people who want to interview you will see it before you arrive.

LinkedIn takes you to your profile page, which looks more or less like Figure 5-4.

Figure 5-3: For most people, Premium is overkill.

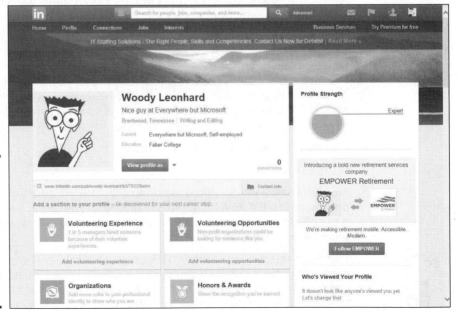

Figure 5-4: On the LinkedIn profile page, it's a good idea to get your profile right early in the game.

9. **If LinkedIn asks you *again* whether you want to log on to your online email accounts (it'll probably also ask whether LinkedIn can scan your Outlook, Apple Mail, or other mail program contacts), ignore it.**

10. **At the top, tap or click the Home link.**

    LinkedIn shows you the main login page, per Figure 5-5.

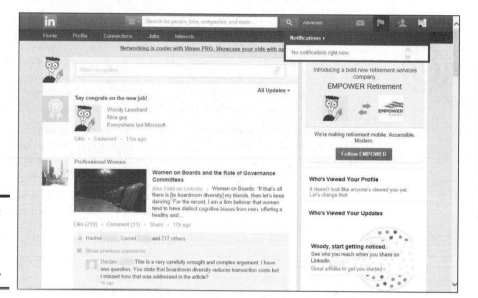

Figure 5-5: LinkedIn returns to the main login page.

Remember that just about anybody can see anything you post.

The social part of LinkedIn involves establishing *connections* — links with people you know, or know of. To start filling in your Connections list, tap or click the Connections link at the top of the home page, choose Add Connections, and add people based on their email addresses. You can also find people you know based on others' connections. Look for the little Connect buttons and links throughout the LinkedIn interface.

Using LinkedIn for Fun and Profit

Using LinkedIn with Windows is both an art and a science. Here are a few hints I've acquired over the years:

✦ **Use your current job title to your advantage.** I'm not sure why, but LinkedIn seems to show your current job title almost everywhere. Anytime someone hovers his mouse over your picture, for example, he sees your current job title and employer, and your location. Stock job titles (CEO, Analyst, Nice Guy — that's the one I use) don't have much sizzle. On the other hand, M2M Executive with Expertise in the Rapid Implementation of CRM Solutions (M.S., Ph.D., O.B.E.) certainly draws attention.

In some contexts LinkedIn truncates your job title. Someone looking at your profile sees the entire title, but someone looking at search results, for example, sees only the first few words.

✦ **Put a different, professional picture on your LinkedIn account.** Don't recycle your Facebook pic — you know, the one your friend took when you were completely plastered at the going-away party. Definitely a no-no in this arena. By all means, wear a suit and tie if you feel more comfortable that way, but casual is okay, too. Just remember that the people you want to impress will look at that mug and make decisions based on it.

✦ **If you graduated with honors, or there's something of note about your degree, include it in the Degree field.** Showing a college degree, such as B.A. Phi Beta Kappa or Summa Cum Laude or M.S. E.E., makes a greater impression than just listing your degree. People will see it.

✦ **Ask for recommendations, but don't use the stock request form.** Recommendations can make a difference in all sorts of situations, so don't be bashful about asking your friends to refer you. But when you do, take a few extra minutes and write a personal request message.

✦ **Start slowly.** Take a few days to get a feel for LinkedIn before you invite everyone to become a Connection. Look around and see how other people set up their profiles. Get a feel for what's acceptable and what's overly pushy. Only when you have your bearings are you really ready to add all those old email contacts to your Connections list. And when you start building your Connections list, go slowly — just a handful of people a day.

Remember six degrees of separation?

After you have a few Connections put together, up at the top, click the Search box's magnifying glass. Look on the left, under Relationship. You may find that you have a whole lot of people connected only two or three steps away; see Figure 5-6.

Social networking works. Even if you don't use LinkedIn very much, having it available "just in case" — just in case you're looking for a new job, or for an expert in a particular field — is well worth the effort.

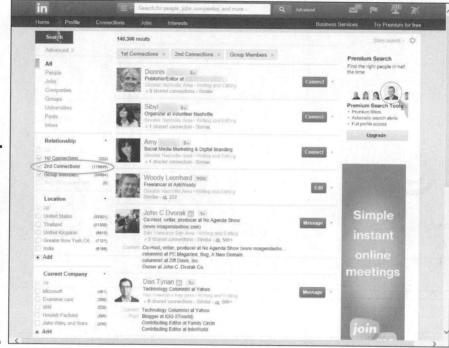

Figure 5-6:
Even if you're only moderately well connected, you can have tens of thousands of people three hops away.

Book VII
Controlling Your System

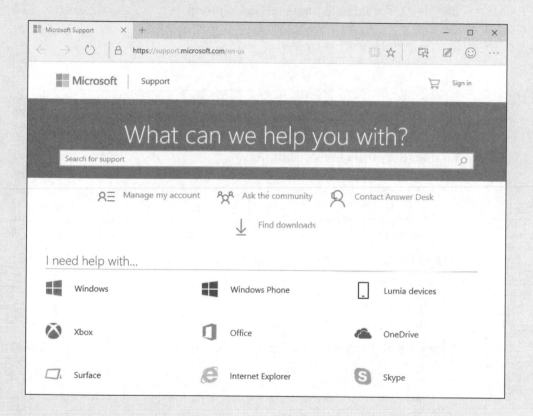

Here's the easy way to remove a program. See www.dummies.com/extras/windows10aio/defenestrate.

Contents at a Glance

Chapter 1: Settings, Settings, and More Settings

In This Chapter

✔ Introducing the Universal Settings app

✔ What's left in the Control Panel

✔ Putting shortcuts to settings on your desktop

✔ "God Mode"

Windows has settings. Boy howdy, does it have settings.

The desktop's Control Panel (shown in Figure 1-1) — long the bastion of Windows settings, through many generations of Windows (see the nearby sidebar) — controls many of the settings on a Windows 10 PC. The new Universal Settings app (shown in Figure 1-2) controls several hundred settings. And — get this — there's a bit of overlap between the two, but some settings can be changed only in the Settings app, and other settings can be changed only on the old-fashioned Control Panel.

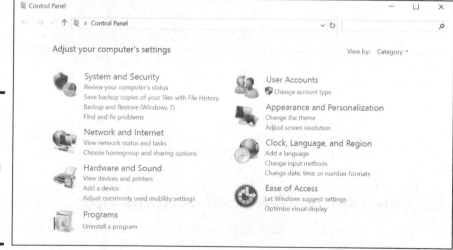

Figure 1-1: The old-fashioned Control Panel is still alive and well — just hard to reach.

What happened to the Control Panel?

Windows has had a Control Panel for as long as Windows has been Windows. It goes all the way back to Windows 1.0. You've probably probed it and sweated over it, as have I, for as long as you've been using Windows.

With Windows 10, Microsoft's clearing out some of the dead wood. I believe they started Windows 10 development hoping to move all those Control Panel settings and applets to a new Universal Windows app called Settings. If that was the intent, Microsoft missed the boat. There are gazillions of settings in the Control Panel. A googolplex of them. Look it up.

Whatever the intent, the final result is a bit schizoid. Some settings are in the Settings app, others are in the Control Panel, and some of them are kind of stretched between the two. Easy example: If you want to change your account from an Administrator account to a Standard account, you have to go into the Control Panel. Want to change your password or your picture? That's in the Settings app.

The Control Panel is definitely headed into the bit bucket. But it remains to be seen if Microsoft will be able to fully eviscerate it this decade.

Figure 1-2:
The new Universal Settings app looks inviting, but it doesn't have all the settings.

This chapter straddles both sides of the fence, both the new Settings app and the old Control Panel. If you want to take control of your machine, unfortunately, you have to learn how to live in both worlds.

Introducing the Universal Settings App

The Universal Settings app (refer to Figure 1-2) is a remarkable collection of settings, arranged in a way that's infinitely more accessible — but arguably less logical — than the old-fashioned desktop Control Panel. Click Start, Settings, and you see these options:

✦ **System:** This includes settings for changing the display and control notifications, analyzing your apps' usage, controlling Snap and multiple desktops, moving in and out of Tablet Mode, kicking in Battery Saver, controlling how long the screen stays active when not in use, analyzing how much storage space is being used, handling downloaded maps, assigning apps to specific filename extensions, and looking at your PC's name and ID. In the Apps & features pane, you can move apps from one drive to another; in Storage (shown in Figure 1-3), you can tell Windows where to store certain kinds of files. There are also links to the Control Panel applets for admin tools, Bitlocker, Device Manager, and Sysinfo.

✦ **Devices:** From here, you can control printers, scanners, and other connected devices; turn Bluetooth on and off; change mouse settings (with a link to the Control Panel app for mice); turn on and off autocorrect and text suggestions; manipulate the pen; and specify what AutoPlay program should kick in when you insert a drive or card.

✦ **Network & Internet:** This lets you turn Wi-Fi off and on, and change your connection, with lots of links to the Control Panel; join or leave a Homegroup (through the Control Panel); set up the Windows Firewall (again through Control Panel); go into Airplane mode, thus turning off both Wi-Fi and Bluetooth connections; track how much data has been sent and received in the past month, by app; set up a VPN; work with a dial-up connection; and manually set a Proxy.

✦ **Personalization:** This catch-all category includes setting your wallpaper (background), choosing accent colors, putting a picture on your lock screen, and controlling the Start menu. There's a link to a Control Panel applet to let you apply desktop themes.

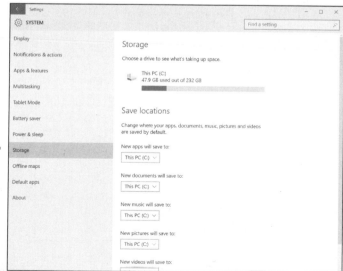

Figure 1-3: System's Storage pane lets you specify where to put new files.

✦ **Accounts:** This lets you disconnect a Microsoft account, set your account picture, and change information about your account with Microsoft's account database in the sky. Find options that enable you to add a new standard user (you have to use the Control Panel to change a standard account into an administrator account), change your password or switch to a picture or PIN password, or switch between a Microsoft account and a local account. You can sync your settings among multiple computers that use your logon (see Figure 1-4). There's also a section that helps you connect to a domain (typically a company or organization network) or Microsoft's Azure Active Directory in the cloud.

✦ **Time & language:** Set your time zone, manually change the date and time, set date and time formats, add keyboards in different languages, control how Windows uses speech and spoken languages, and set up your microphone for speech recognition.

✦ **Ease of Access:** Microsoft has long had commendable aids for people who need help seeing, hearing, or working with Windows. All the settings are here.

✦ **Privacy:** A grandstanding set of settings, with an on/off switch for Cortana and links to Bing's data collection site. You can block app access to your name and picture, turn on and off location tracking, and keep your webcam and microphone locked up. You can also control beacons and other sync proclivities, including giving Windows permission to send your "full health, performance, and diagnostics" information to Microsoft.

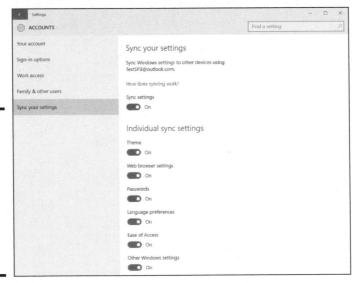

Figure 1-4: Control exactly what gets synced among computers using your Microsoft account.

✦ **Update & Security:** This is an abbreviated form of the Automatic Update settings found in the Control Panel. You can turn File History on and off from this location. The Windows Defender (antivirus) settings live here.

Remarkably, this section also includes (be careful!) links to refresh or reinstall Windows on your PC. Don't accidentally choose one of these, okay?

All in all, it's a well-thought-out subset of the settings that you may want to use. But it's far from complete.

Spelunking through the Control Panel

The inner workings of Windows 10 reveal themselves inside the mysterious (and somewhat haughtily named) Control Panel. You may be propelled to the (sniff) "old" Control Panel via a link in the "aaaah" new Settings app. But if you want to get in directly, of your own volition, right-click (or tap and hold) the Start icon (alternatively press Windows key+X) and choose Control Panel. Figure 1-5 shows the Control Panel window.

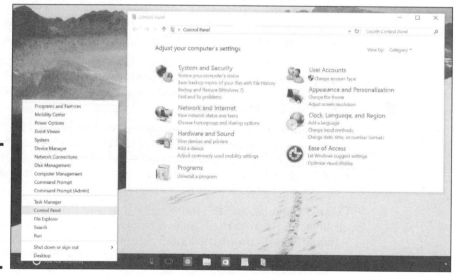

Figure 1-5: The packed Windows 10 Control Panel is a sight to behold.

Book VII
Chapter 1

Settings, Settings, and More Settings

I cover various Control Panel components at several points in this book, but an overview appears in this chapter.

The main categories of the Control Panel span the breadth (and plumb the depths) of Windows 10-dom:

✦ **System and Security:** Use an array of tools for troubleshooting and adjusting your PC and generally making your PC work when it doesn't want to. Check out the components of the Windows 10 Firewall. Change power options, retrieve files with File History, manage Storage Spaces, and rifle through miscellaneous administrative tools. Use this part of the Control Panel with discretion and respect.

✦ **Network and Internet:** Set up a network or a HomeGroup. Set up Internet connections, particularly if you're sharing an Internet connection across a network or if you have a cable modem or digital subscriber line (DSL) service. Deal with conflicting wireless networks. There are even a few hooks for Internet Explorer, which you're not likely to need, because Microsoft Edge has, er, edged it out.

✦ **Hardware and Sound:** The "all other" category. Add or remove printers and connect to other printers on your network. Troubleshoot printers. Install, remove, and set the options for mice, game controllers, joysticks, keyboards, and pen devices. Power settings are here, too.

✦ **Programs:** Add and remove specific features in some programs (most notably, Windows 10 and Office). Uninstall programs. Change the association between filename extensions and the programs that run them (so that you can, for example, have iTunes play WMA audio files).

✦ **User Accounts:** This group is a very limited selection of actions that Microsoft hasn't yet moved to the Settings app. You must go here to change your account type, remove an account, or manage credentials associated with an account

✦ **Appearance and Personalization:** Windows Themes still live here. So do screen savers (which are ignored completely in the Settings app). Oddly, setting the resolution of your screen is still a Control Panel app, as is magnifying text and other items. Font management is in this section, as well as a link to the Ease of Access applet.

✦ **Clock, Language, and Region:** Set the time and date — although double-clicking the clock on the Windows taskbar is much simpler — or tell Windows to synchronize the clock automatically. You can also add support for complex languages (such as Thai) and right-to-left languages, and change how dates, times, currency, and numbers appear.

✦ **Ease of Access:** Change settings to help you see the screen, use the keyboard or mouse, or have Windows flash part of your screen when the speaker would play a sound. You also set up speech recognition here.

Many Control Panel settings duplicate options you see elsewhere in Windows 10, but some capabilities that seem like they should be Control Panel mainstays remain mysteriously absent.

If you want to change a Windows setting, by all means try the Control Panel, but don't be discouraged if you can't find what you're looking for.

Putting Shortcuts to Settings on Your Desktop

Want to see Windows 10's log of your I/O usage — the Data Usage app in Settings — by simply clicking or tapping on the desktop? Enable or disable your microphone with two clicks? Turn off your webcam? Manage your Wi-Fi settings? It's easy.

I came up with a simple extension of a brilliant hack by Lucas (that's the only name we know, @Whistler4Ever on Twitter), published by Sergey Tkachenko at WinAero, and unearthed by Steven Parker at Neowin, gives you a very easy way to put an icon on your Windows 10 desktop that opens to just about any Settings page, where you can change a setting in a nonce.

Here's how to make it work.

1. **Right-click (or tap and hold) any blank place on the Windows 10 desktop.**

2. **Choose New, Shortcut.**

   You see the New Shortcut wizard shown in Figure 1-6.

**Book VII
Chapter 1**

Settings, Settings, and More Settings

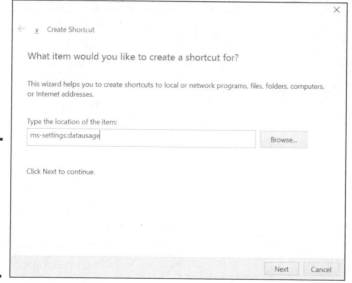

Figure 1-6:
Create a shortcut to the Data Usage pane in the Settings app.

3. **Pick one of the ms-settings apps listed in Table 1-1, and type it into the input box.**

For example, as in Figure 1-6, to go to the Data Usage app, and type `ms-settings:datausage` in the box marked Type the location of the item.

4. **Click Next, give the shortcut a name, and click Finish.**

A new shortcut appears on your desktop. Double-click or tap it, and the Settings app appears, as in Figure 1-7.

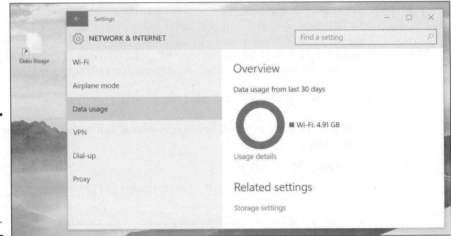

Figure 1-7: The new shortcut takes you straight to the Data Usage pane.

Table 1-1	Shortcuts to Settings App Panels
Settings App Page	*Command*
Battery Saver	ms-settings:batterysaver
Battery Use	ms-settings:batterysaver-usagedetails
Battery Saver Settings	ms-settings:batterysaver-settings
Bluetooth	ms-settings:bluetooth
Colors	ms-settings:colors
Data Usage	ms-settings:datausage
Date and Time	ms-settings:dateandtime
Closed Captioning	ms-settings:easeofaccess-closedcaptioning
High Contrast	ms-settings:easeofaccess-highcontrast

Settings App Page	Command
Magnifier	ms-settings:easeofaccess-magnifier
Narrator	ms-settings:easeofaccess-narrator
Keyboard	ms-settings:easeofaccess-keyboard
Mouse	ms-settings:easeofaccess-mouse
Other Options (Ease of Access)	ms-settings:easeofaccess-otheroptions
Lockscreen	ms-settings:lockscreen
Offline Maps	ms-settings:maps
Airplane Mode	ms-settings:network-airplanemode
Proxy	ms-settings:network-proxy
VPN	ms-settings:network-vpn
Notifications & Actions	ms-settings:notifications
Account Info	ms-settings:privacy-accountinfo
Calendar	ms-settings:privacy-calendar
Contacts	ms-settings:privacy-contacts
Other Devices	ms-settings:privacy-customdevices
Feedback	ms-settings:privacy-feedback
Location	ms-settings:privacy-location
Messaging	ms-settings:privacy-messaging
Microphone	ms-settings:privacy-microphone
Motion	ms-settings:privacy-motion
Radios	ms-settings:privacy-radios
Speech, Inking, & Typing	ms-settings:privacy-speechtyping
Camera	ms-settings:privacy-webcam
Region & Language	ms-settings:regionlanguage
Speech	ms-settings:speech
Windows Update	ms-settings:windowsupdate
Work Access	ms-settings:workplace
Connected Devices	ms-settings:connecteddevices
For Developers	ms-settings:developers
Display	ms-settings:display
Mouse & Touchpad	ms-settings:mousetouchpad

**Book VII
Chapter 1**

**Settings, Settings,
and More Settings**

(continued)

Table 1-1 *(continued)*

Settings App Page	Command
Cellular	ms-settings:network-cellular
Dial-up	ms-settings:network-dialup
DirectAccess	ms-settings:network-directaccess
Ethernet	ms-settings:network-ethernet
Mobile Hotspot	ms-settings:network-mobilehotspot
Wi-Fi	ms-settings:network-wifi
Manage Wi-Fi Settings	ms-settings:network-wifisettings
Optional Features	ms-settings:optionalfeatures
Family & Other Users	ms-settings:otherusers
Personalization	ms-settings:personalization
Backgrounds	ms-settings:personalization-background
Colors	ms-settings:personalization-colors
Start	ms-settings:personalization-start
Power & Sleep	ms-settings:powersleep
Proximity	ms-settings:proximity
Display	ms-settings:screenrotation
Sign-in Options	ms-settings:signinoptions
Storage Sense	ms-settings:storagesense
Themes	ms-settings:themes
Typing	ms-settings:typing
Tablet Mode	ms-settings://tabletmode/
Privacy	ms-settings:privacy

"God Mode"

The Windows Vista-era parlor trick commonly called "God Mode" is alive and well in Windows 10, as shown in Figure 1-8.

I, for one, was quite surprised to see that it made the transition to Win10, because it's based on hooks into the Control Panel — and the Control Panel is being disassembled rapidly in Windows 10.

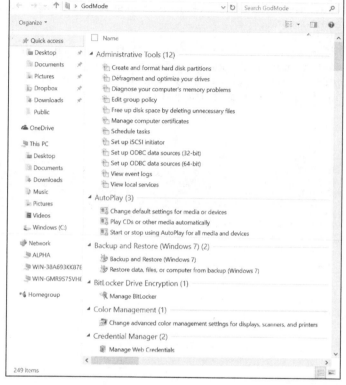

Figure 1-8:
"God Mode"
is a massive
collection
of 262
shortcuts
into all sorts
of Windows
settings,
many of
which
are quite
obscure.

**Book VII
Chapter 1**

Settings, Settings,
and More Settings

The parts of God Mode that appear in Windows 10 are slightly different
from the elements in Windows 8.1 (which, in turn, is slightly different from
Windows 7). But the overall effect is the same.

Follow these steps to access God Mode on your Windows 10 desktop:

1. **Right-click (or tap and hold) any empty spot on the desktop. Choose
New, Folder.**

A new folder appears on your desktop, ready for you to type in a name.

2. **Give the folder the name**

`GodMode.{ED7BA470-8E54-465E-825C-99712043E01C}`

You can use any valid Windows filename instead of "GodMode" — call it
"Parlor Trick" if you like.

3. **Tap or click the folder to bring up the list you see in Figure 1-8.**

   It's a massive list of direct links into all sorts of settings. All of them seem to work.

Some of these may be useful. For example, the AutoPlay option, when accessed through God Mode, brings up the old Windows 7/8 AutoPlay dialog box, which is considerably more advanced than the Windows 10 Settings version of AutoPlay (Start, Settings, Devices, AutoPlay).

Chapter 2: Troubleshooting and Getting Help

*Y*our PC ran into a problem that it couldn't handle, and now it needs to restart. You can search for the error online, but the *error message goes by so fast that you can't possibly read it.*

Wish I had a nickel for every time I've seen that "blue screen" message. People write to me all the time and ask what caused the message, or one like it, to appear on their computers. My answer? Could be anything. Hey, don't feel too bad: Windows couldn't figure it out either, and Microsoft spent hundreds of millions of dollars trying to avoid it.

Think of this chapter as help on Help. When you need help, start here.

Windows arrives festooned with automated tools to help you pull yourself out of the sticky parts. The troubleshooters really do shoot trouble, frequently, if you find the right one. The error logs, event trackers, and stability graphs can keep you going for years — even the experts scratch their heads. Windows abounds with acres and acres — and layers and layers — of Help. Some of it works well. Some of it would work well, if you could figure out how to get to the right help at the right time.

This chapter tells you when and where to look for help. It also tells you when to give up and what to do after you give up. Yes, destroying your PC is an option. But you may have alternatives. No guarantees, of course.

The chapter steps you lightly through the new Windows Contact Support app. It's really just a traffic director, with an opportunity to spend lots of money, but if you're new to Windows, it's worth a quick glance.

This chapter also includes detailed, simple, step-by-step instructions for inviting a friend to take over your computer, via the Internet, to see what is going on and lend you a hand while you watch. I believe that this Remote Assistance capability is the most powerful and useful feature ever built into any version of Windows.

Starting with Contact Support

If you've gone spelunking through your All Apps list, you may have bumped into an oddly named entry called "Contact Support." First time I saw it, I wondered if it was an app for cleaning my contacts, but anyway. . .

Start the app, and you won't be much closer to enlightenment. As Figure 2-1 shows, you really just have two choices.

Figure 2-1: Contact Support is, uh, limited.

If you click the link to Microsoft account & billing, then click to Manage your account on the website, you're taken to www.login.live.com, where you must enter your Microsoft account and password, and then it takes you to the standard Microsoft account maintenance page, shown in Figure 2-2.

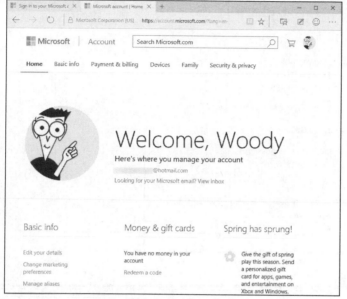

Figure 2-2: Microsoft accounts & billing just takes you to the live.com account maintenance page.

That's probably not what you were expecting. It's not exactly useless, but it's pretty lame.

You have other options under Accounts & billing to contact support staff for Xbox, Skype, Windows Phone, the Store, Windows, Office, or other. From those choices, you can chat online with a Microsoft Answer Tech (have your product key handy), have Microsoft's tech reps call you, or schedule a call for a future time. It's unclear, as we went to press, how much Microsoft will charge for such support.

If you click or tap Microsoft services & apps, you're asked if you want to go to Windows, Internet Explorer or Edge, Office, Office 365, OneDrive, Skype, or Xbox support. Choose Windows, and you're asked if you want help with setting up, technical support, or protecting your PC. In all cases, you get the choices shown in Figure 2-3.

Choose Ask the community, and Edge pops up inside the Microsoft Answers forum, www.answers.microsoft.com — which is a very good source of answers, although it may take a while to get a response to your questions, and the answers you get probably won't be definitive. See the sidebar "Microsoft Answers forum."

Contact Support   — □ ✕

‹ Windows

Ask the community
Get troubleshooting feedback from our
worldwide community

Chat online with a Microsoft Answer Tech

Schedule a call

Call me as soon as possible
Current wait time is 1 minute.

By engaging in support, you agree to the support
Service Agreement terms.

Figure 2-3:
Narrowing
in on
support —
or are we?

Microsoft Answers forum

The Microsoft Answers forum is one of the great resources for Windows customers. There are sections for just about every nook and cranny of every Microsoft product. You post questions, other people post answers, and it's free for everyone.

But it's important that you understand the limitations.

Most of the people on the Answers forum are not Microsoft employees — in fact it's pretty rare to see a Microsoft employee on the forum. (They're identified "Microsoft employee" in their tag line.)

Although the typical forum denizen may be well-intentioned, they aren't necessarily well-informed. You must keep that in mind while wading through the questions and answers.

The Answers forum is a great place to go with immediate problems that may affect other people. It's one of the very few ways that you can register a gripe and expect that, if it's a valid gripe, somebody at Microsoft will actually read it — and maybe respond to it.

In particular, realize that both the Moderators and the Microsoft MVPs (also identified in their tag lines) are all volunteers. No, the Moderators are not Microsoft employees. No, the MVPs aren't paid by Microsoft either. They help on the fora out of the goodness of their hearts. Hard to believe that in this day and age, but it's true. So be kind!

The "Chat online with a Microsoft tech" choice in Figure 2-3 puts you in touch with a real, live, Microsoft support tech and (at least as I write this) their advice is free.

Realize that support techs aren't front-line programmers or testers. Mostly, they're quite familiar with the most common problems and have access to lots of support systems that can answer myriad questions that aren't so common. Some of the techs may even have copies of this book on their desks.

If you have a really, really tough question and the tech you talk to can't solve it, before you hit the reset button, ask to have your question escalated. Support, historically, has had three levels of escalation available, and in very rare cases, some problems are escalated to the fourth level — which is where the product devs (developers) live. Kind of like Dante's *Paradiso.* If your problem is replicable — meaning it isn't caused by bad hardware or cosmic rays — and the tech can't solve it, you should politely ask for escalation.

If you or someone you know is at the beginner stage, do both of you a favor and get Andy Rathbone's *Windows 10 For Dummies* (published by John Wiley & Sons, Inc.). The book/DVD combination, in particular, will answer all your beginner's questions in terminology that you can understand.

Troubleshooting the Easy Way

If something goes bump in the night and you can't find a discussion of the problem and its solution in this book, your first stop should be the Troubleshooters. They don't call 'em Trouble fer nuthin'.

Windows ships with a handful of troubleshooters. *Troubleshooters,* as the name implies, take you by the hand and help you figure out what's causing problems — and, just maybe, solve them.

If you run into a problem and you're stumped, see whether Microsoft has released a pertinent troubleshooter by following these easy steps:

1. **Click in the Cortana search box, next to the Start button, and type (or say) troubleshooter. Tap or click Troubleshooting.**

The Troubleshooting dialog box appears, as shown in Figure 2-4.

2a. ***If you see a troubleshooter that seems to address your problem, tap or click it.***

The selection is limited, but if you're lucky, the Troubleshooting Wizard steps you through the entire process of fixing the problem.

26. ***If you don't see a troubleshooter that seems to address your problem,*** **type a keyword or two in the Search Troubleshooting box and see whether Windows can find one for you.**

Microsoft has dozens of troubleshooters online. You can search for them by using the Search box in the upper-right corner of the Troubleshooting dialog box. For example, there are troubleshooters for power settings, searching and indexing, system maintenance, Windows Update, and many others.

Figure 2-4: Trouble-shooting wizards can cut to the heart of a problem, if you can find one.

Frequently, troubleshooters just can't shoot the trouble, and they end up with an error message dialog box that says something like "This Error Cannot Be Automatically Repaired." You can tap or click Next and end up with informative messages such as "The Error '5' Was Encountered." (I don't make this stuff up — that's exactly the error message I once received while running the connection troubleshooter.)

If you can't find a worthy troubleshooter, you may be able to unearth worthwhile content from your systems log using the Event Viewer, a topic that I tackle in Book VIII, Chapter 4.

System Stability and the Reliability Monitor

The Reliability Monitor's a useful tool that can help pinpoint problems that you can only vaguely identify. Say your computer suddenly starts getting those blue screen messages saying "Your PC Ran into a Problem that It

Couldn't Handle" and now "It Needs to Restart." You know for sure that your PC didn't have those problems last week. But something happened in the past few days, and now, suddenly, Windows encounters more problems than Walter White hits in a season of *Breaking Bad.*

Windows watches all, knows all, sees all — and keeps notes. Windows *events,* as they're called, get stored in a giant database, and you can look into that database with the Event Viewer, which I describe in Book VIII, Chapter 4.

One specific subset of the events get collected into a report — a Reliability Monitor report — that you can understand at a glance.

If you're looking at the Reliability Monitor because somebody on the phone told you that he's trying to help you fix your computer, be very, very suspicious. The Reliability Monitor will show that your computer has problems. Everybody's Reliability Monitor, sooner or later, shows problems. Scammers often use that fact to talk people into paying for services they don't need or allowing them to connect to your computer for nefarious reasons. Don't be conned! It's not unusual to have a string of problems showing in the Reliability Monitor.

Here's the easy way to bring up the Reliability Monitor:

1. **In Cortana's search box, next to the Start button, type or say** reliability. **At the top, tap or click View Reliability History.**

The Reliability Monitor report appears, as shown in Figure 2-5.

2. **Tap or click any item in the list at the bottom of the report to bring up details.**

You can also tap or click an event and merge reports by days or weeks by choosing the appropriate option at the top.

The Reliability Monitor calculates an aggregate score, based on how many problems appear in this graph, taken as a rolling (or in some cases, *roiling*) average. It's the Stability Score, shown as a number between 1 and 10, in the graph at the top.

If you take the Stability score with a small grain of salt, you may be able to glean some useful information from the graph. For example, if you install a new driver and your system goes from ten to five that day, you can bet that the driver had something to do with the decline. The Reliability Monitor shows you significant events for each day and leaves it to you to draw inferences.

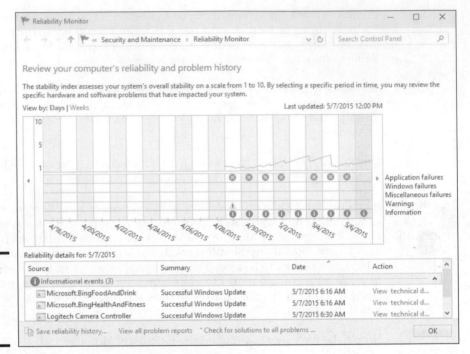

Figure 2-5:
The
Reliability
Monitor
report.

Tricks to Using Windows Help

Slowly, Cortana is getting better at providing some Windows help — Microsoft's busy beefing up its database constantly. If you're very lucky, you can get Cortana to help by simply saying "Hey, Cortana" (or clicking down in the Cortana search bar, to the right of the Start icon) and trying to articulate your problem.

That's much easier said than done, of course.

If you crank up Cortana and say "Windows help," you're directed to the `https://support.microsoft.com` website, as shown in Figure 2-6.

Microsoft hopes to make finding what you need easier for you, even if you don't know the answer to your question in advance — a common problem in all versions of Windows Help.

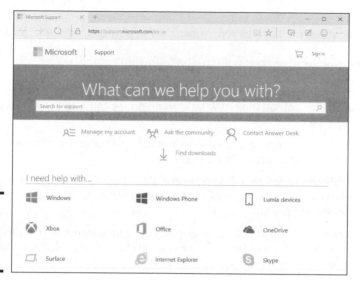

Figure 2-6:
Help from
the Internet
is here!

The problem (s) with Windows Help

Windows Help offers only the Microsoft party line. If a big problem crops up with Windows, you find only a milquetoast report in Windows Help. If a product from a different manufacturer offers a better way to solve a problem, you won't find that information in Windows Help. Want searing insight or unbiased evaluations? That's why you have this book, eh?

Windows Help exists primarily to reduce Microsoft support costs. Microsoft has tried hard to enable you to solve your own problems and to help you connect with other people who may be willing to volunteer. That's good. The new Answer Desk — where you get answers by chatting — is a great idea, but it's still too early to tell how well it will work. And all of it is under the cloud of the Microsoft Party Line. I spill the beans — and give you some much better alternatives — in the section "How to Really Get Help" later in this chapter.

Windows Help puts a happy face on an otherwise sobering (and bewildering!) topic.

Using different kinds of help

Windows Help has been set up for you to jump in, find an answer to your problem, resolve the problem, and get back to work.

Unfortunately, life is rarely so simple. So too with Help. You probably won't dive in to Help until you're feeling lost. And when you're there, well, it's like the old saying, "When you're up to your *<insert favorite expletive here>* in alligators, it's hard to remember that you need to drain the swamp."

Windows Help morsels fall into the following categories:

✦ **Overviews, articles, and tutorials:** These explanatory pieces are aimed at giving you an idea of what's going on, as opposed to solving a specific problem.

✦ **Tasks:** The step-by-step procedures are intended to solve a single problem or change a single setting.

✦ **Walk-throughs and guided tours:** These marketing demos . . . uh, multi-media demonstrations of capabilities tend to be, uh, light on details and heavy on splash.

✦ **Troubleshooters:** These walk you through a series of (frequently complex) steps to help you identify and resolve problems. I talk about troubleshooters earlier in this chapter.

The Windows Help index is quite thorough but, like any index, it relies heavily on the terminology being used in the Help articles themselves. That leads to frequent chicken-and-egg situations: You can find the answer to your question quite readily if you, uh, know the answer to the question — or if you know the terminology involved (which is nearly the same thing, eh?).

How to Really Get Help

You use Windows Help when you need help, right? Well, yes. Sorta.

In my experience, Windows Help works best in the following situations:

✦ You want to understand what functions the big pieces of Windows perform, and you aren't overly concerned about solving a specific problem (for example, *Windows Media Player).*

✦ You have a problem that's easy to define (for example, *my printer doesn't print).*

✦ You have a good idea of what you want to do, but you need a little prodding on the mechanics to get the job done (for example, *touch gestures).*

Help doesn't do much for you if you have only a vague idea of what's ailing your machine, if you want to understand enough details to think your way through a problem, if you're trying to decide which hardware or software to buy for your computer, or if you want to know where the Windows bodies are buried.

For example, if you type **how much memory do I need?**, the answers you see (Figure 2-7) talk about all sorts of things, but they don't tell you how much memory you need.

Figure 2-7: Answers to the question "How much memory do I need?" from the Windows Help website don't always answer the question you asked.

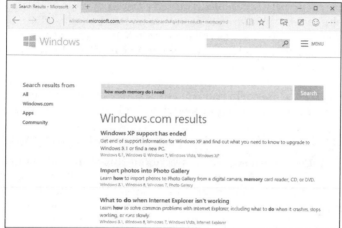

Book VII Chapter 2

Troubleshooting and Getting Help

Beware of "Microsoft" tech support scams!

Somebody calls you, claims to be from Microsoft, and points you to a fancy website that says the caller's a Microsoft Registered Partner. The caller may even know your name or your phone number, or he may act like he knows what version of Windows or what computer you're using. The scammer offers to check whether your system is still under warranty. Invariably, it just went out of warranty, and oh golly, you have to pay $35 or $75 or $150 to get all your problems solved.

These folks are very clever. Many don't live in your home country, although they may sound like it. They may scrape your name from a tech support site and look up your phone number, or they may just make cold calls and figure there's likely to be a warm reception for anyone

who says he's from Microsoft, and he wants to help.

The websites with Microsoft Registered Partner qualifications may look impressive, but anybody — even you — can become a Microsoft Partner; it takes maybe two minutes, and all you need is a free Hotmail or Outlook. com account or other Microsoft account. Drop by `https://mspartner.microsoft. com/en/us/pages/membership/ enroll.aspx`, and sign up!

I have a general explanation of the scam in Book IX, Chapter 1, and a detailed report at `http://windowssecrets.com/ top-story/watch-out-for- microsoft-tech-support-scams`.

For all that, and much more, you need an independent source of information — this book, for example.

My website, AskWoody.com (www.askwoody.com), can come in handy, especially if you're trying to decide whether you should install the latest Microsoft security patch of a patch of a patch. AskWoody.com links to the (absolutely free) Windows Secrets Newsletter Lounge, where hundreds of volunteers help thousands of bewildered Windows victims! You find more than 850,000 searchable posts, absolutely free. Drop by from time to time to see what's happening.

If you can't find the help you need in Windows Help and Support or at AskWoody.com, expand your search for enlightenment in this order:

1. **Use simple bribery, which is far and away the best way to get help.**

Buttonhole a friend who knows about this stuff, and get her to lend you a virtual hand. Promise her a beer, a pizza, a night on the town — whatever it takes. If your friend knows her stuff, it's cheaper and faster than the alternatives — and you'll probably get better advice.

If you can cajole your machine into connecting to the Internet — and get your friend to also connect to the Internet — Windows makes it easy for a friend to take over your computer while you watch with the Remote Assistance feature, which I discuss a little later in this chapter.

2. **If your friend is off getting a tan at Patong Beach, you may be able to find help elsewhere on the Internet.**

See the section "Getting Help Online," later in this chapter.

3. **If you have a problem with a security patch — and can prove it — you may qualify for free support.**

Microsoft used to have a website where you could request a free support ticket, but it has withdrawn the old site. Now, apparently you have to call (see the next step) and convince the person on the other end of the phone that you're having a problem with a security patch, and that your tech support call should be free.

For the life of me, I can't find *any* email address — or pointer to an email address — for tech support at Microsoft.

4. **Use the Contact Support app to start a conversation with a tech support rep.**

You may be pleasantly surprised.

5. As a last resort, you can try to contact Microsoft by telephone.

Heaven help ya.

Microsoft offers support by phone — you know, an old-fashioned voice call — but some pundits (including yours truly) have observed that you'll probably have more luck with a psychic hotline. Be that as it may, the telephone number for tech support in the United States is 800-642-7676, and you may have to press 0 three or more times to get a live person, or 425-635-3311. In Canada, it's 905-568-4494. Have your computer handy. Be prepared to pay.

Snapping and Recording Your Problems

Raise your hand if you've heard the following conversation:

Overworked Geek (answering the phone): "Hi, honey. How's it going?"

Geek's Clueless Husband: "Sorry to call you at work, but I'm having trouble with my computer."

OG: "What kind of trouble?"

GCH: "I clicked the picture, and it went into Microsoft, you know, and I tried to look at this report my boss sent me, but the computer said it couldn't."

OG: "Huh?"

GCH: "I'm sure you've seen this a hundred times. I clicked the picture, but the computer said it couldn't. How do I look at the report?"

OG: "Spfffft!"

GCH: "What's wrong? Why don't you say anything? You have time to help the other people in your office. Why can't you make time for me?"

OG wonders, for the tenth time that day, how she ever got into this crazy business.

At one time or another, you may have been on the sending or receiving end of a similar conversation — probably both, come to think of it. In the final analysis, one thing's clear: When you're trying to solve a computer problem, being able to look at the screen is worth 10,000 words. Or more.

Taking snaps that snap

Since the dawn of WinTime, you could take a snapshot of your desktop and put it on the Windows Clipboard by simply pressing the PrtScr or Print Screen key on your keyboard. Similarly, you can hold down the Alt key and press PrtScr, and Windows puts a screenshot of the currently active window on the Windows Clipboard. From there, you can open Paint (or any of a

**Book VII
Chapter 2**

Troubleshooting and Getting Help

hundred other picture-savvy programs, including Word), paste, and do what you will with the shot. That approach still works in Windows — even in the Windows Universal apps — and in some circumstances, it's exactly the right tool for the job.

Windows Vista introduced the Snipping Tool, which is a more advanced tune on the same theme. With the Snipping Tool (see Figure 2-8), you tap or click New, and then drag and draw a rectangle around the area you want to capture. You can also capture a free-form area anywhere on the screen or automatically capture the current window or the full screen.

Figure 2-8:
The Snipping Tool can take screenshots in a couple of steps.

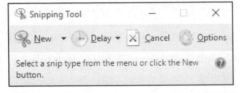

The Snipping Tool has rudimentary tools for drawing on the captured screen, and the result can be copied to the Clipboard and/or saved as a PNG, GIF, JPG, or HTML file, or automatically attached to a newly generated email message.

To bring up the Snipping Tool, click or tap the Windows icon, then All Apps, Windows Accessories, Snipping Tool. The Snipping Tool appears, and if you click New, it lets you click and drag around whatever you want to snip.

Windows has a third screen capture option, and in many circumstances, it's much handier than its two older brethren. If you hold down the Windows key and press PrtScr or Print Screen on your keyboard, Windows takes a screenshot of the entire screen, converts it to a PNG file, and stores it in your Pictures\Screenshots folder. The file is given the name Screenshot (*x*). png, where the number *x* is increased by one with each shot.

Unlike the Snipping Tool, you can't select a part of the screen — you get the whole thing. Also unlike the Snipping Tool, you can't pick a format for the shot or a destination location. Still, for quick screens, it works well.

Recording live

If a screenshot's worth a thousand words, a video of the screen in action must be worth a thousand and one at least, right?

Windows includes the magical *Problem Steps Recorder (PSR),* recently renamed the Steps Recorder, which lets you take a movie of your screen. To a first approximation, anyway, it's actually a series of snapshots, more like an annotated slideshow. You end up with a file that you can email to a friend, a beleaguered spouse, or an innocent bystander, who can then see which steps you've taken and try to sort things out. To read the file, your guru must run Internet Explorer (unless Microsoft has finally updated Edge to read MHTML files).

Steps Recorder creates a slideshow of your screen with automatically generated detailed annotations, good, bad, ugly, problem-infested, or rosy-cheeked. If you have a rosy-cheeked background, anyway.

Steps Recorder is fast and easy, and it works like a champ.

Here's how to record your problems, er, screen:

1. **Make sure you remember which steps you have to take to make the problem (or rosy cheeks) appear.**

   Practice, if need be, until you figure out just how to move the whatsis to the flooberjoober and click the thingy to get to the sorry state that you want to show to your guru friend.

   Realize that anything appearing on the screen, even fleetingly, may be recorded, and your friend may be able to see it. So don't send your salary information, okay?

2. **In the Cortana box to the right of the Start icon, type** steps, **and tap or click Steps Recorder.**

   You can start the Steps Recorder from the Control Panel, but this method is a whole lot easier.

   The Steps Recorder, which resembles a full-screen camcorder, springs to life (see Figure 2-9). It isn't recording yet.

**Book VII
Chapter 2**

**Troubleshooting
and Getting Help**

Figure 2-9:
The
unassuming
Steps
Recorder.

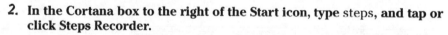

3. **Tap or click Start Record.**

   The recorder starts. You know it's going because the title flashes Steps Recorder — Recording Now.

Note that the recorded slideshow will include the Steps Recorder window, so you may have to move it out of the way in order to show what you want to show.

4. **(Optional) If you want to type a description of what you're doing or why or anything else you want your guru friend to see while she's looking at your home movie:**

   a. *Tap or click the Add Comment button.*

   The recording pauses, and the screen grays out a bit. A Highlight Problem and Comment box appears at the bottom of the screen.

   b. *Tap or click the screen wherever your problem may be occurring and drag the mouse to highlight the problematic location.*

   c. *Type your edifying text in the box, and tap or click OK.*

   Recording continues.

5. **When you're finished with the demo, tap or click Stop Record.**

   Steps Recorder responds with the Recorded Steps dialog box, as shown in Figure 2-10.

   Take a good look at the file because what you see in the Save As box is precisely what gets saved — each of the screenshots, in a slideshow, precisely as presented. Remember, this isn't a video. It's an annotated slideshow.

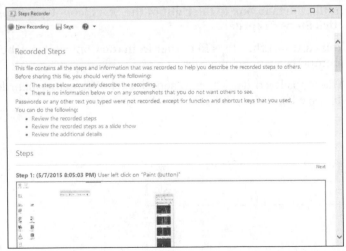

Figure 2-10: Save the recording as soon as you finish it.

6. **Type a name for the file (it's a regular zip file), and tap or click Save.**

    The zip file contains an MHT file, which can be reliably read only by Internet Explorer — although you may have some luck reading the file in Firefox, if it's running the MAFF or UnMHT add-ons. (It's possible, by the time you read this, that Microsoft has built MHTML file reading capabilities into Edge, but don't hold your breath.)

7. **When you're finished, click the red X button to close the Steps Recorder.**

    Magical. Okay, Snagit (`http://techsmith.com/snagit.html`) does the screen recording shtick better, but still.

8. **Send the file to your guru friend.**

    Sneakernet — the old-fashioned way of sticking the file on a USB drive and hand-delivering it — works.

9. **Tell your friend to double-click the zip file when she receives it and then double-click the MHT file inside.**

    Edge appears and shows the MHT file. You have several options; my favorite is to show the file as a slideshow (see Figure 2-11).

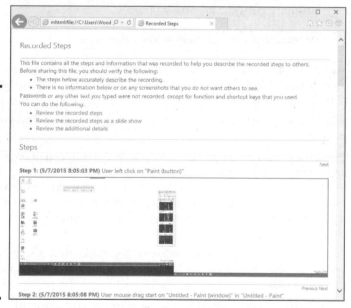

Figure 2-11: The recording appears as a series of snapshots, with detailed accounts of what has been clicked and where.

Book VII Chapter 2

Troubleshooting and Getting Help

Connecting to Remote Assistance

Windows has long boasted the Remote Assistance feature, which lets a person on one computer control a second computer, long distance, while both watch what's on the screen. It's a great puppet/puppet master capability that allows someone to solve your problems remotely while you watch. (Or, if you're the guru, Remote Assistance allows you to solve others' problems while they watch.)

If you're looking at these instructions because someone you don't know wants to get into your computer, stop. Right now. *Seriously. Stop.* Ask yourself how much you know about the person who's trying to look at your PC. Do you trust her to take control of your PC — is it possible she'll pull a fast one on you, even drop an infected file? If you have any qualms at all, DON'T DO IT. Scammers love to talk people into using Remote Assistance because they get full control over the PC, and if they work fast enough (or talk fast enough to convince you that what they're doing is legitimate), they can easily plant anything they want on your computer.

Understanding the interaction

Windows includes the Remote Assistance feature, which lets you call on a friend (or friendly guru) to take over your PC.

The basic interaction goes something like this:

1. You create an invitation file for your guru friend, asking him to look at your computer. Windows creates a password for the invitation and shows it on your screen.

2. You send or give the file to the guru. Separately, you send your guru the password.

   The file can go any way you can imagine: Attach it to an email message, send it via an instant messaging program that allows you to transfer files, put it on a network shared drive, post it on your company's intranet, copy it to a shared folder on OneDrive, copy it to a USB key drive, burn it onto a CD, or strap it to a carrier pigeon. It's just a text file. Nothing fancy.

   Similarly, you can send the password if you like, but it's smarter to call your guru and repeat it over the phone, just in case somebody's scraping your email.

3. Your guru friend receives the message or file and responds by clicking it and then typing the password.

4. Your PC displays a message saying that your guru friend wants to look at your computer.

5. If you give the go-ahead, your guru friend can see what you're doing —
    look, but not touch.

6. Your guru friend may ask whether he can take over your computer. If
    you give your permission, he takes complete control of your machine.

    He can start any program on your computer, bring stuff in from the
    Internet, go into Control Panel . . . the whole nine yards. You watch as
    your friend types and clicks, just as *you* would if you knew what the heck
    you were doing. Your friend solves the problem as you watch.

7. Either of you can break the connection at any time.

The thought of handing your machine over to somebody on an Internet
connection probably gives you the willies. I'm not real keen on it either,
but Microsoft has built some industrial-strength controls into Remote
Assistance. Your guru friend must supply the password that you specify
before he can connect to your computer. He can take control of your computer only if he requests it and you specifically allow it. And you can put a
time limit on the invitation: If your friend doesn't respond within an hour,
say, the invitation is canceled.

Making the connection

When you're ready to set up the connection for Remote Assistance, the following is what you need to do. (I'm writing this from the point of view of the
Dummy requesting assistance from a guru. If you're the guru in the interaction, you have to kind of stand on your head and read backward, but, hey,
you're the guru and no doubt you knew that already, huh?)

1. **Make sure that your guru friend is ready.**

    Call him or shoot him an email and make sure that he will have his
    PC on, connected to the Internet, and running Windows 10, 8 or 8.1,
    7, Vista, XP, Windows Server 2003, Windows Server 2008, or Windows
    Server 2012. Also, make sure that he has his instant messenger program
    cranked up, will check email frequently, and/or will wait for you to hand
    him a file or make one available on your network.

    Make sure that you can contact your guru friend using your selected
    method: If you're using email, make sure that he's in your address book
    and send him a test message to make sure that you have his email
    address down pat; if you're going to send a floppy disk by carrier pigeon,
    make sure the pigeon knows the route and has had plenty of sleep.

2. **Start your machine (the PC that your Remote Assistance friend, the
    guru, will take over), and make sure it's connected to the Internet.**

    Make sure you aren't running any programs that you don't want the guru
    to see. Yes, that includes the Sudoku with the lousy score.

3. **In the Cortana search box next to the Windows icon, type** invite.
   **On the top, choose Invite Someone to Connect to Your PC and Help
   You or Offer to Help Someone Else.**

   The Windows Remote Assistance dialog box appears, as shown in
   Figure 2-12.

4. **Tap or click Invite Someone You Trust to Help You.**

   You don't actually have to trust him but, well, you get the idea.

   Remote Assistance responds with the dialog box shown in Figure 2-13.

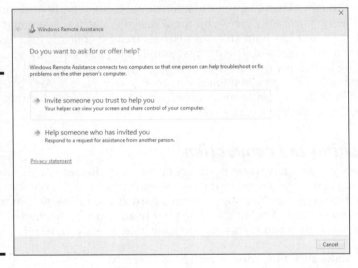

Figure 2-12:
Windows
Remote
Assistance
wants
to know
whether
you're
giving or
getting
advice.

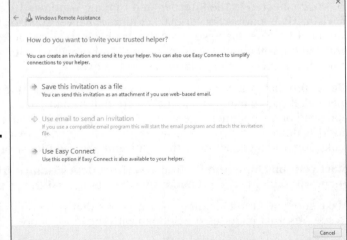

Figure 2-13:
The surest
way is to
save the
invitation as
a file.

Easy Connect is an advanced version of Remote Assistance. It works for some people, if they're connecting with another person who's running Windows 7 or Windows 8, 8.1, or 10. Unfortunately, sometimes network routers get in the way. The big gain with Easy Connect is that you set it up once, and then you can reuse the same connection any time you like, without going through the invitation/password routine.

The method I describe in the following steps works whether your router likes it or not. If you want to try Easy Connect, by all means, choose that option in Figure 2-13 and see whether your guru can connect. If it works, it's, uh, easy.

5. **Choose Save This Invitation as a File.**

   Even if you're going to email the file, it's easier to save the file first and then attach it to an email message.

   Remote Assistance opens the Save As dialog box and prompts you to save the file Invitation.msrcIncident. You can change the name, if you like, but it's easier for your guru friend if you keep the filename extension *msrcIncident*.

6. **Save the file in a convenient place.**

   Remote Assistance responds with an odd-looking dialog box, the Windows Remote Assistance control bar, as shown in Figure 2-14. It advises you to provide your helper (that's your guru friend) with the invitation file and the automatically generated 12-character password.

   Windows waits for your guru friend to contact you. You can continue to work, swear, play Minesweeper, or do whatever it takes to keep you sane until your friend can connect.

**Book VII
Chapter 2**

**Troubleshooting
and Getting Help**

Figure 2-14:
The
Windows
Remote
Assistance
control bar.

7. **Send the invitation file to your guru friend via email, in a shared OneDrive folder, or a USB slipped into his hamburger at lunch.**

8. **Tell your friend to double-click the invitation file to initiate the Remote Assistance session.**

   Your friend's computer asks for the password that's in your Windows Remote Assistance control bar. He types it in the indicated box on his computer and clicks OK.

   Windows Remote Assistance then asks whether it's okay to allow your guru friend to connect to your computer (see Figure 2-15).

Figure 2-15: Remote Assistance requires your explicit permission.

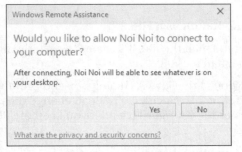

9. **Tap or click the Yes button.**

   Two things happen simultaneously:

   • Your computer's Remote Assistance bar shows that you're connected, as shown in Figure 2-16.

   • Your guru friend's computer sets up a window that shows him everything on your computer, as shown in Figure 2-17.

Figure 2-16: Your computer gets this Remote Assistance bar.

   If your guru friend wants to take control of your PC, he needs to click the Request Control icon on his Remote Assistance bar.

   If he does that, your machine warns you that your guru friend is trying to take control, as shown in Figure 2-18.

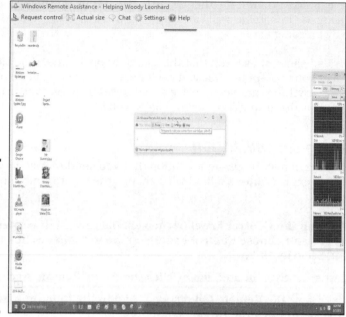

Figure 2-17:
Your guru friend sees your entire desktop in a special Remote Assistance window.

Windows Remote Assistance ✕

Would you like to allow Noi Noi to share control of your desktop?

To stop sharing control, in the Remote Assistance dialog box, click Stop sharing.

☐ Allow Noi Noi to respond to User Account Control prompts   Yes   No

What are the privacy and security concerns?

Figure 2-18:
Allow your guru friend to take over.

10. **On your machine, tap or click Yes to allow your guru friend to take control of your PC.**

Your guru friend can now control your computer, move the mouse cursor, and type while you watch.

11. **Anytime either of you wants to sever the connection, tap or click the Disconnect icon on the Remote Assistance bar.**

In addition, you — the person who requested the session — can cancel the session at any time by pressing Esc.

After a Remote Assistance session is underway and you release control to your friend, your friend can do anything to your computer that you can do — anything at all, except change users. (If either logs off, the Remote Assistance connection is canceled.) Both of you have simultaneous control

over the mouse pointer. If either or both of you type on the keyboard, the letters appear onscreen. You can stop your friend's control of your computer by pressing Esc.

Your friend can rest assured that this is a one-way connection. He can take control of your computer, but you can't do anything on his computer. He can see everything that you can see on your desktop, but you aren't allowed to look at his desktop. Whoever said life was fair?

Limiting an invitation

Unless you change things, an invitation that you send requesting Remote Assistance expires after six hours. To change the expiration time, follow these steps:

1. **Bring up the Control Panel (right-click the lower-left corner of the screen and choose Control Panel); on the left, tap or click the System and Security link.**

2. **Under the System link, tap or click the Allow Remote Access link.**

3. **Make sure the Remote tab displays, and in the Remote Assistance box, tap or click the Advanced button.**

4. **In the Invitations box, choose the amount of time you want invitations to remain open.**

5. **Tap or click OK twice, and then tap or click the X to close the Control Panel.**

Troubleshooting Remote Assistance

Plenty of pitfalls lurk around the edges of Remote Assistance, but it mostly rates as an amazingly useful, powerful tool. The following are among the potential problems:

✦ You and your guru friend must be connected to the Internet or to the same local network. If you can't connect to the Internet — especially if that's the problem you're trying to solve — you're outta luck.

✦ Both of you must be running Windows 10, 8 or 8.1, 7, Vista, XP, Windows Server 2003, Windows Server 2008, Windows Server 2012, or another operating system that supports Remote Assistance. Sorry, your iPad doesn't qualify, but you can mix and match — you can be running Windows 10, while your friend is stuck with Windows 8.1. Go ahead and gloata.

✦ You must be able to give (or send) your guru friend a file so he can use the invitation to connect to your PC.

✦ If a firewall sits between either of you and the Internet, it may interfere with Remote Assistance. Windows Firewall (the firewall that's included in Windows 10, 8, 8.1, 7, and Windows Vista, as well as Windows XP Service Pack 2 and later) doesn't intentionally block Remote Assistance, but other firewalls may. If you can't get through, contact your system administrator or dig in to the firewall's documentation and unblock *Port 3389* — the communication channel that Remote Assistance uses.

You — the person with the PC that will be taken over — must initiate the Remote Assistance session. Your guru friend can't tap you on the shoulder, electronically, and say something like this (with apologies to Dire Straits): "You an' me, babe, how 'bout it?"

Getting Help Online

Microsoft is finally making it easier to chat with a real, live human being. But you may find the answers better (and less conformist to the Microsoft Party Line) if you hop on to the Microsoft Answers forum.

Lots of people join in on the forums to help (see sidebar at the beginning of this chapter). Many of the helpers are *MVPs — Microsoft Most Valued Professionals* — who work without pay, just for the joy of knowing that they're helping people. Microsoft gives the MVPs recognition and thanks, and some occasional benefits such as being able to talk with some people on the development teams. In exchange, the MVPs give generally good — sometimes excellent — support to anyone who asks.

My personal bias, of course, is to direct you to the free online help forum that a bunch of friends and I started 20 years ago. It's at www.windowssecrets.com/forums. I mention it earlier in this chapter.

I also post constantly on www.AskWoody.com. If there's something new and important, I've probably written about it already, most likely for InfoWorld. Check it out. If you're on Twitter, follow @woodyleonhard.

And for ongoing reams of Windows help and advice, subscribe to the weekly Windows Secrets Newsletter, www.windowssecrets.com/. I helped found that newsletter and contribute quite regularly.

**Book VII
Chapter 2**

**Troubleshooting
and Getting Help**

Chapter 3: Working with Libraries

In This Chapter

✔ Understanding Libraries

✔ Customizing and working with Libraries

✔ Building your own Libraries

Windows 8.1 brought several infuriating changes to Windows 8 — I'd list the privacy-busting Smart Search (see Book III, Chapter 6) "feature" as the worst culprit. Smart Search is now part and parcel of Cortana.

In the same infuriated breath, I'd have to mention Microsoft's attempt to make it difficult to use Libraries.

Libraries were a key selling point for Windows 7: They really do make it easier for you to organize and maintain your files. The feature continued untarnished in Windows 8. Unfortunately, Microsoft decided to stunt and bury them in Windows 8.1, and Windows 10 has nothing to make them easier to use. If I were a more cynical soul, I would guess that MS is trying to get you to use OneDrive — and pay the piper for cloud storage.

It's silly, really, because Libraries are the single best way to incorporate SD card storage and external hard drives into your everyday Windows life. When Libraries are set up with the Public folders activated (as should've been the case in Windows 8.1 straight out of the box), they also give you a chance to share data with other people on your computer or on your home network, and you don't have to take a trip through Microsoft's cloud to do it.

In this chapter, I start with some concepts and then show you how to get Libraries working on your Windows 10 machine. Then we can go into the advanced course.

Understanding Libraries

Lots of experienced Windows users get confused when they start thinking about Libraries. That's because they have a long-imprinted misconception that data has to be located in one place. Your files are on your C: drive or on a DVD, or you download them from the Internet. You open a file, and if you don't find what you want, you look in another file in the same folder. If the folder doesn't have what you want, you go up one level and look again.

All those concepts are locked into the idea that your data must be located in just one place.

Although your files have to sit somewhere, Windows 7 introduced a concept that makes it easier to handle collections of files and folders. The concept lives on, half-buried, in Windows 10.

You know what a file is, right? (If not, I talk about it in Book I, Chapter 1.) Files hold data. Typically, you have one photo or video in one file. You have one song in one file. You have one document, spreadsheet, or PowerPoint presentation in one file. Of course, there are lots of nuances, but at its heart, a *file* is just a collection of data that you stick in one place. Files can be empty. They can be huge.

And you know about folders, yes? *Folders* are collections of files and other folders. Folders can also be empty. They can be huge. They can have lots of little files or many big files, or any combination of little and big files and folders. You put a bunch of files and folders together in one place, and that place is a folder.

Note how I said "in one place." The physical details may get a little hairy, but at least conceptually, all the data in the file is in one place. All the files in a folder are in one place. That's how Libraries are different.

Libraries aren't all in one place. Libraries bring together folders that can be sitting just about anywhere: on your C: drive, on your D: drive, on a USB stick, an SD card, on an external drive, in the cloud (which is to say, on the Internet), even someplace else on your network, if you have one. A *Library* is a collection of folders that's broken free of the "in one place" restriction. But Libraries use pointers to make it *seem* like these files are all in one place.

Making Your Libraries Visible

When you bring up File Explorer in Windows 10, you're placed in a make-believe folder called Quick Access, which consists of folders that you have pinned, or that have been pinned for you (Desktop, Documents, Downloads, Music, Pictures, Videos). File Explorer shows your most frequently used folders on top and recently used files on the bottom. See Figure 3-1.

If you've used Windows 7 or 8, you probably wondered what happened to your Libraries — they used to appear on the left side of the screen as links to the Documents, Music, Pictures, and Videos Libraries. Instead, we get the six folders (not Libraries) listed at the top of Figure 3-1.

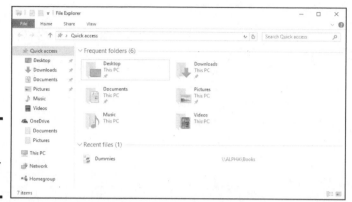

Figure 3-1:
The original
File Explorer
layout.

Here's how to bring back your Libraries:

1. Open File Explorer. Click the View tab.

You see the Ribbon shown in Figure 3-2.

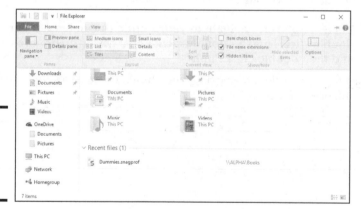

Figure 3-2:
Have File
Explorer
show you
Libraries.

**2. Click or tap the large Navigation Pane icon on the left, and select
Show Libraries.**

Your four default Libraries appear on the left, as in Figure 3-3.

Unfortunately, you aren't finished yet. One of the most important features of
Libraries in Windows 7 and 8 was their ability to hook into the Public folders
on your computer. The Public folders are a good place to put files that you
want to share with other people on your computer or other people on your
network.

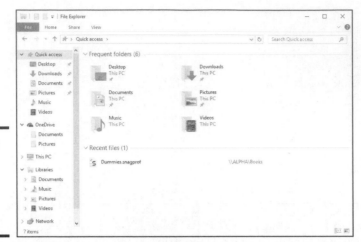

Figure 3-3:
Bringing back the stunted version of Libraries.

In Windows 10, the default Libraries aren't hooked up to the Public folders of the same type. You'll see later in this chapter why that's important. For now, just take my word for it, swear once or twice at Microsoft, and roll your Public folders into your Libraries. Here's how:

1. **In File Explorer, navigate to your Public Documents folder. To do so, double-click This PC, double-click Local Disk (C:), double-click Users, and then double-click Public.**

   After all that double-clicking, you should come to a screen that looks like the one in Figure 3-4.

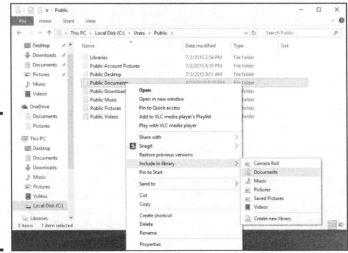

Figure 3-4:
Add the Public Documents folder to your Documents Library.

2. **Right-click the Public Documents folder, choose Include in Library, and then choose Documents.**

   Windows 10 reluctantly puts your Public Documents folder where it belongs.

3. **Repeat the steps for the Public Music folder (put it in the Music Library), the Public Pictures folder (in Pictures), and the Public Videos folder (in Videos).**

4. **Close File Explorer (click the X in the upper-right corner), and restart it. Verify that all the Public folders now appear in their correct Libraries, as in Figure 3-5.**

   Give Microsoft a little epithet for that one.

Figure 3-5: Public folders now appear where they should've been in the first place.

Working with Your Default Libraries

After you've set up your Libraries as described in the preceding section, when you start File Explorer and click Libraries on the left, icons for the four Libraries that you just built appear, along with two others (Camera Roll, Saved Pictures) that may have been added by the Phone Companion app (see Figure 3-6).

You may be tempted to think that Windows magically identifies the kinds of files you're working with and shows them in the appropriate Library — all your pictures appear in the Pictures Library, for example. That isn't how Libraries work.

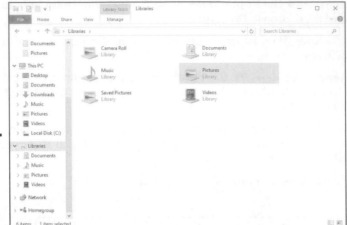

Figure 3-6:
The four
horses of
the Library
apocalypse.

The way we set up Libraries in the preceding section makes them work
this way:

✦ Everything that appears in the Documents Library comes from the
Documents folder, mashed together with the Public\Documents folder,
and the contents of Documents in OneDrive.

✦ The same is true for the Music Library.

✦ Everything in the Pictures Library comes from either the Pictures or
Public Pictures folder, or from OneDrive.

✦ And the same is true for the Videos Library.

The converse is also true. Every file in the Music folder appears in the Music
Library, as does every file in the Public\Music folder. Windows doesn't dig in
to the file and see whether it's a music file. The Music Library doesn't consist of music files, necessarily. It's just a mash-up of all the files in those two
folders.

Why would you want to bother with Libraries? Ends up that they're pretty
powerful after you get used to them. Probably the most valuable timesaver
for most people is in the search that spans across multiple folders. Here are
two examples:

✦ If you want to search all your music for an album by Nickelback, go to the
Music Library and in the upper-right corner search for *Nickelback.*

✦ If you want to search for documents and spreadsheets that contain the
word *defenestrate,* bring up the Documents Library, type **defenestrate**
in the search box, and Windows returns all the documents in both
\Documents and \Public\Documents that contains the word.

Libraries for old Windows hands

If you've used any modern version of Windows Media Player, you already know about Libraries. WMP starts with your Music folder and your PC's Public Music folder, and allows you to add other folders to its Library. So, for example, you can add a folder full of music on an external hard drive to the WMP Library or link to Music folders on other networked computers or even a Music folder on a Windows Home Server server.

When you add a folder to the WMP Library, it doesn't copy the music anywhere. WMP merely provides easy access to all the files (the songs) in the Library, keeps track of them, and lets you search and work with them as a group.

There are no limitations to the folders you can add to a WMP Library: As long as your computer can get at the folders — the external drive is plugged in to the computer, say, or there are no security rules blocking access to another computer — WMP treats the music in those folders more or less the same way they'd be treated if they were sitting on your own PC.

Imagine how that searching can make your life easier if you keep, say, all your music in a folder on one computer that's attached to your network. Set up your Music Library to include that folder, and your searching just got a whole lot easier.

If you have a computer with an SD card, or an external hard drive, set up a \Documents folder on the SD card or external hard drive, and add it to your Documents Library. That makes it easier to find documents on the SD card, store documents on the SD card, and generally keep your system running much, much easier: You don't have to think about where the data's stored because it's all in the Library.

When an application running under Windows looks for the Documents folder, Windows hands it the entire Documents Library. If you start a graphics program and choose File, Open, you don't go to your Pictures folder anymore. Instead, you open the Pictures Library. Imagine. If you have a folder on another computer that contains documents you commonly use, and you add that folder to your Documents Library, every time you crank up Word and choose File, Open, that folder is staring right at you. Unlike earlier versions, Windows Media Player doesn't need separate settings to handle Libraries because Windows takes care of everything.

Yes, Microsoft stacks the deck in more recent versions of Office and some other programs — a File, Open takes you to OneDrive. Blech. But few other programs work that way.

Think of Libraries as Folders: The Next Generation.

Customizing Libraries

You can add more folders to a Library above and beyond the folders that we added in the first section of this chapter. You can also change where a Library saves data when you add items to it. Read on for the details.

Adding a folder to a Library

The most common change I see people make to their Libraries is to add a new folder to the Pictures or Music Library. Typically, you have pictures or maybe music strewn in several locations, either on your computer or on your network. Here's how easy it is to add a folder from far away into your Library:

1. **Using File Explorer, navigate to the folder you want to add.**

   It can be located just about anywhere.

2. **Tap and hold or right-click the folder, select Include in Library, and choose the Library.**

   In Figure 3-7, I add the From iPhone 6 folder — located on a different computer, in a Public location — to my Pictures Library.

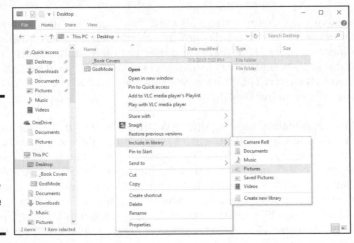

Figure 3-7: Adding a folder to a Library is easy, if you start by going to the folder.

3. **Go back to the Library, and make sure that the folder was added properly.**

   In Figure 3-8, you can see that the From iPhone 6 folder, which sits on a different computer, is now in my Pictures Library.

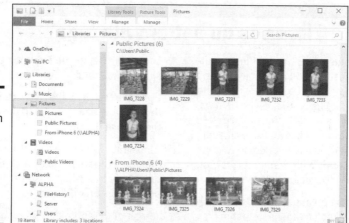

Figure 3-8:
Even though the folder hasn't moved, it's now included in the Library.

It's important to realize that Windows *doesn't move anything.* The pictures are still in their old location — even over on a different computer. But the Library has been expanded to include the folder in the remote location. If you search your Pictures Library, in this case, Windows will not only look at the contents of the \Pictures and \Public\Pictures folders, it will also look inside the From iPhone 6 folder — whether it's on your C: drive, an external hard drive, an SD card, someplace on your network . . . just about anywhere.

Libraries aren't exclusive. You can put one folder in multiple Libraries. You can put a folder in one Library and a subfolder of that folder in a different Library. You can even put a OneDrive folder in your Library.

If you ever want to remove a folder from a Library, tap and hold or right-click the folder's name on the left in the Navigation pane. Choose Remove Location from Library.

Changing a Library's default save location

Want to challenge your brain a bit? Don't short-circuit on this one, but "Libraries" *itself* is a Library — a Library that contains Libraries.

When you drag, copy, or move a file (or folder) into a Library, the file (or folder) must physically go somewhere — it must be placed in a real, physical folder. For example, if you save a new picture called Dummy.pic to the Pictures Library, Windows has to put the file Dummy.pic someplace; it has to stick it in a real folder. Because the Pictures Library isn't a real folder, Windows needs to figure out which folder inside the Pictures Library should get the copy of Dummy.pic.

Libraries go better with tags

Whereas most music files have (at least rudimentary) tags associated with them, photos usually don't come with tags, other than the ones your camera puts on them — *EXIF data,* such as the time and date the picture was taken. Nor do videos. To keep massive amounts of media organized, you have to come to grips with tags, the index data (or *metadata)* that you can stick on every file you own.

Although you can't create a Library based on tags, you can search on tags, and that makes it infinitely easier to keep large Libraries organized.

Windows Media Player and Live Photo Gallery have good tools for handling tags. In general, you can assign your own tags to just about any file (except GIFs) as follows:

1. **Locate the file in File Explorer, and make sure it's selected.**

2. **Open the Details pane (the link is under the Preview pane), and edit the tags in the pane at the right.**

   Alternatively, you can right-click the file, choose Properties, and click the Details tab. Many free programs are available for editing tags on MP3 files, too.

At the risk of paraphrasing Beyoncé (and the Chipettes), if you like it, then you shouldda put a tag on it. Whoa whoa whoa. If you want to find a file, put a tag on it!

The folder is the *default save location* for the Library. If you set up your Libraries as described at the beginning of this chapter, the save location for the Documents Library is your plain old everyday Documents folder. The save location for the Music Library is the Music folder and so on.

It's easy to change the default save location for any of the Libraries.

I, personally, change the save location of the Music Library to the \Public\ Music folder, so when I drag or save music into the Music Library, it automatically ends up in a place where other people who use my PC, and other people on my network, can access that music easily.

Here's how to change the default save location:

1. **Start File Explorer, and click the Libraries link on the left.**

   The Libraries appear, as shown in Figure 3-6.

2. **On the left, tap or click a Library. Then at the top, tap or click the Library Tools tab.**

   The Library Tools Manage tab opens and exposes the Manage Library Ribbon, which looks like Figure 3-9.

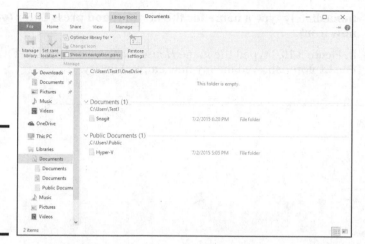

Figure 3-9:
Manage
your
Libraries
from this
Ribbon.

3. **On the left, in the Navigation pane, tap or click whichever Library you want to change.**

4. **At the top, tap or click Set Save Location and choose the folder that you want to set as the default save location.**

Your change takes place immediately.

Creating Your Own Library

At the beginning of this chapter, I showed you how to set up four Libraries — the same four Libraries that ship with Windows 7 and 8 — but you can add as many as you like.

You may want to create your own Library if, for example, you have a bunch of information about a house you want to sell. The info may include Word documents, an Excel spreadsheet, multiple photos, and maybe a video or two. You have the documents in a folder in Documents, the photos are in a separate folder in Pictures, and the video is in a separate folder in Videos. Here's how to make a Library that ties them all together:

1. **Start File Explorer, and make sure your Libraries show (refer to Figure 3-6).**

2. **Tap and hold or right-click any blank location on the right, and choose New, Library.**

Windows creates a new Library, giving it the name New Library.

3. **Immediately type a name for the Library, and press Enter (or tap the new icon).**

   In Figure 3-10, I typed the name *House for Sale* and pressed Enter, and File Explorer showed me my new empty Library.

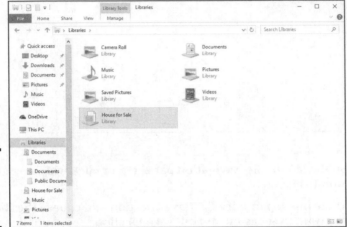

Figure 3-10:
Start your
own custom
Library.

4. **Tap or click the Include a Folder button.**

   Windows lets you out to pick and choose your first folder.

5. **Navigate to the first folder you want to include, and tap or click Include Folder.**

   The first folder becomes the default save folder.

6. **To add additional folders to the Library, navigate to the folder, tap or right-click and hold, choose Include in Library, and choose the name of the new Library.**

   The new Library appears everywhere that the four default Libraries appear, including the Navigation pane on the left of File Explorer and in the right-click menu for folders.

Chapter 4: Storing in Storage Spaces

In This Chapter

- ✔ Virtualizing Storage Spaces
- ✔ Setting up Storage Spaces
- ✔ Care and feeding of Storage Spaces

*F*or people who want to make sure that they never suffer a data loss — in spite of dying hard drives or backup routines that don't run properly — the Windows Storage Spaces feature may, in and of itself, justify buying, installing, and using Windows 10.

If you're using Drobo, ReadyNAS, or some other, expensive, network-attached storage device for file mirroring, you can toss your old hardware. Windows 10 handles it all as part of the operating system itself.

Some people prefer to back up to the cloud, but even if you do stick backups on the Internet, you'll feel a whole lot better knowing that the data you have here on earth is not going to disappear if a hard drive spins its last. On the other hand, if all your data is in the cloud, all the time, you don't need to worry about local drives failing, and you can give this chapter a pass.

In this chapter, I introduce you to the Windows 10 approach to drive virtualization and how it enables Storage Space to work. Then you walk through setting up Storage Spaces and the tips and tricks you need to know to make Storages Spaces work for you. Using Storage Spaces for backup is quick and easy, and it works.

Storage Spaces's roots in Windows Home Server

The crazy thing about Storage Spaces? Microsoft's already shipped a fully functional version, long before Windows 10. The original Windows Home Server, released in July 2007, had a Drive Extender feature that's very, very similar to what Microsoft now offers in Windows 10.

I know. Drive Extender is featured prominently in my book, *Windows Home Server For Dummies;* it's one of the greatest features Microsoft has ever offered to home and small business users.

The really crazy part: Microsoft yanked Drive Extender from the second version of Windows Home Server, which was released in April 2011. The claim, at the time, was that the technology had bugs deep inside that couldn't be exorcised

in the normal course of upgrading from version 1 to version 2. I hollered and moaned at the time to no avail. Drive Extender was one of two really cool features (the other was Automatic Backup) in Windows Home Server that I relied on all the time, and Microsoft threw it away.

I felt so strongly about Microsoft's defenestration of Drive Extender that I refused to upgrade to version 2 of Windows Home Server. Drive Extender really is that cool.

Now I know why MS took Drive Extender out of Windows Home Server 2. It built the same technology, reworked from the ground up, in Windows 8, now 10, and in Windows 2012 Server. You gotta see it to believe it.

Understanding the "Virtualization" of Storage

You're going to get sick of the term *virtualization* sooner or later. People who want to sell you stuff use the term all the time. But if you'll pinch your nose and wade through the offal, there's a solid core of real-world good stuff in this particular kind of virtualization technology.

Windows Storage Spaces takes care of disk management behind the scenes so you don't have to. You'll never even know (or care) which hard drive on your computer holds what folders or which files go where. Volumes and folders get extended as needed, and you don't have to lift a finger.

You don't have to worry about your D: drive running out of space because you don't *have* a D: drive. Or an E: drive. Windows just grabs all the hard drive real estate you give it and hands out pieces of the hard drive as they're required.

As long as you have two or more physical hard drives of sufficient capacity, any data you store in a Storage Spaces pool is automatically mirrored between two or more independent hard drives. If one of the hard drives dies, you can still work with the ones that are alive, and you never miss a beat — not one bit is out of place. Run out and buy a new drive, stick it in the computer, tell Windows that it can accept the new drive into the Storage Spaces borg, wait an hour or two while Windows performs its magic, and all your data is back to normal. You never miss a beat. It's really that simple.

When your computer starts running out of disk space, Windows tells you. Install another drive — internal, external, USB, eSATA, whatever — and, with your permission, it's absorbed into the pool. More space becomes available, and you don't need to care about any of the details — no new drive letters, no partitions, no massive copying or moving files from one drive to another, no homebrew backup hacks. For those accustomed to Windows' whining and whining, the Storage Spaces approach to disk management feels like a breath of fresh air.

When you add a new hard drive to the Storage Spaces pool, everything that was on that new hard drive gets obliterated. You don't have any choice. No data on the drive survives — it's all wiped out. That's the price the drive pays for being absorbed into the Storage Spaces borg.

Here's a high-level overview of how you set up Storage Spaces with data mirroring:

1. Tell Windows that it can use two or more drives as a storage pool.

   Your C: drive — the drive that contains Windows — cannot be part of the pool.

   The best configuration for Storage Spaces: Get a fast solid state drive for your system files, and make that the C: drive. Then get two or more big, hunking drives for storing all your data. The big drives can be slow, but you'll hardly notice. You can use a mixture of spinning disks and solid state disks, if you like.

2. After you set up a pool of physical hard drives, you can create one or more Spaces.

   In practice, most home and small business users will want only one Space. But you can create more, if you like.

3. Establish a maximum size for each Space, and choose a mirroring technology, if you want the data mirrored.

   The maximum size can be much bigger than the total amount of space available on all your hard drives. That's one of the advantages of virtualization: If you run out of physical hard drive space, instead of turning belly up and croaking, Windows just asks you to feed it another drive.

   For a discussion of the available mirroring technologies, see the sidebar "Mirroring technologies in Storage Spaces."

Book VII Chapter 4

Storing in Storage Spaces

Mirroring technologies in Storage Spaces

When it comes to mirroring — Microsoft calls it *resiliency*— you have four choices:

✔ You can choose to *not mirror* at all. That way, you lose the automatic real-time backup, but you still get the benefits of pooled storage.

✔ You can designate a space as a *two-way mirrored* space, thus telling Windows that it should automatically keep backup copies of everything in the space on at least two separate hard drives, and recover from dead hard drives automatically as well. It's important to realize that your programs don't even know the data's being mirrored. Storage Spaces takes care of all the details behind the scenes.

✔ You can use *three-way mirroring,* which is only for the most fanatical people with acres of hard drive space to spare.

✔ There's another form of redundancy called *parity* that calculates check sums on your data and stores the sums in such a way that the data can be reconstructed from dead disks without having two full copies of the original file sitting around. This approach takes up less room than full mirroring, but there's higher overhead in processing input/output. MS recommends that you use parity mirroring only on big files that are accessed sequentially — videos, for example — or on files that you don't update very often.

---

4. If a drive dies, you keep going and put in a new drive when you can. If you want to replace a drive with a bigger (or more reliable) one, you tell Windows to get rid of (or *dismount)* the old drive, wait an hour or so, turn off the PC, yank the drive, stick in a new one, and away you go.

   It's that simple.

If you've ever heard of RAID (Redundant Array of Inexpensive Discs) technology, you may think that Storage Spaces sounds familiar. The concepts are similar in some respects, but Storage Spaces doesn't use RAID at all. Instead of relying on specialized hardware and fancy controllers — both hallmarks of a RAID installation — all of Storage Spaces is built in to Windows itself, and Storage Spaces can use any kind of hard drive — internal, external, IDE, SATA, USB, eSATA, you name it — in any size, mix or match. No need for any special hardware or software.

Setting Up Storage Spaces

Even though you can set up Storage Spaces with just two hard drives — your C: system drive, plus one data drive — you don't get much benefit out of it until you move up to three drives. So in this section, I assume that you have your C: drive, plus two more hard drives — internal, external, eternal, infernal, whatever — hooked up to your PC. I further assume that those two hard drives have absolutely nothing on them that you want to keep. Because they will get blasted. Guaranteed.

Ready to set up a Space? Here's how:

1. **Hook up your drives, log on to Windows using and administrator account (see Book II Chapter 4) and then go into File Explorer and verify that Windows has identified three drives.**

In Figure 4-1, I have three drives. The C: drive has my Windows system on it; C:'s the boot drive. The other two have miscellaneous junk that I don't want to keep.

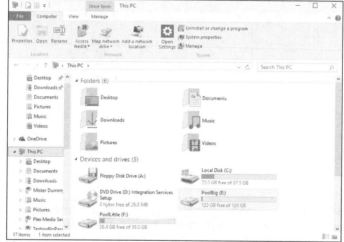

Figure 4-1:
Start with
three drives,
two for your
storage
pool.

**Book VII
Chapter 4**

Storing in
Storage Spaces

2. **Bring up the Control Panel (right-click the lower-left corner of the screen, and choose Control Panel); tap or click System and Security, and then tap or click Storage Spaces.**

Equivalently, you can go to the Metro Start screen, type **storage spaces**, and look under Settings.

If you choose either Storage Spaces or Manage Storage Spaces, you see the Storage Spaces dialog box, as shown in Figure 4-2.

3. **Tap or click the Create a new pool and storage space link.**

You have to create a storage pool first — that is, assign physical hard drives to Windows available pool of hard drives. Windows offers to create a storage pool, as shown in Figure 4-3.

Figure 4-2:
Create a
new storage
pool.

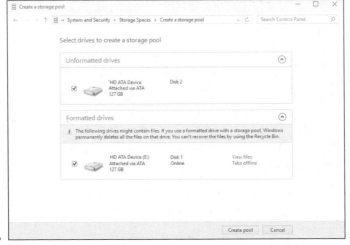

Figure 4-3:
Windows
allows you
to pool any
drives other
than those
that
contain
the boot
and system
partitions.

4. **Select the check boxes next to the drives that you want to include in the storage pool. Note that if you accidentally select a drive that contains useful data, your data's going to disappear. Irretrievably.**

   And I do mean *irretrievably.* You can't use Recuva or some other disk scanning tool to bring back your data. After the drive's absorbed into the storage pool borg, it's gone.

5. **Tap or click Create Pool.**

   Windows whizzes and wheezes and whirs for a while, and then comes up with the Create a Storage Space dialog box, as shown in Figure 4-4.

6. **Give your Storage Space a name and a drive letter.**

   You use the name and the letter in the same way that you now use a drive letter and drive name — even though the Storage Space spans two or more hard drives. You can format the Storage Space "drive," copy data to or from the "drive," and even partition the "drive," even though there's no real, physical drive involved.

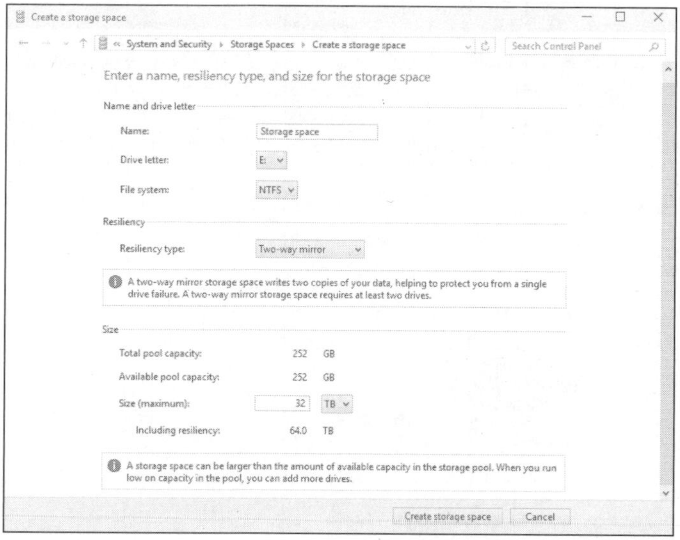

Figure 4-4:
Windows wants you to give the new Storage Space a name and drive letter, and choose the mirroring and the maximum size.

7. **Choose a resiliency.**

   For a discussion of your four choices — no mirroring, two-way, three-way, and parity — see the sidebar "Mirroring technologies in Storage Spaces" earlier in this chapter.

8. **Set a logical size for the Storage Space.**

   As mentioned, the logical size of the Storage Space can greatly exceed the available hard drive space. There's no downside to having a very large logical size, other than a bit of overhead in some internal tables. Shoot for the moon. In this case, I turned less than 1 terabyte of actual, physical storage into a 32TB virtual monstrosity.

9. **Tap or click Create Storage Space.**

   Again, Windows whirs and sets up a freshly formatted Storage Space.

10. **Go back out to File Explorer, and verify that you have a new "drive" which is, in fact, an enormously humongous Storage Space.**

    You see something like Figure 4-5.

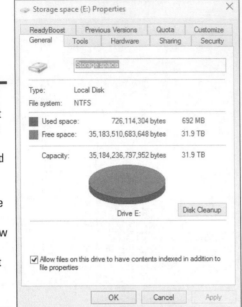

Figure 4-5:
If it weren't
for the fact
that you
just created
it, you
probably
wouldn't be
able to tell
that the new
Storage
Space isn't
a "real"
drive.

Working with Storage Spaces

Have a new Storage Space? Good. Go kick some tires.

First, realize that to the outside world, your Storage Spaces looks just like any other hard drive. You can use the drive letter the same way you'd use any drive letter. The folders inside work like any other folders; you can add them to libraries or share them on your network. You can back it up. If you have a cranky old program that requires a simple drive letter, the Storage Spaces won't do anything to spoil the illusion.

That said, Storage Space "drives" can't be defragmented or run through Checkdisk.

Here's the grand tour of the inner workings of your Storage Spaces:

1. **Bring up the Control Panel (right-click the lower-left corner of the desktop screen, and choose Control Panel); tap or click System and Security, and then tap or click Storage Spaces.**

Equivalently, you can go to the Metro Start screen, type **storage spaces**, and look under Settings.

If you choose either Storage Spaces or Manage Storage Spaces, the Storage Spaces dialog box appears, this time with a Storage Space.

2. **At the bottom, tap or click the down arrow next to Physical Drives.**

   The full Storage Spaces status report appears, as shown in Figure 4-6.

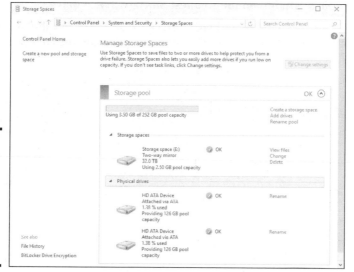

Figure 4-6:
Full details
of your
Storage
Space and
the storage
pool it
sits on.

The Storage Spaces report tells you how much real, physical hard drive space you're using; what the Storage Space looks like to your Windows programs; and how your physical hard drives have been carved up to support all that glorious, unfettered space.

It's quite a testament to the Storage Space designers that all this works so well — and invisibly to the rest of Windows. This is the way storage should've been implemented years ago!

Storage Space Strategies

You can save yourself some headache by following a few simple tricks:

✦ **Use your fastest hard drive as your C: drive.** Don't tie it into a Storage Space.

✦ **If a hard drive starts acting up — you see an error report, in any of a dozen different places – pro-actively remove it from the Storage Space.** See the Take offline option in Figure 4-3. Replace it at your earliest convenience.

✦ **Remember, in a three-drive installation, where two drives are in the Storage Space, the two-way mirror option limits you to the amount of room available on the smallest Storage Space drive.**

✦ **When you need to add more drives, don't take out the other drives.** The more drives in your Storage Space, the greater your flexibility.

Chapter 5: Getting the Most from Homegroups

*I*f you've ever used a house key, you know how to use Homegroups. Okay, that's Microsoft's analogy, and the process isn't quite that easy, but it's close.

The *Homegroup* bundles a bunch of settings in quite a handy — I'm tempted to use the word *brilliant* — way. When your PC joins a Homegroup, Windows strips away lots of the hassle and mind-numbing details generally associated with sharing folders and printers and replaces the mumbo jumbo with a cookie-cutter method of sharing that works quite well, in most home and many small-business networks.

All the computers in a Homegroup share their printers and some other peripherals. When an individual signs up for the Homegroup, their Pictures, Music, and Videos Libraries are shared by default. An extra click adds the Documents Library to the list. (See Book VII, Chapter 3 for a discussion of Libraries and instructions on how to make them visible.)

Other accounts on the computer — ones that haven't been explicitly logged into the Homegroup — only share their printers. In other words, you have to specifically log in to the Homegroup to have your folders shared.

All it takes is a couple of taps. Or clicks.

Don't be put off by the term *Homegroup*. If you have a business and need to share information, a Homegroup may provide exactly what you want.

Preparing a PC for a Homegroup

When you first establish a network connection, Windows asks whether you want to turn on sharing and connect to devices, per Figure 5-1.

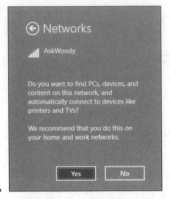

Figure 5-1:
Tell
Windows
if you're
connected
to a friendly
network
or one that
may include
lots of bad
PCs.

Networks

AskWoody

Do you want to find PCs, devices, and content on this network, and automatically connect to devices like printers and TVs?

We recommend that you do this on your home and work networks.

Yes   No

If you turn on sharing and connect to devices, your Windows 10 PC can participate in a Homegroup, if there's one present on your network. If there isn't a Homegroup, you can start one.

To join an existing Homegroup, all you need is the password. Microsoft likens it to having a key to a house. At the risk of stretching a metaphor, if you have the key to the house (the Homegroup password), you can get into anything in the house (printers, folders, and files inside those folders, in particular). If you don't have the password or if there's no Homegroup on your network, you can create a new Homegroup and set a new password. Find out how in the upcoming section, "Setting up a new Homegroup."

A few points to remember as you're getting a PC ready for the Homegroup:

✦ **Homegroups work only with Windows 7, 8, 8.1, and Windows 10 computers.** You can have a zillion computers on your home or office network, running Windows, OS X, Linux, iOS, and Android, laughing and printing and crashing together, but only the ones running Windows 8, 8.1, or 10 with sharing turned on and Windows 7 PCs with a designated Home network type can participate in a Homegroup. (See the sidebar "What happened to home, work, and public networks?")

✦ **Homegroups can exist within a bigger network of Homegroup-incompatible computers.** If you have computers that run something other than Windows 7, 8, or 8.1, you have Windows 7 computers that are set up with work or public networks, or you have Windows 8, 8.1, or 10 computers without sharing turned on, you can think of a Homegroup as a clique inside your network. See the section "Venturing beyond Homegroups" for details.

What happened to home, work, and public networks?

Windows 7 had three specific network "types" that you had to assign to every network connection. As soon as the connection was made, you were required to classify the connection as home, work, or public. Presumably, *home* networks are attached computers that could be trusted; they were allowed to join a Homegroup. *Work* networks were also trusted but not as much — they couldn't participate in Homegroups. *Public* networks were completely locked down — Windows wouldn't broadcast its presence on the networks, and it blocked any unexpected incoming traffic.

When I wrote *Windows 7 All-in-One For Dummies,* I had a very hard time explaining in layman's terms what the big difference was between home and work types. There's a good reason why it was hard to explain: There *isn't* any difference at all between home and work, with the exception that home networks can participate in Homegroups, whereas work networks cannot.

The sins of Windows 7 are visited upon everyone today. The current version of Windows supports Homegroups for systems that have sharing and connect to devices enabled (refer to Figure 5-1). But if you want to put a Windows 7 PC in your Homegroup and let it play with the big boys . . . er, the newer versions of Windows, you must first make sure that the Win7 PC identifies its network connection as a Home connection.

If your Windows 7 PC doesn't identify its network connection as a Home connection, it's easy to change:

1. **Choose Start, Control Panel, and under the Network and Internet heading, click the View Network Status and Tasks link.**

2. **In the View Your Active Networks box, click the link that mentions the network type you now have.**

3. **Click Home, and then click OK.**

    Your network is now a home network.

Connecting to a Homegroup

If you aren't sure whether your machine is ready to join a Homegroup, bring up File Explorer, as shown in Figure 5-2.

If you see Homegoup listed as one of the locations on the left, you're ready to rumble. If you don't see Homegroup listed, you need to change your connection, and tell Windows that you're in a safe location.

If Homegroup isn't listed, and you're running on WiFi, click or tap Start, Settings, Network & Internet. At the bottom, under Additional settings, click or tap Advanced settings. Then on the left, click or tap HomeGroup. You see the dialog box shown in Figure 5-3.

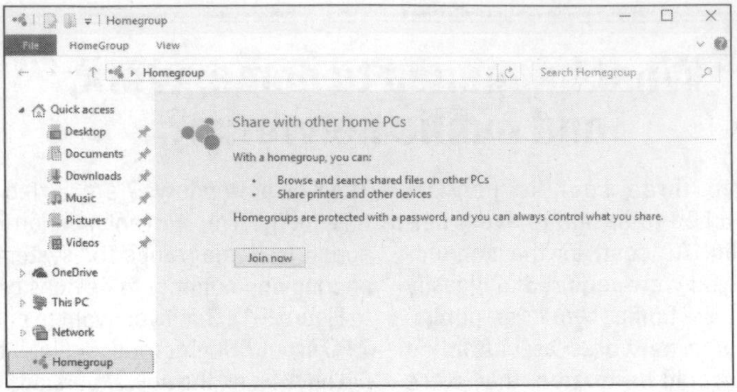

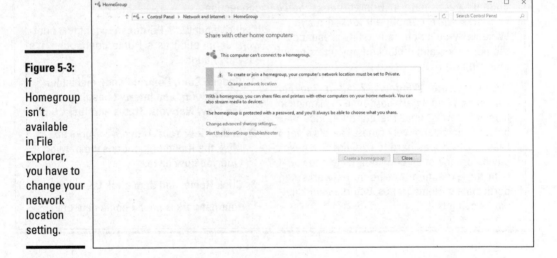

Figure 5-2:
Ready
to join a
Homegroup,
or create a
new one.

Figure 5-3:
If
Homegroup
isn't
available
in File
Explorer,
you have to
change your
network
location
setting.

To change your network type to Private, click the link that says Change network location, and follow the instructions. That will put Homegroup on the left side of your File Explorer listing.

If your computer is attached to a network that doesn't have a Homegroup, clicking Homegroup in File Explorer brings up the offer seen in Figure 5-4.

That's when you need to set up a new Homegroup, the topic of the next section.

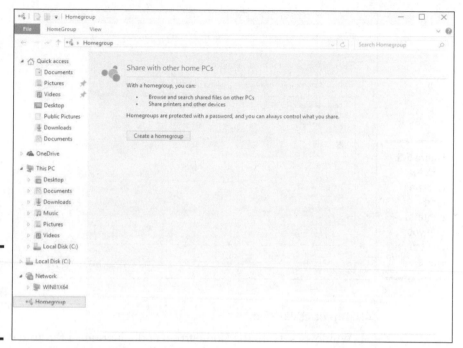

Figure 5-4:
Set up a
Homegroup
on your
network.

Several of you have written to me and complained that PCs newly attached
to a network don't discover an existing Homegroup. The most common
reason? All the PCs in the Homegroup are sleeping. To solve the problem,
make sure at least one of the PCs that belongs to the Homegroup wakes up.
It only takes one.

Setting up a new Homegroup

So you have the first PC in your network that's going to have a Homegroup.
Here's how to set it up if Windows hasn't found a Homegroup:

1. **Tap or click Create a Homegroup in the dialog box (see Figure 5-4).**

   Windows tells you a little bit about Homegroups and tells you that it's
   protected with a password.

2. **Tap or click Next.**

   The Create a Homegroup dialog box appears, as shown in Figure 5-5.

3. **Select which Libraries to offer to other PCs.**

   For most people, the big question about Homegroups is whether you
   want to share your Documents Library with other PCs attached to the
   Homegroup. By default, Windows doesn't put your Documents Library
   out for sharing. You can, if you want. I do.

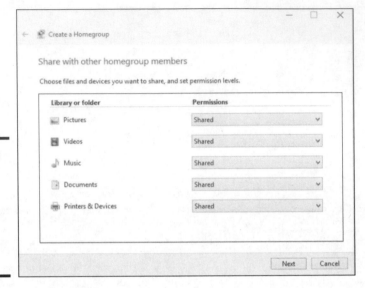

Figure 5-5:
Pick the
Libraries
(and
printers)
that you
want to
share.

4. **Tap or click Next.**

   Windows sets up the Homegroup and generates a random password. The password appears in the Use This Password dialog box. You can safely ignore it — no need to write down the password because you're going to change it.

5. **Tap or click Finish.**

   Homegroup appears on the left of the File Explorer dialog box, with your new Homegroup showing.

   Before you go, change the password to something you'll remember.

6. **Tap or click Start, Settings, Network & Internet, and then at the bottom on the right, choose Advanced settings. Choose Homegroup.**

   The Change Homegroup settings dialog box appears, as in Figure 5-6.

Figure 5-6:
Change the
password
into
something
more
memorable.

7. **Tap or click Change the Password.**

   Windows warns you that changing the Homegroup password will disconnect everyone. Of course, there isn't an "everyone" — you just set up the Homegroup. Now you're going to change the password from the monstrosity that Windows pulled out of thin air and turn it into a password that you can remember.

8. **Tap or click Change the Password (again).**

   Windows offers you a box in which you can type your own password.

9. **Type a new password — one you can remember — and tap or click Next.**

   No need to be Sherlock Holmes about it. Remember this password applies only to people who are *already connected* to your home (or office) network.

   Windows treats you to another shhhhh-super-secret password box like the one in Step 4. You know the password now. And you can always retrieve it. So fuhgeddaboutit.

More than one Homegroup can exist on a single network, but things get complicated quickly. A particular computer can only be part of one Homegroup at a time: You can leave one Homegroup and join another one, but you can't do two at once. By the by, Homegroups work great with Windows Home Server.

Joining an existing Homegroup

If Windows found an existing Homegroup, here's how to get in:

1. **At the bottom of the Share with Other Home PCs dialog (refer to Figure 5-2) or the top of the Change Homegroup Settings dialog box (refer to Figure 5-6), tap or click the Join Now button.**

   Windows tells you that you can join, but you need a password.

2. **Tap or click Next.**

   You see a Share with Other Homegroup Members dialog box, similar to the one in Figure 5-5.

3. **Choose which Libraries you want to share and whether you want to share printers; then tap or click Next.**

   I always share everything, including the Documents Library. Isn't that what sharing's all about?

   Windows asks you for the Homegroup's password. Note that Homegroups don't have names — they only have passwords.

4. **Type the password for the Homegroup, and tap or click Next.**

    Windows advises that you have joined the Homegroup.

5. **Tap or click Finish, and then close the Homegroup Settings dialog box, if you see one.**

If you have the password, joining the Homegroup is very easy. If you don't have the password, go to one of the other PCs in the Homegroup. In Windows 7, 8, or 8.1, bring up Control Panel, and tap or click Change Homegroup Settings on the left under Network and Internet. For a Windows 10 machine, tap or click Start, Settings, Network & Internet, then on the right, tap or click Advanced Settings, Homegroup. Then tap or click the View or Print the Homegroup Password link.

Sharing Files and Printers in a Homegroup

Homegroups are great, and there's more to them than meets the eye. When you dig a little deeper, here's what you find:

✦ **A Homegroup connects computers and printers, but users have to give their permission to share Libraries.** If you attach a Windows PC to a Homegroup, all the people using that PC — all its user accounts — gain access to the data that's available to the Homegroup. They also get access to any printers in the Homegroup. But it doesn't work the other way. Each user, individually, has to give permission for their Libraries to appear in the Homegroup.

✦ **Although you can override the default choices (refer to Figure 5-5), when you join your PC to a Homegroup, you make all Pictures, Music, and Videos Libraries and printers on your PC available to other PCs in the Homegroup.**

I said *Libraries,* not folders. (I talk about Libraries in Book VII, Chapter 3.) If you share the Pictures Libraries on your PC with the Homegroup, for example, all folders in your Pictures Library are shared. If you add a folder from a Windows XP computer to your Pictures Library and your PC is in a Homegroup, that folder on the Windows XP computer becomes accessible to every user on every computer in the Homegroup. That's a very powerful capability, almost as good as connecting an XP computer to the Homegroup (even though XP computers can't participate in Homegroups).

More than that, you can put folders from other Homegroup computers' Libraries into your Libraries. So if a computer in your Homegroup has a Pictures Library that includes a folder from a Windows XP PC, you can simply copy that folder into your Pictures Library, and it works like any other folder in your Pictures Library. Combining Homegroups and Libraries leads to enormously powerful capabilities.

Remarkably, distressingly, you cannot share OneDrive folders in a Homegroup.

When you share a file, it's important to understand whether other people in your Homegroup can open the file, modify its contents, or delete it. The default permissions level for Homegroup-shared folders is a bit convoluted, but it makes sense. Unless you specifically modify the permissions (more about that in the "Caring for Your Homegroup" section, later in this chapter), here's what you get:

✦ **Other users in your Homegroup can open all files in your Libraries (Pictures, Music, Videos, and optionally, Documents).**

✦ **Other users in your Homegroup can't change files in your personal folders (your \Pictures, \Music, \Videos, and, optionally, \Documents folders).** But they can change or delete files in your computer's Public folders (\Public\Pictures, \Public\Music, \Public\Videos, and optionally, \Public\Documents). They can also add new files to the public folders. Book VI, Chapter 1 introduces you to personal versus public folders.

✦ **If you have other folders in your Libraries, the folders inherit the restrictions that are set on the computer containing the folders.**

You can change the permissions level at any time — restrict access to folders, or add new folders on your PC to the Homegroup, for example. I show you how, in the section "Caring for Your Homegroup," later in this chapter.

You can connect to printers on Homegroup computers just as easily as you set up a printer on your own computer. Printers on a Homegroup-connected computer are shared automatically with all other Windows computers on the Homegroup. You may be asked for permission to copy drivers from a different PC in your Homegroup, but it's very easy.

Navigating to a Homegroup Folder

Navigating to a folder or file in a shared Library in a Homegroup, is as easy as navigating to a folder or file on your computer. When your computer is attached to a Homegroup, you see a direct link to the Homegroup on the left side of the File Explorer window (see Figure 5-7). From that jumping-off point, you can easily look at all shared folders on all computers in your Homegroup.

Book VII Chapter 5

Getting the Most from Homegroups

Figure 5-7:
Your
Homegroup
appears
on the left
side of the
Explorer
window.

Homegroups are also baked into every nook and cranny of Windows:

✦ **Windows Media Player:** Homegroup links appear in the Navigation pane on the left. Media streaming from Homegroup computers works in a flash.

✦ **Office applications:** If you fire up Word and choose File, Open, for example, the Homegroups are accessible by clicking Computer.

After the hassles people have had sharing files and printers over the years, I bet you'll find Homegroups like a breath of fresh air. Finally.

Caring for Your Homegroup

So you have a Homegroup with one or more PCs connected to it. This section explains how to change your Homegroup so it suits you to a *T*.

Changing the Homegroup password

Want to know why Windows automatically generates that gargantuan password every time you start a new Homegroup? Because early testers needed it. When the folks at Microsoft watched people trying to use Homegroups for the first time, they discovered that many people would stop, worry, and fret about typing a password. In many cases, that's because the person setting up the Homegroup uses only a small set of passwords, and he didn't want to hand out those passwords to everyone in the house or company. So the testers spent quite a bit of time trying to figure out whether they should create a completely new password and, if so, which one to use. Brain overload.

To make your life easier, Windows assigns a somewhat arbitrary password when you create a Homegroup. If you're smart, you'll change it before you add any more PCs to the Homegroup. That's precisely the procedure I describe in the "Setting up a new Homegroup" section earlier in this chapter.

In fact, you can change a Homegroup's password anytime, and it's easy as long as all the computers in the Homegroup are turned on and you can log on to them all.

To change the Homegroup password, proceed thusly:

1. **Tap or click Start, Settings, Network & Internet, and at the bottom on the right, click Homegroup.**

   In Windows 7, choose Start, Control Panel, Network, Choose Homegroup and Sharing Options.

2. **Tap or click the Change the Password link.**

   Windows warns you that changing the Homegroup password will disconnect everyone. Well, yes, you know that. That's why you've made sure that all the PCs in your Homegroup are awake and that you can log on to them all. If not, well . . . .

3. **Make sure that all computers in your Homegroup are awake (not hibernating or asleep), and make sure that you can log on to them all. When you're ready, tap or click Change the Password.**

   Windows offers a new password for you to use, or you can type one of your own.

4. **Tap or click Next.**

   Your Homegroup password changes dutifully.

5. **One by one, go to each of the other computers in your Homegroup and follow Steps 1 and 2 to Choose Homegroup and Sharing Options.**

   The warning shown in Figure 5-8 may appear. Some scurvy brigand has changed the password on your Homegroup! Avast and alack, and buckle my swash . . . .

6. **Tap or click the Type New Password button, and do precisely that.**

   You reconnect to the Homegroup. By supplying the correct password — the new one — your PC hooks up with the new Homegroup, and all your settings carry across.

**Book VII
Chapter 5**

**Getting the Most
from Homegroups**

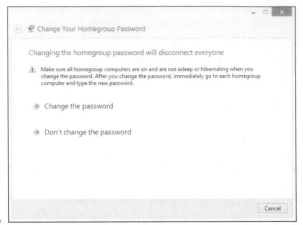

Figure 5-8:
Change the
Homegroup
password
for each
computer
(the warning
in Windows
8.1).

If you have problems reconnecting to the Homegroup, tap or click the link
(refer to Figure 5-6) to leave the Homegroup, and then tap or click the Join
Now button. Continue with Step 2 in the instructions in the "Joining an
existing Homegroup" section, earlier in this chapter.

Adding or blocking folders in the Homegroup

If you want to make a folder available to everyone in your Homegroup, the
simplest approach is to add it to one of your shared Libraries. See Book VII,
Chapter 3 for details.

If you share your Documents Library, for example, adding a folder to your
personal Documents Library makes the folder available so that anybody
attached to the Homegroup can open and read the items in it. Adding the
folder to your Public Documents folder allows everyone in the Homegroup
to read, modify, or delete the items in the folder.

Sometimes, though, you just want to make a folder available to the
Homegroup, and you don't want to go through the steps to add it to a shared
Library. For example, I like to share my Downloads folder so that other
people in my Homegroup can easily copy or run the files I download.

Here's how to add the Downloads folder to your Homegroup, without adding
the Downloads folder to any of your shared Libraries:

1. **Navigate to the folder you want to put in the Homegroup.**

In Figure 5-9, I started File Explorer and navigated to the Camera Roll
folder, on the left.

Figure 5-9:
Adding
a folder
to your
Homegroup
is easy, if
you know
the trick.

2. **At the top, tap or click the Share tab.**

3. **On the Share Ribbon, choose Homegroup (View) if you want to give everyone in your Homegroup read access to the files, or choose Homegroup (View and Edit) if you trust them not to delete or otherwise clobber the files.**

   It can take a few minutes, but eventually the shared folder becomes available across the Homegroup.

**Book VII
Chapter 5**

**Getting the Most
from Homegroups**

Venturing beyond Homegroups

If you have computers on your network that don't work with Homegroups, this section is for you. You find out how to set up fine-grained permissions for folders and documents, whether or not they're in a Homegroup (a task not for the faint of heart). This chapter wraps up with a section about sharing across a mixed network that has computers in and out of a Homegroup clique.

Sharing and granting permissions

Using the Public folder to share files, as described in Book VI, Chapter 1, constitutes a quick 'n dirty approach to sharing: Everybody using your computer gets full access to all the Public files, and people coming from the network either get in or they don't. You have a little bit of fine control over who gets in and what they can do, but by and large, Public is a blunt object.

The Windows ability to establish sharing permissions for individual files and folders on your PC gives you much finer control than the plain ol' Public folder method. You can assign fine-grained permissions for your Homegroup or for individual users with Windows built-in permission levels.

Password-protecting the Public folder

You have fairly complex ways to force people accessing the Public folder from the network to provide a password before opening the folder. If you set a password, anybody on your computer can get at the Public folder without hindrance, but someone coming from the outside has to provide the password. You can also establish read/write permissions for people accessing the Public folder from the network. See *Networking All-In-One For Dummies* (published by John Wiley & Sons) by Doug Lowe for details.

The permission levels come in two flavors:

✦ **View** allows the chosen individuals or groups to open or copy files, but not change or delete them.

✦ **Edit** lets the designated user or group do anything such as open, change, delete, or move the files.

This kind of fine-grained sharing is a minefield that you should not undertake unless you're willing to keep permissions updated. You should also be tolerant of many potential problems because I guarantee you'll bump into them. Rather than assign detailed sharing permissions to a folder, you may find it smarter (and much easier) to put the files you want to share in Public and use the application that created the files to assign read-only or read/write passwords, controlling access to the data in those files. All Office applications, and many others, have heavy-duty password protection available.

Sharing on mixed Homegroup, workgroup, and Apple networks

Sharing with the Public folder is quick and dirty. As long as the person trying to get into your Public folder is connected to your network and he can supply a valid username and password — one that will log on to your computer — he can get at the contents of Public. (Find out about the Public folder in Book III, Chapter 1.)

As I mention earlier in this chapter, Homegroups work only with Windows 7, 8, and Windows 10 computers. That's it. If you have a Vista or (shudder!) XP PC on your network, it can't join the Homegroup so it has to access the shared data directly. Toss a Mac into the mix and, *oy vez!*

Sharing with XP and Vista computers

Windows XP and Vista support *workgroups,* which aren't nearly as fancy as Homegroups. Workgroups and Homegroups coexist peacefully, but you have to jump through some extra hoops to cross from one to another. Here's how:

✦ **If you try to connect a Windows XP or Vista PC to a Windows 7, 8, or 10 PC,** you get a challenge like the one in Figure 5-10. The person using the Windows XP PC must provide a valid username and password for the machine she's trying to access.

Figure 5-10: Windows XP PCs can't get into your Homegroup-protected PC, unless they can provide a username and password.

✦ **If you're using Windows 7, 8, or 10 and trying to get into a PC that isn't in your Homegroup,** you see a challenge like the one in Figure 5-11. Again, the person using the PC must provide a username and password that's valid on the PC he's trying to access.

Figure 5-11: Windows 7 and 8 PCs also get challenged if they aren't part of the same Homegroup.

Sharing with a Mac

Surprisingly, connecting a Mac to a Windows 7, 8, or 10 PC is quite similar. The Mac can't join your Homegroup, no way no how, but it can get into the \Public folder of a specific PC. Here's how:

1. **In the Mac OS X Finder, choose Go, Connect to Server.**

   The Mac responds with the Connect to Server dialog box, shown in Figure 5-12.

Figure 5-12: Connecting from a Mac to a Windows PC is fairly straight forward.

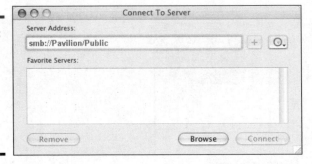

2. **In the Server Address box, type** smb:// **followed by the name of the PC you're trying to connect to, and then type** /Public. **Click Connect.**

   In Figure 5-12, I connected from OS X Mavericks to a Windows 10 PC called Pavilion.

3. **When you see the challenge, enter a username and password that's valid on the computer you're trying to access. If you're asked for a workgroup name, type** workgroup.

   You end up in the Public folder.

You can also enable Windows-style file sharing on your Mac, so you can pull files from the Mac into your PC. At least, theoretically. See www.dummies. com/how-to/content/how-access-file-shares-on-windows- computers-from-y.html for details.

Chapter 6: Running the Built-In Applications

In This Chapter

✓ **Writing with Notepad and WordPad for free**

✓ **Setting alarms**

✓ **Mapping characters**

✓ **Calculating and painting**

✓ **Creating sticky notes**

---

*N*ew Windows Universal apps are just starting to appear in quantity and quality good enough to drive your everyday computing. We're still a long way from the all-Universal desktop, but the trend is definitely in that direction.

In this chapter, I introduce you to a handful of useful programs that you've already paid for. They aren't the greatest, but they're more than adequate in many situations — and when better, free alternatives exist, I tell you about them, too.

Even if they do come from a Microsoft competitor.

Keep your eyes open for new Windows Store Universal apps that can match some of the functions in these free built-in Windows programs. As time goes by, the Universal apps will get better — although it's going to be a little difficult to beat the price on these guys.

Setting Alarms & Clock

The Universal Windows Alarms & Clock app works almost as well as the alarm and clock apps you'll find, free, for iPhones, iPads, and Android phones and tablets. Some paid apps add a few bells and whistles, but for most folks, the built-in free app works well enough.

Permit me to take you on a guided tour through the app:

1. **Click or tap Start, All Apps, and near the top of the list, tap or click Alarms & Clock.**

   The basic Alarm app shows up, as in Figure 6-1. It's not particularly inspiring, but give it a chance and you may be surprised.

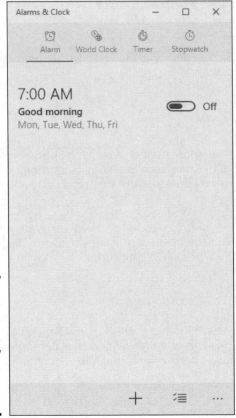

Figure 6-1: The alarm clock starts with a 7:00 am weekday wakeup call, but it's turned off.

2. **Click or tap the + sign at the bottom of the alarm list, to add a new alarm.**

   Alarms & Clock shows you the standard alarm prompt, shown in Figure 6-2.

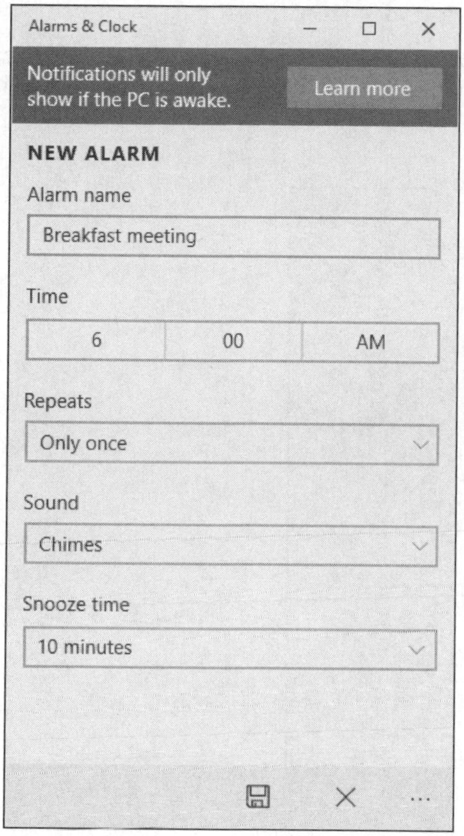

Figure 6-2:
Enter a new
alarm here.

3. **Fill in an alarm — say, for a few minutes from now. Then at the bottom, click the save icon, which looks like a very snappy 1980s-style 3.5-inch diskette.**

   Even if you've never seen a 3.5-inch diskette and can't remember what a joy it was to get one that was stuck out of a diskette drive, the alarm is added to the list in Figure 6-1.

4. **How do you get rid of an alarm? Excellent question. Glad you asked. If you right-click or tap and hold an alarm, nothing happens. But if you click the icon at the bottom that looks like a double-decker hamburger with check marks, you see a list of all the alarms with garbage cans next to them.**

   Yes, that's how you delete an alarm in Universal Windows Universal app land.

5. **Click or tap the World Clock icon.**

   The world clock shows you the current time in your current location and makes it easy to add additional locations. Just click or tap the + sign, as in Figure 6-3.

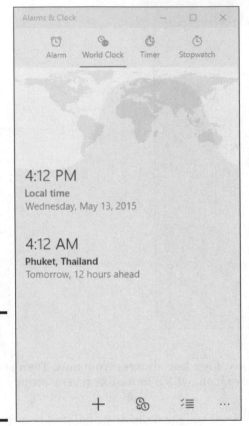

Figure 6-3:
It's easy to add a location to the world clock.

The Compare Times icon at the bottom — the one that looks like two analog clock faces — lets you compare a date and time in one location with another. So, for example, you can input a date and time for Phuket, Thailand, and have the app tell you what the date and time will be in Punxsutawney, Philadelphia.

The double-deck hamburger icon with check marks at the bottom of this tab, like the previous one, lets you delete locations from the list.

6. **Click the Timer tab.**

   You see the rather mundane countdown timer shown in Figure 6-4.

Figure 6-4:
The Timer is a straight-forward countdown timer.

The Timer's main claim to fame: When it's finished counting down, a toaster notification appears on the Windows desktop, and from there travels to the Action Center/Notification Area described in Book II, Chapter 3.

7. Click the Stopwatch tab.

It looks and works much like the Timer tab, except in reverse.

A little word to the wise: Both the countdown Timer and the Stopwatch keep working, even if you minimize the app, or switch tabs.

Getting Free Word Processing

With Office Online (described in Book VI, Chapter 1), you have a free, useful word processor at hand anytime you're connected to the Internet. Word Online (`www.office.com`) doesn't have all the bells and whistles of either the full-blown desktop version of Word, or of the tablet-based mobile version of Word, but it's good enough in almost every situation.

There are two other, free word processing programs that ship with Windows 10:

✦ **Notepad:** For just plain text, use Notepad or its beefed-up (free) brother, Notepad++. I talk about Notepad in this chapter and Notepad++ in Book X, Chapter 5.

✦ **WordPad:** If you need just a little bit of formatting, use WordPad. I talk about WordPad in this chapter.

Someday, one or the other may save your tail.

Running Notepad

Reaching back into the primordial WinOoze, Notepad was conceived, designed, and developed by programmers, for programmers — and it shows. Although Notepad has been vastly improved over the years, many of the old limitations remain. Still, if you want a fast, no-nonsense text editor (certainly nobody would have the temerity to call Notepad a word processor), Notepad's a decent choice.

Notepad understands only plain, simple, unformatted text — basically the stuff you see on your keyboard. It wouldn't understand formatting, such as bold, or an embedded picture if you shook it by the shoulders, and heaven help ya if you want it to come up with links to web pages.

On the other hand, Notepad's shortcomings are, in many ways, its saving graces. You can trust Notepad to show you exactly what's in a file — characters are characters, old chap, and there's none of this froufrou formatting stuff to mess up things. Notepad saves only plain, simple, unformatted text; if you need a plain, simple, unformatted text document, Notepad's your tool of choice. To top it off, Notepad is fast and reliable. Of all the Windows programs I ever met, Notepad is the only one I can think of that has never crashed on me.

The following tidbits of advice are all you'll likely ever need to successfully get in and around Notepad:

✦ **To start Notepad,** click or tap Start, All Apps, scroll way down to Windows Accessories, and choose Notepad. You can also double-click any text (.txt) file in File Explorer. You see something like the file shown in Figure 6-5.

✦ **Notepad can handle files up to about 48MB in size.** (That's not quite the size of the *Encyclopedia Britannica,* but it's close.) If you try to open a file that's larger, a dialog box suggests that you open the file with a different editor.

Figure 6-5:
Notepad rocks in a geriatric sort of way.

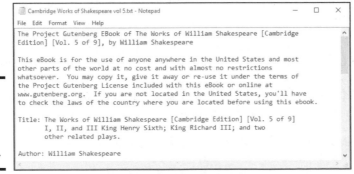

✦ **You can change the font, sorta.** When you first start Notepad, it displays a file's contents in the 11-point Consolas font. That font was chosen by Notepad's designers because it's relatively easy to see on most computer monitors.

Just because the text you see in Notepad is in a specific font, don't assume for a moment that the characters in the file itself are formatted. They aren't. The font you see on the screen is just the one Notepad uses to show the data. The stuff inside the file is plain-Jane, unformatted everyday text.

To change the font that's displayed onscreen, choose Format ➪ Font and pick from the offered list. You don't need to select any text before you choose the font because the font you choose is applied to all text onscreen, and it doesn't affect the contents of the file. The default Notepad font is *monospaced* — all the characters are the same width. If you change the font, text files that are designed for a fixed-width world can look very odd.

✦ **You can wrap text, too.** Usually text extends way off the right side of the screen. That's intentional. Notepad, ever true to the file it's attached to, skips to a new line only when it encounters a line break — usually that means a *carriage return* (or when someone presses Enter), which typically occurs at the end of every paragraph.

Notepad allows you to wrap text onscreen, if you insist, so that you don't have to scroll all the way to the right to read every single paragraph. To have Notepad automatically break lines so that they appear onscreen, choose Format ➪ Word Wrap.

✦ **Notepad has one little geeky timestamp trick** that you may find amusing — and possibly worthwhile. If you type **.LOG** as the first line in a file, Notepad sticks a time and date stamp at the end of the file each time it's opened.

Many, many alternatives to Notepad exist: Programmers need text editors, and many of them take up the mantle to build their own. Over the years, I've used lots of them. Right now, I use Notepad++, — and yes, I do type text quite a bit. Native HTML. But that's another story.

Check out Notepad++ at www.notepad-plus-plus.org. It's free and works very well.

Writing with WordPad

If you really want and need formatting — and you can't get connected to www.office.com for whatever reason — Windows WordPad will do.

WordPad plays nice (at least, reasonably so), with DOCX format documents — the kind that are generated automatically in Word version 2007 and later. But if you have to edit a Word DOC or DOCX file with WordPad, whether it's from Word 97, 2000, 2002, 2003, 2007, or 2010, follow these steps:

1. **Make a copy of the Word document, and open the copy in WordPad.**

   Do not edit original Word doc files with WordPad. You'll break them as soon as you save them. Do not open Word docs in WordPad, thinking that you'll use the Save As command and save with a different name. You'll forget.

2. **When you get Word back, open the original document, on the Review Ribbon, choose Compare, Combine), pick the WordPad version of the document, and click the Merge button.**

   The resulting merged document probably looks like a mess, but it's a start.

3. **Use the Review tab to march through your original document and apply the changes you made with WordPad.**

   This is the only reliable way to ensure that WordPad doesn't accidentally swallow any of your formatting.

WordPad works much the same as any other word processor, only less so. That said, WordPad isn't encumbered with many of the confusing doodads that make Word so difficult for the first-time e-typist, and it may be a decent way to start figuring out how simple word processors work.

To get WordPad going, click or tap Start, All Apps, scroll down to Windows Accessories, and choose WordPad (see Figure 6-6).

Some people like the Ribbon interface across the top of the WordPad window. I find it familiar (like Word 2007) but annoying (like, uh, Word 2007).

WordPad lets you save documents in any of the following formats:

✦ **Rich Text Format (RTF)** is an ancient, circa-1987 format developed by Microsoft and the legendary Charles Simonyi (yes, the space tourist) to make it easier to preserve some formatting when you change word processors. RTF documents can have some simple formatting but nothing nearly as complex as Word 97, for example. Many word processing programs from many manufacturers can read and write RTF files, so RTF is a good choice if you need to create a file that can be moved to many places.

**Book VII
Chapter 6**

Figure 6-6:
WordPad includes rudimentary formatting capabilities and the ability to embed images for free.

**Running the
Built-In
Applications**

✦ **OOXML Text Document (DOCX)** is the new Microsoft document standard file format, introduced in Word 2007. If you're going to use the document in Word, this is the format to choose.

Note that WordPad can read and write DOCX files. Unfortunately, WordPad takes some, uh, liberties with the finer formatting features in Word: If you open a Word-generated DOCX file in WordPad, don't expect to see all the formatting. If you subsequently save that DOCX file from WordPad, expect it to clobber much of the original Word formatting.

✦ **ODF Text Document (ODT),** the OpenDocument format, is the native format for LibreOffice and OpenOffice.

✦ **Text Document (TXT)** strips out all pictures and formatting and saves the document in a Notepad-style, regular old text format. The two alternatives — MS-DOS format and Unicode — control the way WordPad handles non-Roman characters in the document.

If you're just starting out with word processing, keep these facts in mind:

✦ **To format text,** select the text you want to format; then choose the formatting you want from the Font part of the Home Ribbon. For example, to change the font, click the down arrow next to the font name (it's Calibri in Figure 6-2) and choose the font you like.

✦ **To format a paragraph,** simply click once inside the paragraph and choose the formatting from the Paragraph group in the Ribbon.

✦ **General page layout is controlled by settings in the Page Setup dialog box.** General page layout includes things like margins and whether the page is printed vertically or horizontally, for example. To open the dialog box, choose File, Page Setup.

✦ **Tabs are complicated.** Every paragraph starts with tab stops set every half inch. You set additional tab stops by clicking in the middle of the ruler. (You can also set them by clicking the tiny side arrow to the right of the word Paragraph and then clicking the Tabs button.) The tab stops that you set up work only in individual paragraphs: Select one paragraph and set a tab stop, and it works only in the selected paragraph; select three paragraphs and set the stop, and it works in all three.

WordPad treats tabs like any other character: A tab can be copied, moved, and deleted, sometimes with unexpected results. Keep your eyes peeled when using tabs and tab stops. If something goes wrong, click the Undo icon (to the right of the diskette-like Save icon) or press Ctrl+Z immediately and try again.

WordPad has a few features worthy of the term *feature:* bullets and numbered lists; paragraph justification; line spacing; superscript and subscript; and indent. WordPad lacks many of the features that you may have come to expect from other word processors: You can't even insert a page break, much less a table. If you spend any time at all writing anything but the most straightforward documents, you'll outgrow WordPad quickly.

Taming the Character Map

Windows includes the Character Map utility, which may prove a lifesaver if you need to find characters that go beyond the standard keyboard. Using the Character Map, you can ferret odd characters out of any font, copy them, and then paste them into whatever word processor you may be using (including WordPad).

Windows ships with many *fonts* — collections of characters — and several of those fonts include many interesting characters that you may want to use. To open the Character Map, click or tap Start, All Apps, scroll down to Windows Accessories, and choose Character Map. You see the screen shown in Figure 6-7.

You can use many characters as pictures — arrows, check marks, boxes, and so on — in the various Wingdings and Webding fonts. Copy them into your documents and increase the font size as you like.

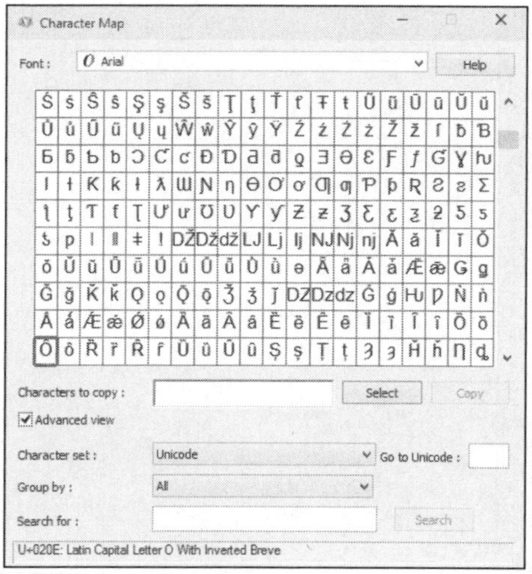

Figure 6-7:
Need a
character
from a
different
language?
Use the
desktop
Character
Map.
Klingon,
anyone?

Calculating — Free

Windows includes a very capable Universal Windows Universal app calculator. Actually, Windows contains three capable calculators with several options in each one, plus a built-in units converter so you can translate furlongs per fortnight into inches per year. Before you run out and spend 20 bucks on a scientific calculator, check out the three you already own!

To run the Calculator, click or tap Start, All Apps, and choose Calculator. You probably see the standard Calculator, as shown in Figure 6-8.

To use the Calculator, just type whatever you like on your keyboard or tap or click the keys, and press Enter when you want to carry out the calculation. For example, to calculate 123 times 456, you type or tap **123 * 456** and press Enter.

The Calculator comes in three modes: Standard, Scientific (which adds *sin* and *tan,* and *x to the y,* and the like), and Programmer (hex, octal, Mod, Xor, Qword, Lsh). You can flip among those modes by clicking the hamburger icon in the upper-left corner.

The Calculator also has very extensive Unit Conversion capabilities. Choose Converter from the hamburger icon, and then choose one of the units converters — Volume, Length, Weight and Mass, Temperature, Energy, Area, or Speed. For example, if you choose Volume, you get something like Figure 6-9.

**Book VII
Chapter 6**

Running the
Built-In
Applications

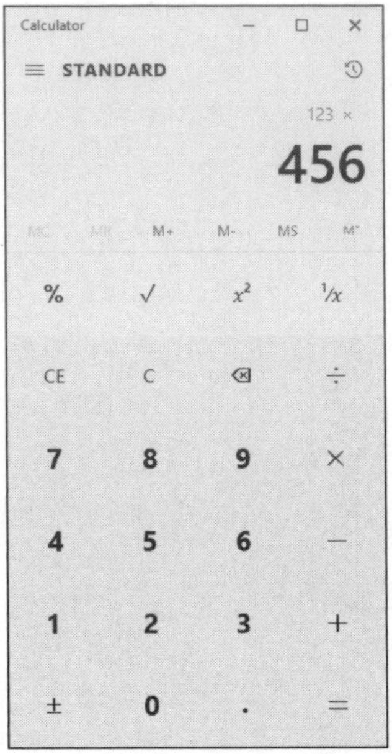

Figure 6-8:
The standard Calculator, with a conventional keyboard.

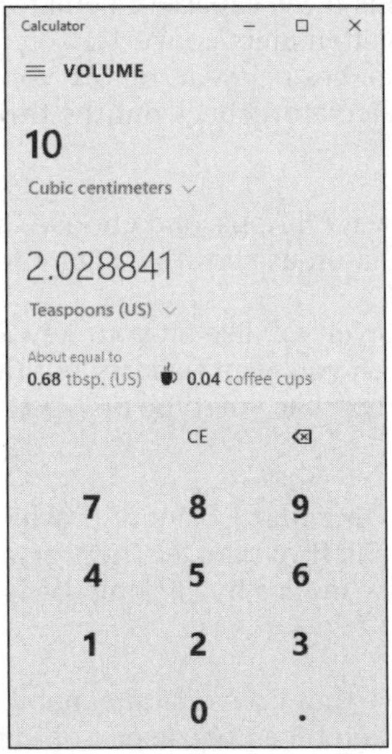

Figure 6-9:
The Volume converter lets you choose from many different measures of volume.

The fun part of the Converters: They have little mind-jogging tips. For example, in Figure 6-9, you can see that 10 cc is about 2 teaspoons, but you can also see that it's about 0.68 tablespoons and 0.04 coffee cups. Play with it a bit, and you can see volumes in cubic yards and bathtubs, lengths in nautical miles, km and jumbo jet-lengths, weight in elephants, and much more.

Personally, I use Google for all the options. You can type **32 C in F** in Google and get the answer back immediately. (Google can calculate *1.2 euro per liter in dollars per gallon,* in one step — way beyond Windows Calculator.) Do a Google search for *mileage, lease payment,* or *amortization,* and you can find hundreds of sites with far more capable calculators.

A couple Calculator tricks:

✦ Nope, an X on the keyboard doesn't translate into the times sign. I don't know why, but computer people have had a hang-up about this for decades. If you want to say "times," you have to tap the asterisk on the Calculator, or press the asterisk key (*) or Shift+8.

✦ You can use the number pad, if your keyboard has one, but to make it work, you have to get Num Lock going. Try typing a few numbers on your number pad. If the Calculator sits there and doesn't realize that you're trying to type into it, press the Num Lock key. The Calculator should take the hint.

Painting

The Windows Paint program has taken many hard knocks for many years, but it can actually do a few things that you may need. It's a just-barely-good-enough application for manipulating existing pictures, and it helps you convert among the various picture file formats (JPEG or GIF, for example). But it's certainly no competition for a real drawing tool like Adobe Photoshop or Illustrator, or even a free graphics editor like IrfanView (www.irfanview.com) or www.paint.net (see Book X, Chapter 5). And, if you want to correct red-eye or adjust for a bad exposure, Windows Photos has the tools that you need (see Book IV, Chapter 3).

That said, you can have lots of fun with Windows Paint. To bring it to life, click or tap Start, All Apps, Windows Accessories, and choose Paint. You see a screen like the one shown in Figure 6-10.

Opening, saving, and closing pictures in Paint is a snap; it works just like any other Windows program, after you figure out that you have to tap or click the File tab.

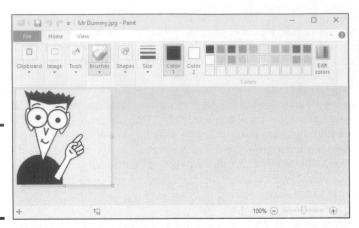

Figure 6-10:
Paint offers
a handful
of useful
features.

Scanning pictures into Paint goes like a breeze: Choose File, From Scanner or Camera. To draw one of the prebuilt shapes, just tap or click the shape, and then tap/click and drag the drawing paper to adjust the size. Crop, resize, or rotate by choosing the corresponding icon in the Image group of the Ribbon. Easy.

Where you're bound to get in the most trouble is in free-form drawing, which can be mighty inscrutable until you understand the following points:

✦ You select a line color (used by all the painting tools as their primary color) by tapping or clicking the Color 1 icon and choosing the color in the Colors group on the Ribbon.

✦ You select a fill color (used to fill the inside of the solid shapes, such as the rectangle and oval) by tapping or clicking the Color 2 icon and choosing a color in the Colors group on the Ribbon.

✦ Many painting tools let you choose the thickness of the lines they use — in the case of the spray can, you can choose the heaviness of the spray — in the Size drop-down list on the Ribbon.

General rules for editing are much like what you see in the rest of Windows — select, copy, paste, delete, and so on. The only odd editing procedure I've found is for the Free-form Selection tool, which hides behind the Select icon on the Image group on the Ribbon. If you tap or click this tool and draw an area on the picture, Paint responds by selecting the smallest rectangle that encloses the entire line you drew. It's . . . different.

Sticking Sticky Notes

Do you really like little yellow sticky notes on your screen? Really? I guess the electronic ones are better than the meatspace version — at least they won't get your screen gummy.

Anyway, if you really want one, here's how to make a yellow sticky note to yourself:

1. **Click or tap Start, All Apps, Windows Accessories, and choose Sticky Notes.**

2. **Start typing.**

   Really. That's all there is to it.

Your new sticky note appears, as shown in Figure 6-11.

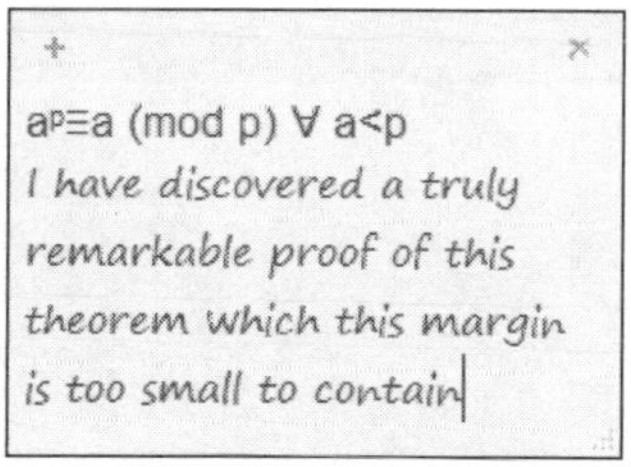

Figure 6-11: Sticky notes are cool, but the margin is too small for the proof.

$a^p \equiv a \pmod{p}\ \forall\ a < p$
I have discovered a truly remarkable proof of this theorem which this margin is too small to contain

After you have a sticky note, you can create a new one by tapping or clicking the + sign in the upper-left corner.

You can change the color to something other than that eyestrain-inducing cadmium yellow by right-clicking the note (or tap and hold) and choosing a new color.

Sticky notes live on your desktop. You can drag and move them like any other denizen of the desktop. They're easy to resize. You can alternately show or hide all sticky notes on your desktop by tapping or clicking the Sticky Notes icon on the toolbar.

Hate the sticky note font? I don't blame you. If you open any program that'll format text — Word, or even WordPad, for example — type the text you want, format it the way you like it, and then copy and paste the text into a sticky note; the formatting stays. That's how I created Fermat's Last Theorem in Figure 6-11.

And you thought sticky notes didn't have any hidden secrets . . .

Chapter 7: Working with Printers

In This Chapter

↙ **Attaching a new printer to your PC or network**

↙ **Solving print queue problems**

↙ **Troubleshooting other problems with printers**

↙ **Stopping a runaway printer**

*A*h, the paperless office. What a wonderful concept! No more file cabinets bulging with misfiled flotsam. No more hernias from hauling cartons of copy paper, dumping the sheets 500 at a time into a thankless plastic maw. No more trees dying in agony, relinquishing their last gasps to provide pulp as a substrate for heat-fused carbon toner. No more coffee-stained reports. No more paper cuts.

No more . . . oh, who the heck am I trying to kid? No way.

Industry prognosticators have been telling people for more than two decades that the paperless office is right around the corner. Yeah, sure. Maybe around *your* corner. Around *my* corner, I predict that PC printers will disappear about the same time as the last *Star Trek* sequel. We're talking geologic time here, folks.

The biggest problem? Finding a printer that doesn't cost two arms and three legs to, uh, print. Toner cartridges cost a fortune. Ink costs two fortunes. That bargain-basement printer you can get for $65 will probably print, oh, about ten pages before it starts begging for a refill. And four or five refills can easily cost as much as the printer.

Gillette may have originated the razor-and-blades business model, but it took the likes of HP, Brother, Canon, and Samsung to perfect it. Thank heavens Gillette hasn't figured out a way to put a microchip in the blades to guarantee their obsolescence.

There has been one important — even exciting — development in the laser/inkjet printer arena during the past ten years. Network connected printers — ones that attach to a network router, either through a wire or a WiFi connection, bypassing PCs entirely — are finally affordable. Relatively. In my experience anyway, network attached printers have fewer problems than the ones that are tethered to a specific machine.

And 3D printers? Whoa, Nelly! They're coming — and from what I've seen, they hook up just as easily as laser printers. Running them is another story, of course.

Windows has excellent printer support. It's easy after you grasp a few basic skills.

Installing a Printer

You have three ways to make a printer available to your computer:

✦ Attach it directly to the computer.

✦ Connect your computer to a network and attach the printer to another computer on the same network.

✦ If the printer can attach directly to a network, connect your computer to a network and attach the printer directly to the network's hub, either with a network cable or via a wireless connection.

Having used all three attachment methods for many years, I can tell you without reservation that, if you have a home network, it's worth an extra $20 or $40 or more to get a wireless-connecting printer.

Connecting a computer directly to a network hub isn't difficult, if you have the right hardware. Each printer controller is different, though, so you have to follow the manufacturer's instructions.

Although choosing a new printer is beyond the scope of this book, you can find free tips — inkjet or laser, basic or multifunction? — at www.dummies.com.

Attaching a local printer

So you have a new printer and you want to use it. Attaching it *locally* — which is to say, plugging it directly into your PC — is the simplest way to install a printer, and it's the only option if you don't have a network.

All modern printers have a USB connector that plugs in to your computer. In theory, you plug the connector into your PC's USB port and turn on the printer, and then Windows recognizes it and installs the appropriate drivers. You're done.

If you're watching the desktop while Windows is doing its thing, you see an icon flashing. If you're curious, click the flashing icon, and you see something like Figure 7-1.

I *don't* recommend that you install the manufacturer's software right off the bat, no matter what the instructions in the box with the printer may say. Most printers come with a CD loaded with . . . junk. Far better is to use the standard Windows drivers — in other words, just plug the thing in and print away — and resort to the manufacturer's CD only if it absolutely, definitely has something you need.

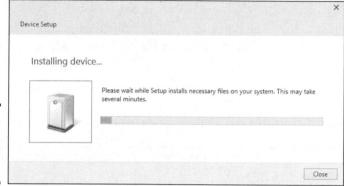

Figure 7-1:
Let
Windows do
all the work.

When the printer is installed properly, you can see the printer in your Devices list. (See Book VII, Chapter 1 for details on the Devices list.) To see your devices, click or tap Start, Settings, and then click Devices. You see a list similar to the one in Figure 7-2.

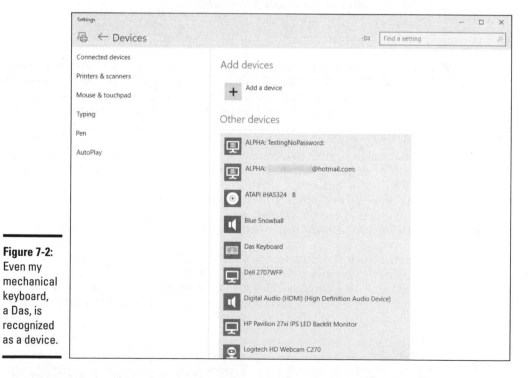

Figure 7-2:
Even my
mechanical
keyboard,
a Das, is
recognized
as a device.

Once in a very blue moon, and sometimes with very new or very old models of printers, Windows may have trouble locating a driver. If that happens, you can use the CD that came with your printer or, better, go to the manufacturer's website and download the latest driver. Table 7-1 has a list of websites.

Table 7-1	Driver Sites for Major Printer Manufacturers
Manufacturer	*Find Drivers at This URL*
Brother	`http://brother-usa.com/downloads/default.aspx?ProductGroupID=1`
Canon	`http://usa.canon.com/cusa/consumer/standard_display/support`
Dell	`http://www.dell.com/support/article/us/en/19/SLN115154/EN`
Epson	`http://epson.com/cgi-bin/Store/support/SupportIndex.jsp`
HP	`http://www8.hp.com/us/en/drivers.html`
Samsung	`http://www.samsung.com/us/support/downloads`

Connecting a network printer

Windows networks work wonders. When they work. Say that ten times real fast.

If you have a network, you can attach a printer to (almost) any computer on the network and have it accessible to all users on (almost) all computers in the network. You can also attach different printers to different computers and let network users pick and choose the printer they want to use as the need arises.

If you attach a printer to a computer in your HomeGroup, Windows automatically recognizes it and offers to make it accessible on your computer. You can turn off the automatic sharing of printers in your HomeGroup (see Book VII, Chapter 5), but unless you changed something, every printer attached to every computer in your HomeGroup is automatically identified and added to the Devices list on every computer in the HomeGroup. Very slick.

If you have printers attached to your network but not in your HomeGroup — for example, you may have a printer on a Windows Vista or Windows XP machine, or on a Windows 7 or 8/8.1 or 10 machine that isn't set up to share devices — you can still add it to your collection of shared printers. Here's how:

1. **Click Start, Settings, and choose the Devices link.**

2. **On the left, choose Printers & scanners.**

   The Printer list appears (refer to Figure 7-3).

Figure 7-3:
All the printers accessible to this machine — most of which aren't really printers at all, but they can work like printers.

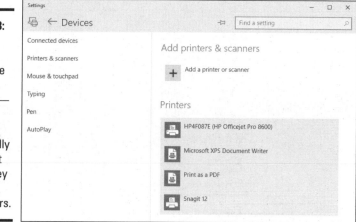

3. **At the top, tap or click the Add a printer or scanner button.**

   Windows looks all through your network — not just your HomeGroup — to see whether any printers are available. If any printers are available, you get a notification that lists the printer.

4. **Tap or click the printer to add it.**

   Windows looks to see whether it has a driver handy for that particular printer. If there's no driver immediately available, it asks Do You Trust This Printer?

5. **Check to see whether a button says, "Golly, it's always been a good printer to me, but you never really know if it suddenly acquired subversive tendencies — right? — so how can I tell for sure?" If you don't find that button, tap or click Install Driver.**

   Windows whirs and clanks for a while and then tells you that you've successfully added the printer.

6. **Tap or click Next.**

   You're asked whether you want to make the new printer your *default* printer (the one that an application uses unless you explicitly tell it otherwise).

7. **If you want to make the printer your default, tap or click Yes.**

8. **Tap or click Finish.**

   Your new printer appears in the Printers & scanners list, as shown in Figure 7-4.

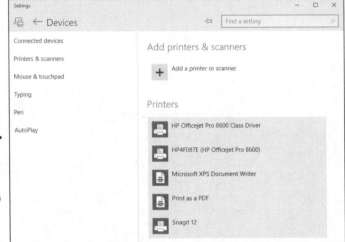

Figure 7-4:
Windows adds the Officejet Pro printer to the list.

Using the Print Queue

You may have noticed that when you print a document from an application, the application reports that it's finished before the printer finishes printing. If the document is long enough, you can print several more documents from one or more applications while the printer works on the first one. This is possible because Windows saves printed documents in a *print queue* until it can print them.

If more than one printer is installed on your computer or network, each one has its own print queue. The queue is maintained on the *host PC* — that is, the PC to which the printer is attached.

If you have a network-attached printer, the printer itself maintains a print queue.

Windows uses print queues automatically, so you don't even have to know that they exist. If you know the tricks though, you can control them in several useful ways.

Displaying a print queue

You can display information about any documents that you currently have in a printer's queue by following these steps:

1. **Bring up the Control Panel by right-clicking the Start screen in the lower-left corner of the screen and choosing Control Panel.**

Or you can type Windows + X.

2. **Under the Hardware and Sound category, choose View Devices and Printers.**

You see the list of devices like the one shown in Figure 7-5. Looks better than the modern-looking list in 7-4, doesn't it?

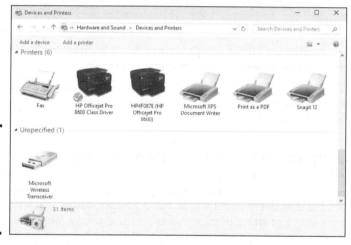

Figure 7-5: This is a typical Devices and Printer listing.

3. **Double-click (or tap and hold) the printer you're interested in. Then tap or click See What's Printing.**

The print queue appears, as shown in the lower right of Figure 7-6. If you have documents waiting for more than one printer, you get more than one print queue report.

4. **To cancel a document, tap and hold or right-click the document you want to cancel; choose Cancel.**

In many cases, Windows must notify the printer that it's canceling the document, so you may have to wait awhile for a response.

The Owner column tells you which user put the document in the print queue. The jobs in the print queue are listed from the oldest at the top to the newest at the bottom. The Status column shows which job is printing.

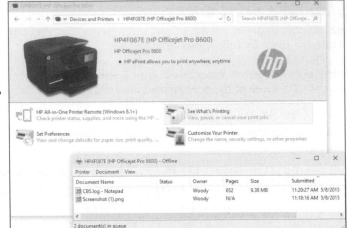

Figure 7-6:
All the
documents
you have
waiting to
print display
in the
queue.

5. **Keep the print queue window open for later use, or minimize the print queue window and keep it in the taskbar.**

That can be quite handy if you're running a particularly long or complex print job; Word mail merges are particularly notorious for requiring close supervision.

Pausing and resuming a print queue

When you *pause* a print queue, Windows stops printing documents from it. If a document is printing when you pause the queue, Windows tries to finish printing the document and then stops. When you *resume* a print queue, Windows starts printing documents from the queue again. Follow these guidelines to pause and resume a print queue:

✦ **To pause a print queue,** when you're looking at the print queue window (refer to the lower-right corner of Figure 7-6), choose Printer, Pause Printing.

✦ **To resume the print queue,** choose the same command again. The check mark in front of the Pause Printing line disappears, and the printer resumes.

Why would you want to pause the print queue? Say you want to print a page for later reference, but you don't want to bother turning on your printer to print just one page. Pause the printer's queue, and then print the page. The next time you turn on the printer, resume the queue, and the page prints.

Sometimes, Windows has a hard time finishing the document — for example, you may be dealing with print buffer overruns (see the "Troubleshooting Printing" section, later in this chapter) — and every time you clear the printer, it may try to reprint the overrun pages. If that happens to you, pause the print queue and turn off the printer. As soon as the printer comes back online, Windows is smart enough to pick up where it left off.

Also, depending on how your network is set up, you may or may not be able to pause and resume a print queue on a printer attached to another user's computer or a network attached printer.

Pausing, restarting, and resuming a document

If you've followed along so far, here are some other reasons you may want to pause a document. Consider the following:

✦ Suppose you're printing a web page that documents an online order you just placed, and the printer jams. You've already finished entering the order, and you have no way to display the page again to reprint it. Pause the document, clear the printer, and restart the document.

✦ Here's another common situation where pausing comes in handy. You're printing a long document, and the phone rings. To make the printer be quiet while you talk, pause the document. When you're finished talking, resume printing the document.

Here's how pausing, restarting, and resuming work:

✦ **Pause a document:** When you pause a document, Windows is prevented from printing that document. Windows skips the document and prints later documents in the queue. If you pause a document while Windows is printing it, Windows halts in the middle of the document and prints nothing on that printer until you take further action.

✦ **Restart a document:** When you restart a document, Windows is again allowed to print it. If the document is at the top of the queue, Windows prints it as soon as it finishes the document that it's now printing. If the document was being printed when it was paused, Windows stops printing it and starts again at the beginning.

✦ **Resume a document:** Resuming a document is meaningful only if you paused it while Windows was printing it. When you resume a document, Windows resumes printing it where it paused.

To pause a document, right-click the document in the print queue, or tap and hold and choose Pause. The window shows the document's status as Paused. To resume or restart the paused document, right-click or tap and hold that document, and choose Resume.

**Book VII
Chapter 7**

Working with Printers

Canceling a document

When you *cancel* a document, Windows removes it from the print queue without printing it. You may have heard computer jocks use the term *purged* or *zapped* or something totally unprintable.

Here's a common situation when document canceling comes in handy. You start printing a long document, and as soon as the first page comes out, you realize that you forgot to set the heading. What to do? Cancel the document, change the heading, and print the document again.

To cancel a document, select that document. In the print queue window, choose Document, Cancel. Or tap and hold, or right-click the document in the print queue window and choose Cancel. You can also select the document and press Delete.

When a document is gone, it's gone. No Recycle Bin exists for the print queue.

Conversely, most printers have built-in memory that stores pages while they're being printed. Network attached printers can have sizable buffers. You may go to the print queue to look for a document, only to discover that it isn't there. If the document has already been shuffled off to the printer's internal memory, the only way to cancel it is to turn off the printer.

Troubleshooting Printing

The following list describes some typical problems with printers and the solutions to those sticky spots:

+ **I'm trying to install a printer. I connected it to my computer, and Windows doesn't detect its presence.** Be sure that the printer is turned on and that the cable from the printer to your computer is properly connected at both ends. Check the printer's manual; you may have to follow a procedure (such as push a button) to make the printer ready for use.

+ **I'm trying to install a printer that's connected to another computer on my network, and Windows doesn't detect its presence. I know that the printer is okay; it's already installed and working as a local printer on that system!** If the printer is attached to a Windows XP or Vista PC, the printer may not be shared. If it's attached to a Windows 7 or 8/8.1 PC, the PC may be set to treat the network as a public network — in which case, it doesn't share anything. To rectify the problem, right-click the printer and choose Sharing. (For details, see *Windows XP All-in-One Desk Reference For Dummies* or *Windows Vista All-in-One Desk Reference For*

Dummies, Windows 7 All-in-One For Dummies, Windows 8 All-in-One For Dummies, or *Windows 8.1 All-in-One For Dummies* all by yours truly and published by John Wiley & Sons.)

If the printer is attached to a Windows 7, 8/8.1, or 10 PC and it's part of your HomeGroup, make sure that the HomeGroup is working. If it isn't part of your HomeGroup, read Book VII, Chapter 5 and get with the system!

✦ **I can't use a shared printer that I've used successfully in the past. Windows says that it isn't available when I try to use it, or Windows doesn't even show it as an installed printer anymore.** This situation can happen if something interferes with your connection to the network or the connection to the printer's host computer. It can also happen if something interferes with the availability of the printer, for example, if the host computer's user has turned off sharing.

If you can't find a problem or if you find and correct a problem (such as file and printer sharing being turned off), but you still can't use the printer, try restarting Windows on your own system. If that doesn't help, remove the printer from your system and reinstall it.

To remove the printer from your system, click Start, Settings. Choose the Devices icon, and on the left, choose Printers & scanners. On the right, double-click or tap and hold on the device. A Remove Device box appears. Click it. Windows asks whether you're sure you want to remove this printer. Tap or click the Yes button.

Book VII Chapter 7

To reinstall the printer on your system, use the same procedure you used to install it originally. (See the "Connecting a network printer" section, earlier in this chapter.)

Working with Printers

✦ **I printed a document, but it never came out of the printer.** Check the printer's print queue on the host PC (the one directly attached to the printer), if it's attached to just one PC, or the print queue on any attached PC if it's a network printer. Is the document there? If not, investigate several possible reasons:

- *The printer isn't turned on, or it's out of paper.* Hey, don't laugh. I've done it. In some cases, Windows can't distinguish a printer that's connected but not turned on from a printer that's ready, and it sends documents to a printer that isn't operating.

- *You accidentally sent the document to some other printer.* Hey, don't laugh — you've heard that one.

- *Someone else unintentionally picked up your document and walked off with it.*

- *The printer is turned on but not ready to print, and the printer (as opposed to the host PC) is holding your whole document in its internal memory until it can start printing.* A printer can hold as much as several hundreds — even thousands — of pages of output internally, depending on the size of its internal memory and the complexity of the pages. Network attached printers frequently have 16MB or more of dedicated buffer memory, which is enough for a hundred or more pages of lightly formatted text.

If your document is in the print queue but isn't printing, check for these problems:

- *The printer may not be ready to print.* See whether it's plugged in, turned on, and properly connected to your computer or its host computer.

- *Your document may be paused.*

- *The print queue itself may be paused.*

- *The printer may be printing another document that's paused.*

- *The printer may be "thinking."* If it's a laser printer or another type of printer that composes an entire page in internal memory *before* it starts to print, it appears to do nothing while it processes photographs or other complex graphics. Processing may take as long as several minutes.

- Look at the printer, and study its manual. The printer may have a blinking light or a status display that tells you it's doing something. As you become familiar with the printer, you develop a feel for how long various types of jobs should take.

- *The printer is offline, out of paper, jammed, or unready to print for some other reason.*

Catching a Runaway Printer

This topic must be the most common, most frustrating problem in printer-dumb.

You print a document, and as it starts to come out the printer, you realize that you're printing a zillion pages you don't want. How do you stop the printer and reset it so that it doesn't try to print the same bad stuff, all over again?

Here's what you do:

1. **Turn off the printer. Pull the paper out of the printer's paper feeder.**

   Be careful with this step to avoid roller damage or paper tears that cause problems later.

   This step stops the immediate problem, uh, immediately.

2. **On the desktop, in the lower-right corner, look among the notification icons for one that looks like a printer; tap and hold it or double-click it.**

   The print queue appears (refer to Figure 7-6).

3. **Right-click (or tap and hold) the runaway print job, and choose Cancel.**

   If this step deletes the bad print job, good for you.

4. **If it doesn't delete the bad print job, wait a minute and then turn off the printer and unplug it from the wall. (Really.) Reboot Windows. When Windows comes back, wait another minute, plug the printer back in, and turn the printer back on.**

   Your bad job is banished forever.

Book VIII

Maintaining Windows 10

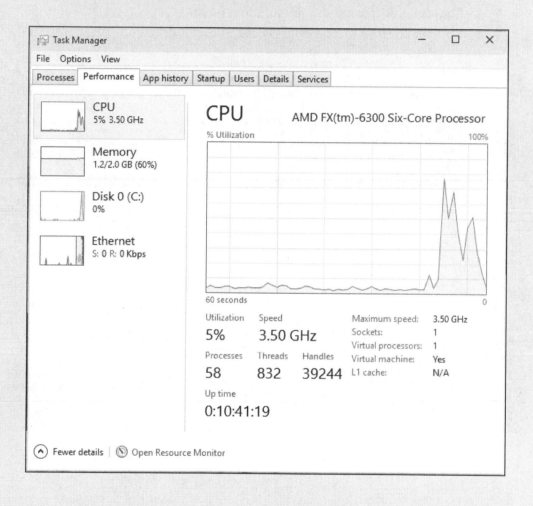

Tired of Windows? Want to throw your machine out the, uh, garbage chute? Check here first: www.dummies.com/extras/windows10aio/calmdown.

Contents at a Glance

Chapter 1: File History, Backup, Data Restore, and Sync

In This Chapter

✔ Discovering what happened to the Windows 7 backup

✔ Backing and restoring your data

✔ Can you make a full-disk "ghost" backup?

✔ Storing via the cloud

*I*f you're accustomed to using earlier versions of Windows to back up or restore data, to "ghost" a whole drive, or to set restore points, you're probably in this chapter looking for something that no longer exists.

Although you can set manual restore points — much the same process as it was in Windows ME, many moons ago — the way to do so is buried deep inside the new Windows, and frankly, your need for them is highly debatable.

Microsoft has, in one stroke, made backup and restore much simpler and much less controllable. Or perhaps I should say *micro-manageable*.

In this chapter, I talk about how to back up your data: running backups, restoring them, being smart about where to store them, and accessing them if something goes wrong. (In Chapter 2 of this minibook, I talk about Refresh and Reset, two ways of bringing Windows back to life. Refresh keeps all your data. Reset wipes out everything and returns your PC to its out-of-the-box state.)

In this chapter and Chapter 2 of this minibook, I don't talk much about old Windows topics that just don't apply anymore. These include system repair discs, restore points, image backups, recovery mode, and safe mode. You can find vestiges of those features in Windows 10 if you look hard enough. But they aren't recommended anymore — and they're rarely supported.

What Happened to the Windows 7 Backup?

If you're an experienced Windows 7 user, you may be looking for specific features that have been renamed, morphed, or axed in the current version of Windows. Here's a little pocket dictionary to help you figure out the landmarks:

+ **Shadow Copies (or Previous Versions) of files are now called File History.** It's functionally very similar to the Apple Time Machine — just not as cool, visually.

+ **Image Backup (or System Image or Ghosting) is buried deep.** If you really want to use Windows 10 to create a full disk image, tap or click Start, Settings, Update & security. On the left, choose Backup, then on the right, click the link to Go to Backup and Restore (Windows 7). On the left, click Create a System Image, and go from there.

+ **Windows Backup and the Backup and Restore Center are there, but they're hard to find.** They were in Windows 8, got tossed out of Windows 8.1, and now they're back in Windows 10. Click Start, Settings, Update & security, Backup. Click the link to Go to Backup and Restore (Windows 7). Most of the time it's much smarter to use File History anyway, but if you're nostalgic — or you don't want to learn new tricks — the old way still works.

+ **You can boot into safe mode if you really want to, but Microsoft makes it very difficult to get there.** Follow the instructions in Book VIII, Chapter 2 to get into the Windows Recovery Environment.

Microsoft is *deprecating* (killing, zapping) all the old backup, restore, system restore, and safe mode options, in favor of completely new (and much easier-to-use) backup and restore options.

All the while, the subtle push is there to store everything in OneDrive, so Microsoft can take care of backing up and restoring.

The Future of Reliable Storage Is in the Cloud

Microsoft wants you to put your data in the cloud.

It's more than a question of letting you shoot yourself in the foot. Microsoft has turned into a bigtime fan of cloud storage. New features in Windows 10 are designed to make it easier for you to put your data in the cloud — preferably Microsoft's cloud, OneDrive, of course. Yes, part of the motivation is to get you to pay for cloud storage, or at least lock you in to Microsoft's cloud offerings. But a big part of the reason for steering you to cloud storage is that it's better.

Replicating Windows Home Server backup

Many people use Windows Home Server. I love it. Even wrote a book about it, *Windows Home Server For Dummies*. But Microsoft has given up on WHS, and it isn't coming back.

With the new version of Windows, though, I'm not going to miss WHS too much. The absolutely best feature in WHS was its ability to back up data on connected PCs and keep redundant copies of the data. That way, any drive on the server or on my PC could fail, and all it took was a new drive and an hour or two to restore all my data as if nothing had happened.

And you can do all that and more by combining Storage Spaces (see Book VII, Chapter 4) with File History (see the nearby section "Backing Up and Restoring Files with File History").

WHS has one more significant feature that isn't replicable in Windows 10: It not only backs up your data, it backs up the entire contents of all your drives. When I was using WHS, if my C: drive decided to crack into a million pieces, restoring it was quite simple. Without WHS, but using Windows 10 and File History, I can restore everything except my desktop applications.

Yes, you read that right. I'm telling you that cloud storage is better than local storage, for most people in most situations. One of the big reasons why: backup. You don't have to sweat backup when your data is in the cloud. I admit that there are rare examples of people who have lost data saved on one of the cloud storage systems — OneDrive, Google Drive, iCloud, Dropbox, Box, and so on.

Contrast that with local storage. If you've been using computers for any length of time at all, chances are good that you've lost some data. If you know ten people who store data on their own PCs, I'd guess that ten of them have lost data.

So scoff at cloud storage if you like. Worry about the privacy problems. Fret over maintaining an internet connection. But contrast that with the possibility — no, the likelihood — that you'll lose data by managing it yourself. No contest, from my point of view.

I cover cloud storage later in this book, in the section "Storing to and through the Cloud."

Backing Up and Restoring Files with File History

Windows File History not only backs up your data files, it also backs up many versions of your data files and makes it very easy to retrieve the latest version and multiple earlier versions.

**Book VIII
Chapter 1**

**File History,
Backup, Data
Restore, and Sync**

By default, File History takes snapshots of all the files in your Libraries (see Book VII, Chapter 3), your desktop, your Contacts data, and your browser (Microsoft Edge, Internet Explorer) favorites. It does not take snapshots of anything in OneDrive; that's the cloud's duty. The snapshots get taken once an hour and are kept until your backup drive runs out of space.

You can change those defaults. I explain how later in this section.

Setting up File History

To use File History, Windows demands that you have an external hard drive, a second hard drive, or a network connection that leads to a hard drive. In this example, I connect to a drive on my home network. You could use a cheap external hard drive, which you can pick up at any computer store.

If you have lots of photos in your Photos Library or a zillion songs in the Music Library, the first File History backup takes hours and hours (or longer!). If you have lots of data and this is your first time, don't even try to set up things until you're ready to leave the machine for a long, long time.

If you haven't yet set up your Libraries, made them visible in File Explorer, and put the Public folders inside your Libraries, mosey over to Book VII, Chapter 3 and bring back the Library stuff Microsoft knocked out.

To get the desktop version of File History going, follow these steps:

1. **Bring up the Control Panel by right-clicking in the lower-left corner of the screen and choosing Control Panel. Click or tap System and Security and then File History.**

   The File History applet appears in the desktop Control Panel, as shown in Figure 1-1.

   If you don't have a drive set up for File History, you see the banner that starts, We Recommend That You Use an External Drive for File History . . . .

2. **Attach your external drive, or tap or click the User Network Location link and navigate to a networked drive.**

   If you're using a clean hard drive, the banner disappears. If data's on your drive or your drive installs a driver of some sort, you may need to tap or click Use Network Location, then Add Network Location, and point to the drive.

   After your drive is connected, File History presents you with the dialog box shown in Figure 1-2.

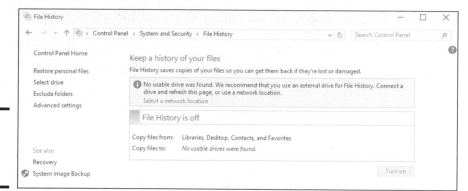

Figure 1-1:
Set up File
History
here.

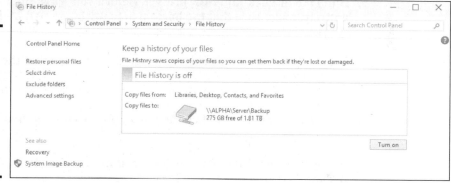

Figure 1-2:
With an
external or
networked
drive
connected,
time to
turn on File
History.

3. Tap or click the Turn On button.

If you have a HomeGroup, File History asks whether you want to recommend the drive to other members of your HomeGroup.

4. If you have a HomeGroup and want to recommend the drive to other members, so they can also use it for File History, tap or click Yes; if you don't want to recommend the drive, tap or click No.

File History goes out to lunch for a long time. Possibly a very long time. It gathers everything in your libraries (see Book VII, Chapter 3), everything on your desktop, all your Contacts, and your IE and Spartan favorites.

You can go back to work, or grab a latte or three. Go home. Take a nap. If you have lots of pictures in your Library, you may want to consider rereading *War and Peace*. When File History is good and ready, a Run Now link appears in the dialog box under Files last copied, per Figure 1-3.

**Book VIII
Chapter 1**

**File History,
Backup, Data
Restore, and Sync**

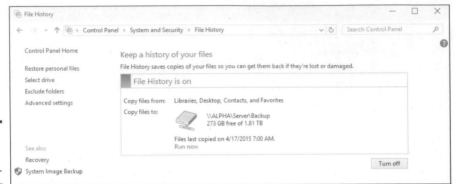

Figure 1-3:
File History
is on the job.

5. **Don't tap or click Run Now just yet. Before you leave the topic entirely, make sure that the backup actually happened by following the next steps.**

Instead of relying on the File History program to tell you that the backup occurred, take matters into your own hands and look for the backup with File Explorer. To find the backup files with File Explorer, follow these steps:

1. **On the desktop, tap or click the File Explorer icon on the taskbar.**

   File Explorer opens.

2. **Navigate to the drive that you just used in the preceding steps for a backup.**

   This may be an external or a networked drive; it may even be a second drive on your PC, although I don't recommend that.

3. **Tap or double-click your way through the folder hierarchy:**

   - *FileHistory*
   - *Your username*
   - *Your PC name*
   - *Data*
   - *The main drive you backed up* (probably `C:`)
   - *Users*
   - *Your username* (again)
   - *Desktop* (assuming you had any files on your desktop that you backed up), or *Pictures*, or some other folder of interest.

   A File Explorer screen like the one in Figure 1-4 appears.

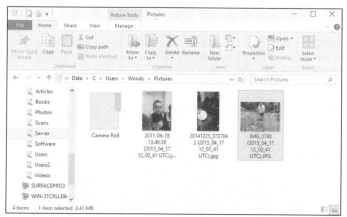

Figure 1-4:
Your
backup data
appears
waaaay
down in a
chain of
files; they're
stored on
the hard
drive.

4. **Check whether the filenames match the files that are on your desktop, or in your Pictures folder, with dates and times attached.**

5a. *If the files match,* **you can close File Explorer and close the File History dialog box.**

Although you can restore data from this location via File Explorer, it's easier to use the File History retrieval tools. (See the next section for details.)

5b. *If you don't see a list of filenames that mimics the files on your desktop,* **go back to Step 1 of the preceding steps list and make sure you get it right!**

File History doesn't run if the backup drive gets disconnected or the network connection to the backup drive drops — but Windows produces File History files anyway. As soon as the drive is reconnected or the network starts behaving, File History dumps all its data to the correct location.

Restoring data from File History

File History stores snapshots of your files, taken every hour, unless you change the frequency. If you've been working on a spreadsheet for the past six hours and discovered that you blew it, you can retrieve a copy of the spreadsheet that's less than an hour old. If you've been working on your résumé over the past three months and decide that you really don't like the way your design changed five weeks ago, File History can help you there too.

If you're accustomed to the Windows 7 way of bringing back Shadow Copies, you need to unlearn everything you think you know about bringing back old files. Windows 10 works differently.

**Book VIII
Chapter 1**

**File History,
Backup, Data
Restore, and Sync**

Here's how to bring back your files from cold storage:

1. **Bring up the Control Panel by right-clicking in the lower-left corner of the screen and choosing Control Panel. Click or tap System and Security; then under File History, click or tap Restore Your Files with File History.**

The File History Restore Home page, as shown in Figure 1-5, appears.

Figure 1-5:
You need to find the file you want to restore, starting at the top.

2. **Navigate to the location of the file you want to restore.**

In Figure 1-5, I went to the Pictures library, where the file I want to resuscitate is stored.

You can use several familiar File Explorer navigation methods inside the File History program, including the up arrow to move "up one level," the forward and back arrows, and the search box in the upper-right corner. See Figure 1-6.

3. **Check the time and date in the upper-left corner.**

4a. ***If that's the time and date of the file you want to bring back,*** **tap and hold or right-click the file, and then choose Restore or (usually easier, if you have a mouse) simply click and drag the file to whatever location you like.**

You can even preview the file by double-clicking it.

Figure 1-6:
First, find
the location.
Then find
the correct
version.

4b. *If this isn't the right time and date,* **at the bottom, tap or click the left arrow to take you back to the previous snapshot.**

Tap or click left and right arrows to move to earlier and later versions of the files, respectively.

5. If you want to restore all the files you can see, at any given moment, tap or click the arrow-in-a-circle at the bottom of the screen.

You're given options to replace the files (which deletes the latest version of each file) or to choose which files you want to replace, as in Figure 1-7.

Personally, I always restore by clicking and dragging. It's much easier to see exactly what's happening and avoid mistakes before they happen.

If you accidentally replace a good file, be of good cheer. There was a snapshot of that file taken less than an hour ago. You just have to find it. Kinda cool how that works, eh? And that old copy stays around for a long time — years, if you have enough disk space, and your backup drive doesn't die.

**Book VIII
Chapter 1**

**File History,
Backup, Data
Restore, and Sync**

Changing File History settings

File History has several settings you may find valuable.

File History backs up *every file in every Library* on your computer. If you have a folder that you want to have backed up, just put it in a Library. Any Library. Invent a new Library if you want. You don't have to *use* the Library; just put the folder in a Library. File History takes care of all the details.

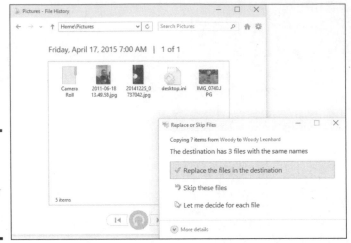

Figure 1-7:
You can
restore an
entire folder
full of files
all at once.

Microsoft makes it hard to find File History, just as they've made it hard
to find Libraries. Kind of goes hand in hand with trying to get you to use
OneDrive.

I have an extensive discussion of libraries in Book VII, Chapter 3, but if you
only want to stick an existing folder in a newly minted Library, it's easy: Tap
and hold or right-click the folder, choose Include in Library, Create New
Library, and give your new Library a name. You're finished.

Here's how to change some other key settings:

1. **Bring up the Control Panel by right-clicking in the lower-left corner
   of the screen and choosing Control Panel. Click or tap System and
   Security, and then tap or click File History.**

   The File History main page appears (refer to Figure 1-3).

2. **If you want to exclude some folders in your libraries so they don't get
   backed up, on the left, choose Exclude Folders.**

   File History opens a simple dialog box with an Add button that lets you
   put folders on the exclude list. For example, in Figure 1-8, I exclude a
   folder in the Documents Library that I don't want to have backed up.

3. **Tap or click the back arrow to get back to the File History applet.**

4. **To change how backups are made, on the left, tap or click the
   Advanced Settings link.**

   The Advanced Settings dialog box in Figure 1-9 appears.

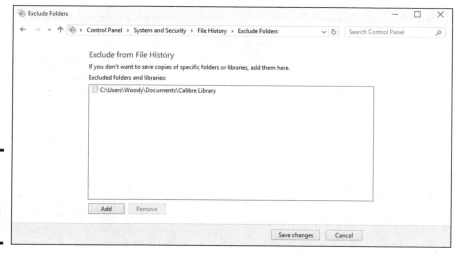

Figure 1-8:
Exclude
individual
folders from
File History.

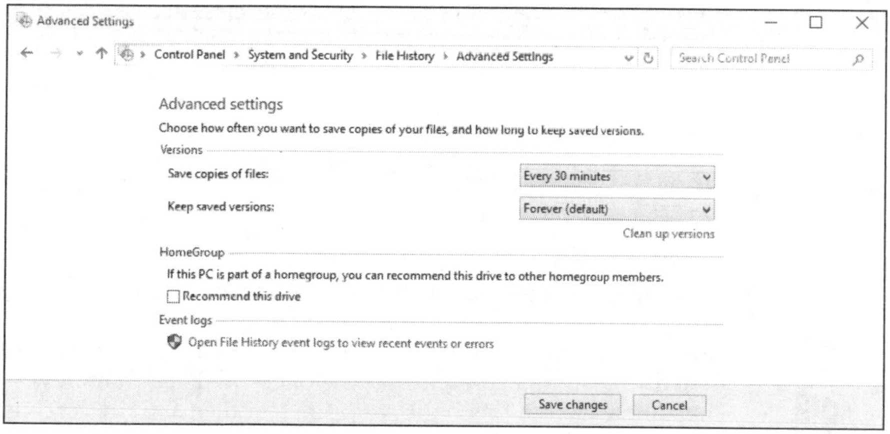

Figure 1-9:
Take control
of your
backups
here.

In this dialog box, you can change the frequency of backups and how long versions should be kept.

5. **See my recommendations for these settings in Table 1-1, and choose accordingly.**

6. **Tap or click Save Changes.**

Your next File History backup follows the new rules.

Table 1-1	File History Advanced Settings	
Setting	*Recommendation*	*Why*
Save Copies of Files	Every 30 Minutes	This is mostly a tradeoff between space (more frequent backups take a tiny bit of extra space) and time — your time. If you have lots of back-ups, you increase the likelihood of getting back a usable version of a file, but on the other hand, you have to wade through many more versions. I find 30 minutes strikes the right balance, but you may want to back up more frequently.
Keep Saved Versions	Forever (default)	If you choose Until Space Is Needed, File History won't raise a holy stink if you run out of room on your backup drive. By leaving it at Forever, File History sends notifications when the hard drive gets close to full capacity, so you can run out and buy another backup drive.
If This PC Is Part of a HomeGroup	Checked	Other people who use your PC and other people in your HomeGroup probably need backups too.

Storing to and through the Cloud

File History's a great product. I use it religiously. But it isn't the be-all and end-all of backup storage. What happens if my office burns down? What if I really, really need to get at a file when I'm away from the office?

The best solution I've found is to have File History do its thing, but I also keep my most important files — the ones I'm using right now — in the cloud. That's how I wrote this book, with the text files and the screenshots both in Dropbox. I also handed off the files to my editors, and received edited versions back, through Dropbox.

The only question with the editorial team nowadays is which cloud storage vendor to use. Believe me, things have really changed.

I also back up data, from time to time, to the Internet. Doing so is fast, cheap, and easy — but it does have problems. I talk about the mechanics of using OneDrive in Book IV, Chapter 4, and OneDrive's certainly a good choice. But other choices are available, and I want you to know about them.

Backing up to the Internet has one additional, big plus: Depending on which package you use and how you use it, the data can be accessible to you, no matter where you need it — on the road, on your iPad, even on your phone. You can set up folders to share with friends or coworkers, and in some cases, have them help you work on a file while you're working on it, too.

Six years ago, only one big player — Dropbox — was in the online storage and sharing business. Now there's Dropbox, Microsoft OneDrive, Google Drive, the Apple iCloud (which is a bit different), and Amazon Cloud Drive — all from huge companies — and SugarSync, Box (formerly Box.net), SpiderOak, and many smaller companies.

What happened? People have discovered just how handy cloud storage can be. And the price of cloud storage has plummeted to nearly nothing.

There are other online storage places. Mega (formerly known as Megaupload and now relocated to New Zealand) gives 50GB free. They and RapidShare, Hotfile.com, Soundcloud, and many others specialize in offering parking places for large files and making it easy to download single files. I use Mega all the time.

The cloud storage I'm talking about is specifically designed to allow you to store data on the Internet and retrieve it from just about anywhere, on just about any kind of device — including a phone or tablet. They also have varying degrees of interoperability and sharing, so, for example, you can upload a file and have a dozen people look at it simultaneously. Some cloud storage services (notably OneDrive and Google Drive) have associated programs (such as Microsoft Office and Google Apps) that let two or more people edit the same file simultaneously.

Considering cloud storage privacy concerns

I don't know how many times people have told me that they just don't trust putting their data on some company's website. But although many people are rightfully concerned about privacy issues and the specter of Big Brother, the fact is that the demand for storage in the cloud is growing by leaps and bounds.

The concerns I hear go something like this:

✦ **I have to have a working Internet connection in order to get data to or from the online storage.** Absolutely true, and there's no way around it. If you use cloud storage only for offsite backup, it's sufficient to be connected whenever you want to back up your data or restore it. Some of the cloud storage services have ways to cache data on your computer when, say, you're going to be on an airplane. But in general, yep, you have to be online.

**Book VIII
Chapter 1**

**File History,
Backup, Data
Restore, and Sync**

✦ **The data can be taken or copied by law enforcement and local governments.** True. The big cloud storage companies get several court orders a day. The storage company's legal staff takes a look, and if it's a valid order, your data gets sent to the cops. Or the feds. Or the tax people.

Unless, of course, you're talking about the U.S. National Security Agency and programs like PRISM, which basically allows the NSA to take any data it likes and prohibits the storage company from even talking about it. With a little luck, that's going to change, but it's hard to say how, or when, or even if.

Moral of the story: If you're going to store data that you don't want to appear in the next issue of a certain British tabloid, it would be smart to encrypt the file before you store it. Word and Excel 2007 and later use very effective encryption techniques. Couple that with a strong password, and your data isn't going anywhere soon. Unless, of course, you're required by the court to give up the password, or the NSA sets one of its teraflops password crackers to the job.

✦ **Programs at the cloud storage firm can scan my data.** True, once again, for most (but not all) cloud storage firms. With a few notable exceptions — Mega, Spider Oak, and others — cloud storage company programs can see your data. There's been a big push in the past few years to hold cloud storage companies responsible for storing copyrighted material: If you upload a pirate copy of *Men in Black 4,* the people who hold the copyright are going to get very upset.

Different cloud storage companies handle the task differently, but with the takedown of Megaupload in January 2012, everybody's concerned about incurring the wrath of the *MPAA* and *RIAA,* the companies that defend movie and music copyrights, respectively. Mega packed up, moved to New Zealand, and lives again, but the legal problems continue. The net result is that most cloud storage companies will be performing routine scans — either now or in the not-too-distant future — to see whether you're trying to upload something that's copyright-protected.

✦ **Employees at the cloud storage firm can look at my data.** True again. Certain cloud storage company employees *can* see your data — at least in the larger companies (Mega, Spider Oak, and a few others excepted). They must be able to see your data, in order to comply with court orders.

Does that mean Billy the intern can look at your financial data or your family photos? Well, no. It's more complicated than that. Every cloud storage company has very strict, logged, and monitored rules for who can authorize and who can view customer data. Am I, personally, absolutely sure that every company obeys all its rules? No, not at all. But I don't think my information is interesting enough to draw much attention from Billy, unless he's trying to swipe the manuscript of my next book.

✦ **Somebody can break in to the cloud storage site and steal my data.** Well, yes, that's true, but it probably isn't much of a concern. Each of the cloud storage services scrambles its data, and it'd be very, very difficult for anyone to break in, steal, and then decrypt the stolen data. Can it happen? Sure. Will I lose sleep over it? Nah. That said, you should enable two-factor authentication when it's offered (so the backup service sends an entry code to your email address, or sends you a message on your phone, requiring the entry code in order to get into your data). And if you want to be triple-sure, you can encrypt the data before you store it — 7Zip, among many others (see Book X Chapter 5), makes it easy to encrypt files when you zip them.

Reaping the benefits of backup and storage in the cloud

So much for the negatives. Time to look at the positives. On the plus side, a good cloud storage setup gives you:

✦ **Offsite backups** that won't get destroyed if your house or business burns down.

✦ **Access to your data from anywhere,** using just about any imaginable kind of computer, including phones and tablets.

✦ **Controlled sharing** so you can password-protect specific files or folders. Hand the password to a friend, and he can look at the file or folder.

✦ **Broadcast sharing** from a Public folder that anyone can see.

✦ **Direct access from application programs that run in the cloud.** Both Google Apps and the many forms of Microsoft Office are good examples. That includes iWork, if you're using Apple's iCloud. Office apps now have direct access to Dropbox data, too.

✦ **Free packages, up to a certain size limit,** offered by most of the cloud storage services.

Choosing an online backup and sharing service

So which cloud storage service is best? Tough question. Personally, I use four of them — three for PCs and Android, and iCloud for my Mac, iPad, and iPhone stuff — different services for different purposes.

Dropbox, Microsoft OneDrive, and Google Drive have programs that you run on your PC or Mac to set up folders that are shared. Drag a file into the shared folder, and it appears on all the computers you have connected (with a password) to the shared folder. Go on the web and log on to the site, and your data's available there too. Install an app on your iPhone, Android, or

Blackberry phone or tablet, and the data's there as well. Here's a rundown of what each cloud storage service offers:

✦ **Dropbox,** as shown in Figure 1-10, offers 2GB of free storage, with 1TB for $10 per month. It's very easy to use, reliable, and fast. I use it for synchronizing project files — including the files for this book. Dropbox also connects to Facebook to retrieve or post pictures (www.dropbox.com).

✦ **OneDrive** has 15GB of free storage, with 100GB for $4 per month or 1TB for $7 per month. The amounts on offer change from time to time. Also note that many Office 365 subscription levels have unlimited OneDrive storage, free, for as long as you're an Office 365 subscriber. Yes, that's unlimited, as in infinite, for free as in beer. I talk about OneDrive in Book VI, Chapter 2 (www.OneDrive.com).

✦ **Google Drive,** as shown Figure 1-11, has 15GB of free storage, with 100GB for $2 per month and 1TB for $10 per month. Google Drive isn't as slick as the other two, and there's no Facebook connection, but it works well enough. There's an optical character recognition facility and the ability to launch web apps directly. Most of all, it's fall-down simple to use Google Drive with Google Apps, which includes Gmail, and several not-very-compatible writing and spreadsheet apps. See Book X, Chapter 3 (www.drive.google.com). All the apps, to a greater or lesser extent, work while you aren't connected to the Internet.

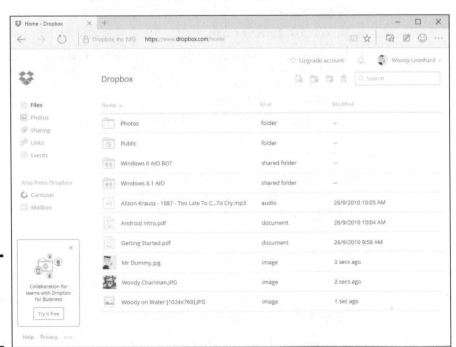

Figure 1-10: Dropbox popularized cloud storage.

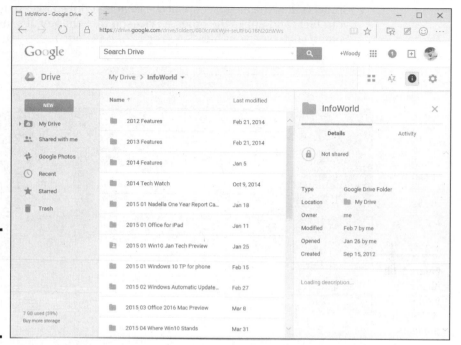

Figure 1-11:
Google
Drive works
very well
with Google
Apps.

✦ **Apple iCloud,** as shown in Figure 1-12, is really intended to be an Apple-centric service. The first 2GB is free, and then it's $20 per year for an additional 10GB. It works great with iPads and iPhones and even my new Mac, with extraordinarily simple backup of photos. In fact, photo and video backup and sharing take place automatically, and I don't have to do a thing. Music goes in easy as can be, and anything you buy from the iTunes store is in your storage, free, forever. But it's not really set up for open data sharing (www.icloud.com). Apple, too, is trying to bring its cloudy offerings down to the desktop. Stay up on the latest, if you're thinking about going with Apple.

The other services have specific strong points:

✦ **Amazon Cloud Drive** ties in with Amazon purchases and the Kindle but not much else (www.amazon.com/clouddrive).

✦ **SugarSync** lets you synchronize arbitrary folders on your PC. That's a big deal if you don't want to drag your sync folders into one location (www.sugarsync.com).

✦ **Box** is designed for large companies. It gives companies tools to control employee sharing (www.box.com).

**Book VIII
Chapter 1**

**File History,
Backup, Data
Restore, and Sync**

✦ **SpiderOak** is the most secure of the bunch: It doesn't keep the keys to your files, and unlike the other services in this chapter, it's impossible for SpiderOak to see your files (www.spideroak.com).

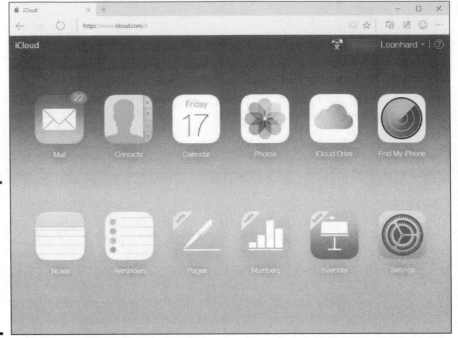

Figure 1-12: iCloud works with Apple products, but makes it difficult to share files among PCs.

 Like so many other things in the PC business, cloud storage is changing very, very rapidly. If you're interested in backing up to the cloud — and sharing files on the Internet, too, by the way — stay on top of the latest at my site, AskWoody.com (www.askwoody.com).

Chapter 2: A Fresh Start: Restore and Reset

In This Chapter

✔ **Refreshing, resetting, and restoring your PC**

✔ **Creating and using a System Image**

✔ **Introducing the Windows Recovery Environment**

In this chapter, I look at how you can bring back to life a computer that's been possessed. (This chapter doesn't talk about bringing files back from the dead. That's the purview of Book VIII, Chapter 1.)

If you've worked with Windows for any length of time at all, you know that from time to time Windows PCs simply go out to lunch . . . and stay there. The problem could stem from a bad drive, a scrambled Registry entry, a driver that's suddenly taken on a mind of its own, a revolutionary new program that's throwing its own revolution, or that dicey tuna sandwich you had for lunch.

Windows is a computer program, not a Cracker Jack toy, and it will have problems. The trick lies in making sure that *you* don't have problems too. This chapter walks you through the important tools you have at hand to make Windows do what you need to do, to solve problems as they (inevitably!) occur.

If you're the family's resident voodoo doctor — or the Windows go-to-gal in the office — this chapter can save your hide.

Microsoft has gone through a great deal of effort to make restoring a recalcitrant PC much simpler than ever before. The goal is to keep *you* out of the details and let Windows handle it: Computer, heal thyself, as it were. To a large degree, Microsoft has succeeded.

The Three R's — and an SI and RE

When resuscitating a machine with Windows gone bad, consider the three R's — Remove, Refresh, and Restore. Two of them are readily available, but they make major changes to your machine. One's not nearly so destructive, but it's harder to understand and use.

Here are the three R's that every Windows medic needs to know, starting with the most destructive:

✦ **Remove** (some people call it, confusingly, Reset) removes everything on your PC and reinstalls Windows. Your programs, data, and settings all get wiped out — they're irretrievably lost. This is the most drastic thing you can do with your computer, short of shooting it. (Did you see that viral video of the guy shooting his daughter's laptop? I digress.) If you like, you can tell Remove to do a *thorough* reformatting of the hard drive, in which case, random patterns of data are written to the hard drive to make it almost impossible to retrieve anything you used to store on the disk.

✦ **Refresh** keeps some Windows settings (accounts, passwords, the desktop, Microsoft Edge and IE favorites, wireless network settings, drive letter assignments, and BitLocker settings) and all personal data (in the User folder). It wipes out all programs and then restores the apps available in the Windows Store (primarily the tiled apps). This one's pretty drastic too, but at least it keeps the data stored in the most common locations — Documents folder, the desktop, Downloads, and the like. And as an added bonus, the Refresh routine keeps a list of the apps it zapped and puts that list on your desktop, so you can look at it when your machine's back to its chirpy self.

If you've tried to bring back an older Windows machine from purgatory, in previous years, you may have encountered System Restore. In fact, System Restore still exists, but Microsoft really doesn't want you to use it. Refresh is a combination of System Restore, safe mode, Recovery Console, and all sorts of minor earlier system recovery techniques, wrapped into one neat one-click bundle — with none of the hassles, but none of the old controls.

✦ **Restore (I prefer "Rollback")** is very hard to find — Microsoft doesn't want everyday users to find it — but it rolls Windows back to an earlier *restore point,* which I describe in the section "Restoring to an Earlier Point" later in this chapter. Restore/rollback doesn't touch your data or programs; it simply rolls back the Registry to an earlier point in time. If your problems stem from a bad driver or a problematic program change you made recently, Restore/rollback may do all you need. If you're familiar with Windows 7 or earlier versions, Windows 10 Restore/rollback is almost identical to Restore in the earlier version; you just access it a little differently.

Why does Microsoft make it hard to find Restore? As far as I know, the logic goes something like this: If you don't use Restore/rollback right, you can shoot your machine; in which case, you'll bother the folks at Microsoft mercilessly and accuse them of all sorts of mean things. Even if you *do* use Restore right, it fixes only a small percentage of all Windows-breaking problems, so if you try Restore/rollback and it doesn't work, you'll also bother the folks at Microsoft mercilessly — a classic lose-lose situation for the company. Importantly, there's nothing analogous to Restore/rollback with any competing operating system, tablet, or phone. The iPad doesn't have anything that resembles Restore; Android tablets and phones aren't in any shape to Restore; OS X wouldn't know a Restore from a hole in the ground; and my Linux friends start tittering obnoxiously anytime I say "Restore." In short, only Windows has a Registry, and Restore/rollback works almost exclusively on the Registry, so only Windows needs a Restore. There's not much competitive benefit to offering Restore to the average Windows consumer — and lots of downside.

All three of these resuscitation methods play out in the *Windows Recovery Environment (WRE),* a special proto-Windows system. If you run Reset or Refresh, you won't even know that WRE is at work behind the scenes, but it's there.

When there's trouble and Windows can't boot normally, Windows instead boots into WRE, not into Windows itself. WRE has the special task of giving you advanced tools and options for fixing things that have gone bump in the night.

Remove, Refresh, and Restore/rollback — and several more (Recycle, Reuse, Reduce?) are available in WRE.

I talk about WRE — and your advanced boot options — toward the end of this chapter.

A note about terminology

I *hate* the terminology Microsoft uses for its Windows-resuscitation technology.

If you and I get confused about Remove, Refresh, Restore/rollback, Recovery Environment, and Recombobulate (okay, I made up that last one), just imagine how confused normal, everyday users are going to get when they're confronted with choices that could, quite literally, obliterate all their data.

Further confusing the issue, Restore also applies to bringing back files. Refresh applies to network settings, in a different way. Recovery,

in the Windows world, is a Console that helps step you through the process.

It's very important that you watch carefully when you apply any of these R's. The implications of your actions are spelled out reasonably well on all the screens that Windows uses. But you can still very easily get confused.

And for heaven's sake, don't tell your mom to reset (or Remove) her PC when you meant to tell her to refresh it. You may not get invited over for dinner next Thanksgiving.

Book VIII
Chapter 2

A Fresh Start:
Restore and Reset

Resetting Your PC

You don't really know or care about restore points, and you don't want to dig in to Windows to make it work right. Mostly, you just want a one-tap (or click) solution that reams out the old, replaces it with known good stuff, and might or might not destroy your files in the process — at your option. That's what Microsoft has tried to offer with Reset.

Reset runs in two different ways:

✦ The **Keep my files** option tries to work its magic without disturbing any of your personal data files.

✦ The **Remove everything** option blasts everything away, including your data. It's the scorched-earth approach, to be used when nothing else works.

That's the view from 30,000 feet. Here are the details that you really need to know.

Running a Keep my files reset *keeps* all these:

✦ **Many of your Windows settings:** These include accounts and passwords, backgrounds, wireless network connections and their settings, BitLocker settings and passwords, drive letter assignments, and your Windows installation key.

✦ **Files in the User folder:** That includes files in every user's Documents folder, the desktop, Downloads, and so on. Refresh also keeps folders manually added to the root of the C: drive, such as C:\MyData. Reset with Keep my files keeps File History versions, and it keeps folders stored on drives and in partitions that don't contain Windows (typically, that means Refresh doesn't touch anything outside of the C: drive).

Files that *aren't* kept can be retrieved for several weeks from the C:\Windows.old folder. Yes, Microsoft keeps a secret stash of the files that it really wants to delete — and it's up to you to find them, if something disappears unexpectedly.

✦ **Windows Apps from the Windows Store:** Their settings are saved too. So if you're up to the 927th level of Cut the Rope before you run a Reset with Keep my files, afterward, you're still at the 927th level. Confusingly, if you bought a Windows Desktop app in the Windows Store, its settings get obliterated. Only your Windows/Universal/Metro apps come through unscathed.

Running Reset with the Keep my files option *destroys* all these:

✦ **Many of your Windows settings:** Display settings, firewall customizations, and file type associations are wiped out. Windows has to zap most of your Windows settings because they could be causing problems.

✦ **Files — including data files — not in the User folder:** If you have files tucked away in some unusual location, don't expect them to survive the Reset.

✦ **Windows Desktop apps:** Their settings disappear too, including the keys you need to install them, passwords in such programs as Outlook — everything. You need to reinstall them all.

The Reset routine, helpfully, makes a list of the programs that it identifies on the kill list and puts it on your desktop.

Here's how to run a Reset with the Keep my files option:

1. **Make very, very sure you understand what will come through and what won't.**

See the preceding bullet lists.

2. **Click or tap Start, Settings, Update & security.**

3. **At the bottom, choose Recovery.**

You see the Reset options shown in Figure 2-1.

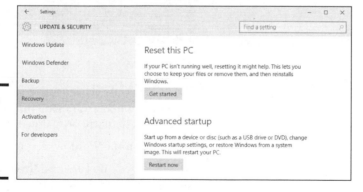

Figure 2-1: Run Reset from the Settings app.

4. **Under the heading Reset this PC, tap or click Get Started.**

Windows asks if you want to keep your files, or obliterate everything. See Figure 2-2.

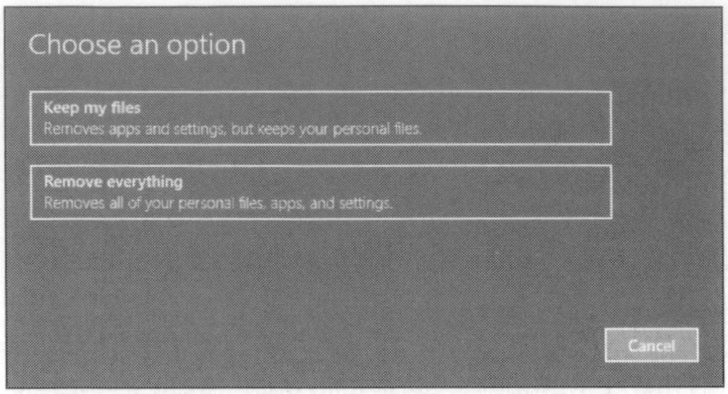

Figure 2-2:
Well,
whaddya
say, punk?
Keep 'em
or blast 'em
away?

5. Unless you're going to recycle your computer — give it to charity, or the kids – first try the less-destructive approach. Click or tap Keep my files.

If you have apps that won't make it through a Reset with Keep my files option, a list appears on your screen, as shown in Figure 2-3.

Figure 2-3:
These
apps —
yes, even
apps from
Microsoft —
won't
survive a
Refresh.

6. Tap or click Next, and then tap or click Reset.

The whole process takes about ten minutes on a reasonably well-seasoned PC, but it can take longer, particularly on a slow tablet.

When Refresh is finished, you end up on the Windows log in screen.

7. Log on to Windows. Tap or click the Desktop tile, and then tap or double-click the new Removed Apps file on the desktop.

Your default browser appears and shows you a list of all the programs it identified that didn't make it through the Refresh.

If Windows 10 can't boot normally, you're tossed into the Windows Recovery Environment. See the preceding section in this chapter for a description of how to start Refresh from the Windows Recovery Environment.

Resetting Your PC and Removing Everything

Reset with the Remove everything option is very similar to running Reset with Save my files except . . .

Warning! Warning! Danger, Will Robinson! Resetting with Remove everything on your PC wipes out everything and forces you to start all over from scratch. You even have to enter new account names and passwords, and reinstall everything, including Windows Universal apps.

If you're selling your PC, giving it away, or even sending it off to a recycling service, Reset with Remove everything is a good idea. If you're keeping your PC, only attempt Reset with Remove everything when you've run two or more Resets with Keep my files, and they haven't solved the problem. Reset with Remove everything is very much like a clean install (which I discuss in Book I, Chapter 4). You're nuking everything on your PC.

With that as a preamble, here's how to nuke, er, Reset your PC with Remove everything:

1. **Make very, very sure you understand that your PC will turn out like a brand-new PC, fresh off the store shelves. Also make sure that you have your 25-character Windows installation key.**

   Absolutely nothing survives the wipeout.

2. **Click or tap Start, Settings, Update & security.**

3. **At the bottom, choose Recovery.**

   You see the Reset options shown in Figure 2-1.

4. **Under the heading Reset this PC, tap or click Get Started.**

   Windows asks if you want to keep your files, or obliterate everything. See Figure 2-2.

5. **Tap or click Remove everything.**

   Reset asks whether you want to merely delete your old files or whether you want to positively nuke them, as shown in Figure 2-4.

   - The *Just Remove My Files* option reformats the hard drive, but as you no doubt know, data can be recovered from a reformatted hard drive.

   - The *Fully Clean the Drive* option writes random data on every sector of the hard drive. Although, in theory, the NSA may be able to reconstruct what's on the hard drive, in practice, it'll be very difficult (but not impossible!) to retrieve anything.

   PCs with solid state drives will be handled correctly, in accordance with your instructions.

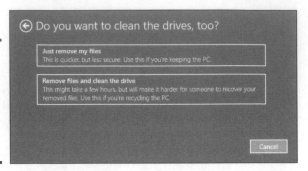

Figure 2-4:
How
thoroughly
do you want
to wipe out
your old
hard drive?

6. **Tap or click the Just Remove My Files option or the Fully Clean the Drive option, depending on your intended disposition of the PC.**

   The Just Remove My Files option takes about five minutes on a PC with a small hard drive. The Fully Clean the Drive option can take hours. Many hours.

   Regardless of which option you choose, when Reset is finished, you end up staring at a screen that asks for your product key. Now *that's* a complete, scorched-earth install.

Restoring to an Earlier Point

If you've used Windows 7 or earlier, you may have stumbled upon the System Restore feature. Windows 10 has full support for System Restore and restore points; it just hides all the pieces from you.

Why? Because Microsoft spends a fortune every year answering phone calls and email messages from people who bork System Restore. Instead of trying to handle all the picayune questions — and there are hundreds of thousands of them — Microsoft said, "That's enough!" and invented Reset, with and without Keep my files.

With a few exceptions (see the next section on System Image), Reset takes you all the way back in time to when you first set up your PC; it adds the Windows 10 Universal apps that ship with Windows, and it's careful not to step on your data. Aside from a few Windows settings, that's about it. Reset is a sledgehammer, when sometimes the tap of a fingernail may be all that you need.

Smashing with a sledgehammer is easy. Tapping your fingernail requires a great deal more finesse. And that brings me to System Restore in Windows 10.

System Protection and Restore points

Windows 7 created restore points for your system drive (usually C:) by default. Windows 10 doesn't. Restore points take up space on your hard drive, and Microsoft would rather that you just trust in their cloud-based recovery options. But if you want to take your system into your own hands, properly maintained and used restore points can change a gut-wrenching Refresh or Reset into a simple rollback to an earlier restore point.

See the section on Creating a restore point to see how to knock Windows upside the head and get it to start System Protection.

If you've enabled System Protection (see Book VIII Chapter 1), Windows takes snapshots of its settings, or *restore points,* before you make any major changes to your computer — install a new hardware driver, perhaps, or a new program. You can roll back your system settings to any of the restore points. (See sidebar on System Protection and Restore points.)

A restore point contains Registry entries and copies of certain critical programs including, notably, drivers and key system files — a *snapshot* of crucial system settings and programs. When you roll back (or *restore)* to a restore point, you replace the current settings and programs with the older versions.

When Windows can tell that you're going to try to do something complicated, such as install a new network card, it sets a restore point — as long as you have System Protection turned on. Unfortunately, Windows can't always tell when you're going to do something drastic — perhaps you have a new CD player and the instructions tell you to turn off your PC and install the player before you run the setup program. So it doesn't hurt one little bit to run System Restore — er, System Protection — from time to time, and set a restore point, all by yourself.

Creating a restore point

Here's how to create a restore point:

1. **Wait until your PC is running smoothly.**

   No sense in having a restore point that propels you out of the frying pan and into the fire, eh?

2. **Down in the search bar, where Cortana lives, type** restore point.

   The first result in Windows Search is Create a Restore Point.

3. **Tap or click the Create a Restore Point link.**

   Windows brings up the System Properties Control Panel dialog box, and opens it to the System Protection tab. (Cool, huh? Sometimes it's much easier to use Cortana.) See Figure 2-5.

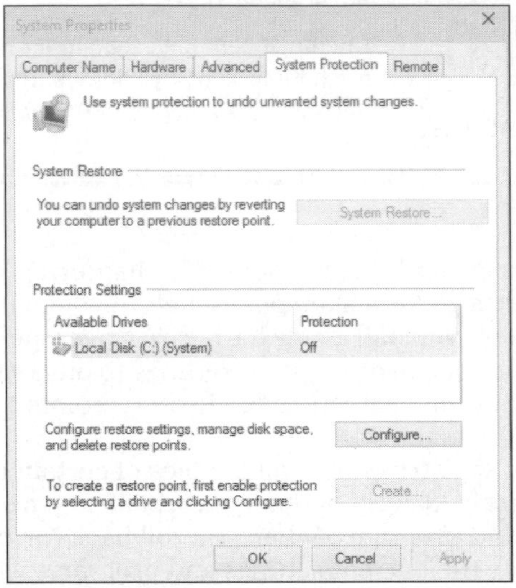

Figure 2-5: The hard-to-find System Restore command point.

4. **If Windows hasn't enabled restore points yet (the Protection column says Off, as it does in Figure 2-6), click the Configure button, click Turn on System Protection, and click OK.**

   That sets the Protection column to On and activates restore points for that particular drive.

5. **At the bottom, next to Create a Restore Point Right Now, tap or click the Create button.**

   The Create a Restore Point dialog box appears (see Figure 2-6).

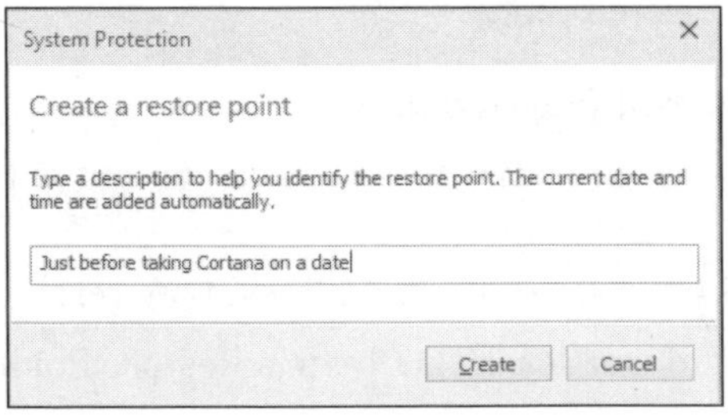

Figure 2-6: Give your restore point a name.

6. **Type a good description, and tap or click Create.**

   Windows advises that it's creating a restore point. When it's finished, it shows a message that says The Restore Point Was Created Successfully.

7. **Tap or click Close on the message, and then tap or click the X button to close the System Properties dialog box.**

   Your new restore point is ready for action.

Rolling back to a restore point

If you don't mind getting your hands a little dirty, the next time you think about running Refresh, see whether you can roll your PC back to a previous restore point, manually, and get things working right. Here's how:

1. **Save your work, and close all running programs.**

   System Restore doesn't muck with any data files, documents, pictures, or anything like that. It works only on system files, such as drivers, and the Registry. Your data is safe. But System Restore can mess up settings, so if you recently installed a new program, for example, you may have to install it again after System Restore is finished.

2. **Down in the Search box, type** restore point.

   The first result in Windows Search is Create a Restore Point.

3. **Tap or click the Create a Restore Point tile.**

   Windows flips you over to the desktop, brings up the System Properties Control Panel dialog box, and opens it to the System Protection tab (refer to Figure 2-6). Protection for your main drive should be "On." (If it isn't "On," you don't have any restore points.)

4. **Near the top, tap or click the System Restore button.**

   The System Restore wizard appears, as shown in Figure 2-7.

5. **Tap or click Next.**

   A list of recent restore points appears, as shown in Figure 2-8.

6. **Before you roll your PC back to a restore point, tap or click to select the restore point you're considering and then tap or click the Scan for Affected Programs button.**

   System Restore tells you which programs and drivers have system entries (typically in the Registry) that will be altered and which programs will be deleted if you select that specific restore point. See Figure 2-9.

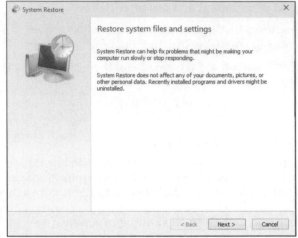

Figure 2-7:
See, wizards are in Windows 10.

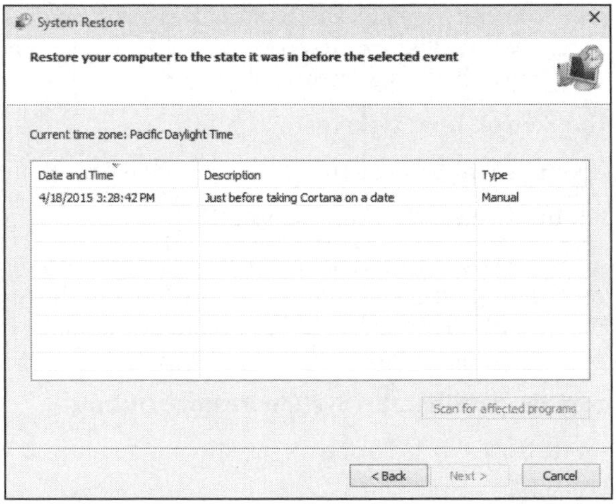

Figure 2-8:
The latest restore point isn't always the best restore point.

7. **If you don't see any major problems with the restore point — it doesn't wipe out something you need — tap or click Close, and then tap or click Next.**

(If you do see a potential problem, go back and choose a different restore point, or consider using Refresh, as I describe earlier in this chapter.)

System Restore asks you to confirm your restore point. You're also warned that rolling back to a restore point requires a restart of the computer and that you should close all open programs before continuing.

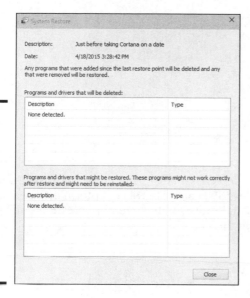

Figure 2-9:
Windows
can scan
the restore
point to
see what
programs
will be
affected
by rolling
back to it.

8. **Follow the instructions to save any open files, close all programs, and tap or click Finish.**

   True to its word, System Restore reverts to the selected restore point and restarts your computer.

System Restore is a nifty feature that works very well. The folks at Microsoft figure it's too complicated for the general computer- and tablet-buying consumer public. They may be right but, hey, all it takes is a little help and a touch of moxie, and you can save yourself a Refresh — as long as System Protection is turned on.

Entering the Windows Recovery Environment

In Windows 10, the Windows Recovery Environment has become a very sophisticated, almost eerily intelligent fix-everything program that works very well.

Except, of course, when it doesn't.

You know you're in the Windows Recovery Environment if you see a blue Choose an Option screen or a blue Troubleshoot screen like the one in Figure 2-10. (If you find yourself facing a blue Choose an Option screen, choose Troubleshoot!)

Figure 2-10:
The
hallmark
of the
Windows
Recovery
Environment.

Figure 2-10:
The
hallmark
of the
Windows
Recovery
Environment.

From the Troubleshoot screen, you can run Refresh or Reset directly: They behave precisely as I describe earlier in this chapter. You can also choose Advanced Options, which brings you to several interesting — if little-used — options, as shown in Figure 2-11.

Figure 2-11:
The
advanced
boot
options.

You can also get to this screen by choosing Advanced Startup from the Recovery list (refer to Figure 2-1). After you choose Advanced Startup, choose Troubleshoot and then choose Advanced Options.

Here's what the Advanced Options can do:

✦ **System Restore** puts your system back to a chosen restore point, following the same steps in the section "Rolling back to a restore point" earlier in this chapter. It won't work, though, unless you've turned on System protection/restore points for one or more drives on your computer.

✦ **System Image Recovery** requires a system image file that you can make only by using the DOS command line in a very geeky way. The particular command you need is recimg.exe. Details at the Windows 10 forums `www.tenforums.com/tutorials/4254-refresh-custom-recovery-image-create-windows-10-a.html`.

✦ **Startup Repair** reboots into a specific Windows Recovery Environment program known as Start Repair and runs a diagnosis and repair routine that seeks to make your PC bootable again. I've seen this program run spontaneously when I'm having hardware problems. A Start Repair log file is generated at `\Windows\System32\Logfiles\Srt\SrtTrail.txt`. If you find yourself running Automatic Repair, you can't do anything: Just hold on and see whether it works.

✦ **Command Prompt** brings up an old-fashioned DOS command prompt, just like you get if you go into Safe Mode. Only for the geek at heart. You can hurt yourself in there.

✦ **Startup Settings** reboots Windows and lets you go into Safe Mode, change video resolution, start debugging mode or boot logging, run in Safe Mode, disable driver signature checks, disable early launch anti-malware scans, and disable automatic restart on system failure. Definitely not for the faint of heart.

If you ever wondered how to do an old-fashioned "F8" boot into Safe Mode, now you know.

Chapter 3: Monitoring Windows

In This Chapter

✔ Watching Windows with the built-in tools

✔ Finding and fixing problems

✔ Working with the Event Viewer

✔ Tracking reliability over time

*W*indows 10 ships with a small array of tools designed to help you look at your system and warn you if something's wrong. In this chapter, I talk about two of them: Event Viewer and Reliability Monitor.

One long-time monitoring tool is gone. RIP. Windows Vista included a rag-tag, system performance benchmarking routine known as the Windows Experience Index. It continued through Windows 7 and 8. I used WEI all the time as a quick way to check PCs in shops to see which ones were great and which ones were merely mediocre. It wasn't the best test, but it was good enough for quick comparisons, and every Windows PC had a copy.

Microsoft dropped the WEI in Windows 8.1. One of its biggest motivations: The original Surface Pro — Microsoft's flagship Windows machine — scored a meager 5.9 on a scale from 1 to 9.9, which put it below just about any laptop or desktop you could mention. For years, I used a slapped-together Pavilion with a WEI of 4.8. It cost less than $300.

Instead of improving the Surface Pro — or changing the benchmark — Microsoft simply dropped the Windows Experience Index.

In Microsoft's zeal to make Windows less intimidating to new users, some of those tools are tucked away in rather obscure corners. But if you know what you're doing, you can find them and use them to help make your machine hum.

Or at least burble.

One of the tools, the *Event Viewer,* is a favorite foil of scammers and charlatans, who use it to convince you that your PC needs fixing (for a fee, of course) when it's just fine. I talk about that in this chapter, too.

Viewing Events

Every Windows user needs to know about Event Viewer, if only to protect themselves from scammers and con artists who make big bucks preying on peoples' fears.

As I explain in Book IX, Chapter 1, scammers are calling people in North America, Europe, Australia, and other locations all around the world, trying to talk Windows users into allowing these con artists to take over victims' systems via Remote Assistance. The scammers typically claim to be from Microsoft or associated with Microsoft. They may get your phone number by looking up names of people posting to help forums.

Some of them just cold call: Any random phone call to a household in North America or Europe stands a very good chance of striking a resonating chord when the topic turns to Windows problems. If you randomly called ten people in your town and said you were calling on behalf of Microsoft to help with a Windows problem, and you sounded as if you knew what you were talking about, I bet at least one or two of your neighbors would take you up on the offer. In my neighborhood, it'd probably be closer to nine. Maybe eleven or twelve.

The scam hinges around the Windows Event Viewer feature. It's an interesting, useful tool — but only if *you* take the initiative to use it, and don't let some fast talker use it to bilk you out of hundreds of bucks.

Using Event Viewer

Windows has had an Event Viewer for almost a decade. Few people know about it. At its heart, the Event Viewer looks at a small handful of logs that Windows maintains on your PC. The logs are simple text files, written in XML format. Although you may think of Windows as having one Event Log file, in fact, there are many — Administrative, Operational, Analytic, and Debug, plus application log files.

Every program that starts on your PC posts a notification in an Event Log, and every well-behaved program posts a notification before it stops. Every system access, security change, operating system twitch, hardware failure, and driver hiccup all end up in one or another Event Log. The Event Viewer scans those text log files, aggregates them, and puts a pretty interface on a deathly dull, voluminous set of machine-generated data. Think of Event Viewer as a database reporting program, where the underlying database is just a handful of simple flat text files.

In theory, the Event Logs track "significant events" on your PC. In practice, the term "significant" is in the eyes of the beholder. Or programmer. In the normal course of, uh, events, few people ever need to look at any of the Event Logs. But if your PC starts to turn sour, the Event Viewer may give you important insight to the source of the problem.

Here's how to use the Event Viewer:

1. **Right-click or tap and hold the Start icon. Choose Event Viewer.**

    The Event Viewer appears.

2. **On the left, choose Event Viewer, Custom Views, Administrative Events.**

    It may take a while, but eventually you see a list of notable events like the one in Figure 3-1.

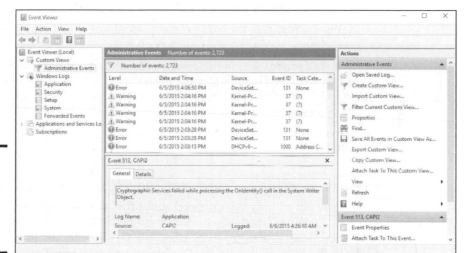

Figure 3-1: Events are logged by various parts of Windows.

3. **Don't freak out.**

    Even the best-kept system (well, my production system anyway) boasts reams of scary-looking error messages — hundreds, if not thousands of them. That's normal. See Table 3-1 for a breakdown.

Table 3-1	Events and What They Mean
Event	*What Caused the Event*
Error	Significant problem, possibly including loss of data
Warning	Not necessarily significant, but might indicate that there's a problem brewing
Information	Just a program calling home to say it's okay

The Administrative Events log isn't the only one you can see; it's a distillation of the other event logs, with an emphasis on the kinds of things a mere human might want to see.

Other logs include the following:

+ **Application events:** Programs report on their problems.

+ **Security events:** They're called "audits" and show the results of a security action. Results can be either successful or failed depending on the event, such as when a user tries to log on.

+ **Setup events:** This primarily refers to domain controllers, which is something you don't need to worry about.

+ **System events:** Most of the errors and warnings you see in the Administrative Events log come from system events. They're reports from Windows system files about problems they've encountered. Almost all of them are self-healing.

+ **Forwarded events:** These are sent to this computer from other computers.

Events worthy — and not worthy — of viewing

Before you get all hot and bothered about the thousands of errors on your PC, look closely at the date and time field. There may be thousands of events listed, but those probably date back to the day you first installed the PC. Chances are good that you can see a handful of items every day — and most of the events are just repeats of the same error or warning. Most likely, they have little or no effect on the way you use Windows. An *error* to Windows should usually trigger a yawn and "Who cares?" from you.

For example, looking through my most recent Event Log, I see a bunch of error id 10010 generated by a source called DistributedCOM, telling me that the server didn't register with DCOM within the required timeout. Really and truly, no biggie. Fugeddaboutit.

That's exactly my advice. If you aren't experiencing problems, don't sweat what's in the Event Viewer. Even if you *are* experiencing problems, the Event Viewer may or may not be able to help you.

How can Event Viewer help? See the Event ID column? Make note of the ID number and look it up at www.eventid.net. They may be able to point you in the right direction or at least translate the event ID into something resembling plain English. Figure 3-2 shows the results when I went looking for event ID 10010 — the DCOM problem.

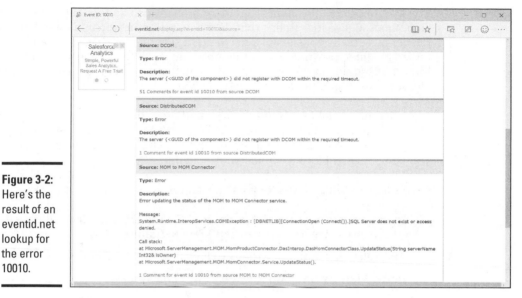

Figure 3-2:
Here's the result of an eventid.net lookup for the error 10010.

You can click at the bottom of each description to see comments left by someone else who's tackled the problem.

If you're trying to track down a specific problem, and you see an event that may relate to the problem, use Google to see whether you can find somebody else who's had the same problem. Event Viewer can also help you nail down network access problems because the Windows programs that control network communication spill a large amount of details into the Event Logs. Unfortunately, translating the logs into English can be a daunting task, but at least you may be able to tell where the problem occurs — even if you haven't a clue how to solve it.

Gauging System Reliability

Every Tom, Dick, 'n Hairy Windows routine leaves traces of itself in the Windows Event Log. Start a program, and the ignoble event gets logged. Stop it, and the Log gets updated. Install a program or a patch, and the Log knows all, sees all. Every security-related event you can imagine goes in the Log. Windows Services leave their traces, as do errors of many stripes. Things that should've happened but didn't get logged, as well as things that shouldn't have happened but did. Soup to nuts.

Book VIII
Chapter 3

Monitoring Windows

The Event Log contains items that mere humans can understand. Sometimes. It also logs things that only a propeller head could love. The Event Log actually consists of a mash-up of several files that are maintained by different Windows system programs in different ways. The Event Viewer, discussed in the preceding section, looks at the trees. The Reliability Monitor tries to put the forest in perspective.

The Windows Reliability Monitor slices and dices the Event Log, pulling out much information that relates to your PC's stability. It doesn't catch every-thing — more about that in a moment. But the stuff that it does find can give you instant insight into what ails your machine.

Here's how to bring up the Reliability Monitor:

1. **In the Ask me anything Cortana box, next to the Start icon, type** reli. **At the top of the list, click or tap View Reliability History.**

The Reliability Monitor springs to life, as shown in Figure 3-3.

2. **In the View By line, flip between Days and Weeks.**

Reliability Monitor goes back and forth between a detailed view and an overview.

Again, please don't freak out. There's a reason why Microsoft makes it hard to get to this report. It figures if you're sophisticated enough to find it, you can bear to see the cold, hard facts.

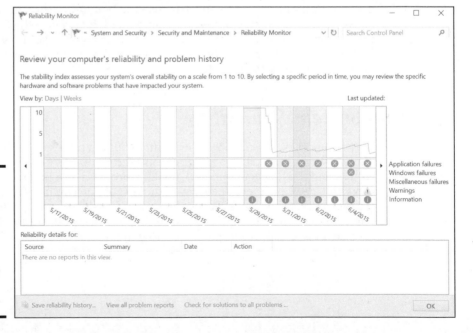

Figure 3-3:
When something goes out to lunch, it leaves a trace in the Reliability Monitor.

The top line in the monitor is supposed to give you a rating, from one to ten, of your system's stability. In fact, it doesn't do anything of the sort, but if you see the line drop like a wood barrel over Victoria Falls (as it has in Figure 3-3), something undoubtedly has gone bump in the night.

Your rating more or less reflects the number and severity of problematic Event Log events in four categories: Application, Windows failures, Miscellaneous failures, and Warnings. The Information icons (circled i's) generally represent updates to programs and drivers; if you installed a new printer driver, for example, there should be an Information icon on the day it was installed. Microsoft has a detailed list of the types of data being reported in its TechNet documentation at `http://bit.ly/HW3rSF`. Here's what they say:

Since you can see all of the activity on a single date in one report, you can make informed decisions about how to troubleshoot. For example, if frequent application failures are reported beginning on the same date that memory failures appear in the Hardware section, you can replace the faulty memory as a first step. If the application failures stop, they may have been a result of problems accessing the memory. If application failures continue, repairing their installations would be the next step.

If you tap or click a day (or a week), the box at the bottom shows you the corresponding entries in your Windows Event Log. Many events at the bottom have a more detailed explanation, which you can see by tapping/clicking the View Technical Details link.

If you click the View all problem reports link at the bottom of the screen, you get a summary like one shown in Figure 3-4.

The Reliability Monitor isn't meant to provide a comprehensive list of all the bad things that have happened to your PC, and in that respect, it certainly meets its design goals. It isn't much of a stability tracker, either. The one-to-ten rating uses a trailing average of daily scores where more recent scores have greater weight than old ones, but in my experience, the line doesn't track reality: My system can bounce like a Willy's in four-wheel drive, and it doesn't affect the rating; conversely, my system can be purring like a cat while my rating score goes to the dogs.

The real value of the Reliability Monitor lies in showing you a time sequence of key events — connecting the temporal dots so you may be able to discern a cause and effect. For example, if you suddenly start seeing blue screens repeatedly, check the Reliability Monitor to see whether something untoward has happened to your system. Installing a new driver, say, can make your system unstable, and the Reliability Monitor can readily show you when it was installed. If you see your rating tumble on the same day that a driver update got installed, something's fishy, and you may be able to readily identify the scaly culprit.

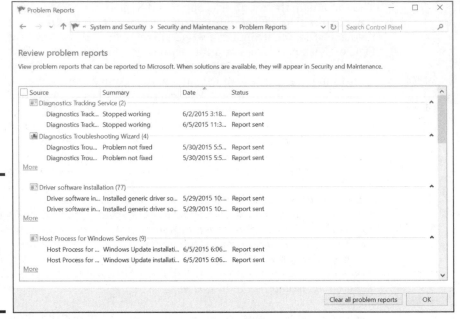

Figure 3-4:
Here, you
can find
the key
deleterious
events and
what they
mean.

The proverbial bottom line: The Reliability Monitor doesn't keep track of everything, and some of it is a bit deceptive, but it can provide some worthwhile information when Windows starts kicking. The Reliability Monitor is well worth adding to your Win bag of tricks.

Other performance monitors

Windows has two other monitors — *perfmon,* the Performance Monitor, and *resmon,* the Resources Monitor — that largely have been rendered obsolete because of the new (and very cool!) Task Manager. I talk about Task Manager in Chapter 5 of this minibook. If you really want to see either perfmon or resmon in

action, type the appropriate name on the Start screen and then tap or click the only app that appears.

But I think you're going to like the new Task Manager much better.

Chapter 4: Using System Tools

In This Chapter

✔ **Unveiling the super Task Manager**

✔ **Installing a new hard drive**

✔ **Running Hyper-V**

***W**indows abounds with tools that can help you do everything from taking out the dog to making the perfect espresso — at least, if your computer runs hot. In this chapter, I step you through three specific tools that can come in very handy:*

✦ The new-in-Windows-8, better-in-Windows-10 greatly improved and expanded *Task Manager* has turned into the Swiss Army knife of Windows applications. In Windows 7, you had to bring up, navigate to, and download and/or install a half dozen different tools to even come close to what the Win10 Task Manager does right out of the box. In earlier versions of Windows, many of the tools existed only in vestigial form.

✦ Windows includes all the tools you need to install a new hard drive, and the steps are easier than you think. All it takes is a trip to the *Disk Management* application. In this chapter, I show you how.

✦ Finally, I have a bonus section on the virtual machine generator (*Hyper-V*) that ships with Windows 10 Pro only. (Sorry, if you have Windows 10 Home, you don't get it.) A *virtual machine* is a make-believe, fully contained PC that runs inside your regular PC. You can use it to run Windows XP programs, for example, without setting up a dual boot on your Windows 10 system. You can also use a VM to check out new tricks or try some different Windows settings, without gumming up your working machine. Hyper-V works like a treat, if you know how to treat it.

Tasking Task Manager

Windows has a secret command post that you can get to if you know the right handshake, uh, key combination. Whatever. The key combination (or tap sequence) works all the time, unless Windows is seriously out to lunch.

Task Manager can handle any of these jobs:

✦ **Kill a program.** That comes in very handy if, say, Spartan freezes and you can't get it to do anything. Doesn't matter if you're trying to kill a Windows (formerly Universal, formerly Metro) app or an old-fashioned Windows Desktop app. Either way, one trip to Task Manager and *zap!*

Windows tries to shut down the application without destroying any data. If it's successful, the application disappears from the list. If it isn't successful, it presents you with the option of summarily zapping the application (called End Now to the less imaginative) or simply ignoring it and allowing it to go its merry way.

✦ **Switch to any program.** This is convenient if you find yourself stuck somewhere — in a game, say, that doesn't "let go" — and you want to jump over to a different application. You can easily go to a Windows app or Windows desktop program.

✦ **See which processes are hogging your CPU.** There's a bouncing list of program pieces — called *processes* — and an up-to-the-second ranking of how much computer time each one's taking. That list is invaluable if your PC is working like a slug, and you can't figure out which program is hogging the processor.

✦ **See which processes take up most of your memory, use your disk, or gab over the network.** Sometimes, it's hard to figure out which program's at fault. Task Manager knows all, sees all, and tells all.

✦ **Get running graphs of CPU, memory, disk, or network usage.** They're cool and informative, and may even help you decide whether you need to buy more memory.

✦ **See which tiled Windows Store apps use the most resources over a specified period of time.** Did the Camera take up the most time on your PC in the past month? Pinball?

✦ **Turn off auto-starting programs.** This used to be a huge headache, but now it's surprisingly easy. The simple fact is that almost everybody has automatically starting programs that take up boot time, add to your system overhead, cause aggravation, and may even be dangerous. Task Manager shows you major programs that start automatically and gives you the option to disable the programs.

✦ **Send a message to the other users on your PC.** The message shows up on the lock screen when you log off.

✦ **Force Task Manager to stay on top of all other windows.** This includes "immersive" full-screen windows.

Who da man?

Here's how to bring out the full glory of the Swiss Army knife version of Windows Task Manager:

1a. ***If you have a keyboard,* press Ctrl+Alt+Delete; tap or click the Task Manager link in the screen that appears. Or right-click in the lower-left corner of the screen, and choose Task Manager.**

1b. ***If you don't have a keyboard,* in the Search box, type task, and at the top of Cortana's list, tap or click Task Manager.**

In either case, the Task Manager appears with a list of all running applications (see Figure 4-1). (You may need to click or tap More Details at the bottom to get the full list.) Notably, the list includes all the running tiled apps, as well as all the running desktop programs.

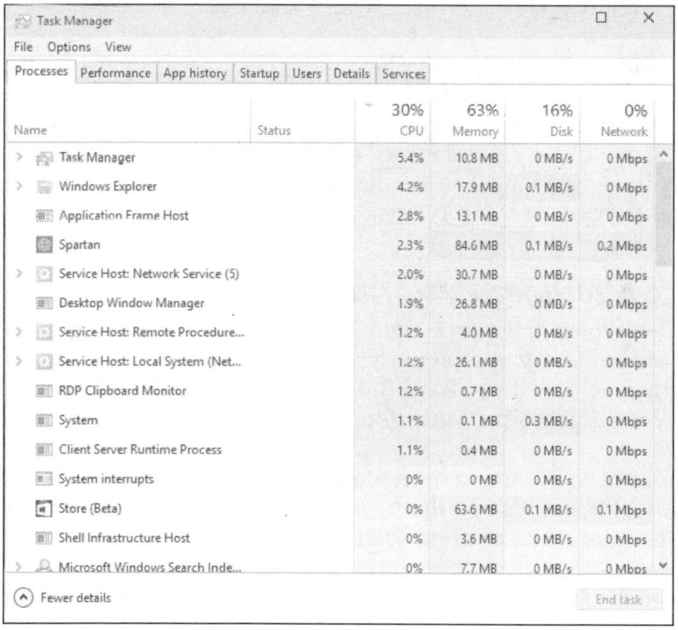

Name	Status	30% CPU	63% Memory	16% Disk	0% Network
Task Manager		5.4%	10.8 MB	0 MB/s	0 Mbps
Windows Explorer		4.2%	17.9 MB	0.1 MB/s	0 Mbps
Application Frame Host		2.8%	13.1 MB	0 MB/s	0 Mbps
Spartan		2.3%	84.6 MB	0.1 MB/s	0.2 Mbps
Service Host: Network Service (5)		2.0%	30.7 MB	0 MB/s	0 Mbps
Desktop Window Manager		1.9%	26.8 MB	0 MB/s	0 Mbps
Service Host: Remote Procedure...		1.2%	4.0 MB	0 MB/s	0 Mbps
Service Host: Local System (Net...		1.2%	26.1 MB	0 MB/s	0 Mbps
RDP Clipboard Monitor		1.2%	0.7 MB	0 MB/s	0 Mbps
System		1.1%	0.1 MB	0.3 MB/s	0 Mbps
Client Server Runtime Process		1.1%	0.4 MB	0 MB/s	0 Mbps
System interrupts		0%	0 MB	0 MB/s	0 Mbps
Store (Beta)		0%	63.6 MB	0.1 MB/s	0.1 Mbps
Shell Infrastructure Host		0%	3.6 MB	0 MB/s	0 Mbps
Microsoft Windows Search Inde...		0%	7.7 MB	0 MB/s	0 Mbps

Figure 4-1: Windows Task Manager lets you control running programs.

Book VIII Chapter 4

Using System Tools

2. **To kill one of your running programs, tap or click it and then tap or click End Task.**

The program may continue for a minute or two — some programs hold on tenaciously — but in the end, almost every program succumbs to the preemptive force.

Task Manager Processes

On the Processes tab, Task Manager groups running programs depending on the type of program:

✦ **Apps** are just regular, everyday programs. They're ones you started or ones that are set up to start automatically. (You may think that "apps" means "Windows Desktop apps" or "Universal apps" — but no. These are just programs, of any stripe — whatever happens to be running.)

✦ **Background processes** keep the pieces of your programs and drivers working.

✦ **Windows processes** are similar to background processes, except they're parts of Windows itself.

You can tap or click a column heading (such as CPU, Memory, Disk, or Network), and Task Manager sorts on that particular value. To update the report, choose View, Refresh Now.

As you start new programs, they appear on the Apps list, and any background programs that they bring along appear on the Background processes list. Universal apps, in particular, go to sleep when they aren't being used, so they drop off the Task Manager list. One glance at the Processes tab should give you a good idea if any programs are hogging your machine — for CPU processor cycles, memory, disk access, or tying up the network.

Task Manager Performance

The Performance tab (see Figure 4-2) gives you running graphs of CPU usage, allocated memory, disk activity, and the volume of data running into and out of your machine. If you have Bluetooth turned on, it'll also show you activity over your Bluetooth connection.

If you want to see much more detailed information — including utilization of each of the cores of a multi-core CPU — tap or click the Open Resource Monitor link at the bottom. See Figure 4-3.

Personally, I keep the Resource Monitor scrunched down and running on my desktop all the time, as in Figure 4-4. It tells me about my current sorry state of affairs at a glance.

Resource Monitor is my go-to app when anything starts acting wonky. Which is not all that uncommon in Windows, eh?

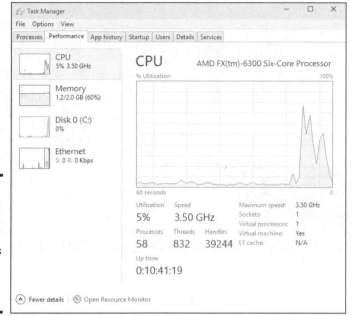

Figure 4-2:
Keep tabs
on the
four key
components
of your PC's
perfor-
mance.

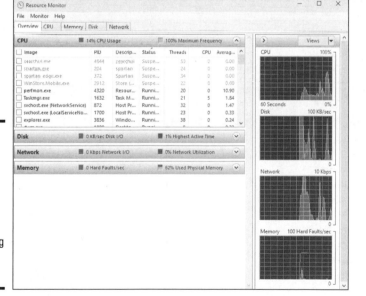

Figure 4-3:
The
Resource
Monitor
tells you at
a glance
what's
going wrong
with your
machine.

**Book VIII
Chapter 4**

Using System Tools

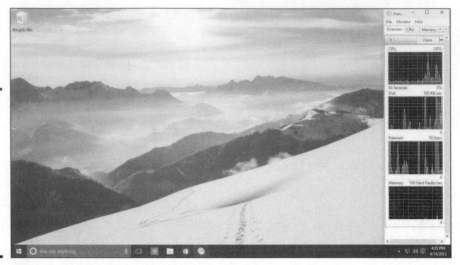

Figure 4-4: You can dock the Resource Monitor on your screen and refer to it constantly. I do.

Task Manager App History

The App History tab (see Figure 4-5) keeps a cumulative count of all the time you've spent on each of the various tiled Universal apps from the Windows Store. Tap or click a column header to sort.

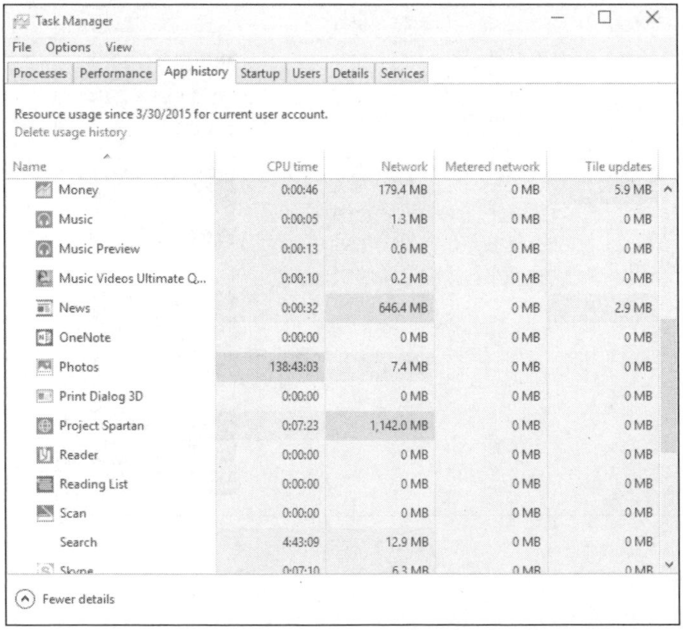

Name	CPU time	Network	Metered network	Tile updates
Money	0:00:46	179.4 MB	0 MB	5.9 MB
Music	0:00:05	1.3 MB	0 MB	0 MB
Music Preview	0:00:13	0.6 MB	0 MB	0 MB
Music Videos Ultimate Q...	0:00:10	0.2 MB	0 MB	0 MB
News	0:00:32	646.4 MB	0 MB	2.9 MB
OneNote	0:00:00	0 MB	0 MB	0 MB
Photos	138:43:03	7.4 MB	0 MB	0 MB
Print Dialog 3D	0:00:00	0 MB	0 MB	0 MB
Project Spartan	0:07:23	1,142.0 MB	0 MB	0 MB
Reader	0:00:00	0 MB	0 MB	0 MB
Reading List	0:00:00	0 MB	0 MB	0 MB
Scan	0:00:00	0 MB	0 MB	0 MB
Search	4:43:09	12.9 MB	0 MB	0 MB
Skype	0:07:10	6.3 MB	0 MB	0 MB

Figure 4-5: A comprehensive list of all the time you've spent playing, er, using each of the Universal (Metro) apps.

Task Manager Startup and Autoruns

No doubt you know that Windows automatically runs certain programs every time you start it and that those programs can prove, uh, cantankerous at times. The Startup tab, as shown in Figure 4-6, represents a giant step forward for Windows usability. It shows you all the programs that are started automatically each time you log on to Windows.

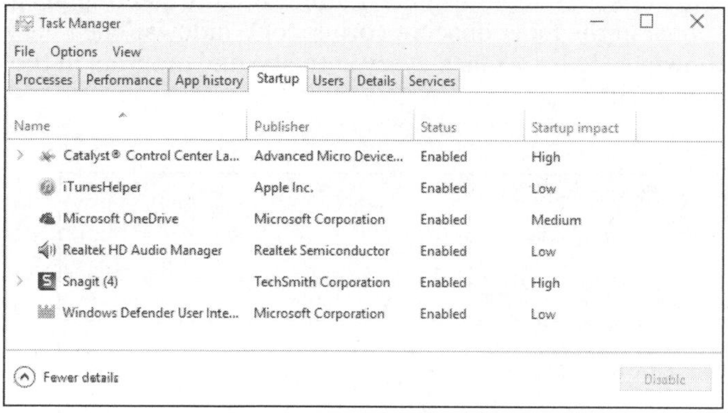

Figure 4-6:
A subset of those cycle-stealing auto-startup programs.

If you want to disable an autorunning program, tap or click the program, choose Disable, and then reboot Windows.

The Task Manager Startup tab shows you the application programs, their helper programs, and sometimes problematic programs that use well-known tricks to run every time Windows starts. Unfortunately, really bad programs frequently find ways to squirrel themselves away, so they don't appear on this list.

Microsoft distributes an Autoruns program that digs in to every nook and cranny of Windows, ferreting out autorunning programs — even Windows programs.

Autoruns started as a free product from the small Sysinternals company and owes its existence to Mark Russinovich (now a celebrated novelist) and Bryce Cogswell, two of the most knowledgeable Windows folks on the planet. In July 2006, Microsoft bought Sysinternals. Mark became a Microsoft Demigod, er, Fellow. Microsoft promised that all the free Sysinternals products would remain free. And wonder of wonders, that's exactly what happened.

**Book VIII
Chapter 4**

Using System Tools

To get Autoruns working, download it as a zip file from `http://technet.microsoft.com/en-us/sysinternals/bb963902.aspx` and extract the zip file. Autoruns.exe is the program you want. Tap or double-click to run it; no installation is required.

After Autoruns is working on your computer, the following tips can help you start using the program:

✦ **Autoruns lists an enormous number of auto-starting programs.** Some appear in the most obscure corners of Windows. The Everything list shown in Figure 4-7 lists every auto-starting program in the order they're run.

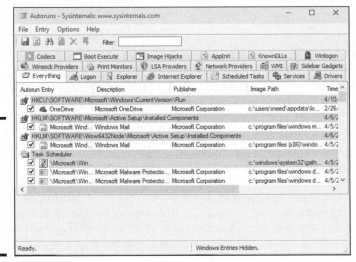

Figure 4-7: Autoruns shows you every program that starts auto-matically.

✦ **Autoruns has many options.** You can get a good overview on the Microsoft Ask the Performance Team blog, `http://blogs.technet.com/b/askperf/archive/2009/02/10/who-s-that-hiding-in-my-windows.aspx`. The one I use most is the ability to hide all the auto-starting Microsoft programs. It's easy. Choose Options, Filter Options, and then select the Hide Microsoft Entries box. The result is a clean list of all the foreign stuff being launched automatically by Windows.

✦ **Autoruns can suspend an auto-starting program.** To do so, deselect the box to the left of the program and reboot Windows. If you zap an auto-starting program and your computer doesn't work right, run Autoruns again and select the box. Easy.

Of course, you shouldn't disable an auto-starting program just because it looks superfluous, or even because you figure it contributes to global warming or slow startups, whichever comes first. As a general rule, if you don't know *exactly* what an auto-starting program does, don't touch it. It's not nice to fool with the support for those tiled apps, in particular.

On the other hand, if you concentrate on auto-starting programs that don't come from Microsoft, you may find a few things that you don't want or need — items that deserve to get consigned to the bit bucket.

Which programs deserve to die? Any that provided services you don't want. They go by various names, which change from time to time. Look for the Apple update checker, any utilities you no longer need or want, and perhaps the sync routines for cloud data services you no longer use. I've seen leftovers of antivirus programs that had been terminated with extreme prejudice long ago, game program helpers, communication tools for messaging systems long forgotten, and much more.

Task Manager Users

If you're using an administrator account, the Users tab lets you look at what's happening with every person who's currently logged on to your computer, as shown in Figure 4-8.

Task Manager		5%	60%	0%	0%
File Options View					
Processes Performance App history Startup **Users** Details Services					
User	Status	CPU	Memory	Disk	Network
⌄ ineedawindowsliveid@live.c...		2.6%	401.7 MB	0 MB/s	0 Mbps
Adobe® Flash® Player Uti...		0%	2.0 MB	0 MB/s	0 Mbps
Application Frame Host		0%	14.9 MB	0 MB/s	0 Mbps
Browser_Broker		0%	2.4 MB	0 MB/s	0 Mbps
Client Server Runtime Proc...		0%	0.4 MB	0 MB/s	0 Mbps
Desktop Window Manager		0%	26.8 MB	0 MB/s	0 Mbps
Host container for Unistac...		0%	0.4 MB	0 MB/s	0 Mbps
Host Process for Setting Sy...		0%	4.1 MB	0 MB/s	0 Mbps
Host Process for Windows ...		0%	1.5 MB	0 MB/s	0 Mbps
InstallAgent		0%	1.0 MB	0 MB/s	0 Mbps
LicenseManager		0%	1.8 MB	0 MB/s	0 Mbps
Microsoft OneDrive (32 bit)		0%	2.3 MB	0 MB/s	0 Mbps
Microsoft Web Cache		0%	14.0 MB	0 MB/s	0 Mbps
Project Spartan		0%	42.2 MB	0 MB/s	0 Mbps
Project Spartan		0%	94.7 MB	0 MB/s	0 Mbps
Project Spartan		0%	14.8 MB	0 MB/s	0 Mbps
RDP Clipboard Monitor		0%	0.7 MB	0 MB/s	0 Mbps
⌃ Fewer details					Disconnect

Figure 4-8:
See what other users are doing right now.

Book VIII
Chapter 4

Using System Tools

Tap or click the wedge to the left of the user's name, and you see a full list of processes.

Task Manager Details and Services

If you used Task Manager in Windows 7 or earlier, you've seen this version, shown in Figure 4-9. The Details tab shows all the running processes, regardless of which user is attached to the process.

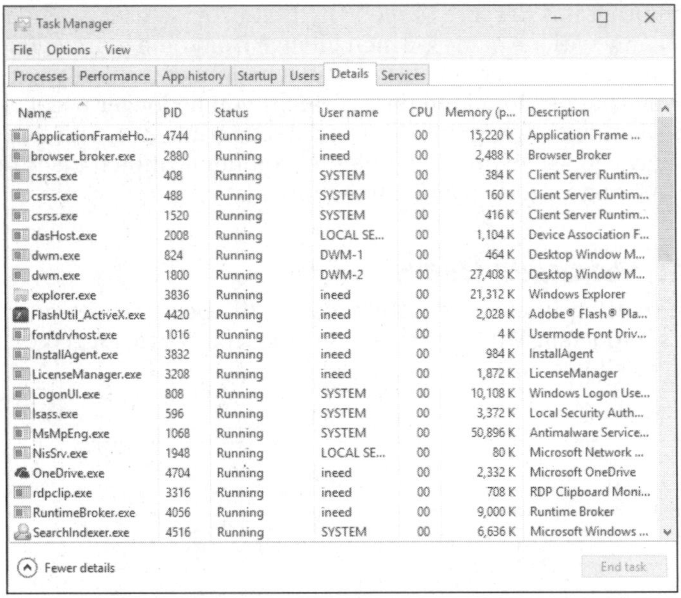

Figure 4-9:
All the details about every process appear here.

The Services tab, similarly, shows all the Windows services that have been started. Once in a blue moon, you may find a Windows error message that some Windows service or another (say, the printer service, or some sort of networking service) isn't running. This tab is where you can tell whether the service is really running.

Installing a Second Hard Drive

You probably know how hard it is to install an external hard drive in a Windows 10 PC. Basically, you turn off the computer, plug the USB or eSATA cable into your computer, turn it on . . . and you're finished.

Yes, external hard drive manufacturers have fancy software. No, you don't want it. Windows knows all the tricks. If you install one additional hard drive, internal or external, you can set up File History (see Book VIII, Chapter 1). Install two additional drives, internal or external, and you can turn on Storage Spaces (see Book VII, Chapter 4). None of the Windows programs need or want whatever programs the hard drive manufacturer offers.

Installing a second *internal* hard drive into a PC that's made to take two or more hard drives is only a little bit more complex than plugging an external drive into your USB port. Almost all desktop PCs can handle more than one internal hard drive. Some laptops can, too.

Here's how to do it:

1. **Turn off your PC. Crack open the case, put in the new hard drive, attach the cables, and secure the drive, probably with screws. Close the case. Turn on the power, and log in to Windows.**

   If you need help, the manufacturer's website has instructions. Adding the physical drive inside the computer case is really very simple — even if you've never seen the inside of your computer.

2. **Right-click in the lower-left corner of the screen, and choose Disk Management.**

   The Disk Management dialog box appears, as shown in Figure 4-10.

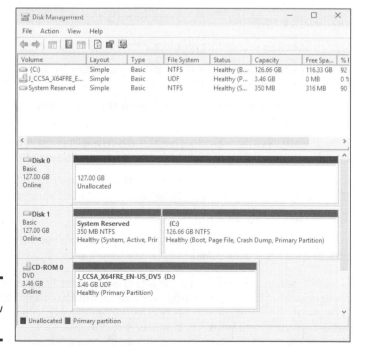

Figure 4-10:
Add the new drive here.

**Book VIII
Chapter 4**

Using System Tools

3. **Scroll down the list, and find your new drive, probably marked Unallocated.**

   In Figure 4-10, the new drive is identified as Disk 0.

4. **On the right, in the Unallocated area, tap and hold or right-click, and choose New Simple Volume.**

   The New Simple Volume wizard appears, as shown in Figure 4-11.

Figure 4-11: The wizard takes you through all the steps.

5. **Tap or click Next.**

   You're asked to specify a volume size.

6. **Leave the numbers just as they are — you want to use the whole drive — and tap or click Next.**

   The wizard asks you to specify a drive letter. `D:` is most common, unless you already have a D: drive.

7. **If you really, really want to give the drive a different letter, go ahead and do so (most people should leave it at `D:`). Tap or click Next.**

   The wizard wants to know whether you want to use something other than the NTFS file system, or to set a different allocation unit. You don't.

8. **Tap or click Next; then tap or click Finish.**

   Windows whirs and clunks, and when it's finished, you have a spanking new drive, ready to be used.

If you have three or more drives in or attached to your PC, consider setting up Storage Spaces. It's a remarkable piece of technology that'll keep redundant copies of all your data and protect you from catastrophic failure of any of your data drives. See Book VII, Chapter 4 for details.

Changing your C: drive

Whoa nelly! If you've never seen a Windows 10 PC running an SSD (Solid State Drive) as the system drive, you better nail down the door and shore up the, uh, windows. Changing your C: drive from a run-of-the-mill rotating platter to a fast, shiny new Solid State Drive can make everything work so much faster. Really.

Unfortunately, getting from an HDD (hard disk drive) C: to an SSD C: ain't exactly 1-2-3.

Part of the problem is the mechanics of transferring your Windows 10 system from an HDD to an SSD: You need to create a copy (not exactly a clone) that'll boot Windows. Part of the problem is moving all the extra junk off the C: drive, so the SSD isn't swamped with all the flotsam and jetsam you've come to know and love in Windows.

Most of the drive cloning/backup/restore techniques developed over the past decade work when you want to move from a smaller drive to a bigger one. However, replacing your HDD C: drive with an SSD C: drive almost always involves going from a larger drive to a smaller one.

The website LifeHacker has an excellent rundown of the steps you need to take to get your old hard drive removed and have everything copied over to your new SSD, using a backup program called EaseUS Todo Backup Free. It's not a simple process. Check out `www.lifehacker.com/5837543/how-to-migrate-to-a-solid+state-drive-without-reinstalling-windows`.

Running a Virtual Machine

At its heart, a virtual machine (or VM) is a sleight of hand. A parlor trick. You set up a "machine" inside Windows that isn't really a machine; it's a program. Then you stick other programs inside the virtual machine. The programs think they're working inside a real machine, when they aren't — they're working inside another program.

Windows 10 Pro (and Enterprise) includes Hyper-V and all the ancillary software (drivers and such) you need to run a virtual machine inside Windows. If you only have the "regular" version of Windows 10, you need to look elsewhere. (Hint: Use Google, and find a copy of VirtualBox.)

In addition, to get the Hyper-V program going, you must be running the 64-bit version of Windows 10 Pro, with at least 2GB of memory. The hardware itself must be fairly up to date because it must support the *Second Level Address Translation (SLAT)* capability. You can find a good overview of testing for SLAT on the How-To Geek site, `www.howtogeek.com/73318/how-to-check-if-your-cpu-supports-second-level-address-translation-slat`.

Why would you want to use a VM? Many reasons:

✦ Suppose you have an old program that runs only under Windows XP or Windows 95 (or even DOS, for that matter). You set up a VM, install XP or 95 (or DOS) and then stick the old program inside the VM. The old program doesn't know any better — it's fat, dumb, and happy working inside of XP. But you're watching from the outside. You can interact with the old program, type inside it, click inside it, give it disk space to play with, or attach it to a network interface card. A fake ("virtual") one, of course, that works just like the real thing.

✦ You want to try a different operating system. Maybe you want to play with Linux for a while or take Windows Server 2012 for a ride. Or you get nostalgic for the days of Windows Me. Or Microsoft Bob. Set up a virtual machine for each of the operating systems, and install the operating system in the VM. Then close each VM and save it. When you want to play with one of the OSs, just crank up the right VM, and you're on your way.

✦ You need to isolate your "real" system while you try something that's tricky or experimental or potentially dangerous. If you have a VM that gets infected with a virus, the virus doesn't necessarily spread to your main machine. If you try a weird program inside a VM and it crashes, restarting the VM is much easier than restarting your PC, and if there are any bizarre side effects — say, weird Registry changes — they won't affect your main machine.

✦ I use VMs when I'm experimenting with hooking computers together. It's pretty easy to set up several VMs, one running XP, say, another with Win7, another with Win 8.1, and one more with Win10. Each of them thinks that it's connected to the other two. That way, I can test settings and figure out how to get them to communicate with each other.

Hyper-V is a complex product, worthy of a book unto itself. In this chapter, I just get you started and then point you to some sources of information that'll help you take full advantage of the product.

Here's how to turn on Hyper-V:

1. **On the Start screen, in the Search box, type** Hyper-V.

2. **Tap or click the Turn Windows Features On or Off link.**

   The Windows Features dialog box appears, as shown in Figure 4-12.

3. **Select the Hyper-V box and the two boxes below it, and then tap or click OK.**

   Windows installs two programs: the Hyper-V Manager and the Hyper-V Virtual Machine Connection.

4. **Reboot after the installation finishes.**

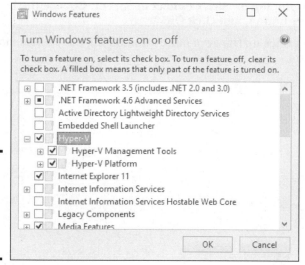

Figure 4-12:
Hyper-V
must be
turned on
before you
can use it.

When Windows comes back, you're ready to set up your first virtual
machine. Here's how:

1. **Tap or click Start, All Apps, and then tap or click Hyper-V
Management Tools and then Hyper-V Manager.**

Hyper-V brings up the rather intimidating screen shown in Figure 4-13.

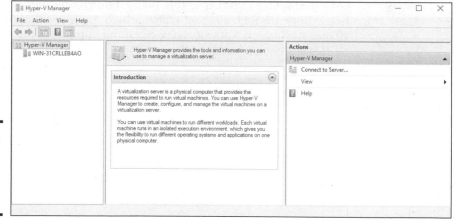

Figure 4-13:
Create
new virtual
machines
here.

2. **On the right, tap or click Connect to Server. Choose the Local Computer button, and click OK.**

   Hyper-V brings up the even-more-intimidating dialog box shown in Figure 4-14.

Figure 4-14:
Hyper-V
shows you
its main
options.

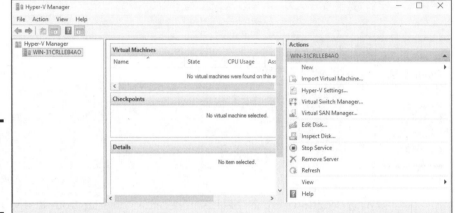

3. **On the right, tap or click Virtual Switch Manager.**

   The Virtual Switch Manager for your PC appears, as shown in Figure 4-15.

   I assume you want your new VM to be able to communicate with the outside world — for an Internet connection, if nothing else — and it's easiest to set up that connection before you create the VM. The connection is done through a *virtual switch,* which ties a connection inside the virtual machine to a physical device on the outside, in the real world.

Figure 4-15:
Set up
a virtual
switch now,
while it's
easy.

4. **In the drop-down list, choose External. On the right, click Create Virtual Switch.**

   You're asked to set up properties for the new virtual switch, as shown in Figure 4-16.

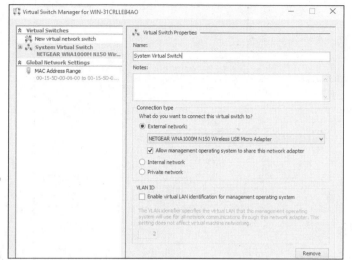

Figure 4-16:
Flesh out
the virtual
switch here.

5. **At the top, give the new virtual switch a name, and tap or click OK.**

   Chances are good that you want your VM to connect to a physical network adapter in the outside world, so leave the default selections the way they are.

   Hyper-V goes back to the Hyper-V Manager dialog box (refer to Figure 4-14).

6. **On the right, choose New, Virtual Machine.**

   The New Virtual Machine Wizard starts.

7. **Tap or click Next.**

   You're asked to specify a name and location for the VM, as shown in Figure 4-17.

8. **Type a name that will immediately tell you what you're running on this VM; if you need to move the location of the VM (remember the VM is a program, and it needs to store its files somewhere), change the location.**

9. **Tap or click Next. Choose Generation 1, and then click Next again.**

   VMs take up lots of room, and each time you take a "snapshot," you store away the entire status of the VM — including any data on the disks, copies of installed programs, and all settings.

   The wizard asks how much memory you want to assign for startup.

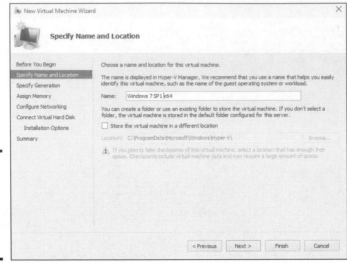

Figure 4-17:
Start by
giving the
VM a name
you will
recognize.

10. If you're going to run Windows 7, 8.1, or 10, set startup memory at 2048MB and select the Use Dynamic Memory for this Virtual Machine box.

Linux fans can get by with 512MB and no Dynamic Memory.

11. Tap or click Next.

You want enough memory so the VM doesn't start thrashing, but you don't want to specify too much in case you try to start many VMs at the same time.

Hyper-V wants to know whether you want to connect the VM to a network adapter. You set up the virtual connection already, so it's easy.

12. In the Connection box, choose the name of the connection that you created in Steps 3 and 4. Tap or click Next.

Hyper-V wants you to set up the virtual hard disk.

In case you're wondering, the virtual hard disks inside Hyper-V are quite different from the disk virtualization done in Windows Storage Spaces. Don't be confused. They work in completely different worlds.

13. Type a new name if you like, and tap or click Next.

The defaults here are fine.

You see the final key step in the wizard, which asks you how you want to install the operating system on the VM, as shown in Figure 4-18.

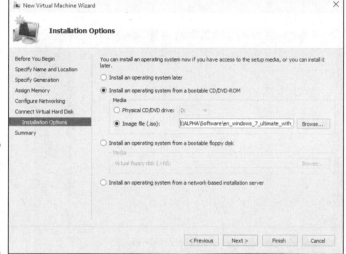

Figure 4-18:
Every VM needs an operating system. Pick yours here.

14. **If you have a Windows installation disk or file, select Install an Operating System from a Boot CD/DVD-ROM and tell Hyper-V where to find the Boot CD/DVD (or ISO file, if you have one).**

15. **Tap or click Next.**

    Hyper-V gives you a last look at your settings.

16. **Tap or click Finish.**

    Your new VM appears in the list of virtual machines shown on the main window, Figure 4-14.

To start the VM, tap or double-click it and, if necessary, choose Action, Start. You see something like the VM in Figure 4-19, which runs Windows 7 in a VM inside Windows 10.

The first thing you want to do with your new VM is add an Integration Services Setup Disk, so you can control the VM more readily. To do so, choose Action, Insert Integration Services Setup Disk.

That just barely scratches the surface of Hyper-V. For more info, start at Microsoft's Hyper-V support center at `http://technet.microsoft.com/en-us/windowsserver/dd448604`.

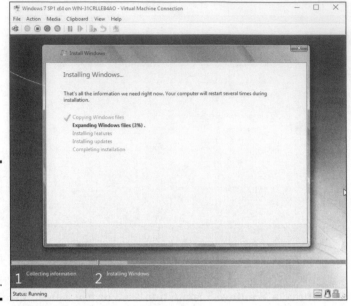

Figure 4-19:
A
Windows 7
virtual
machine
running
inside
Windows 10.

Book IX

Securing Windows 10

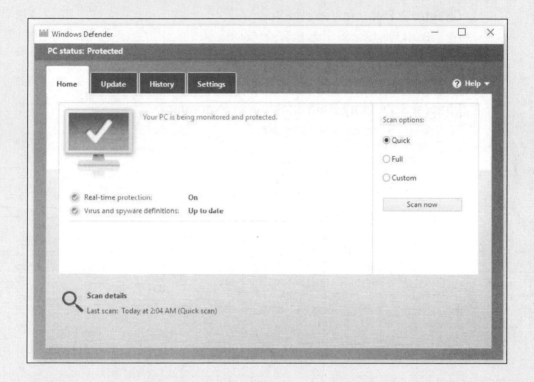

Think you have a virus? Take a deep breath, and look here: www.dummies.com/
extras/windows10aio/truthaboutviri.

Contents at a Glance

Chapter 1: Spies, Spams, Scams — They're Out to Get You

In This Chapter

✔ **Determining which hazards and hoaxes to look out for**

✔ **Keeping up to date with reliable sources**

✔ **Figuring out whether you're infected**

✔ **Protecting yourself**

*W*indows XP had more holes than a prairie-dog field. Vista was built on top of Windows XP, and the holes were hidden better. Windows 7 included truly innovative security capabilities; it represented the first really significant break from XP's lethargic approach to security.

Windows 8 included marginal security improvements to Windows itself, but better safety nets to keep you from shooting yourself in the foot. Also a fully functional, very capable antivirus program was built in. That's important. Windows 8.1's security improvements over Win8 were marginal, but at least we didn't go backwards.

Windows 10's biggest contribution to your security? Microsoft finally, finally got rid of Internet Explorer. "Got rid of" is a bit of an overstatement; IE is still around, sitting in a formaldehyde jar, ready to be used if you really need it for compatibility. But Microsoft Edge doesn't suffer from many of the IE deficiencies we've all encountered over the years.

The single best security recommendation I can give you: Don't run Internet Explorer. Ever. Funny, that's the same advice I've been handing out since *Windows XP All-In-One For Dummies.*

When you hear about a mass infection, it's invariably on XP computers. There's a reason why. It's getting harder and harder to take out Windows. Of course, the bad guys are getting smarter and smarter — and they have more money these days.

Targeted infections, though, are another story. There's lots of money to be made — and important governments to please — with very narrowly defined information-gathering techniques. Unless you work for a defense contractor or a Tibetan relief organization, you probably don't have much to worry about. But it doesn't hurt to keep your guard up.

In this chapter, I explain the source of real threats. (More details follow in the upcoming chapters in this minibook.) I bet it'll surprise you to find out that Adobe and Oracle let more bad guys into Windows boxes than Microsoft. I also take you outside the box, to show you the kinds of problems people face with their computer systems and to look at a few key solutions. And I look even farther outside the box, to mass password leaks — think Target, Home Depot, MasterCard, Visa, Yahoo, Facebook, LinkedIn, and the billion-plus compromised accounts (many with deciphered passwords, credit card numbers, and personal info) that are being sold every day like electronic trading cards.

Most of all, I want you to understand that (1) you shouldn't take a loaded gun, point it at your foot, aim carefully, and pull the trigger, and (2) if you're smart and can control your clicking finger, you don't need to spend a penny on malware protection.

Understanding the Hazards — and the Hoaxes

Many of the best-known Internet-borne scares in the past two decades — the Rustocks, Waledacs, Esthosts, Confickers, Mebroots, Bagles, Netskys, Melissas, ILOVEYOUs, Blasters and Slammers, and their ilk — work by using the programmability built in to the computer application itself or by taking advantage of Windows holes to inject themselves into unprotected machines (see Figure 1-1).

Fast-forward a dozen years, and the concepts have changed. The old threats are still there, but they've taken on a new twist: The scent of money, and sometimes political motivation, has made *cracking* (or breaking in to PCs for nefarious ends) far more sophisticated. What started as a bunch of miscreants playing programmer one-upmanship at your expense has turned into a profitable — sometimes highly profitable — business enterprise.

Where's the money? At least at this moment — and for the foreseeable future — the greatest profits are made by using botnets and phishing attacks. That's where you should expect the most sophisticated, most damnably difficult attacks. Unless you're running a nuclear reactor or an anti-government campaign, of course. You get to choose the government.

The primary infection vectors

How do people *really* get infected?

According to Microsoft's Security Intelligence Report 11, the single greatest security gap is the one between your ears. See Figure 1-2. (Pro tip: You can find the latest MS Security Intelligence Report at www.microsoft.com/sir. They're always intriguing.)

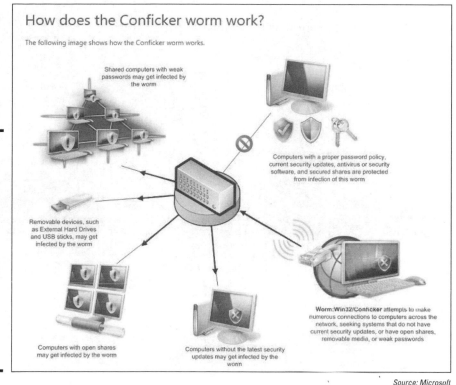

Figure 1-1:
The Conficker worm employed programmability built in to Windows or security holes that had been patched months earlier.

Source: Microsoft

Many years ago, the biggest PC threat came from newly discovered security holes: The bad guys use the holes before you get your machine patched, and you're toast. They traded 'em like baseball cards. Those holes still get lots of attention, especially in the press, but they aren't the leading cause of widespread infection. Not even close. A very large majority of infections happen when people get tricked into clicking something they shouldn't.

Narrow, targeted infections, though, tend to rely on previously unknown security holes. It's hard for the big boys to protect against that kind of attack. Little folks like you and me don't really stand a chance.

In the last couple of years, security holes in Windows have fallen by the wayside, when it comes to infecting Windows machines. Depending on whose statistics you read, something like 70 to 90 percent of all Windows infections in recent years came through Java, Flash, and Adobe Reader. You go to a malicious website; click something you shouldn't click; and Java, Flash, or a bad PDF file processed by Adobe Acrobat Reader jumps out and takes over your machine. Sometimes you don't need to click, especially if you're using older versions of Internet Explorer.

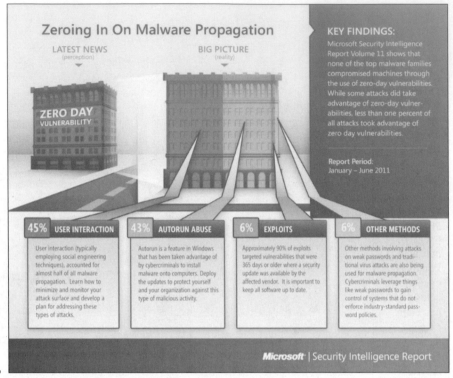

Source: Microsoft

Figure 1-2: Most infections happen when people don't think about what they're doing.

Zombies and botnets

Every month, Microsoft posts a new Malicious Software Removal Tool that scans PCs for malware and, in many cases, removes it. In a recent study, Microsoft reported that 62 percent of all PC systems that were found to have malicious software also had backdoors. That's a sobering figure.

A *backdoor* program breaks through the usual Windows security measures and allows a scumbag to take control of your computer over the Internet, effectively turning your machine into a zombie. The most sophisticated backdoors allow creeps to adapt (upgrade, if you will) the malicious software running on a subverted machine. And they do it by remote control.

Backdoors frequently arrive on your PC when you install a program you want, not realizing that the backdoor came along for the ride.

What's a buffer overflow?

If you've been following the progress of malware in general, and the beatings delivered to Windows in particular, you've no doubt run across the term *buffer overflow* or *buffer overrun*— a favorite tool in the arsenal of many virus writers. A buffer overflow may sound mysterious, but it is, at its heart, quite simple.

Programmers set aside small areas in their programs to transfer data from one program to another. Those places are buffers. A problem arises when too much data is put in a buffer (or if you look at it from the other direction, when the buffer is too small to hold all the data that's being put in it). You may think that having ten pounds of offal in a five-pound bag would make the program scream bloody murder, but many programs aren't smart enough to look, much less cry uncle and give up.

When too much data exists in the buffer, some of it can spill into the program itself. If the bad guy who's stuffing too much data into the buffer is very clever, he/she/it may be able to convince the program that the extra data isn't data but is instead another part of the program, waiting to be run. The worm sticks lots of data in a small space and ensures that the piece that flops out will perform whatever malicious deed the worm's creator wants. When the offal hits the fan, the program finds itself executing data that was stuffed into the buffer — running a program that was written by the worm's creator. That's how a buffer overrun can take control of your computer.

Every worm that uses a buffer-overrun security hole in Windows takes advantage of a stupid programming error inside Windows, but nowadays it's more common for the buffer overflows to happen in Flash or Java.

Less commonly, PCs acquire backdoors when they come down with some sort of infection: The ZeuS, Rustock, Waledac, TDL4/Alureon, Conficker, Mebroot, Mydoom, and Sobig worms installed backdoors. Many of the infections occur on PCs that haven't kept Java, Flash, or the Adobe Acrobat Reader up to date. The most common mechanism for infection is a *buffer overflow* (see the nearby "What's a buffer overflow?" sidebar).

An evildoer who controls one machine by way of a backdoor can't claim much street "cred." But someone who puts together a *botnet* — a collection of hundreds or thousands of PCs — can take his zombies to the bank:

✦ A botnet running a *keylogger* (a program that watches what you type and sporadically sends the data to the botnet's controller) can gather all sorts of valuable information. The single biggest problem facing those who gather and disseminate keylogger information? Bulk — the sheer volume of stolen information. How do you scan millions of characters of logged data and retrieve a bank account number or a password?

✦ Unscrupulous businesses hire botnet controllers to disseminate spam, "harvest" email addresses, and even direct coordinated distributed denial-of-service (DDoS) attacks against rivals' websites. (A *DDoS attack* guides thousands of PCs to go to a particular website simultaneously, blocking legitimate use.)

There's a fortune to be made in botnets. The Rustock botnet alone was responsible for somewhere between 10 and 30 *billion* pieces of spam per day. Spammers paid the Rustock handlers, either directly or on commission, based on the number of referrals.

The most successful botnets run as *rootkits,* programs (or collections of programs) that operate deep inside Windows, concealing files and making it extremely difficult to detect their presence.

You probably first heard about rootkits in late 2005, when a couple of security researchers discovered that certain CDs from Sony BMG surreptitiously installed rootkits on computers: If you merely played the CD on your computer, the rootkit took hold. Several lawsuits later, Sony finally saw the error of its ways and vowed to stop distributing rootkits with its CDs. Nice guys. (The researchers, Mark Russinovich and Bryce Cogswell, were later hired by Microsoft.)

Microsoft deserves lots of credit for taking down botnets in innovative, lawyer-laden ways. In October 2010, 116 people were arrested worldwide for running fraudulent banking transactions, thanks to Microsoft's tracking abilities. When the folks of Microsoft went after the ZeuS botnet, they convinced a handful of companies whose logos were being used to propagate the botnet to go to court. The assembled group used the RICO laws — the racketeering laws in the United States — to get a takedown order. On March 23, 2012, U.S. Marshals took out two command centers — one in Illinois, the other in Pennsylvania — and effectively shut down ZeuS. Microsoft also led the efforts to take down the Waledac, Rustock, and Kelihos botnets.

That said, Microsoft has been roundly criticized by members of the security community for "hampering and even compromising a number of large international investigations in the United States, Europe, and Asia" while trying to dispense swift justice (`www.krebsonsecurity.com/2012/04/microsoft-responds-to-critics-over-botnet-bruhaha`).

Botnets on Windows 8 and Windows 8.1 aren't common, but somebody, someday, is going to figure out how to shoehorn them in.

What about Stuxnet?

Few computer topics have sucked in the mainstream press as thoroughly as the Stuxnet worm — the Windows-borne piece of malware that apparently took out several centrifuges in Iran's uranium enrichment facility.

Here's what I know for sure about Stuxnet: It's carried by Windows but doesn't do anything dastardly until it finds that it's connected to a specific kind of Siemens computer that's used for industrial automation. When it finds that it's connected to that specific kind of Siemens computer, it plants a rootkit on the computer that disrupts operation of whatever the computer's controlling. And that specific Siemens

computer controlled the centrifuges at Iran's enrichment plant.

The people who wrote Stuxnet are very, very adept at both Windows infection methods and Siemens computer programming. David Sanger, chief Washington correspondent for *The New York Times,* claims convincingly in his book *Confront and Conceal* (published by Crown) that Stuxnet originated as a collaboration between the U.S. National Security Agency and a secret Israeli military unit, and subsequent revelations have confirmed that's almost undoubtedly the case.

Phishing

Do you think that message from Wells Fargo (or eBay, the IRS, PayPal, Citibank, a smaller regional bank, Visa, MasterCard, or whatever) asking to verify your account password (Social Security number, account number, address, telephone number, mother's maiden name, or whatever) looks official? Think again.

Did you get a message from someone on eBay saying that you had better pay for the computer you bought or else he'll report you? Gotcha. Perhaps a notification that you have received an online greeting card from a family member — and when you try to retrieve it, you have to join the greeting card site and enter a credit card number? Gotcha again.

Phishing — sending email that attempts to extract personal information from you, usually by using a bogus website — has in many cases reached levels of sophistication that exceed the standards of the financial institutions themselves. Some phishing messages, such as the bogus message in Figure 1-3, warn you about the evils of phishing, in an attempt to persuade you to send your account number and password to a scammer in Kazbukistan (or New York).

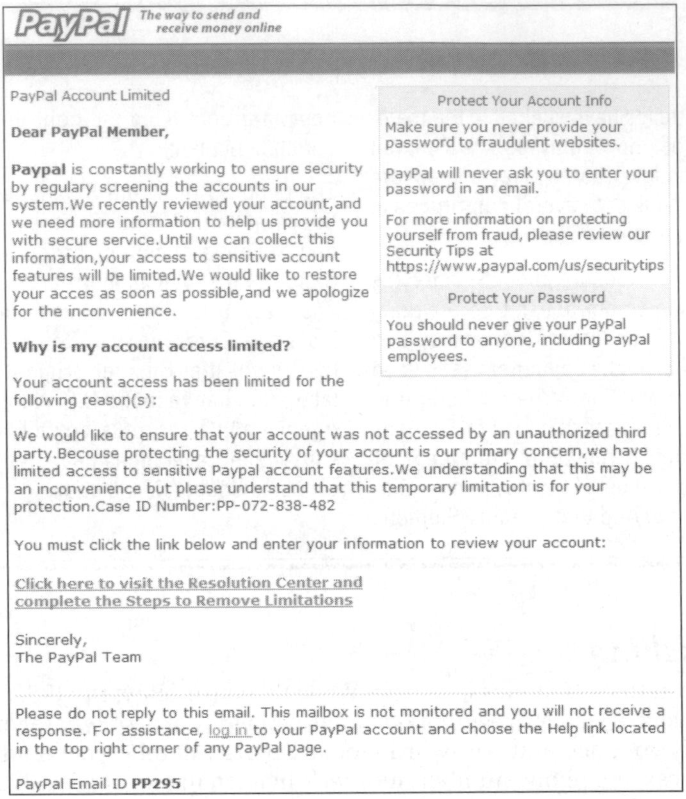
PayPal The way to send and receive money online

PayPal Account Limited

Dear PayPal Member,

Paypal is constantly working to ensure security by regulary screening the accounts in our system.We recently reviewed your account,and we need more information to help us provide you with secure service.Until we can collect this information,your access to sensitive account features will be limited.We would like to restore your acces as soon as possible,and we apologize for the inconvenience.

Why is my account access limited?

Your account access has been limited for the following reason(s):

We would like to ensure that your account was not accessed by an unauthorized third party.Becouse protecting the security of your account is our primary concern,we have limited access to sensitive Paypal account features.We understanding that this may be an inconvenience but please understand that this temporary limitation is for your protection.Case ID Number:PP-072-838-482

You must click the link below and enter your information to review your account:

Click here to visit the Resolution Center and complete the Steps to Remove Limitations

Sincerely,
The PayPal Team

Protect Your Account Info

Make sure you never provide your password to fraudulent websites.

PayPal will never ask you to enter your password in an email.

For more information on protecting yourself from fraud, please review our Security Tips at https://www.paypal.com/us/securitytips

Protect Your Password

You should never give your PayPal password to anyone, including PayPal employees.

Please do not reply to this email. This mailbox is not monitored and you will not receive a response. For assistance, log in to your PayPal account and choose the Help link located in the top right corner of any PayPal page.

PayPal Email ID **PP295**

Figure 1-3: If you click the link, you open a page that looks much like the PayPal page, and any information you enter is sent to a scammer.

Here's how phishing works:

1. A scammer, often using a fake name and a stolen credit card, sets up a website.

   Usually it's quite a professional-looking site — in some cases, indistinguishable from the authentic site.

2. The website asks for personal information — most commonly, your account number and password or the PIN for your ATM card. See Figure 1-4 for an example.

3. The scammer turns spammer and sends hundreds of thousands of bogus messages.

   The messages include a clickable link to the fake website and a plausible story about how you must go to the website, log on, and do something to avoid dire consequences. The From address on the messages is spoofed so that the message appears to come from the company in question.

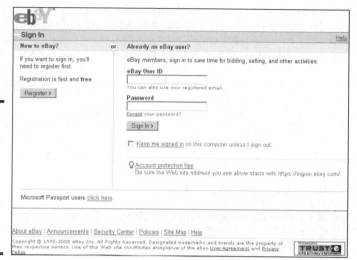

Figure 1-4:
This is a
fake eBay
sign-on
site. Can
you tell the
difference
from the
original?

The message usually includes official logos — many even include links to the real website, even though they encourage you to click through to the fake site.

4. A small percentage of the recipients of the spam email open it and click through to the fake site.

5. If they enter their information, it's sent directly to the scammer.

6. The scammer watches incoming traffic from the fake website, gathers the information typed by gullible people, and uses it quickly — typically, by logging on to the bank's website and attempting a transfer or by burning a fake ATM card and using the PIN.

7. Within a day or two — or sometimes just hours — the website is shut down, and everything disappears into thin ether.

Phishing has become hugely popular because of the sheer numbers involved. Say a scammer sends 1 million email messages advising Wells Fargo customers to log on to their accounts. Only a small fraction of all the people who receive the phishing message will be Wells Fargo customers, but if the hit rate is just 1 percent, that's 10,000 customers.

Most of the Wells Fargo customers who receive the message are smart enough to ignore it. But a sizable percentage — maybe 10 percent, maybe just 1 percent — will click through. That's somewhere between 100 and 1,000 suckers, er, customers.

If half the people who click through provide their account details, the scammer gets 50 to 500 account numbers and passwords. If most of those arrive within a day of sending the phishing message, the scammer stands to make a pretty penny indeed — and she can disappear with hardly a trace.

I'm not talking about using your credit card online. Online credit card transactions are as safe as they are face to face — more so, actually, because if you use a U.S.-based credit card, you aren't liable for any loss caused by somebody snatching your card information or any other form of fraud. I use my credit cards online all the time. You should, too. (See "Using your credit card safely online," later in this chapter, for more information.)

Here's how to fight against phishing:

✦ **Use the latest versions of Edge, Firefox, or Chrome.** All three contain sophisticated — although not perfect — antiphishing features that warn you before you venture to a phishy site. See the warning in Figure 1-5.

Figure 1-5:
If enough people report a site as being dangerous, you see a warning like this one from Firefox.

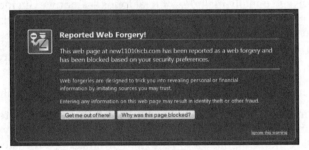

✦ **If you encounter a website that looks like it may be a phishing site, report it.** Use the tools in Edge, Firefox, or Chrome. Use all three, if you have a chance! Chrome and Firefox use the same malicious site database. To report a site, go to www.google.com/safebrowsing/report_phish/.

✦ **If you receive an email message that contains any links to the web, don't click them.** Nowadays, almost all messages with links to commercial sites are phishing come-ons. Financial institutions, in particular, don't send messages with links any more — and few other companies would dare. If you feel motivated to check out a dire message — for example, if it looks like somebody on eBay is planning to sue you for something you didn't do — open your favorite browser and type the address of the company by hand.

You can see which site a link *really* points to by hovering your mouse over the link. There's no tap equivalent just yet.

✦ **Never include personal information (for example, your address, Social Security or government id number, passport number, phone number, or bank account information) in an email message and send it.** Don't give out any of your personal information unless you manually log on to the company's website. Remember that unless you encrypt your email messages, they travel over the Internet in plain-text form. Anybody (or any government) that's "sniffing" the mail can see everything you've written. It's roughly analogous to sending a postcard, with the NSA as the addressee, and Google and Microsoft on the cc list.

✦ **If you receive a phishing message that may be new or different, check** www.millersmiles.co.uk **to see whether it's a well-known, uh, phish.** If you don't see your phish listed, submit a copy using the instructions at www.millersmiles.co.uk/submit.php. Hold on to the message for a while to see whether the authorities need a copy of the message header: If so, it'll send you instructions.

MillerSmiles (see Figure 1-6) has a wealth of information on phishing — more than 2 million samples of phishing messages, at last count — including an invaluable description of the steps you should take if you accidentally give your personal information to a phisher. See www.millersmiles.co.uk/identitytheft/oah-6.htm.

419 scams

Greetings,

I am writing this letter to you in good faith and I hope my contact with you will transpire into a mutual relationship now and forever. I am Mrs. Omigod Mugambi, wife of the late General Rufus Mugambi, former Director of Mines for the Dufus Diamond Dust Co Ltd of Central Eastern Lower Leone . . .

I'm sure you're smart enough to pass over email like that. At least, I hope so. It's an obvious setup for the classic 419 ("four one nine") scam — a scam so common that it has a widely accepted name, which derives from Nigerian Criminal Code Chapter 38, Article 419.

Much more sophisticated versions of the 419 scam are making the rounds today. The basic approach is to convince you to send money to someone, usually via Western Union. If you send the money, you'll never see it again, no matter how hard the sell or dire the threatened consequences.

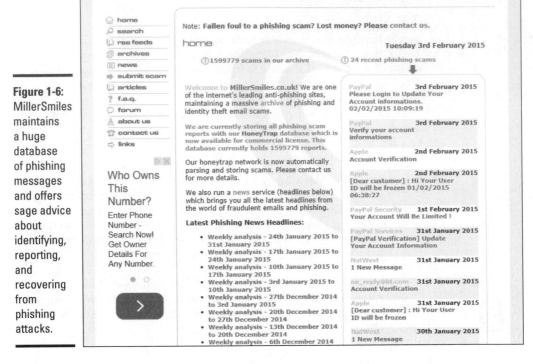

home
search
rss feeds
archives
news
submit scam
articles
f.a.q.
forum
about us
contact us
links

Who Owns This Number?
Enter Phone Number - Search Now! Get Owner Details For Any Number.

Note: Fallen foul to a phishing scam? Lost money? Please contact us.

home   Tuesday 3rd February 2015

1599779 scams in our archive   24 recent phishing scams

Welcome to MillerSmiles.co.uk! We are one of the internet's leading anti-phishing sites, maintaining a massive archive of phishing and identity theft email scams.

We are currently storing all phishing scam reports with our HoneyTrap database which is now available for commercial license. This database currently holds 1599779 reports.

Our honeytrap network is now automatically parsing and storing scams. Please contact us for more details.

We also run a news service (headlines below) which brings you all the latest headlines from the world of fraudulent emails and phishing.

Latest Phishing News Headlines:

- Weekly analysis – 24th January 2015 to 31st January 2015
- Weekly analysis – 17th January 2015 to 24th January 2015
- Weekly analysis – 10th January 2015 to 17th January 2015
- Weekly analysis – 3rd January 2015 to 10th January 2015
- Weekly analysis – 27th December 2014 to 3rd January 2015
- Weekly analysis – 20th December 2014 to 27th December 2014
- Weekly analysis – 13th December 2014 to 20th December 2014
- Weekly analysis – 6th December 2014

PayPal   3rd February 2015
Please Login to Update Your Account informations.
02/02/2015 10:09:19

PayPal   3rd February 2015
Verify your account informations

Apple   2nd February 2015
Account Verification

Apple   2nd February 2015
[Dear customer] : Hi Your User ID will be frozen 01/02/2015 06:38:27

PayPal Security   1st February 2015
Your Account Will Be Limited !

PayPal Services   31st January 2015
[PayPal Verification] Update Your Account Information

NatWest   31st January 2015
1 New Message

no_reply@bt.com   31st January 2015
Account Verification

Apple   31st January 2015
[Dear customer] : Hi Your User ID will be frozen

NatWest   30th January 2015
1 New Message

Figure 1-6: MillerSmiles maintains a huge database of phishing messages and offers sage advice about identifying, reporting, and recovering from phishing attacks.

There's a reason why everybody gets so much 419 scam email. It's a huge business. Some people reckon it's the third to fifth largest revenue-generating business in Nigeria. I have no way of verifying independently whether that's true, but certainly these folks are raking in an enormous amount of money. And they don't all work out of Nigeria: 419 scams are a significant source of foreign exchange in Benin, Sierra Leone, Ghana, Togo, Senegal, and Burkina Faso, plus just about anywhere else you can mention. Some even originate in the United States although, as you see shortly, there are big advantages to working out of small countries.

Here's one of the new variations of the old 419. It all starts when you place an ad that appears online. It doesn't really matter what you're selling, as long as it's physically large and valuable. It doesn't matter where you advertise — I've seen reports of this scam being played on Craigslist advertisers and major online sites, tiny nickel ad publishers, local newspapers, and anywhere else ads are placed.

The scammer sends you an email from a Gmail address. I got one recently that said, "I will like to know if this item is still available for sale?" I wrote back and said, yes, it is, and he'd be most welcome to come and look at it. He wrote back:

"Let me know the price in USD? I am OK with the item it looks like new in the photos I am from Liverpool U.K., i am sorry i will not be able to come for the viewing, i will arrange for the pickup after payment has been made, all documentation will be done by the shipper, so you don't have to worry about that. Thanks"

Three key points:

+ The scammer is using a Gmail address, which can't be traced with anything short of a court order.

+ He claims to be out of the country, which makes pursuing him very difficult.

+ He claims that he has a shipper who will pick up the item. The plot thickens.

Also, his grammar falls somewhere between atrocious and unintelligible. Unfortunately, that isn't a sure sign, but it's not bound to inspire confidence.

I wrote back and gave him a price, but I expressed concern about the shipper. He wrote that he would send the shipper from the U.K. for pickup and said, "I will be paying the PayPal charges from my account and i will be paying directly into your PayPal account without any delay, and i hope you have a PayPal account."

I gave him a dormant PayPal account, listing my address as that of the local police station. He wrote back quite quickly:

"I have just completed the Payment and i am sure you have received the confirmation from PayPal regarding the Payment. You can check your paypal email for confirmation of payment.a total of 25,982usd was sent, 24,728usd for the item and the extra 1,200usd for my shipper's charges, which you will be sending to the address below via western union" and then he gave me the name of someone in Devon, U.K. "You should send the money soon so that the Pick Up would be scheduled and you would know when the Pick Up would commence, make sure you're home. I advice you to check both your inbox or junk/spam folder for the payment confirmation message."

I then received a message that claimed to be from Service-Intl.PayPal.Com:

"The Transaction will appear as soon as the western union information is received from you,we have to follow this procedure due to some security reason. . . the Money was sent through the Service Option Secure Payment so that the transaction can be protected with adequate security measures for you to be able to receive your money. The Shipping

Company only accept payment through Western Union You have nothing to doubt about, You are safe and secured doing this transaction and your account will be credited immediately the western union receipt of *1,200USD* is received from you."

There's the hook. Of course, the message didn't come from PayPal, much less from `www.paypal.com`. I strung the scammer along for several days. Ultimately he threatened me with legal action, invoking PayPal and the FBI as antagonists, see Figure 1-7.

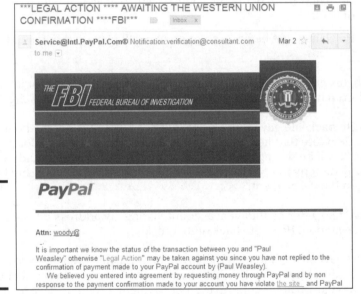

Figure 1-7: Oh me, oh my, he's going to send the FBI.

In the end, the scammer and his cohorts were quite sloppy. Most of the time when scammers send email from "PayPal," they use a virtual private network (VPN; see Book IX, Chapter 4) to make it look like the mail came from the United States. But on three separate occasions, the scammer I was conversing with forgot to turn on the VPN. Using a very simple technique, I traced all three messages back to one specific Internet service provider in Lagos, Nigeria.

So I had three scamming messages with identified IP addresses, the name of a large Internet service provider in Nigeria, and a compelling case for PayPal (to defend its name) and Western Union (which was being used as a drop) to follow up.

I sent copies of the messages to Western Union and PayPal. I got back form letters — it's unlikely that a human even read them. I wrote to the ISP, MTN Nigeria. They responded, but the upshot is disheartening:

"All our 3G network subscribers now sit behind a small number of IP addresses. This is done via a technology called network address translation (NAT). In essence, it means that 1 million subscribers may appear to the outside world as one subscriber because they are all using the same IP address."

So now you know why Nigerians love to conduct their scams over the Nigerian 3G network. No doubt MTN Nigeria could sift through its NAT logs and find out who was connected at precisely the right time, but tracing a specific email back to an individual would be difficult, if not impossible — and it would certainly require a court order.

If you know anybody who posts ads online, you may want to warn him.

I'm from Microsoft, and I'm here to help

This kind of scam really hurts me, personally, because I've made a career out of helping people with Microsoft problems.

Someone calls and says she's been referred by Microsoft to help with your Windows problem. She's very convincing. She says that she heard about your problem from a post you made online, or from your Internet service provider, or from a computer user group. She even gives a website as reference, a very convincing site that has the Microsoft Registered Partner logo.

You explain the problem to her. Then one of two things happens. Either she requests your 25-character Windows activation key or she asks for permission to connect to your computer, typically using Remote Assistance (see Book VII, Chapter 2).

If you let her onto your machine, heaven knows what she'll do. (Believe me, these guys are fast and convincing: It's like playing three-card Monte with a tech support guru.)

If you give her your activation key — or she looks up your validation key while she's controlling your PC — she'll pretend to refer to the "Microsoft registration database" (or something similar) and give you the bad news that your machine is all screwed up, and it's out of warranty, but she can fix it for a mere $189.

As proof positive that your machine's on its last legs, she'll probably show you the Event Viewer. As I mention in Book VIII, Chapter 4, the Event Viewer on a *normal* machine shows all sorts of scary warnings. And that Microsoft Registered Partner stuff? Anybody can become a Microsoft Registered Partner — it takes maybe two minutes, and all you need is a Microsoft account — a Hotmail, Live, or Outlook.com ID. Don't believe it? Go to `https://mspartner.microsoft.com/en/us/pages/membership/enroll.aspx` and fill out the forms.

The overwhelming con give-away — the big red flag — in all this: *Microsoft doesn't work that way.* Think about it. Microsoft isn't going to call you to solve your problems, unless you've received a very specific commitment from a very specific individual in the organization — a commitment that invariably comes only after repeated phone calls on your part, generally accompanied by elevation to lofty levels of the support organization on multiple continents, frequently in conjunction with high-decibel histrionics. Microsoft doesn't respond to random online requests for help by calling a customer. Sorry. Doesn't happen.

If you aren't sure whether you're being conned, ask the person on the other end of the line for your Microsoft Support Case *tracking numbe*r — every MS tech support interaction has a tracking number or Support ID. Then ask for a phone number and offer to call him back. Con artists won't leave trails.

If the con is being run from overseas — much more common in these days of nearly-free VoIP cold calling — your chances of nailing the perpetrator runs from extremely slim to none. So be overly suspicious of any "Microsoft Expert" who doesn't seem to be calling from your country.

Microsoft knows all about the tech support scams — a recent blog post claimed that "three million [Microsoft] customers this year alone" had been hit by scummy scammers. In the first legal action of its kind, in late December 2014, Microsoft sued Omnitech Support, a division of Customer Focus Services, "and related entities," claiming unfair and deceptive business practices and trademark infringement.

Microsoft's filing says the scammers "have utilized the Microsoft trademarks and service marks to enhance their credentials and confuse customers about their affiliation with Microsoft. Defendants then use their enhanced credibility to convince consumers that their personal computers are infected with malware in order to sell them unnecessary technical support and security services to clean their computers."

The Customer Focus Services website says it's "A pioneer in India-based off-shoring with over a decade of experience in call center outsourcing. . . [with] Multi-location delivery (offshore and onshore) centers in India (Bangalore)." Wonder how long it'll take for them to fold up their company in the U.S., and continue overseas?

If you've already been conned — given out personal information or a credit card number — start by contacting your bank or the credit card issuing company and follow its procedures for reporting identity theft.

0day exploits

What do you do when you discover a brand-new security hole in Windows or Office or another Microsoft product? Why, you sell it, of course.

When a person writes a malicious program that takes advantage of a newly discovered security hole — a hole that even the manufacturer doesn't know about — that malicious program is a *0day exploit*. (Fuddy-duddies call it "zero-day exploit." The hopelessly hip say "zero day," or "sploit.")

0days are valuable. In some cases, very valuable. HP has a subsidiary — *TippingPoint* — that buys 0day exploits. TippingPoint works with the software manufacturer to come up with a fix for the exploit, but at the same time, it sells corporate customers immediate protection against the exploit. "TippingPoint's goal for the Zero Day Initiative is to provide our customers with the world's best intrusion prevention systems and secure converged networking infrastructure." TippingPoint offers up to $10,000 for a solid security hole.

Rumor has it that several less-than-scrupulous sites arrange for the buying and selling of new security holes. Apparently, the Russian hacker group that discovered a vulnerability in the way Windows handles WMF graphics files sold its new hole for $4,000, not realizing that it could've made much more. In 2012, *Forbes Magazine* estimated the value of 0days as ranging from $5,000 to $250,000. You can check it out at the following URL:

```
http://www.forbes.com/sites/andygreenberg/2012/03/23/
shopping-for-zero-days-an-price-list-for-hackers-secret-
software-exploits/
```

Bounties keep getting bigger. Google's Pwnium competition offers up to $2.7 million for hacks against their ChromeOS, and "significant bonuses" for other cracks. HP's Zero Day Initiative (latest incarnation of TippingPoint) now offers more than $500,000 in prize money for the best cracks in the Pwn2Own contest — and an additional $400,000 for the separate Mobile Pwn2Own.

According to Forbes, some government agencies are in the market. Governments certainly buy 0day exploits from Vupen, a notorious 0day brokering firm. The problem (some would say "opportunity") is getting worse, not better. Governments are now widely rumored to have thousands — some of them, tens of thousands — of stockpiled 0day exploits at hand.

How do you protect yourself from 0day exploits? In some ways, you can't: By definition, nobody sees a 0day coming, although most antivirus products employ some sort of heuristic detection that tries to clamp down on exploits based solely on the behavior of the offensive program. Mostly, you have to rely on the common-sense protection that I describe in the section "Getting Protected," later in this chapter. You must also stay informed, which I talk about in the next section.

Staying Informed

When you rely on the evening news to keep yourself informed about the latest threats to your computer's well-being, you quickly discover that the mainstream press frequently doesn't get the details right. Hey, if you were a newswriter with a deadline ten minutes away and you had to figure out how the new Bandersnatch 0day exploit shreds through a Windows TCP/IP stack buffer — and you had to explain your discoveries to a TV audience, at a presumed sixth-grade intelligence level — what would you do?

The following sections offer tips on getting the facts.

Relying on reliable sources

Fortunately, some reliable sources of information exist on the Internet. It would behoove you to check them out from time to time, particularly when you hear about a new computer security hole, real or imagined:

✦ **The Microsoft Security Response Center (MSRC) blog** presents thoroughly researched analyses of outstanding threats, from a Microsoft perspective (`http://blogs.technet.com/msrc`).

The information you see on the MSRC blog is 100-percent Microsoft Party Line — so there's a tendency to add more than a little "spin control" to the announcements. Nevertheless, Microsoft has the most extensive and best resources to analyze and solve Windows problems, and the MSRC blog frequently has inside information that you can't find anywhere else.

✦ **SANS Internet Storm Center (ISC)** pools observations and analysis from thousands of active security researchers. You can generally get the news first — and accurately — from the ISC (`http://isc.sans.org`).

✦ **Windows Secrets newsletter,** the most-read Windows weekly ever, contains excellent recaps of all the latest problems. Also, my site, AskWoody.com (`www.askwoody.com`), strives to present the latest security information in a way that doesn't require a Ph.D. in computer science (`www.windowssecrets.com`).

Take a moment right now to look up those sites and add them to your Firefox or Chrome Bookmarks or Edge Favorites. Unlike the anti-malware software manufacturers' websites, these sites have no particular ax to grind or product to sell. (Well, okay, Microsoft wants to sell you something, but you already bought it, yes?)

From time to time, Microsoft also releases security advisories, which generally warn about newly discovered 0day threats in Microsoft products. You can find those, too, at the MSRC blog.

It's hard to keep all the patches straight without a scorecard. I maintain an exhaustive list of patches and their known problems and also the Microsoft patches of the patches (of the patches) on www.AskWoody.com. I also write about them frequently in InfoWorld, and tweet about them all the time @woodyleonhard.

Ditching the hoaxes

Tell me whether you've heard any of these:

✦ "Amazing Speech by Obama!" "CNN News Alert!" "UPS Delivery Failure," "Hundreds killed in *[insert a disaster of your choice],*" "Budweiser Frogs Screensaver!" "Microsoft Security Patch Attached."

✦ A virus hits your computer if you read any message that includes the phrase "Good Times" in the subject line. (That one was a biggie in late 1994.) Ditto for any of the following messages: "It Takes Guts to Say 'Jesus'," "Win a Holiday," "Help a poor dog win a holiday," "Join the Crew," "pool party," "A Moment of Silence," "an Internet flower for you," "a virtual card for you," or "Valentine's Greetings."

✦ A deadly virus is on the Microsoft *[or insert your favorite company name here]* home page. Don't go there or else your system will die.

✦ If you have a file named *[insert filename here]* on your PC, it contains a virus. Delete it immediately!

They're all hoaxes — not a breath of truth in any of them.

Some hoaxes serve as fronts for real viruses: The message itself is a hoax, a red herring, designed to convince you to do something stupid and infect your system. The message asks (or commands!) you to download a file or run a video that acts suspiciously like an .exe file.

I'm not talking about YouTube videos, or Vimeo, or links to any of the other established video sites. Steer clear of attachments that appear to be videos, but in fact turn out to be something else. If you tell Windows to show you filename extensions (see Book III Chapter 1), you have most of the bases covered.

Other hoaxes are just rumors that circulate among well-intentioned people who haven't a clue. Those hoaxes hurt, too. Sometimes, when real worms hit, so much email traffic is generated from warning people to avoid the worm that the well-intentioned watchdogs do more damage than the worm itself! Strange but true.

Do yourself (and me) a favor: If somebody sends you a message that sounds like the following examples, just delete it, eh?

✦ A horrible virus is on the loose that's going to bring down the Internet. (Sheesh. I get enough of that garbage on the nightly news.)

✦ Send a copy of this message to ten of your best friends, and for every copy that's forwarded, Bill Gates will give *[pick your favorite charity]* $10.

✦ Forward a copy of this message to ten of your friends and put your name at the bottom of the list. In *[pick a random amount of time],* you will receive $10,000 in the mail, or your luck will change for the better. Your eyelids will fall off if you don't forward this message.

✦ Microsoft (Intel, McAfee, Norton, Compaq — whatever) says that you need to double-click the attached file, download something, don't download something, go to a specific place, avoid a specific place, and on and on.

If you think you've stumbled on the world's most important virus alert, by way of your uncle's sister-in-law's roommate's hairdresser's soon-to-be-ex-boyfriend (remember that he's the one who's a really smart computer guy, but kind of smelly?), count to ten twice and keep these four important points in mind:

✦ No reputable software company (including Microsoft) distributes patches by email. You should never, ever, open or run an attachment to an email message until you contact the person who sent it to you and confirm that she intended to send it to you.

✦ Chances are very good (I'd say, oh, 99.9999 percent or more) that you're looking at a half-baked hoax that's documented on the web, most likely on the Snopes urban myths site (www.snopes.com).

✦ If the virus or worm is real, Brian Krebs has already written about it. Go to www.krebsonsecurity.com.

✦ If the Internet world is about to collapse, clogged with gazillions of email worms, the worst possible way to notify friends and family is by email. D'oh! Pick up the phone, walk over to the water cooler, or send a carrier pigeon, and give your intended recipients a reliable web address to check for updates. Betcha they've already heard about it anyway.

Try hard to be part of the solution, not part of the problem, okay? And if a friend forwards you a virus warning in an email, do everyone a big favor: Shoot him a copy of the preceding bullet points, ask him to tape it to the side of his computer, and beg him to refer to it the next time he gets the forwarding urge.

Am I Infected?

So how do you know whether you're infected?

The short answer is this: Many times, you don't. If you think that your PC is infected, chances are very good that it isn't. Why? Because malware these days doesn't usually cause the kinds of problems people normally associate with infections.

Whatever you do, don't fall for the scamware that tells you it removed 39 infections from your computer but you need to pay in order to remove the other 179 (see "Shunning scareware," a little later in this chapter).

Evaluating telltale signs

Here are a few telltale signs that may — *may* — mean that your PC is infected, or that one of your online accounts has been hacked:

✦ **Someone tells you that you sent him an email message with an attachment — and you didn't send it.** In fact, most email malware these days is smart enough to spoof the From address, so any infected message that appears to come from you probably didn't. Still, some dumb old viruses that aren't capable of hiding your email address are still around. And, if you receive an infected attachment from a friend, chances are good that both your email address and his email address are on an infected computer somewhere. Six degrees of separation and all that.

✦ **You suddenly see files with two filename extensions scattered around your computer.** Filenames such as kournikova.jpg.vbs (a VBScript file masquerading as a JPG image file) or somedoc.txt.exe (a Windows program that wants to appear to be a text file) should send you running for your antivirus software.

Always, always, always have Windows show you filename extensions (see Book III, Chapter 1).

✦ **Your antivirus software suddenly stops working.** If the icon for your antivirus product disappears from the notification area (near the clock), something killed it — and chances are very good that the culprit was a virus.

✦ **You can't reach websites that are associated with anti-malware manufacturers.** For example, Firefox or Edge or Chrome works fine with most websites, but you can't get through to www.microsoft.com, www.symantec.com, or www.mcafee.com. This problem is a key giveaway for several infections.

Where did that message come from?

In my discussion of 419 scams, I mentioned that I can trace several scammer messages back to Nigeria. If you've never traced a message before, you'll probably find it intriguing — and frustrating.

You know that return addresses lie. Just like an antagonist in the TV series *House*. You can't trust a return address because "spoofing" one is absolutely trivial. So what can you do?

If you receive a message and want to know where it came from, the first step is to find the header. In the normal course of events, you never see message headers. They look like the gibberish in Figure 1-8.

Figure 1-8: The header for the 419 message in Figure 1-7.

Here's how to find a message's header:

+ **If you're using Outlook 2003 and earlier,** open the message and choose View ⇨ Options.

+ **In Outlook 2007,** you must open the message and click the tiny square with a downward, right-facing arrow in the lower-right corner of the Options group.

+ **Outlook 2010 and Outlook 2013** will show you the header, but only if you know the secret handshake. Open the message. In the message window, click File and then Properties. The header is listed in the box marked Internet Headers.

+ **In Gmail,** click the down arrow next to the message subject and choose Show Original. That shows you the entire message, including the header.

+ **In Hotmail or Outlook.com,** click the down arrow next to Reply, which is near the sender and subject.

    Other email programs work differently. You may have to jump on to Google to figure out how to see a message's header.

After you have the header, copy it, and head over to the ipTracker site, `www.iptrackeronline.com/header.php`. Paste the message's header into the top box, and tap or click Submit Header for Analysis. A report like the one in Figure 1-9 appears.

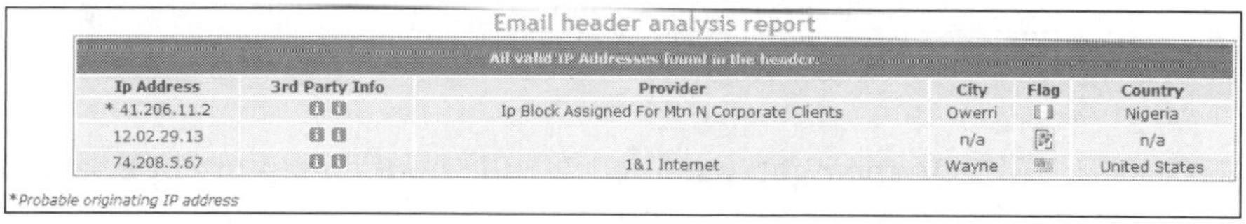

Figure 1-9:
Confirmation
that a
message
came from
Nigeria.

Email header analysis report

All valid IP Addresses found in the header.

Ip Address	3rd Party Info	Provider	City	Flag	Country
* 41.206.11.2		Ip Block Assigned For Mtn N Corporate Clients	Owerri		Nigeria
12.02.29.13			n/a		n/a
74.208.5.67		1&1 Internet	Wayne		United States

*Probable originating IP address

Realize that the header can be faked, too. Really clever scammers can disguise the origin of a message by faking the header. It's difficult, though, and scammers tend not to be, uh, the brightest bulbs on the tree.

What to do next

If you think that your computer is infected, follow these steps:

1. **Don't panic.**

Chances are very good that you're not infected.

2. **DO NOT REBOOT YOUR COMPUTER.**

   You may trigger a virus update when you reboot. Stay cool.

3. **Run a full scan of your system. If you're using Windows Defender, go to the Search box to the right of the Start icon, type** `windows def`, **and choose Windows Defender.**

   If you aren't using Windows Defender, get your antivirus package to run a full scan.

   The Windows Defender main interface appears (see Figure 1-10). See Book IX, Chapter 3 for details about Windows Defender.

Figure 1-10:
Windows
Defender,
ready for
action.

4. **On the right, tap or click Full and then tap or click Scan Now.**

   A full scan can take a long time. Go have a latte or two.

5. **If Step 4 still doesn't solve the problem, go to the Malwarebytes Removal forum at** `http://forums.malwarebytes.org/index.php?showforum=7` **and post your problem on the Malware Removal forum.**

   Make sure that you follow the instructions precisely. The good folks at AumHa are all volunteers. You can save them — and yourself — lots of headaches by following their instructions to the letter.

6. **Do not — I repeat — do not send messages to all your friends advising them of the new virus.**

Messages about a new virus can outnumber infected messages generated by the virus itself — in some cases causing more havoc than the virus itself. Try not to become part of the problem. Besides, you may be wrong.

In recent years, I've come to view the mainstream press accounts of virus and malware outbreaks with increasing skepticism. The antivirus companies are usually slower to post news than the mainstream press, but the information they post tends to be much more reliable. Not infallible, mind you, but better. I also cover security problems at www.AskWoody.com.

Shunning scareware

A friend of mine brought me her computer the other day and showed me a giant warning about all the viruses residing on it (see Figure 1-11). She knew that she needed XP Antivirus, but she didn't know how to install it. Thank heaven.

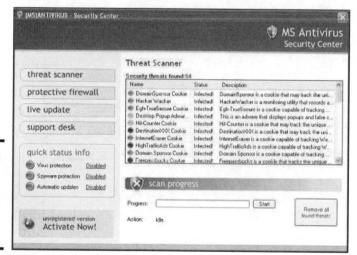

Figure 1-11: Rogue anti-malware gives you reason to pay.

Another friend brought me a computer that always booted to a Blue Screen of Death that said

```
Error 0x00000050 PAGE_FAULT_IN_NON_PAGED_AREA
```

It took a whole day to unwind all the junkware on that computer, but when I got to the bottom dreck, I found Vista Antivirus 2009.

I've received messages from all over the world from people who want to know about this fabulous new program, Security Essentials 2010 or Antivirus 2012 (or XP Antivirus or MS Antivirus Security Center or Total Win7 Security or similar wording). Here's what you need to know: It's malware, plain and simple, and if you install it, you're handing over your computer to some very sophisticated folks who will install keyloggers, bot software, and the scummiest, dirtiest stuff you've ever seen on any PC.

Here's the crazy part: Most people install this kind of scareware voluntarily. One particular family of rogue antivirus products, named Win32/FakeSecSen, has infected more than a million computers; see Figure 1-12.

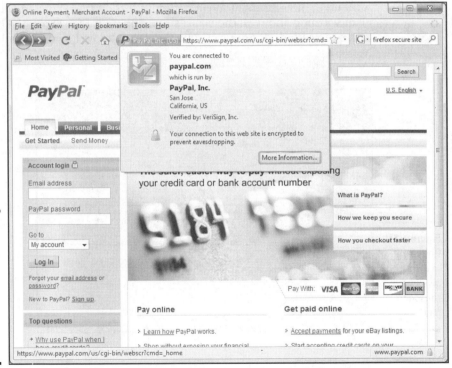

Figure 1-12: Win32/FakeSecSen scares you into thinking you have to pay to clean your computer.

The exact method of infection can vary, as will the payloads. Almost always, people install rogue antivirus programs when they think they're installing the latest, greatest virus chaser — and they're hastened to get it working because they just *know* there are 179 more viruses on their computers that have to be cleaned.

If you have it, how do you remove it? For starters, don't even bother with Windows Add or Remove Programs. Any company clever enough to call a piece of scum Antivirus 2012 won't make it easy for you to zap it. Personally, I rely on `www.malwarebytes.com` — but removing some of these critters is very difficult (see Book IX, Chapter 4).

One of my favorite anti-malware industry pundits, Rob Rosenberger, has an insightful analysis of this type of scareware in the article "Two decades of virus hysteria contributes to the success of fake-AV scams," at `www.vmyths.com/2009/03/22/rogue-av`.

Getting Protected

The Internet is wild and woolly and wonderful — and, by and large, it's unregulated, in a Wild West sort of way. Some would say it cannot be regulated, and I agree. Although some central bodies control basic Internet coordination questions — how the computers talk to each other, who doles out domain names such as Dummies.com, and what a web browser should do when it encounters a particular piece of HyperText Markup Language (HTML) — no central authority or Web Fashion Police exists.

In spite of its Wild West lineage and complete lack of couth, the Internet doesn't need to be a scary place. If you follow a handful of simple, common-sense rules, you'll go a long way toward making your Internet travels more like Happy Trails and less like *Grand Theft Auto V*.

Protecting against malware

"Everybody" knows that the Internet breeds viruses. "Everybody" knows that really bad viruses can drain your bank account, break your hard drive, and give you terminal halitosis — just by looking at an email message with *Good Times* in the Subject line. Right.

In fact, botnets and keyloggers can hurt you, but hoaxes and lousy advice abound. Every Windows user should follow these tips:

✦ **Don't install weird programs, cute icons, automatic email signers, or products that promise to keep your computer oh-so-wonderfully safe.** Unless the software comes from a reputable manufacturer whom you trust and you know precisely *why* you need it, you don't want it. Don't be fooled by products that claim to clean your Registry or clobber imaginary infections.

You may think that you absolutely must synchronize the Windows clock (which Windows does amazingly well, no extra program needed), tune up your computer (gimme a break), use those cute little smiley icons (gimme a bigger break), install a pop-up blocker (Edge, Firefox, and Chrome do that well), or install an automatic email signer (your email program already can sign your messages — read the manual, pilgrim!). What you end up with is an unending barrage of hassles and hustles.

✦ **Never, ever, open a file attached to an email message until you contact the person who sent you the file and verify that she did, in fact, send you the file intentionally.** You should also apply a bit of discretion and ask yourself whether the sender is smart enough to avoid sending you an infected file. After you contact the person who sent you the file, don't open the file directly. Save it to your hard drive and run Windows Defender on it before you open it.

✦ **Follow the instructions in Book III, Chapter 1 to force Windows to show you the full name of all the files on your computer.** That way, if you see a file named something.cpl or iloveyou.vbs, you stand a fighting chance of understanding that it may be an infectious program waiting for your itchy finger.

✦ **Don't trust email.** Every single part of an email message can be faked, easily. The return address can be spoofed. Even the header information, which you don't normally see, can be pure fiction. Links inside email messages may not point where you think they point. Anything you put in a message can be viewed by anybody with even a nodding interest — to use the old analogy, sending unencrypted email is much like sending a postcard. Those of you who live in the United States or send mail to or from the United States now know that Uncle Sam himself has been looking at all your mail — the NSA has been sharing the information with the DEA and IRS and lying about it (see the *Forbes* magazine series by Jennifer Granick).

✦ **Check your accounts.** Look at your credit card and bank statements, and if you see a charge you don't understand, question it. Log on to all your financial websites frequently, and if somebody changed your password, scream bloody murder.

Disabling Java and Flash

As I'm fond of saying, "It's time to run Java out of town." More precisely, I think developers should stop developing programs that require the Java Runtime Environment, or JRE, to run on your computer.

I also salute the rapid change from Flash, for automating websites, to HTML5, which does a better job in a faster and more secure way.

If you use Firefox, get the free NoScript Firefox extension (www.noscript.net), which automatically blocks both Java and Flash in Firefox. You can allow Java and Flash to run, on a case-by-case basis, but for general surfing, NoScript and Firefox are the safest ways to go.

Google's browser Chrome has some serious malware-blocking capabilities, combined with custom-built Java and Flash engines that make surfing with Chrome (debatably) the safest choice of the Big Three.

When I talk about Java, I'm not talking about JavaScript. Although the two names are very similar, they're as different as chalk and cheese. JavaScript is a language that automates actions on web pages. Java (in our case, the JRE) is a set of programs inside your computer that web pages can call. JavaScript is relatively benign (although it has been exploited). Java has led to millions of infections.

Using your credit card safely online

Many people who use the web refuse to order anything online because they're afraid that their credit card numbers will be stolen and they'll be liable for enormous bills. Or they think the products will never arrive and they won't get their money back.

If your credit card was issued in the United States and you're ordering from a U.S. company, that's simply not the case. Here's why:

✦ **The Fair Credit Billing Act protects you from being charged by a company for an item you don't receive.** It's the same law that governs orders placed over the telephone or by mail. A vendor generally has 30 days to send the merchandise, or it has to give you a formal written chance to cancel your order. For details, go to the Federal Trade Commission (FTC) website (www.ftc.gov/bcp/edu/pubs/ consumer/credit/cre28.shtm).

✦ **Your maximum liability for charges fraudulently made on the card is $50 per card.** The minute you notify the credit card company that somebody else is using your card, you have no further liability. If you have any questions, the Federal Trade Commission can help (www.consumer. ftc.gov/articles/0213-lost-or-stolen-credit-atm-and- debit-cards).

The rules are different if you're not dealing with a U.S. company and using a U.S. credit card. For example, if you buy something in an online auction from an individual, you don't have the same level of protection. Make sure that you understand the rules before you hand out credit card information. Unfortunately, there's no central repository (at least none I could find) of information about overseas purchase protection for U.S. credit card holders: Each credit card seems to handle cases individually. If you buy things overseas using a U.S. credit card, your relationship with your credit card company generally provides your only protection.

Some online vendors, such as Amazon, absolutely guarantee that your shopping will be safe. The Fair Credit Billing Act protects any charges fraudulently made in excess of $50, but Amazon says that it reimburses any fraudulent charges under $50 that occurred as a result of using its website. Many credit card companies now offer similar assurances.

Regardless, take a few simple precautions to make sure that you aren't giving away your credit card information:

✦ **When you place an order online, make sure that you're dealing with a company you know.** In particular, don't click a link in an email message and expect to go to the company's website. Type the company's address into Edge or Chrome or Firefox, or use a link that you stored in your Edge Favorites or the Chrome or Firefox Bookmarks list.

✦ **Type your credit card number only when you're sure that you've arrived at the company's site and when the site is using a secure web page.** The easy way to tell whether a web page is secure is to look in the lower-right corner of the screen for a picture of a lock (see Figure 1-13). Secure websites scramble data so that anything you type on the web page is encrypted before it's sent to the vendor's computer. In addition, Firefox tells you a site's registration and pedigree by clicking the icon to the left of the web address.

Figure 1-13:
Major
browsers
show a lock
to indicate a
secure site.

🔒 https://plus.google.com/u/0/

Be aware that crafty web programmers can fake the lock icon and show an `https://` (secure) address to try to lull you into thinking that you're on a secure web page. To be safe, confirm the site's address and click the icon to the left of the address at the top to show the full security certificate.

✦ **Don't send your credit card number in an ordinary email message.** Email is just too easy to intercept. And for heaven's sake, don't give out any personal information when you're chatting online.

✦ **If you receive an email message requesting credit card information that seems to be from your bank, credit card company, Internet service provider, or even your sainted Aunt Martha, don't send sensitive information back by way of email.** Insist on using a secure website, and type the company's address into your browser.

Identity theft continues to be a problem all over the world. Widespread availability of personal information online only adds fuel to the flame. If you think someone may be posing as you — to run up debts in your name, for example — see the U.S. government's main website on the topic at `www.ftc.gov/bcp/edu/microsites/idtheft`.

Defending your privacy

"You have zero privacy anyway. Get over it."

That's what Scott McNealy, former CEO of Sun Microsystems, said to a group of reporters on January 25, 1999. He was exaggerating — Scott has been known to make provocative statements for dramatic effect — but the exaggeration comes awfully close to reality. (Actually, if Scott told me the sky was blue, I'd run outside and check. But I digress.)

I continue to be amazed at Windows users' odd attitudes toward privacy. People who wouldn't dream of giving a stranger their telephone numbers fill out their mailing addresses for online service profiles. People who are scared to death at the thought of using their credit cards online to place an order with a major retailer (a very safe procedure, by the way) dutifully type their Social Security numbers on web-based forms.

I suggest that you follow these few important privacy points:

+ **Use work systems only for work.** Why use your company email ID for personal messages? C'mon. Sign up for a free web-based email account, such as Gmail (`www.gmail.com`), Yahoo! Mail (`www.mail.yahoo.com`), or Hotmail/Outlook.com (`www.hotmail.com` and `www.outlook.com`).

  In the United States, with few exceptions, anything you do on a company PC at work can be monitored and examined by your employer. Email, website history files, and even stored documents and settings are all fair game. At work, you have zero privacy anyway. Get over it.

+ **Don't give it away.** Why use your real name when you sign up for a free email account? Why tell a random survey that your annual income is between $20,000 and $30,000? (Or is it between $150,000 and $200,000?)

  All sorts of websites — particularly Microsoft — ask questions about topics that, simply put, are none of their dern business. Don't put your personal details out where they can be harvested.

+ **Follow the privacy suggestions in this book.** You turned off Smart Search already, right? (See Book II, Chapter 6.) You know that Google keeps track of what you type in to the Google search engine, and Microsoft keeps track of what you say to Cortana or type in to Bing. You know that both Google and Microsoft scan your email — and that Google, at least, admits to using the contents of emails (on free accounts) in order to direct ads at you. You know that files stored in the cloud can be opened by all sorts of people, in response to court orders, anyway.

✦ **Know your rights.** Although cyberspace doesn't provide the same level of personal protection you have come to expect in *meatspace* (real life), you still have rights and recourses. Check out www.privacyrights.org for some thought-provoking notices.

Keep your head low and your powder dry!

Reducing spam

Everybody hates spam, but nobody has any idea how to stop it. Not the government. Not Bill Gates. Not your sainted aunt's podiatrist's second cousin.

The Doubleclick shtick

A website plants a cookie on your computer. Only that website can retrieve the cookie. The information is shielded from other websites. ZDNet.com (the *PCMag* website) can figure out that I have been reading reviews of digital cameras. Dealtime.com knows that I buy shoes. But a cookie from ZDNet can't be read by Dealtime and vice versa. So what's the big deal?

Enter Doubleclick.net, which is now a division of Google. For the better part of a decade, both ZDNet.com and Dealtime.com have included ads from a company named Doubleclick.net. Don't believe it? Use Internet Explorer to go to each of the sites, press the Alt key, and choose View, Web Page Privacy Policy. (In Firefox, you can do the same thing by choosing Tools, Options, Privacy, Show Cookies and watching the bottom of the list.) Unless ZDNet or Dealtime has changed advertisers, you see Doubleclick.net featured prominently in each site's privacy report.

Here's the trick: You surf to a ZDNet web page that contains a Doubleclick.net ad. Doubleclick

kicks in and plants a cookie on your PC that says you were looking at a specific page on ZDNet. Two hours (or days or weeks) later, you surf to a Dealtime page that also contains a Doubleclick.net ad — a different ad, no doubt — but one distributed by Doubleclick. Doubleclick kicks in again and discovers that you were looking at that specific ZDNet page two hours (or days or weeks) earlier.

Now consider the consequences if a hundred sites that you visit in an average week all have Doubleclick ads. They can be tiny ads — 1 pixel high or so small that you can't see them. All the information about all your surfing to those sites can be accumulated by Doubleclick and used to "target" you for advertising, recommendations, or whatever. It's scary.

Want to look at who's watching you? Install the Ghostery browser (www.ghostery.com/download). It shows you exactly which cookies are tracking you on every page you visit.

You think legislation can reduce the amount of spam? Since the U.S. CAN-SPAM Act (www.fcc.gov/cgb/consumerfacts/canspam.html) became law on January 7, 2003, has the volume of spam you've received increased or decreased? Heck, I've had more spam from politicians lately than from almost any other group. The very people who are supposed to be enforcing the antispam laws seem to be spewing out spam overtime.

By and large, Windows is only tangentially involved in the spam game — it's the messenger, as it were. But every Windows user I know receives email. And every email user I know gets spam. Lots of it.

Why is it so hard to identify spam? Consider. There are 600,426,974,379,824,381,952 different ways to spell *Viagra.* No, really. If you use all the tricks that spammers use — from simple swaps such as using the letter *l* rather than *i* or inserting e x t r a s p a c e s in the word, to tricky ones like substituting accented characters — you have more than 600 quintillion different ways to spell Viagra. It makes the national debt look positively tiny.

Hard to believe? See www.cockeyed.com/lessons/viagra/viagra.html for an eye-opening analysis.

Spam scanners look at email messages and try to determine whether the contents of the potentially offensive message match certain criteria. Details vary depending on the type of spam scanner you use (or your Internet service provider uses), but in general, the scanner has to match the contents of the message with certain words and phrases stored in its database. If you've seen lots of messages with odd spellings come through your spam scanner, you know how hard it is to see through all those sextillion, er, septillion variations.

Spam is an intractable problem, but you can do certain things to minimize your exposure:

+ **Don't encourage 'em.** Don't buy anything that's offered by way of spam (or any other email that you didn't specifically request). Don't click through to the website. Simply delete the message. If you see something that may be interesting, use Google or another web browser to look for other companies that sell the same item.

+ **Opt out of mailings only if you know and trust the company that's sending you messages.** If you're on the Costco mailing list and you're not interested in its email anymore, click the Opt Out button at the bottom of the page. But don't opt out with a company you don't trust: It may just be trying to verify your email address.

✦ **Never post your email address on a website or in a newsgroup.**
Spammers have spiders that devour web pages by the gazillion, crawling around the web, gathering email addresses and other information automatically. If you post something in a newsgroup and want to let people respond, use a name that's hard for spiders to swallow: `woody (at) ask woody (dot) com`, for example.

✦ **Never open an attachment to an email message or view pictures in a message.** Spammers use both methods to verify that they've reached a real, live address. And, you wouldn't open an attachment anyway — unless you know the person who sent it to you, you verified with her that she intended to send you the attachment, and you trust the sender to be savvy enough to avoid sending infected attachments.

✦ **Never trust a website that you arrive at by "clicking through" a hot link in an email message.** Be cautious about websites you reach from other websites. If you don't personally type the address in the Edge address bar, you may not be in Kansas anymore.

✦ Most important of all, if spam really bugs you, stop using your current email program and **switch to Gmail or Hotmail/Outlook.com.** Both of them have superb spam filters that are updated every nanosecond. You'll be very pleasantly surprised, I guarantee.

Ultimately, the only long-lasting solution to spam is to change your email address and give out your address only to close friends and business associates. Even that strategy doesn't solve the problem, but it should reduce the level of spam significantly. Heckuva note.

Dealing with Data Breaches

In recent months we've seen a breathtaking rise in the number of data breaches — where scumbags have broken into company computers and stolen data for millions of customers. Home Depot, 56 million. JP Morgan Chase, 76 million. Target, 70 million. Ebay, 145 million. Adobe, 36 million. Evernote, 50 million. Activision, 14 million. Sony, 77 million (and almost every key internal document). Tj Maxx, 94 million. AOL, 92 million, then 20 million more. Kmart, 7-Eleven, JC Penney, Dow Jones, Snapchat, Staples, Facebook, Twitter, and on and on.

Usually the thieves get away with email addresses and some personal information. If you're one of the unfortunate victims and your password was stolen, you can hope that the password was stored in a very secure way. Sometimes you're lucky. Sometimes you're not.

Researchers recently found a database with 1.2 *billion* stolen IDs.

Lots of people want to know what they can do to keep from being the next statistic. The short answer is, mostly you need to constantly monitor your credit card statements, bank statements, and other financial accounts, to catch problems as quickly as you can. That's a fatalistic analysis of the situation: You can't do much to stop it, so you have to watch to see if the cows have run out of the barn.

That said, there are a few things you should be doing to keep the bad guys guessing as much as possible:

1. **Don't use the same password twice.**

   Yeah, I know. *Everybody* reuses passwords. I do, too. But I try to reuse passwords on sites that aren't important — and leave the unique passwords for financial sites.

2. **Use a password remembering program such as LastPass, 1Password, Dashlane, RoboForm, or IronKey.**

   The only chance you have at remembering passwords *just on your financial sites* is to rely on some computer assistance. There are plenty of pros and cons to the products and methods — do you want to trust the cloud, can you remember to take a USB drive everywhere, where and how securely should the master password be manipulated — but the bottom line is that you need some sort of automated password helper.

   I use LastPass. See Book X Chapter 5.

3. **Assume that the bad guys have your email address and some additional identifying information.**

   They may even have the passwords to your not-sensitive websites. Act accordingly.

4. **If you receive notification that your account has been compromised, don't worry so much about changing the password on the hacked account — look to your other accounts, to see if any of those need changing.**

   After the deed's done, there isn't much you can do — kind of like putting the toothpaste back in the tube. But you can, and should, take a hard look at what might've been taken, and move to mitigate the disclosure.

Want to know if your email address has appeared in public? Drop by www.pwnedlist.com and check (see Figure 1-14).

PwnedList has almost a billion compromised email addresses on file.

The check is free — and, no, they won't spam you.

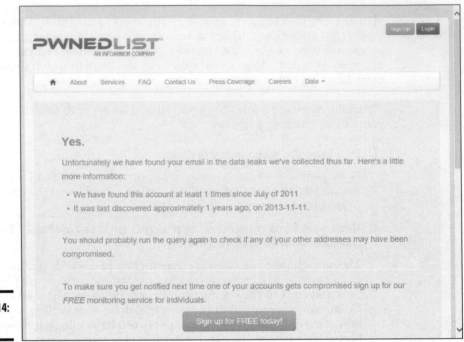

Figure 1-14:
Nailed.

Chapter 2: Fighting Viri and Scum

In This Chapter

✔ **Quick security checklist — do's and don'ts**

✔ **Getting the lowdown on malware**

✔ **Understanding how Windows Defender works**

✔ **Scanning for rootkits via Windows Defender Offline**

✔ **Deciphering your browser's cryptic security signs**

Windows 8 was the first version of Windows to ship with a complete antivirus/anti-spy/anti-malware package baked right into the product. Windows 10 brings along all those goodies — and they're more than enough for just about anybody except spies and organizations that have ticked off Anonymous.

You don't need to buy an antivirus, firewall, or anti-everything product. Windows 10 has all you need. It's already installed and working, and it doesn't cost a penny.

On the other hand, you need to hold up your end of the bargain by not doing anything, uh, questionable. I wanted to say "stupid," but some of the tricks the scummeisters use these days can get you even if you *aren't* stupid. Book IX, Chapter 1 helps you understand the tactics online creeps use and keep your guard up.

I start this chapter with a very simple list of do's and don'ts for protecting your computer and your identity. They're important. Even if you don't read the rest of this chapter, make sure you read — and understand, and follow — the rules in each list.

Basic Windows Security Do's and Don'ts

Here are the ten most important things you need to do, to keep your computer secure:

✦ **Check daily to make sure Windows Defender is running.** If something's amiss, a red "X" appears on the Action Center flag, down in the desktop's notification area, near the time. To check Defender's status, click in the

Search box (that's Cortana's hiding place) to the right of the Start button, type **def**, and choose Windows Defender. If Defender's running, a green check mark appears, as shown in Figure 2-1.

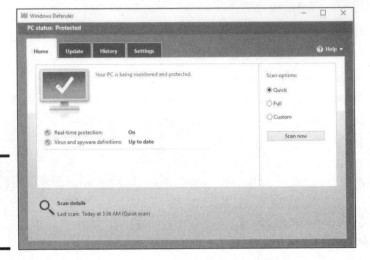

Figure 2-1: Windows Defender is up and running.

Actually, Windows should tell you if Defender stops, either via a toaster notification from the right side or a red X on the flag in the lower-right corner of the desktop. But if you want to be absolutely sure, there's no better way than to check it yourself. Only takes a second.

✦ **Don't use just any old browser.** Edge is infinitely better than Internet Explorer, when it comes to security exposures, but I usually run Chrome (realizing that Google keeps track of where I'm going, all the better to serve me ads) because Chrome has superior Java and Flash support built-in. I switch to Firefox from time to time, but I use it with NoScript or a similar Java and Flash blocker installed and working. That said, Edge is getting better quickly.

Most Windows infections come in the door through Java, Flash, or Adobe Reader (see Book IX, Chapter 1), and they usually get in through Internet Explorer.

✦ **Use anything other than Adobe Reader to look at PDF files.** All the major browsers have their own PDF readers, just because Adobe Reader has caused so many infections. For a standalone reader, download and install an alternative to Adobe Reader. See Book X Chapter 5 for alternatives.

✦ **Every month or so, run Windows Defender Offline.** WDO scans for rootkits. I talk about WDO later in this chapter.

✦ **Every month or so, run Malwarebytes.** The Malwarebytes program gives you a second opinion, possibly pointing out questionable programs that Windows Defender doesn't flag. I talk about Malwarebytes in Book IX, Chapter 4.

✦ **Delete chain mail.**

I'm sure that you'll be bringing down the wrath of several lesser deities for the rest of your days, but do everyone a favor and don't forward junk. Please.

If something you receive in an email sounds really, really cool, it's probably fake — an urban legend or a come-on of some sort. Look it up at www.snopes.com.

✦ **Keep up to date with Windows patches and (especially) patches to other programs running on your computer.** Windows 10 should be keeping itself updated. For help keeping your other programs updated, use Secunia Personal Software Inspector, which I describe in Book IX, Chapter 4.

✦ **Check your credit cards and bank balances regularly.**

I check my charges and balances every couple of days and suggest you do the same.

✦ **If you don't need a program any more, get rid of it.** Use the Windows Uninstaller that I describe in Book VII, Chapter 1. If it doesn't blast away easily, use Revo Uninstaller in Book X, Chapter 5.

✦ **Change your passwords regularly.** Yeah, another one of those things everybody recommends, but nobody does. Except you really should. See the admonitions in Book II, Chapter 4 about choosing good passwords, but especially look at LastPass and RoboForm, which I describe in Book IX, Chapter 4.

Here are the ten most important things you *shouldn't* do, to keep your computer secure:

✦ **Don't trust any PC unless you, personally, have been taking close care of it.** Even then, be skeptical. Treat every PC you may encounter as if it's infected. Don't stick a USB drive into a public computer, for example, unless you're prepared to disinfect the USB drive immediately when you get back to a safe computer. Assume that everything you type into a public PC is being logged and sent to a pimply-face genius who wants to be a millionaire.

✦ **Don't install a new program unless you know precisely what it does, and you've checked to make sure you have a legitimate copy.**

Yes, even if an online scanner told you that you have 139 viruses on your computer, and you need to pay just $49.99 to get rid of them.

If you install apps from the Windows Store, you're generally safe — although the Windows Store has its share of crappy programs. But any programs you install from other sources should be vetted ten ways from Tuesday, downloaded from a reputable source (such as www.cnet.com, www.softpedia.com, www.majorgeeks.com, www.tucows.com, www.snapfiles.com), and *even then* you need to ask yourself whether you really need the program, and *even then* you have to be careful that the installer doesn't bring in some crappy extras like browser toolbars.

Similarly, Firefox and Chrome add-ons are generally safe.

✦ **Don't use the same password for two or more sites.** Okay, if you reuse your passwords, make sure you don't reuse the passwords on any of your email or financial accounts.

True confession time. Yes, I reuse passwords. Everybody does. LastPass (see Book IX, Chapter 4) makes it easier to create a different password for every website, but I'm lazy sometimes.

Email accounts are different. If you reuse the passwords on any of your email accounts and somebody gets the password, he may be able to break into everything, steal your money, and besmirch your reputation. See the nearby "Don't reuse your email password" sidebar.

✦ **Don't use Wi-Fi in a public place unless you're running exclusively on HTTPS-encrypted sites or through a virtual private network (VPN).**

If you don't know what HTTPS is and have never set up a VPN, that's okay. Just realize that anybody else who can connect to the same Wi-Fi station you're using can see *every single thing* that goes into or comes out of your computer. See Book IX, Chapter 4.

✦ **Don't fall for Nigerian 419 scams, "I've been mugged and I need $500 scams," or anything else where you have to send money.** There are lots of scams — and if you hear the words "Western Union" or "Postal Money Order," run for the exit. See Book IX, Chapter 1.

✦ **Don't tap or click a link in an email message or document and expect it to take you to a financial site.** Take the time to type the address into your browser. You've heard it a thousand times, but it's true.

✦ **Don't open an attachment to any email message until you've contacted the person who sent it to you and verified that she intentionally sent you the file.** Even if she did send it, you need to use your judgment as to whether the sender is savvy enough to refrain from sending you something infectious.

No, UPS didn't send you a non-delivery notice in a Zip file, Microsoft didn't send you an update to Windows attached to a message, and your winning lottery notification won't come as an attachment.

Don't reuse your email password

Say you have a Gmail account. You run over to an online classified advertising site and sign up for an account there. You're lazy, so you use the same password for both accounts.

A day, month, or year later, you place an ad on the classified advertising site. You have to provide your email address. Hey, no problem.

The next week, somebody breaks into the classified advertising site and steals the information from 10,000 accounts. Unbeknownst to you, the people who created and maintain the classified advertising site stored the passwords and email addresses in a way that can be cracked.

The person who broke into the site posts his booty on some underground file-sharing site, and within minutes of the break-in, two dozen

people are trying every combination of your Gmail address and password, trying to break into banking sites, brokerage sites, PayPal, whatever.

If they hit on a financial site that requires only an email address in order to retrieve the account information, bingo, they use your Gmail address and ask for a new password. They log on to Gmail with your password and wait for the password reset instructions. Thirty seconds later, they're logged in to the financial site.

The site doesn't have to be financial. Just about any site that stores your Social Security number, or includes sensitive information like a hospital site, might be similarly vulnerable.

Happens every day.

✦ **Don't forget to change your passwords.** Yeah, another one of those things everybody recommends, but nobody does. Except you really should.

 ✦ **Don't trust anybody who calls you and offers to fix your computer.** The "I'm from Microsoft and I'm here to help" scam has gone too far. Stay skeptical, and don't let anybody else into your computer, unless you know who he is. See Book IX, Chapter 1.

✦ **Don't forget that the biggest security gap is between your ears.** Use your head, not your tapping or clicking finger.

Making Sense of Malware

Although most people are more familiar with the term *virus,* viruses are only part of the problem — a problem known as malware. *Malware* is made up of the elements described in this list:

✦ **Viruses:** A computer virus is a program that replicates. That's all. Viruses generally replicate by attaching themselves to files — programs, documents, or spreadsheets — or replacing "genuine" operating system files with bogus ones. They usually make copies of themselves whenever they're run.

You probably think that viruses delete files or make programs go belly-up or wreak havoc in other nefarious ways. Some of them do. Many of them don't. Viruses sound scary, but most of them aren't. Most viruses have such ridiculous bugs in them that they don't get far "in the wild."

✦ **Trojans:** Trojans (occasionally called Trojan horses) may or may not be able to reproduce, but they always require that the user do something to get them started. The most common Trojans these days appear as programs downloaded from the Internet, or email attachments, or programs that helpfully offer to install themselves from the Internet: You tap or double-click an attachment, expecting to open a picture or a document, and you get bit when a program comes in and clobbers your computer, frequently sending out a gazillion messages, all with infected attachments, without your knowledge or consent.

✦ **Worms:** Worms move from one computer to another over a network. The worst ones replicate very quickly by shooting copies of themselves over the Internet, taking advantage of holes in the operating systems (all too frequently, Windows).

Viruses, Trojans, and worms are getting much, much more sophisticated than they were just a few years ago. Lots of money can be made with advanced malware, especially for those who figure out how to break in without being detected.

Some malware can carry bad *payloads* (programs that wreak destruction on your system), but many of the worst offenders cause the most harm by clogging networks (nearly bringing down the Internet itself, at times) and by turning PCs into zombies, frequently called *bots,* which can be operated by remote control. (I talk about bots and botnets in Book IX, Chapter 1.)

The most successful pieces of malware these days run as *rootkits* — programs that evade detection by stealthily hooking into Windows in tricky ways. Some nominally respectable companies (notably, Sony) have employed rootkit technology to hide programs for their own profit. Rootkits are extremely difficult to detect and even harder to clean. Windows Defender Offline, discussed later in this chapter, is your best bet to clobber the beasts.

All these definitions are becoming more academic and less relevant, as the trend shifts to *blended-threat* malware. Blended threats incorporate elements of all three traditional kinds of malware — and more. Most of the most successful "viruses" you read about in the press these days — Conficker, Rustock, Aleuron, and the like — are, in fact, blended-threat malware. They've come a long way from old-fashioned viruses.

Lies, damn lies, and malware statistics

Computer crime has evolved into a money-making operation, with some espionage tacked on for good measure, but when you hear statistics about how many viruses are out and about and how much they cost everyone, take those statistics with a grain of salt.

As *The New York Times* puts it so accurately, "A few criminals do well, but cybercrime is a relentless, low-profit struggle for the majority . . ." (`www.nytimes.com/2012/04/15/opinion/sunday/the-cybercrime-wave-that-wasnt.html`)

Here's what you need to know about those cost estimates:

✔ There's no way to tell how much a virus outbreak "costs." You should expect that any dollar estimates you see are designed to raise your eyebrows, nothing more.

✔ Although corporate cyberespionage certainly takes place all the time, it's very hard to identify — much less quantify. For that matter, how can you quantify the effects of plain-old, everyday industrial espionage?

✔ Instead of flinging meaningless numbers around, it's more important to consider the amount of hassle people and companies encounter when they have to clean up after a group of cybercretins. One hundred thousand filched credit card credentials may not lead to lots of lost money, but it'll certainly cause no end of mayhem for lots of people.

Although the major antivirus companies release virus-catching files that identify tens of millions of signatures, most infections in any given year come from a handful of viruses. The threat is real, but it's way overblown.

Scanning for Rootkits with Windows Defender Offline

Windows Defender Offline (WDO) sniffs out and removes rootkits. WDO should occupy a key spot in your bag of tricks. It works like a champ on Windows XP, Vista, Windows 7, Windows 8, and Windows 10 systems and should be able to catch a wide variety of nasties that evade detection by more traditional methods.

Windows Defender Offline can help in two very different situations:

✦ When Windows won't boot, you can boot your machine with a WDO CD or USB drive and have WDO perform a malware scan.

✦ If you think you may have a rootkit — or even if you're just curious — WDO can scan your system and remove many different kinds of rootkits.

It's important to understand that, even though Microsoft makes and distributes WDO, it is *not* a Windows application; it doesn't use the copy of Windows installed on your PC. Rather, it's completely self-contained — you boot with the WDO CD or USB drive, and WDO looks at your system without any interference from the installed copy of Windows.

To find rootkits, a rootkit detector has to do its job when Windows isn't running. If the rootkit detector was running on Windows, it would never be able to see underneath Windows to catch the rootkits.

To get WDO up and running, make sure you have a blank CD, DVD, or USB flash drive with at least 250MB of free space. Then follow these steps:

1. **Figure out the "bittedness" of the computer that's going to get scanned.**

   If you don't already know whether your PC is running 32-bit or 64-bit Windows, right-click the lower-left corner of the screen and choose System. (If you don't have a mouse, flip to the desktop, swipe from the right, choose the Settings charm, and at the top, tap Control Panel. Tap the System and Security link, and then tap the System link. And consider buying a mouse.) Windows responds with the System window, as shown in Figure 2-2, and near the middle, it tells you whether you have a 32-bit or 64-bit system.

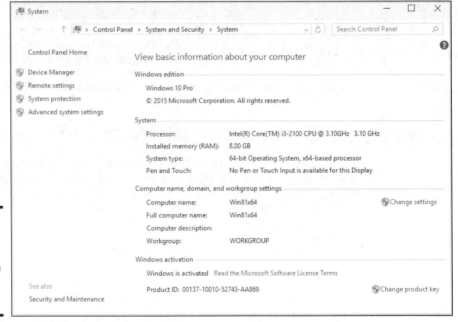

Figure 2-2:
The System window tells you the bittedness of your PC.

You can use any Windows computer for the following steps — you don't have to use the PC that's going to get scanned.

If you're going to create a CD or DVD to boot WDO, you do have to use a PC with a CD or DVD writer. To create a bootable USB drive, the downloading computer has to have a USB port.

2. **Go to the Windows Defender Offline site, and click to download either the 32-bit or 64-bit version, depending on the bittedness of the system you're going to scan. Tap or double-click to run the downloaded file.**

   The WDO site can be found at `http://windows.microsoft.com/ en-us/windows/windows-defender-offline-faq`.

   The welcome pane appears, as shown in Figure 2-3.

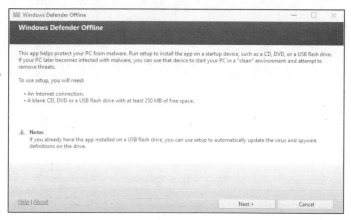

Figure 2-3: You need to sacrifice a CD, DVD, or USB drive to hold the WDO booter.

3. **Tap or click Next, accept all the defaults, choose whether you want to use a CD, DVD, or USB drive, and then tap or click Finish.**

   The ISO file option is primarily for people who are going to run WDO on systems that can boot from an ISO file, which usually means a virtual machine.

   If you're going to create a bootable USB drive, be aware that this installer wipes out everything on the drive.

   The installer downloads the latest version of the software and signature files (about 210MB for the 32-bit version or 230MB for the 64-bit version) and then creates the boot drive, or the ISO file.

4. **With a bootable CD, DVD, or USB drive properly inserted, boot the PC you want to examine from the device.**

   If you've never booted the machine from CD or USB before and can't figure out how to jimmy the BIOS to make it work, Microsoft has some suggestions for getting it to work at www.windows.microsoft.com/en-US/windows/windows-defender-offline-faq.

5. **If you have a multiboot system, choose which OS you want to scan.**

   WDO scans only one system at a time.

   With the OS chosen, you see a Windows 7-like startup screen that dissolves into the Windows Defender Offline screen, as shown in Figure 2-4.

Figure 2-4: Windows Defender Offline may need to be updated before it scans your system.

6. **Update the definitions if need be, by tapping or clicking the Update button. Choose a Quick, Full, or Custom scan, and then tap or click the Scan Now button.**

   The Full scan option is very thorough — it looks inside all the files on the system, including ancient backed-up emails — and can run for six or eight hours. The Custom option lets you select drives and folders for scanning. In my tests on a fresh Windows 10 machine, the Full scan took only 30 minutes.

   If WDO finds potential a threat, it displays a warning identical to the warning dialog box in Windows Defender.

7. **Choose to Remove, Quarantine, or Ignore the threat.**

   See Book IX, Chapter 3 for a discussion of the options and what they mean. *Hint:* Unless you have an overwhelming need to do otherwise, choose Remove.

Understanding how Windows Defender works

Windows Defender in Windows 10 is a fully functional, very capable, fast, small anti-malware program that works admirably well. There's absolutely no reason to spend any money on any other anti-malware/anti-whatever program. You have the best inside Windows 10, already working, and you don't have to lift a finger, or pay a penny.

Windows Defender in Windows 10 is built on the Microsoft Security Essentials foundation,

which I've raved about for years. It incorporates all the MSE pieces (so there's no reason to install Microsoft Security Essentials on a Win10 machine), while adding new features, including the ability to work with the new UEFI boot system to validate secure boot operating systems.

I talk about Windows Defender, UEFI, and secure boot in Book IX, Chapter 3.

Deciphering Browsers' Inscrutable Warnings

One last trick that may help you head off an unfortunate online incident: Each browser has subtle ways of telling you that you may be in trouble. I'm not talking about the giant Warning: Suspected Phishing Site or Reported Web Forgery signs. Those are supposed to hit you upside the head, and they do.

I'm talking about the gentle indications each browser has that tell you whether there's something strange about the site you're looking at. Historically, if you're on a secured page — where encryption is in force between you and the website — you see a padlock. That simple padlock indicator has grown up a bit, so you can understand more about your secure (or not-so-secure) connection with a glance.

Chrome

Chrome browsers have four different icons that can appear to the left of a site's URL, as shown in Figure 2-5.

Here's what they mean:

✦ The world icon doesn't look like a padlock because it indicates that the site isn't secure. As long as you don't have to type anything into a site, there's no great reason to require a secure site. If you're asked to provide information on an unsecure site, be intensely aware that it can be seen by anybody who's snooping on your connection.

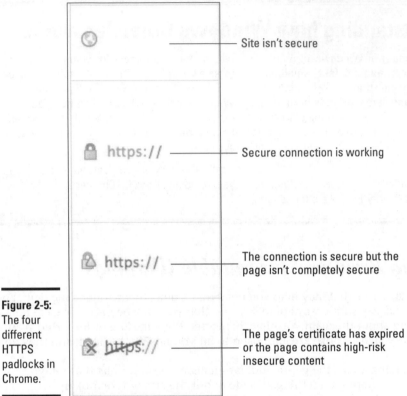

Site isn't secure

https:// — Secure connection is working

https:// — The connection is secure but the page isn't completely secure

https:// — The page's certificate has expired or the page contains high-risk insecure content

Figure 2-5:
The four
different
HTTPS
padlocks in
Chrome.

+ The green padlock says that there's a secure connection in place, and it's working. As long as you're looking at the correct domain — you didn't mistype the domain name, for example — you're safe.

If the site has an Extended Validation certificate (see the nearby "What is Extended Validation?" sidebar), you also see green highlighting in the address bar.

+ The yellow warning on a padlock says that Chrome has set up a secure connection, but there are parts of the page that can, conceivably, snoop on what you're typing. That's what the "insecure content" warning means.

+ The red X on a padlock tells you that there are problems with the site's certificate or that "insecure content" on the page is known to be high risk. When you hit a red X, you have to ask yourself whether the site's handlers just let the certificate lapse (I've seen that on banking sites and other sites that shouldn't go bad) or if there's something genuinely wrong with the site.

Firefox

Firefox handles things a little differently. Firefox puts a box to the left of the URL — called a Site Identity Button (see Figure 2-6) — that's color-coded to give you an idea of what's in store. If you tap or click the button, you see detailed information about the security status of the site.

The three colors indicate

+ **Gray:** Not a secure site

+ **Blue:** Basic security information

+ **Green:** Complete security information, including an Extended Validation certificate (see the "What is Extended Validation?" sidebar)

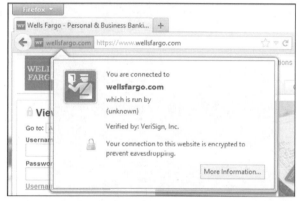

Figure 2-6:
Firefox gives detailed, site security information, like the fact that Wells Fargo doesn't identify its site.

What is Extended Validation?

Companies have to pay to get a secure certificate and use it correctly on their sites before the major browsers will display a padlock for those sites.

Unfortunately, in recent years, there have been many problems with faked, stolen, or otherwise dubious certificates. Part of the difficulty lies in the fact that just about anybody can get a website security certificate. Several years ago, a couple people applied for a security certificate for Microsoft.com. They sweet-talked their way into having a certificate issued.

Starting in April 2008, a second level of certification, an *Extended Validation certificate,* was put into effect. In order to buy an EV certificate, the organization or individual applying for the certificate has to jump through many hoops to establish its legal identity and physical location, and prove that the people applying for the certificate do, in fact, own the domain name that they're trying to certify.

EV certificates aren't infallible, but they're much more trustworthy than regular certificates.

Chapter 3: Running Built-In Security Programs

In This Chapter

✔ **Making Windows Defender work your way**

✔ **Coping with SmartScreen**

✔ **Working with UEFI and Secure Boot**

✔ **Controlling User Account Control**

✔ **Understanding Windows Firewall**

*W*indows 10, right out of the box, ships with a myriad of security programs, including a handful that you can control.

This chapter looks at the things you can do with the programs on offer: Windows Defender, SmartScreen, UEFI (don't judge it by its name alone), User Account Control, and Windows Firewall. What you find in this chapter is like a survey of the tip of an iceberg. Even if you don't change anything, you'll come away with a better understanding of what's available, and how the pieces fit together. With a little luck, you'll also have a better idea of what can go wrong, and how you can fix it.

Working with Windows Defender

Fast, full-featured, and free, Microsoft Windows Defender draws accolades from experts and catcalls from competitors.

If you've ever put up with a bloated and expensive security suite exhorting/ extorting you for more money, or you've struggled with free AV packages that want to install a little toolbar here and a funny monitoring program there — and *then* ask you for money — you're in for a refreshing change . . . from an unexpected source.

Windows Defender takes over antivirus and antispyware duties and tosses in bot detection and anti-rootkit features for good measure. In independent tests, Microsoft has consistently received high detection and removal scores for Windows Defender (and Microsoft Security Essentials, Windows Defender's kissin' cousin) for years.

Windows Defender conducts periodic scans and watches out for malware in real time. It vets email attachments, catches downloads, deletes or quarantines at your command, and in general, does everything you'd expect an antivirus, anti-malware, and/or anti-rootkit product to do.

Is Windows Defender the "best" antivirus package on the market? No. It depends on how you define "best," but Microsoft has no intention of coming out on top of the competitive anti-malware tests. I think Fred Langa said it best, in his Windows Secrets Newsletter article (`windowssecrets.com/langalist-plus/questions-about-ms-security-essentials`) in November, 2013:

"Microsoft Security Essentials' relatively low scores in recent anti-malware tests prompted several Windows Secrets readers to question whether it's advisable to use Microsoft's free AV tool. . . MSE [now Windows Defender] is probably not the best for novice users and those who rarely think about PC security — users who click any link that interests them and who ignore security warnings. Those users need lots of protection — mostly from themselves! For the most part, Windows Secrets readers tend to be experienced and involved PC users. They take security seriously. For that type of user, I still consider MSE an excellent choice."

I think *Windows 10 All-In-One For Dummies* readers tend to be experienced and involved, and agree wholeheartedly with Fred's assessment.

The beauty of Windows Defender is that it just works. You don't have to do anything — although you should check from time to time to make sure it hasn't been accidentally (or maliciously) turned off. To check whether Windows Defender is running, go to the search box next to the Start button, where Cortana lives, type **def**, and below the Search box choose Windows Defender. If you see the green check mark, you're doing fine. (You can see the check mark in the upcoming Figure 3-1.)

Microsoft maintains a very active online support forum for Windows Defender at Microsoft Answers, `www.answers.microsoft.com/en-us/windows/forum/windows_8-security`.

When you use Windows Defender, you should be aware of these caveats:

✦ It's *never* a good idea to run two antivirus products simultaneously, and Windows Defender is no exception: If you have a second antivirus product running on your machine, Windows Defender has been disabled, and you shouldn't try to bring it back.

If you don't like your AV product and don't particularly want to keep paying and paying and paying for it, use the Windows tool to get rid of it. Click or tap on Start, Settings, System. On the left choose Apps & features. Wait for the list to fill out. Then pick the program you want to remove and choose Uninstall. Reboot your machine, and Windows Defender returns.

In summary, Windows Defender works great, but if you get a second anti-virus program that's designed to run continuously, do *not* run Windows Defender and the usurper at the same time.

You may see updates listed for Windows Defender, if you go into Windows Update and look. Just leave them alone. They'll install all by themselves.

✦ No matter how you slice it, real-time protection eats into your privacy. How? Say Windows Defender (or any other antivirus product) encounters a suspicious-looking file that isn't on its zap list. In order to get the latest information about that suspicious-looking file, Windows Defender has to phone back to Mother Microsoft, drop off telltale pieces of the file, and ask whether there's anything new. You can opt out of real-time protection, but if you do, you won't have the latest virus information — and some viruses travel very fast.

Adjusting Windows Defender

Unlike many other antivirus products, Windows Defender has a blissfully small number of things that you can or should tweak. Here's how to get to the settings:

1. **In the Search bar, to the right of the Start button, type** windows def **and then at the top, tap or click Windows Defender.**

The main Windows Defender screen appears, as shown in Figure 3-1.

2. **Tap or click the Settings tab.**

Here you can make minor changes in Windows Defender's behavior.

It's rare that you would want to change any of these settings, except the Microsoft Access Protection Services (MAPS), as shown in Figure 3-2.

3. **Adjust the MAPS setting if you want by tapping or clicking the MAPS entry on the left.**

Generally, I don't like it when Microsoft gathers information about my system, but in this case I make an exception and set MAPS at Turn on Cloud Protection, which is the default. That's the only way to get the full benefit of real-time checking for updated definitions. As I explain earlier in this chapter, you're caught between a rock and a hard place.

For a manual scan, choose level of scanning

Check mark on green icon means everything is okay

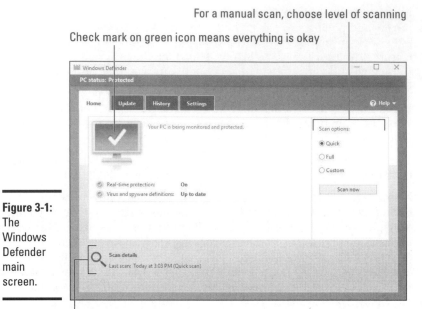

Figure 3-1:
The
Windows
Defender
main
screen.

Results of most recent scan

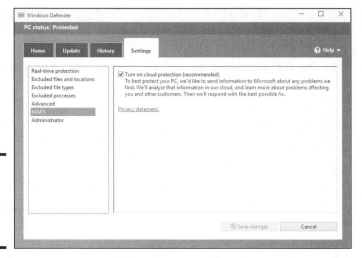

Figure 3-2:
The MAPS
settings for
Windows
Defender.

4. **If you change anything on the Settings tab, tap or click Save Changes and then tap or click X to close Windows Defender. (If you didn't change anything, just tap or click X.)**

   Your changes take effect immediately.

Running Windows Defender manually

Windows Defender works without you doing a thing, but you can tell it run a scan if something on your computer is giving you the willies. Here's how:

1. **In the Search bar to the right of the Start button, type** def **and at the top, tap or click Windows Defender.**

The main Windows Defender screen appears (refer to Figure 3-1).

2. **On the Update tab (see Figure 3-3), to get the latest anti-malware definitions, tap or click Update.**

When you tap or click Update, Windows Defender retrieves the latest signature files from the Microsoft site, but it doesn't run a scan. If you want to run a scan, you need to go back to the Home tab and run it.

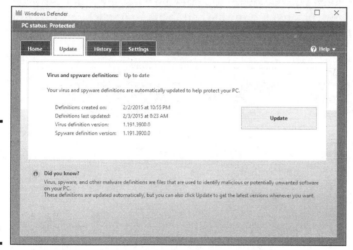

Figure 3-3:
The current
status of
Windows
Defender
signature
file updates.

3. **To perform a manual scan, tap or click one of the three buttons on the left and then tap or click Scan Now.**

Here's what the Scan options mean:

- *Quick* looks in locations where viruses and other kinds of malware are likely to hide.

- *Full* runs a bit-by-bit scan of every file and folder on the PC.

- *Custom* is like Full, but you get to choose which drives and folders get scanned.

4. **To see what Windows Defender has caught and zapped, historically, tap or click the History tab (see Figure 3-4).**

Once upon a time, Windows Defender would flag infected files and offer them up for you to decide what to do with the offensive file. It appears as if that behavior has been scaled back radically. As best I can tell, in almost all circumstances, when Windows Defender hits a dicey file, it *quarantines* the file — sticks it in a place you won't accidentally find — and just keeps going. You're rarely notified, (although a toaster notification may slide out from the right side of the screen), but the file just disappears from where it should've been.

If you just downloaded a file, and it disappeared, there's a very good chance that it's infected, Windows Defender has whisked it away to a well-guarded location, and the only way you'll ever find it is in the History tab of the Windows Defender program.

Should you decide to bring the file back, for whatever reason, select the check box next to the file and then tap or click Restore. Rub your lucky rabbit's foot a couple of times while you're at it.

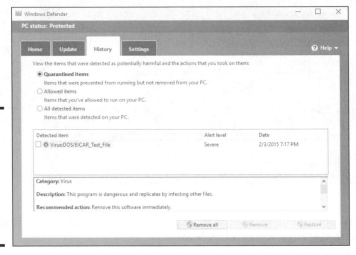

Figure 3-4:
A full history of the actions Defender's taken appear here.

Judging SmartScreen

Have you ever downloaded a program from the Internet, then clicked to install it — and then, a second later, thought, "Why did I do that?"

Microsoft came up with an interesting technique it calls SmartScreen that gives you an extra chance to change your mind, if the software you're trying to install has drawn criticism from other Windows customers. It was built in to the older version of Internet Explorer, version 8. It's now part of Windows 10.

SmartScreen is not the same as Smart Search. SmartScreen, discussed here, offers some real benefits to most Windows users. Smart Search, on the other hand, is a pernicious piece of snooping malware (did I put you off sufficiently?) that Microsoft sneaks into Windows 10. You have to turn off Cortana in order to disable Smart Search — and that isn't easy. Follow along here to use SmartScreen.

One part of SmartScreen works in conjunction with Windows Defender. In fact, sometimes I've seen an infected file trigger a toaster notification from Windows Defender, and later had the same infected file prompt the SmartScreen warning shown in Figure 3-5.

Figure 3-5: Smart-Screen may take the credit for the bust, but Windows Defender did the work.

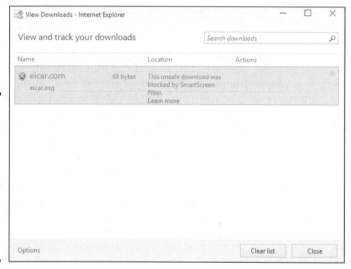

If you don't run the program, it gets stuffed into the same location that Windows Defender puts its quarantined programs — out of the way where you can't find it, unless you go in through Windows Defender's History tab (refer to Figure 3-4).

There's a second part of SmartScreen that works completely differently. Something like this:

1. You download something — anything — from the Internet.

Most browsers and many email programs and other online services (including instant messengers) put a "brand" on the file that indicates where the file came from.

2. When you try to launch the file, Windows checks the name of the file and the URL of origin to see whether they're on a "trusted" white list.

3. If the file doesn't pass muster, you see the notification in Figure 3-5.

4. The more people who install the program from that site, the more "trusted" the program becomes.

Again, Microsoft is collecting information about your system — in this case, about your downloads — but it's for a good cause.

How-To Geek has an excellent description of the precise way the tracking mechanism works: `www.howtogeek.com/128199/learn-where-windows-8-stores-smartscreen-filter-information-for-downloaded-files`.

Microsoft claims that SmartScreen helped protect IE9 users from more than 1.5 billion attempted malware attacks and 150 million phishing attacks. Microsoft also claims that, when a Windows user is confronted with a confirmation message, the risk of getting infected is 25-70 percent. Of course it's impossible to independently verify those figures — and the gap from 25-70 percent gapes — but SmartScreen does seem to help in the fight against scumware.

So what can go wrong? Not much. If SmartScreen can't make a connection to its main database when it hits something phishy, er, fishy, you see a green screen like the one in Figure 3-6 telling you that SmartScreen can't be reached right now. The connection can be broken for many reasons, such as the Microsoft servers go down or maybe you downloaded a program and decided to run it later. When that happens, if you can't get your machine connected, you're on your own.

Figure 3-6:
If Smart-
Screen
can't phone
home, it
leaves you
on your
own.

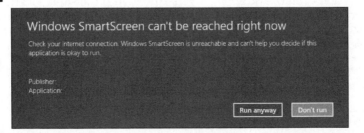

Windows SmartScreen can't be reached right now

Check your internet connection. Windows SmartScreen is unreachable and can't help you decide if this application is okay to run.

Publisher:
Application:

Run anyway   Don't run

Turning off SmartScreen is an option when you install Windows. You can also turn it off manually. Normally, overriding a SmartScreen warning requires the okay of someone with an administrator account. You can change that, too. Here's how:

1. **In the Cortana search box, to the right of the Start button, type** smartscreen. **At the top of the resulting list, click or tap Change SmartScreen settings.**

   The old Control Panel's Security and Maintenance pane appears.

2. **On the left, click or tap the Change Windows SmartScreen settings link.**

   The Windows SmartScreen dialog box appears, as shown in Figure 3-7.

Figure 3-7:
Think twice
before
turning
off Smart-
Screen.

3. **Tap or click the appropriate button to drop the requirement for an administrative account in order to okay a SmartScreen warning override or to turn off SmartScreen entirely.**

4. **Tap or click OK.**

   If you disabled SmartScreen, you see a near-immediate reaction in the desktop's notification area, warning you that SmartScreen has been turned off.

Booting Securely with UEFI

If you've ever struggled with your PC's BIOS — or been knee-capped by a capable rootkit — you know that BIOS should've been sent to the dugout a decade ago.

Windows 10 will pull the industry kicking and screaming out of the BIOS generation and into a far more capable — and controversial — alternative,

Unified Extensible Firmware Interface (UEFI). Although UEFI machines in the time of Windows 7 were unusual, starting with Windows 8, every new machine with a Runs Windows 8 sticker is required to run UEFI; it's part of the licensing requirement. Windows 10 continues the same requirement. 'Tis a brave new world.

A brief history of BIOS

To understand where Windows is headed, it's best to look at where it's been. And where it's been with BIOS inside PCs spans the entire history of the personal computer. That makes PC-resident BIOS more than 30 years old. The very first IBM PC had a BIOS, and it didn't look all that different from the inscrutable one you swear at now.

The Basic Input/Output System, or *BIOS*, is a program responsible for getting all your PC's hardware in order and then firing up the operating system — in this case, Windows — and finally handing control of the computer over to the OS. BIOS runs automatically when the PC is turned on.

Older operating systems, such as DOS, relied on BIOS to perform input and output functions. More modern OSs, including Windows, have their own device drivers that make BIOS control obsolete, after the OS is running.

Every BIOS has a user interface, which looks much like the one in Figure 3-8. You press a key while the BIOS is starting and, using obscure keyboard incantations, take some control over your PC's hardware, select boot devices (in other words, tell BIOS where the operating system is located), overclock the processor, disable or rearrange hard drives, and the like.

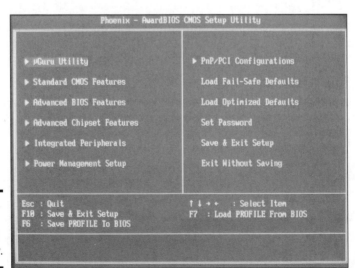

Figure 3-8:
The
AwardBIOS
Setup Utility.

The PC you're using right now may or may not have UEFI, and even if it does have UEFI, you may not be able to get to it. Windows 10 runs just fine on BIOS systems, but it can protect you even better — especially from rootkits — if your PC supports UEFI.

How UEFI is different from/better than BIOS

BIOS has all sorts of problems, not the least of which is its susceptibility to malware. Rootkits like to hook themselves into the earliest part of the booting process — permitting them to run underneath Windows — and BIOS has a big Kick Me sign on its tail.

UEFI and BIOS can coexist: UEFI can run on top of BIOS, hooking itself into the program locations where the operating system may call BIOS, basically usurping all the BIOS functions after UEFI gets going. UEFI can also run without BIOS, taking care of all the run-time functions. The only thing UEFI can't do is perform the *POST* power-on self-test or run the initial setup. PCs that have UEFI without BIOS need separate programs for POST and setup that run automatically when the PC is started.

Unlike BIOS, which sits inside a chip on your PC's motherboard, UEFI can exist on a disk, just like any other program, or in non-volatile memory on the motherboard or even on a network share.

UEFI is very much like an operating system that runs before your final operating system kicks in. UEFI has access to all the PC's hardware, including the mouse and network connections. It can take advantage of your fancy video card and monitor, as shown in Figure 3-9. It can even access the Internet. If you've ever played with BIOS, you know that this is in a whole new dimension.

Compare Figure 3-8 with 3-9, and you'll have some idea where technology's been and where it's heading.

BIOS — the whole process surrounding BIOS, including POST — takes a long, long time. UEFI, by contrast, can go by quite quickly. The BIOS program itself is easy to reverse-engineer and has no internal security protection. In the malware maelstrom, it's a sitting duck. UEFI can run in any irascible, malware-dodging way its inventors contrive.

Dual boot in the old world involves a handoff to a clunky text program; in the new world, it can be much simpler, more visual, and controlled by mouse or touch.

More to the point, UEFI can police operating systems prior to loading them. That could make rootkit writers' lives considerably more difficult by, for example, refusing to run an OS unless it has a proper digital security

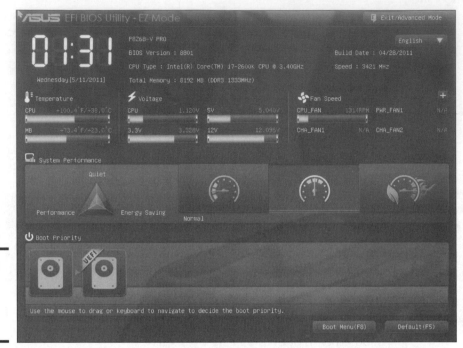

Figure 3-9:
The UEFI
interface
on an
ASUS PC.

signature. Windows Defender can work with UEFI to validate OSs before they're loaded. And that's where the controversy begins.

How Windows 10 uses UEFI

A UEFI *Secure Boot* option validates programs before allowing them to run. If Secure Boot is turned on, operating system loaders have to be "signed" using a digital certificate. If you want to dual boot between Windows 10 and Linux, the Linux program must have a digital certificate — something Linux programs have never required before.

After UEFI validates the digital key, UEFI calls on Windows Defender to verify the certificate for the OS loader. Windows Defender (or another security program) can go out to the Internet and check to see whether UEFI is about to run an OS that has had its certificate yanked.

So, in essence, in a dual boot system, Windows Defender decides whether an operating system gets loaded on your Secure Boot-enabled machine.

That curls the toes of many Linux fans. Why should their operating systems be subject to Microsoft's rules, if you want to dual boot between Windows 10 and Linux?

If you have a PC with UEFI and Secure Boot and you want to boot an operating system that doesn't have a Microsoft-approved digital signature, you have two options:

+ **You can turn off Secure Boot.**
+ **You can manually add a key to the UEFI validation routine, specifically allowing that unsigned operating system to load.**

Some PCs won't let you turn off Secure Boot. So if you want to dual boot Windows 10 and some other operating system on a Windows 10-certified computer, you may have lots of hoops to jump through. Check with your hardware manufacturer.

Controlling User Account Control

User Account Control *(UAC)* is a pain in the neck, but then again, it's supposed to be a pain in the neck. If you try to install a program that's going to make system-level changes, you see the obnoxious prompt in Figure 3-10.

Figure 3-10:
User
Account
Control tries
to keep
you from
clobbering
your system.

UAC's a drama queen, too. The approval dialog box in Figure 3-10 appears front and center, but at the same time, your entire desktop dims, and you're forced to deal with the UAC prompt.

UAC grabs you by the eyeballs and shakes once or twice for a good reason: It's telling you that a program wants to make changes to your system — not piddling things like changing a document or opening a picture, but earth-shaking things like modifying the Registry or poking around inside system folders.

If you go into your system folders manually or if you fire up the Registry Editor and start making loose and fancy with Registry keys, UAC figures you know what you're doing and leaves you alone. But the minute a program tries to do those kinds of things, Windows whups you upside the head, warns you that a potentially dangerous program is on the prowl, and gives you a chance to kill the program in its tracks.

Windows lets you adjust User Account Control so it isn't quite as dramatic — or you can get rid of it entirely.

To bring up the slider and adjust your computer's UAC level, follow these steps:

1. **In the Cortana search box, next to the Start button, type** `user account`**. At the top of the ensuing list, choose Change User Account Control Settings.**

The slider shown in Figure 3-11 appears.

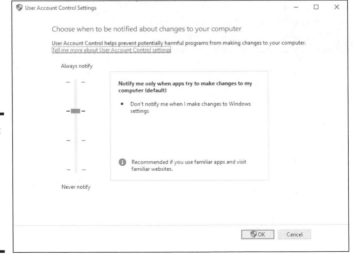

Figure 3-11:
Windows
allows you
to change
the level
of UAC
intrusive-
ness.

2. **Adjust the slider according to Table 3-1, and then tap or click OK.**

   Perhaps surprisingly, as soon as you try to change your UAC level, Windows hits you with a User Account Control prompt (refer to Figure 3-10). If you're using a standard account, you have to provide an administrator username and password to make the change. If you're using an administrator account, you have to confirm the change.

Table 3-1　　　　　User Account Control Levels

Slider	What It Means	Recommendations
Level 1	Always brings up the full UAC notification whenever a program tries to install software or make changes to the computer that require an administrator account, or when you try to make changes to Windows settings that require an administrator account. You see these notifications even if you're using an administrator account. The screen blacks out, and you can't do anything until the UAC screen is answered.	This level offers the highest security but also the highest hassle factor.
Level 2	Brings up the UAC notification whenever a program tries to make changes to your computer, but generally doesn't bring up a UAC notification when you make changes directly.	The default — and probably the best choice.
Level 3	This level is the same as Level 2 except that the UAC notification doesn't lock and dim your desktop.	Potentially problematic. Dimming and locking the screen present a high hurdle for malware.
Level 4	UAC is disabled — programs can install other programs or make changes to Windows settings, and you can change anything you like, without triggering any UAC prompts. Note that this doesn't override other security settings. For example, if you're using a standard account, you still need to provide an administrator's ID and password before you can install a program that runs for all users.	Choosing Level 4 automatically turns off all UAC warnings — not recommended.

3. **Tap or click Yes.**

   Your changes take effect immediately.

This description sounds simple, but the details are quite complex. Consider. Microsoft's Help system says that if your computer is at Level 2, the default setting in Windows, "You will be notified if a program outside of Windows tries to make changes to a Windows setting." So how does Windows tell when a program is "outside of Windows" — and thus whether actions taken by the program are worthy of a UAC prompt at Levels 2 or 3?

UAC-level rules are interpreted according to a special Windows security certificate. Programs signed with that certificate are deemed to be part of Windows. Programs that aren't signed with that specific certificate are "outside of Windows" and thus trigger UAC prompts if your computer is at Level 1, 2, or 3.

Poking at Windows Firewall

A *firewall* is a program that sits between your computer and the Internet, protecting you from the big, mean, nasty gorillas riding around on the information superhighway. An *inbound firewall* acts like a traffic cop that, in the best of all possible worlds, allows only "good" stuff into your computer and keeps all the "bad" stuff out on the Internet, where it belongs. An *outbound firewall* prevents your computer from sending bad stuff to the Internet, such as when your computer becomes infected with a virus or has another security problem.

Windows includes a usable (if not fancy) inbound firewall. It also includes a snarly, hard-to-configure, rudimentary outbound firewall, which has all the social graces of a junkyard dog. Unless you know the magic incantations, you never even see the outbound firewall — it's completely muzzled unless you dig in to the Windows doghouse and teach it some tricks.

Everybody needs an inbound firewall, without a doubt. You already have one, in Windows 10, and you don't need to do anything to it.

Outbound firewalls tend to bother you mercilessly with inscrutable warnings saying that obscure processes are trying to send data. If you simply click through and let the program phone home, you're defeating the purpose of the outbound firewall. On the other hand, if you take the time to track down every single outbound event warning, you may spend half your life chasing firewall snipes.

I have a few friends who insist on running an outbound firewall. They uniformly recommend Comodo Firewall, which is available in a free-for-personal-use version at `http://personalfirewall.comodo.com`.

Hardware firewalls

Most modern routers and wireless access points include significant firewalling capability. It's part and parcel of the way they work, when they share an Internet connection among many computers.

Routers and wireless access points add an extra step between your computer and the Internet. That extra jump — named network address translation — combined with innate intelligence on the router's part can provide an extra layer of protection that works independently from, but in conjunction with, the firewall running on your PC.

I think outbound firewalls are a complete waste of time. Although I'm sure some people have been alerted to Windows infections when their outbound firewall goes bananas, 99.99 percent of the time, the outbound warnings are just noise. Outbound firewalls don't catch the cleverest malware, anyway.

Understanding Firewall basic features

All versions of Windows 10 ship with a decent and capable, but not fool-proof, *stateful* firewall named Windows Firewall (WF). (See the nearby side-bar, "What's a stateful firewall?")

The WF inbound firewall is on by default. Unless you change something, Windows Firewall is turned on for all connections on your PC. For example, if you have a LAN cable, a wireless networking card, and a 3G USB card on a specific PC, WF is turned on for them all. The only way Windows Firewall gets turned off is if you deliberately turn it off or if the network administrator on your Big Corporate Network decides to disable it by remote control or install Windows service packs with Windows Firewall turned off.

In extremely unusual circumstances, malware (viruses, Trojans, whatever) have been known to turn off Windows Firewall. If your firewall kicks out, Windows lets you know loud and clear with balloon notifications near the system clock on the desktop, toaster notifications from the right on the Start screen, and a crescendo from Ride of the Valkyries blaring on your speakers.

You can change WF settings for inbound protection relatively easily. When you make changes, they apply to all connections on your PC. On the other hand, WF settings for outbound protection make the rules of cricket look like child's play.

WF kicks in before the computer is connected to the network. Back in the not-so-good old days, many PCs got infected between the time they were connected and when the firewall came up.

What's a stateful firewall?

At the risk of oversimplifying a bit, a *stateful* firewall is an inbound firewall that remembers. A stateful firewall keeps track of packets of information going out of your computer and where they're headed. When a packet arrives and tries to get in, the inbound firewall matches the originating address of the incoming packet against the log of addresses of the outgoing packets to make sure that any packet allowed through the firewall comes from an expected location.

Stateful packet filtering isn't 100-percent foolproof. And you must have some exceptions so that unexpected packets can come through for reasons discussed elsewhere in this chapter. But a stateful firewall is a fast reliable way to minimize your exposure to potentially destructive probes from out on the big bad Internet.

Speaking your firewall's lingo

At this point, I need to inundate you with a bunch of jargon so that you can take control of Windows Firewall. Hold your nose and dive in. The concepts aren't that difficult, although the lousy terminology sounds like it was invented by a first-year advertising student. Refer to this section if you become bewildered when wading through the WF dialog boxes.

As you no doubt realize, the amount of data that can be sent from one computer to another over a network can be tiny or huge. Computers talk with each other by breaking the data into *packets* (or small chunks of data with a wrapper that identifies where the data came from and where it's going).

On the Internet, packets can be sent in two ways:

✦ **User Datagram Protocol (UDP):** UDP is fast and sloppy. The computer sending the packets doesn't keep track of which packets were sent, and the computer receiving the packets doesn't make any attempt to get the sender to resend packets that vanish mysteriously into the bowels of the Internet. UDP is the kind of *protocol* (transmission method) that can work with live broadcasts, where short gaps wouldn't be nearly as disruptive as long pauses, while the computers wait to resend a dropped packet.

✦ **Transmission Control Protocol (TCP):** TCP is methodical and complete. The sending computer keeps track of which packets it has sent. If the receiving computer doesn't get a packet, it notifies the sending computer, which resends the packet. Almost all communication over the Internet these days goes by way of TCP.

Every computer on a network has an *IP address,* which is a collection of four sets of numbers, each between 0 and 255. For example, 192.1610.2 is a common IP address for computers connected to a local network; the computer that handles the Dummies.com website is at 208.215.179.139. You can think of the IP address as analogous to a telephone number. See Book II, Chapter 6 for details.

Peeking in to your firewall

When you use a firewall — and you should — you change the way your computer communicates with other computers on the Internet. This section explains what Windows Firewall does behind the scenes so that when it gets in the way, you understand how to tweak it. (You find the ins and outs of working around the firewall in the "Making inbound exceptions" section, later in this chapter.)

When two computers communicate, they need not only each other's IP address but also a specific entry point called a *port* — think of it as a telephone extension — to talk to each other. For example, most websites respond to requests sent to port 80. There's nothing magical about the number 80; it's just the port number that people have agreed to use when trying to get to a website's computer. If your web browser wants to look at the Dummies.com website, it sends a packet to 208.215.179.139, port 80.

Windows Firewall works by handling all these duties simultaneously:

✦ **It keeps track of outgoing packets and allows incoming packets to go through the firewall if they can be matched with an outgoing packet.** In other words, WF works as a stateful inbound firewall.

✦ **If your computer is attached to a private network, Windows Firewall allows packets to come and go on ports 139 and 445, but only if they came from another computer on your local network and only if they're using TCP.** Windows Firewall needs to open those ports for file and printer sharing. WF also opens several ports for Windows Media Player if you've chosen to share your media files, as you might within a HomeGroup (see Book VII, Chapter 5), for example.

✦ **Similarly, if your computer is attached to a private network, Windows Firewall automatically opens ports 137, 138, and 5355 for UDP, but only for packets that originate on your local network.**

✦ **If you specifically told Windows Firewall that you want it to allow packets to come in on a specific port and the Block All Incoming Connections check box isn't selected, WF follows your orders.** You may need to open a port in this way for online gaming, for example.

✦ **Windows Firewall allows packets to come into your computer if they're sent to the Remote Assistance program, as long as you created a Remote Assistance request on this PC and told Windows to open your firewall (see Book VII, Chapter 2).** Remote Assistance allows other users to take control of your PC, but it has its own security settings and strong password protection. Still, it's a known security hole that's enabled when you create a request.

✦ **You can tell Windows Firewall to accept packets that are directed at specific programs.** Usually, any company that makes a program designed to listen for incoming Internet traffic (Skype is a prime example, as are any instant-messaging programs) adds its program to the list of designated exceptions when the program is installed.

✦ **Unless an inbound packet meets one of the preceding criteria, it's simply ignored.** Windows Firewall swallows it without a peep. Conversely, unless you've changed something, any and all outbound traffic goes through unobstructed.

Making inbound exceptions

Firewalls can be absolutely infuriating. You may have a program that has worked for a hundred years on all sorts of computers, but the minute you install it on a Windows 10 machine with Windows Firewall in action, it just stops working, for absolutely no apparent reason.

You can get mad at Microsoft and scream at Windows Firewall, but when you do, realize that at least part of the problem lies in the way the firewall has to work. (See the "Peeking in to your firewall" section, earlier in this chapter, for an explanation of what your firewall does behind the scenes.) It has to block packets that are trying to get in, unless you explicitly tell the firewall to allow them to get in.

Perhaps most infuriatingly, WF blocks those packets by simply swallowing them, not by notifying the computer that sent the packet. Windows Firewall has to remain "stealthy" because if it sends back a packet that says, "Hey, I got your packet, but I can't let it through," the bad guys get an acknowledgment that your computer exists, they can probably figure out which firewall you're using, and they may be able to combine those two pieces of information to give you a headache. It's far better for Windows Firewall to act like a black hole.

Some programs need to "listen" to incoming traffic from the Internet; they wait until they're contacted and then respond. Usually, you know whether you have this type of program because the installer tells you that you need to tell your firewall to back off.

If you have a program that doesn't (or can't) poke its own hole through the Windows Firewall, you can tell WF to allow packets destined for that specific program — and *only* that program — in through the firewall. You may want to do that with a game that needs to accept incoming traffic, for example, or for an Outlook extender program that interacts with mobile phones.

To poke a hole in the inbound Windows Firewall for a specific program:

1. **Make sure that the program you want to allow through the Firewall is installed.**

2. **In the Search box, next to the Start button, type firewall. Choose Allow an App Through Windows Firewall.**

   Windows Firewall presents you with a lengthy list of programs that you may want to allow (see Figure 3-12): If a box is selected, Windows Firewall allows unsolicited incoming packets of data directed to that program and that program alone, and the column tells you whether the connection is allowed for private or public connections.

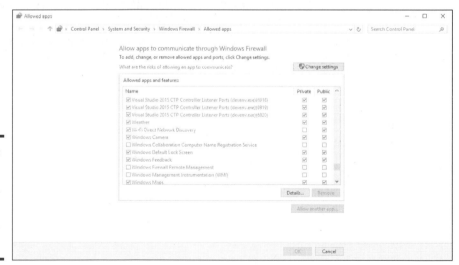

Figure 3-12: Allow installed programs to poke through the firewall.

These settings don't apply to incoming packets of data that are received in response to a request from your computer; they apply only when a packet of data appears on your firewall's doorstep without an invitation.

In Figure 3-12, the tiled Weather app is allowed to receive inbound packets whether you're connected to a private or public network. Windows Media Player, on the other hand, may accept unsolicited inbound data from other computers only if you're connected to a private network: If you're attached to a public network, inbound packets headed for Windows Media Player are swallowed by the WF Black Hole (patent pending).

3a. ***If you can find the program that you want to poke through the firewall listed in the Allow Programs list,*** **select the check boxes that correspond to whether you want to allow the unsolicited incoming data when connected to a home or work network and whether you want to allow the incoming packets when connected to a public network.**

It's rare indeed that you'd allow access when connected to a public network but not to a home or work network.

3b. ***If you can't find the program that you want to poke through the firewall,*** **you need to go out and look for it. Tap or click the Change Settings button at the top, and then tap or click the Allow another App button at the bottom.**

You have to tap or click the Change Settings button first and then tap or click Allow another Program. It's kind of a double-down protection feature that ensures you don't accidentally change things.

Windows Firewall goes out to all common program locations and finally presents you with the Whack a Mol . . . er, Add an App list like the one shown in Figure 3-13. It can take a while.

Figure 3-13:
Allow a
program
(that you've
thoroughly
vetted!)
to break
through the
firewall.

4. **Choose the program you want to add, and then tap or click the Add button.**

Realize that you're opening a potential, albeit small, security hole. The program you choose had better be quite capable of handling packets from unknown sources. If you authorize a renegade program to accept incoming packets, the bad program could let the fox into the chicken coop. If you know what I mean.

You return to the Windows Firewall Allowed Apps list (refer to Figure 3-12), and your newly selected program is now available.

5. **Select the check boxes to allow your poked-through program to accept incoming data while you're connected to a private or a public network. Then tap or click OK.**

Your poked-through program can immediately start handling inbound data.

In many cases, poking through the Windows Firewall doesn't solve the whole problem. You may have to poke through your modem or router as well — unsolicited packets that arrive at the router may get kicked back according to the router's rules, even if Windows would allow them in. Unfortunately, each router and the method for poking holes in the router's inbound firewall differ. Check the site `www.portforward.com/routers.htm` for an enormous amount of information about poking through routers.

Chapter 4: Top Security Helpers

In This Chapter

↙ **Deciding whether to pay for BitLocker**

↙ **Keeping on top of all those passwords**

↙ **Watching your programs for updates**

↙ **Blocking Java and Flash in your browser**

↙ **The ultimate antiscumware scan**

*I*n Chapter 3 of this minibook, I talk about built-in Windows programs that are available to every Windows 10 owner. In this chapter, I cast the web out a bit further to include one Microsoft encryption program you have to pay for — *BitLocker* which is in Windows 10 Pro — and a handful of free-for-personal use programs that belong on every Windows 10 user's desktop.

Windows covers lots of security bases, but it doesn't touch them all.

Two very good programs will store all your passwords and automatically fill in the username/password prompts at the websites you visit. One of them, *LastPass,* is based in the *cloud,* which means you can get at it even when you're on a dive boat in the Similans. The other, *RoboForm,* stores its data on your computer or on a USB drive. I take you through the pros and cons of both approaches in this chapter.

Sometimes you — or one of your friends — will get an infection that even Windows Defender (and Windows Defender Offline) can't handle. Usually it's because you (or, say, "they") installed a program they didn't research. If you (er, *they*) get hit bad, there's one place to turn. *Malwarebytes,* a combination of software and a very competent website, can crack just about any infection.

Secunia Personal Software Inspector is free and does an amazing job of helping you keep all your software up to date.

If you want to connect to a website and make sure nobody can snoop on your connection — particularly important if you access financial sites from public WiFi setups, like in a coffee shop or, urp, a bank — you should figure out how to use a VPN. I've been using *VyprVPN* for years, and although it isn't free, it works great.

Finally, I know of one specific Java and Flash blocker that works very well in the Firefox browser. *NoScript* can be customized in many ways. Although there are more-or-less similar choices for Chrome and Edge, NoScript works the best of them all. It's the primary reason why I use Firefox as my main browser.

All these programs are free (or nearly so), well known, and tested — and they need to be part of your Windows system.

Deciding about BitLocker

BitLocker encrypts an entire drive. (Actually, it encrypts a *volume* — typically a piece of a drive that's been lopped off to treat as if it were a drive all by itself.) Unlike the Encrypting File System (see the nearby "The Encrypting File System [EFS]" sidebar), you have to encrypt full drives (or, more accurately, volumes) or nothing at all. BitLocker runs *underneath* Windows: It starts before Windows starts. The Windows partition on a BitLocker-protected drive is completely encrypted. Even if a thief gets his hands on your laptop or hard drive, he can't view anything on it — not even your settings or system files.

BitLocker To Go is quite similar to BitLocker, except it works on USB drives.

BitLocker is part of Windows 10 Pro. It is not part of the regular version of Windows 10. If you have Windows 10 and you want to get BitLocker, you have to upgrade to Windows 10 Pro. There's no other way to get it.

The Encrypting File System (EFS)

The Microsoft *Encrypting File System* works with or without BitLocker. EFS is a method for encrypting individual files or groups of files on a hard drive. EFS starts after Windows boots: It runs as a program under Windows, which means it can leave traces of itself and the data that's being encrypted in temporary Windows places that may be sniffed by exploit programs. The Windows directory isn't encrypted by EFS, so bad guys (and girls!) who can get access to the directory can hammer it with brute-force password attacks. Widely available tools can crack EFS if the cracker can reboot the, uh, crackee's computer. Thus, for example, EFS can't protect the hard drive on a stolen laptop/notebook. Windows has supported the Encrypting File System since the halcyon days of Windows 2000.

BitLocker and EFS protect against two completely different kinds of attacks. Given a choice, you probably want BitLocker.

I talk about the various versions of Windows 10 in Book I, Chapter 3. Suffice it to say that some people feel their information is sufficiently valuable that BitLocker, all by itself, justifies paying the extra bucks for Windows 10 Pro.

Here's how to encrypt your hard drive with BitLocker:

1. **Wait until you have several hours free.**

   Encrypting a drive can take a long, long, long, time.

2. **In the Search box, next to the Start button, type** bitlocker; **then click or tap Manage BitLocker.**

   The BitLocker Drive Encryption dialog box appears, as shown in Figure 4-1.

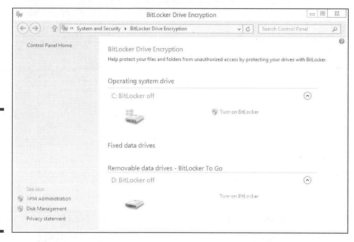

Figure 4-1:
Encrypt
full drives
(actually,
volumes)
using a key
you specify.

3. **Next to the drive (volume) you want to encrypt, tap or click Turn On BitLocker.**

4. **If you get a message asking you to verify, choose Yes.**

   If your PC doesn't have a built-in Trusted Platform Module system, you see a message that says *Your administrator must set the 'Allow BitLocker without a compatible TPM' option.* The only easy way to solve that problem is to run the Local Group Policy Editor program, gpedit. msc. If you need advice, check out the TechNet article at `http://technet.microsoft.com/en-us/library/cc732725(v=ws.10).aspx#BKMK_S5`.

   The BitLocker Drive Encryption setup dialog box appears.

5. **Tap or click Next.**

   On Operating System drives (such as your drive C:), the Preparing Your Drive dialog box appears.

6. **Tap or click Next.**

   On removable drives, BitLocker asks how you want to unlock the drive, as shown in Figure 4-2.

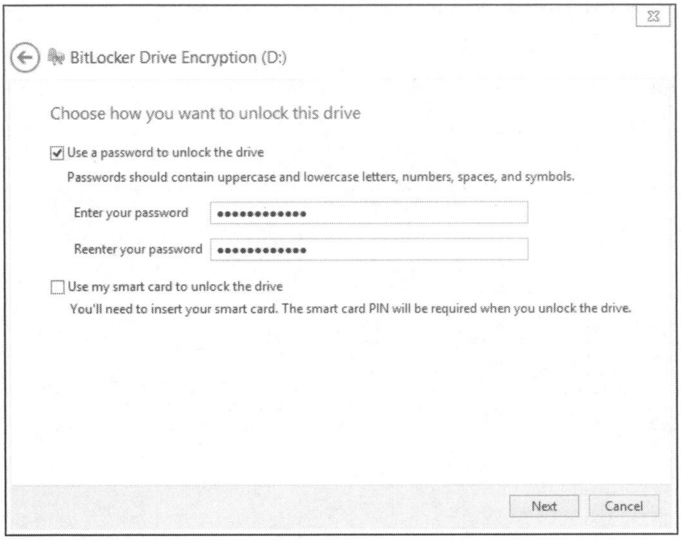

Figure 4-2:
Enter your
password.

7. **Enter your password twice, and tap or click Next.**

   On an operating system drive, BitLocker asks how you want to unlock the drive.

8. **Tap or click Require a Startup Key at Every Startup.**

   This ensures that data on a stolen laptop can't be purloined.

   On an operating system drive, BitLocker asks how you want to store your recovery key.

9. **Choose Save the Recovery Key to a USB Flash Drive.**

   The wizard takes you through the steps.

10. **Select the Run BitLocker System Check check box, and choose Continue.**

    BitLocker asks for your permission and then reboots your system. After rebooting, it starts encrypting — a process that can take a few minutes on a USB drive or many hours on a full C: drive.

If you encrypted your operating system drive — typically your C: drive — keep that USB drive in a safe place. You need it every time you want to boot your computer.

Oh. In case you were wondering. Yes, you can use BitLocker on Storage Spaces. BitLocker encrypts the whole Storage Space.

Managing Your Passwords

You can find no end of advice on creating strong passwords, using clever tricks, stats, mnemonics, and such. But all too frequently people (myself included in this rebuke) tend to reuse little passwords at what people think are inconsequential sites. It's a big mistake. If somebody hacks into that small-time site and steals your password — a process that's frighteningly common these days — any other place where you've used that same password is immediately vulnerable.

There have been some spectacular examples of ultra-secure sites getting hacked in the past few years, where the hacker stole a username and password off a little inconsequential site and then discovered that the same username and password opened the doors to a trove of top-secret — even politically sensitive — corporate email or customer bank account information. The usernames and passwords were stolen from seasoned security professionals and admins at sensitive sites. You'd think they'd know better.

Using password managers

I don't know about you, but I have dozens of usernames and passwords that I use fairly regularly. There's just no way I can remember them all. And my monitor isn't big enough to handle all the yellow sticky notes they'd demand.

That's where a password manager comes in. A *password manager* keeps track of all your online passwords. It can generate truly random passwords with the click of a button. Most of all, it remembers the username and password necessary to log on to a specific website.

Every time I go to www.ebay.com, for example, my password manager fills in my username and password. Amazon, too. Facebook. Twitter. My bank. Stock brokerage house. I have to remember the one password for the password manager, but after that, everything else gets filled in automatically. It's a huge timesaver.

A password manager won't log on to Windows for you, and it won't remember the passwords on documents or spreadsheets. But it does keep track of every online password and regurgitates the passwords you need with absolutely no hassle.

Which is better: Online or in-hand?

I have used two password-remembering programs for many years. I like — and trust — them both. The big difference between them? One was originally designed to run on a USB drive; the other has always been in the cloud, which is to say, on the Internet:

✦ **RoboForm Desktop,** which can store passwords on your hard drive or on a USB drive, works with all the major web browsers and has simple tools for synchronizing passwords between your hard drive and a USB drive.

✦ **LastPass,** which stores passwords on its website, uses an encryption technique that guarantees your passwords won't get stolen or cracked. I talk about the encryption method in the section "Liking LastPass," later in this chapter.

Although it started as a USB-toting application, RoboForm now offers **RoboForm Everywhere,** which synchronizes in the cloud, like LastPass.

Which one is better? It depends on how you use your computer.

If you always use the same computer or you can always remember to sync and take your RoboForm2Go USB drive with you, RoboForm works great.

Unfortunately, I don't meet either of those two criteria, so in recent years, I've been using LastPass. Of course, there's an additional security concern because your data's stored on LastPass's servers and not on the USB drive in your pocket. In addition, you need an Internet connection to get to LastPass — but then if you don't have an Internet connection, you probably don't need LastPass, either.

The new RoboForm Everywhere syncs to the cloud, too.

Opinions run all over the place, but I personally prefer LastPass's interface, as opposed to RoboForm Everywhere's. You should feel comfortable using either.

Rockin' RoboForm

RoboForm Desktop (`www.roboform.com`) has all the features you need in a password manager. It manages your passwords, of course, with excellent recognition of websites, automatically filling in your login details, but it'll also generate random passwords for you, if you like, fill in forms on the web, and create backups either on a USB drive or on another computer on your network.

What is AES-256?

The most effective encryption method that's commonly used on PCs conforms to the U.S. National Institute of Standards and Technology's Advanced Encryption Standard 256-bit specification.

AES is the first widely available, open encryption technique (yes, you can look at the program) that's been approved by the U.S. National Security Agency for Top Secret information. Of course, that fact has led to speculation that the NSA has cracked the algorithm, so it can decrypt AES-256 data, but there doesn't seem to be any corroboration. I guess the conspiracy theory makes for good beer-drinking banter but not much more.

It's been estimated that if you took all the computer horsepower currently on the face of the earth and set it to work on a single AES-256 encrypted file, cracking the encryption would take far longer than the age of the universe.

RoboForm stores all its data on a disk in AES-256 encrypted format. If somebody steals your RoboForm database, you needn't worry. Without the master key — which only you have — the whole database is gibberish.

RoboForm has versions for Windows, Mac, Linux, iPhone, iPad, Android phones and tablets, and BlackBerry. You need to buy a separate license for each computer, device, or USB drive.

The evaluation version of RoboForm (which can store up to ten passwords) is free. The Pro version, with form-filling, unlimited storage and several additional features, runs $29.95.

The new RoboForm Everywhere will store all your information on RoboForm's servers, so you can download it and use it anywhere — even on an unlimited number of computers. The trick is the price: Unlike the other versions, where you pay once and have a license for that specific version forever, RoboForm Everywhere costs $19.95 per year. (The first year's discounted to $9.95.) After you've paid for RoboForm Everywhere, if you want all the RoboForm Desktop features, including form-filling, you have to pay $29.95 per desktop. Prices may change, of course.

Liking LastPass

LastPass (www.lastpass.com) stores everything "in the cloud" on LastPass's servers. Like RoboForm, LastPass keeps track of your user IDs, passwords, automatic form-filling information (think name, address, phone, credit card number), and other settings and offers them to you with a click.

Using LastPass can't be simpler. Download and install it, and it'll appear with a red asterisk in the upper-right corner of your browser (see Figure 4-3).

LastPass

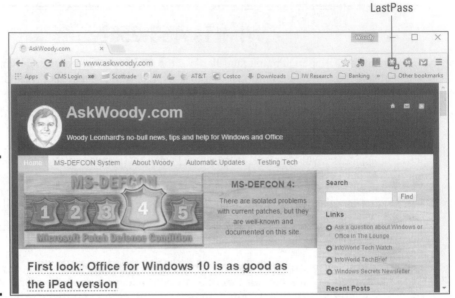

Figure 4-3:
LastPass is on the job if you can see a red asterisk in the upper-right corner.

You don't really need to do anything. LastPass will prompt you for the master password when you start using your browser. If LastPass is turned off, the star icon turns gray. Tap or click it, provide the master password, and the LastPass icon turns red again, ready to roll.

When you go to a site that requires a username and password, if LastPass recognizes the site, it fills them both in for you. If LastPass doesn't recognize the site, you fill in the blanks and click, and LastPass remembers the credentials for the next time you surf this way.

Form filling works similarly.

You can maintain two (or more) separate usernames and passwords for any specific site — say, you log on to a banking site with two different accounts. If LastPass has more than one set of credentials stored for a specific site, it takes its best guess as to which one you want but then gives you the option of using one of the others. In this screen shot, I have four separate credentials for the site — that's why there's a "4" on the LastPass icon.

Any time you want to look at the usernames and passwords that LastPass has squirreled away, tap or click the red LastPass icon. You have a chance to look at your *Vault* — which is your password database — or look up recently used passwords and much more. You can even keep encrypted notes to yourself.

The way LastPass handles your data is quite clever. All your passwords are encrypted using AES-256. They're encrypted and decrypted *on your PC.* Only you have the master password. So if the data is pilfered off LastPass's servers or somebody is sniffing your online communication, all the interlopers get is a bunch of useless bits.

LastPass is free for individual use. If you want versions for iPhone, iPad, Android, Windows Phone, or to run LastPass without installing a plug-in (important for the "universal" versions of Windows 10 web browsers, including Edge), you need the Premium edition, which costs $12 a year.

Keeping Your Other Programs Up to Date

You have Windows Update to keep Windows working and patched.

But what about all the other programs on your PC? Considering that something like 80 percent of all new infections come from *third-party* programs (read: software written by some company other than Microsoft), keeping those other programs updated is a crucial task.

That's where Secunia Personal Software Inspector — Secunia PSI to its friends — comes into play. Secunia PSI keeps tabs on every program in your computer. (Well, some really weird programs may not make the cut.) Secunia PSI keeps on top of the latest patches for every single program, and it warns you if the software you have is out of date.

If you use the Automatic Update features — which I recommend — Secunia PSI even installs updates for you as they become available.

Here's how to install Secunia Personal Software Inspector:

1. **Go to the Secunia main site (`www.secunia.com`), tap or click Products, and then under Consumer, tap or click the Personal Software Inspector (PSI) link.**

2. **Tap or click the Download button, and depending on your browser, either save or run the file.**

    The Setup Wizard starts.

3. **Accept all the defaults, and when the wizard asks whether you want to Install Updates Automatically, make sure you select the box before choosing Install.**

    Automatic updates are an important feature of Secunia PSI.

    After the wizard ends, it asks whether you want to Launch Secunia PSI now.

4. **Choose Yes.**

   The first run can take a long, long time, so be patient.

5. **If PSI prompts you to run a scan, do so.**

   When the scan finishes, you see a screen like Figure 4-4.

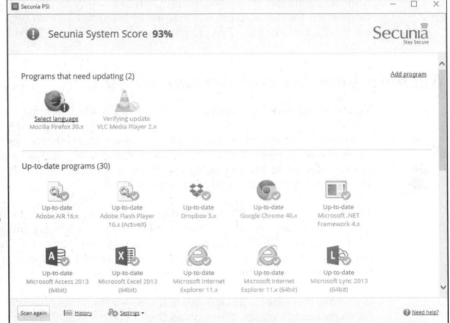

Figure 4-4:
Secunia
PSI's first
scan usually
brings
surprises.

6. **If any programs in the upper part of the screen need attention —
   for example, if you need to select the language for a particular
   program — tap or click the program and follow the instructions.**

   Secunia PSI may take a few minutes, it may take a few hours, but when
   it's done, all your applications are updated.

PSI offers only two options, under the Settings wheel:

✦ **Start on Boot:** You may or may not want to because it does tie up your
  machine for a while.

✦ **Install Updates Automatically:** Almost everybody needs this.

Blocking Java and Flash in Your Browser

Giorgio Maone has done the world a favor by bringing the NoScript add-on to the Firefox browser. NoScript selectively blocks Java, JavaScript, Flash, and other plug-ins — you control when and how. NoScript doesn't work in Chrome or Edge.

NoScript is so good that I use Firefox as my main browser on the desktop, simply because it's the only browser that supports NoScript. I also like the fact that Firefox doesn't have any particular interest in keeping track of where I go on the Internet.

Google has a new improved "sandbox" in Chrome that effectively keeps Flash safely tied up in a separate cocoon, where Flash can't crash or control the PC. I use Chrome, too, extensively — but only when I don't particularly care if Google's watching over my shoulder.

Edge has a simple switch that lets you turn off Java (actually the Java Runtime Environment). See Book V Chapter 1 for details.

Although Java and Flash may or may not be able to poke through their sandboxes in tiled, Windows Ultimate app versions of browsers, there's no question you have to worry about Java, Flash, and Acrobat — the three leading sources of Windows infections, by far — if you use a browser on the desktop.

Installing and using NoScript is easy. Here's how:

1. **Start Firefox, and in the upper-right corner, tap or click the Hamburger icon (three lines) and choose Add-Ons.**

   The standard Firefox add-ons page appears.

2. **In the search box, in the upper right, type** noscript **and press Enter or tap the magnifying glass icon.**

   Firefox comes up with a list of about a zillion add-ons, and the first is NoScript.

3. **To the right of NoScript, tap or click Install.**

   Firefox downloads and installs NoScript. You have to restart Firefox.

   The NoScript S appears in the upper-right corner of Firefox.

4. **Tap or click the NoScript S icon and choose Options, or tap or click the Options button and choose Options. Then tap or click the Embeddings tab.**

   The NoScript Options dialog box appears, as shown in Figure 4-5.

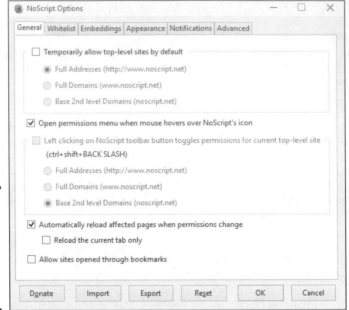

Figure 4-5:
NoScript's
default
configu-
ration really
locks things
down.

5. **Consult Table 4-1, and decide whether you want to change any of the settings. If you do, select or deselect the appropriate box(es) and tap or click OK.**

The NoScript Release Notes page may appear. If it does, ignore everything about running Registry cleaners.

6. **Review the annotated directions at** `www.noscript.net/screenshots`.

You may have to click the S icon and select Temporarily Allow All on This Page for the video to run.

By the time you've gone through the video and the tutorial, you're in very good shape.

Getting used to NoScript may take a while. You're going to find that some of the sites you visit all the time — including financial sites and most sites with ordering baskets — won't work unless you allow scripts on the site. You may even hate me for recommending it to you. Fair enough.

At the same time, you should feel much more secure, knowing that the largest source of Windows infections are being blocked before they even have a chance to get into your PC.

Table 4-1	NoScript Restrictions
Forbid	*And You Block*
Java	Both JavaScript and Java. In spite of the names, Java (which is a complex programming language that interacts with the Java Runtime Environment on your PC) and JavaScript (which is a much simpler language that runs on your PC all by itself) are very different. Historically, JavaScript was used by malicious websites to wreak havoc. More recently, Java — particularly aided by bugs in the Java Runtime Environment — has become a very fertile ground for attacks. Shopping sites, such as Amazon and eBay, use Java programs to keep track of your shopping cart and purchases. Email sites, such as Hotmail/ Outlook.com and Gmail, also need Java, as do forums. You have to tell NoScript to back off on those sites.
Flash	Any Flash videos on a site won't play. If you think that means you can't watch videos on YouTube, you're wrong: YouTube has spent years converting the vast majority of its videos to other formats, including formats that work with NoScript. If you have NoScript set to block Flash and you go to a YouTube site, YouTube is smart enough to understand that it can't play Flash, and will switch to a different format if it's available. The web is finally getting rid of Flash. Slowly.
Silverlight	Microsoft's answer to Flash is so bad that Microsoft *itself* isn't allowing Silverlight into the tiled full-screen part of Windows 10. That should tell you something. Don't need it. Don't want it.
Other Plugins	A motley assortment of plug-ins get stopped in their tracks including, notably, any PDF rendering plugins. Select this box, and you can't read PDF files directly in your browser; you have to go through the extra step of downloading the PDF file and opening it in a viewer, preferably one other than Adobe Acrobat Reader, which has been plagued with security holes for years. Choosing this box also blocks QuickTime files.

NoScript is absolutely free. The effort's supported a little bit by those cloying Clean Your Registry and other ads, when they appear, but primarily by donations from people like you and me. If you use NoScript, take a minute to make a donation via the Donate button in the upper-right corner. You'll be helping to make the web a safer place for everybody. And, yes, PayPal is already on NoScript's "allowed" white list.

Fighting Back at Tough Scumware

Windows Defender works great. But sometimes you need a second opinion. Sometimes you get hit with an infection that's so nasty, absolutely nothing will clean it up.

That's when you want to check out Malwarebytes (`www.malwarebytes.org`).

Malwarebytes is a last resort. If your system is running normally, there's no reason to bother with it. In fact, if your system is really messed up, you can probably fix things with a full scan in Windows Defender (see Book IX, Chapter 3) or Windows Defender Offline — or even a System Refresh (see Book VIII, Chapter 2). If you've tried all that and still can't get your furshlinger machine to work properly, time to haul out the big guns.

Malwarebytes has long been my software (and site) of choice for going after absolutely intractable infections — viruses, Trojans, scumware, spyware, retroware, introware, sticky gooey messyware, you name it, Malwarebytes can probably get rid of it.

When you're ready to tear out your hair, you've run Windows Defender and Windows Defender Offline, and performed Refresh, and you *still* can't get rid of the beast that's plaguing your system, here's what to do:

1. **Go to the Malwarebytes support forum, `http://forums.malwarebytes.org`, see whether anyone has the same problem, and if so, log on and talk to him.**

2. **If that doesn't work, go to the Malwarebytes Anti-Malware Free site, `http://malwarebytes.org/products/malwarebytes_free`, and install the free version of its anti-malware package.**

During the installation phase, Malwarebytes disables parts of Windows Defender. Not to worry. You don't want to run two antivirus packages at the same time.

3. **Run Malwarebytes and, if it doesn't get rid of your problem, post your results on the support forum.**

Start at `http://forums.malwarebytes.org/index.php?showtopic=9573`, and follow the instructions precisely.

4. **If Malwarebytes fixes your problem, pay for its Pro package.**

Even if you only use it occasionally. It's only $24.95, and you're helping to keep the Malwarebytes effort solvent.

You should run Malwarebytes manually: Don't let it run all the time because you'll hit inevitable conflicts with Windows Defender. When Malwarebytes is finished with a manual scan, it returns Windows Defender to its full and upright position.

Securing Your Communication with VyprVPN

If you're serious about protecting your surfing from prying eyes, and you ever use a public, unencrypted WiFi connection, the onus is on you to lock your connections down. The best way I know to protect against surreptitious sniffing — and a dozen other problems — involves a technology known as Virtual Private Networking, or VPN.

Firesheep (see sidebar) has raised the hackles — and the awareness — of WiFi users all over the world.

Https isn't the only way to subvert Firesheep in particular and sidejacking in general. If you connect to a wireless access point that uses WPA2 encryption, you're protected. (At least at this point, nobody I know has figured out a way to sidejack over a WPA2 encrypted WiFi connection.) But if you're using a public hotspot with no password required, you're definitely at risk.

Put simply, if you use an unencrypted WiFi hotspot, you need to take the bull by the horns and protect your own transmissions. Fortunately, that's reasonably easy, using a technology called Virtual Private Networking, or VPN.

What's a VPN?

You may have heard of VPN, but figured it was just too difficult for regular Windows users to hook together. Big companies have VPN, but they also

---

Firesheep and Sidejacking

In October 2010, white hat hacker Eric Butler released a startling Firefox add-on called Firesheep. If you run Firesheep on your computer, and other people using the same network aren't careful, you can "sniff" other people logging into websites. Click a link inside Firefox, and you can take over the logon credentials for the other person.

Eric Butler describes it this way: "When logging into a website, you usually start by submitting your username and password. The server then checks to see if an account matching this information exists and if so, replies back to you with a "cookie" which is used by your browser for all subsequent requests. While most websites protect your username and password by forcing you to log on over a secure (https) connection, many websites immediately drop back into unsecure (http) communication. If the cookie comes back to you over an unsecured connection, anybody snooping on your conversation can make a copy of the cookie and use it to interact with the website in precisely the same way you do — a process known as sidejacking. Firesheep makes it point-and-click easy to monitor WiFi signals, looking for cookies shouted out in the clear. It specifically sidejacks interactions with Amazon, CNET, Dropbox, Facebook, Flickr, Windows Live (including Hotmail), Twitter, WordPress, and Yahoo, among many others."

have experts to keep them running. Ends up that we little guys have good choices now, too.

VPN started as a way for big companies to securely connect PCs over the regular phone network. It used to take lots of specialty hardware, but if you worked for a bank and had to get into the bank's main computers from a laptop in Timbuktu, VPN was the only choice. Times have changed. Now you can get free or low-cost VPN connections that don't require any special hardware on your end, and they work surprisingly well.

When you set up a VPN connection with a server, you create a secure "tunnel" between your PC and the server. The tunnel encrypts all the data flowing between your PC and the server, provides integrity checks so no data gets scrambled, and continuously looks to make sure no other computer has taken over the connection.

VPNs prevent sidejacking because the connection between your PC and the wireless access point runs inside the tunnel: Firesheep or any other sniffer can see the data going by, but can't decipher what it means. VPNs do much more than simply foil Firesheep attacks: They provide complete end-to-end security, so nobody — not even your Internet service provider — can snoop on your communication, or look to see if you're using a service such as BitTorrent that may give them conniption fits. If you're traveling in a country subject to governmental eavesdropping, VPN is a must.

With a VPN, data goes into the tunnel from your PC, out of the tunnel at the VPN server, then to whatever location you're accessing, back into the VPN server, and out at your PC. There's a very effective cloaking device that hides your data everywhere in between. The people running the VPN server can match you up with your data stream, but nobody else can.

Setting up a VPN

I've used free VPNs from OpenVPN and ItsHidden. They both work, but I've had problems with speed in both cases. I'm also getting to the point (Saints preserve me) where I would like to have VPN protection for my mobile phone connection. There are also times when I would like to connect to a VPN server in Europe, not in the States.

I've been using VyprVPN, from Golden Frog, for several years (`www.goldenfrog.com/vyprvpn`). VyprVPN runs on Windows, of course, but it also runs on Mac OS/X, Linux Ubuntu, iPhone, iPad, and Android phones. They have server clusters located in 50 different countries, all over the world.

It isn't free. The basic package runs $6.67 a month. VyprVPNPro for $8.33 a month adds three additional VPN protocols. Those protocols can come in handy if you have an ISP or if you travel or live in a country that tries to block VPN: The VPN blockers snag the older PPTP protocol, but they don't catch the newer OpenVPN, L2TP/IPsec, or Chameleon protocols, the ones provided in VyprVPNPro.

Here's how hard it is to get VPN running on your computer (or phone, for that matter). Go to the order site, and sign up. You get an email message with a link. Click the link, and you go to your account's control panel. Click the link to Get Started. On the left, click the link for the protocol you want to install. Installing PPTP is easy — the instructions step you through a simple trip to PC Settings — but the other protocols take more work. That's it. Windows does all the heavy lifting.

Once installed, you turn on VyprVPN by bringing up the app (unless you leave it running on the desktop; see Figure 4-6), clicking Log In, and entering your credentials. You can choose the location of the VPN server. Click Connect, and you're finished. From that point on, your communication is cloaked. Easy.

Figure 4-6:
VyprVPN
makes
industrial-
strength
protected
communi-
cation easy.

Book X
Enhancing Windows 10

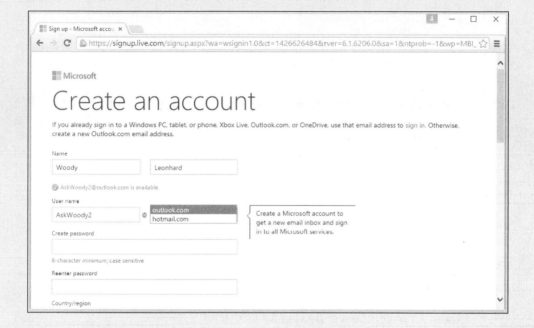

Windows can play nicely with your phone, tablet, and TV. Find a quick overview of digital detente at www.dummies.com/extras/windows10aio/worktogether.

Contents at a Glance

Chapter 1: Using Your iPad and iPhone with Windows

In This Chapter

✔ **Discovering the best peripheral your PC ever had**

✔ **Running iTunes on Windows**

✔ **Breaking the iTunes link with iCloud**

✔ **The inside story on Office for iPad and iPhone**

✔ **Recommending great iPad apps to use with Windows**

✔ **Letting your kids use iPads and iPhones**

*L*ike it or not — and I know that many don't — tablets are changing the way the world works and plays. Whether it's an iPad, a Kindle, a Nook, an Android, or even a Windows tablet or phone, mobile devices are rolling over the computing landscape like rainclouds over Redmond. Big rainclouds.

Some people moan about the way "toy computers" are taking over. I, for one, relish it. A tablet is vastly superior to a notebook — even an ultrabook, or any other kind of book — in performing very specific tasks. And they're tasks I do all the time: surfing the web, watching videos, keeping up on Facebook and Twitter, even doing light email.

Sure, I would never use a tablet or a phone to write a book or build a complex investment-tracking spreadsheet. But (appearances to the contrary) I don't write books all day, every day. And online investment-tracking software is so good now that I have very little reason to futz with obtuse Excel formulas.

(A friend insists that you can write a book on a tablet. I assume he used it to hold down the writing paper and stow his pen.)

Although Microsoft certainly disagrees with me, I see the iPad as the best peripheral a Windows PC ever had. And, yes, I include Windows 10 in that assessment, too. Although I can flip back and forth from the desktop to the Metro Start screen when necessary in Windows 10, I find it much simpler to just walk away from Windows 10 and pick up the iPad when I need to do something the iPad does well.

In this chapter, I'm not going to try to turn you to the iPad Side of the Force. But I do want to point out places where real, live everyday Windows users such as yourself should seriously consider using an iPad — or an Android tablet — if you have one. I explain how to wrangle with iTunes, but only when you have to, and point you to apps and techniques for combining Windows and the iPad.

I also won't try to introduce you to the iPad or take you through an iPad tutorial. *iPad For Dummies* by Edward Baig and Bob LeVitus does a great job with the basics, and *Exploring iPad For Dummies* by Galen Gruman and *iPad All-In-One For Dummies* by Nancy Muir (all published by John Wiley & Sons) tackle deeper subjects. Instead, I'm going to concentrate on how you can use your iPad with Windows 10 and vice versa.

Running iTunes on Windows, or Maybe Not

iTunes is Apple's program originally designed to sync your Windows PC or Mac with iPods and later other mobile devices. Apple's iDevices used to be like dumb boxes that wouldn't work without iTunes on a computer to sync and organize contacts, playlists, and the like. You don't really *need* iTunes for your iPad or iPhone anymore. Apple has made the iPad and the iPhone free-standing devices, ready to connect directly to the iCloud. But if you overlook the fact that iTunes is simply one of the worst Windows applications ever created, it has some good points, too.

Never mind me. I've been complaining about the iTunes program running on Windows for more than a decade now. (iTunes on the Mac is a completely different kettle of fish.) And iTunes on Windows does have a sharing capability that allows one PC on your home network to play music that's available to iTunes on another. Still, as a Windows program, iTunes leaves much to be desired.

I'm most assuredly not dissing the iTunes Store, the online shop where you can buy music, video, apps, and more from Apple, all of which are formatted to work on Apple's devices. The iTunes Store has its own problems, but it's revolutionized the way I buy music. In 2009, in response to Amazon's launching a DRM-free MP3 store, iTunes put one of the final nails in the coffin of music *Digital Rights Management* — where the people who sell music control how it's played, even after you buy it. Apple made an incredible array of music relatively affordable and easy to access, to lots of people, and it's made a bundle of money out of the effort.

iCloud is fine as long as everything you own is from Apple. But just try to sync something outside of the iCloud domain, like songs from iTunes. Back up your songs that originated outside iTunes and you should plan on paying the iTunes Match piper. Apple has built a walled garden. Truth be told, all three of the cloud consumer giants — Apple, Google, and Microsoft — have spent just as much effort building walls as building bridges.

Why you may need or want iTunes for Windows

As long as all your iPhone/iPad music, videos, or books reside in (or can be retrieved from) the iTunes Store, you're better off starting and staying with the iCloud. (iCloud is Apple's storage service that can store and sync your iPhone or iPad data over the Internet.) Don't install the Windows iTunes app, and don't even try to understand it. Just follow the instructions to set up iCloud at `www.apple.com/icloud/setup`.

Switching your iPad or iPhone over to using iCloud is simple: In the iPad or iPhone Settings app, on the left, tap iCloud. Make sure you have the right account set up (believe me, you don't want to hassle with mismatched accounts), on the right at the bottom, tap Storage and Backup. Slide the iCloud Backup setting to On. Then wait — my initial backup took two hours.

If you have some music, videos, or books on your computer that aren't in iCloud, or if you want to be able to pull your iCloud stuff (especially music) into your PC, the iTunes app is something you have to bear with. Two reasons why you may want iTunes:

+ **iTunes is the easiest way to sideload non-iTunes stuff from your PC onto your iPad.** For example, if you've acquired books, movies, or TV shows from someplace other than the iTunes Store, it's easier to use the iTunes Windows app to put them on an iPad.

+ **If you've paid for iTunes Match, running iTunes on your PC is the only way to pull music from iCloud and use it on your PC.** If you have a sizable collection of music, see the nearby sidebar "Music on iCloud — iTunes Match."

Installing iTunes

Fair warning. iTunes is one of the snarliest Windows programs I've ever used: It takes over the computer and doesn't let go until it's good and ready. It's slow to switch services (links on the left side). Double-clicking anything can result in really odd behavior. All in all, it doesn't look or work like a Windows app. And it's been like that for 15 years.

Music on iCloud — iTunes Match

If you're willing to pay $24.99 per year, and you have lots of (upload) time on your hands, iTunes Match lets you upload *all* your music — it doesn't matter where it came from. That music becomes available on all your iPhones and iPads, and it's available through iTunes for Windows on all your PCs. (Not to mention iTunes on the Mac as well.)

Yes, that's a good reason to install iTunes on your Windows PC. But it's also a good reason to hook your iPad directly into iCloud, so you can retrieve all your music, all the time.

Apple doesn't copy your music, *per se*. It uses sophisticated matching software to identify the music you have on your PC and match it with the 43 million songs Apple already has on file — millions of exceedingly high-quality recordings. If Apple can't match your music (live recordings of Juice Newton, anyone?), it stores the unidentified tracks on Apple's servers and makes them available to you directly. Those unidentified tracks are counted against your free allowance of 5GB of iCloud storage.

Ship too many oddball songs to iCloud, and you end up paying for storage. But the songs that iTunes Match identifies get stored without eating into your free 5GB.

After you sign up for the service and let iTunes scan your music, you can download up to 25,000 matching tracks — all in 256KB (high-quality) MP3 files. When you download those matching tracks, you can either replace your current tracks or keep the old ones — up to you. If you stop paying $25 per year, the music's all yours; you just can't pull it down from the iCloud anymore — so you can't stream to your iPhone, iPad, or iTunes.

iTunes Match is one of the great bargains on the Internet. And one of the few good reasons for installing iTunes for Windows.

Google Play's Music app is pretty righteous, too, as an iOS app. Your music gets stored on the Google side of the fence, of course, but it's free (for now) and reasonably easy to use.

iTunes uses another Apple program, QuickTime — a video-playing program that I've sworn at for many years. When you install iTunes, you install QuickTime, whether you want to or not.

From time to time, Apple also tries to get you to install other pieces of software, such as Safari, Bonjour Services, the Apple Updater, and MobileMe, and it's been known to use sneaky techniques to convince you to install other software. So keep your guard up and keep your clicking finger at bay. The idea is to install iTunes because you have to — and nothing extra. If that friendly Apple update reminder appears miraculously on your screen three months from now and says you need to install another wonderful Apple product, you have my permission to guffaw and obliterate the reminder.

Here's how to get your Windows PC iTuned:

1. **Crank up your favorite browser and head to `www.itunes.com`.**

   Apple redirects your browser to a different page, but that's okay. You end up in the right place, which looks like Figure 1-1.

**Book X
Chapter 1**

Using Your iPad
and iPhone with
Windows

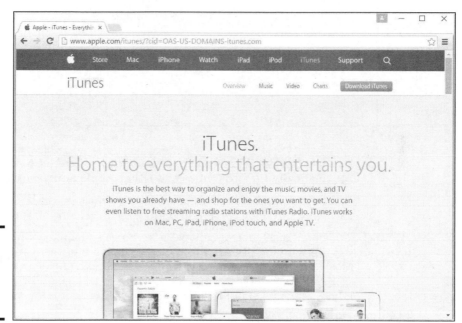

Figure 1-1:
The landing
page for
installing
iTunes.

2. **Tap or click the Download itunes button.**

   Apple kindly offers you an opportunity to sign up for its spam, er, mailing lists, and requests your email address. Don't give it to them.

3. **Deselect any boxes, and don't type your email address, but do tap or click the Download Now button.**

   Your browser downloads the correct version — 32-bit or 64-bit. Depending on which browser you're using, you may have to tap or click something to save and run the downloaded file.

4. **In the standard splash screen that appears, tap or click Next.**

   The options in Figure 1-2 appear.

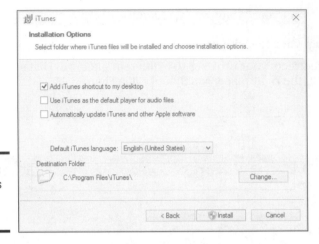

Figure 1-2:
The iTunes
installer
options.

5. **Deselect the Use iTunes as the Default Player for Audio Files and the Automatically Update iTunes and Other Apple Software check boxes.**

   In the past, Apple has used the update "permission" to bother iTunes users into installing Safari and putting ten new icons on the desktop.

   If you let iTunes take over all your audio files, it appears in all sorts of weird places and does things that aren't at all intuitive — to me, anyway. Most importantly, if iTunes is your default audio player, every time you click an audio file, you have to wait and wait and wait and wait for iTunes to get itself put together and start playing the tune.

6. **Tap or click Install.**

   The installer splashes an ad on your screen, does its thing, and ends several minutes later with a Congratulations! message.

7. **Tap or click Finish.**

   You can quit at this point, or you can continue on to start iTunes for the first time. See the next section.

Setting up iTunes

Before you use iTunes for the first time, you run through the iTunes Setup Assistant program. Here's how to minimize your ongoing headaches:

1. **If you quit immediately after iTunes is installed (see the preceding section) or if iTunes was preinstalled on your PC, tap the iTunes tile on the Start menu's All Apps list or double-click the iTunes icon on the desktop to run iTunes for the first time.**

   If you didn't quit iTunes, you automatically come to this step after iTunes has been successfully installed.

2. **Tap or click through another license agreement, which is considerably longer than the U.S. Constitution. Choose I Agree, Yer Honor (or words to that effect).**

While you're waiting, head over to YouTube and look up the *South Park* episode where Butters reads the iTunes agreement, or development of the HUMANCENTiPAD. You don't want to mess with these people.

The iTunes Tutorials home page appears, as shown in Figure 1-3.

Figure 1-3: Take the quick tour. It's worth the effort.

3. **When the tutorials are done, close the Tutorials home page and click Agree (again). If you have music on your computer that you want iTunes to see, click or tap Scan for Media.**

Depending on how much music you have stored in your Music library, the scan can take minutes or hours.

The initial iTunes Music page appears, as shown in Figure 1-4.

If you're curious about what iTunes actually does with your music, don't be overly concerned. Unlike earlier versions, the latest version of iTunes doesn't move any files. Instead, it builds a database that points to your music and stores it in the new \Music\iTunes folder. Still worried? Crank up File Explorer and go look. And breathe a sigh of relief.

You may or may not want to use iTunes to import *(rip)* music CDs—ripping is much less common now than it once was. But even if you don't want to use iTunes to rip CDs, it's a good idea to make one simple change, right now.

Figure 1-4:
Automat-
ically
scanned
and
analyzed,
the iTunes
way.

4. **Way up in the upper-left corner, click the small down arrow next to the icon that looks like an open book. Choose Preferences. Tap or click the Import Settings icon near When You Insert a CD.**

   The Import Settings dialog box appears, as shown in Figure 1-5.

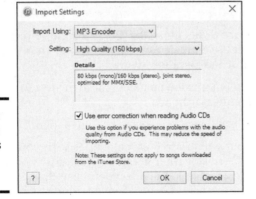

Figure 1-5:
Make sure
iTunes rips
to MP3
format.

5. **Choose MP3 Encoder in the Import Using drop-down list.**

That ensures the ripped music files appear as MP3 files. You may prefer AAC format (or WMA format, for that matter), but there's nothing as clean — or as ubiquitous — as MP3. Keep in mind that AAC uses less space for high quality sound, and that iTunes doesn't speak the Microsoft-proprietary WMA format.

6. **Unless you rip many CDs every day, select the Use Error Correction When Reading Audio CDs check box.**

Although using error correction may make the ripping process run a little slower — okay, much slower — it'll guarantee that you get the best recordings possible from those old, dirty scratched CDs. You know you have them.

7. **Tap or click OK, and then tap or click OK again.**

You end up back in iTunes.

If you ever discover that iTunes failed to pick up a new song — one that you ripped from a CD, downloaded from the Internet, or bought from an online service — simply locate the song file or album folder in File Explorer and drag it into iTunes.

Pulling Internet videos onto your iPad

Most (but not all) of the videos that you can see on the Internet can be *scraped* and stored permanently on your iPad or iPhone. That can be very useful if you're going to be someplace that doesn't have an Internet connection for your iPad, or if you're going to watch the same video over and over (hey, you have kids, yes?) and you don't want to pay for repeatedly downloading the same clip.

Many products will scrape videos off the Internet. KeepVid (www.keepvid.com) was one of the first, and it works well for most videos on YouTube, DailyMotion, Megavideo, Metacafe, and Vimeo. To use the free version of KeepVid, go to the KeepVid website and paste in the URL of the video you want to save.

My personal preference is the Firefox Video DownloadHelper add-in (http://addons.mozilla.org/en-US/firefox/addon/video-downloadhelper). When you install Video DownloadHelper in Firefox, it watches to see whether scrapable videos are on the page you're viewing. If there are, a little icon starts rotating. Tap or click the icon, and download the video. Easy.

The trick with KeepVid, Video DownloadHelper, or any other video scraper you find is that you need to have it produce videos in MP4 format. Although MP4 isn't a format as much as it's a group of formats (details too boring to recount here), most of the time, MP4 files play just fine on an iPad. Or anywhere else, for that matter.

Of course, you don't do this for copyrighted material or on sites that otherwise expressly forbid it.

Here's how to get videos off the Internet and into your iPad. Follow these steps:

1. **Use Video DownloadHelper or a similar scraper to produce MP4 files.**

2. **Start iTunes. On the left, under Library, tap or click the Movies line.**

   iTunes doesn't have any way to make a playlist of movies just yet, but you can still play individual movies with your iPad's built-in Video app.

3. **Locate the MP4 files in File Explorer. Switch iTunes over to the Movies folder by clicking the strip in the upper left that looks like a couple of movie frames. Then drag and drop the movie files into the iTunes Movies folder.**

   A thumbnail of the movie appears if you click Home Videos, as shown in Figure 1-6.

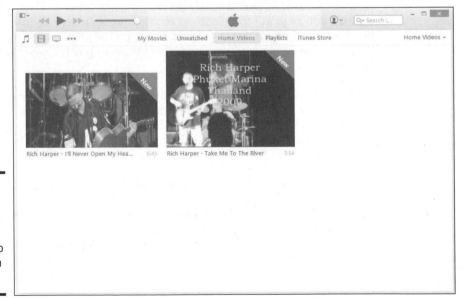

Figure 1-6: Drag MP4 movies into iTunes, and then sync to get them on your iPad.

4. **When you're finished dragging all your MP4 files into the Movies folder, connect your iPad or iPhone and sync.**

   If the movie will play on your iPad or iPhone, it gets copied over to the device.

Once in a while, the movie won't sync properly. I have no idea why, but I've found that if you drag the movie from the iTunes\Library\Movies folder to the iPad Movies folder, it gets copied onto the iPad.

The Inside Story on Office for iPad

People ask me frequently about running Office on the iPad. To a first approximation, it works well, if you realize that running Office on a touch-first device is quite different from running it on a desktop or laptop. To a second approximation, Microsoft's done a more than credible job translating the big ol' Office we've all known and loved for decades into a svelte and quick thing that does justice to the touch approach.

You may have heard that Microsoft released Office on the iPad even before it released Office on Windows tablets. It's true — and remarkable. Office for iPad and Office for Windows/Mac share a few idiosyncrasies, but by and large they're completely different programs. Although you can pick up a document in one and use it in the other — going both ways — and some of the concepts carry across, there's a big gulf between the desktop/laptop versions of Office and the touch-first transmogrification on the iPad.

If you've ever tried to tap your way through the desktop version of Office on a mouseless machine, Office for iPad will blow you away. The interface runs rings around the desktop Office we've known for decades, for touch-first situations. But if you're looking for a specific feature that's in desktop Office, you may well come up empty-handed — in the move from desktop to iPad and other touch devices, wide swathes of features were cut.

I know it's confusing, but the free version of Office for iPad is slightly different from the paid version of Office for iPad. For most people, the difference isn't enough to sneeze at. If you want a detailed list of the differences between the free and paid ("Premium") versions of Office for iPad, look at the official list at `http://products.office.com/en-US/office-resources#table8`.

Here's what you need to know about getting Office for iPad.

Fire up your iPad, hop over to the AppStore, search for "Office," and install Word, PowerPoint, and Excel. That gives you the free version. When you first start Word, Excel, or PowerPoint for iPad, you're asked to provide either a Microsoft account or an Office 365 account (see Figure 1-7). If you (or your organization) haven't yet paid for an Office 365 subscription, or if you'd rather save that Office 365 license for a different device, you should ask yourself if you really need to pay for your copy of Office for iPad.

Figure 1-7: Office for iPad wants a Microsoft account or an Office 365 account. Surprisingly, the paid Office 365 account only gives you a few more features.

Note that you get one Office for iPad license when you buy Office 365 Personal, five when you buy Office 365 Home or Office 365 Business or Business Premium, but you don't get any licenses with Office 365 Home & Student or with Office 365 Business Essentials.

After you have Office for iPad working, there's a whole world of new but familiar features — fonts, page layouts, picture manipulation. The commands are arranged a little different from what you may know on the desktop side of the fence, but most of what you use is right there, lurking somewhere (see Figure 1-8). For example, tracked changes work just fine.

I've had very few problems working with Office for iPad. It's highly recommended, even the free version, for every iPad owner.

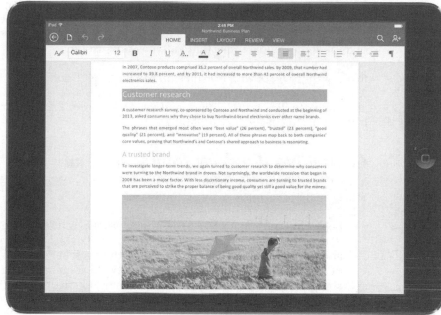

Figure 1-8:
Word for
iPad, with
all sorts
of familiar
capabilities,
including
tracked
changes.

Great iPad Apps to Use with Windows

Full disclosure: I love my new iPad. Don't know how I ever lived without it.

On the other hand, as you have probably surmised by a quick perusal of the thousand or so pages in this book, I have a complex love-hate relationship with Windows. The PC runs rings around the iPad in a dozen different areas. The converse is just as true. How to get the best out of both? It ain't easy.

If you're like me, you've been using Windows for a long time but got an iPad on something of a lark — it's cute, does a few things very well, and it's very good with kids and not-so-computer-savvy members of the family. I talk about that at length in the next section.

The iPad is also hell for a touch typist, incompatible with many Windows-friendly programs, and too expensive to just sit in a closet most of the time. Unlike a smartphone with a camera, an iPad doesn't have any compelling, redeeming social graces.

So now that you have it, what do you do with it — how can you make your iPad work within your Windows-centric life?

I don't claim to have The Answer. In fact, everything's changing so quickly, I doubt that anybody caught straddling both the Win and iPad worlds has more than a tiny piece of the equation figured out. But I've found a handful of apps and a couple tricks that you may find useful.

If you want to work with PDF files on the iPad, get GoodReader, $4.99 in the App Store. GoodReader lets you read PDFs, but it also allows you to mark up and annotate PDF and TXT files, and sync with Dropbox or remote servers. It's an amazing, legendary program.

Controlling Windows from your iPad

More than a dozen PC remote control apps are available in the Apple App Store. Some of them work surprisingly well:

✦ **LogMeIn Ignition:** A favorite among reviewers, although at $29.95 for the iPad application, it's pricey. You have to run LogMeIn on both the iPad and the Windows machine. If you go with LogMeIn Free on the Windows PC, you can't transfer files, print remotely, hear sounds from the PC, or share desktops. To do any of that, you have to spend an additional $69.95 per year for the Windows PC's software.

✦ **GoToMyPC:** Another name that should sound familiar to Windows aficionados, it also draws good reviews, but it turns even pricier quickly. Figure on spending $9.99 per month per computer after the initial, 30-day, free trial period.

✦ **Desktop Connect:** A lesser-known product that demands you run a Virtual Network Computing (VNC) program on your Windows PC. You also have to connect with a hard-coded IP address.

✦ **Splashtop:** Another lesser-known product works well on a Wi-Fi system, connecting to PCs on the same network, but going outside the local network can get more difficult. I use Splashtop to play videos on my iPad that aren't in MP4 format.

✦ **TeamViewer:** My favorite, remote control program (free for non-commercial use) can run in one of two ways. You can either install the TeamViewer program on your Windows PC and let it control the interaction or simply run the program on your PC, manually, anytime you want to be able to access the Windows PC from your iPad (see Figure 1-9). When you run the program manually on your Windows PC, it generates a random user ID and password, which you use on the iPad to initiate the session.

After TeamViewer is connected, it lets you use the iPad keyboard, pinch to expand or reduce the size of the screen, tap with two fingers to emulate a right-click, use the buttons on the top of the screen for Alt and Ctrl and Esc, and much more. Even Flash animations come through remarkably quickly.

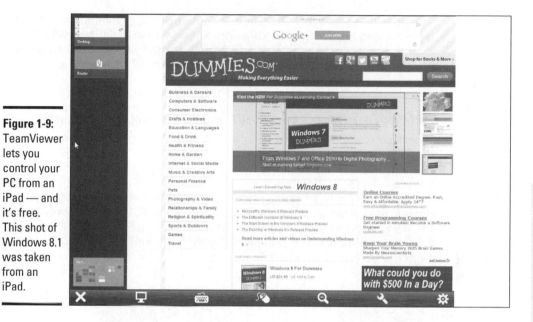

Book X
Chapter 1

Using Your iPad and iPhone with Windows

Figure 1-9:
TeamViewer lets you control your PC from an iPad — and it's free. This shot of Windows 8.1 was taken from an iPad.

Delivering PowerPoint presentations with your iPad

I'll never forget the first time I saw a PowerPoint presentation delivered from an iPad. Actually, it combined a laptop, a projector, and an iPad. The presenter had a reasonably good PowerPoint presentation, running on a plain-vanilla Win7 laptop connected to a projector. Instead of hiding behind his laptop and mousing his way through the slides, or staring at the projector screen and using a clicker, he was actually looking at the audience, glancing at the slides and notes on the iPad in front of him, swiping his way through the presentation. The presentation went extraordinarily well because the presenter interacted with the audience, not with his PC, not with the projector screen. He had the right tools for the job.

If you have a Windows 10 tablet that weighs less than a Volkswagen and doesn't overheat, you can use the tablet to make the presentation from the desktop. But if you're running Win10 on a laptop, holding the computer while delivering the presentation just isn't in the cards. I know. I've tried.

If you haven't yet seen, or delivered, a PowerPoint presentation with an iPad, you're in for a treat. The liberating little tablet changes the entire dynamic of making PowerPoint presentations.

The presenter was using Slideshow Remote from LogicInMind. It's $4.99 from the App Store. Slideshow Remote shows you the slides on your iPad, of course, but it also shows notes and it previews the next slide. You can even bring up a full slide thumbnail list, just like in PowerPoint itself, and jump to specific slides with a swipe and a tap.

Extending your Windows display with iDisplay

What? You didn't know that you can use your iPad to extend your Windows PC's display?

iDisplay — $4.99 in the App Store — works using Wi-Fi, not a cable, and you don't have to invest in a fancy video card with two outputs. Instead, you download and run the iDisplay app on both your iPad and your Windows PC. Go into the Windows app, find the iPad, and start the iDisplay app on it. Stick the monitors side by side (see Figure 1-10), and you can click and drag from one screen to the other.

Figure 1-10: iDisplay extends your Windows PC's desktop without a fancy video card.

iDisplay is best suited for shuffling relatively static information off to the side of your screen — all the bits have to travel by Wi-Fi, and they don't move quickly. I use iDisplay to run TweetDeck on the side of my screen.

Moving files between your PC and the iPad

The iPad's file system can best be described as, uh, rudimentary. Actually, *nonexistent* comes to mind. Be that as it may, from time to time, you may want to transfer a file other than a typical iTunes file — music, video, podcast, photo, or book — to or from your iPad.

My personal favorite? Dropbox. I talk about Dropbox in Book VIII, Chapter 1, in the context of cloud backup. But for normal, everyday files, the Dropbox iPad app (free, from the App Store) works fine. Download and install the app, give it your username and password, and you're finished. Dropbox handles syncing across multiple platforms, invisibly and reliably. Even if your Internet connection goes down, the files are still in the box.

If you have a Dropbox account, and Dropbox is working on your iPad, get the account hooked into the Office for iPad apps. To do so, start one of the Office for iPad apps. On the left, tap Open, then tap the + Add a Place icon in the left column. Dropbox appears as one of your options. Tap Dropbox (Figure 1-11), and you're sent over to the Dropbox app. The app asks if you want to allow the Office app access to the files and folders in your Dropbox. Tap Allow, and the Office for iPad app can work with Dropbox files.

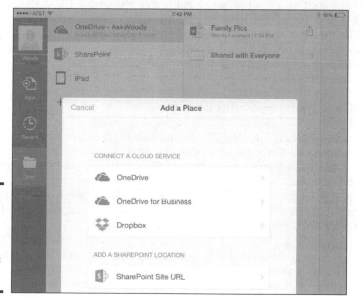

Figure 1-11:
Adding
Dropbox to
Office for
iPad apps is
easy.

After you've connected the Office for iPad apps, Dropbox becomes aware of the new link. From that point onward, every time you tap an Office file inside Dropbox, the action box in the lower-right corner gets a new "pencil on a sheet of paper" icon that allows you to open the file directly in the corresponding Office for iPad app.

You can use iCloud to transfer files, but it's considerably more complicated than Dropbox. Transferring with OneDrive is like falling off a log; it's built in to Office for iPad. While it's possible to use Google Drive to transfer files to the iPad and thus to Office, you'll find it to be a process only a contortionist could endorse.

Playing with Kids on Your iPad or iPhones

Permit me to end this chapter with a bit of personal advice, aimed at the parents (and grandparents!) in the crowd.

In 2010 and 2011, there was a rash of articles in the popular press saying that iPads and iPhones would rot your kids' brains. I mean, it's hard to wade through a bunch of headlines like these from *The New York Times* and not feel like an iPad's the root of all kiddy evil: "Growing Up Digital, Wired for Distraction" and "The Risks of Parenting While Plugged In" and "An Ugly Toll of Technology: Impatience and Forgetfulness." I forgot what the other headlines said, but you get my drift. Typical admonishment: People are raising a generation of kids whose brains are going to be wired differently for staring at small screens.

Well, yes. That's exactly the point.

When I was a kid, the child development experts said that any more than 45 minutes of television per day would make a kid irresponsible, incapable of concentrating, unable to interact with people, and a developmental basket case. Look what happened to me. Oh, wait. That isn't a good comparison. Look at what happened to the entire generation. Perhaps everyone suffered from short attention spans and terminal halitosis. But somehow I think we all pulled through it, give or take a few politicians.

I don't claim to be a child development expert. But I do know this. Putting an iPad (or Android, Kindle, Windows tablet, whatever) into your child's hands isn't a brain cell death sentence. It's opening an important new world.

Yes, I've read about the studies that show toddlers who grow up on tablets don't develop vocabularies until a later age. I know about the teen tech idiot savants, who can't write a sentence but spin out programs to solve algebra problems. The high schoolers who send 20,000 SMSs a month but can't find time to finish a homework assignment. The kids who play so many games they forget to sleep at night.

On the other hand, I've seen the toddlers who spend hours and hours practicing their letters and numbers, shapes and words, colors and coordination, exploring with their parents' help, and going right back to the iPad at every opportunity — because it's fun. And I know a whole lot of people in Silicon Valley who make a living, not by writing book reports, but by churning out miles of incredible code. The best of the bunch started as teenagers. Young teenagers.

The trick, in my opinion, is to use the technology to interact with your kids. Sure, my toddler and I still read books — real, dead tree books — every day. But most of the day when we're playing indoors, the topics are generally educational, and they're frequently on the iPad or the PC.

Am I setting up my toddler for having his brain wired the wrong way? Pshaw. Will his interpersonal skills suffer? Not if he gets some time playing with other kids. Will he be able to use all the tools he'll need as he gets older? Yeah, I think so. Most of all, he won't be intimidated by these talking pieces of glass. It'll be second nature, and when the time comes, he'll be able to start standing on the shoulders of giants. It's just that, in the meantime, he has to learn that he can't tap or swipe a TV screen and get it to change channels, or slide his finger on a magazine and expect it to move forward a page.

**Book X
Chapter 1**

Using Your iPad and iPhone with Windows

So I say take your kids to the library. Watch TV with them. Make sure they have time with other kids their own age. And get a tablet into their hands at an early age, so you can play with them.

A friend of mine asked me to come up with a list of iPad apps that my wife and I like to play with our toddler. Here's the list:

- The Cat in the Hat
- Dr. Seuss Band
- Anything by the GiggleBellies
- Any Sandra Boynton books
- Pat the Bunny
- Twinkle Twinkle (Super Simple Learning)
- My First Words Baby Picture dictionary
- Starfall ABCs
- Elmo Loves ABCs
- Any Duck Duck Moose stories
- Nighty Night!
- Pepi Bath
- The Little Critter books

If you own an Xbox, look for the SmartGlass app for iPad and iPhone in the Apple App Store.

You can also scrape videos off YouTube. I leave it to your search skills to find videos on YouTube for your kids. And, of course, you can watch YouTube directly, if you hook the iPad up to your Wi-Fi.

All the apps I listed are in the Apple App Store — immediately accessible from the iPad, or if you want to surf, go to www.apple.com/itunes. The YouTube app comes preloaded on your iPad or iPhone.

Computers are going to give your kids (and grandkids and their grandkids) abilities I can hardly dream about today. Don't be afraid to teach them well. In spite of what the experts say.

Chapter 2: Android, Chromecast, Roku, Kindle, and Windows 10

In This Chapter

✔ **Making Windows 10 cooperate with your Android device**

✔ **Driving your TV with Chromecast and Windows 10**

✔ **The Roku connection between Windows and your TV**

✔ **Demystifying book file formats**

✔ **Getting media from your PC to your Kindle**

I love my iPad. (Actually, iPads.) My wife loves her iPhone. I also love my Android-based Samsung Galaxy Tab, and our various Android tablets, including the best reading tablet around, the Amazon Kindle. I "cut the cord" (stopped paying for cable TV) a decade ago, substituting a Roku several years ago, driving downloaded media to the Roku from Plex, which runs on my Windows computers. And in the past couple of years, I find myself using a Chromecast more and more to let the family watch what I'm seeing on my Windows laptop.

How do I reconcile all that technological promiscuity with my decades-long Windows-centric background? That's easy. I don't.

I say pick the right tool for the job, and if you don't like what's happening now, wait a few months and see what crops up. It's never been more true than it is right now: There's more than one way to skin the computing cat. As long as you don't get bogged down in the "Windows first and best" mentality, or hide behind a fear of learning new things, there's a big, exciting world out there. Yes, even if you use Windows. Let me steer you through it.

If you think that the iPhone rules the smartphone roost, you're wrong. Android phones (that is, smartphones that run the Android operating system) outsell iPhones by a very wide margin, in almost every country. That's true for tablets, too — although the numbers change from version to version, location to location.

iPhone outsells Android in the U.S., and the Apple App Store certainly dwarfs Google's Play Store for both number of apps and profitability for developers — people just spend more on Apple apps than on Google apps.

Android and iOS run neck-and-neck by most ways of reckoning, but iOS certainly commands more public attention and money.

he e-reader market helps: Few people realize it, but the Amazon Kindle is an Android tablet. Inside the understated exterior and behind the gorgeous eye-friendly display beats a heart of pure Android.

Android's market share is increasing, too. As I write this chapter, more than 1 billion Android devices are in use. In 2013, more than 1,500,000 were being activated every day. That's a whole lotta Android.

This area is seeing lots of activity right now — in fact, with so many people doing so many things, Android may be the target of more change than any other platform in history, including the iPad and (emphatically) Windows. So my emphasis in this chapter is on showing you Android techniques that are likely to survive as long as Windows 10 remains on the market.

Which could be an eternity, in Internet time.

Android isn't Android isn't Android. The Android device you buy today may not be capable of running the new Android of tomorrow. Actually, that's true of Windows Phone, Windows tablets (just ask a Surface 2 customer), iPad, and iPhone, too. But Android seems to be less upgradable than its competitors. Be careful.

What, Exactly, Is Android?

You know all about Windows — at least if you've managed to get this far in the book — and you probably have at least a nodding acquaintance with Mac OS X (pronounced "oh ess ten"), the operating system that runs on Macs, and iOS ("eye oh ess"), the operating system that drives iPads and iPhones.

Android is different. Just for starters, it's open source, at least to some degree, based on a modified version of Linux. That means individuals and companies have free access to the programs that make up Android; they can modify the code and release their own versions of Android, on devices of their own devising.

That's both a blessing and a curse: Upgrading some Android devices is easy; others are difficult, and for some it's impossible. Apple doesn't promise that older hardware will run newer software, in all cases, but the Android situation is fractured and confusing.

Apple's walled garden versus Android's open source

When you deal with iPhones and iPads (and the iCloud, iMacs, iTVs, iPods, and all those other iThingies), you're living in a walled garden. Apple controls it from beginning to end. That's one of the reasons why all the different iDevices work together so well — the hardware and software come from the same company, they're designed to fit together, and Apple's designers are absolutely first-class. But you pay for the privilege.

On the other hand, Android devices come from a huge array of manufacturers, many with very different ideas of what's right and what's

almost right. Although Google is in the driver's seat — Google bought Android, give or take a patent claim or two or ten, and has released Android to the world — hardware manufacturers, to a first approximation, are free to take Android in any direction they like.

Android is open source under the Apache License, which means that not only is the program free, the source code for the program is free and readily available as well. (It's a little more complicated than that; for details, see `www.apache.org`.)

**Book X
Chapter 2**

**Android, Chrome-
cast, Roku, Kindle,
and Windows 10**

Android started in 2003, envisioned as an advanced operating system for digital cameras. By 2004, the core group — Andy Rubin, Rich Miner, Nick Sears, and Chris White, all experienced developers — had run out of money. One of Rubin's friends, Steve Perlman, loaned the group $10,000 out of his own pocket, wired them an undisclosed additional amount, simultaneously turning down a stake in the company.

Both Rubin and Perlman worked for Apple in the early 1990s. Perlman's a very wealthy entrepreneur and inventor. He says he handed over the $10,000 cash "to help Andy."

Google's Larry Page learned about Rubin's project, and the two companies started a six-month-long mating dance that ended in July 2005, with the Android team moving over to Google, a rumored $50 million changing hands.

Getting clear on Android

Android isn't free-as-in-beer.

Microsoft claims to hold patents on certain parts of Linux, and claims (with varying degrees of justification) that those patents are violated in Google's implementations of Android. Microsoft thus demands ransom, er, royalty payments from large hardware vendors that use Android. In 2013, Samsung alone paid more than a billion dollars to Microsoft, just to avoid a patent court battle.

More than that, manufacturers running Android still have to pay the Google piper: Details are top secret, but apparently Google requires phone and tablet manufacturers to preinstall more than 20 Google apps on every Android device. A recent scan of a Samsung phone came up with these obvious Google apps: Drive, Gmail, Google, Google Settings, Google+, Hangouts, Play Books, Play Games, Play Movies & TV, Play Music, Play Newsstand, Photos, and Voice Search.

You can uninstall individual apps, of course, but few people do.

Apparently, there are even requirements about where some of those apps must appear on the fresh-out-of-the-box phone and tablet screens. Ka-ching.

Making Windows talk to your Android phone or tablet

If you're trying to get your Android phone or tablet to interact with your Windows 10 PC, you need to know several tricks.

First, just plug it in. Every Android device I know about can connect to a USB port. Chances are good that Windows will recognize the device and install a driver for it. You get a dialog box like the one in Figure 2-1.

Figure 2-1: With any luck at all, your Android device installs itself. All you have to do is plug it in.

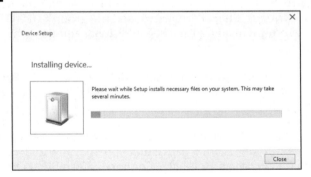

After it's installed, you can access all the files on the Android device through File Explorer. My Samsung Galaxy Note 3 looks like Figure 2-2. Photos are in the folder \Phone\DCIM\Camera.

The Android device shows up in the Computer folder. Depending on what kind of device you attached, you may see one or two folders: The one marked Internal Storage is for the phone or tablet itself; the other, marked SD card, is for any additional storage you have on the phone or tablet. (There is no additional storage on an iOS device.)

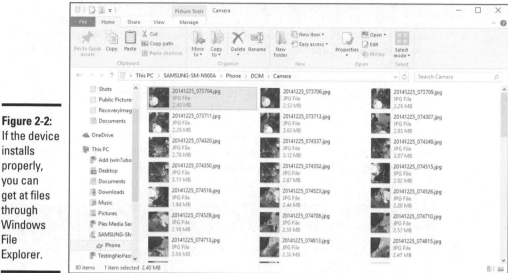

**Book X
Chapter 2**

**Android, Chrome-
cast, Roku, Kindle,
and Windows 10**

Figure 2-2:
If the device installs properly, you can get at files through Windows File Explorer.

From File Explorer, you can cut or copy files, moving them to your PC. You can edit or delete them. And you can print them.

Copying files from your computer onto your Android device, using File Explorer, usually works. I've had no problems with more recent Android phones and tablets, but your device, and mileage, may vary. Don't delete any precious photos until you know for sure that they've been transferred properly.

Connecting TVs with Roku, Plex, and Chromecast

If you haven't yet heard the term "Over-the-top content," you better get used to it. "Over-the-top" refers to using the Internet to bypass the entrenched companies that used to control all media access. If you use Facebook to make a long distance phone call, that's over-the-top. Skype has been over-the-top since its beginning years ago. If you watch a TV show from a website, you're over-the-top. Netflix, HBO, Hulu — as long as you don't subscribe to a cable TV channel to get them — are likewise OTT.

So is Roku. At least inside the U.S., it's a fantastic, cheap, and capable OTT thing. Outside the U.S., your results may vary, but I managed to coax my Roku into submission while in Asia, with a U.S. credit card and a VPN (see Book IX, Chapter 4).

The Roku box connects to your home network (either through WiFi or plugged in with an Ethernet cable), plugs into an HDMI port on your TV, and handles all the stuff in between. You get a remote. (If you're smart, you'll get a remote with headphones.) You supply the Internet service. And you're off to the races.

The Roku interface (see Figure 2-3) couldn't be simpler. Buttons for up, down, left, and right let you navigate like a champ.

The Roku is a Linux device that gives you access to (as you can see in Figure 2-3) Amazon Instant, Netflix, HuluPlus, YouTube, HBOGo, PBS, Pandora, Google Play Movies, and much, much more.

Figure 2-3:
Getting around Roku.

Not all of those channels are free, but they're not expensive. I pay for Netflix ($8/month through `Netflix.com`), Hulu Plus ($8/month thru Roku), and Amazon Plus (free with my Amazon Prime membership, which costs $99/ year or less, and covers many benefits besides the Amazon channel). Because I get Internet service through Comcast/Xfinity, I would have to pay Comcast to get HBO GO. One relatively new channel, called Sling, offers ESPN, TNT, TBS, Food Network, Disney Channel, and CNN through local TV stations, starting at $20 per month.

You can control the Roku with its remote, or with apps for iOS, Android, or even (we're promised) with its own Windows 10 tile.

The best way I've found to connect media stored on my PC — home movies, ripped DVDs, and stuff pulled from all over the web — involves a nifty product called Plex. Highly recommended, especially for Roku owners.

Plex is something of a media hub, repository, and player. You can call it a media server, if you promise not to get freaked out by the techie terminology. It allows you to keep your video, photos, and music organized on your Windows PC, and to stream them to your Roku and other kinds of streaming boxes, other computers, phones, and tablets. The base configuration is free, or you can spend $30 per year and get management tools, automatic photo uploading, movie trailers, and lots of little extras; see Figure 2-4.

Any way you get media onto your PC, by hook or by crook, you can store it there and serve it up with Plex through Roku onto your TV. The videos, pictures, and songs transfer themselves over your home network. Setup takes a few seconds, after you add the Plex "channel" to your Roku. Fast, cheap, and easy.

Increasingly, I find myself bypassing Plex and Roku entirely and using a remarkable little dongle called Chromecast. Although it's only been around since 2013, at $35 it's an amazing product.

Using the Chromecast couldn't be simpler. You plug the little critter (it's about the size of a USB drive) into an empty HDMI port on your TV. Crank up your Chrome browser, and you're ready. Install the Chromecast extension.

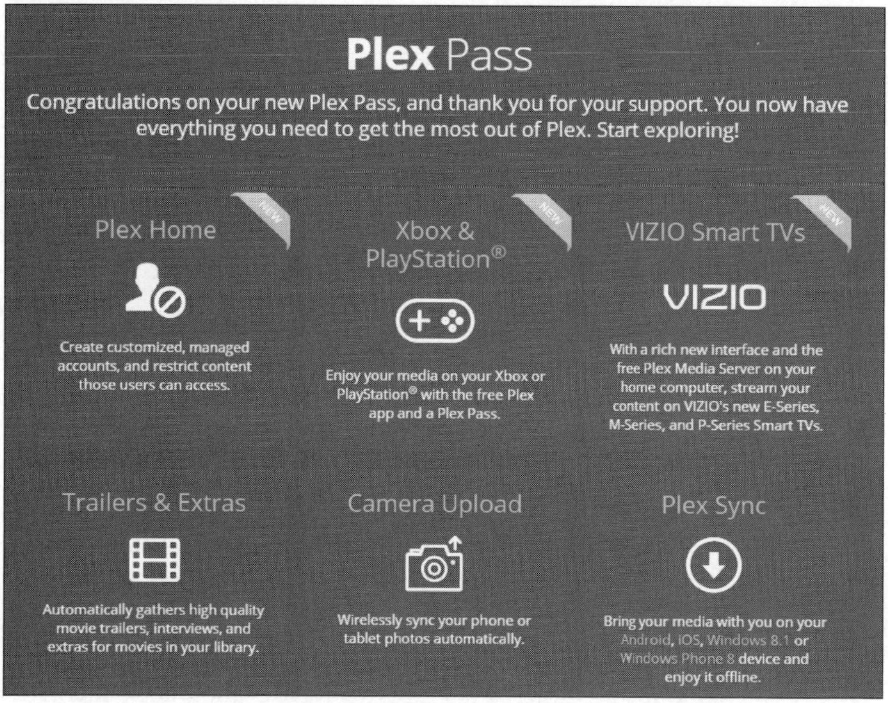

Figure 2-4:
The basic
Plex is
free and
powerful
enough
to feed
your Roku
everything
that sits on
your PC.
PlexPass
costs $30
per year
and brings
some useful
extras.

Plex Pass

Congratulations on your new Plex Pass, and thank you for your support. You now have everything you need to get the most out of Plex. Start exploring!

Plex Home
Create customized, managed accounts, and restrict content those users can access.

Xbox & PlayStation®
Enjoy your media on your Xbox or PlayStation® with the free Plex app and a Plex Pass.

VIZIO Smart TVs
VIZIO
With a rich new interface and the free Plex Media Server on your home computer, stream your content on VIZIO's new E-Series, M-Series, and P-Series Smart TVs.

Trailers & Extras
Automatically gathers high quality movie trailers, interviews, and extras for movies in your library.

Camera Upload
Wirelessly sync your phone or tablet photos automatically.

Plex Sync
Bring your media with you on your Android, iOS, Windows 8.1 or Windows Phone 8 device and enjoy it offline.

The Chromecast extension looks out on your home network, searching for a Chromecast. When it finds the dongle, click a couple of times and your computer is connected to the TV.

Bring up anything at all in your browser — say, a YouTube video — and click the Chromecast button, and voilà. What's on your screen appears, full-screen, on your TV. In high definition, too.

Chromecast works on much more than the Chrome browser. If you use the Netflix app on an iPad or iPhone, or on an Android phone or tablet, there's a Chromecast button. TED. HBO GO. Showtime. NPR, Hulu Plus, MLB.TV, PBS Kids, and on and on. Of course, you have to pay to get the app to work — Netflix doesn't let you freeload in an iPad app. But when the app can see it, you can broadcast the show straight to your TV.

Microsoft has a wannabe dongle setup called Miracast. (More accurately, Miracast is an open standard that's supported by Windows 10, if your video hardware can handle it.) Miracast works in much the same method as the Chromecast. Miracast has a few advantages, but it just doesn't have Google's reach. Not all Windows machines support Miracast — their hardware doesn't talk to Miracast receivers. Check before you buy anything new.

Using Office for Android

I have a detailed report on Office for iPad in Book X, Chapter 1. Suffice it to say that I'm very impressed by Office for iPad, and I'm equally impressed with Office for Android. The two are nearly identical, except for a few interface tweaks.

Remarkably, the free version of Office for Android is almost identical to the "premium" version (which is only available to Office 365 subscribers).

If you have a reasonably capable Android tablet (1GB of RAM, Android 4.4 KitKat or later), you should give it a try. Look for Word, Excel, and PowerPoint in the Play Store. And read my review in Book X, Chapter 1.

Wrangling E-Book Files

Most popular e-book readers, including, notably, the Kindle line, are based on a modified fork of Android. That's why I put this discussion in the Android chapter.

Someday, a single format will exist for all electronic books. In my utopian future, you will buy a book in one format, and that format will just work, no matter what device you want to use to read it.

Unfortunately, the world isn't at that point yet. In fact, it isn't even close. The single biggest headache you're likely to have with electronic books revolves around book formats, and how to get one device to show you books that were made for a competing device.

If you can afford to stick with just one device and bookstore — only buy books from Amazon and read them on the Kindle, for example, or only buy books from the iTunes Store and read them on the iPad — I salute you. Your life will be considerably less complicated. Most people aren't so lucky.

If you're one of them, you can simplify e-book management by buying your books online through your PC's web browser, using a program called calibre to convert files into whatever format your reader requires, and then syncing your e-books with your e-reader on your PC. (You can also read any e-book on your Windows computer, but that may be beside the point, huh?)

Book X
Chapter 2

Android, Chrome-cast, Roku, Kindle, and Windows 10

Introducing popular e-book formats

Here are the most popular book file formats:

✦ **EPUB** comes closest to being a universal format. The iPhone and iPad handle EPUB natively, there are many third-party Windows EPUB readers (more about that after this list), the almost-disappeared Nook reads EPUB natively, and many Android apps read EPUB. The only major holdout for the EPUB format, as this book went to press, was Kindle — and it's entirely possible that Kindle will be able to accept EPUB format books by the time you read this.

Given a choice, unless you live in a Kindle-only world, get your books in EPUB format.

✦ **MOBI** and **PRC** formats are the Kindle's bread and butter. Amazon has a format converter — *KindleGen* — that changes EPUB files into MOBI. It works surprisingly well.

✦ **PDF** is the original format for publications that have to survive a transition from one kind of computer to another. Although every common device can read PDF, most readers just display the original document without trying to reflow pages or add any features, such as note-taking. Reading a PDF file in most readers is a frustrating and headache-inducing experience.

Reading e-book files on your PC

Whether or not you have e-books you bought with an e-reader, you can read anything on a Windows 10 PC. Sometimes, though, you have to get a little creative and bring in apps that can do the heavy lifting.

Windows EPUB readers are a dime a dozen. Actually, they're free. Before you try to download and install one on the desktop, run through the Windows Store (just tap or click the Store tile on the Metro Start screen) and see whether any highly rated EPUB readers are available. Just use the Search box to look for the text *EPUB*. Details in Book III, Chapter 2.

If you can't find a tiled Metro EPUB reader that you like, you have several choices for desktop apps that can read EPUB files. Arguably the best of the bunch is Adobe Digital Editions (ADE), which is free, from `www.adobe.com/products/digitaleditions`. ADE does yeoman's work of rendering EPUB and PDF/A files accurately, and it includes note-taking features.

ADE also allows you to read files that have been copy-protected with the ADEPT (Adobe Digital Experience Protection Technology) technique. Barnes & Noble uses a form of ADEPT copy-protection on its books. ADEPT was reverse-engineered years ago, and several programs (including programs called *inept* and *ignoble*) can crack the encryption.

PDF viewers are also a dime a dozen. The viewer that Microsoft built into Microsoft Edge, shown in Figure 2-5, works reasonably well, although it doesn't have any bookmarking or note-taking ability.

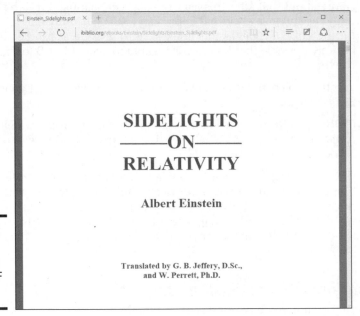

Figure 2-5:
Microsoft Edge has a built-in PDF viewer.

Organizing your e-book files with calibre

Before you lose any sleep over different book file formats, realize that one desktop app has been translating among the formats for years. In fact, calibre's more than a Babel fish; it's also a book manager — for free. See Figure 2-6.

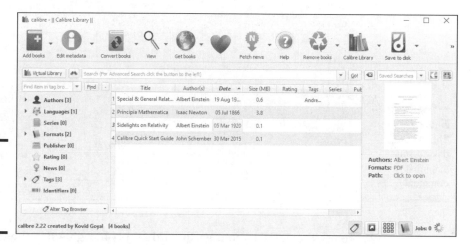

Figure 2-6: calibre translates and organizes.

Much like Windows Media Player or iTunes, calibre keeps track of all your books, translates them into the correct format if need be, and offers the files up for easy transfer to the reader of your choice.

Here's a quick look at calibre's capabilities:

1. **Bring up your favorite browser, go to** `http://calibre-ebook.com`, **and download and install calibre.**

   The installer doesn't have any options.

2. **Tap or click Finish, and run calibre for the first time.**

   When calibre asks for your e-book device (see Figure 2-7), don't panic — it converts any format to any other. This just sets up things so calibre knows which format you favor and makes it easier to choose your most common format.

   calibre scans your Documents library for books — just about any format you can imagine — and lists each book (refer to Figure 2-6).

   Note that calibre lists books, not files. If you have a book that's in two different formats — say, a MOBI file and an EPUB file — it appears only as one book on this main screen.

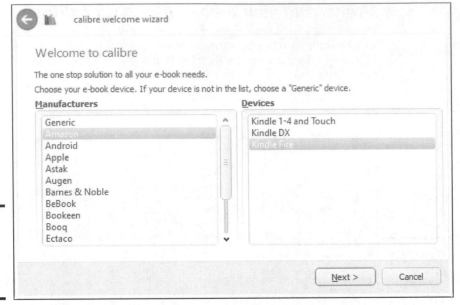

Figure 2-7:
Choose the
device you
use most
commonly.

3. **To see the details about an individual book, right-click it and choose Edit Metadata, Edit Metadata Individually.**

   (Someday, calibre will have a touch option; for now, it's mouse only.)

   calibre shows you an enormous amount of information about the book, including the formats that are available. See Figure 2-8.

4. **When you're finished looking at, or modifying, the data, close the book's dialog box.**

   You return to calibre library (refer to Figure 2-6).

5. **To convert a book to a different format, right-click the book and choose Convert Books, Convert Individually.**

   A Convert dialog box appears, similar to Figure 2-9.

6. **In the upper right, choose the format you want to convert the book to; in the lower right, tap or click OK.**

   calibre converts the book to the format you choose and places the new file next to the old ones.

This just touches on calibre's capabilities; it's an amazingly versatile program. For a more detailed rundown of what calibre can do, start at `http://manual.calibre-ebook.com/gui.html`. Keep in mind that caliber translates from one format to another. It doesn't relax digital rights restrictions: If you translate a pirated book from MOBI to PDF, it's still a pirated book.

Figure 2-8: calibre shows, and allows you to edit, an enormous amount of data about each book.

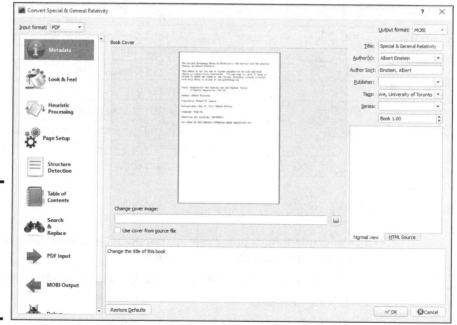

Figure 2-9: Pick the new book format in the Output Format box, in the upper right.

Getting Media from Your PC to Your Kindle

If you use your PC to manage your books and music, you need a way to get those files onto your e-reader or tablet. This section is here to help. Unfortunately, the methods for each device are specific to that device. So I focus on the Kindle e-reader in this section because the Kindle is the most popular e-reader out there.

If you use a Nook or other Android tablet and you need help syncing files, check out the articles and tutorials available at www.dummies.com.

Emailing books from your PC to your Kindle

The easiest way to transfer books to your Kindle? Email them via the Kindle Personal Documents Service. As long as you need to transfer a file type listed in Table 2-1, emailing is the best, quickest way.

Table 2-1	Documents That Can Be Emailed to a Kindle
File Type (Filename Extension)	**Description**
MOBI	Kindle native MOBI format
TXT	Plain text files (looks surprisingly good on the Kindle)
DOC, DOCX	Doesn't handle complex Word documents very well, but simple ones are fine
RTF	Rich Text Format
HTML	Web pages
ZIP, X-ZIP	Kindle unpacks the files
PDF	Second-generation Kindle devices (Kindle 2 or later, Fire, and so on) show PDF files directly
JPG, GIF, BMP, PNG	Images show up fine

Here's how to transfer a file:

1. **On your Kindle's home screen, tap the gear settings icon in the upper right and choose More on the right.**

   Kindle shows you several settings options, starting with Help & Feedback.

2. **Tap My Account.**

   Kindle shows you the registration information, including an email address, such as woody_217b64@kindle.com.

3. **Write down the email address.**

4. **In Windows (or on any computer for that matter), send a message to that email address, from the email address that you use to log into Amazon, and attach to the message the file you want to transfer.**

   The file ends up in your Kindle's Documents folder.

Amazon has a Send to Kindle application that lets you right-click a file in the desktop File Explorer and choose Send To, Kindle. That sends the file to your Kindle, using the email method described earlier. You can also print from any desktop application and choose Send to Kindle. I don't use either because emailing is very simple and clean, and I don't have to worry about the Amazon application gumming up things.

Receiving emailed books from a friend

If you want a friend to send books or documents to your Kindle, you have to give her permission by adding her email address to your allowed list. Here's how to let others email books and documents directly to your Kindle:

1. **Sign on to www.amazon.com with the same ID you use on your Kindle.**

   If you're already logged in, your personalized Amazon screen appears, as shown in Figure 2-10. (If you aren't logged in, click Sign in and get with the system.)

**Book X
Chapter 2**

**Android, Chrome-
cast, Roku, Kindle,
and Windows 10**

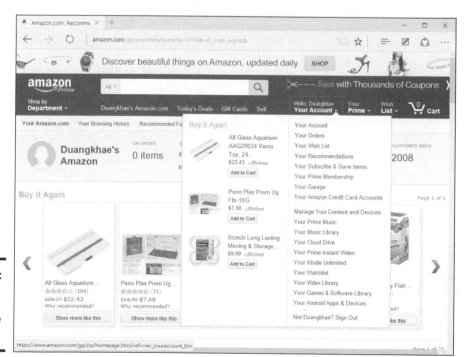

Figure 2-10:
Your
Account
settings are
here.

2. **Click, tap and hold, or hover your mouse over Your Account, and choose Manage Your Content and Devices.**

   Amazon shows you a list of all the titles you've bought and placed on your Kindle.

3. **At the top, click the Settings tab and scroll down to the section marked Personal Document Settings.**

   You see the options shown in Figure 2-11.

4. **At the bottom, tap or click the Add a New Approved Email Address link.**

   A box that lets you add email addresses appears.

5. **Type the address of anyone you want to allow to send stuff directly to your Kindle, and tap or click Add Address.**

   To add multiple addresses, simply repeat the preceding steps.

   The changes take effect immediately.

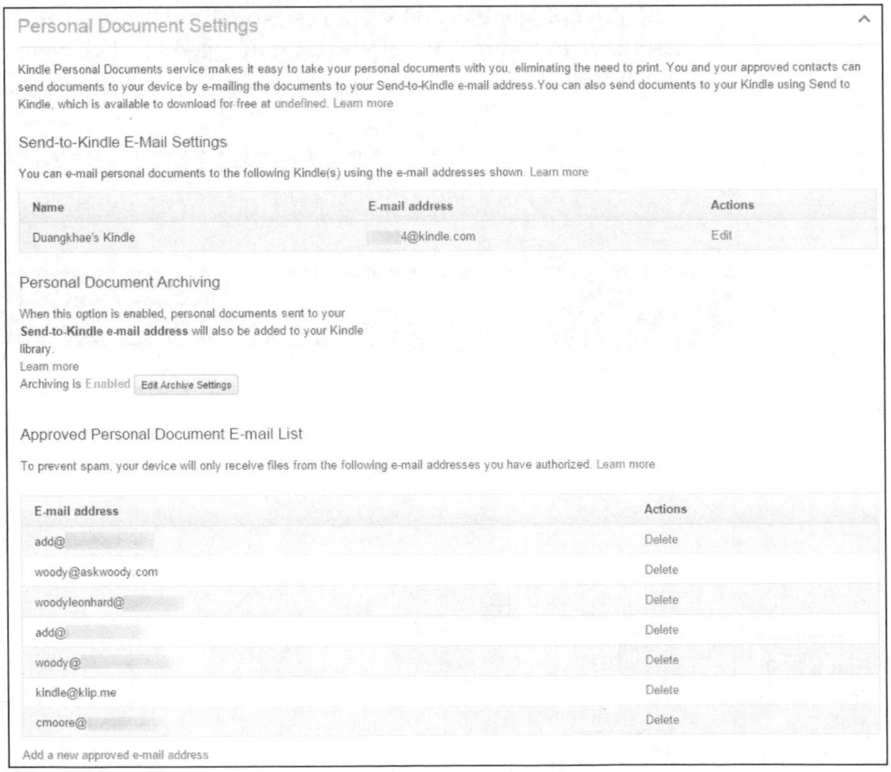

Personal Document Settings ⌃

Kindle Personal Documents service makes it easy to take your personal documents with you, eliminating the need to print. You and your approved contacts can send documents to your device by e-mailing the documents to your Send-to-Kindle e-mail address. You can also send documents to your Kindle using Send to Kindle, which is available to download for free at undefined. Learn more

Send-to-Kindle E-Mail Settings

You can e-mail personal documents to the following Kindle(s) using the e-mail addresses shown. Learn more

Name	E-mail address	Actions
Duangkhae's Kindle	4@kindle.com	Edit

Personal Document Archiving

When this option is enabled, personal documents sent to your
Send-to-Kindle e-mail address will also be added to your Kindle
library.
Learn more
Archiving is Enabled [Edit Archive Settings]

Approved Personal Document E-mail List

To prevent spam, your device will only receive files from the following e-mail addresses you have authorized. Learn more

E-mail address	Actions
add@	Delete
woody@askwoody.com	Delete
woodyleonhard@	Delete
add@	Delete
woody@	Delete
kindle@klip.me	Delete
cmoore@	Delete

Add a new approved e-mail address

Figure 2-11:
Add your
send-
enabled
friends to
this list.

Adding music to your Kindle

To get music into the Kindle, you need to connect it to your PC and drag the files across. Follow these simple steps:

1. **Plug a standard mini-USB cable into your Kindle (one may have come with the device), and stick the other end in your PC.**

2. **Slide the Start Screen slider on your Kindle.**

   A screen appears telling you that You Can Now Transfer Files from Your Computer to Kindle.

   Windows hums and haws for a while and may ask (in a toaster notification on the right side) what you want to do with newly inserted hard drives.

3. **If a Windows notification appears, ignore it.**

4. **Bring up File Explorer by tapping or clicking the Explorer icon on the taskbar.**

   It may take a minute, or two, or even three, but sooner or later, your Kindle appears on the left side of File Explorer, somewhere on the list of other hard drives on your computer.

5. **Find a favorite MP3 file, or folder full of MP3 files, and drag it from your PC into the Kindle \Music folder.**

   All the music in the \Music and \Audible folders is available to the Kindle music player.

6. **When you've transferred all the music that's fit to play, tap Disconnect on the Kindle and unplug the USB cable.**

   Your music is loaded and ready to rock.

7. **On the Kindle's home page, tap Music.**

   A list of all the MP3 files appears in either the \Music or \Audible folders.

8. **(Optional) To create a playlist, tap the Playlists link and follow the instructions to build a playlist.**

9. **To simply play your music, tap the Shuffle and Play button, or simply tap a song.**

   The song starts playing. Individual controls are available for volume, pause, fast-forward, rewind, shuffle, and cycle. After the music starts, you can go back to the Kindle's home page and read books. The music keeps going even after the screen has gone dark.

10. **To turn off the music, tap Music and, at the bottom of the screen, tap the Pause button.**

You can also copy your music to the Amazon Cloud Drive and play it on your Kindle from there: To play iTunes music, for example, download it to your computer and upload to your cloud drive. See the Cloudplayer website, www.amazon.com/cloudplayer, for details.

If you own a Kindle, Amazon gives you free Amazon Cloud Drive storage for everything you've bought from Amazon, plus 5GB of free storage for things you've acquired elsewhere — even songs from iTunes. Very slick.

If you're an Amazon Prime member, you qualify for the lending library. See the Cloudplayer website, www.amazon.com/cloudplayer, for details.

Chapter 3: Getting Started with Gmail, Google Apps, and Drive

In This Chapter

✓ **Using Google alternatives to Microsoft products**

✓ **Setting up your Gmail account**

✓ **Using Google Docs (Drive)**

✓ **Moving your domain to Google**

*I*n spite of the rivalry between Microsoft and Google, Google's so important to today's computer users that Microsoft builds hooks into Windows 10 that try to get you to add your Gmail account to the Windows Universal Mail app and add your Gmail contacts to the Windows Universal People app. Of course, Google is happy to return the favor, with easy ways to put your Hotmail/Outlook.com mail inside Gmail, and to import your Hotmail/Outlook.com contacts into Gmail.

There's a reason why Microsoft wants you to put your Google eggs in its basket. Google has very good competitors to the Microsoft online stable, er, stables, including the following:

✦ *ChromeOS,* as explained in the nearby sidebar, obviates the need to run Windows for many people.

✦ *Microsoft Hotmail/Outlook.com,* the *Windows 10 Universal Mail app,* the mail part of Microsoft's Outlook and Outlook 365, the *Outlook Web App,* and a zillion other Microsoft mail programs all compete with *Google Gmail,* in different ways.

✦ The *Microsoft Windows Universal Calendar app* and the various *Office Outlook calendars* compete with *Google Calendar.*

✦ The *Microsoft Windows Universal People app* and *Hotmail/Outlook.com contacts* compete with *Google Gmail contacts.*

Worth noting: Every app in *italics* in the preceding list is *free* if you're running Windows 10. Absolutely free. Microsoft and Google give away the apps to draw you in to their corners, with the hope of selling you something in the future.

You can use Gmail to send and receive mail using your own private domain, and it's free for up to ten mailboxes. So, for example, I can use Gmail to handle all the mail coming into and going out of AskWoody.com without changing my email address and without anyone knowing that I'm using Gmail: All the mail going out says it's from `Woody@AskWoody.com`, and all the mail sent to `Woody@AskWoody.com` ends up in my Gmail Inbox. It's a feature in Google Apps, and except for one step, it's pretty easy. See the last section in this chapter, "Moving Your Domain to Google," for details.

All this wrangling takes place against a backdrop of increased competition from Apple and new assaults from Facebook. All the companies really want to get you hooked on their ways of working.

Don't forget that "free" services aren't free in the sense of being zero-sum. The companies offering the "free" service gather information about you, unabashedly, and show you targeted ads, in the hope of selling you something. As a poster named *blue_beetle* on the site MetaFilter (`www.metafilter.com/95152/Userdriven-discontent#3256046`) put it so succinctly, "If you're not paying for it, you're not the customer; you're the product being sold."

In the following section, I very briefly look at Google alternatives to Microsoft products from the perspective of a Windows user.

Finding Alternatives to Windows with Google

Google has a handful of free online products and offerings that warrant your attention. Microsoft has two or three handfuls, but that's the subject of the rest of this book.

Here are the five Google products, other than ChromeOS, that serve as alternatives to Microsoft offerings:

✦ **Gmail:** A free, online mail program, similar to Microsoft's Hotmail/Outlook.com. Features change constantly, but it's fair to say that if you find a feature you like in Hotmail/Outlook.com, it'll be in Gmail soon — and vice versa. Some people prefer one interface over the other; I'm ambivalent but for now I've settled on Gmail, primarily because I prefer the interface. If you use Google's Chrome web browser, you can even use Gmail when you aren't connected to the Internet.

✦ **Google Drive:** A service from Google that gives you up to 15GB of free online storage, similar to Microsoft OneDrive's 15GB free allotment, with occasional discounts for various promotions. I talk about the different online storage services in Book VIII, Chapter 1. Google Drive's main advantage is its ability to work easily with Google Apps.

ChromeOS — the Windows killer

In the course of a few years, Chromebooks have jumped from scoffed-at toys to genuine Windows rivals. I talk about ChromeOS and the Chromebooks that run them in Book I Chapter 1. In general, if I know somebody who's looking for a computer and they don't need to do anything that's directly tied to Windows (which describes, oh, 80% of my friends or more), I usually recommend that they get a Chromebook. They're easier to use, less prone to infection, and all-in-all a whole lot less hassle for me to support.

Chromebooks run ChromeOS which is, to a first approximation, just the Chrome browser you've used before.

To a second approximation, ChromeOS can support overlapping resizable windows (each resembling a Chrome window on Windows or OS X), as well as apps built to the Google Package App Platform. That's what gives specific apps (such as Gmail, Sheets, Docs) the ability to run even when the OS is offline. ChromeOS also includes a built-in media player and a file manager.

My wife and I went shopping for a car last month. At one dealership we met a salesman who was carrying a Chromebook, using it to make the sale. I asked him how he liked it and was bowled over by the response. He not only liked it; he loved it. Bought one to use at home.

As he stepped me through the virtues of the Chromebook — it's like he was trying to sell me one — he showed me how the corporate IT guys had built a Chrome-based support system for salespeople at the dealership. "We used to have PCs, and they sucked." Alas, that's a refrain I hear dozens of times a day. You probably do, too. "The Chromebook works all the time. The PCs would go up and down, or get slower as they got older. I don't have to worry about updates. The printer's always there. No waiting when I start the machine, it takes like two seconds and it's ready to go. And if I can't find this computer, like I forgot it in the meeting room or in a car, I pick up another one, log in, and everything's just the way I left it."

I asked him if he missed Office. You could've heard the snort at the other end of the showroom. "You're joking, right?" He has one sales spreadsheet to fill out every week, and his boss prefers that he use Google's Gsheets, which is one click away on a Chromebook. "I don't need to worry about messing up anything or emailing an attachment. Hell, I don't even need to save it." As for email? "We use Gmail, like I've been using at home for years."

Then the kicker. "One of the guys at corporate told me they saved enough on the maintenance contract to pay for the system." Probing a little deeper, I discovered that the car manufacturer had hardware maintenance agreements with a large national chain. When the salespeople had problems with their old PCs, they called "The Computer Guy," who promptly ran out and fixed it. Several times a week, on average. With the Chromebooks, The Computer Guy only shows up when the secretary's machine goes down or when the Service Department needs fixing. Now, if a Chromebook starts misbehaving, the salespeople just pick up a different one, log on and they're off to the races.

If that anecdote reverberates with you in your environment, Chromebooks may be a good alternative to Windows laptops.

✦ **Google Docs:** Contains online programs for creating and editing word processing documents, spreadsheets, fill-in-the-blank forms, presentations, and drawings. Although the programs are rudimentary, they can work collaboratively — two or more people can edit the same document at the same time, with no ill effect and no weird restrictions. And you can get at your docs from your PC, Mac, tablet, or phone. Very slick, and you don't need to do a thing.

Google is gradually phasing out the use of the terms *Google Docs* and rolling all the programs into the umbrella *Google Drive*. In this chapter, I talk about Google Docs occasionally to give you a reference point for when you see instructions (even from Google!) that refer to Google Docs. But the distinction between Google Docs and Google Drive is fading fast. You can use the terms interchangeably.

✦ **Google Apps for Work:** A combination of several web apps — Gmail, Docs, Calendar, Groups (see the next bullet), and Sites (team collaboration) — and 30GB of Google Drive storage with a framework that lets you run your own domain name through Google's programs.

(The "for Work" part means it's a paid account. Everything except the domain name parking is free for personal use.)

Think of Google Apps for Work as a way to leverage Google's software and servers for your organization. It's $5 per person, per month (or $50 a year), for business users, free for non-profits and schools, and there's a special setup for government organizations.

Google Apps competes more or less with Microsoft Office 365 (see the nearby "Office 365 in a nutshell" sidebar).

✦ **Google Groups:** If you belong to an organization, Google Groups offers an alternative to a Facebook page for keeping the members of the organization updated on what's happening and to give members of the organization a chance to talk to each other.

One person, the *manager,* sets up a group at `http://groups.google.com`. The manager then sends invitations to people, who can respond by joining the group. The invitations can go to any email address — they don't have to go to `@gmail.com` addresses. Members can post messages to the group, which are then emailed to every member of the group.

The manager can set herself up as *moderator* for the group — in which case, she must approve each message before it's relayed to the members — or whether the group should be allowed to receive messages unmoderated. She also has control over each individual, such as who can post messages and who will receive them, and she can remove an individual from the group.

Technologically, Google Groups has been more or less upstaged by Facebook private pages and by Google Hangouts (a real-time video meeting place). But for people who feel more comfortable dealing with email than with Facebook — or cameras — it's a good option.

There's one big difference between Google Docs and Google Apps for Work/Education/Nonprofits. If you don't pay for using the Google apps, Google takes a peek inside your emails and your stored files, scanning them in order to target ads in your direction. If you pay for Google Apps for Work, or if you have an official, free Google for Education or Google for Nonprofits account, Google does *not* scan your email or your stored data to target ads.

There are some if's, and's, and but's. For one, *every* online email program (Outlook.com/Hotmail, Yahoo! Mail, AOL, whatever) scans your mail for viruses, spam and scams — some more thoroughly than others. The online storage providers also scan for malware than can clobber their systems. That's part of the ballgame. Scanning, in and of itself, isn't bad. The email provider is protecting both you and them.

Office 365 in a nutshell

Microsoft's entry in the office application wars is *Office 365*. Over the years, Office 365 has grown from a stub of an offering into a multi-billion-dollar baby. Depending on the subscription level — and the amount of money you pay — Office 365 can include web-only apps which aren't very exciting, full-blown installed versions of the Office apps, click-to-run versions of the Office apps that are updated continuously, and/or touch-centric Office apps, including the full-blown version of Office for Windows 10, Office for iPad, and Office for Android.

I have a lengthy analysis of the differences between Google Apps and Office 365 in the InfoWorld review, http://www.infoworld.com/article/2609136/cloud-computing/review--microsoft-office-365-vs--google-apps.html. The short version goes like this.

Google Apps is small and easily administered; it covers the high points; and it doesn't try to reach into the more obscure corners. Office 365, on the other hand, offers the best (and most complex) support in the business. I'm continually amazed at how well Microsoft has built out Office 365, rolling feature upon feature into the mix, yet keeping the whole package remarkably stable, usable, and manageable.

If you need to create complex Office-standard documents, Office 365 has no equal. But if you have less-stringent requirements and a willingness to part with 100% absolute Office document compatibility, Google Apps offers a good, inexpensive, and reliable alternative.

Pull out your calculator (or your Google Sheet), and do the math. On the Google side, personal use is free; in business settings, it costs $50 per year per person, plus the price of the necessary copies of Office (rent or buy). On the Microsoft side, if you want all the standard Office apps installed on your PC, plan on paying at least $100 per person per year. (Each copy can be installed on up to 5 machines.) For business, plan on $150 per person per year for up to 25 users, or $180 per person for up to 300 users — $240 per seat to get all the bells and whistles.

I cover Office 365, Office for Windows 10, for iPad and for Android, as well as the desktop Office apps at www.askwoody.com.

Second, Google's snooping is expressly for the purpose of directing ads. They aren't sniffing for your bank account numbers, and any organization that wants access to your data has to go through the usual channels — which usually involve a search warrant.

Third, if you use encryption to either protect the body of your email message or to lock up files stored in Google's cloud, Google won't go to the trouble of cracking the encryption. If you want something safe, lock it up yourself.

Setting Up Gmail

If you don't yet have a Gmail account, get one. Doing so is free and easy. Besides, every new Gmail account gets 15GB of free cloud storage. Here's how to set up an account:

1. **With your favorite browser, go to www.gmail.com.**

   At the bottom or on the left is the Create an Account button.

2. **Tap or click the Create an Account button.**

   The sign-up form in Figure 3-1 appears.

Figure 3-1:
Signing up for a Google account is free and easy.

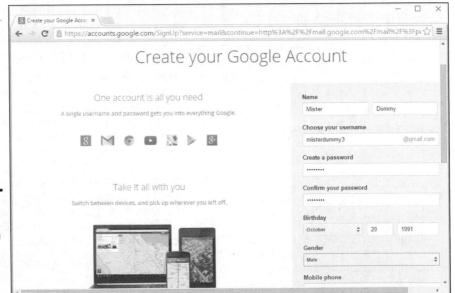

3. Fill in the form as creatively as you wish.

If you type a real phone number, Google can use it to help you get into your account if you're locked out, or for two-factor authorization. Similarly, your current email address may help you get back into your account if somebody hijacks it.

In some countries, you're required to give a valid mobile number, and Google sends you an SMS to verify that phone number before you can sign in. Currently, the United States, most of the countries in Europe, and India require valid mobile numbers, but the requirement can change from day to day. If you're reticent to give Google your phone number, remember that it could save your tail one day, if you get locked out, or if you elect to have two-factor authorization added to your account (challenging you with an SMS message every time you log on from a new computer). Google says it "won't use this number for anything else besides account verification."

4. At the bottom, tap or click Next Step.

5. Tap or click Continue to Gmail.

You now have an official Google account and a new Gmail address. Google dangles the default Gmail screen in front of you (see Figure 3-2), and it's already populated with three email messages.

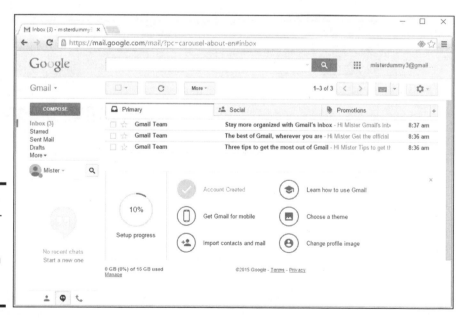

Figure 3-2:
Your brand-new Gmail account comes with three email messages.

A good way to get started is to simply send an email to yourself. Follow these simple steps for an orientation:

1. **In the upper-left corner, tap or click Compose.**

   The mail composition pane shown in Figure 3-3 appears.

2. **In the To field, type your new Gmail address, add a subject, write a message, and try formatting parts of the message using the string of formatting icons at the top of the typing box.**

3. **When you tire of talking to yourself, in the upper-left corner, tap or click Send.**

   Wait a minute or two. If you get bored, click the round arrow at the top, to force your browser to look again.

4. **When the message arrives, play with it a bit.**

   Gmail is different from other mail programs. For starters, it groups messages by the subject. With one click, change to a conversation view that looks like the list seen in forum messaging. Its folders — called *labels* — work differently from other mail programs. Some people like the organization, some people hate it, but it's well worth taking some time to see whether this method feels better to you than the method you're using now.

Figure 3-3: Create a new email message here.

After you have a few messages under your belt, hop over to the Gmail learning center at `http://support.google.com/mail` and figure out the options Gmail has to offer. They're extensive and impressive. It probably won't surprise you to know that Gmail has search down cold — you can find any message in seconds, if you know the tricks. But you may be surprised to see how Gmail can work offline — when you aren't connected to the Internet (but you have to use the Chrome browser) — and its support for huge (25MB!) messages.

I have detailed instructions for moving your existing email accounts to Gmail at `http://windowssecrets.com/top-story/going-google-apps-part-1-move-your-mail/`. Yes, it's easy to keep your current email address. People you write to will never know that you switched to Gmail.

And while you're looking at Gmail, try the new service called Inbox. I'm gradually getting used to it, and can't believe how some smarts on the Google side make my email burden much easier.

Using Google Docs/Drive

After you get a free Google account (see the preceding section), take a few minutes to see what Google Drive can do for you. Remember that Google Docs and its applications — for creating documents, spreadsheets, presentations, fill-in-the-blanks forms, and drawings — are being absorbed into Google Drive. If you see the name *Google Docs* or *Google Apps* while working with *Google Drive,* it's only because Google is slow in getting its names sorted out.

Everything's free, of course.

Here's how to start with Google Docs, er, Drive:

1. **With your favorite browser, go to www.drive.google.com.**

2. **If you aren't logged in to Google, provide your Google account and password. Tap or click Get Started.**

There's a short tutorial that you can click through. Then the Google Drive download page appears, with an interface that's uncannily similar to Gmail. See Figure 3-4.

If you already have a Google account, you can spread the goodness to other machines by clicking Install Drive for your computer.

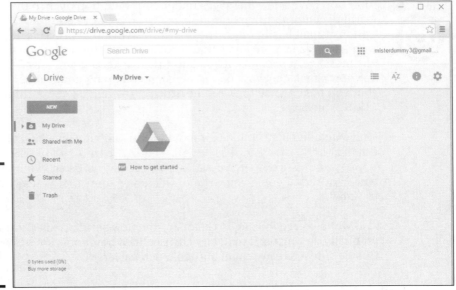

Figure 3-4:
Google
Drive is
familiar
to anyone
who's seen
Gmail.

3. **Open File Explorer and note that you have a new folder called Google Drive. Drag an assortment of files into the Google Drive folder.**

Try grabbing a simple Word document, a spreadsheet, some graphics files, some PowerPoint slides, and maybe a PDF. Get a handful of them so you can experiment with the Google Drive apps.

4. **Go back to your browser, and again go to `www.drive.google.com`.**

All the files you put in the Google Drive folder appear, as shown in Figure 3-5.

5. **Open one of the documents (a Word document, Excel spreadsheet, or PowerPoint slide, if you have one) that you copied into the Google Drive folder.**

If you have the corresponding Office program installed and working on your computer, Google Drive opens the document inside the correct program.

If you didn't spend the exorbitant amount of money for Office — there's no Office or Office-wannabe on your computer — and the document's fairly simple, as you can see in Figure 3-6, Google Drive does a reasonably good job of *rendering* it — showing it on the screen.

More complex documents, though, can have all sorts of problems, from missing pieces to jumbled text. Although Google Drive does yeoman's work trying to display Office documents, it's far from 100-percent accurate — and it doesn't play well with complex templates, and doesn't work at all with macros.

Figure 3-5:
Files you drag or copy into the Google Drive folder on your desktop appear inside Google Drive on the Internet.

6. **To edit the document, click or tap the Open button at the top (see Figure 3-6).**

A copy of the document is saved in Google format (Word documents become .gdoc; Excel files become .gsheet; and PowerPoint slides become .gslides, for example), which you can then edit.

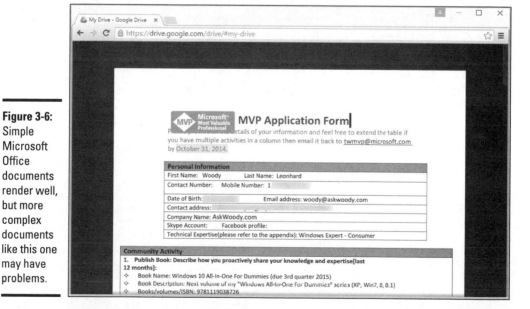

Figure 3-6:
Simple Microsoft Office documents render well, but more complex documents like this one may have problems.

At this point, converting from the Office format to the Google format is a one-way trip. At least as of this writing, you can't change a Google document back to an Office document, although Google has at times offered a File, Export as Word option. Although you can treat Google documents just like any other file — copy or e-mail them, for example — they can be edited only by Google Drive applications.

Don't be surprised if the Google applications fall over when converting documents from Microsoft format (or even PDF) to Google format. You'll see something like *An error has occurred and we cannot save your changes.* The conversion feature is very much a work in progress.

7. **To create a new document, on the Google Drive home page, tap or click the New button and choose what kind of document you want.**

   You can create a new document, presentation, spreadsheet, fill-in-the-blanks form (which is stored as a spreadsheet), or drawing (which is stored as a .gdraw file). See Figure 3-7.

8. **Edit the file using the Google Drive apps' comparatively limited tools (although the spreadsheet app does support Pivot Tables).**

   In fact, more than one person can edit the file simultaneously.

9. **When you're finished, close the browser tab.**

   Your files are saved automatically, and the latest versions appear almost immediately in the Google Drive folder on your desktop.

Figure 3-7: It's safer to create new documents from inside Google Drive, rather than importing and switching from Microsoft Office format.

After you play with Google Drive a bit, take a few minutes to read the manual. You can find the Google Docs (ooops — there's that word again) help system at `http://support.google.com/docs`.

I have an extensive discussion about setting up Google Drive in the second part of my Windows Secrets Newsletter series on Going Google at `http://windowssecrets.com/top-story/going-google-apps-part-2-move-your-docs/`.

Moving Your Domain to Google

The terminology's confusing. Permit me to review quickly.

Google Docs, now Google Drive, has a bunch of apps — word processing, spreadsheet, presentation, drawing, and fill-in-the-blanks forms. The apps are tied together with a Dropbox-like, online file storage and synchronization app.

Google Calendar, which I didn't cover in this chapter, is a standalone calendar with lots of advanced features, including the ability to sync with many other calendars. I use Google Calendar exclusively because it's easy to use on all my devices — desktop, laptops, MacBooks, iPhone, Galaxy phone, iPad — and it fits in nicely with calendars that are maintained by local governments and my son's school. To read more about Google Calendar, go to `www.google.com/calendar`.

All those apps — word processing, spreadsheet, presentation, forms, drawing, and calendar — together with Google Groups (which is being edged out by other technologies), and 15GB or more of online synced storage, are available free for anybody, anytime. I talk about most of the apps in this chapter.

Google used to have a free, ad-support version called Google Apps Free. It was similar to Google Apps for Work (see next), but if you only had ten or fewer users, it didn't cost anything. Unless you were grandfathered in, that version is gone.

The basic Google Drive and apps, as mentioned earlier in this chapter, are all free for personal use, all the time. The next level up, Google Apps for Work ties together organizations (companies, yes, but charities and clubs and all sorts of other kinds of organizations), and it's particularly useful for organizations that operate with a single domain, such as AskWoody.com or Dummies.com. When your organization (and your domain) hooks up with Google Apps, you get to use Gmail for handling all your mail and you aren't tied to `@gmail.com` email addresses.

You're most likely to be interested in these Google Apps for Work packages:

+ **Google Apps for Work:** Costs $50 per email address per year. It includes all the free stuff, such as running your domain through Gmail and shared calendars. The $50 also buys your organization 30GB of storage in each account and 24/7 phone support. You aren't limited to just a few email addresses — you can have tens of thousands.

+ **Google Apps for Education:** Free for schools, colleges, and universities with up to 30,000 users.

+ **Google Apps for Non-Profits:** Free for up to 30,000 users in a 501(c)3 organization; same service as Google Apps for Work. If your organization needs more than 30,000 email addresses, being a non-profit means you automatically qualify for a 40-percent discount on the Google Apps for Work price.

Why would an individual or small group want Google Apps for Work? Good question. The most persuasive arguments I know are these:

+ It's simple, effective, cheap (or free), and easy, especially if you know and like Gmail.

+ If the Google Drive apps do everything you need — straightforward documents, spreadsheets, presentations — you can save yourself and your organization a ton of money by not buying Microsoft Office.

This, to me, is the crucial question: Do you need to spend the money to get all the frills in the Office apps, or do the Google Drive apps give you enough of what you need? Tough question, and one only you can answer after you try it for a while.

+ If you set things up properly, you can share documents with everyone in your group, and it doesn't take any extra work. In fact, you can all collaborate on a document at the same time with basically zero effort.

+ Everyone can work on the device they prefer; whether the device is a PC, a Mac, an iPad, a Nexus, or an abacus (okay, I exaggerated a little bit), Google Apps has you covered. And you can switch from machine to machine, location to location, without any concerns about syncing or dropping files.

+ Google's reliability is second to none. It isn't up 100 percent of the time, but it's mighty close.

Before you go screeching to your terminal to sign up for Google Apps, understand that, although the day-to-day use of Google Apps is as simple as using Gmail, setting it up has a couple of gotchas. Converting to the free version of Google Apps isn't too difficult, but it'd be wise to make sure you understand the steps before you commit yourself.

Also ensure that you understand what will and won't happen with your email after you switch. For example, Google Apps doesn't move your old messages over to Gmail: If you want your old messages to come across, you have to run its migration program. You can find a comprehensive discussion about moving to Google Apps Gmail at `http://learn.googleapps.com/gmail`.

I assume that you already have a domain name for yourself or your organization. If not, you can register a domain name with thousands of different, web-hosting companies. I use `www.greengeeks.com`, but your friends may have better recommendations.

In general terms, here's how to get your domain grafted onto the free version of Google Apps (read all the steps before you get started):

1. **Go to `www.google.com/work/apps/business/pricing.html`, and in the Google Apps column, tap or click the Get Started button.**

Google hides the free version, but it's there if you know where to look.

The sign-up sheet appears, as shown in Figure 3-8.

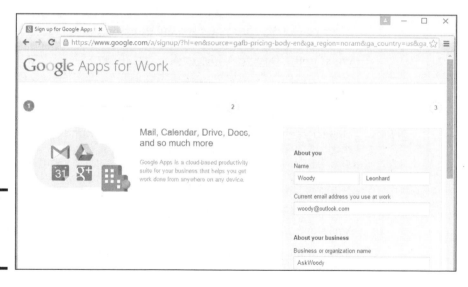

Figure 3-8:
Sign up for the free service.

2. **Tap or click Next. Google asks if you would like to use a domain name you already have, or if you want to buy a new domain through Google (at $8/year, which is quite reasonable).**

If you already have a domain that you're very attached to, you'll have to jump through some hoops to prove that you own the domain.

On the other hand, if you aren't very infatuated with your domain name and would like to start with a new one, buying it from Google is much simpler — Google will even set up your email automatically.

Choose your preference, and click Next.

3. **Type your chosen username and password for the Google Apps for Work account, and click Next.**

4. **You will have three weeks to verify that you do, in fact, own the domain that you're moving over to Google Apps for Work.**

   You have to put a unique identifier inside a file that you upload to your web site. That unique number tells Google that you do, indeed, own your domain.

   Look at the video at `http://support.google.com/a/bin/answer.py?hl=en&answer=60216` for details.

   Although you may be uncomfortable performing the upload yourself, if you have a person who helps you with your website, he may well find it to be a piece of cake. Google has detailed instructions for more than 50 different web hosts. Yes, it has step-by-step instructions for Go Daddy, in case you were wondering.

5. **After you verify that you own the domain and Google confirms that it's received the verification, change your site so it starts routing email to the Google Apps servers.**

   You do that by changing the so-called MX Records that are associated with the domain.

   This part's easier than Step 3, but it takes some concentration, especially if you're not accustomed to bumping around inside your domain's records. Details are at `http://support.google.com/a/bin/answer.py?hl=en&answer=140034`.

6. **Wait for the changes to take effect.**

   Usually that's less than an hour. In my case, it took only a few minutes.

   Mail starts flowing to your Gmail account, and you can use it immediately.

7. **If you want to move any mail over from your current program to Gmail, follow the instructions at** `http://learn.googleapps.com/gmail`.

All in all, setting up Google Apps is a bit of a pain — it's definitely non-trivial, takes time and jumping some difficult hurdles — but after you're over the hump, using Gmail for all your mail can be a liberating experience.

Chapter 4: Using Web-Based Outlook.com (nee Hotmail)

In This Chapter

✔ Getting the scoop on Hotmail's long and tortured history

✔ Starting out with Outlook.com

✔ Organizing Outlook.com

✔ Finding out if Outlook.com went down

✔ Getting some advanced Outlook.com tips

Two months before Microsoft shipped the original Windows 8, the folks in Redmond dropped a bomb on the online email world. Hotmail — one of the best-recognized brands on the planet — would be put out to pasture, replaced by something completely different. Yes, Microsoft tossed out a brand as well known as "Coca-Cola" or "taxi" or "Visa" and replaced it with . . . Outlook.com.

If you think that the name Outlook.com was chosen because Microsoft's new flagship online email service-formerly-known-as-Hotmail looks or acts like Outlook in Office, or Outlook Express, or the Outlook Web App, or Outlook on the iPad, or the Universal "Metro" Outlook app, or anything else that's ever been called "Outlook," you'd be wrong, of course. Outlook.com is just the old Hotmail, with a few internal changes and a new, tiled-style boxy interface.

It's all marketing, folks.

How thorough is the change? Well, right now, if you point your web browser to `www.hotmail.com`, you end up at `login.live.com` — the former Windows Live login location. (Windows Live IDs are now called Microsoft accounts, and Windows Live itself was abandoned during the days of Windows 7, but whatever.) After you log in, you're directed to `mail.live.com`, which is the current home of what used to be Hotmail and is now Outlook.com — except it isn't really *at* Outlook.com. It's located at `mail.live.com`. It's been that way for years, in spite of Microsoft getting rid of the "Live" brand.

Doesn't make any sense, does it?

In this chapter, I step you through Outlook.com, with a nod and a wink to Hotmail, which is now officially dead.

Getting Started with Outlook.com

When working with Outlook.com, any Microsoft account will do. I talk about Microsoft accounts in Book II Chapter 5. If you already have an @hotmail. com, @live.com, @outlook.com, or an older @msn.com email address, it's already a Microsoft account. If you don't yet have a @hotmail.com or @outlook.com email address, getting one is easy. Follow these steps:

1. **On the old-fashioned desktop, with your favorite web browser, go to www.outlook.com.**

The main screen asks whether you have a Microsoft account.

2. **To get a new Microsoft account, down at the bottom, tap or click Sign Up Now.**

The sign-up form appears, as shown in Figure 4-1.

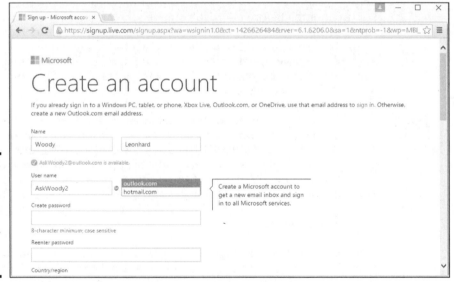

Figure 4-1: Sign up for an @ hotmail.com or @outlook. com email address.

3. **Fill out the form creatively, and think hard about whether you want to enable two-factor authentication by giving Microsoft your phone number (for texting password reset info only) or an alternate email address (not for spam — this is only to email you a password reset message). Type the CAPTCHA codes (if you can figure them out), deselect the Send me promotional offers check box, and tap or click Create Account.**

Part of the signup includes Microsoft's two-factor authentication. In short, you are offered two ways to identify yourself: Provide a phone number where MS can send an SMS (text) message, or provide an email address where MS can send a verification email. Although the form doesn't make it clear, you don't need to give a phone number, as long as you give an alternate email address — and you don't have to give an email address as long as you give a phone number. Either or both can be fake.

Microsoft doesn't use either of those authentication routes right now, while you're signing up. It'll keep your answers and use them if you're trying to retrieve your password.

Having a phone number and/or alternate email address on file with Microsoft makes it easier and more secure to reset your password if you lose it; Microsoft sends an SMS to your phone or an email with a reset key. Only you can decide if the additional convenience (and greater security) of having a working SMS phone number or alternate email address on file is worth the dent in your privacy.

Outlook.com whirrs for a minute or so, asks you to click a Continue to inbox button, and then shows you the Outlook.com welcome screen (see Figure 4-2).

The ads are free.

**Book X
Chapter 4**

Using Web-Based Outlook.com (nee Hotmail)

Figure 4-2:
Your new Outlook. com email address is alive and working.

Axing the advertising

Yes, the entire third column of your Outlook. com home page is taken up by advertising. Want to get rid of the ads? That's gonna cost you, bucko.

If you upgrade to Ad-Free Outlook.com for the princely sum of $20 a year, Microsoft gives you the right column back. Sorta. If you pay to get rid of the ads, the rightmost column contains either a search link, or if the mail came from someone on your Windows 10 People contact list, you see a picture of the sender along with her latest Twitter tweets and Facebook posts. Saints preserve.

If you really want to spend the money, click the gear icon near your name, choose Options, and at the bottom of the Manage Your Account list, click the link to Upgrade to Ad-free Outlook.

Or you can get Office 365, for $70 or so a year.

You can now use your new Outlook.com account as a Windows logon ID. You can use it for email, Xbox, just about anything. It's just another Microsoft account.

Take a quick spin around Outlook.com, starting from the welcome screen, which you see when you log on to Outlook.com (`www.outlook.com`) using your favorite `@hotmail.com`, `@live.com`, or `@outlook.com` email address (refer to Figure 4-2):

✦ **The default folders on the left are Inbox, Archive (which you may not be able to see, if you're using an older account), Junk, Drafts, Sent, and Deleted.** You click each folder to open it. Make sure you understand what each one is supposed to contain:

- *Inbox* gets all your mail as it comes in. If you don't do anything with it, the message stays in your inbox.

- *Archive* is where you drag messages that you want to keep forever. Microsoft, uh, borrowed the idea of an archive from Google.

- *Junk* holds mail that was sent to you but that Outlook.com has identified as being junk. Outlook.com and Gmail have very effective junk identifiers, but occasionally a message will get tossed in here that really isn't junk. If that happens, tap or click the box next to the "good" junk message, and at the top, choose Move To ➪ Inbox.

You can also drag and drop the message into whatever folder you like.

If you get a piece of junk mail in your Inbox, don't delete it. You can help the Hotmail filters and other Hotmail users by marking the message as Junk. Just check the box next to the message, and at the top, tap or click Junk.

- *Drafts* holds mail that you were working on but didn't send.

- *Sent* contains copies of everything that's gone out.

- *Deleted* is the place where messages go when you "delete" them.

  You can create new folders. Just tap or click the New Folder link.

✦ **The search box in the upper left is the most important location on the Outlook.com main page.** People go nuts trying to organize their mail. The Search function finds things amazingly quickly. But that's the topic for the next section.

✦ **The Sweep feature enables you to move all the messages sent from a specific address into a folder.** Select one message from the sender you want to move, choose Sweep, and then choose how you want to sweep.

- *Delete (or Archive) all from Inbox* takes the action on all mail sent from this sender that's currently residing in the Inbox.

- *Delete (or Archive) all from Inbox and block future email* — the future messages end up in the Junk folder.

- *Always keep the latest one, Delete (or Archive) the rest*

- *Always delete (Archive) email older than 10 days* applies only to mail from this particular sender. It does, however, apply to all current and future messages from the sender. Discretion advised.

Bringing back Quick Views/Categories

Earlier versions of Outlook.com had a feature called Quick Views, which let you sort your incoming email, using Microsoft's filters to pick out what's what. For example, in the good old days, you could click Documents in the navigation pane on the left, and Outlook.com would only show you incoming emails with attached documents.

You can bring those Quick Views back in a new navigation technique known as Categories (see Figure 4-3).

Here's how to set up Categories:

1. **From the Outlook.com main screen (see Figure 4-2), in the upper-right corner, click or tap the gear and choose Manage categories.**

Outlook.com shows you a list of Categories, as in Figure 4-4. Some are obvious — Unread, for example, contains all the messages you haven't read. But others aren't so obvious.

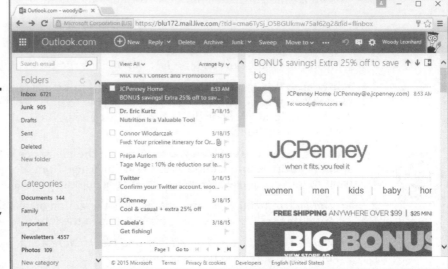

Figure 4-3:
Categories, in the lower-left corner, can make navigation much faster, particularly if you have lots of mail.

Figure 4-4:
Use Outlook.com's built-in categories.

Here's how the most useful predefined categories work:

- *Documents:* If you receive a message with a "document" attachment that Outlook.com recognizes — primarily Word, Excel, or PowerPoint documents — the message appears in the Documents Quick Views list until you delete it. Strangely, PDF files don't qualify.

- *Flagged:* If you flag a message by clicking the flag icon, the message gets elevated to the top of your Inbox list, and it also appears in the Flagged quick view. There doesn't appear to be any difference between looking at the list of flagged messages at the top of the Inbox and the list of flagged messages in the Flagged Quick Views category, and apparently you can't assign different kinds of flags.

- *Photos:* If you receive a message with an attachment that Outlook.com recognizes as a photo, the message appears in the Photos Quick Views until you delete it.

- *Shipping Updates:* Arguably most bizarre of all, if an inbound message contains text that Outlook.com recognizes as a tracking number (UPS, FedEx, and so on), the message appears in the Shipping Updates Quick Views until you delete it.

2. **Check the box in the Show in folder pane column for categories that you want to appear on your main Outlook.com screen.**

Book X
Chapter 4

Using Web-Based
Outlook.com
(nee Hotmail)

A brief history of Hotmail

Hotmail blazed new ground as the first, major, free, web-based email service when Sabeer Bhatia (a native of Bangalore and a graduate of Caltech and Stanford) spent $300,000 to launch it in 1996.

On December 31, 1997, Microsoft bought Hotmail for $400 million, and the service has never been the same. Microsoft struggled with Hotmail for many years, adding new users like flies, but always suffering from severe performance problems and crashes heard round the world. Ultimately, Hotmail was shuffled under the Microsoft Network (MSN) wing of the corporate umbrella, its free services were clipped, and its user interface was subjected to more facelifts than an aging Hollywood actor, which is saying something.

As MSN lost its luster and competitors, such as Gmail and Yahoo! Mail, battered at the, uh, Gates, the Hotmail, subscription-based, income model died almost overnight, and the company's market share fell precipitously.

Why pay for 20MB of Hotmail message storage when Google gave away 1GB for free? Hotmail became the number-one candidate for a "Live" makeover and the poster child for Microsoft's entire Live effort. Now that "Live" is dead, Hotmail has to stand on its own.

Microsoft has gone through a series of well-intentioned but horrendously implemented rebrandings and a few minor upgrades, passing through (get out your scorecard) MSN Hotmail, Windows Hotmail, Windows Live Hotmail, Microsoft Hotmail, and now Outlook.com. Hotmail's final facelift, pre-Outlook.com, came in early 2012. Few people cared, and among the ones who did, the reaction was not universally positive.

Although email as a whole isn't an endangered species, it isn't growing very quickly. Social networking sites are starting to pick up a substantial portion of traditional, one-to-one email traffic, and instant messages, SMSs (texts), and VoIP/Skype calls eat away at the numbers.

3. **When you're finished, click the left arrow in the upper-left corner.**

   Outlook.com should have a Categories list, such as the one in Figure 4-3.

With the addition of a few obvious features that you see when you poke around — tapping or clicking a column heading, for example, sorts that column — that's the extent of navigating in Outlook.com.

In the next section, I talk about organizing mail so you can use it effectively.

Bringing Some Sanity to Outlook.com Organization

Here's my number-one tip for Outlook.com users:

   If you have an Archive folder, don't create any new folders.

That way lies madness.

Yes, you can create a folder hierarchy that mimics the filing cabinets in the Pentagon. You can fret for an hour over whether an email about your trip to the beach should go in the Trips folder or the Beaches folder — or both. You can slice and dice and organize 'til you're blue in the face, and all you'll have in the end is a jumbled mess.

If you want to save that message about your trip to the beach, just click the Archive tab at the top of the Outlook.com window, or drag it into the Save/Archive folder.

The first time you click Archive at the top of the Outlook.com window, Outlook.com offers to set up a new Archive folder for you. After that, anything you archive goes into that folder.

If you want to find all the messages about Trips, use the Search box. If you want to find all the messages about Beaches, use the Search box. And if you want to find all the messages about Trips *and* Beaches . . . wait for it . . . use the Search box!

People get caught up in flags (you can tap or click the silhouette of a flag next to a message to set it) as a way to organize and sort mail. If you work well that way, hey, knock yourself out. But note that there's only one kind of flag; you can't set up different flag colors as you can in many other email programs. My general approach is to blast through email as quickly as I can, responding to what needs responding and filing the rest immediately. *De gustibus non est disputandum.*

Handling Outlook.com Failures

Although any computer system in general — and any online system in particular — has failures, Outlook.com, and Hotmail before it, seems (at least to me) to be more susceptible than Gmail.

I recall one particular incident in January 2011, when Hotmail went down and took all the mail from 17,000 users with it. In the grand Hotmail scheme of things, 17,000 users is a very tiny drop in the 300-million-plus subscribers bucket. But if you're one of the 17,000, your opinion may well vary. Ultimately, all those customers got their mail back, but it took up to three days to restore from tape backups (yes, tape!).

If Outlook.com starts acting up on you, here are two websites you should consult:

✦ **The Microsoft Hotmail, er, Outlook.com Service Status site** (see Figure 4-5) gives you the latest information about Outlook.com's current health — from Microsoft's point of view. Unfortunately, in the past, the site has been criticized for being very slow to recognize reality. In the past few years, Microsoft's network going down has, at times, also taken the status reporting sites down (`http://status.live.com/detail/outlook`).

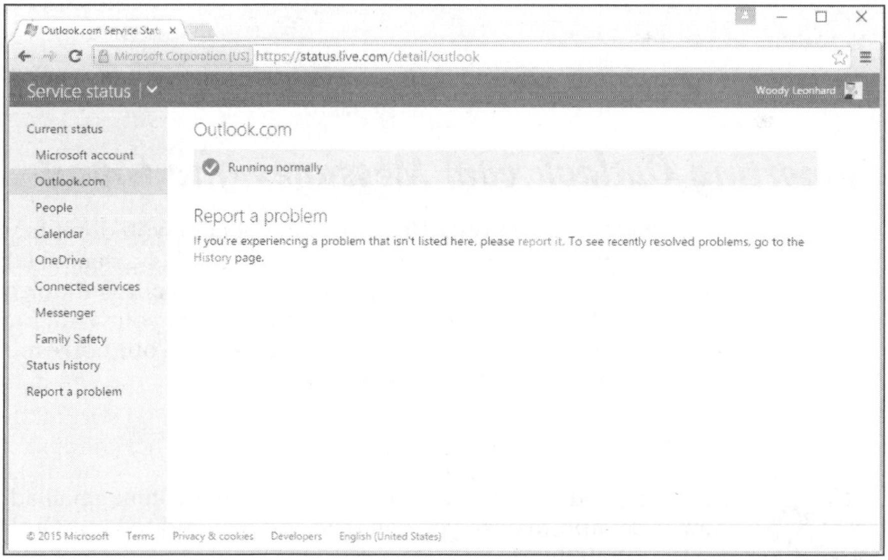

Figure 4-5: Microsoft's Outlook Service Status site gives a very broad overview of current Outlook.com status.

✦ **downrightnow,** which isn't aligned with Microsoft, gives you a crowd-sourced consensus view of what's really happening with Outlook.com/ Hotmail. downrightnow (shown in Figure 4-6) not only actively solicits comments from people who visit the site but also has a Twitter monitoring program that finds some (not all) of the tweeted complaints in real time (www.downrightnow.com/hotmail). Yes, it's Hotmail, not Outlook.

Figure 4-6:
Compare the Microsoft Party Line with the crowd-sourced downright-now (which still calls Outlook.com "Windows Live Hotmail").

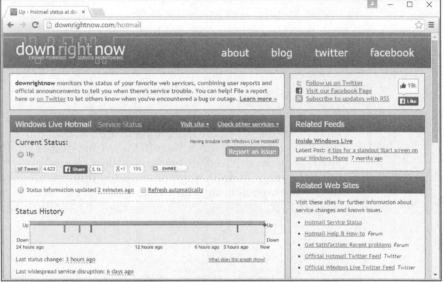

Importing Outlook.com Messages into Gmail

If you find that you prefer Gmail to Outlook.com, you don't have to give up your @hotmail.com, @live.com, or @outlook.com email address. Gmail gladly — I'm tempted to say "gleefully" — takes your Outlook.com mail, pulls it into Gmail and, if you reply to a message, tacks your @hotmail.com, @live.com, or @outlook.com address onto it. Your correspondents won't know that you've switched email providers.

I know. I've been doing it for years.

Assuming you have both a Gmail and an Outlook.com email address, here's how to set up Gmail so you can read and respond to your Outlook.com mail via the Gmail interface:

1. **Fire up Gmail, and log in with your account.**

2. **In Gmail, tap or click the gear settings icon and choose Settings.**

The Settings page appears, as shown in Figure 4-7.

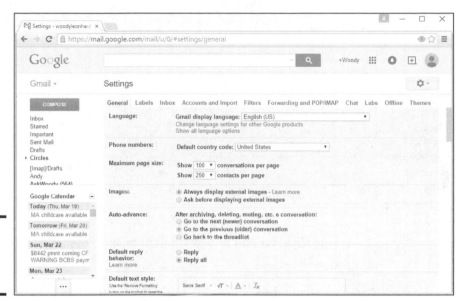

Figure 4-7:
The Gmail
Settings
page.

3. **At the top, tap or click Accounts and Import; then under the heading Check Mail from Other Accounts (Using POP3), tap or click Add a POP3 Mail Account You Own.**

Gmail asks for the email address.

4. **Type your @hotmail.com, @live.com, or @outlook.com email address — the full address — and then tap or click Next Step.**

Gmail fills in all the details for hooking into an Outlook.com (or Hotmail) account, as shown in Figure 4-8, and asks for your password.

5. **Type your password, and tap or click Add Account.**

Gmail asks whether you want to be able to send email using your @hotmail.com, @live.com, or @outlook.com address.

6. **Choose Yes, I Want to Be Able to Send Mail, and tap or click Next Step.**

7. **Accept the rest of the default responses.**

Gmail sends a message to your Outlook.com account to make sure you own it.

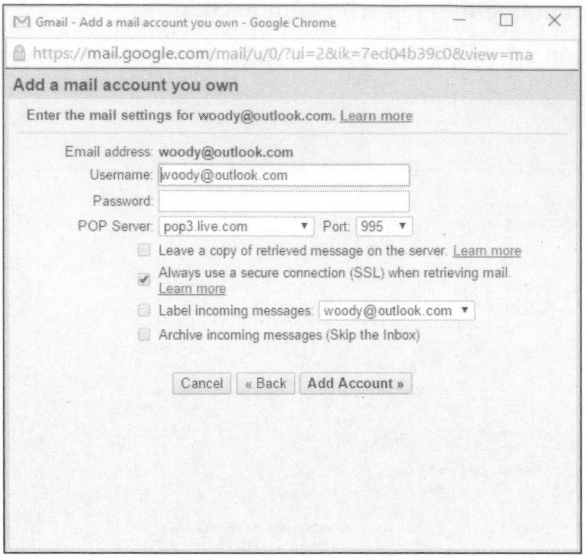

Figure 4-8: Enter the details for your Outlook.com account here.

8. **Tap or click the link in that email message.**

   You're all set up.

Gmail's melding onto your Outlook.com account doesn't change anything inside Outlook.com: You still get your mail in Outlook.com and can respond to it there, if you don't want to use Gmail.

Questions about Outlook.com? Go to `http://answers.microsoft.com`.

Weighing the Alternatives

In Book IV, Chapter 1, I talk about choosing an email program. Hotmail, er, Outlook.com is just one of many, many email programs. At this moment, Microsoft offers about a dozen different email programs:

✦ The tiled, Windows 10 Universal Mail app (see Book IV, Chapter 1)

✦ Outlook.com, formerly Hotmail (this chapter)

✦ Outlook inside Office (many flavors in various versions of Office, some of them Exchange Server-based, some on Windows, Mac, iPad, iPhone, or Android tablet or phone)

✦ The Outlook Web App

✦ The desktop program Windows Live Mail, now pretty much defunct

✦ The nearly identical twins Outlook Express (for Windows XP) and Windows Mail (for Vista and Windows 7)

With the exception of Outlook Express and Windows Mail, and to a lesser extent the various versions of Office Outlook, no two Microsoft email programs look even vaguely similar. In particular, Outlook.com doesn't look or act anything at all like Outlook inside Office.

Microsoft isn't the only email game in town, of course. Yahoo! Mail still has lots of users, especially in the United States. Gmail's in the same league, although its appeal reaches worldwide. Microsoft's been trying to catch up with Gmail for years, and its latest switch to Outlook.com is widely viewed as an attempt to shore up Hotmail's rapidly declining market share.

In Chapter 3 of this minibook, I cover Gmail in some depth and branch out to show you how Gmail, Google Drive, and Google Apps cooperate.

Outlook.com doesn't tie in with the other Microsoft apps the same way that Gmail ties in with Google Apps. Microsoft's approach to an all-encompassing application solution, Office 365, uses Outlook and its variants for managing mail, not Outlook.com. (Confusing, yes, I know.) Although you can get your Outlook.com messages fed into Outlook, and you can coerce the Windows 10 tiled Universal Mail program to grab your Outlook.com messages, Outlook. com isn't integrated into Microsoft's Grand Scheme. Yet.

I go through a metric ton of email. I use Gmail, and I'm in the process of moving over to Gmail's new Inbox app. If you're shopping for an email program, make sure you check them out.

Chapter 5: Windows' Best Free Add-Ons

In This Chapter

✔ Finding out which Windows add-ons you must have

✔ Getting the lowdown on the best of the (free) rest

✔ Figuring out what software you don't need

Much as I love — and hate, and love to hate — Windows 10, it has a few glaring holes that can be fixed only by non-Microsoft software.

In this chapter, I step you through two different kinds of software. First come the (few) programs that you need to fix holes in Windows. Second is a much larger group of programs that just make Windows work better. Both of the collections have two things in common: They're absolutely free for personal use, with one exception (which costs $5), and they all run on the desktop side of Windows 10.

Windows 10 titled "Universal" apps are still in their infancy. A year or two from now, I hope to include many of them in this Hall of Cheap Charlie Honor.

At the end of this chapter, I turn to one of my favorite topics: Software that you *don't* need and should never pay one cent to acquire. There are lots of snake oil salesmen out there. This chapter tells you why they're just blowing smoke.

Windows Universal Apps You Absolutely Must Have

Depending on what kind of Windows machine you have, there's a short and sweet list of free software that you definitely need.

File History

It isn't an add-on. There, I fooled you to get your attention.

I don't know how Windows users miss this one, but File History (see Figure 5-1) is a fantastic backup application; it's easy to use, and it's part of Windows. You already own it.

Figure 5-1:
File
History, the
Windows
version
of Time
Machine.

Microsoft's telemetry says that more than 80 percent of all Windows 7 users missed the analogous feature in the older version of Windows. Now you have no excuse. All it takes is a USB drive or a hard drive.

Think of File History as the Windows version of Apple's long-admired Time Machine. You get full backups, automatically, and it's easy to retrieve all the earlier copies of a file.

Granted, if you store all your data on OneDrive, your need for File History goes way down. But for most of us who still stick things on our PCs, it's a godsend.

If you haven't yet turned on File History, drop everything, head over to Book VIII, Chapter 1, and turn it on.

I apologize for the deception. From this point on, I turn to add-ons.

VLC Media Player

Although Microsoft made a few minor improvements to its media handling in Windows 10 — adding the ability to play FLAC lossless audio, MKV video, and a handful of less interesting media formats — it remains woefully under-powered in its ability to work with common media files.

Find a DVD movie somewhere — if you don't have one, rent one . . . if you can find a place to rent them now — and stick the DVD in your PC. A Windows notification appears, and you can tap or click that notification and play the DVD. It ought to be like falling off a log.

Unfortunately, many Windows 10 PCs — brand-spanking new machines — won't play DVD movies. Why? Microsoft decided that, even though it shipped the DVD-playing capability in previous versions of Windows, putting that capability in Windows 8 and later just cost too much. You can read the details on my blog at `http://www.infoworld.com/article/2616896/ microsoft-windows/update--windows-8-won-t-be-able-to-play-dvds.html`.

Some PC makers step in and provide the DVD movie-playing software with their new machines, but they're under no obligation to do so. That's why I suggest you get a DVD movie and see whether it'll play.

If it won't play, a simple solution is the free VLC Media Player program. In fact, VLC is so good that I use it and recommend it for all media playing — music and movies. VLC includes the small translation programs (called *codecs*) that let you play just about any kind of music or video on your Windows 10 PC.

Another poster child for open source, VLC Media Player plays just about anything — including YouTube Flash FLV files — with no additional software, downloads, or headaches.

Unlike other media players, VLC sports simple, Edge controls; built-in codecs for almost every file type imaginable; and a large, vocal online support community. VLC plays Internet streaming media with a click, records played media, converts between file types, and even supports individual-frame screenshots. VLC is well-known for tolerating incomplete or damaged media files. It will even start to play downloaded media before the download is finished.

Hop over to VLC (`www.videolan.org`) and install it (see Figure 5-2). Yeah, it's ugly. But it works very well indeed.

PSI Inspector

Every system — absolutely every Windows system — should run Secunia's Personal Software Inspector (`www.secunia.com/vulnerability_ scanning/personal`). It keeps track of all the software on your PC and alerts you when updates are needed. It'll even install those updates for you, if you let it.

The security intelligence company Secunia makes PSI available free to advertise its other services; just make sure you tell the PSI installer that it's for personal use.

Figure 5-2:
VLC Media
Player
plays every
song and
video type
imaginable,
even your
video DVDs.

Secunia PSI knows about thousands of programs (see Figure 5-3). It scans your computer and advises you on which ones need security patches, and then it installs most of the updates automatically. Details in Book IX, Chapter 4.

LastPass

In Book IX Chapter 4, I talk about two password managers, LastPass and Roboform. Both are excellent choices. Most people, in my experience, prefer LastPass, but you ought to look at Book IX Chapter 4 and see if your circumstances are different.

LastPass (Figure 5-4) keeps track of your user IDs, passwords, and other settings; stores them in the cloud; and offers them to you with a click. LastPass does its AES-256 encrypting and decrypting on your PC, using a master password that you have to remember. The data that gets stored in the cloud is encrypted, and without the key, the stored passwords can't be broken, unless you know somebody who can crack AES-256 encryption.

LastPass works as a browser add-on for IE, Firefox, or Chrome – Microsoft Edge support expected soon — so all your passwords are stored in one place, accessible to any PC you happen to be using — if you have the master password.

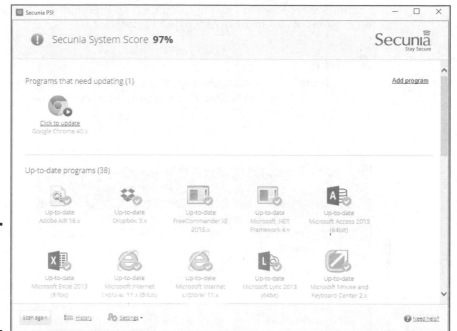

Figure 5-3:
Every
Windows
PC needs to
run Secunia
PSI.

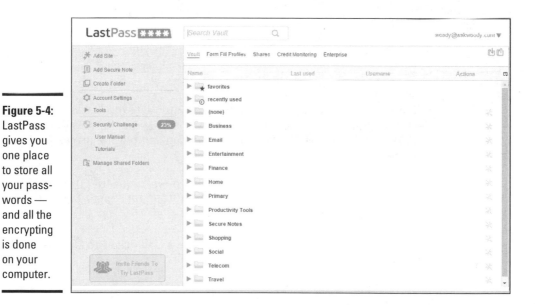

Figure 5-4:
LastPass
gives you
one place
to store all
your pass-
words —
and all the
encrypting
is done
on your
computer.

LastPass is free for personal use on PCs. The Premium version, which works on all sorts of mobile devices, costs $12 per year.

Recuva

File undelete has been a mainstay PC utility since DOS. But there's never been an undeleter better than Recuva (pronounced "recover"), which is fast, thorough, and free. See Figure 5-5.

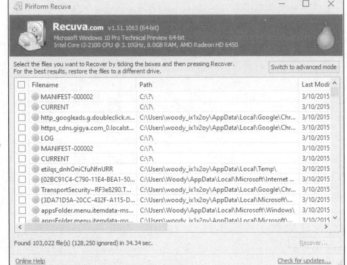

Figure 5-5:
Recuva
undeletes
files — even
on your
phone or
camera.

When you throw out the Windows Recycle Bin trash, the files aren't destroyed; rather, the space they occupy is earmarked for new data. Undelete routines scan the flotsam and jetsam and put the pieces back together.

As long as you haven't added new data to a drive, undelete (almost) always works; if you've added some data, there's still a good chance you can get most of the deleted stuff back.

Recuva can also be used to undelete data on a USB drive, an SD card, and many phones that can be attached to your PC.

Powerful stuff.

The Best of the Rest — All Free

Here are my recommendations for useful software that you may or may not want, depending on your circumstances.

Hey, the price is right.

Revo Uninstaller

Revo Uninstaller (www.revouninstaller.com) well and truly uninstalls programs, and it does so in an unexpected way.

When you use Revo, it runs the program's uninstaller and watches while the uninstaller works, looking for the location of program files and for Registry keys that the uninstaller zaps. It then goes in and removes leftover pieces, based on the locations and keys that the program's uninstaller took out. Revo also consults its own internal database for commonly left-behind bits and roots those out as well.

Revo gives you a great deal of flexibility in deciding just how much you want to clean and what you want to save. For most programs, the recommended Moderate setting strikes a good balance between zapping problematic pieces and deleting things that really shouldn't be deleted.

The not-free Pro version monitors your system when you install a program, making removal easier and more complete. Pro will also uninstall remnants of programs that have already been uninstalled.

If you uninstall programs — whether to tidy up your system or to get rid of something that's bothering you — it's worth its weight in gold.

Paint.net

In Book VII, Chapter 6, I talk about the Microsoft Paint program, which can help you put together graphics in a pinch.

For powerful, easy-to-use photo editing, with layers, plugins, and all sorts of special effects, along with a compact and easily understood interface, I stick with Paint.net.

The program puts all the editing tools a non-professional may reasonably expect into a remarkably intuitive package.

With dozens of good — even great — free image editors around, it's hard to pick one above the others. Irfanview, for example, has tremendous viewing, organizing, and resizing capabilities.

Although Paint.net requires the Windows .Net Framework, the program puts all the editing tools a nonprofessional might reasonably expect into a remarkably intuitive package.

Download it at `www.getpaint.net` and give it a try.

7-Zip

Another venerable Windows utility, 7-Zip (`www.7-zip.org`) still rates as a must-have, even though Windows supports the Zip format natively.

Why? Because some people of the Apple persuasion will send you RAR files from time to time, and 7-Zip is the fast, easy, completely free way to handle them.

7-Zip also creates self-extracting EXE files, which can come in handy (although heaven help you if you ever try to email one — most email scanners won't let an EXE file through). And it supports AES-256 bit encryption. The interface rates as clunky by modern standards (see Figure 5-6), but it gets the job done with Zip, RAR, CAB, ARJ, TAR, 7z, and many lesser-known formats. It even lets you extract files from ISO CD images.

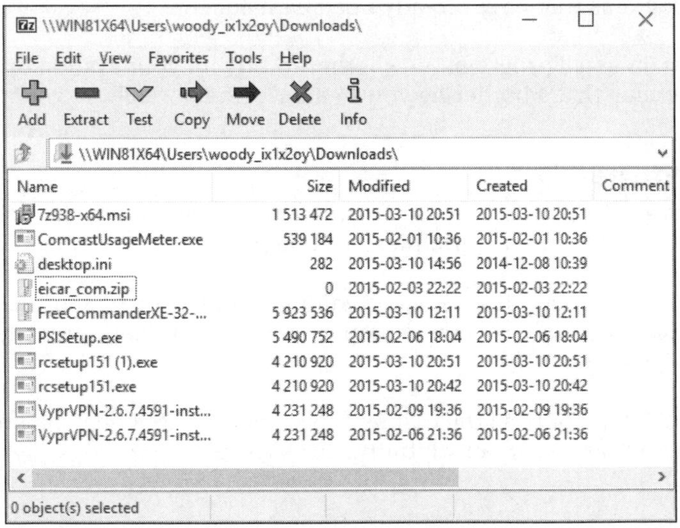

Figure 5-6: 7-Zip may not have the greatest interface, but it's a workhorse.

Name	Size	Modified	Created	Comment
7z938-x64.msi	1 513 472	2015-03-10 20:51	2015-03-10 20:51	
ComcastUsageMeter.exe	539 184	2015-02-01 10:36	2015-02-01 10:36	
desktop.ini	282	2015-03-10 14:56	2014-12-08 10:39	
eicar_com.zip	0	2015-02-03 22:22	2015-02-03 22:22	
FreeCommanderXE-32-...	5 923 536	2015-03-10 12:11	2015-03-10 12:11	
PSISetup.exe	5 490 752	2015-02-06 18:04	2015-02-06 18:04	
rcsetup151 (1).exe	4 210 920	2015-03-10 20:51	2015-03-10 20:51	
rcsetup151.exe	4 210 920	2015-03-10 20:42	2015-03-10 20:42	
VyprVPN-2.6.7.4591-inst...	4 231 248	2015-02-09 19:36	2015-02-09 19:36	
VyprVPN-2.6.7.4591-inst...	4 231 248	2015-02-06 21:36	2015-02-06 21:36	

\\WIN81X64\Users\woody_ix1x2oy\Downloads\

File   Edit   View   Favorites   Tools   Help

Add   Extract   Test   Copy   Move   Delete   Info

0 object(s) selected

Another poster boy for the open-source community, 7-Zip goes in easily, never nags, and wouldn't dream of dropping an unwanted toolbar on your system. Enlightened.

You don't need to register or pay for 7-Zip. Don't fall for a website with a similar name. To get the real, original, one and only free 7-Zip, with a crapware-free installer, go to 7-zip.org. There's support on the 7-Zip SourceForge page, `http://sourceforge.net/projects/sevenzip/`.

PicPick

If you've ever tried to use the Windows Snipping Tool to capture fleeting images on the screen — notification boxes that go away when you click, or popover menus that disappear the minute you move your mouse — you're in for a treat.

Book X
Chapter 5

Windows' Best
Free Add-Ons

PicPick (Figure 5-7) lets you take screenshots with the press of a key, and pressing the key doesn't make ephemeral items on the screen run for cover.

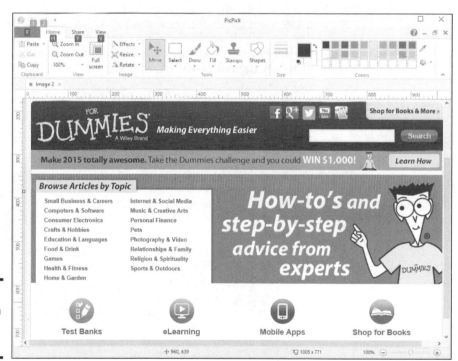

Figure 5-7:
Easy screen shots with PicPick.

After you've taken the shot, PicPick pops your screen into an editor with tools for resizing and editing. Add automatic file naming, on-screen magnification at selectable levels, a pixel ruler, color picker, and a half-dozen other screen-shooting aids, and you end up with a versatile, everything-but-the-kitchen-sink shooter.

Tixati

If you aren't yet using torrents, now's the time to start. Torrents have taken a bad rap for spreading illegal, pirate software. Although that reputation is entirely deserved, it's also true that many torrents are absolutely legitimate. Torrents are the single most efficient way to distribute files that exists.

For years I've used and recommended uTorrent, but the current version's installer includes crapware — and in previous versions, it's installed some really obnoxious crapware. Worse, the uTorrent "Date hot Russians" ads and their ilk make it tough to torrent in mixed company.

Instead, try Tixati, shown in Figure 5-8. It's simple (no Java, no .Net), fast, and easy to use, and it supports magnet links (which really simplify downloads), with extensive bandwidth reporting and management. Be careful when you navigate the download site. You may see an ad at the top of the page that says Download. If so, don't click it — horrendous crapware may lurk. Instead, follow the link farther down the page to an official mirror site.

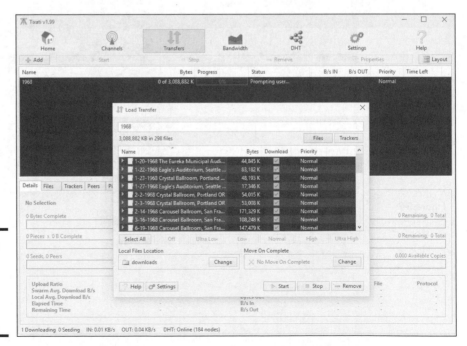

Figure 5-8: Tixati doesn't have uTorrent's baggage.

Dropbox, Google Drive, OneDrive, or . . .

Even if the thought of putting your data on the Internet drives you nuts, sooner or later you're going to want a way to store data away from your main machine, and you're going to want an easy way to share data either with other people, or with other computers (desktops, laptops, tablets, and phones).

I give you an overview of the options available in Book IV, Chapter 4. There's no obvious winner — no cloud storage that's inherently better than any of the others. Just pick one and get it set up. Someday, it'll save your tail.

They all have free introductory options, and some give you an enormous amount of storage for free, for a small fee, or even an infinite amount of storage if you subscribe to a related service – that's the Office 365 shtick.

Other interesting free software

If you connect over public WiFi, like in a coffee shop, you really should use a Virtual Private Network (VPN). I talk about VPNs in Book IX Chapter 4. Session hijacking, pioneered by the program Firesheep, can let others pose as you, even while your session is in progress. Using secure sockets (SSL) helps, but even those can be subverted in certain circumstances. Best bet is to stick with VPN.

Need to rip a DVD? Forget trying to use Windows. Get the open source, free and junk-free Handbrake, `https://handbrake.fr`. Works like a champ on any DVD.

Wonder what programs run whenever you start Windows? Look at Microsoft's venerable and free-as-a-breeze Autoruns, `https://technet.microsoft.com/en-us/sysinternals`. Autoruns finds more autostarting programs (add-ins, drivers, codecs, gadgets, shell extensions, whatever) in more obscure places than any other program, anywhere. AutoRuns not only lists the autorunning programs, it lets you turn off individual programs. It has many minor features, including the ability to filter out Microsoft-signed programs, a quick way to jump to folders holding autostarting programs, and a command-line version that lets you display file hashes. AutoRuns doesn't require installation. It's a program that runs and collects its information, displays it (with a rather rudimentary user interface), lets you wrangle with your system, and then fades away.

Want to know what hardware you have? It's a common question that's easily answered with a nifty, free utility called HWiNFO, available at `www.hwinfo.com`. HWiNFO delves into every nook and cranny. From the summary to detailed Device Manager-style trees of information — entire forests of information — HWiNFO can tell you everything anyone could want to know about your machine. There's a separate real-time monitoring panel that tells you the current status of everything under the sun: temperatures, speeds, usage, clocks, voltages, wattages, hard drive SMART stats, read rates, write rates, GPU load, network throughput, and on and on.

You may not need to buy Microsoft Office

Maybe.

If your needs are simple and you don't have to edit fancy documents created in Word, Excel, or PowerPoint, you may be able to get by with Google Apps (which I discuss in Book X, Chapter 3) or LibreOffice. The web-based Office Online apps are also good — and free for personal use. If you're moonlighting with a Mac, the iWork apps might do, too.

Do the math: LibreOffice, free. Google Apps, free for personal use. iWork apps, free. Office 365 Home (which includes five licenses) $100/year, forever. Office 2013 Home & Student (for personal use only, no Outlook), $150. Home & Business, $220. Office Online, free for personal use.

The big advantage to Office 365: You not only get five licenses of the latest versions of the Office programs — Word, Excel, PowerPoint, Outlook, OneNote, Access, Publisher — for PCs or Macs, you also get licenses for five tablets (including Office for iPad, which is a tremendous product), and five licenses for phones (largely forgettable). In addition, you get 1TB of OneDrive online storage per user for up to five users. Unless you have a visceral reaction to renting Office — I can sympathize — Office 365 at $100/year or less comes across as quite a bargain.

Whenever somebody asks me, "Why do you recommend Office when OpenOffice/LibreOffice does everything for free?", I have to cringe. It's true that Microsoft Office is expensive, and with Office 365 you're locked in to the annual fee. It's also true that good, but not great, alternatives exist — including Google Drive or Google Apps (which I discuss in Chapter 3 of this minibook), among many others.

Here are two substantial problems:

✦ As much as I would love to recommend a free replacement for Word, Excel, or PowerPoint, the simple fact is that the free alternatives (other than Office Online) aren't 100-percent compatible. In fact, for anything except the simplest formatting and most basic features, they aren't compatible at all. Even Microsoft's free Office Online Apps aren't as full-featured as the real Word, Excel, or PowerPoint. If your needs are modest, by all means, explore the alternatives. But if you have to edit a document that somebody else is going to use and it has any unusual formatting, you may end up with an unusable mess.

✦ Many people don't realize it, but OpenOffice.org isn't the same organization it used to be. In fact, there's an ongoing debate about the superiority of the new OpenOffice.org (which now belongs to Apache) and the renegade offshoot LibreOffice (`www.libreoffice.org`). Basically, some feel that OpenOffice.org moved away from its open-source roots when Oracle owned it, so a new organization, LibreOffice, forked the code and has released several new versions that are not associated with OpenOffice.org or Oracle. So you're left with two organizations, slightly different products, and no clear indication of which version (if either) will be around for the long term.

Don't Pay for Software You Don't Need!

If you've moved to Windows 10, there's a raft of software — entire *categories* of software — that you simply don't need.

Why pay for it?

Many people write to ask me for recommendations about antivirus software, utility programs, Registry cleaners, or backup programs. They cite comparative reviews — even articles that I wrote a few years ago — debating the merits and flaws of various packages.

Time and again, I have to tell them that all the information they know is wrong. On second thought, I guess the accumulated knowledge isn't so much wrong as obsolete.

The simple fact is, if you moved up to Windows 10, you wouldn't need lots of that stuff — and the old reviews are just that. Old reviews.

In this, the last section of the last chapter of this book, I'm going to lay it on the line — point out what you don't need, in my considered opinion — and try to save you a bunch of money. With any luck at all, this handful of tips will save you the price of the book.

Windows 10 has all the antivirus software you need

Windows Defender works great. And it doesn't cost a cent.

I've railed against the big antivirus companies for years. And I'll rail once again. You don't need to pay a penny for antivirus, antispyware, anti-anything software, and you don't need a fancy outbound firewall, either.

I talk about Windows Defender and the Windows Firewall in Book IX, Chapter 3.

There are *other* security programs you need, however. I list those in Book IX, Chapter 4. They're free.

Windows 10 doesn't need a disk defragger

Because of the way Windows stores data on a hard drive and reclaims the areas left behind when deleting data, your drives can start to look like a patchwork quilt, with data scattered all over the place. *Defragmentation* reorganizes the data, plucking data off the drive and putting files back together again, ostensibly to speed up hard drive access.

Although it's true that horribly fragmented hard drives — many of them handcrafted by defrag software companies trying to prove their worth — run slower than defragged drives, in practice the differences aren't that remarkable, particularly if you defrag your hard drives every month or two or six. (Note that you should never defrag a Solid State Drive.) In practice, even moderately bad fragmentation doesn't make a noticeable difference in performance, although running a defrag every now and again helps.

With Windows 10, you don't need to run a defrag. Ever. Windows runs one for you, by default, one day every week at 1:00 a.m. You can check that your defrags are running properly by looking at the Task Scheduler, as I describe in Book VIII, Chapter 5.

Windows 10 doesn't need a disk partitioner

I personally hate disk partitioning, but rather than get into a technical argument (yes, I know that dual-boot systems with a single hard drive need multiple partitions), I limit myself to extolling the virtues of Windows 10's partition manager.

No, Windows 10 doesn't have a full-fledged, disk partition manager. But it does everything with partitions that most people need — and it gets the job done without messing up your hard drive. Which is more than I can say for some third-party disk partition managers.

For details, see Book VIII, Chapter 5.

Windows 10 doesn't need a Registry cleaner

I've never seen a real-world example of a Windows 10 machine that improved in any significant way after running a Registry cleaner. As with defraggers, Registry cleaners may have served a useful purpose for Windows XP, but nowadays, I think they're useless (correction: worse than useless). I've never found a single run of a single Registry cleaner that caused anything but grief.

There's a great quote that (as best I can tell) originated on the DSLReports forum in March 2005. A poster who goes by the handle Jabarnut states, "The Registry is an enormous database, and all this cleaning really doesn't amount to much . . . I've said this before, but I liken it to sweeping out one parking space in a parking lot the size of Montana." And that's the long and short of it.

Jabarnut is correct: The Registry is a giant database — a particularly simple one. As with all big databases, sooner or later some of the entries get stale; they refer to programs that have been deleted from the system or to settings for obsolete versions of programs. Sure, you can go in and clean up the pointers that lead nowhere, but why bother? Registry cleaners are notorious for messing up systems by cleaning things that shouldn't be touched.

Windows 10 doesn't need a backup program

The built-in backup options, which I discuss at length in Book VIII, Chapter 1, work very well.

The only possible exception is if you're paranoid enough to want a full "ghost" backup of your hard drive. In that case, yes, you have to acquire (possibly buy) a backup program. But why bother? Windows 10's Restore works very well indeed.

Don't turn off services or hack your Registry

I just love it when someone writes to me, all excited because he's found a Windows service that he can turn off, with no apparent ill effect. Other people tell me about this really neat Windows pre-fetch hack they've found, in which a couple of flipped bits in the Registry can significantly speed up your computer. Before they changed, Windows boot times were sooooo slow. Now, with the hack, it's like having a new PC all over again!

Meh.

I call it the Registry Placebo Effect. If you find an article or a book or a YouTube video that shows you how to reach into the bowels of Windows to change something, and the article (or book or video) says that this change makes your machine run faster, well — by golly — when you try it, your machine runs faster! I mean, just try it for yourself: Your machine will run *so* much better.

Yeah. Sure. Once upon a time, when dinosaurs walked the earth, it's possible that turning off a few Windows *services* (little Windows subprograms that run automatically every time you boot) may have added a minuscule performance boost to your daily Windows ME routine. Bob may have jumped up faster, or Clippy could have offered his helpful admonitions a fraction of a millisecond more quickly. But these days, turning off Windows services is just plain stupid. Why? The service you turn off may be needed, oh, once every year. If the service isn't there, your PC may crash or lock up or behave in some strange way. Services are tiny, low-overhead critters. Let them be.

That covers the high points. I hope this chapter alone paid for the book — and the rest is just gravy!

Index

Notes

Notes

Dedication

To Add and Andy, for putting up with an obsessed writer.

Author's Acknowledgments

Many thanks to everyone involved in the process of bringing this book to light in spite of horrendous deadlines — and those who worked on previous Windows All-In-One books, refining the format and tightening the approach. It's been quite a road from Windows XP to Windows 10, and you all deserve enormous praise.

Thanks to David Weinraub, who repeatedly had to dive into the AskWoody.com website and fend off attackers.

GreenGeeks provided tremendous support for AskWoody.com, even in our darkest hours. Good people, very competent.

Finally to the folks at 2bee2, www.2bee2.com, for giving us a sneak peek at the new game. Positively addictive. Due on Windows 10 soon, I hope.

Publisher's Acknowledgments

Acquisitions Editor: Amy Fandrei

Project Editor: Martin V. Minner

Copy Editor: Gwenette Gaddis

Technical Editor: Ryan Williams

Editorial Assistant: Claire Brock

Production Editor: Kinson Raja

Cover Image: © iStock.com/mihau

le & Mac

 For Dummies,
Edition
-1-118-72306-7

ne For Dummies,
Edition
-1-118-69083-3

s All-in-One
Dummies, 4th Edition
-1-118-82210-4

X Mavericks
Dummies
-1-118-69188-5

gging & Social Media

ebook For Dummies,
Edition
-1-118-63312-0

ial Media Engagement
Dummies
-1-118-53019-1

rdPress For Dummies,
Edition
-1-118-79161-5

iness

ck Investing
Dummies, 4th Edition
-1-118-37678-2

sting For Dummies,
Edition
-0-470-90545-6

Personal Finance
For Dummies, 7th Edition
978-1-118-11785-9

QuickBooks 2014
For Dummies
978-1-118-72005-9

Small Business Marketing
Kit For Dummies,
3rd Edition
978-1-118-31183-7

Careers

Job Interviews
For Dummies, 4th Edition
978-1-118-11290-8

Job Searching with Social
Media For Dummies,
2nd Edition
978-1-118-67856-5

Personal Branding
For Dummies
978-1-118-11792-7

Resumes For Dummies,
6th Edition
978-0-470-87361-8

Starting an Etsy Business
For Dummies, 2nd Edition
978-1-118-59024-9

Diet & Nutrition

Belly Fat Diet For Dummies
978-1-118-34585-6

Mediterranean Diet
For Dummies
978-1-118-71525-3

Nutrition For Dummies,
5th Edition
978-0-470-93231-5

Digital Photography

Digital SLR Photography
All-in-One For Dummies,
2nd Edition
978-1-118-59082-9

Digital SLR Video &
Filmmaking For Dummies
978-1-118-36598-4

Photoshop Elements 12
For Dummies
978-1-118-72714-0

Gardening

Herb Gardening
For Dummies, 2nd Edition
978-0-470-61778-6

Gardening with Free-Range
Chickens For Dummies
978-1-118-54754-0

Health

Boosting Your Immunity
For Dummies
978-1-118-40200-9

Diabetes For Dummies,
4th Edition
978-1-118-29447-5

Living Paleo For Dummies
978-1-118-29405-5

Big Data

Big Data For Dummies
978-1-118-50422-2

Data Visualization
For Dummies
978-1-118-50289-1

Hadoop For Dummies
978-1-118-60755-8

Language &
Foreign Language

500 Spanish Verbs
For Dummies
978-1-118-02382-2

English Grammar
For Dummies, 2nd Edition
978-0-470-54664-2

French All-in-One
For Dummies
978-1-118-22815-9

German Essentials
For Dummies
978-1-118-18422-6

Italian For Dummies,
2nd Edition
978-1-118-00465-4

 **Available in print and e-book formats.**

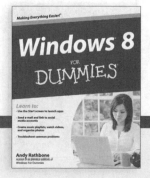

Available wherever books are sold. **For more information or to order direct visit www.dummies.com**

Math & Science

Algebra I For Dummies,
2nd Edition
978-0-470-55964-2

Anatomy and Physiology
For Dummies, 2nd Edition
978-0-470-92326-9

Astronomy For Dummies,
3rd Edition
978-1-118-37697-3

Biology For Dummies,
2nd Edition
978-0-470-59875-7

Chemistry For Dummies,
2nd Edition
978-1-118-00730-3

1001 Algebra II Practice
Problems For Dummies
978-1-118-44662-1

Microsoft Office

Excel 2013 For Dummies
978-1-118-51012-4

Office 2013 All-in-One
For Dummies
978-1-118-51636-2

PowerPoint 2013
For Dummies
978-1-118-50253-2

Word 2013 For Dummies
978-1-118-49123-2

Music

Blues Harmonica
For Dummies
978-1-118-25269-7

Guitar For Dummies,
3rd Edition
978-1-118-11554-1

iPod & iTunes
For Dummies, 10th Edition
978-1-118-50864-0

Programming

Beginning Programming
with C For Dummies
978-1-118-73763-7

Excel VBA Programming
For Dummies, 3rd Edition
978-1-118-49037-2

Java For Dummies,
6th Edition
978-1-118-40780-6

Religion & Inspiration

The Bible For Dummies
978-0-7645-5296-0

Buddhism For Dummies,
2nd Edition
978-1-118-02379-2

Catholicism For Dummies,
2nd Edition
978-1-118-07778-8

Self-Help & Relationships

Beating Sugar Addiction
For Dummies
978-1-118-54645-1

Meditation For Dummies,
3rd Edition
978-1-118-29144-3

Seniors

Laptops For Seniors
For Dummies, 3rd Edition
978-1-118-71105-7

Computers For Seniors
For Dummies, 3rd Edition
978-1-118-11553-4

iPad For Seniors
For Dummies, 6th Edition
978-1-118-72826-0

Social Security
For Dummies
978-1-118-20573-0

Smartphones & Tablets

Android Phones
For Dummies, 2nd Edition
978-1-118-72030-1

Nexus Tablets
For Dummies
978-1-118-77243-0

Samsung Galaxy S 4
For Dummies
978-1-118-64222-1

Samsung Galaxy Tabs
For Dummies
978-1-118-77294-2

Test Prep

ACT For Dummies,
5th Edition
978-1-118-01259-8

ASVAB For Dummies,
3rd Edition
978-0-470-63760-9

GRE For Dummies,
7th Edition
978-0-470-88921-3

Officer Candidate Tests
For Dummies
978-0-470-59876-4

Physician's Assistant Exam
For Dummies
978-1-118-11556-5

Series 7 Exam For Dummies
978-0-470-09932-2

Windows 8

Windows 8.1 All-in-One
For Dummies
978-1-118-82087-2

Windows 8.1 For Dummies
978-1-118-82121-3

Windows 8.1 For Dummies
Book + DVD Bundle
978-1-118-82107-7

 Available in print and e-book formats.

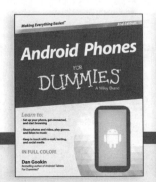

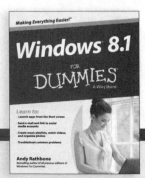

Available wherever books are sold. **For more information or to order direct visit www.dummies.com**

Take Dummies with you everywhere you go!

Whether you are excited about e-books, want more from the web, must have your mobile apps, or are swept up in social media, Dummies makes everything easier.

Visit Us

bit.ly/JE0O

Like Us

on.fb.me/1f1ThNu

Follow Us

bit.ly/ZDytkR

Watch Us

bit.ly/gbOQHn

Join Us

.in/1gurkMm

Pin Us

bit.ly/16caOLd

Circle Us

bit.ly/1aQTuDQ

Shop Us

bit.ly/4dEp9

For Dummies is the global leader in the reference category and one of the most trusted and highly regarded brands in the world. No longer just focused on books, customers now have access to the For Dummies content they need in the format they want. Let us help you develop a solution that will fit your brand and help you connect with your customers.

Advertising & Sponsorships

Connect with an engaged audience on a powerful multimedia site, and position your message alongside expert how-to content.

Targeted ads • Video • Email marketing • Microsites • Sweepstakes sponsorship

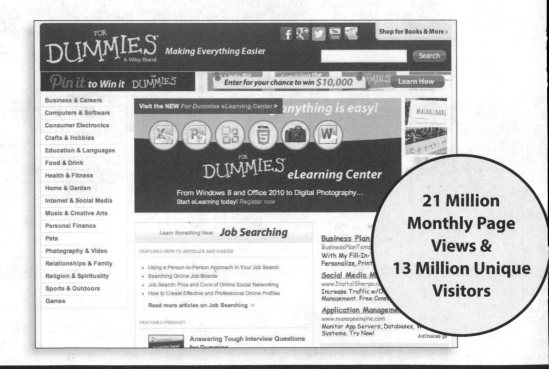

For Dummies is a registered trademark of John Wiley & Sons, Inc.

of For Dummies

Custom Publishing

Reach a global audience in any language by creating a solution that will differentiate you from competitors, amplify your message, and encourage customers to make a buying decision.

Apps • Books • eBooks • Video • Audio • Webinars

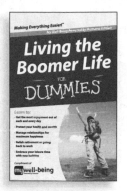

Brand Licensing & Content

Leverage the strength of the world's most popular reference brand to reach new audiences and channels of distribution.

For more information, visit www.Dummies.com/biz

FOR
DUMMIES
A Wiley Brand

Dummies products make life easier

- DIY
- Consumer Electronics
- Crafts
- Software
- Cookware
- Hobbies
- Videos
- Music
- Games
- and More!

DISCARD

005.446 LEONHARD

Leonhard, Woody.
Windows 10 all-in-one
for dummies

METRO

R4001929312

METROPOLITAN
Atlanta-Fulton Public Library

For more info... ...tore by category.

For Dummies is a registered trademark of John Wiley & Sons, Inc.

FOR DUMMIES
A Wiley